# OF SINGULAR BENEFIT

". . . *the good education of children is of singular benefit to any Commonwealth.*"

—MASSACHUSETTS CODE OF 1648

# OF SINGULAR BENEFIT

*The Story of Catholic Education*
*in the United States*

by HAROLD A. BUETOW

*The Macmillan Company*
*Collier-Macmillan Ltd., London*

The Macmillan Company
866 Third Avenue, New York, N.Y. 10022
Collier-Macmillan Canada Ltd., Toronto, Ontario

Library of Congress Catalog Card Number: 74-103683

First Printing

Printed in the United States of America

# Acknowledgments

OBVIOUSLY, SO MAMMOTH a task, though intended only as a beginning, could not be done completely alone. Through years of research, the author is sincerely grateful to many people. At the Catholic University of America, these would include especially the Revs. Christian Ceroke, O. Carm.; Aubert J. Clark. O.F.M. Conv.; Joseph N. Moody, Carl J. Peter, Robert J. Trisco, J. Whitney Evans, and Sister Teresita Dobbin, R.S.M. In the local Washington, D.C., area at the University of Maryland we owe a special debt of gratitude to Margaret Carthy; at the National Catholic Educational Association to the Rev. C. Albert Koob, O. Praem., and Mrs. Winifred R. Long; and in the Archdiocese of Washington to the Very Rev. Thomas W. Lyons.

The National Catholic Educational Association and His Eminence Terence Cardinal Cooke, through their kind assistance, made possible many aspects of research that would otherwise have been difficult at best. Among other things, this assistance enabled the author to contact every Catholic diocesan superintendent of schools in the United States, through the mails, by phone, or in person, and to travel 10,000 miles to most of the relevant archives, libraries, and depositories throughout the country. On this trip the following were particularly helpful: Rt. Rev. Msgr. Carl J. Ryan and the Rev. James Shappelle, Cincinnati, Ohio; Rt. Rev. Msgr. Felix N. Pitt, Louisville, Kentucky; Sister Ramona Mattingly, S.C.N., Nazareth, Kentucky; Sister Edwarda Ashe, S.L., Loretto, Kentucky; Sister Julia, O.P., St. Catherine's, Kentucky; the Rev. Leo Conti and Miss Ruth Ostendorf, Vincennes, Indiana; the Rev. William Faherty, S.J., and John J. O'Brien, St. Louis University; the Rev. R. Stafford Poole, C.M., Perryville, Missouri; in New Orleans, Louisiana,

Rt. Rev. Msgr. Henry C. Bezou, Sister St. Pierre Rivet, O.S.U., Ursuline Academy, Sisters Consuela Marie Duffy, S.B.S., and Stanislaus Dalton, S.B.S., both of Xavier University, and Miss Connie Griffith of Tulane University Library; Sister Antonia Plauché, R.S.C.J., Academy of the Sacred Heart, Grand Coteau, Louisiana; Sister M. Claude Lane, O.P., Houston, Texas; in Austin, Texas, Miss Mary Pound of the University of Texas, and Sister Loretta Raphael, O.P.; in San Antonio, Texas, the Misses Carmen Perry, St. Mary's University, and Catherine McDowell, The Alamo Research Library; in El Paso, Texas, Jess Duggan of the University of Texas, Brother George Murphy, S.J., Cleofas Calleros, and Joseph Rochford; the Rev. Francis J. Weber, San Fernando, Calif.; the Rev. Pierre DuMaine, San Francisco, Calif.; Fray Angelico Chavez, Peñablanca, New Mexico; Sister Maura McDonald, O.P., Albuquerque, New Mexico; Rt. Rev. Msgr. Philip Cassidy, Santa Fe, New Mexico; Rt. Rev. Msgr. William H. Jones, Denver, Colorado; the Rev. Charles Forsyth, O.S.B., University of Colorado, Boulder; Robert L. McCaul, Jr., University of Chicago; at St. Mary's College, South Bend, Indiana, the Rt. Rev. Msgr. John J. McGrath and the Rev. John J. Zemanick, S.S.E.; the Rev. Thomas T. McAvoy, C.S.C., and Philip J. Gleason, University of Notre Dame; Rt. Rev. Msgr. Edward J. Hickey, Detroit, Michigan; Rt. Rev. Msgr. Albert W. Low, Boston, Massachusetts; in New York City, Rt. Rev. Msgrs. Edward M. Connors and Joseph O'Keefe, and the Rev. Henry J. Browne; the Most Rev. Charles R. Mulrooney, Brooklyn, New York; Patricia C. Deeley, Adelphi University; in Philadelphia, Pennsylvania, Brother Thomas J. Donaghy, F.S.C., of La Salle College, and the Revs. John Shellem of St. Charles Seminary Archives in Overbrook and Hugh J. Nolan of Immaculata College; and in Baltimore, Maryland, the Revs. John J. Tierney, S.S., of the Baltimore Chancery Archives, and Charles G. Neuner, S.J., of the Jesuit Provincial Archives.

H.B.

# Contents

# Introduction

### Some Reflections on the Title

THE "STORY" OF our title refers to history, which a humorist has defined as "a story of events that never happened by people who weren't there." Hopefully, one can do better than that. Etymologically from the Greek *historia*, meaning an inquiry or narrative, history is, according to Webster, different from annals and chronicles, and is "a systematic written account comprising a chronological record of events . . . and usually including a philosophical explanation of the cause and origin of such events." [1] It is, in the words of the *Harvard Guide to American History*, "a . . . particular way of studying the record of human experience." [2] Henri-Irénée Marrou asserts that the historian is delegated "by men, his brethren, to conquer truth." [3] Pope Leo XIII gave its underlying principle when, citing Cicero, he said on August 18, 1883, in making the Vatican Archives available to historians: "The first law of history is neither to say anything false, nor to keep silent about the truth." [4]

The "United States" will, of course, vary in space and in time. With regard to space, this book will refer to this country in its present boundaries. With regard to time, because history is a continuum and not a mere succession of events like acts on a stage with a rising and falling curtain separating one part from another, historical divisions are somewhat false and arbitrary. They are nevertheless necessary, and there are reasons for the chronological divisions in this work. The first section, "Colonial Period of Transplantation," extends to 1783, with the Treaty of Paris a logical breaking point. It looks eastward, to the countries from which the Spanish, French, and English settlers transplanted their educational ideas. The next period, "Formative Foundations," beginning in 1784 and ending in 1828, looks more within these shores; witnesses the beginnings of organization of Catholic life in this country and of the realization of plans for Catholic education; and includes the writing of the Constitution and the legal considerations attached to it, a story in itself in a history of this kind. The "Transition" from 1829 to 1884 includes all of the Councils of Baltimore, many of which had an important and ongoing influence on the history of Catholic education in this country. Seven of these Councils were designated as "Provincial," embracing only a part of the Church, and three were "Plenary," major Councils that included all of the Church in this country. The period from 1885 witnessed "Further Growth," because of quantitative increase and a finer delineation of qualitative excellence through implementation of Conciliar decrees and findings arrived at through controversy. The years from 1918 to 1957 displayed a "Maturing Process" for the country at large, the Church, and Catholic education. "Contemporary Soul-searching and Ferment" begins in 1958, the year of intense criticism of both public and private education in this country because of the success of Russia's Sputnik the year before, and because of other criticisms internal to the Catholic Church.

The word "Catholic" in our title refers to those aspects of education and life which refer specifically and uniquely to the doctrine of beliefs and practices professed by that Church. The *corpus* of these beliefs and practices is many-splendored, the emphases of which will vary, like the reflections of a diamond, from place to place and from time to time. Pertaining to education, there is no such thing as a Roman Catholic *system*, uniform and identical for all times and places. There is only a Roman Catholic *pattern*, about which these pages speak.

Education, an experience different from any other in human life, is very frequently confused with such other terms as *teaching, instruction, training, discipline, schooling,* and *formation.* Etymologically, *education* comes from the two cognate Latin words, *educere* and *educare,* meaning to lead forth or draw out. A real definition in modern times adds nothing essential to Pythagoras, who spoke of education as that which enables a person to become what he is, and education,

although it implies or presupposes teaching or instruction as the means, in discriminating use stresses the intention or the result, the bringing out or development of qualities or capacities latent in the individual or regarded as essential to his position in life.[5]

Other disciplines refer to it also as acculturation and socialization. Essentially it has six aspects, differing from one theorist to another both in terminology and in order of importance. *Conditions* comprise such directly relevant aspects as buildings, equipment, finances, social climate, etc. On *goals*, aims, and purposes, everything else depends, and it is only when outcomes and achievement are measured in comparison with these that the success or failure of education can be ascertained. In this connection, Catholics have ever been mindful that, as they state before the Lord's Prayer in every Mass, they are "formed by the word of God," while at the same time remembering the words of the Psalm, "I have seen the limits of all fulfillment." [6] The goals of the Catholic pattern of education have varied in their emphasis as the Church's emphases have varied—from the eschatalogical, for example, to the incarnational.

*Curriculum*, too, is very important, containing as it does in its modern definition all of the pupil's experiences that are under the direction of the school. Underlying the curriculum for the Catholic is an acceptance of the existence of objective truth and the possibility of achieving it.[7] Underlying the social aspects of the curriculum are the assumptions that a person must be brought to understand and live basic relationships with God, his neighbor, and his environment; and that there is possible a social integration, based on a recognition of the essential unity of all men and on an acceptance of responsibilities toward the kingdom of God. Education also has its *agents*—those who are responsible for bringing it about. Among these are the State, for which the common welfare of all its citizens posits responsibilities, one being education; the Church, which is concerned with man's natural well-being as well as his supernatural destiny; and most importantly the Family, the basic unit of society, which has prior rights and duties in the education of all its children. Another essential component is the *teacher*, who represents the agents of education and through whose person flows all of its other aspects. Finally, there are those for whom the entire process exists: the *students*. How the entire program proceeds depends upon how one understands the nature of the student. Here, too, Catholic education has reflected the Church and its Founder; to the extent that such mundane practicalities as financing have allowed, it has appealed to the *anawim*—society's downtrodden and needy. Underlying the Church's procedures here are such foundational assumptions as the spiritual nature of the soul; the inherent dignity of every person; the redemptive plan of God; and the possibility of an integrated personality through the development of one's physical and spiritual, individual and social, and natural and supernatural powers.

This story, like all other histories of education, must by its nature bear a close relationship to other areas of history, without which it cannot be understood. It is related, for example, to *intellectual* history, wherein the direction of the schools is frequently shown to be tied in with the thinking and influence of philosophers of a time and place. It is also related to *social* history—e.g., the importance of the family, the position of the persons in the home, the degree of stratification of society, the condition of the masses making possible or impossible universal education, etc. *Economic* history has its place too, for educational institutions are influenced by what men do for a living, and times of financial prosperity or depression greatly influence a nation's learners. *Political* history plays its part as well, involving such areas as controversies as well as cooperative enterprises between schools and governments. For the purpose of practical limitation, this book concentrates upon the elementary and middle levels of education; it touches upon higher education where it has affected lower—e.g., where it began as lower education, such as Georgetown University, or had a raison d'être intertwined with lower, such as The Catholic University of America, or was involved with teacher training, such as diocesan teacher training colleges, or had goals that spilled over into the entire Catholic educational pattern.

## Why We Wrote

The constant criterion of the busy, time-pressed, and pragmatic modern American—as of others—for the choice of any such time-consuming operation as the reading of a book is what he calls "relevancy." To speak to this criterion as applied to history in general, T. S. Eliot said that

Time present and time past
Are both perhaps present in time future
And time future contained in time past.[8]

The American historian John Hicks put it aptly:

It is impossible to understand our times without a knowledge of the conditions which brought them about; and it is equally impossible to make intelligent decisions for the future if we have only an uncomprehending view of the age in which we live.[9]

The English theorist R. G. Collingwood expressed it interestingly when he asserted:

Knowing yourself means knowing what you can do; and since nobody knows what he can do until he tries, the only clue to what man can do is what man has done. The value of history, then, is that it teaches us what man has done and thus what man is.[10]

Marrou said essentially the same thing, adding an appreciation of history as a "meeting with others": a meeting that "reveals to us infinitely more things—on all the aspects of being and of human life—than we could discover in only one lifetime." [11] Only the most imprudent would plunge blindly into the problems of the present or future without attempting to view past experience.

The relevancy of the history of education in particular cannot be overestimated. With regard to the past, it familiarizes one with education's mistakes so that one need not be condemned to repeat them. "Almost all current educational problems and issues," observes Edgar W. Knight, "have their roots in the past. These problems can be met and solved only by understanding them. They can be understood only in the light of their origin and development." [12] With regard to the present, a knowledge of the history of education enables us to see today's "innovations" in proper perspective, and teaches the teacher much that otherwise he would have to learn by long and painstaking experience. As one of the advantages of the history of education, the Most Rev. John Lancaster Spalding spoke of "culture of mind, without which the teacher always works at a disadvantage,"[13] and remarked that "the history of education may be said to be the history of human progress and culture."[14] The "Report of the Sub-Committee on the Training of Teachers" to the National Education Association in 1895 agreed, saying that the "history of education . . . gives breadth of view."[15] With regard to the future, a knowledge of the history of education facilitates the avoidance of more flagrant abuses such as are reported in daily newspaper items and makes possible the building of a more solid foundation.

All of that had to do with *relevancy*. It is just possible, however, that *relevant* does not necessarily rank highest among the many adjectives to be prefixed to such nouns as *knowledge, book,* or *course of study*. It has little to do with truth, and history sometimes changes one's mind about what is relevant at a given moment. It takes effort to differentiate it from the fad (which effort is also helped by history). Relevance inheres not in the subject matter, but in the mind of the onlooker, and the onlooker has to be on his guard lest his attempt is to become fashionable instead of learned. Relevance is at best a criterion of timeliness; if clear and decisive, it is "pertinent." Finally, there are worse things than being irrelevant—being dishonest, for example, or wrong. A criterion at least as necessary as relevancy is *importance*. Relevancy contains a note of urgency, immediacy, and youth—but importance carries notes of inner weight and more timelessness.

All of this brings us to the question of why we wrote this book. First, the subject is both relevant and important—not only because it shares in the advantages of history in general and in the history of education, but inherently. True scholarship recognizes that there has always been more than one pattern of education in this country, and at the present time the largest sector of American private education is the Roman Catholic. This establishment—tens of thousands of schools, hundreds of thousands of religious and lay teachers and staff, and many billions of dollars—is responsible for educating about one out of nine children in the United States, a sizeable proportion of the future of our country. Interest in it does not imply less interest in, or criticism of, the public school pattern of education in the U.S., which has done an extremely fine job in fulfilling its goals and has made major contributions to the history of education in the western world. Interest in its history is at the present time necessary, as well as being relevant and important, because of the controversies swirling around it and within it, and because, if it is true that "conduct is the key to nature," its history will provide a key to its nature that will add to the information provided by other disciplines.

Another reason for writing is that, strangely enough, very little litera-
ture exists in the field. There have, of course, been histories of the
Church in the United States, such as those of John Gilmary Shea, Peter
Guilday, John Tracy Ellis, and Thomas T. McAvoy.[16] Specifically in
Catholic education, primary source documentation is not lacking. Going
over the entire field lightly is Neil G. McCluskey, *Catholic Education in
America: A Documentary History*. There are the Jesuit *Woodstock Letters* and *Records* for the early period; the published decrees of the
Councils of Baltimore; Peter Guilday's *National Pastorals of the Ameri-
can Hierarchy, 1792–1919*, and Raphael M. Huber's updating of this to
1951, and subsequent statements of the U.S. hierarchy on education; the
very interesting ideas on Catholic education of Orestes A. Brownson in
*Brownson's Quarterly Review*; the publications on education of such
eminent bishops as John England, John Ireland, and John Lancaster
Spalding; the pamphlets in the Bouquillon controversy; and such state-
ments from Rome as Pius XI's encyclical *On the Christian Education of
Youth* and *The Documents of Vatican II*.[17] Among secondary sources,
there have been articles and books on one or another aspect of Catholic
education. Among the notable articles that come to mind are Thomas T.
McAvoy on "Public Schools *vs.* Catholic Schools and James McMaster";
Francis P. Cassidy, "Catholic Education in the Third Plenary Council of
Baltimore"; Henry J. Browne's 1953 article on "The American Parish
School in the Last Half Century"; James A. Burns, "The Development
of Parish School Organization"; and, of the plethora of current articles
on federal aid, William B. Ball's "The Constitutionality of the Inclusion
of Church-Related Schools in Federal Aid to Education." [18]

Among books, although many have been written in various areas of
United States Catholic education, there is an insufficient number of
monographs and other works to be put together easily into one adequate
history. There are, for example, biographies of individuals who are important to this history. Some of these have concerned members of the
hierarchy, such as John Tracy Ellis' *John Lancaster Spalding* and his two-
volume *Life and Times of James Cardinal Gibbons*; and Sister M.
Salesia Godecker's work on Bishop Simon William Bruté. Other biographies have been written on founders and foundresses of teaching
religious communities, such as Annabelle M. Melville's *Elizabeth Seton*.
Among the countless histories of religious communities that come to
mind are Sister Mary Agnes McCann's history of the Sisters of Charity
of Cincinnati, Ohio, Anna B. McGill's *Sisters of Charity of Nazareth,
Kentucky*, and Louise Callan's work on the Society of the Sacred Heart.
Many have written about particular sections of the country, such as
Edward M. Connors on New York State, William H. Jones on Colorado,
Sister M. Salesia Godecker on Indiana, Louis Walsh on Lowell and
Boston, Mass., and some master's theses and doctoral dissertations. Still
others have focused on aspects of the curriculum and textbooks, such as

George Johnson on the Catholic elementary school curriculum, Judah Harris' *The Treatment of Religion in Elementary School Social Studies Textbooks*, and Sister Marie Leonore Fell, *The Foundations of Nativism in American Textbooks, 1783–1860*.[19] There have been only three attempts, however, at putting together a complete history, and these a long time ago: the Rev. James A. Burns' *The Catholic School System in the United States: Its Principles, Origin, and Establishment*, published in 1908; the same author's *The Growth and Development of the Catholic School System in the United States*, published in 1912; and Bernard J. Kohlbrenner's revision of these into *A History of Catholic Education in the United States*, published in 1937.[20] The present author hopes that his book will be a good beginning, and that in turn it will mark further beginnings, of more research into this important field.

## CHAPTER I

# To 1783: Colonial Period
# of Transplantation

THE PATTERN OF EDUCATION in Colonial America—of *all* education—was one of transplantation: the schools were modeled after those in the mother countries from which the colonists came. The history of Catholic education within the present territorial United States began long before the sucessful English foundation at Jamestown, Virginia, in 1607. The Spanish were not only the first explorers but also the first Catholic colonists in America. From Columbus' discovery in 1492, "three G's" impelled the Spaniards westward—glory, God, and gold. The French, too, left their mark: explorations which began successfully with Jacques Cartier in 1534 eventually gave the French claim to the Hudson Bay region, the St. Lawrence River basin, the Great Lakes, and the Ohio and Mississippi valleys.

## Spanish Missions

Isabella of Castille and Ferdinand of Aragon, under whose flags Columbus sailed in 1492, immediately set the stage for the preaching of the gospel in the newly found land. Exploration and evangelization went hand in hand, first to the West Indies and Mexico and finally northward into the regions of the present United States. No settlement of the Spanish in North America was ever densely populated; their settlements were borderlands forming the "Rim of Christendom." [1] Towns grew up around Spanish Catholic missions, and their methods of dealing with the Indians in the conquered frontiers were those of New Spain. Missionary endeavors were tied to military and civil administration. The missionaries were paid agents of the state who were expected to civilize and Christianize the natives in the interests of Spain. Rippy states four main objectives in Spain's policy in dealing with the Indians in the Americas: reduction to village life, Christianization, civilization, and final racial fusion with the colonists.[2] In 1497 the Spanish crown had begun the practice of allotting lands to Spaniards on which natives would be forced to labor. In 1503 Spain gave the order that the Indians of the New World should be congregated in permanent villages and put under protectors (*encomenderos*) who had the right to exact Indian labor but also the duty to protect and teach the Indians. This was known as the encomienda system, which was designed to protect, civilize, and Christianize the native—as well as to exploit him.[3]

The Spanish missions of the Colonial period in the present United States make for fascinating study. There are still marks of Spanish days on our southern border. Some states—Florida, Colorado, Nevada, Texas, New Mexico, and California—boast names that are Spanish in form. The Spanish tongue is spoken in many southern towns and by the southwestern Indians who prefer it to English. Scattered all the way from Georgia to San Francisco are Spanish mission ruins. The Southwest retains quaint church customs brought from Spain or Mexico by early pioneers. Las Posadas is still enacted at Christmas time. California has her Portolá festival, her rodeos, and her Mission Play.[4] The Spanish missions extended, held, and promoted the frontier. Spain utilized her missionaries as a means of changing the social order of the natives in order that, lacking colonists, she would colonize the frontier with aborigines.

If a part of education is acculturation, then the missionaries contributed a great deal. The Franciscan friar Sebastián de Aparicio, for example, can be considered to have contributed to both Mexico and the missions within the present United States with his invention of the yoke at Vera Cruz, Mexico, in 1531, and with his first oxcart (*carreta*), introduced into Texas in 1540.[5] Also, the first to introduce classical music to the present United States was Fray Cristobal de Quinoñez, who came in 1620. Spain gave to the Indians the Catholic faith, Spanish blood (intermarriage was favored), and protection. Spain expected in return labor, loyalty, and the extension of Spanish dominions. Contrasted to the English in Colonial North America, to whom the only good Indians were dead Indians, Spain preserved the natives—a noted feature of Spain's frontiering genius.

The catechisms in use in Mexico City were no doubt used by the Franciscan missionaries in the "Rim of Christendom." The first Bishop of Mexico City, the Right Rev. Juan Zumárraga, O.F.M., exerted educational leadership in Mexico from the time of his arrival in 1528 and, zealous and eager to bring education and Christianity to the Mexican Indian tribes, published at his own expense *Doctrina Breve*, the earliest book to issue from the press in the Western Hemisphere. There is one perfect copy of this historic volume included among the treasures collected by Archer M. Huntington for the library of the Hispanic Society of America in New York City. The Henry Huntington Library of San Marino, Calif., contains the original copy. Freely translated, the title page of America's oldest textbook reads:

A brief and very valuable compendium of the facts that pertain to the Catholic faith in our Christianity, in simple style, for the average intelligence. Compiled by the Most Reverend Sr. Don Fray Juan Zumárraga, first Bishop of Mexico and one of his Majesty's Council. Published in the said City of Mexico by his direction and at his expense in the year 1543.[6]

Zumárraga believed that simple, direct methods should be used in teaching the poor and ignorant in New Spain. Other catechisms in Mexico City followed his—that of Alonso de Molina, O.F.M., for example, in the mid-sixteenth century, and that of Pedro de Palacio, O.F.M., in the 1570's. The missionaries of New Mexico followed their example.

Spain set importance on the educational work of her missionaries. It was provided for in the plans of the Franciscan Cardinal Ximenes de Cisneros, who, together with Hadrian of Utrecht, ruled the Spanish Empire after the death of King Ferdinand in 1516. Ximenes was aware of the needs of New Spain and of the human dignity of the natives of the New World. At his instigation the following seven-point Indian charter was drawn up:

1. The Indians are free persons.
2. They are to be Christianized.
3. They can be compelled to work, but this labor may not interfere with the program of the friars nor impede the higher welfare of the state.
4. The work may not be excessive.
5. The Indians should possess private property.
6. They should be allowed to mingle with the public and should be given an education, especially in Christian doctrine.
7. The Indians should receive wages, not in money, but in goods that are necessary and useful to them.[7]

By the terms of this plan each village in New Spain was to have its own school and church, and it was the duty of the missionaries to see that each individual was taught according to his abilities and needs and instructed in the Catholic faith. At least this was the ideal system of education described by the first *custos* of New Mexico, Fray Alonso de Benavides, O.F.M., and planned by the great Ximenes. This ideal would work out differently in different times and places, however, and the student of Spanish colonial education must examine in detail the historical factors that were decisive in all aspects of the frontier's life and culture.[8]

## FLORIDA

The earlier stages of Spain's activities in Florida consisted of exploring expeditions and repeated attempts at colonization. The Franciscans came first with Narvaez when he reached Florida's western shore in 1528 and perished in the expedition. Four friars and eight secular priests accompanied De Soto in 1539-1543. One of the friars was a Trinitarian, Francisco de la Rocha; two of them were Dominicans, Luis de Soto and Juan Gallegos; the fourth was Juan Torres, a Franciscan.[9] This expedition, too, was doomed to failure. When Pedro Menendez de Ávilés, one of Spain's greatest conquerors, founded the city of St. Augustine in 1565, Florida's history took on the character of permanence. Menendez secured three Jesuits for his conquered Florida. Another band arrived in 1568, and went to Santa Elena, Orista, and Gualé (Georgia), where they founded missions. At first they were successful, but in 1573 they were driven out by native oppression. In that same year nine Franciscans began work in this uncompromising territory and labored in Florida until 1763.[10] Then Florida changed to English hands and the missions of the Franciscans were no more.

Franciscan missionary activity appears to have been limited during the first years of settlement in Florida, and it was not until 1594 that educational work began on a systematic scale. In that year twelve Franciscans arrived from Spain to help the four friars already there.[11] The Gualé Revolution in 1597, however, in which the Indians rose in revolt and killed the Franciscan friars, almost ended the missionaries' work in Florida. Gradually the missions were rejuvenated and extended, and by 1606 they had nearly regained the status they had had before 1597. Personnel was increased. Florida was raised to the dignity of an independent province. Santa Elena comprised all the friars in Cuba, Florida, Georgia, and South Carolina. New churches and mission schools were built. By 1633, with preparations made for the conversion of the Apalache in the interior of northwestern Florida, Geiger claims that the Florida missions entered upon their Golden Age.[12] The Golden Age was followed by a decline that began toward the end of the seventeenth century. Economically, Florida had had troubled times from its beginnings. The colony was never self-supporting and often was actually poverty stricken. This was Spain's one New World colony where she may be said to have done her duty as a Christian mother country without expecting material return. Only because of royal support did the Florida missions exist.

Florida's educational activities were in Franciscan hands from 1573 until 1763. The friars used the same methods of instruction as prevailed elsewhere in New Spain, but not with as much success. The Indians were savage and treacherous, and the French and English were a constant threat to mission peace and security. The friars did, however, make some progress. As early as 1606, a year before the founding of Jamestown and some thirty years before the establishment of a school in English North America, the Franciscans had a classical school and preparatory seminary at St. Augustine for the Spanish.[13] Evidence of this school's activity may be seen in the fact that the Dominican auxiliary bishop of Havana, Juan de Las Cabezas de Altamirano, made a confirmation tour and conducted the first known episcopal visitation in what is now the United States. The report of the bishop's notary shows the number of confirmations conferred as 370 upon Spaniards or Creoles and 2,074 upon Indians.[14] Also twenty candidates for the priesthood, some of whom were educated by the Franciscans at the friary of St. Augustine, may have been ordained.[15]

Wherever possible, the missions had schools. There were missions and *doctrinas* along hundreds of miles of the Atlantic Coast (Florida, Georgia, South Carolina), administered from St. Catherine's Island, Franciscan provincial headquarters. By 1650, fifty Franciscan priests, not counting novices and attachés, were caring for fifty missions and numerous stations with 25,000 Indian converts, with government assistance.[16] After the middle of the seventeenth century there was little of educational interest in Florida. In 1736, the Franciscan Bishop Francis de San Buenaventura Tejada, of Tricali, Yucatan and Guadalajara, and first resident bishop of St. Augustine, reopened a classical school at St. Augustine. Shea quotes from several letters of Tejada to the King in 1736, telling His Majesty of the clerics trained in this school. In a letter of 1737 to Governor Justiz, Tejada remarks that this school is the only one of its kind in Florida at the time.[17]

A manuscript dated 1753 preserved in the John Carter Brown Library of Providence, Rhode Island, throws further light on the classical school at St. Augustine and shows that it was still in existence in that year. Regulations for religious teachers in the convent at St. Augustine are given, and salaries of two hundred pesos annually are claimed to have been assigned to the Superior and to each of the five priests and three lay brothers. One of the brothers was "to teach the children Christian doctrine, reading and writing." The Rev. Francisco Gomez, O.F.M., was appointed Master Teacher of the jurisdiction of Florida.[18] The school appears to have continued for only a few years, and no mention of it is found after 1753.

### LOUISIANA

Louisiana was French territory in Colonial times and only for a short period came under Spanish rule. Spain acquired Louisiana by necessity, not by choice, for its value as a buffer against England. England was advancing to the Mississippi, and her settlers were pushing over the Alleghenies; France, smarting from the English capture of Quebec in 1759, wanted to rid herself of Louisiana and the probable humiliation of English seizure. French rule came to an end in 1762. Seven years later Spain reluctantly, but with no other course to follow, took hold of the vast region of Louisiana; she held it from 1769 until October 1, 1800, when by the treaty of San Ildefonso she retroceded it to France, which kept it until the Louisiana Purchase, April 30, 1803. Although Louisiana politically passed over to Spanish rule, the colonists remained French in heart and mind.

A Spanish school was established in New Orleans in 1772 but received little support from French parents. Pupils never exceeded thirty, and the number dwindled to as low as six. The records of Spanish Franciscan education in the colony show a few attempts by Spanish Recollect Franciscans operating out of Cuba,[19] but language difficulties hindered their work. On April 1, 1788, Governor Don Estevan Miro made a report to the Spanish Crown in which he reviewed the educational situation in the province. He reported six schools in the city—a Spanish school, four French private schools, and the Ursuline academy. The Spanish school had excellent professors, chosen from the universities of Spain, but few pupils. Inasmuch as most educational developments of colonial Louisiana took place under French influence, we shall discuss them there.

### NEW MEXICO

Francesco Vasquez Coronado is acclaimed as the discoverer of New Mexico: in a search for first the Seven Golden Cities of Cíbola and then the Gran Quivira in 1540, he and his party, equipped at royal expense, set out from Compostela, Mexico, and passed through the area. Fray Marcos de Niza, O.F.M., and four other Franciscans accompanied the party, and after Coronado and the others returned to Mexico three Franciscans remained to work among the Indians, but were martyred. The actual establishment of the New Mexico missions began in 1598 when Don Juan de Oñate took possession of New Mexico in the name of Spain. The Franciscans who accompanied him laid the foundation of their work in that area. Their first mission was at San Gabriel, but the center of activities was soon transferred to Santa Fe.[20]

Information on the educational activities of the missionaries in New Mexico can best be gleaned from the writings of Benavides. He kept two *memorials* of his visitation, one in 1630 and the other in 1634, both of which were addressed to King Philip IV of Spain and were no doubt colored by optimism as he tried to induce the King to give more missionaries and money to New Mexico. But they are an "on the scene" report and for that reason invaluable. Benavides made projections of the educational activities of the Franciscans in each pueblo and among each nation. A few examples will set a definite picture of education. Of the Teoas nation, he said:

At these [the monasteries of San Francisco de Sandia, and San Antonio de la Isleta] there are schools of reading and writing, singing, and playing all instruments; and the pupils are well taught in the Doctrine [*dotrinados*], and with much care in the polite [or civilized, political] life.[21]

The Tanos nation had four thousand souls baptized. Benavides stated that "there are here training schools of all trades, as in the rest of the pueblos." The Indians of the Queres nation, according to Benavides' *Memorial,* were "very dexterous in reading, writing, and playing on all instruments, and craftsmen in all the crafts, thanks to the industry of the Religious who converted them." [22] Benavides portrayed the Indians of New Mexico as a people who led a community life, learned civilized ways by living them, acquired the skills of irrigation along with crafts and other arts, learned to read, white, paint, sing, and play musical instruments, and over and above all became versed in Christian doctrines and in the Christian way of life.

These improvements, however, meant work, and Indian men were not accustomed to work. Daily there was a program of spiritual exercises, which must have jarred upon the Indians who, before the friars, came and went as they pleased. A fight between the military and the ecclesiastical in 1680 added loss of respect to the Indians' discontent (of which the Spaniards seemed unaware), leading to an Indian revolt on August 9, 1680, which brought the flourishing Indian mission to a surprised and disastrous end. "At that time," Ellis remarks, "there were approximately 2,800 Spaniards in New Mexico with thirty-two Franciscans spread through the pueblos where they were ministering to around 35,000 Christion natives." [23] Twenty-one Franciscans were murdered and the missions destroyed. Eleven years later, the Spaniards took control of New Mexico again. The Franciscans returned, but the glory was somewhat dimmed.

The methods of instruction in New Mexico were not unlike those of Old Mexico. For example, Vasco de Quiroga, a layman who later became the first bishop of Michoacan, Mexico, worked in Mexico on the education of orphans, which led him into adult education, and finally into cooperatives for both production and selling. Some of his Indians migrated north with a knowledge of his concepts. Also, the father of Mexican education, Brother Peter of Ghent, referred to in Mexico as Fray Pedro, had come to Mexico City in 1527 and continued his educational work there until his death in 1572. His instructional methods were ahead of his time and rightly may be termed democratic and progressive. He objectified his teachings by means of visual aids as a way to hold the interest of his pupils. He composed a hieroglyphic catechism for the instruction of Mexican children, a copy of which still exists in the National Library in Madrid. "Gante" did not neglect the teaching of industrial arts. As far as possible he sought to harmonize the Aztec and Spanish cultures, by building on a common base of Christianity. He emphasized civic virtues. Gante steered the Indians' love of music and art into Christian channels as he taught the natives to use such talents in the service of the Church. But perhaps the main reason for Gante's success was his concern for the Indian as a human being, a person to be treated kindly, loved, and led to eternal salvation. In such a work no effort was too great. The Indian as a child of God mattered to the missionary; Gante found ways to make God matter to the Indian, and the missionaries in New Mexico made Gante's goals and methods their own. Church and State, however, did not always agree in New Mexico—or, indeed, in many parts of New Spain—and there were hints of Spanish cruelty to the Indians, all of which left the natives confused and scornful. In 1776, the only books in New Mexico were those of the Franciscan custody at Santo Domingo, New Mexico.[24] For all that, the educational achievements of the missionaries in New Mexico were great.

### TEXAS

Spain made pioneering expeditions into Texas—the vast area stretching east from New Mexico [25]—all through the years 1535 to 1675. Catholic education first appeared in 1682 when the Franciscan missionaries established a mission at Ysleta near El Paso.[26] It was not until 1685, however, with the immediate danger of a French settlement by Robert Cavelier, Sieur de la Salle, that Spain became really interested and attempted permanent occupation. Franciscan missionaries had been present in each of the early Spanish explorations of Texas, according to the *Memorial* of Benavides, who hoped that the King of Spain would open a port "between the Cape of Apalache and the coast of Tampico," whence the friars would operate in Texas. Texan Spanish missions numbered twenty-five in all, and the last, Nuestra Señora del Refugio, was founded in 1793.[27] During this time, old records show that in 1746 Cristobal de los Santos Coy was a teacher in a parochial school in San Antonio, and in 1759 the Most Rev. Francisco Tejada, Bishop of Guadalajara, in his episcopal visitation ordered the maintenance of a parochial school in San Antonio.[28] Also, one of the most outstanding missionaries of Texas lived during this time: Pedro Ramirez de Arellano, O.F.M. Contemporaneous with Junipero Serra in California, Ramirez was Father President of the Zacatecan mission in Texas for about nine years and of all Texas missions for about eight years more (1764-1781).[29] None of this meant success, however: Texas was a buffer state between New Spain and the French colonial empire, and the Indians were very hard to instruct or convert.

An excellent picture of the Indians of Texas and the Texan Franciscan missions is given in the *Diary of Fray Gaspar José De Solis*. Solis made a visitation of the missions in the years 1767-1768. On the whole he found the Indians a dangerous lot. He penned:

They are cruel, inhuman and ferocious. When one nation makes war with another, the one that conquers puts all of the old men and old women to the knife and carries off the little children for food to eat on the way; the other children are sold; the vagabonds and grown women and young girls are carried off to serve them, with the exception of some whom they reserve to sacrifice in the dance before their gods and saints. This is done in the following manner: they set a nailed stake in the ground in the place where they are to dance the *mitote*; they light a big fire, tying the victim who is to be danced about or sacrificed to that stake. All assemble together and when the harsh instrument, the *cayman*, begins to play they begin to dance and to leap, making many gestures and very fierce grimaces with funereal and discordant cries, dancing with well sharpened knives in their hands. As they jump around they approach the victim and cut a piece of flesh off his body, going to the fire and half roasting it in sight of the victim, they eat it with great relish, and so they go on cutting off pieces and quartering him until they take off all of the flesh and he dies. . . . They do the same with the priests and Spaniards if they catch any.[30]

Some of the missions, however, succeeded in civilizing the Indian to some extent, and in Christianizing and educating him. Solis describes the Mission of El Rosario:

The workshop and dwellings for the ministering Fathers, as well as for the Indians, are good and adequate. Its stockade of strong stakes, which defends the mission from its enemies, is very good. A very nice church made of logs lined with mud on the inside, whitewashed walls and roofed with good beams skillfully made, which seem like a carved panel very neat and clean; . . . Its minister, who is as I have said, Fray Joseph Escovar, works hard for its advancement. . . . He conducts himself toward the Indians with great love, charity and gentleness.[31]

Solis then gives us a glance at the daily routine of the mission:

He [Fray Escovar] makes them work, he teaches them to pray, he tries to catechize them and instruct them in civilized customs and the rudiments of our Holy Faith; he assists and aids them as well as he can in all of their necessities, physical and spiritual, giving them something to eat and to wear. Above all he gets them together, young and old, in the cemetery at the ringing of the bell before prayers at night and makes them say their prayers and the Christian doctrine. On Saturdays he gets them together to pray the rosary with its mysteries and hymns of praise. On Sundays and feast days he makes them recite the prayers and the doctrine before Mass, and afterwards he preaches to them, explaining the doctrine and what they ought to know and understand.[32]

The daily exercises were the same in all the missions, with certain changes to suit particular localities. Agriculture was the principal occupation. Implements were crude, but grain was sown and irrigation installed where needed. The friars taught the Indians such trades as pottery, carpentry, masonry, blacksmithing, and spinning. The existence of catechisms and primers of Christian doctrine show that the elements of religion received formal attention and that the friars must also have taught reading.[33]

White settlers in Texas were few. San Antonio was the main Spanish settlement, and some years before 1789 it had a school for the children of Spanish colonists which continued for about thirty years.[34] But by that time the end was already beginning. The first mission to "travel [the] road to oblivion [secularization] was San Antonio de Valero [the present 'Alamo' site in San Antonio]." [35] With regard to San Antonio, it would be decided as early as 1785 that, because the local Indian tribes were gradually becoming exterminated, not all the missions were needed. Proprietary rights and administrative affairs were taken from the friars and put into the hands of the military. Though no proprietary rights were at first given to the Indians, this would be corrected by an Act of February 25, 1793. The other missions would suffer the same fate shortly thereafter.

### ARIZONA

In Spanish colonial times there was no such province as Arizona. Arizonac, whence probably the name Arizona is derived, had vague boundaries.[36] Bancroft claims that nearly all of what we now call Arizona has no other history before 1846 than the record of exploring *entradas* from the south and east. Both Shea and Englehardt give credit for the discovery of Arizona to Marcos de Niza, a Franciscan friar who crossed the territory from southwest to northeast in 1539. He passed over the same ground again in 1540, but there is no record that he preached to the Indians or made any conversions among them. The first to come formally were the Jesuits, who in the late 1680's extended their missions across the border from Sonora. Their work in Arizona is admirably exemplified by the celebrated Eusebio Francisco Kino, S.J., who in 1687 established the Nuestra Señora de los Dolores mission about 100 miles south of Tucson. It was to remain his headquarters for twenty-four years, during which he explored, did mission work, and kept records of his experiences. He knew the country well. Bancroft declares: "Over and over again, often alone, sometimes with associates, guides, and a guard, this indefatigable missionary traversed the valleys bounding the region on the south, east and north." [37] Kino wrote happily of his successes in Arizona:

With all these expeditions or missions which have been made to a distance of two hundred leagues in these new heathendoms in these twenty-one years, there have been brought to our friendship and to the desire of receiving our holy Catholic Faith, between Pimas, Cocomaricopas, Yumas, Quiquimas etc., more than 30,000 souls, there being sixteen thousand of Pimas alone. I have solemnized more than 4,000 baptisms, and I could have baptized ten or twelve thousand Indians more if the lack of farther laborers had not rendered it impossible for us to catechise them and instruct them in advance.[38]

In 1700 Kino founded the mission of San Xavier de Bac and within two years the missions of Guevavi and Tumacácori, all within present-day Arizona. To support them he established flourishing stock ranches. Bolton marks him as the "cattle king of his day and region." [39] He was a map maker too, who made numerous maps and sketches of the regions in which he labored, several of which are extant. His writings leave us a picture of the born explorer, but always the missionary predominates.[40] Bolton observed that Indians dot the pages of Kino's letters. He delighted in giving them instruction, in showing them his compass, sundial, and the lens with which he started fires, but nothing gave him as much pleasure as some sign that the Indians wanted to become Christians.

Arizona's Jesuit mission stagnated after Kino's death in 1711, and the end of Jesuit hopes in Pimería Alta came with King Charles III's decree in 1767 which suppressed the Society of Jesus in all Spanish possessions. The missions of Sonora were transferred from Jesuit to Franciscan hands. The "Kino" of the Franciscans was to be the Rev. Francisco Garcés, who after more than a decade of labors among the Indians of Arizona was among four friars murdered by them on July 19, 1781, in their uprising against the Spanish soldiers. Missionary educational endeavors in Arizona were ever difficult. The foundations were far apart, the missioners few, the country vast, and the tribes scattered, and there was a royal decree that Christian doctrine should be taught in the Spanish language [41] —all of which made fulfillment well-nigh impossible.

## CALIFORNIA

Not to the Spanish military but to the Jesuits must go the credit for establishing the first permanent European settlement in Lower (Baja) California—at Loreto in 1697. The missionaries' years there were difficult ones, for they had no state support. With characteristic efficient Jesuit economy they established the Pious Fund of the Californias, which provided for donations from devout persons.[42] Among others to whom Englehardt gives high praise is the Rev. Juan de Ugarte who, during Lower California's early years, was associated with the three missions of Loreto, San Juan de Londó, and San Xavier de Viggé-Biamundo,[43] and labored for Indian education. He writes of the missioner:

His interest for the education of the young made him convert his dwelling into a school for boys, where he instructed them in religion and morals, and taught the necessary mechanical arts with remarkable patience and devotedness. This was the first school on the peninsula and proved of much benefit to the missions later on. For the girls, especially the orphans, Ugarte erected another house, where under the watchful eye of an elderly woman, instructed by himself, they were gradually initiated into the work and duties peculiar to their sex.[44]

The general system of education was uniform in all mission establishments. The missionaries lavished their first attention on the children, for they realized that ultimate success resided in the youth. From outlying *visitas* they brought the more talented boys to the main mission center at Loreto where they taught them Spanish, reading, writing, and ecclesiastical singing. Their teachers were often imported from Mexico and paid by the Jesuits. These boys were later utilized as teachers of the *Doctrina,* and as general assistants of the missionaries.[45] Jesuit educational achievements came to an end in Lower California, as in Arizona, when Charles III expelled the Jesuits from every part of the Spanish dominions in 1767. Sixteen Franciscan Fathers, under the famous Fray Junípero Serra, of whom we shall hear more, came to replace the Jesuits. The work was hampered by a waning Spanish empire, internal conflicts with the local Spanish administration, and the civil oppression of the natives. Serra looked northward.

The rumor of a Russian advance into Upper (Alta) California was among the motivations that hastened Spain's occupation of the area in 1769. The mother country selected the Franciscans to go into the area, and Serra inaugurated the first missionary center at San Diego on July 16, 1769. The first year was discouraging. Serra made no converts; but perseverance won out, and by 1772 five missions had been established: San Diego (1769), San Carlos Borromeo (1770), San Antonio (July 14, 1771), San Gabriel (1771), and San Luis Obispo (1772). Support for the missions came from the Jesuits' Pious Fund of the Californias in Lower California; Spain did back them with detachments, however, for protection. Actually the soldiers often gave scandal to the Indians and concern to the priests by their immoral conduct. In spite of troubles the California missions made real progress, extending their numbers to twenty-one establishments and Christianizing thousands of Indians before 1833, when mission secularization would set in.[46] Berger had this to say of the Franciscan missions:

Certainly no episode in the white man's conquest of the present United States is more amazing. In contrast to the procedure of deliberate extermination as carried out along the Eastern seaboard, the Spanish conquerors of California made a valiant effort to raise the native Indians to their own standards of civilization. The instrument employed in this ambitious venture was the marvelous mission system developed by the Jesuits and adopted by the Franciscans. Although the whole futile undertaking lasted only sixty-five years, the Mission Period gave California an historical background unsurpassed in interest and romance by the local traditions of any other section of this nation. Nor can any locality boast of better preserved monuments to its pioneers than the remains of its twenty-one missionary stations.[47]

The proposals framed by the Franciscan Cardinal Ximenes were the ideal of the friars in California, as of other members of their order in New Spain. The subjects of instruction were to include Christian doctrine, reading, writing, music, and simple trades. The goals of Serra incorporated the same ideals of education, missionization, culturization, and socialization evident in all the Spanish missions—that is, the formation of Christian character. The means were modified somewhat to avoid the excesses of earlier missions and to follow a realistic bent. Religious instruction and industrial crafts prevailed. The California Indians were a primitive and lazy group who had first to push aside their Stone Age way of life. The friars knew that education must be adapted to the condition and prospects of the pupil. They did not make reading and writing compulsory, but offered the opportunity of learning those subjects only to boys expressing a willingness to do so. They insisted on manual labor for all without exception.[48] Unmarried girls, residing at the mission in quarters segregated from the boys, were taught the traditional domestic skills. The teaching of agriculture as well as industrial and mechanical arts helped, according to the friars' view, in adjusting the natives to civilized living. Such organization of labor, eventually resulting in a modicum of material prosperity, brought about the envy of the state and hastened the onset of secularization.[49]

## French Missions

The first quarter of the sixteenth century had hardly ended before France began to contest Spain's right to the New World. French fishermen had been plying their trade off the coast of Newfoundland probably since the beginning of the sixteenth century, but no explorations had been made with the sanction and support of the French government.[50] The expeditions of Giovanni de Verrazano in 1524 and Jacques Cartier in 1534, 1535, and 1542 stimulated a desire in France to extend westward and to propagate the Faith in the New World. As a result of Cartier's first voyage, Francis I of France issued a royal commission for the founding of a permanent colony—but the attempt of 1542 ended unsuccessfully. Owing to France's involvement in Continental affairs and her internal strife and religious wars, nearly a century elapsed before a permanent settlement sprang up on the Saint Lawrence. In the interim, the Huguenots attempted to found in the New World places of refuge from religious persecution. Admiral Gaspard de Coligny, a Huguenot of political influence, convinced the king that the Americas offered a way to weaken France's enemies in Europe.[51] Coligny formed a settlement in 1562 on what is now Parris Island, South Carolina—shortly abandoned in favor of Fort Caroline, Florida. In 1565 the Spaniards destroyed Fort Caroline, and the Huguenot colony disappeared.

The credit for the first permanent French settlement in North America goes to Samuel de Champlain. He founded Quebec in 1608, but before this time had joined with Sieur De Monts in the settlement of Acadia. In 1615 Champlain brought Recollect priests of the Franciscan Order to Quebec. They had little success among the Indians and, feeling unequal to the task, called the Jesuits to their aid. In 1625 six Jesuits arrived in New France under the Rev. Charles Lalemant. These priests were very active, learning the language and customs of the natives in order to find means to convert them. The Rev. Paul Le Jeune, S.J., began the publication of the *Jesuit Relations,* a series of letters relating life in New France, aiming to inspire members of his Society at home, encourage vocations, and interest the laity to give material support. His appeals for help brought the Ursuline Sisters and the Hospital Sisters from France in 1639 to work in Quebec.

There is no doubt that the promotion of religion was a prime factor throughout the development of New France. Montreal was founded in 1642 by Sieur de Maisonneuve, accompanied from Quebec by the Rev. Barthelmy Vimont, S.J., who celebrated the first Mass at Villemarie. The Jesuits ministered to the spiritual needs of Montreal until the coming of the Sulpicians in 1657. Under their guidance Marguerite Bourgeoys founded the great teaching congregation of Notre Dame and provided a school for the colony.

The establishment of a bishopric in New France was a great step forward for the Catholic Church in North America. Pope Alexander VII appointed François de Montmorency Laval as Vicar-Apostolic of Canada. Laval, who arrived in Quebec in June 1659, encouraged and promoted mission work within the borders of the present United States. The founding of the Church in Canada set the stage for missionary endeavors in this country—in Maine, New York, the old Northwest, the Illinois country, Detroit, and down the Mississippi to New Orleans.[52]

MAINE

During the Colonial period, the missionary activities of the French in New England were confined to Maine. Sieur De Monts granted Acadia to his associate Baron de Pourtrincourt, while he and Champlain located a colony on Saint Croix Island within the present site of Maine in 1604. When the site was found unfit for habitation, the entire group moved to Port Royal in Acadia (present-day Nova Scotia) and joined Pourtrincourt. It is interesting that, though De Monts was a Huguenot, his commission provided for the propagation of the Catholic Faith among the natives, for which purpose the Rev. Nicholas Aubry and another priest (name unknown) accompanied the expedition. Aubry had the distinction of being the first priest to celebrate Mass in New England.

Another French colony was organized by Madame de Guercheville in 1613 for the purpose of Christianizing the Indians. Mount Desert Island —again within the present state of Maine—was the site selected. The expedition was accompanied from France by the Jesuit Jacques Quentin. He was joined by two other Jesuits, Pierre Biard and Enemond Massé, from Acadia. An English ship, commanded by Captain Samuel Argall of

Virginia, raided the colony, taking all of them prisoners. The north-eastern boundary line between the French in Quebec and the English in Massachusetts remained an unsettled question for a long time, both countries insisting on claims to Maine. Ellis adds that

a widespread ignorance of geography contribut[ed] to the confusion. The fact that the area changed hands nine times in a century and a quarter is sufficient evidence of its instability and of the deleterious effects that these constant military and political changes had upon the Catholic missions.[53]

The Capuchins were Maine's Catholic missionaries during the first half of the seventeenth century. Between 1632 and 1654 the French Capuchins established seven missions in Acadia and New Brunswick in Canada and in Maine. After the English seized Fort Pentagot (now the town of Castine, Maine) in 1654, the Capuchins closed their missions and the schools they had established for their Indian charges.

Prior to the English conquest of 1654, the Rev. Gabriel Druillettes, S.J., laid the foundation for the Jesuit Mission of the Assumption on the Kennebec in 1646. He stayed there for a year and made two visits to the place afterwards. It was not, however, until the late seventeenth century that missionary work was resumed in Maine, and the missions became localized on the three principal rivers: Kennebec, Penobscot and Saint John. In 1694, the Jesuit Sébastian Râle (Père Sébastien Rasles) arrived in Maine to work among the Abenaki on the Kennebec. The French and English were at war at the time (King William's War of 1689-1697) and Massachusetts held that Râle was a French intruder. In spite of strong opposition, he established one of the most ideal of the French Indian missions, working there for thirty years surprised and killed by the English in 1724. Death at English hands actually came as no surprise to Râle. On October 12, 1723, he wrote to his brother an account of his work among the Abenaki, and his concluding words were:

Doubtless you will judge that I have most to fear from the English Gentlemen of our neighborhood. It is true that they long ago resolved my death; but neither their ill will toward me, nor the death with which they threatened me, can ever separate me from my old flock.[54]

Râle's Indians loved him. In a letter from Father de la Chasse, Superior-General of the Missions in New France, to a priest of the same Society, Râle is extolled in death:

He was not content with instructing the Savages almost every day in the Church; he often visited them in their cabins. His familiar conversations charmed them; he knew how to blend with them a holy cheerfulness which is more pleasing to the Savages than a serious and melancholy manner. He had also the art of winning them to do whatever he wished. . . . We were surprised at his facility and his perseverance in learning the different Savage tongues; there was not one upon this continent of which he had not some smattering.[55]

The Maine missions finally fell into English hands in 1763. There would be no further missionary activity of any consequence there until the last decade of the nineteenth century. The steadfast adherence of the Maine Indians to the Roman Catholic faith, however, was a worthy testimony of the accomplishment of the French missionaries.[56]

NEW YORK

The efforts of French missionaries in what is now New York State were almost entirely confined to the work of the Jesuits among the Iroquois. Missionary activity began in a very dramatic fashion in 1642 when a band of Mohawk Indians of the Iroquois confederacy surrounded and captured a group of Hurons near Trois Rivières (Three Rivers) in Canada. They took captive the Rev. Isaac Jogues, S.J., and his faithful companion René Goupil, and brought them to an Indian village near present-day Auriesville, N.Y., where they murdered Goupil and subjected Jogues to prolonged torture. Jogues managed to return to France but came back in 1646, only to be tomahawked to death on October 18, 1646. An attempt to plant a French mission among the Onondaga Indians in 1656 near what is now Lake Onondaga ended in failure within a year because of the unrest among the Iroquois. It was not until 1668 that a mission was able to be established in the Iroquois confederacy, and in the decade after that some 2,000 converts were made, among them Kateri Tekakwitha, who became an Indian martyr.

The deep rivalry that developed between England and France ended with the cession of New France to England at the close of the French and Indian War in 1763. The Jesuit missionaries during this time were looked upon as French agents. Thomas Dongan, Catholic governor of New York from 1683 to 1688, was able to provide the Jesuits a modicum of protection on the northern frontier, but beginning in 1687, for the sake of peace he requested the French Jesuits not to work among the Iroquois. The Jesuit Iroquois mission was apparently a failure. The only other partially successful effort to establish a Christian community in New York was made by the Sulpician François Piquet, who established the Indian mission, La Présentation, on the present site of Ogdensburg, in 1758. In the course of time, over four hundred families became physically, spiritually, and educationally dependent on this mission, but this settlement also dispersed with the fall of New France.

GREAT LAKES

In the Northwest, the French established missions first in the upper Great Lakes region, and from there extended into the interior of what are now the states of Wisconsin, Michigan, and Illinois. The Jesuits called their mission the Ottawa, because the tribe was the first to have a permanent station. Except for the Sulpician and Recollect explorers, and the chaplains of Detroit, the Northwest was a Jesuit field.[57]

To the area around the trade centers at Michilimackinac (Mackinac), Green Bay, and Sault Sainte Marie during the 1640's and 1650's came several French Jesuits including Charles Raymbault, Isaac Jogues, Léonard Garreau, and Gabriel Druillettes. Since the Sault was the converging point for Indians and fur traders, the mission at Sainte Marie became a center of missionary activities. Claude Dablon, S.J., made it the residence of the Jesuit superior upon his arrival in 1669. When Dablon was recalled in 1671 to become the superior of all the Jesuits in New France, the Ottawa mission consisted of Sault Sainte Marie (with the dependent mission of the Islands in Lake Huron), Saint Ignace at Mackinac, and Saint François Xavier (with the Stations of Saint Jacques, Saint Marc, and Saint Michel Archange). These missions were abandoned, however, before the English and French struggle for the control of the continent set in. The distance from Quebec and the shortage of priests explain why the Ottawa mission was not pursued with greater success.[58]

ILLINOIS

The Jesuits shared the Illinois mission in the beginning with the Recollects and later with Quebec seminary priests. French villages of consequence developed in the Illinois area, and there were many whites as well as natives. Jacques Marquette, S.J., and Louis Jolliet were the first Frenchmen to visit the Illinois Indians on their way to explore the Mississippi River to determine its source. They found the Peorias on a western tributary of the Mississippi now identified as Des Moines, Iowa. On their return they visited the Kaskaskia village, and to both Des Moines and Kaskaskia Marquette promised priests to instruct the Indian in Christian ways. Marquette dedicated the Immaculate Conception Mission among the Kaskaskia tribe. After Marquette's death in 1675, Claude Jean Alouez, S.J., took over the Kaskaskias and worked with them till his death in 1689. Claude Dablon, S.J., Alouez's superior, estimated that Alouez in his mission among the western Indians had instructed almost 100,000 and baptized some ten thousand.[59] Another well-regulated mission was estabilshed at Cahokia, but Kaskaskia was the principal station of the Jesuits throughout the French regime.

In 1663, at the city of Quebec, Bishop Laval set up missionary seminaries whose students went out into the Illinois area among the whites and the Indians. Unfortunately, disputes arose between the secular priests and the Jesuits over who would have jurisdiction in individual cases. During the eighteenth century several villages were established along the Illinois River which were generally administered by the Jesuits, and those communities thrived—probably because of the more tractable character of the Illinois Indians—until the end of the French and Indian War in 1763. Vincennes, the last French post established in the Illinois country, and now in Indiana, is the only one of lasting importance. Its ecclesiastical history started when the priests began to come over from Kaskaskia. Some sixty French settlers had gathered about the fort by 1763, and they formed the nucleus of a future episcopal See.[60] A letter that Pierre Gibault, S.J., the pastor sent to Bishop Joseph-Oliver Briand of Quebec in 1786 claimed that he was teaching the children at least religion. It was Gibault's boast that "the smallest boys in the village know not only how to serve Mass but also the ceremonies of festivals and Sundays and the entire catechism, small and large." [61] Gibault had reason to boast of any small success, for the Illinois had been reduced to a state of savagery with the expulsion of the Jesuits, which coincided with the fall of French political power. It was Gibault and the ailing Father Sébastian Meurin who kept some semblance of religion and civilization alive among the Illinois until Bishop John Carroll would send help in 1791.

DETROIT

Detroit was the last center of French influence in the Northwest. Morel de la Durantaye took possession of that locality on June 7, 1687. The strategic importance of the fort, however, was realized by Antoine de la Mothe Cadillac, who was appointed as commandant at Michilimackinac in 1694. Cadillac planned to concentrate the various tribes of the Northwest about Detroit, where they would come under the influence of the Jesuits and of the Ursulines to be provided. Cadillac's plans had no religious motive, but rather that of attracting the northern Indians away from the English and the trading influence of the Hudson's Bay Company. Cadillac made recommendations to Comte de Louis Pontchartrain concerning the missionaries, the school system, and the fur trade which he envisioned for Detroit. He saw his school system already in operation and wrote:

It would be well for the Governor, with his officials, to visit the classes from time to time and give prizes to the children. This will make them ambitious, and will greatly please their parents.

It would be well for the King to create a fund for Indian boarding children to be entrusted to the care of the missionaries, provided this is done in concert with the governor. This would keep the Indians in check, for they would never dare start anything while their children were in the French fort, and suspicion would be aroused were they to try to take them out. . . .

It would be necessary also to establish a house of Sisters or Ursulines [*sic*], to teach French to the Indian girls, and to instruct them in our religion. . . .

Thus the Indian children, thrown together with the French children, will engage in conversation, and the same thing will happen that has happened everywhere, namely, the Indians will speak French, and the French Indian, for if ten children, each speaking a different language were often together, every one of them would learn the ten languages.[62]

The Jesuits did not share Cadillac's views. They feared the mixing of the races, for they questioned the bad moral influence of the whites on the natives. Cadillac and the Jesuits parted ways, but the commandant did succeed in getting a Recollect chaplain, the Rev. Constantin Delhalle, for Detroit. Cadillac's plans for an Indian Utopia were doomed to failure. The tribes warred among themselves and Cadillac's school system existed only on paper. There is no doubt, however, that the chaplains at the Detroit post gave religious instruction. Paré observes:

But it must not be lost sight of, that the children were never deprived of schooling in the most important branch of all, religion. The successive priests at the post could not have been derelict in this most essential duty of their ministry. We may take for granted that from the time of Father Delhalle no child ever went without a course of catechetical instruction, and this even without such a delightful bit of intimation as that found in Chaussegros de Lery's journal: "A stag entered the fort through a breach in the palisade at 4 o'clock this afternoon, and wandered about. The children coming out of catechism class chased after him until he got out by another breach and made for the woods." [63]

While Cadillac remained at Detroit a Jesuit mission was out of the question, for their policies conflicted. With Cadillac's transferral to the governorship of Louisiana in 1710, the Jesuits contemplated a return to their beloved Huron missions. We know that Armand de la Richardie, S.J., was in charge of the Hurons at Detroit in 1728.[64] Parish posts in Detroit continued to be held by Recollects and secular priests throughout the French and Indian War and the American Revolution until the area would come under the jurisdiction of the first Bishop of the United States, John Carroll.

### LOUISIANA

The ambitious French explorer, Robert Cavelier, Sieur de La Salle, disregarded the prior claim of the Spanish to the Mississippi valley when on April 9, 1682, he and his party took formal possession of the entire region in the name of King Louis XIV of France. Three years earlier, in 1679, La Salle had given the name of Louisiana to the area in honor of the French king; in 1682 he established Fort St. Louis among the Illinois, and on his return to France in the following year was received with honor and given a group of some 280 colonists to plant a permanent colony in French Louisiana. La Salle, however, was never to see that plan realized, for he was murdered by his companions on March 19, 1687. La Salle's colonists were massacred by Indians, and it was left for Pierre Le Moyne, Sieur d'Iberville, and Jean Baptiste Le Moyne, Sieur de Bienville, to colonize Louisiana.[65]

Iberville established the first permanent French settlement in the lower Mississippi country at Biloxi in 1699. In 1702 this settlement was moved to Fort Louis de la Louisiane on Mobile Bay, the present site of Mobile, Alabama. Iberville, unlike La Salle, who preferred Sulpician and Franciscan priests to accompany his expedition, wanted Jesuits for his new colony. He brought Paul Du Ru, S.J., to Louisiana in 1700. The priests of the Society of Foreign Missions had been doing missionary work there among the Indians since 1699, and the Jesuits and secular priests clashed because the Jesuits wanted separate jurisdiction and the appointment of one of their own members as vicar general. This quarrel resulted in the departure of the Jesuits from the region for twenty years. During this time, educational efforts were individual, under such concerned and self-sacrificing people as Mlle. Françoise de Boisrenaud, whose instruction was probably catechetical for the most part, and who personally consecrated herself to the education of the little Indian slave girls as well as the daughters of the French.[66]

In 1718, Bienville succeeded in establishing a settlement on the Mississippi River itself. He named it New Orleans, and in 1722 it was made the capital of Louisiana. To Pierre F. X. de Charlevoix, S.J., journeying down the Mississippi river in that year, New Orleans presented a dismal picture. An old warehouse served as a church at first "and was scarce appropriated for that purpose," observed Charlevoix, "when it was removed to a tent."[67] New Orleans was a far cry from being true to the report to the mother country boasting that the city had "eight hundred fine houses, and . . . five parishes." Instead Charlevoix saw "a hundred barracks, placed in no very great order, . . . a large storehouse built of wood, . . . two or three houses which would be no ornament to a village in France"[68]—an unattractive settlement from a Frenchman's point of view. But Charlevoix looked into the future and saw New Orleans as the capital city of a large and rich colony.

If the physical set-up of the city was deplorable, its moral condition was even more so. The majority of the white inhabitants were from the outcast and criminal classes in France, and Negro slaves outnumbered the whites. Bienville saw the need for Christian education. He arranged to bring Capuchin friars from France to care for the parish and open a school. Bienville faced difficulties in this attempt, for neither the Company of the Indies nor the colonists made any efforts to provide for education. The few families of wealth sent their sons to colleges in France, but the education of girls and of those boys who could not attend schools in France constituted a serious problem. Two Capuchins came from France in 1722, and three studies[69] tell of their difficulties in starting a school. Father Cecil, a Capuchin monk whose correct name according to Claude L. Vogel, O.F.M. Cap., was Frater Cyril, is credited by many writers as being the first teacher to open a school for boys in the colony. The school building was a small house near the priests' dwelling in New Orleans. Father Raphael, the Capuchin Superior, was the founder of the first "petit collège," as is shown by his letter to Abbé Gilles Bernard Raquet, Ecclesiastical Director of the Company of the Indies, in which he stated that "un petit collège" at New Orleans had been established. Father Raphael recommended that no fees be charged for admission and that the Company furnish catechisms, primers, elementary books, grammars, and other material for advanced work. He worked hard for a new school as the original schoolhouse was too small and in debt from its beginnings. The Company turned a deaf ear to his pleadings, and the majority of the colonists looked upon his work with indifference. Baudier writes a sad closing sentence to the Capuchin story: "The efforts of the Capuchin Fathers to provide Catholic education for the children not only of the city but of the rural sections as well, came to naught after a self-sacrificing effort of five or six years." [70]

The first successful and permanent school in the whole of New France in what is today the central United States was opened in New Orleans by the Ursulines in 1727. At the request of Governor Bienville and the Company of the Indies, Nicolas Ignace de Beaubois, S.J., invited the Ursulines of Rouen, France, to undertake the education of girls in Bienville's colony. Ten Ursuline Sisters under the direction of Mère Marie de St. Augustine Tranchepain set sail for New Orleans on February 22, 1727.[71] After five perilous months at sea their vessel, the *Gironde*, reached the mouth of the Mississippi on July 23, 1727. They had yet to endure two weeks of rough canoe life—making their way up the river as best they could in small boats by day and sleeping in the forest at night —before they finally arrived in New Orleans on August 7, 1727.[72] Even then there were few material comforts; Ellis comments that "for seven years they lived in cramped quarters in a makeshift residence, and only in July, 1734, was a new and adequate convent ready for their occupancy." [73] Undaunted, the Ursulines went about the work which they had come to do. Three months after their arrival, in November 1727, they opened a school for girls. The school comprised a day school which was free of charge and a boarding school which was actually a part of the house set aside for the education of the better classes. They gave religious instruction to Negro and Indian children; rich and poor alike were accepted, taught, and loved. Speaking of the Ursuline boarding school in Colonial days, Shea says: "The daughters of the better class were educated in their Academy, many in time marrying French and Spanish officials of rank, and doing honor in other lands to their training by the exhibition of Christian graces." [74] The *Rule* [75] for the Ursuline Order printed at Paris in 1705 was the rule that the Ursuline Sisters brought to New Orleans in 1727; it is still preserved in the Ursuline convent there. From the typed copy which this author was particularly fortunate in obtaining, we learn that the same ideas and methods of teaching prevailed in the primitive parish school for girls in New Orleans as had been used by the Ursuline teachers throughout Europe since the Ursulines' foundress Angela Merici.

The school day was very short in the early period—only four hours. Vacation time, too, was brief—only three weeks. There were many feast days, however, and every Saturday was free. The spirit which the teachers inherited from their great foundress was one of motherliness. The aim of the Ursuline school was instruction in Christian dogma and Christian conduct. Pupils must be taught to think and act in an intelligent, Christian way. The *Constittuions of the Ursuline Order* stressed teacher preparation. "All the teaching religious," stated the *Constitutions,* "ought to prepare themselves in the sciences and arts, so as to be always capable of meeting the exigencies of the times and to be thoroughly master of all they may be called on to teach." [76]

The order of the day in the Ursuline school at New Orleans was marked by regularity. There were special detailed rules for boarders and day scholars.[77] Reading, writing, and a little arithmetic, together with the catechism and industrial training, made up the simple program for this pioneer town. Religious instruction was the most important part of the curriculum. Reading was regarded as central and the subject around which all other secular instruction revolved. In teaching it, the teacher read a passage first, slowly and distinctly. The pupils followed along in a low tone and then one after another, beginning with the more advanced, repeated the part the teacher had read. Spelling was taught in connection with reading. Writing was done at a long table supplied with quill pens and inkstands, the teacher writing a model which the children copied.

The Ursulines employed pupil-teachers, called in the *Rule* "dixainiè-res," chosen from the brightest and best-behaved girls. It was their duty to assist in class-work and discipline. They taught prayers to beginners, questioned their own groups of ten or more pupils, and admonished their assigned pupils of their faults, reporting misconduct to the sister-teacher only when it was grave enough to call for her correction. The "dixainiè-res" had the particular duty of distributing textbooks to their pupils at the beginning of the class and of locking up the books before class dismissal.[78] Textbooks were free, but the pupils were never permitted to take them home; in those days books were hard to come by. This system was in many ways like the monitorial system which Joseph Lancaster would later initiate in England and which would be introduced into the United States in 1806. Another feature of the Ursuline school program was vocational work. The pupils learned to sew, knit, and make their own clothing—"musts" in those days for every good housewife. They learned, too, ornamental work—fine needlework, the making of artificial flowers, crocheting, and the like. The sister in charge of industrial training read some instructive story to the pupils as they worked. The social value of the vocational program in itself was important, not to speak of

the Sisters' refining influence upon the poor girls of that rough city.
The Spanish assumed control of Louisiana in 1769 and held the area until Spain retroceded it to France in 1800. Changes in government, a different language, and new types of immigrants presented difficult problems
for the educator, French Louisiana for some time resenting this transfer
and refusing to accept the mores of a different regime, as we mentioned
above. Baudier, describing the turmoil that beset Louisiana by the time
the United States purchased the territory in 1803, accounts for the dismal demoralization with these words:

One must consider also the almost complete lack of Catholic educational institutions of learning in Louisiana for this whole period of a century and a
quarter, and for that matter, a lack of any educational facilities of any consequence. . . . From 1727 to 1821, there was just one Catholic school in
Louisiana—the Ursuline convent. The Capuchin school for boys unfortunately
did not last a decade. . . . The Spanish school was likewise short-lived.[79]

## English Colonies

The English were the last of the European nations to establish settlements in the New World. Starting with the first colony at Jamestown
in 1607 and ending with Georgia in 1732, thirteen English colonies in all
were founded. By the end of the Colonial period, there were no more
than 35,000 Catholics, forming a very small minority, and the Catholic
Church was being persecuted in every colony except Pennsylvania.
Even in Maryland, which had been conceived as a refuge for Roman
Catholics, a hostile attitude to Catholicism prevailed. Nevertheless,
Catholic educational developments in the colonies were restricted pretty
much to Maryland and Pennsylvania. We shall therefore confine our remarks here to these two colonies.

### MARYLAND

Maryland was founded by the first two Lords Baltimore, both Catholics in an anti-Catholic age. To George Calvert, the first Lord Baltimore, Charles I of England gave a patent for a large tract of land en-
closing the northern half of Chesapeake Bay. To this new province the
king gave the name of Maryland in honor of his queen, Henrietta Marie.
Sir George died before the charter was sealed, but his son Cecilius, the
second Lord Baltimore, carried out his father's plans. He founded Maryland in 1634 as a refuge for Catholics; blending tolerance with common sense, however, and realizing that no colony could thrive in that
age on Catholics alone, he directed his plea for settlers to all Englishmen regardless of religion. Catholics were a minority of the Maryland
population, but the charter promised all Maryland colonists political

security and religious liberty.[80] It was a religious experiment of which Andrews observes that

in no other colony of the period was the experiment even tried of Roman Catholics and Protestants actually living side by side on terms of equality, amity, and forbearance. In that respect the settlement of Maryland holds a unique place in the history of English colonization.[81]

At first a measure of success attended the attempts, but the experiment proved to be an ideal that failed in application. Ellis states the reasons simply:

The chief source of trouble arose from William Claiborne of Virginia, whose deep hatred of Catholics made him resentful of their proximity in Maryland, and who likewise harbored a personal grudge against the Calverts for their claim to Kent Island on which he had a plantation. . . . The fact that Baron Baltimore had permitted several hundred Puritans, unwelcome in Virginia, to cross into Maryland in 1648 added a further complication, since the newcomers soon showed how little they appreciated the proprietor's hospitality by making common cause with Claiborne.[82]

Claiborne played on the strengthening of the Protestant element through the migration of the Puritans to Maryland. Religious differences and dissatisfaction with proprietary land policy there caused much dissension. An "Act Concerning Religion" was issued in 1649 with the hope of bringing religious tolerance, but in vain: in 1692 the Church of England was established by law, a result of the Revolution of 1688 in the mother country, and Catholics were taxed for its support. In the years after 1689 Cecilius Calvert would not have recognized Maryland as the colony provided for by the Charter of Charles I.[83]

It is not our purpose here to make a study of the legislation and of assembly and court proceedings of Maryland during the years from the "Glorious" Revolution in England to the Revolutionary War in this country. During this critical period for Roman Catholics in the colony, they were deprived of their rights as citizens, and of all opportunities of advancement in educational, social, and economic life. Some legislation, however, directly affected Catholic education; this must be considered as the chief impediment to the establishment of Catholic schools in colonial Maryland. An example was the legislation of September 30, 1704, by which Catholics were not permitted to practice their religion, priests were forbidden to perform the duties of their office, and Catholic children were not allowed to be educated in their faith. This law's ruling on education was strong. It provided that

if any Papist or Person making profession of the Popish Religion shall keep school or take upon themselves the Education, Government or Boarding of youth in any place within this Province such person or persons being thereof lawfully convicted . . . [must] be transported out of this Province.[84]

Another such piece of legislation, this one related at least indirectly to the education of Catholic children, was enacted in 1715. It was an attempt to break up Catholic homes and curtail the growth of Catholicism in Maryland, and stated:

Provided always, that where any person, being a Protestant, shall die and leave a widow and children, and such widow shall intermarry with any person of the Romish Communion, or be herself of the opinion and profession, it shall and may be lawful for his Majesty's Governor and Council, within this Province, upon application to them made, to remove such child or children out of the custody of such parents, and place them where they may be securely educated in the Protestant religion.[85]

The anti-Catholic attitude persisted, and especially Protestant determination that Catholic education have no beginnings in Maryland. The Protestant Committee on Grievances in 1754 even went so far as to bring to England the complaint that Popish schoolmasters were publicly and openly teaching school and even Protestant children.[86] The result was an order from the mother country which required the licensing of teachers and their taking of the Oath of Abhorrency against Catholicism.[87] No Catholic teacher could, of course, take such an oath.

In such a climate the illegal and irregular attempts of Catholics to educate their children were of necessity carried out in stealth and silence. McCluskey observes:

As a group, Catholics were suspected and feared; as individuals, they lived their lives almost completely outside the principal cultural and political currents. They were denied freedom of worship, to take part in civic affairs, and to educate their children.[88]

Ellis deplores the lack of Catholic educational activities in such a climate: "As for the intellectual life of the Maryland Catholics," he says, "there was, indeed, very little. . . ." And he continues:

Parents of means, however, paid as little heed as they dared to the law about sending their children outside the country with the result that a considerable number of youth—both boys and girls—enjoyed as good, if not better, educational advantages than their American contemporaries at the schools maintained by both the male and female English religious communities on the continent.[89]

It was in Maryland, nevertheless, that Catholic educational work in the English colonies had its beginnings. That work dates back to the arrival of the original Maryland Jesuit missionaries, the Revs. Andrew White and John Altham, accompanied by the Jesuit lay brother Thomas Gervase.[90] White, the superior of the group, was a noted scholar who had filled the offices of Prefect of Studies, and Professor of Sacred Scripture, Dogmatic Theology, and Hebrew in the English colleges of Valladolid and Seville.[91] (A monument erected June 10, 1934, on the Father

Andrew White Memorial Road at St. Mary's City, Maryland, refers to him as the "first historian of the colony.") Lord Baltimore deserves the credit for obtaining these Jesuit missionaries and teachers in the very first days of his colony's founding. With the first expedition, the Jesuits landed on St. Clement's Island on March 25, 1634, celebrated Mass, and lived for a while in a little Indian hut in the first settlement of St. Mary's until a church adjoining the fort was erected. They quickly began to evangelize the neighboring Indians and to buy from them new grants of land. To Lord Baltimore this was a violation of his rights, and he appealed to the authorities at Rome, asking that the Jesuits be recalled and secular priests sent in their stead. The priests were sent as requested in 1642, but the Jesuits remained. Their quarrel with Calvert dragged on, but it was settled when the Jesuits agreed to give up their lands and hold them as tenants of the proprietor. Nevertheless, the dispute hindered the Jesuits' activities in early Maryland.

Despite these disagreeable events, the first years of the Jesuits in the colony met with some success in their instruction of the Indians. The King of the Patuxent tribe, Maquacomen, whose influence among the neighboring savages was strong, was converted to Christianity. Another converted chieftain, KittamaquuND, brought his little daughter to St. Mary's "to be educated among the English." [92] The conditions of the colony, with its problems of settlement, were not conducive to the establishment of schools at first, but we are amazed to find as early as 1640 the Jesuits envisioning a college for Maryland. Writing on September 15, 1640, to the Rev. John Brooks, then Superior of the Maryland mission, the superior-general of the Jesuits spoke encouragingly of the plan: "The hope held out of a college I am happy to entertain, and when it shall have matured, I will not be backward in extending my approval." [93] The Jesuits set about with remote preparations by their involvement in education on an elementary level.

The first Catholic school in Maryland of which we have any knowledge opened about 1640. In that year Ralph Crouch came from Europe and began a service to education and to the Catholic Church that would last for twenty years. He had been a Jesuit novice preparing for the priesthood, but had left the novitiate honorably in 1639. He was a man of no mean educational attainments, full of zeal and charity. On his arrival in Maryland, Jesuit activity was centered at Newtown, where the Jesuits had a manor house and where there was a concentration of Catholics. It was here that Crouch set up the Newtown Manor school, and financed it out of the endowments of local wealthy Catholics. Among these was Edward Cotton, a rich planter who gave a herd of cattle and their increase forever as an endowment for a school.[94] Crouch, and the school at Newtown, were mentioned directly in his will, which was made on April 4, 1653, and was the first bequest in favor of Catholic education in Maryland. In part, it read as follows:

Thirdly I doe appoint my Loving Friends, Thomas Matthews and Ralph Crouch my Executors Equally to have power to take and dispose of all my whole Estate whatsoever in manner and forms as followeth. . . . Ninthly I doe give all my female Cattle and their increase for Ever to be disposed of . . . unto charitable uses . . . the Stocks to be preserved and the profits to be made use of to the use of a Schooll. . . . Twelfthly, my desire is if they shall think Convenient that the Schooll be kept at Newtowne.[95]

Crouch continued to teach in Maryland until 1659, when he returned to Europe and was readmitted into the Jesuit novitiate as a coadjutor Brother. In a letter dated September 4, 1662, he wrote:

I affirme boldly allsoe that on my part I did (as appeared to all the neighbors) as much as lay in mee, fulfill the will of the Deceased [Cotton], in removeing my teaching of schoole to the New Towne; & there was ready some yeares to teach eyther Protestant or Catholikes.[96]

He died in Liège, Belgium, on November 18, 1679. Henry S. Spalding speaks with Jesuit pride when he writes that Crouch

seemed to have every qualification for the duties of a teacher, and won the esteem and admiration of the priests with whom he worked. . . . He must have instilled into these children a knowledge of their religion and the necessity of its practice, for when they became grown men and women they were remarkable for their fidelity under the most trying conditions. From him, too, they must have learned the value of an education, for a generation later we find them as fathers and mothers of families making every sacrifice to secure an education for their children.[97]

It is difficult to find any satisfactory account of the school at Newtown. The character of the curriculum can be arrived at only through meager sources. At first, it probably encompassed no more than learning the truths of religion and how "to write and read and cast accompt." [98] The Jesuit *Records*, however, refer to Crouch as having "opened schools for teaching humanities." [99] The actual opening of Crouch's school at Newtown cannot be dated accurately and precisely, and a perusal of the few sources on the subject calls for agreement with Treacy, who claims that for many years Crouch instructed Catholic children in their religion, finally climaxing his good works by opening the Newtown School, where humanities were taught.[100] It seems that Newtown School did not have a continuous existence. We find in the annual letter of the English Provincial to the higher Superiors in Europe, dated 1683, a reference to a school for humanities that had opened in 1677. It reads:

Four years ago, a school for humanities was opened by our Society in the centre of the country, directed by two of the Fathers; and the native youth, applying themselves assiduously to study, made good progress. Maryland and the recently established school sent two boys to St. Omer who yielded in abilities to few Europeans, when competing for the honor of being first in their class.[101]

The sending of students to St. Omer's (a college established in Belguim for the education of Catholic youth of English-speaking countries) indicates that at Newtown a full collegiate curriculum was not developed. We can only conclude from available fragmented sources that the school was a combination of elementary and preparatory school that had greatly strengthened its faculty and curriculum by 1682. Of that time Shea writes of Newtown that "the college was evidently prospering. It had good teachers, and even Protestants sent their sons there." [102]

Penal legislation after 1688 forced the closing of the school. [103] Catholic parents tried to evade the unjust laws by having Catholic teachers tutor their children at home; but prying persecutors were everywhere, and any Catholic conducting a school was liable to perpetual imprisonment. That Catholics would seek to evade the laws was anticipated and interdicted. A Catholic parent was liable to a fine of forty shillings per day if any but a Protestant teacher instructed his child. If he sent his son to a Jesuit college in Europe, he became liable to a fine of £100. Catholics who were poor were therefore deprived of the opportunity to give their children a Catholic education, except to the extent that they were able to teach them at home. Wealthy Catholics, in spite of Protestant vigilance and the harshness of the laws, sent their sons to Europe. These harsh laws barring Catholic schooling appear all the more unjust when one realizes that there was little done to further the cause of public education during the period. The first positive move in that direction came in 1694 when Governor Francis Nicholson implored the Assembly, then convened at Anne Arundel Town, now Annapolis, "that a way be found out for the building a free-schoole for the province and a maintenance for a Schoole Master and Usher and a Writeing Master that can cast Accounts." [104] The Assembly passed a law providing for the "Incouragement of Learning and Advancement of the natives of this province," [105] to materialize in the erection of a free school in each county of the colony. The law remained on paper, however, for it was difficult to raise money for schools. Again in 1696, Nicholson presented the "Petitionary Act" to the Assembly for presentation to the King, asking

That for the Propagation of the Gospel and the Education of the Youth of this Province in good Letters and Manners, a certain Place or Places, for a Free-School or Schools or Place of Study of Latin, Greek, Writing and the like, consisting of One Master, One Usher, One Writing Master or Scribe to a school . . . may be made, erected, founded, propagated and established under your Royal Patronage . . . And that the Most Reverend Father in God, Thomas by Divine Providence, Lord Archbishop of Canterbury . . . may be chancellor of the said schools and that to perpetuate the Memory of your Majesty, it may be called King William's School.[106]

It was not, however, until 1701 or 1704 that a free school opened in Annapolis. It was called King William's School and continued to be the only public school in Maryland until 1723. Catholics were excluded from any share in the school's management. The Anglican rector of the parish was the chairman of the school board, and all teachers had to be members of the Church of England. Donations were solicited for the school's upkeep which, in the main, was financed by private generosity, although taxes for the same purpose were placed on all sorts of things from tobacco to imported Irish Catholic servants.[107] In 1723, the Assembly again enacted a law that furthered the founding of county free schools in Maryland.[108] Gradually such schools were introduced—the law had called for one free school in each of the twelve counties—and they were under the strict regulation of the Established Church. Capable, approved teachers, however, were hard to recruit, and so the teachers often had to be servants, and at times even Irish indentured criminals and servants.[109] Guilday deplores "the immoral conditions of these schools," and remarks on "the abhorrence in which such educational masters must have been held by Catholic Maryland women." [110]

It was in this situation that the Jesuits made one last important educational effort in colonial Maryland. They opened a new school on the northeastern shore of the colony, at Herman's Manor in Bohemia. Devitt has described its location as follows:

Bohemia Manor was the immense tract of land in Cecil County, Maryland, that was granted to Augustine Herman; but, the name "Bohemia" was also locally and generally applied to the Catholic Church and residence of the Jesuit Fathers, and their property was known as "Bohemia Manor." The true title of the church is St. Francis Xavier, and the original tract of land was named St. Xaverius. It is situated near the head of Little Bohemia creek, at a short distance from the village of Warwick, in Cecil County; the nearest station on the Peninsular Railroad is Middletown, Delaware. The spot is very secluded and is surrounded by well-cultivated farms which were the property of the Mission.[111]

The Bohemia Mission was founded in 1704 by the Rev. Thomas Mansell, S.J., but it was during the pastorate of the Rev. Thomas Poulton, S.J., that the school was begun in 1745 or 1746. Spalding sets the opening date as 1741, and writes that the school's location near the Pennsylvania border "was chosen on account of its isolation, for the anti-Catholic laws were still pressing upon this class of people." [112] Hughes agrees with this reason for the location, adding the further note of the friendlier Pennsylvania neighbors.[113] In further addition, whatever itinerant schoolmasters had existed had undoubtedly been put out of business by the French and Indian War, and consequently it probably appeared to Poulton that his estate was just the place for a primary school for boys. We have scanty information on the school at Bohemia Manor. We cannot state accurately its opening and closing dates. We are not certain if it had a continuous existence or if it opened at intervals and by stealth, but the latter would seem to be the case in view of the aforementioned hostile legislation. A fragment of an old account book in the George-town University Archives is our only primary source; it reads:

1745–6.  Peter Lopez to your son's board. Feb. 17.
  "    May 20. Daniel Carroll to your son's board.
  "    June 24. Edward Neale, to board of your two sons, £43-16-3.
1748.    April 22. Daniel Carroll, 2nd time, son John came here.
    Jackey Carroll went to Marlborough, July 8.
    August 5. Robert Brent.
    August 20. Bennett Neale, Archibald Richard.
    June 24. Ben. Neale, Ed. Neale, John Carroll, James
      Heath went first to school.
N. B.   All those that learn Latin at 40 currency pound.
The rest at 30 £ as by agreement this day.[114]

The above names were those of prominent Catholic families in Mary-land. "Jackey Carroll" became the first Catholic bishop of the United States. Relating to this, Devitt observes:

The historians and chroniclers of Georgetown College, and writers on Catholic education in the United States, are wont to refer to this academy of Bohemia as the predecessor of Georgetown College, or the "germ" from which was evolved the oldest academic institution, under Catholic direction, for young men, in the United States. The connection between the Bohemia school and the "Academy on the Patowmack" is that they were projected and conducted under Jesuit auspices; and that John Carroll, the Founder of Georgetown, was numbered amongst the pupils of Bohemia; he is the link, moral and personal, between Georgetown and the earlier school.[115]

There is little more that can be said of the school at Bohemia. Shea claims that prying persecutors found this secluded spot and relates that the Anglican rector of St. Stephen's Parish, near Bohemia, made vigorous efforts to secure the enforcement of the laws against the Jesuit teachers at Bohemia Manor.[116] We have no knowledge of the curriculum of the school and may only conjecture on the subjects taught. The fragment of the old account book which states that each boy who studied Latin paid forty pounds, whereas the other students paid thirty, has been taken as an indication of the preparatory and elementary character of the school.[117] We do know that for further studies the students went to Europe to further their education. Guilday quotes the *Maryland Gazette* of October 17, 1754, as recording that "a great number of their [Catho-lic] youth were sent this year to foreign Popish seminaries." [118] But again we have to admit that "a few faded lines of antique writing" [119] are scant evidence on which to estimate the influence of Jesuit educators at Bohemia Manor. The same anti-Catholic legislation that makes infor-mation uncertain here results in the same difficulty concerning other Jesuit educational efforts. The Jesuits apparently did what they could to educate, but under cover—for example, in 1735 at St. Inigo's there is mention of one Vitus Herbert, for whose schooling a legacy of 250 pounds of tobacco had been left.[120]

The pattern of education, however, in colonial Maryland is not difficult to discern. There was a strong religious motivation for schools among the colonists generally. The Established Anglican Church after 1688 made attempts, with government help and private donations, to found free county schools, of which Anglican clergymen acted as supervisors. In most cases, the standards of these schools were low, as funds and competent teachers were scarce. They published descriptions of their teachers in an effort to entice parents to place their children in the school's care. One such notice appeared in the *Maryland Gazette* on December 13, 1764. It not only exemplifies the procedure followed, but states the aim of the school as well. It reads:

This is to inform the Public, that William Kean who had a regular University Education in Trinity College, Dublin, and had been Employed for many Years in the most noted Academies in England and Ireland has opened School in the above mentioned place (Queen Anne's County). . . . Any Gentleman who favors him with the care of his children, may be assured, that there will be the most punctual care observed both as to their Principles of Virtue and Morality, as well as their School Education.[121]


### PENNSYLVANIA

In March, 1681, Charles II of England gave to his friend William Penn, a Quaker, a charter conferring upon him proprietary rights in the New World to a large tract of land comprising an area as great as England and Wales combined: Pennsylvania. Its limits overlapped those of both New York and Maryland, resulting in boundary disputes until 1760.[122] (It was a happy controversy for the Jesuits of Maryland, who established Bohemia Manor at the disputed boundary line, thereby seeking to evade the anti-Catholic laws of Baltimore's colony.) Penn, who for his Quaker beliefs had endured "ridicule, parental disapproval, and persecution"[123] in England, determined that in his colony—his "holy experiment"—freedom of worship and civil rights would prevail and be the privilege of all law-abiding citizens who believed in God. It was this generous religous policy that made the colony the asylum of many persecuted sects from Europe, and the sole refuge for Roman Catholics, enabling it to show more promise than Catholic-founded Maryland. "In many ways," writes Ellis, "the story of the Catholics in Pennsylvania is the most pleasant and positive of any of the original colonies. The fact is due largely to the spirit of broad tolerance that informed the Quaker settlements from the outset."[124]

During the Colonial period, Pennsylvania prospered and its inhabitants increased. By the middle of the eighteenth century it had a population of about two hundred thousand, and by the outbreak of the Revolutionary War had doubled that number. Philadelphia, its chief city, was the largest in the English colonies, the most important in commerce and culture, and by 1750 boasted a population of nearly eighteen thousand.[125] The "List of all the Roman Catholicks in Pennsylvania (that is of all such, as receive the sacraments), beginning from twelve years of age, or thereabouts," [126] which the Rev. Robert Harding, S.J., submitted on April 29, 1757 in response to a demand of Lord Loudoun, indicated a total of 1,365, of whom only about 403 were "in and about Philadelphia." The colony attracted immigrants of all religious persuasions. Some were German Catholics who came with German Protestants after Penn visited Germany seeking colonists. The Germans settled on farming land to the west and northwest of Philadelphia. The Scots-Irish came in large numbers, most of them Protestant. There are frequent references to Irish schoolmasters in Pennsylvania during the first half of the eighteenth century.[127] The Catholic community in Philadelphia included "many who had fled from Maryland to the kinder rule of the Quaker province, and others who had been driven from New York after the revolt of Jacob Leisler in 1689." [128] Pennsylvania became a haven for oppressed Catholics, and Griffin speaks of its religious toleration towards them:

Pennsylvania was the only colony except Maryland from which Papists were not excluded from the first hour of their settlement. After 1692, it was the only colony that did not prohibit the public exercise of the Catholic religion, and for forty years prior to that time our Religion was not free even in Maryland.[129]

Penn's benign attitude gave favorable opportunity to the Jesuits. Before 1729, Jesuit missionaries visited Pennsylvania to attend to the spiritual needs of scattered Catholics, but in that year, the Rev. Joseph Greaton, S.J., took up residence in Philadelphia. By 1734, he was able to erect a tiny chapel. This was old Saint Joseph's in Philadelphia, then the only place of public worship for Catholics in the English colonies. Again as a sign of Quaker tolerance and friendship for Catholics, the location of Greaton's chapel was, according to Griffin, "right beside the Quaker Almshouse, back of Walnut Street." [130] Greaton was concerned for the Catholic immigrants from Germany, and wrote to his superiors pleading for German-speaking priests. His appeal was heard, and in 1741 two great Jesuit missionaries, the Revs. William Wappeler and Theodore Schneider, arrived.[131] Carroll would write of Wappeler (of the Lower German Province of the Jesuits), after having visited him while he was teaching in retirement in Bruges, that "Fr. Wappeler's candor and artless disposition of heart always endeared him to me"; [132] spiritually oriented, he was definitely not interested in material things. Schneider (of the Upper German Province of the Jesuits) "was a tall, strong man

[with] a striking forehead, light complexion dotted with red spots and a cheerful, calm and serene countenance." [133] Apart from being devoted and zealous missionaries, they were teachers who would not be satisfied until schools were established. In the Centennial Volume published by the Diocese of Harrisburg, Pennsylvania, in 1968, the diocese delved into its Colonial past, and treated of the teaching accomplishment of Wappeler and Schneider. It states:

Father Wappeler, only thirty years old when he came to America, had already acquired a degree of Master of Arts and had taught the humanities in Buren College and Munster College. Father Schneider, thirty-eight years old, after serving as Professor of philosophy and theology at the Jesuit Seminary in Liège, Belgium, at the time his call came to the missions of America, had attained the exalted post of Rector Magnificus of the famous University of Heidelberg. The success of men of such caliber on the missions is not to be wondered at.[134]

Wickersham also gives credit to Wappeler and Schneider. He states that Wappeler probably started a school near Conewago a few years after the priest's arrival there, and that at Goshenhoppen, Schneider's "residence was a two-storied building, in a small room of which on the first floor he taught school. Living on the most friendly terms with all denominations, his school was largely attended by children from the whole neighborhood." [135] Something of the nature of Goshenhoppen can be ascertained from its name: although it had at least twenty spellings, it very onomatopoetically described a person in a springless wagon travelling its rutted road *das macht die Goschen hoppen*—"that makes the jaws hop up and down." Of the character and personality of Schneider, one can ascertain something from a letter written by Ferdinand Farmer, S.J., to Germany:

Fr. Schneider often went hungry and ate cheap food, which indeed broke his fast, but did not still his hunger; he traversed the inhospitable woods and mountains, sought out very remote towns, taught the ignorant, attending to the spiritual needs of the people, imbuing all with faith and concern for their welfare. He took particular care of the little ones whom he gathered around him, founding schools in many places. He himself initiated them in writing and drawing lines.[136]

For these trips, he had to pack into his saddle bags the materials needed for saying Mass, his breviary, and books to set up school. Because all of this made his bags overcrowded, he used the parts of the winter in which he was snowed in to copy the large Roman Missal by hand into two 5" x 6" books.

Pertaining to Farmer's reference to the founding of schools, Schneider undoubtedly perceived that a fruitful apostolate could center about the towns built around the local iron forges and furnaces. Near Goshenhoppen were four of them with "Furnace" appended to their names—

Colebrookdale, Mayberry, Pine, and Pool Furnaces—and not too far away were two more, the little towns of Warwick Furnace and Coventry. A Catholic school teacher, John Mulcastor, was present in Coventry Town in 1742 and in Warwick Furnace in 1748. He could have been the one to whom the Anglican Parson Richard Backhouse ("Parson Bacchus" in the Warwick Day Book) was referring in a letter to the Society for the Propagation of the Gospel back in England:

I the more earnestly recommended him [Charles Fortesque, an Anglican] to the honourable board [of Concord, Chester County], not only because he is a fit person, but because what I am sorry to acquaint you with, the Quakers with all their powers and ill offices have endeavored to drive him away and set up another, not one of their own set truly, but a native biggoted Papist in opposition to him.[137]

Another likely spot for Schneider to open a school would have been Haycock, where there were sufficient Catholics to support a schoolmaster. At any rate, at Goshenhoppen people of all denominations held Schneider in great love and esteem, and sent their children to his school. In gratitude for his work, more than a century later the public school authorities of the district would provide for the education of children of this school at public expense.[138] We have no record of the curriculum or of the texts he used. Catholic elementary schools in Colonial times, however, differed little in these respects from other schools of the period. Protestants as well as Catholics felt that it was the first duty of the school to impart religious instruction, and each denomination took pains to ensure that this was done. The school also presented reading, writing, spelling, and a little arithmetic. Pupils were of all ages, and the school term was short.

It is not far-fetched, therefore, to consider Schneider as the founder of the parochial school system in the archdiocese of Philadelphia. At the same time, one must admit that there is no documentary proof establishing when the first Catholic schools were founded in Pennsylvania. Local traditions hold that in nearly every case the organization of a Catholic parish was attended, if not preceded, by the organization of the parish school, and that the priest of the parish was usually the first schoolmaster. The earliest known bequest made in behalf of Catholic education in the colony was that of James White, a merchant, who in 1767 provided in his will that 30 pounds be given "toward a schoolhouse." [139]

Two other famous figures in the history of the Catholic Church and of Catholic education in Pennsylvania during the Colonial period were the Jesuits Ferdinand Farmer (real name Steinmeyer) and Robert Molyneux. Farmer came to Pennsylvania from Germany in 1752, and after spending six years at Lancaster was called to Philadelphia to minister to the Germans there. Like Schneider at Goshenhoppen, Farmer's genial temperament and charity for all endeared him to Protestants and Catholics alike. He moved in educational circles, and was a member of the famous Philosophical Society of Philadelphia. Upon the reorganization of the University of Pennsylvania by the Assembly in 1779, Farmer became a trustee under the provisions of the law that, in addition to the persons named, trustees could consist of the senior pastors of the six principal denominations. Farmer was the one who served as trustee, even though Molyneux was Superior of the Jesuit mission.[140] When Farmer died in 1786, all the local newspapers carried the information; typical was the account in the *Philadelphische Correspondenz*, which referred to "the funeral being attended by the Protestant clergy, the members of the Philosophical Society and the faculty of the University of Pennsylvania and a large gathering of people of all religions." [141]

St. Joseph's Church, which as we observed first opened in 1734, grew and prospered, so that almost twenty years later another parish was established from it, with the name of St. Mary's. To this new parish the fat and jovial Molyneux came as pastor in 1773, Farmer being already there; and under their able direction Catholic education made rapid progress in Philadelphia. The Catholic population there "increased so that during the Revolutionary War the parish of Saint Mary alone gave to the service of the struggling colonies such great men as Commodore John Barry, George Meade, Thomas Fitzsimmons and Stephen Moylan." [142] Their first years were the trying times of the Revolutionary War, but "in the assurance of peace that came with Cornwallis's surrender," [143] Molyneux carried out his plans for parish improvement—the renovation of the church and the establishment of a parish school. With regard to the church, in 1782 Molyneux installed pews for which parishioners had to bid at auction and thereafter pay annual rental. Possession of a pew became socially significant and set up a Catholic society in the city, based on wealth. For Molyneux such a distinction between classes was natural because of his background in England, where society had existed that way for centuries. For the American emerging from the Revolution and unwilling to admit that he had fought for an English stratification of society, there was undoubtedly some resentment.

The procedure solved the vexing financial problem, however, and now Molyneux, for whom the education of Catholic children was a matter of great importance, turned his attention to the establishment of a school "where the young might be instructed in their religion and receive a secular education as well." [144] Molyneux eyed the Quaker school, a large and spacious house that stood northeast of St. Joseph's Church. Inasmuch as the Quakers could not maintain it after the war, Molyneux bought the building on February 17, 1781, for 400 pounds.[145] The new school house, a source of pride to the Catholics of the city, was ready for occupation in August, 1782. It was two stories high, and divided into two sections—the upper schoolroom for the younger children and the lower for "such as shall be fit for Writing and Cyphering." The Minute Book of St. Mary's Church contains an entry for September 12, 1782, telling of the administration of Church and school. It reads, in part:

12th. That eight Managers be appointed, with one of the Clergy as President, and one as vice President, who shall have full and absolute power, to carry the foregoing rules and regulations into execution, and to Superintend order and direct, all other Publick affairs belonging to the Church & School.[146]

The concern of the managers for the efficient functioning of the school is evidenced in a Minute Book entry of September 1, 1783, which states:

1783 Sepr 1st. At a Meeting of the Managers, it was agreed
That, as an encouragement to the Childrens improvement at School, premiums be given them four times in the year, Viz. the first Mondays in February, May, August & November, to the Value of Twenty shillings each time.
That, Firewood be supply'd the Schools by the Managers, at the Publick expense.
That, The Schoolmasters pay Twelve Pounds yearly rent each, for their dwelling house, in quarterly payments, from and after the first day of April next, and that in Consideration of the School-rooms, each School-Master shall instruct Six poor Scholars, and be paid for as many as he shall instruct over that Number.
That, the poor scholars be recommended by the Clergy, only.
That in future, no Scholars shall be receiv'd in the lower school-room, but such as shall be fit for Writing & Cyphering.[147]

St. Mary's School in Philadelphia has been termed the mother-school of all parochial schools in the English colonies. It may not have been the first of Catholic educational attempts in Philadelphia, but was certainly the first Catholic schoolhouse of any importance in that city, boasting an upper and lower school, a board of managers, and even a scholarship system whereby cash premiums were given pupils of high academic standing.

Another evidence of the concern and determination of the Jesuits in Pennsylvania to give their best for the furtherance of education is seen in their anxiety for the instruction of the children of exiled Acadians in their midst. These were 454 persons who had become separated from the 6,000 pathetic French Catholics whom the British in 1755 strategically transported from the region of Nova Scotia to the coastal colonies in the south and whom Longfellow's "Evangeline" made memorable. This particular group arrived by ship at the City of Brotherly Love on November 19, 1756—hardly a worse time—and were finally permitted to land three months later. In 1771, a petition was made to the General Assembly of Pennsylvania, begging relief for some poor Acadians, and among others for Ann Bryald, a Catholic, "who acts as Schoolmistress to the Children, and on that account is in need of assistance, as she can not work for a livelihood, her whole time being taken up in the care of them." [148]

## Evaluations, Parallels and Contrasts, and Conclusions

Among other purposes, Spanish missions within the present United States were established for extending the mother country's frontier. The missionaries had one chief aim—spreading the Catholic faith; but since the provisions of the *Patronato Real* also regarded missionaries as agents of the state, the two goals were fused and furthered by the system of education implemented in New Spain. This overall system was democratic, in that it accepted all who voluntarily agreed to submit to the program; realistic, for it considered time, place, and needs of the moment; recognized individual differences, as it drew upon the divergent abilities of the various American Indian tribes; and at least rivalled the mother country in being representative, progressive, and Christian. With regard to the mother country, some would say that the missioners went even beyond contemporaneous education, and if "free air makes free people," they may be right.

The missionaries regarded the City of Mexico as the central office of Spain's outposts of empire. The missioners' enthusiasm for education brought it about that wherever the priests went, a school was established for the instruction of the Indians or a college for its clerics. Half a century before Jamestown was founded by the English, the University of Mexico was conferring degrees—on Europeans, at any rate—in law and theology.[149] As far as the Indian schools were concerned, they were to discipline the native, civilize him, make him self-supporting, and bring him the truths of Christianity, all within the Spanish way of life. These were the ideals, which the missioners realized to a moderate extent. They deplored the exploitation of the Indian which the implementation of Spanish ambitions often occasioned. As far as religion was concerned, the missionaries taught the Indians how to live good Christian lives in their own environment.

Mission schools had, then, a civilizing function. Bolton writes:

While the Church was ever the centre of the establishment, and the particular object of the minister's pride and care, it was by no means the larger part. Each fully developed mission was a great industrial school, of which the largest, as in California, sometimes managed more than 2,000 Indians. There were weaving room, blacksmith shop, tannery, wine-press, and warehouses; there were irrigating ditches, vegetable gardens, and grain fields; and on the ranges roamed thousands of horses, cattle, sheep and goats. Training in the care of fields and stock not only made the neophytes self-supporting, but afforded the discipline necessary for the rudiments of civilized life. The women were taught to cook, sew, spin and weave; the men to fell the forest, build, run the forge, tan leather, make ditches, tend cattle, and shear sheep.[150]

The missions preserved the Indian, and the missioners loved him as a child of God. When possible and advantageous for the natives they taught them to read and write, but for a people moving from primitive living into civilization the missionaries considered technical training as the most suited system of education. The Spanish missions may perhaps fall short of our twentieth century educational standards. "Sometimes," says Bolton, "and to some degree, they failed as has every human institution." [151] It is true that they represented Spain and Spanish conquests, but their educational goal was that of preparing the natives to live in such a way in this world as to ensure their eternal destiny. In these missions of Spanish North America are the beginnings of the history of our West.

Historians claim that on the whole the French regarded the Indian with respect and sought to accept him on his own terms. The missionaries, however, found the Indians difficult to educate and christianize. One of the earliest French missioners, Jean de Brebeuf, S.J., in an account written in 1637, told how he would advise his fellow missioners to conduct themselves among the savages. After explaining the ways of accommodating to savage life, he said:

All the fine qualities which might make you loved and respected in France are like pearls trampled under the feet of swine, or rather of mules, which utterly despise you when they see that you are not as good pack animals as they are. If you go naked, and carry the load of a horse on your back, as they do, then you would be wise according to their doctrine and would be recognized as a great man. Otherwise not.[152]

The Rev. Louis Hennepin of the French Recollects described typical difficulties:

These miserable dark Creatures listen to all we say concerning our Mysteries, just as if 'twere a Song; they are naturally very vitious [sic], and addicted to some Superstitions that signifie nothing; there [sic] Customs are savage, brutal and barbarous; they will suffer themselves to be baptized ten times a Day for a Glass of Brandy, or a Pipe of Tobacco, and offer their Children to be baptiz'd, but without any Religious Motive.[153]

Indian aversion to anything abstract or spiritual, together with a nomadic way of life, made any stable educative influence very difficult. Even the French fur traders and their families followed the Indian way of life, abandoning one trading post after another, so that education was practically impossible among them too. However, not all Indians can be grouped together indiscriminately: of the Illinois, for example, a letter from Gabriel Marest, S.J., to Barthelemy Germon, S.J., provided this account:

The Illinois are much less barbarous than other savages. Christianity and intercourse with the French have by degrees civilized them. This is to be noticed in our village of which nearly all the inhabitants are Christians. It is this also which has brought many Frenchmen to settle here and very recently we married three of them to Illinois women. These savages do not lack intelligence. They are naturally inquisitive.[154]

In addition, Marest expressed the opinion in the *Jesuit Relations* that a change had taken place in the Illinois due in part to the influence of the Christian religion.[155]

Priests on those Indian missions have described their methods of instruction, which was mostly in religion. In the Illinois village of Kaskaskia, for example, Marest described his teaching methods: "Very early in the morning the Catechumens are called to the Church where they offer up prayers. They listen to an instruction and sing a few hymns." [156] Marest would at that point dismiss the Indians and have Mass only for the Christians. The rest of the morning was spent in various kinds of work. Later in the afternoon there were catechism instructions, which everyone was expected to attend. There were no books of religion in the Indian language, necessitating completely verbal instructions. Marest was deeply interested in learning the Indian language, however, in order to improve his facilities for telling the savages about God. When he lived among the Hudson Bay Indians in 1694, he made a dictionary of many words of their language, and he wrote of "translating the Sign of the Cross, the Pater, the Ave, the Credo and the Commandments of God." [157] At the mission of the Kaskaskias, where Marest worked in 1712, he used hymns for instruction because "the words are set to airs which they [the Indians] know, and which are pleasing to them." [158]

In instructing the more difficult Hurons, Brebeuf relates how he called together the Indians with the help of their chief, usually referred to as the captain. Opening the sessions, the Indians chanted, one couplet at a time, the Pater Noster translated into Huron verse. The children then listened to a review of the previous lesson and an explanation of a new one. This was followed by the missioners asking questions and giving a prize of a glass bead or porcelain for correct answers (which the parents were very happy to see their children win). The final part of the session consisted of two young French boys retracing the lesson by asking each other the questions, which motivated the Indians to admire the French. Discipline was usually harsh. Recalcitrant boys were punished by the schoolmaster, and girls by a reliable matron.[159]

Priestley remarks that "amid white and red men alike the Church sought to raise the level of civilization by educational ministrations." [160] Into the wilderness the Jesuit followed his nomad flock and, even though the results may have been meager, the efforts were great. The primitive Indians were not the only source of mission difficulties. Gallicanism, which greatly curtailed the power of the Pope and which held the Church tightly within the State's grasp, was strong in New France. Bishop Laval of Quebec saw its evils in France, where Gallicanism, set firmly in the policy of Louis XIV, made the royal power supreme over national life. On this side of the Atlantic Ocean, Laval faced fearlessly his greatest Gallican opponent, Louis de Baude Frontenac, appointed governor of New France in 1672, Laval giving the order that his priests were to disavow any other jurisdiction than his. After Laval's resignation on January 24, 1688, the struggle of church and state continued. It was only with the crushing of French power in North America by the English in 1759 that the Church of New France wrenched itself from the shackles of Gallicanism. Although the Church in New France, through the influence of Laval and succeeding French bishops, kept on the ultramontanist side of the national church controversy, this struggle had hindering effects on education. The Jesuits, in opposition to state views, believed in teaching the Indian in his own tongue and favored building up a native culture. Priestley observes that "Gallicization produced the *coureur-de-bois* and lapse into savagery, not the elevation of the redskin." [161]

Another weakening movement within the French Church at the time was Jansenism, which emphasized predestination and the irresistibility of God's grace with its working upon the individual soul. Commenting on the confusion, Ellis observes that "the Jesuits vigorously opposed the theological pessimism of the Jansenists with its harshness and moral rigorism, only to have their opponents, in turn, assail them with equal vigor as laxists." [162] Nevertheless, Jansenistic tendencies and beliefs were present even among some members of the clergy. Perhaps the rigorist tradition of spirituality which even to this day pervades certain villages of French extraction in Illinois may well have had its origin in these times. French seminary priests who worked in the Illinois region in the eighteenth century brought with them personal libraries far out of proportion to the immediate needs of the frontier. One of these libraries, which portrayed Jansenist beliefs, was that of the Rev. Domic Marie Varlet, who was sent directly from the Foreign Seminary in Paris to Cahokia in 1712 and who is noted for lending some ninety books to the Tamarois Mission. (Varlet, soon after his return to France in 1718, broke with the Church because of his Jansenist beliefs.) Also remarkable among the mission libraries of that time were those of the Rev. Antoine Davion, who was sent to the Mississippi valley from the Quebec Seminary in 1698 and had 300 volumes,[163] and of the Rev. Pierre Gibault, who came to the Illinois country in 1768 and brought with him a library of 211 volumes.[164] For the masses of French Colonial society, however, educational facilities were lacking and books were few. Illiteracy was prevalent.

In terms of lasting results, perhaps the French educational activity discussed in this chapter was a failure. In spite of the fact that hundreds of priests—Jesuits, Franciscans, Sulpicians, Carmelites, Capuchins, and secular priests—spent a great part of their lives and often their blood in its behalf, the authorities at home and in the colonies were frequently uncooperative. The immorality of whites and natives, the unpredictability of the Indians, tribal warfare, and the continuous wars between England and France were a hindrance to any process of acculturation of either the immigrant or of the native Indians. In New France as in New Spain the government played a major role in missionary activity. French concern for the Indians was economic, built upon the fur trade and political diplomacy in gaining Indian allies against the English. The French Crown, of course, desired the Christianization of the natives and was determined that New France must be a Catholic colony. But education outside of Quebec and Montreal was fragmentary, consisting in religious instruction and means to win the friendship of the Indians in line with the State's objectives.

The missionaries in New France worked with the Indian in the latter's environment and did not attempt to form the natives into well-knit communal groups, as did the missioners of New Spain. Since educational progress requires a certain measure of stability, no mission ruins remain in New France to speak of Indian skill and training. In the new Canadian towns, schools had been established, but the program of study was of an elementary character. Missionary activity consisted mainly in blazing the trail into the unknown frontiers which the trader followed. The Indian tribes encountered on the way were given the missionary's care and concern as he labored to bring them to baptism and to some semblance of Christian civilization. It was not a situation conducive to educational progress or to the foundation of a system that could have lasting effects. (It is from the pens of the missionaries—used in shaky canoes or in dark forests or in smoky wigwams—that we gain a knowledge of the educational endeavors in the wilderness which, for the most part, was New France.) Munroe claimed that the English conquest of 1763 found New France in almost utter stagnation as far as education was concerned. He further commented:

Intellectually, the people of New France comprised on the one hand a small elite and on the other a great unlettered mass. There was no middle class between. Yet the population of the colony always contained, especially among its officials and clergy, a sprinkling of educated and scholarly men. These have given us a literature of travel and description which is extensive and of high quality. No other American colony of the seventeenth and eighteenth centuries put so much of its annals into print; the *Relations* of the Jesuits alone were sufficient to fill forty-one volumes and they form but a small part of the entire literary output.[165]

There are many parallels as well as interesting contrasts between the French and Spanish missionary efforts during the colonial period. Ellis records similarities, for example, in their origins and in their fields of activity:

As Mexico and the West Indies provided the base from which there was launched the Spanish missionary drive on American soil, so it was Canada that furnished the starting point for the advance of the French missionaries into what is today the United States. Likewise as there were five principal areas wherein the Spanish missions occupied a major role in American colonial history, so too, there were five regions of this country whose earliest civilized settlements owed much to the French missionaries, namely, Maine, New York, the Great Lakes, the Illinois country and Louisiana.[166]

The same author draws upon another similiarity when he writes:

The same concept of the Indian as a man whose soul had equal value in the sight of God with that of the white man, motivated the French Jesuit and Recollect around the Great Lakes and through the Mississippi Valley as much as it did their Spanish brethren further south.[167]

If judged by outward success, the missionaries in New Spain were more successful than the missionaries of New France. There were many factors, however, which make such a comparison unfair. New Spain counted its inhabitants in the millions, whereas New France's population never reached more than 80,000. The wilderness was the home of the French missionaries within the limits of the present United States, but there were very different conditions for the mission centers of New Spain. As Bolton put it:

The very mission plants were even built and often served as fortresses, not alone for padres and neophytes, but for near-by settlers, too. Every well-built mission was ranged around a great court or patio, protected on all sides by the buildings, whose walls were sometimes eight feet thick. In hostile countries these buildings were themselves enclosed within massive protecting walls.[168]

The missionaries in Spanish North America attempted to change the social order of the Indians and succeeded to a great degree in destroying the Indians' primitive value systems, which conflicted with those of Catholic Spain. Missionaries in French North America, who worked in a difficult land of harsh climate and savage Indian tribes, were happy when the natives were friendly and embraced Catholicity. There were many diverse motives for the colonization of America: gold for the Spaniards, furs for the French, and national and individual glory for both, but always the propagation of the Catholic Faith in the New World was taken seriously. For the missionaries, who were also the educators, the greatest single objective was the extension of God's kingdom on earth—i.e., of His Church—and this essentially involved the extension of western civilization as well. If this goal did not always succeed in ways one might like, this was because of many complex factors and because of the imperfection of the human vessels who were the instruments—a factor that is still with us.

The thirteen original colonies that were to be the nucleus of the United States inherited the typical English attitude toward education at the time: namely that it was the responsibility of the parents, and the formal schools were to be church-controlled. Education was therefore a church and family affair, and the education of the religious minority groups who were not of the Established Church was of little concern to the Colonial government. Families who could afford it sent their children abroad. Hughes observes:

In the history of the old colonies, and indeed of the new States also, we do not think a parallel can be found to the liberality with which Maryland Catholics provided an expensive education for their children, simply because they wished that education to be Catholic. Nor was there any time, during more than a century previous to the American Revolution, when good parents were not sending their children to the continental colleges and convents of Europe. It was chiefly the boys, however, that they trusted to the perils of a long voyage and journey by land and sea, from the banks of the Potomac to St. Omer's College in French Flanders.[169]

Entrance into European colleges required preparation, however, and the Jesuits were trying to supply this in such places as Newtown Manor and Bohemia.

The educational pattern in the thirteen original colonies was different from that among the Spanish and French colonials, in that it could not be as much equated with Indian education. Also, the English colonies were to have the greatest permanence and influence. This would be especially true ecclesiastically, about which Ellis remarked that

it was the minority group along the Atlantic coastline that set the pattern for future Catholic development, a development destined to reach out to the West and South in the early nineteenth century and there be joined by the descendants of the Spaniards and French where Catholic elements fused on the distant frontiers.[170]

In contrast, when the time arrived for transition to the rule of the New Republic, all that was left of the Church's attempts at education in the Spanish areas were some illiterate Indians around ruined mission compounds. Also, no school survived French entries into the national period, other than the Ursuline school in New Orleans.

## CHAPTER II

# 1784-1828: Formative Foundations

## Relevant Conditions of the Church

THE AMERICAN WAR OF INDEPENDENCE was a struggle for man's sacred rights and liberties. The colonists felt that the British Crown had violated the God-given rights of man. Upon these acknowledged rights and the derived conclusion that they should not permit taxation without representation, they began, fought, and won the war. The American people in the Declaration of Independence expressed unequivocally their belief in the dignity of man, made a solemn act of loyalty to human reason, and founded their new republic on freedom and truth. Catholics were among the first and staunchest patriots in the war for independence and among the first, too, to proclaim religious freedom.[1] During the colonial period, they had been an unimportant minority group in the English colonies. They had been legally and socially discriminated against by the bulk of the population, who reflected prevailing attitudes in the mother country: transformation rarely accompanies transplantation, and the majority of settlers in the new country had brought with them the same prejudices against Roman Catholicism which had prevailed in England. Now, as religious freedom gained ground on an uneven front in the new republic, Catholics won recognition. This new liberty, nominal as it was, raised Catholics to a heretofore unenjoyed equality with their countrymen. Such acceptance was not an overnight accomplishment, but would remain an ongoing struggle for generations: legislation, like transplantation, does little to change men's attitudes.

The period, however, between the Treaty of Paris (1783) and the convening of the first provincial Council of Baltimore (1829) laid the foundations that would be formative for the Church in the United States. To appreciate fully the Church's progress in this era, it is important to keep in mind the difficulties which it faced. Key among them were poverty and insecurity, divisions among clergy and laity, too few priests and teachers to minister to the spiritual and instructional needs of the faithful, need for integration and organization, and some continuation of restrictions upon civil liberties. The man who dominated and shaped the Church within the new republic was John Carroll, S.J., who in 1789 became the first bishop of the Catholic Church in the United States. He was a friend of Benjamin Franklin and an associate of his, invited by Congress to encourage the Canadians to be at least neutral if they were not ready to join the American effort for independence. His appointment to the See of Baltimore tended greatly to ameliorate the Catholic position, and came at an opportune moment. George Washington, with his characteristic impartiality, had publicly acknowledged at the close of the war the patriotic part which Catholics as a group had taken in the great struggle for liberty.[2] Tolerance was dawning, and the Catholic Church needed a leader. It acquired one in Carroll. His personality and his famous name made him acceptable to non-Catholics who might otherwise have been reluctant to accept a representative of Catholicism.

Carroll's task was arduous. Among the scattered 25,000 Catholics,[3] there was only a handful of highly educated men. There was virtually no literary tradition among them, and the typical Catholic citizen of the youthful republic was quite inarticulate.[4] Most Catholics were poorly or inadequately educated—no different in this from their compatriots, with the additional factor that for them educational opportunities during the Colonial period had been furtive and disallowed. The Revolution, with its call to battle, had captured the energies of Americans and had been of graver moment than the building of schools or the promotion of educational ideas. Illiteracy had increased as education had been neglected.[5]

Carroll was concerned over the plight of Catholic education in the new republic. In his first report to Rome on the state of Catholicism in America, March 1, 1785, he expressed the hope of establishing institutions—colleges in particular—"in which Catholics can be admitted as well as others. . . . We hope that some educated there will embrace the ecclesiastical state."[6] In his first pastoral letter as bishop, May 28, 1792, he addressed his flock on the subject of education. "I have considered," he said, "the virtuous and Christian instruction of youth as a principal object of pastoral solicitude."[7] He emphasized "the necessity of a pious and Catholic education of the young to insure their growing up in the faith."[8] He was determined that no longer would it be necessary for American Catholic youth to go to Europe for secondary training.

On December 15, 1791, three-fourths of the states of the young republic ratified the Bill of Rights; its First Amendment to the Constitution assured all Americans that "Congress shall make no law respecting an establishment of religion or prohibiting the free exercise thereof." Nine of the original states, however, had not accepted the principles of religious freedom for all citizens. Guilday asserted:

The Constitutional Congress had done all it could to ordain liberty of conscience throughout the land, but years were to pass before all the States were to accept the principle of complete religious freedom. Some of the dates are significant: Massachusetts (1833); Connecticut (1818); New York (1806); New Jersey (1844); South Carolina (1790), and Georgia 1798).[9]

Colonial education had been a private matter and under the control of the churches, and the writers of the Constitution did not deem it necessary to make any mention of education. The First Amendment, however, freed the Catholic Church, at last, to organize and to extend its work. This freedom of operation was not complete—the worst period of anti-Catholicism in the United States was to come between 1830 and 1860.[10]

Catholic population increased by immigration. The double incentive of freedom of worship and a chance to earn a livelihood in a new land proved powerful attractions to numbers from abroad. The Germanies, disunited at the time, contributed many who fled before the invasion of Napoleon Bonaparte. Although mostly Lutherans, these Germans numbered many Catholics too, and all tended to settle together, retaining their language and customs. The influx of Germans en masse, however, would not begin until the 1840's. French increase in population was not so much in terms of the laity (unless one considers the acquisition of Louisiana in 1803) as it was of the clergy. The French government's demand in July 1790 that clergy subscribe to the oath of the Civil Constitution of the Clergy caused many priests to go into exile. Many came to America and in the following years filled the gap when priests were lacking in this new republic. A number were among the learned churchmen of their day and devoted themselves especially to the cause of education in this country. History during this time reveals an array of French names among the American hierarchy—Bishops Jean Cheverus of Boston, Massachusetts; Benedict Flaget of Bardstown, Kentucky; William DuBourg of New Orleans, Louisiana; Jean Portier of Mobile, Alabama; and Jean DuBois of New York. The successor of Archbishop Leonard Neale to the see of Baltimore in 1818 was the French-born Sulpician, Ambrose Maréchal. During this period and for a long time afterward the largest immigrant Catholic group was the Irish, of whom the famine-ridden counties of southern Ireland yielded the chief portion. Out of a net Catholic immigration of 54,000 for the decade 1820-1830, 35,356 were Irish.[11] (The total Catholic population at the end of 1830 was 318,000. Immigration was occurring at all times from the beginning of the Republic, but it was difficult to estimate growth from 1784 to 1820, as there were no recorded government statistics within those years.)

The bulk of the Catholic population stemmed from largely peasant agricultural backgrounds. A deep conservatism and loyalty to traditional forms allowed little or no hospitality to a free play of the intellect.[12] Different strains of tradition set Catholics apart even from one another. In some cases parishioners were irked by national differences, wherein their assigned pastors were sometimes foreign to them in language and custom. There were also those who, following the lead of ambitious and strongly-willed clergymen, yielded to the persuasion of extreme lay rule and precipitated the early struggle with trusteeism. The system of trusteeism placed financial control of parishes in the hands of laymen selected by the congregation. Property deeds were invested in the hands of lay trustees, and the salaries of pastors depended on the trustees' good will. An example of one of the ways in which it could affect Catholic education came to a climax in New York in 1829, when the plans of Bishop Dubois to secure religious brothers for the teaching of boys seemed ready to come to a conclusion. An organization of brothers from Ireland had agreed to teach both a pay and a free school, all without compensation provided that funds from the former could be used to pay for the latter. The brothers requested a house both for their novitiate and the schools, and asked to be subject exclusively to the bishop. The trustees refused to purchase the house unless they would retain control over both the property and the society, and Dubois abandoned the plan rather than submit.

The Catholic Church in the United States was in a precarious state when the new republic began, not only with reference to the law of the land, but in her internal organization as well. Shaugnessy describes the situation:

Insubordinate priests, a rebellious and haughty laity, high-minded in pride and insolence when their bishop was concerned, but pusillanimous and cringing when they faced their enemies; a Church poor in material resources, and from a legal point of view tolerated only under sufferance; . . . such was the flock of which John Carroll was called to be chief shepherd and pastor.[13]

Then, too, as Diffley observes,[14] there was always the danger of priests forming a national church. There were members of the clergy, however, whose devotion and assistance figured greatly in the progress which the Church made during the early national period. These were few in number and grossly overworked. In Carroll's report on the state of religion in the United States in 1785, he deplored the fact that his priests numbered twenty-four, five of whom were over seventy or very near it. "Some are in very bad health," Carroll wrote, "and there is one recently approved by me for a few months, only that in the extreme want of priests I may give him a trial." [15] By the time Carroll died in 1815, thirty priests had been ordained, and America had become the refuge and new home for many others from foreign lands. In 1818, Maréchal stated in his first report that "there are fifty-two priests exercising the sacred ministry." [16] Maréchal's report indicates not only an increase, but a remarkable one—referring as it does to a proportionately smaller territorial area than had Carroll's. In 1790, the limits of Carroll's vast diocese embraced the entire country. Carroll realized from the beginning the difficulties of ruling this vast See and requested Rome to divide the diocese. Accordingly, in 1808 the diocese of Baltimore was made an archdiocese with four suffragan sees: [17] Boston, New York, Philadelphia, and Bardstown (from 1841, Louisville), Kentucky. Together with westward expansion, this Church reorganization was a key factor setting the stage for the steady growth of Catholic education in this country.

The Catholic Church in the new republic was a poor and pioneer church, and for assistance its hierarchy had to turn to Europe. Three mission societies were organized there which were to help the Church in America over a period of one hundred years. With regard to the first of these, William DuBourg, consecrated bishop of Louisiana in 1815, asked assistance of France, to which country he was no stranger, in building up his diocese, which, as he explained, was larger than France. His request sparked a charitable movement by his wealthy friends which in 1822 resulted in the creation of the Society for the Propagation of the Faith. By the third year of its existence, it was able to send a substantial sum of money to the United States.[18] The second society, the Leopoldinen-Stiftung, was formed in 1829 in Austria to help the missions in North America, and the third, the Ludwig-Missionsverein, originated in 1838 in Bavaria to help the missions of Asia and America, but with special attention to those in the United States.

Priests and bishops were concerned with preserving the faith of their people, the erection of churches, vocations to the priesthood, and—above all—Catholic education. At first there had been the hope that separate Catholic schools would not be necessary, but it soon became clear that Catholics and Protestants could not unite in a schooling that would be satisfactory to all. Many Catholic schools took root in poverty—abandoned buildings or log cabins—set up under the poorest conditions. Teacher shortage presented a grave problem. Priests turned schoolteachers, tending to their flocks on Sundays and instructing classes during the week. Carroll planned help for education in outlying regions when, in these words, he urged parents to send their sons to Georgetown: "Some after being educated at George-Town, and having returned into their neighborhood, will become, in their turn, the instructors of the youths who cannot be sent from home." [19]

The growth of the Church and of Catholic education under these adverse circumstances is related with justifiable pride in the Letter which the American Bishops addressed to Pope Pius VIII, at the closing of the First Provincial Council of Baltimore, in 1829:

Six ecclesiastical seminaries, the hope of our churches, have already been established, and are governed in holy discipline by pious and learned priests; nine colleges under ecclesiastical control, the glory of the Catholic name, have been erected in different states to train boys and young men in piety, arts, and higher branches of science; three of these have been chartered as universities by the legislatures; thirty-three monasteries and houses of religious women of different Orders and Congregations, Ursulines, Visitandines, Carmelites, Sacred Heart, Sisters of Charity, Loretto, etc., are everywhere established in our dioceses, whence emanate not only the observance of the ecclesiastical counsels, and the exercise of all other virtues, but "the good odor of Christ" in the pious training of innumerable girls; houses of religious of the Order of Preachers and the Society of Jesus, of secular priests of the Congregation of the Mission and of St. Sulpice, from which as centres priests are sent out to missions; many schools where the poor of both sexes are taught gratuitously, hospitals where the examples of Christian charity which were formerly unknown, are now daily given by religious women to the great benefit of our souls and of religion. These, Most Holy Father, are the signal benefits which God has bestowed upon us within a few years.[20]

A concept of the progress of Catholic education during this period can perhaps best be gotten by a look at the individual dioceses.

## Educational Conditions

### ARCHDIOCESE OF BALTIMORE

The archdiocese of Baltimore was the action base and center of Catholic education in the United States during the early national period. As early as Colonial times, the Jesuits had hoped to establish a college in Maryland for the education of Catholic youth. Discrimination against the Catholic minority, however, made such a venture but a dream. Then, too, the Jesuits had been suppressed in 1773 by Pope Clement XIV. The Revolution brought a new era of religious freedom and revived in Carroll, a Jesuit himself, the dream of Colonial times. After a journey through the newly formed states, in which he observed the strongly Protestant atmosphere of the existing educational institutions, he wrote on December 15, 1785:

The object nearest my heart now and the only one that can give consistency to our religious views in this country, is the establishment of a school, and afterwards of a seminary for young clergyman.[21]

### GEORGETOWN COLLEGE

The college project was discussed informally among the priests. Some of the Southern District clergy feared that the erection of the college would involve the alienation of the property on the site of Georgetown which originally belonged to the Society of Jesus and which, they thought, should be kept until such time as the Order would be restored. These objections were finally overruled, however, in 1786 at the Second General Chapter of the Clergy held at Whitemarsh, Maryland. Carroll recommended the site in Georgetown, and the assembled clergy passed the following resolutions concerning the school:

1. That a school be erected for the education of youth and the perpetuity of the body of clergy in this country.
2. That the following plan be adopted for the carrying out of the same into execution:

### Plan of the School

1. In order to raise the money necessary for the erecting the aforesaid school, a general subscription shall be opened immediately.
2. Proper pensions shall be appointed in different parts of the continent, West India Islands, and Europe, to solicit subscriptions and collect the same.
3. Five Directors of the school, and the business relative thereto, shall be appointed by the General Chapter.
4. The moneys collected by subscription shall be lodged in the hands of the aforesaid Directors.
5. Masters and tutors to be procured and paid by the Directors quarterly and subject to their directions.
6. The students are to be received by the Managers on the following terms:

### Terms of School

1. The student shall be boarded at the Parent's expense.
2. The pension for tuition shall be £ 10 currency per annum, and is to be paid quarterly, and always in advance.
3. With the pension the students shall be provided with masters, books, paper, pens, ink and firewood in the school.
4. The Directors shall have power to make further regulations, as circumstances may point out necessary.

### Other Resolves Concerning the School

1. The General Chapter, in order to forward the above Institution, grants 100 sterling towards building the school, which sum shall be raised out of the sale of a certain tract of land.
2. The residue of the monies arising out of the sale . . . shall be applied by the General Chapter to the same purpose if required to complete the intended plan.
3. That the Procurator General be authorized to raise the said sum to lay it out for the above purpose as the Directors shall ordain.
4. The General Chapter orders this school to be erected in Georgetown, in the State of Maryland.
5. A clergyman shall be appointed by the Directors to superintend the masters and teachers of the students, and shall be removable by them.
6. The said Clergyman shall be allowed a decent living.

7. The General Chapter has appointed the RR. Messrs. John Carroll, James Pellentz, Robt. Molyneux, John Ashton and Leonard Neale Directors of the school.[22]

Although the erection of the first building of the academy was begun in 1788, Georgetown was not ready for students until 1791. The first student was received on November 22, 1791; he was William Gaston of North Carolina, who would later represent his state in the United States Congress. Jesuits and Sulpicians at first shared the teaching and administrative duties, and in 1798 the Jesuits took over the administration completely. The year 1805 saw Georgetown placed officially in Jesuit charge, to continue under the Society's control until the present time. The early years of Georgetown College were not prosperous ones, but it stubbornly kept its doors open and by 1815 was authorized by Congress to grant academic degrees.[23] By the 1820's it was counted as one of the "outstanding institutions in the country offering a liberal education." [24] As "the oldest Catholic literary establishment," [25] Georgetown University deserves some detailed description of its early years.

Georgetown "University," at the time of its founding, had three divisions—elementary, comparable to today's elementary schools; preparatory, a high school; and the college, corresponding to our liberal arts college. For many years, Georgetown's lowest division was open to any literate eight-year-old of respectable behavior. By the close of 1792, there were sixty-six students in the three divisions, and seven teachers. In the beginning, the students lived in houses in Georgetown and not at the college, where there were no dormitory quarters. The students were, however, under the control and supervision of college authorities. The *College Prospectus* of 1798, probably the first printed catalogue of the college, listed the following itemized rates: "Board: $100.00; Tuition: $26.67; Mending linen and stockings: $4.00; Washing: $6.00; Doctors' fees, remedies, nursing: $3.00; Firewood for schools: $2.00; Pew in Church: $1.00; Entrance Money: $4.00." [26] In the case of some students in special courses, there were specific charges. Dancing, for example, was noted as an extra at $8.00 for a three-month course.

Although most of the students were Catholic, the College was open also to non-Catholics. The latter would board in a separate house, according to the *Prospectus* of 1814, under the inspection of the President and Supervisor, and "would be subjected to the same Rules (Religion excepted) and enjoy the same advantages for their improvement in science with the boarders in the college." [27] Day students were also admitted. They could enter the college yard at 8:00 A.M. and 2:00 P.M., and there is a suggestion of an abuse forestalled or possibly remedied in the rule forbidding them to "take out letters for the boarders without the knowledge and consent of the President of the College."

The curriculum of Georgetown College throughout the early national period was essentially classical. Six years of study were required. "To

sketch, even in outline," comments Daley, "the syllabus of this period
taxes the paper with its weight." [28] But relying on the *Prospectus* of 1820,
the same author describes the study load of the student at that time:

The first class, requirement for which was that the student be able to read,
was Rudiments. Here the young scholars studied English and French grammar, arithmetic, etc., and at the conclusion of the year, were expected to be
able to read and write English correctly. In the following year, Third Grammar, English and French grammar was continued and one of the easier French
authors was read. Composition in French was begun in this year, and toward
the close of the year the students began the study of Latin grammar. Second
Grammar concentrated on the addition of Latin to the curriculum. (The English and French studies continued throughout the six years.) Latin exercises
were done, and the students read "several books of the easy Latin and French
authors, as Caesar, Bossuet's Universal History, etc." A course in Geography
also occupied a part of the year. By the time a student reached First Grammar
he was reading portions of Cornelius Nepos, Sallust, Livy, Cicero's minor
works, and some of Ovid's *Elegies*. In this year, besides Latin and French, he
was introduced to the study of Greek, and before the end of the year was reading portions of the Scripture in Greek, the *Dialogues* of the satirist, Lucian,
and Xenophon's history. History and algebra also took up some of his "leisure"
hours. In Humanities, normally the fifth year, Cicero's minor works and ora-
tions were read, as well as Virgil, Horace, Homer and Livy. History, algebra,
and geometry were continued and "a treatise of mythology learned." The final
year, or Rhetoric, busied the scholars with the rules of rhetoric, Cicero's ora-
tions, Homer, Virgil, Horace, history, and mathematics. Always the emphasis
was on composition. In 1820 it was announced that there would "also be a
class of bookkeeping, for the convenience of those who wish to learn it."[29]

The student took three examinations on this curriculum during the year
—before Christmas, Easter, and the summer vacation. Two days were set
aside for public academic exercises—one in March, and the final exercise
of Commencement at the end of July. The same *Prospectus of Georgetown College, 1820* shows that the academic year ran from September
15 to July 31.[30]

Discipline was strict. Rising was at 5:00 A.M. in summer and at 5:30
A.M. in winter. No one was permitted to rise before the Prefect. Morning
prayers were at 5:45 A.M., followed by Mass at 6:00 A.M. Breakfast was
still more than two hours away. Classes began at 8:15 A.M. and continued
until 11:15 A.M., when the boys walked in single file, according to their
height, to dinner.[31] During this meal, as well as supper, conversation was
customarily barred. Instead, a student read a book or, on appointed
days, delivered a Latin poem or declaimed in English or French. In the
afternoon, there was a study period from 1:15 to 2:15 and classes from
2:15 until 4:45 followed by a half-hour's recreation. Rosary was in common at 5:45 P.M., after which the students studied until seven o'clock, the

hour of supper. The students said their prayers in common at eight o'clock, and at 8:30 all retired to the dormitories.[32]

Only on rare occasions were students allowed to leave the college unattended. Students could visit parents and guardians once a month, but they had to return by 5:00 P.M. The regulations frowned upon students' having much pocket money. The *Prospectus* of 1814 declared:

As long experience has convinced the directors that a profusion of pocket money is very prejudicial, not only to good order, but even to study and application, they therefore request that parents will not be too indulgent to their children, in allowing more than one dollar per month at most and whatever is allowed must be deposited in the hands of the procurator of the house.[33]

In the usual Jesuit manner, teachers encouraged their students to study by the system of emulation. They gave tangible rewards for superior work. Class rank counted and was coveted. Corporal punishment was not unknown, but class demotion and the reading of an offender's faults before the assembled school body proved effective punishments to stir lazy students to greater achievements.[34] Teaching at Georgetown was guided by the principles laid down in the Jesuit *Ratio Studiorum* ("Plan of Studies"),[35] of which Shea writes:

To the methods and spirit of the *Ratio Studiorum* Georgetown University has always been faithful, so far as the circumstances of time and place and available material in scholars and teachers would permit; and in this fact is found the explanation of her great success, and of the exceptionally large proportion of her graduates who have attained distinguished positions no less in literary and learned professions than in the practical management of affairs.[36]

During the years 1784–1828, Georgetown College had fifteen presidents (or superintendents as they were called). The Rev. Robert Plunkett, a man of Carroll's own choosing, was imported from England and installed as first president in the summer of 1791. Although the physical expansion of Georgetown was gradual and the early years discouraging because of lack of funds and students, the College finally prospered, loyal to the fundamental principles of its founder.[37]

SAINT MARY'S COLLEGE, BALTIMORE

The founding in 1803 of the second Roman Catholic college in the confines of the present United States, St. Mary's in Baltimore, was also initiated by Carroll, and has a relationship to Georgetown College. According to Carroll's design, Georgetown was to provide the basic college education which would equip young men to continue their studies at St. Mary's. The initial intention was that Georgetown be a college open to all young men, regardless of creed, and that St. Mary's be reserved exclusively as a seminary for college graduates who wished to study for the priesthood. In ten years only a handful of students transferred to

St. Mary's Seminary from Georgetown, while a quarter of the seminary student body transferred to Georgetown. Clearly, Georgetown was not to be the source of vocations for the newly founded American seminary.[38] When the French Revolution caused some members of the Society of Saint Sulpice to flee to the United States, and Carroll's desire for a seminary brought them to Baltimore, their primary objective was the education of young men destined for the priesthood. Students came slowly, and the Sulpicians decided to open an academy in the seminary building. In 1793, they gathered a few boys of the city for French and Latin,[39] but Carroll disapproved of this procedure because he was afraid it might interfere with Georgetown's enrollment.

In 1799, the Sulpician William DuBourg brought from Havana three Cuban students for whom he opened a school in the seminary. This action was more to Carroll's liking, and he agreed that the school might be continued if it did not enroll American students. Within the same year a new building was erected—St. Mary's College. Carroll, realizing that it was useless to oppose further this educational venture of Du-Bourg's, permitted St. Mary's to be opened in 1803 to all American students, boarders or day students, irrespective of creed.[40] On January 19, 1805, a law was passed by both Houses at Annapolis and signed by Governor Robert Bowie, granting permission to DuBourg and others associated with him in the Baltimore institution of learning "to hold public commencements and confer degrees in any of the faculties which are usually permitted to be conferred in a College or University in America or Europe."[41] St. Mary's College, therefore, held the distinction of being the first *chartered* Catholic university in the United States.[42] In the Commencement of August 13, 1806, the institution conferred academic degrees for the first time. Until the opening of classes in September 1809, only boarders or semi-boarders were admitted to St. Mary's, but in that year day students were permitted to enroll for the various courses. A copy of the printed rules for these day scholars in the Archives of St. Mary's Seminary shows a rigidly strict regimen and discipline similar to Georgetown's.[43]

As for the boarders, their life was well regulated. The daily exercises included rising at 5:30 on weekdays. Twenty minutes later, they had morning prayers, followed by Mass. Study began at 6:30 and lasted to 7:55, followed by recreation for a quarter of an hour. They received breakfast at 8:10, then another short recreation, during which they were permitted no sort of game. Classes began at 8:30 and lasted until 12:55, after which there was a 20-minute recreation until dinner at 1:15. After the afternoon recreation, classes were renewed at 3:00, and continued until 5:00. Supper, preceded by a 20-minute spiritual reading, was served at 7:30. After supper, there was recreation for a half hour, followed by night prayers, after which the students retired to their dormitories. Some of the more interesting dormitory rules were as follows:

1. The students will rise immediately, will dress promptly and modestly. In their dress, they will avoid anything that might suggest peculiarity, anything that might not be in conformity with the rules of modesty.
2. From the beginning of the year until May 1st, no one shall leave his room before the signal is given for prayer. The bell will ring for prayer twenty minutes after rising, after which all the students will go down to the prayer-hall.
3. From the first of May until vacation, the students may obtain permission to rise before the appointed hour. Those who will have obtained that permission will immediately go to the southern campus, and will not remain in the dormitories after leaving their rooms. Permission to rise before five will be given to no one. Those who have the privilege of early rising will keep silence on the way down to the campus and will walk without making any noise, in order not to disturb the sleep of their schoolmates. When they are on the campus, they will remember the purpose for which they rise before the appointed hour is that they might have more time for study.
4. The dormitories will be locked during the day. Everyone is forbidden to go there without special permission.[44]

All the students wore uniforms. The *Rules* prescribed:

The uniform of the College is a blue suit, with a velvet collar, blue trousers, black or dark vest, and a black hat. During the summer, the students will wear a white vest and white trousers. They will wear that uniform whenever they go into the city, whenever they are in the chapel on Sundays and Holy Days, and on all solemn occasions.[45]

There were detailed descriptions of all the rules concerning the dormitories, ranks (all students had to keep ranks, which was the way they moved silently to the chapel or refectory), refectory, study-hall, classes, punishments, permissions, infirmary, chapel, and recreations. It is interesting to note the type of punishment meted out to offenders:

The customary punishments at the college are: a written work to be done in the study-hall; to be deprived of something at meals; to be deprived of some recreation, or of permission to go into the city; to be put into the college jail; finally, to be expelled from the college.[46]

Herbermann claims that St. Mary's College ranked high academically. Its teaching staff was more than adequate, and the proportion of students to instructors was less than in State institutions.[47]

The text of the *Statutes of the Faculty of St. Mary's College, Baltimore,* which went into effect with the 1819 school year, gives a fair idea of the curriculum and the requirements for degrees. The text of the *Statutes,* dealing with Graduation, reads as follows:

No student of the College shall be entitled to the degree of Bachelor of Arts, before having gone through a regular course of studies, including: *Arithmetic, Algebra, Geometry, Trigonometry, Conick Sections, Geography, Natural Phi-*

*losophy*, including, at least, *Pneumatics, Electricity, Galvanism, Chemistry, Opticks* and *Astronomy.*

The *Greek* and *Latin* languages, Rhetoric and Moral Philosophy, including *Logic, Metaphysics* and *Ethics.*

They, besides, shall undergo all examinations that shall take place during their stay at the College. The last year, unless they have begun Divinity, or are about to begin it, they shall write and deliver a speech on a literary, scientific or moral subject, a copy of which shall be left to the College.

Students from other colleges, in order to be admitted to the degree of Bachelor of Arts, must have attended the classes of the College at least during the year. And previous to their being admitted amongst the students, they shall undergo a general examination on what they have studied before.

The degree of Master of Arts shall be conferred on the students of the College, who, two years, at least, after having received that of Bachelor of Arts, will apply for it to the President of the Faculty, provided they can prove, that from the time they left College, they applied to literary or scientific pursuits, produce certificates of moral deportment. [*sic*] [48]

The texts they used during this period show clearly that the chief discipline was intellectual training. Store account-books for the years 1806 to 1808 reveal the following titles:

Kombert, *Arithmetic;* Comby, *English Grammar;* Comby, *Spelling Book;* Young, *Dictionary of English;* Murray, *Grammar;* Murray, *Exercise Book; Visites au St. Sacrament; Manuel du Chrétien; Spanish Grammar;* Fénélon, *Télémaque; Dictionnaire Espagnol* de Ormon; *Mathematical Manual; Oeuvres* de Baileau; Perrin, *Grammar;* Perrin, *Exercises;* A. B. C. *Française;* Scott, *Lessons;* Fleury, *Cathéchisme;* Dommard, *French Grammar; Sallust; Virgil; Fables Françaises;* Gough, *Arithmetic;* Goldsmith, *History of Greece and Rome;* Ross, *Grammar;* Sequet, *English Reader; Cornelius Nepos;* Nugent, *Dictionary; Exhibition de Géométrie; Compendio de Historia Espagna; Novum Testamentum; Imitation de Jésus-Christ; Blossoms of Morality;* Snowden, *History of America; Graeca Minora;* Webster, *Spelling Book; Geometrical Computation; Atlas; Ecolier Chrétien;* St. Jerome, *Liber de viris illustribus;* Glouster, *Greek Grammar; Epitome Historiae Sacrae;* Chambaud, *Fables;* Davidson, *Grammar;* Jackson, *Bookkeeping; Horatius; Tacitus;* Bossat, *Géométrie;* Juvenal, *Satires, Beauties of the Spectator; Orationes Ciceronis;* Ross, *Latin Grammar;* Blair, *Lectures; Xenophon;* Clark, *Homer; Ovid; Beauties of Chesterfield;* Racine, *Grècques; Moralistes Gracie; L'Ami de L'Enfance; L'Etude de L'Enfance; Combat Spirituel; El Hombre Felix; El Tesoro Espagnol; Cours d'Hydrodinanique* [sic]; *Le Modèle des Jeunes Gens;* Bossat, *Higher Mathematics.*[49]

In 1849, the French superiors of St. Sulpice would arrive at the opinion that the college was an undertaking out of harmony with the Sulpician vocation, and arrangements were made with the Jesuits that they should open a college in Baltimore to replace St. Mary's. St. Mary's College, Baltimore, would close its doors in 1852, after having served as an educational center for prominent Catholic and non-Catholic families in Maryland and in the South. When St. Mary's College was permanently closed, the Jesuit institution, Loyola College, would take its place.

## MOUNT ST. MARY'S COLLEGE, EMMITSBURG, MARYLAND

The third Catholic College in the United States was founded by another priest fleeing the terrors of the Revolution in his native France, the Rev. John Dubois. He came to the United States in 1791. By September 24, 1808, he had cleared a tract of land on "St. Mary's Mount" near Emmitsburg, Maryland, about seventy miles north of Washington, D.C., to begin construction of the college that would be known as Mount St. Mary's College and Seminary. Although it was the third Catholic college founded in the United States, in years of service the college is second only to Georgetown University, the seminary second only to St. Mary's of Baltimore. The histories of the college and seminary are so closely interwoven that it is impossible to speak of one without the other. The college history, related in summary fashion in the *Catalogue* for the academic year 1900-1901, states:

> MOUNT ST. MARY'S COLLEGE was founded in 1808 by Rev. John Dubois, afterward Bishop of New York.
>
> In 1812 Rev. Simon G. Brute, afterward the first Bishop of Vincennes, was associated with the founder in conducting the College. The College obtained its first charter from the Legislature of the State of Maryland in 1830, during the presidency of Rev. John B. Purcell, afterward Archbishop of Cincinnati. From the year 1833 Very Rev. John McCaffrey, D. D., presided over the College.
>
> During the first century of its existence many men distinguished in Church and State have been educated at Mount St. Mary's College.
>
> Since its foundation by Bishop Dubois, there has been maintained, in connection with the College, an Ecclesiastical Seminary for the education of missionary priests. Many of the theological students defray their expenses wholly, or in part, by teaching classes in the College.
>
> The institution is under the direction and control of an association of clergymen, and in addition to the clergy, there are in the faculty several eminent lay professors. The number of teachers and tutors furnished by the Seminary is such that classes are limited in membership, so that more than ordinary attention can be given to each pupil.[50]

Actually, Mount St. Mary's history is linked with Pennsylvania. On August 15, 1806, Very Rev. François C. Nagot, S.S., founder and first Superior of St. Mary's Seminary in Baltimore, started a preparatory seminary at Pigeon Hill near Hanover, Pennsylvania. This proved unsuccessful, and the Sulpician Fathers encouraged Dubois, who had not yet been received into their Society, to undertake the humanities aspect of the education of those who expressed a desire to enter the priesthood. The school at Pigeon Hill was transferred to Mount St. Mary's, and Dubois' handful of students increased until by the end of the school year in 1809 there were fifty students in attendance paying $80 per year.[51] Thus began the academic organization of Mount St. Mary's College and Seminary. It must be remembered that the "seminary" was a preparatory seminary, and as soon as preparatory studies were finished the young men were transferred to St. Mary's Seminary in Baltimore. After the arrival of the Rev. Simon Gabriel Bruté, the "Ángel Guardian of the Mount," Mount St. Mary's Seminary became a school of divinity as well as of philosophy and the humanities. He brought his private library with him—a valuable collection amounting to nearly five thousand volumes—and permitted the students to use it.[52] The connection of the Mount with the Society of St. Sulpice was terminated during the administration of Dubois in 1823, and from that time to the present Mount St. Mary's has been under the control of secular priests, who form a corporation, the president of which *ex officio* is the archbishop of Baltimore.

The first rules for the College were published in 1810. The seminarians and those old enough to attend meditations had to get up in silence and begin meditation and prayers at 5:20 A.M. At six o'clock study began, lasting until 7:30 A.M. Then there was Mass on certain days. On Sunday the schedule was not too different: rising was at 6:00 A.M. in the winter and 5:00 A.M. in the summer; nine o'clock catechism was followed by Mass, after which the students filed out two by two to the dormitory; in the afternoon, recreation was permitted until vespers; and in the evening there was spiritual reading and catechism again, followed by supper and night prayers.[53] Included in the daily schedule were prayers, rosary, and spiritual reading, and during these exercises the students sat in their assigned seats in chapel. Every evening the meditation for the next day was read. Class rules were also specified. An interesting one was a rule requiring "good and bad points" to be read after dinner every Tuesday. Those students having bad notes were to be deprived of recreation, while those having none were to have "extra recreation on Saturday night."

The farm was an important part of the college. Its profits in 1811, for example, were $481.00. The old day-book gives us some idea of the great variety of business Dubois had to look after: cattle, hogs, land, rent, annuity taxes, wages, slaves, and everything connected with running the parish, boarding school, and farm.[54] The diary of Dr. William Seton, a student in 1809, indicated that there were not many comforts at Mount St. Mary's. Unbuttered bread and coffee were served for breakfast. For dinner, meat and gravy was provided in abundance. Supper was the same as breakfast, with the occasional addition of a little butter.[55] An account of the college in 1822 included the expenses of the student. Rates were $135 per year, and an extra fee for French was $10. Pens, ink, mending, etc., were $4.50 for the year; use of bedding (unless brought by the pupil) cost $8.00; doctor's fees were $3.00, and 12½ cents were allowed the student per week for pocket money.[56] The Mount enrollment grew: in 1809 sixteen students were enrolled, in 1811 forty, and in 1812 sixty. *The Laity's Directory* of 1822 made the observation that "the number of students amounts to eighty; that of the tutors who are all young men intended for the ministry, amounts to twenty-one, besides three clergymen." [57]

RELIGIOUS COMMUNITIES OF TEACHING SISTERS

The bishop of Baltimore's next care was to introduce into Maryland religious communities of women to instruct young girls and to care for the sick and orphans. Carroll knew that his hope for the Catholic Church in America lay in good schools, and especially in good teachers. The latter was the one great demand: teachers, especially trained teachers—and in many instances the practical steps of religious communities to train teachers preceded those in public schools. The religious congregations had in great measure, due to such catastrophes as the French Revolution, come from Europe. Their ties were there, and they remained in close touch with home. Many Catholic teaching communities date from the founding of the Brothers of the Christian Schools in 1684 by St. John Baptist de la Salle, who may possibly have been the founder of the first normal school of any kind. The Jesuits had behind them the *Ratio Studiorum*, which had appeared in finalized form in 1599, and which recommended a carefully planned teacher-training program. Jesuit teachers were expected to have high mental ability, a liberal education, interest in youth, the ability to work with school authorities, mastery of teaching skills, creativity in new teaching situations, and a high moral character.[58] In the main, Catholic education on this continent followed the European pattern of turning over the work of teaching to religious communities. Two motives prompted this tendency—religious and financial. That those responsible for the formation and training of youth be religious seemed fitting and right. The financial benefits were obvious— that the religious teachers gave little consideration to financial remuneration was of particular advantage in the poverty of the early days of the American Republic.

The first effort made by religious women in the United States during the national period was that of the Carmelite Nuns, of whom the Rev. Charles Neale brought four from Antwerp, Belgium, to found a convent at Port Tobacco, Maryland, in 1790. They had been a cloistered community and were therefore hindered by their rule from opening an academy for girls, which had been Carroll's hope. Carroll wrote Rome for permission to have the Sisters teach school. The Sisters did not act on the permission until 1830, when the community, then numbering twenty-four, moved to Baltimore and opened a school. About 1792, some Poor Clares, driven from France by the horrors of the Revolution, sought a refuge in Maryland. They had a house at Frederick, Maryland, and in 1801 purchased a lot on Lafayette Street in Georgetown, where they opened a school but had a constant fight against poverty. On the death of the abbess in 1804, the community returned to Europe,[59] their early efforts here a failure.

The first community of religious women of *American* origin devoted to Catholic education was the American Visitation Nuns. The Rev. Leonard Neale, then president of Georgetown College, acquired the property of the Poor Clares, and then conveyed it to a group of religious-minded women under the leadership of Miss Alice Lalor, who had been teaching previously in a "free school" (a school open to all) nearby. By 1814, Neale permitted the "Pious Ladies," as they were then called, to take simple vows to be renewed every year. When Nearle became archbishop of Baltimore he petitioned the Holy See for power to erect the community into a convent of the Visitation Order. The Holy See granted the request in 1816, and permitted the Sisters to make solemn vows the following year. Thirty-five Sisters were then in community.[60] The Academy of the Visitation initiated the work of educating girls in the new republic. Its first years were stalked by paucity of funds, few students, and scarcity of vocations. Only the commonest branches of the curriculum were taught—reading, writing, arithmetic, and geography. But the teachers at Georgetown Visitation were fortunate in that they had the guidance and teaching experience of the priests from Georgetown College, especially the concern of the College's president. When the Rev. Joseph Picot de Clorivière, a learned Sulpician, succeeded Neale as the Sisters' director, he also trained the nuns as teachers, and he did it well. In 1828, the Academy received its official charter, signed by President John Quincy Adams.[61] The course of study in 1836 would include the following:

Orthography, Reading, Writing, Arithmetic, Grammar, English Composition, Sacred and Profane History, Ancient and Modern Chronology, Mythology; [sic] most important and interesting experiments in Philosophy and Chemistry, Rhetoric, Versification and Poetic Composition, Geography, Astronomy, the Use of the Maps and Globes, French and Spanish Languages, Music on the Harp and Piano Forte, Vocal Music, Painting in Water Colours, Painting on Velvet, Plain and Ornamental Needlework, Tapestry, Lace Work or Embroidery on Bobbinet, Bead Work, etc. The young ladies in the first class are taught Domestic Economy.[62]

By 1832, the enrollment at Georgetown Visitation Academy would rise to one hundred, and the academy would become one of the most prominent schools for girls in the country.[63]

The second American community of women dedicated to Catholic education was the Sisters of Charity, which came into being through the zeal of Mrs. Elizabeth Bayley Seton. After the death of her husband and her subsequent conversion to Catholicism she planned to offer her services to one of the religious communities devoted to education in Montreal. During a visit to New York, the Rev. William DuBourg met the zealous young widow and, in view of Baltimore's pressing educational needs, suggested that she found a new religious institute by uniting a group of pious women under the rule of some order already in existence.[64] Mrs. Seton went to Baltimore in 1808 and took possession of a little house on Paca Street that DuBourg, then president of St. Mary's Seminary, had prepared for her and her three daughters.[65] Mrs. Seton's view was to begin by opening a boarding school for young ladies, leaving to God and time the formation of a society especially consecrated to religion. In December of the same year, 1808, Cecelia O'Conway, "Philadelphia's first nun," joined her. In the spring of 1809 other aspirants came—Miss Maria Murphy of Philadelphia, a niece of Mathew Carey, and the Misses Mary Ann Butler and Susan Clossy of New York.[66] Formal steps were taken for the organization of the religious community in June 1809. Mrs. Seton was admitted to annual vows, a religious habit selected, and provisional rules adopted. The sisters at first called themselves Sisters of St. Joseph, but then decided to take the name of Sisters of Charity, after the religious Order of St. Vincent de Paul.[67] As the Visitation Academy had been founded in the shadow of Georgetown College, so now the Sisters of Charity's educational endeavors flourished in connection with St. Mary's Seminary in Baltimore.

In 1809, Mother Seton founded the motherhouse of old St. Joseph's in the valley not more than a half mile from Emmitsburg, and established a convent boarding school for young ladies. Thus began the extensive work in education destined for the Daughters of Mother Seton in the United States. Guilday writes:

> The prominent ecclesiastics of the day—Bishop Carroll and Fathers Cheverus, Matignon, DuBourg, David, Dubois, and Bruté, all eminent educators, saw in her [Mother Seton's] conversion and in her devotion to the training of the young the solution of the educational problem which dated back to the earliest Jesuit schools in Maryland.[68]

The primary educational aim of Mother Seton's community was the establishment of free common schools for the poor. The first free parochial school taught by the Sisters and open to children of both sexes was established at St. Joseph's Parish, Emmitsburg, Maryland, on February 22, 1810. Twenty pupils came on the first day. The Sisters habitually gave their needy pupils free meals and free textbooks.[69] The Sisters had to pay for this and for their own upkeep, however, and in addition Emmitsburg was heavily in debt. The Sisters therefore had to open academies for the well-to-do to acquire the tuition fees of those who could afford it; their academy at Emmitsburg was the second permanent academy for girls in the United States. Mother Seton's work extended on every side. A list of the schools founded by the Sisters of Charity of Emmitsburg, Maryland, during this period shows clearly her

deep concern for the free instruction of the poor and her agreement
with the growing movement in America for the establishment of free
schools for those who could not afford to pay tuition:

| Place | School | Foundation Date |
|---|---|---|
| Emmitsburg, Md. | St. Joseph's Academy | July 13, 1809 |
| Philadelphia, Pa. | St. Joseph's Orphan Asylum | October 6, 1814 |
| New York, N. Y. | New York Orphan Asylum and Pay School | August 13, 1817 |
| Philadelphia, Pa. | Free School for German Catholics | October 10, 1818 |
| New York, N. Y. | Free School | May 13, 1820 |
| Baltimore, Md. | St. Mary's Asylum and School (Free) | July 4, 1821 |
| New York, N. Y. | The Lancasterian School | April 30, 1822 |
| Frederick, Md. | St. John's School and Asylum | December 23, 1824 |
| Washington, D.C | St. Vincent's School and Asylum | October 4, 1825 |
| Harrisburg, Pa. | Free School and Asylum | March 4, 1828 [70] |

When Mother Seton died in 1821, in her forty-seventh year, her sisters
numbered nearly fifty and were rapidly increasing.

At St. Joseph's Academy, the primary aim of instruction was the formation of Christian character. Proper environment was a key factor. The
entire order of the day revolved around Christian living, and every
moment of the day was scheduled.[71] Mother Seton, an excellent administrator who kept abreast of the educational trends of the day, and a
practical woman, made her first care the appointment of teachers' duties
and the delegation of authority. There was to be one sister appointed as
head, another as mistress of discipline, and four school mistresses. She
demanded monthly reports on the students; a copy of an original
monthly report card gives an idea of the curriculum set up at St. Joseph's,
and of Mother Seton's desire to develop the entire personality of her girls.

## MONTHLY REPORT

Miss . . .

| | |
|---|---|
| Religion | Exemplary |
| English | |
|   Spelling | Very well |
|   Reading | Very good |
|   Grammar | Very well |
| Writing | Very good |
| Arithmetic | Very good |
| French | |
| Music | |
| History | Very well |
| Bookkeeping | |
| Printing on velvet | |
| Plain work | Very good |
| Fancy work | |
| Embroidery | |

| | |
|---|---|
| Behavior | Very good |
| Talents | Very good |
| Judgment | Very good |
| Memory | Good |
| Temper | Fretful, and has much pride to contend with |
| Application | Good |
| Manners | At times amiable, yet frequently influenced by temper |
| Health | Not good [72] |

Catholics and non-Catholics alike attended St. Joseph's. *The Catholic Almanac* of 1822, referring to the system of education at St. Joseph's, states that although the Catholic religion is the only one taught, young ladies professing any other religion are not excluded, provided that they attend Divine Service and the customary exercises, adding that such a measure was necessary for the good order of the house.[73]

Mother Seton's novices received professional training for their work as teachers almost twenty years before the first public normal school was opened at Lexington, Massachusetts, in 1837. An entry in the Daughters of Charity's first Council Book, dated July 20, 1818, reads as follows:

Finding it advisable to bring forward some Sisters in their education so as to establish to teach the pupils we have resolved to hire women for ironing and washing. . . . Mother, the Assistant and the Treasurer were requested to form a plan of who should be taught, whom to teach and what to do.[74]

This entry may be considered the beginning of Mother Seton's Teacher-Training School at Emmitsburg. Believing firmly in thorough preparation for teachers, she employed the principles of the modern "practice" school, including visitation of classrooms for the purpose of constructive supervision:

Once a month Mother will endeavor to attend every class herself, choosing for it the time which will suit her best and the least foreseen either by the girls or even by the Sisters, in order to witness herself not only the talents, application, and dispositions of the children, but also the capacity, mode of teaching, attention, and success of the different teachers—on the whole, she will take notes that she may be able to judge better of those which will be taken by the Sisters.[75]

Mother Seton used her notes as a basis for a conference with the individual teacher.

### OTHER EDUCATIONAL VENTURES IN BALTIMORE

All these developments gave the archdiocese of Baltimore at this time pre-eminence in education as well as in other ecclesiastical pursuits. Surprisingly for the conditions of this time, even the children of the poor were not forgotten. This was especially true in Baltimore city. The first "common school," as the elementary schools of that day were called, in the entire city of Baltimore was that in connection with St. Patrick's Church. There were at that time no public schools in Baltimore, so this was not only a "first" for Catholics, but also for education in general in that city. It came about in 1815, when the Rev. John Francis Moranville, a Frenchman who came to the United States in 1794 during the French Revolution, opened a school for poor children in connection with St. Patrick's parish, of which he was pastor. He organized "St. Patrick's Benevolent Society," a group of charitable ladies, to provide funds for the school's support. The pupils were admitted without distinction of creed. Almost from the start, there were registered between sixty and seventy pupils. Many, in addition to being admitted to the school, were also clothed by the Society. For a time the Society declined, but Moranville revived it and kept it up even though the parish was quite poor.[76]

The second Catholic school in the city of Baltimore was St. Mary's Free School. Although Carroll as early as 1795 requested a free school in the cathedral parish, it was not until 1817 that this was carried out. The girls' school was opened in February of that year, the boys' school the following December. The girls' school was supported by an association of ladies organized for the purpose, which association also made an appropriation of $200.00 the first year to provide clothing for the pupils. In 1821 the Sisters of Charity from Emmitsburg took charge of the school, and in connection with it opened also an orphan asylum. In 1822 *The Laity's Directory* stated that there were then two free schools in Baltimore,

in which the children are carefully instructed in the various branches of useful knowledge, and at a proper age are apprenticed to such trades as they themselves may incline to, or are supposed to be most advantageous to their future prospect in life. They are generally supported by private donations, and stated collections in the different churches.[77]

The city of Baltimore also established its first school for Negroes during this period. In 1825, when there were only four Catholic churches in the city of Baltimore, the Rev. James Joubert, S.S., founded a religious order of nuns called the Oblate Sisters of St. Francis. Its first three members, all Negro, were Elizabeth Lange, Frances Balis, and a Miss Bogue. They immediately started a school for Negro children. By 1834 there would be twelve sisters. Girls were received both as boarders and as day students. The board and tuition was $4.00 a month. The school, being essentially for the poor, at first concentrated on "industrial" work, but the *Catholic Almanac* for 1835 and 1838 indicates that the curriculum consisted of "English, French, cyphering and writing, Sewing in all its branches, embroidery, Washing and Ironing."[78]

## DIOCESE OF DETROIT

Other signs of Roman Catholic ecclesiastical and educational growth were being shown in Detroit in particular, and in Michigan in general. The Treaty of Paris in 1783 gave the Northwest Territory, including Michigan, to the United States. The British were reluctant to part with Detroit, by then the hub of the Lake District. On the grounds that America had not fulfilled all treaty obligations, a British garrison occupied Detroit. By the Jay Treaty of 1794, the British agreed that the frontier parts in the Northwest Territory would be evacuated, but it was not until 1796 that the Canadian authorities authorized the transfer of Detroit to American control.[79] Ecclesiastically Detroit then came under the jurisdiction of the archbishop of Baltimore. Actually, the Illinois country had been Carroll's responsibility since 1791, when he and Bishop Jean François Hubert of Quebec submitted the problem of jurisdiction to the Propaganda Congregation in Rome.[80] Where was Carroll, already hard-pressed for priests, to find clergy for the Illinois country and now for Detroit? The need was filled by the providential appearance of the Sulpicians, one of whom, Michael Levadoux, set out for Detroit in 1796. In a letter to Carroll, he described the town as not very much:

English traders form practically the entire population. But the shores of the river are inhabited for twelve leagues on both sides making this parish extremely difficult to care for. I have already partially covered it. . . . There are about 110 families, nearly all farmers. . . . A plot of 120 acres has been set aside for the use of the priest on which they have built a pretty rectory whose upper story serves as a church. They have already written you concerning their ardent desire to have a priest sent them.[81]

The historian Stanley Pargellis agrees, indicating that at the time, "French fashions could be seen in Detroit shops in the same year that hounds chased a bear down the main street." [82] Getting back to Levadoux, he expressed the hope that his priest-friend, the Sulpician Gabriel Richard, a refugee from the French Revolution who had been assigned to Kaskaskia in 1792, would be sent to Detroit to assist him. Carroll heeded the request, and Richard came to Detroit in 1798. When in 1801 Levadoux left Detroit because of ill health, Richard became pastor, with the Rev. John Dilhet, S.S., as his assistant.[83]

To trace the history of Catholic, or any and all, education in Detroit during this period is to dwell on the educational contributions of Richard. He was an extraordinary man—a man of inquiring mind and practical approach to problems, as befitted a pioneer priest in Michigan's wilderness —a man who, in the words of Quebec's Bishop Joseph-Octave Plessis, "had the talent of doing almost simultaneously, ten entirely different things."[84] Plessis, who had observed Richard at work, continues his characterization:

Provided with newspapers, well informed on all political matters, ever ready to argue on religion when the occasion presents itself, and thoroughly learned in theology, he reaps his hay, gathers the fruits of his garden, manages a fishery fronting his lot, teaches mathematics to one young man, reading to another, devotes his time to mental prayer, establishes a printing press, confesses all his people, imports carding and spinning wheels and looms to teach the women of his parish how to work, leaves not a single act of his parochial register unwritten, mounts an electrical machine, goes on sick calls at very great distances, writes letters and receives others from all parts, preaches every Sunday and holyday both lengthily and learnedly, enriches his library, spends whole nights without sleep, walks for whole days, loves to converse, receives company, teaches catechism to his young parishioners, supports a girls' school under the management of a few female teachers of his own choosing whom he directs like a religious community, while he gives lessons in plain-song to young boys assembled in a school he had founded, leads a most frugal life, and is in good health, as fresh and able at fifty as one usually is at thirty.[85]

Pargellis, a non-Catholic, goes even further, comparing him to Thomas Jefferson and Benjamin Franklin. Of the comparison with Jefferson, he explained:

Jefferson, probably the most versatile, philosophic and enlightened man ever to be called to the White House, and this gaunt unknown priest from a frontier village were brothers under the skin. Here is the priest, a representative of the Catholic Church, reputedly one of the most conservative of institutions, whose altars had been replaced in the French Revolution by an altar to the Goddess of Reason. . . . And here on the other hand is Jefferson, believing that men were created equal . . . championing "natural" religion or something like it, and helping form in this country a political party that adhered to the doctrines of the French Revolution. Opposites! Yet in their educational philosophy —and I believe that the quickest way to find out what a man really thinks about any great subject is to ask him what he thinks about education—Jefferson and Richard were disciples of the same master.[86]

Of the comparison with Franklin, Pargellis elaborated:

Benjamin Franklin has been called the father of almost everything; father of circulating libraries, father of American spelling reform, father of daylight saving, inventor of bifocal lenses, of the United States Postal Service, of the lightning rod, father of fire insurance. Father Richard was a father in more than name in Michigan, and would have fathered much more had his resources matched his restless spirit.[87]

Richard, working in the largest city west of the Alleghenies, had education in his blood. Inasmuch as he was a Sulpician, one would expect that he would have been interested in the education of seminarians alone. The truth is that he was interested in the education of all—boys and girls, Indians and whites. He wanted to educate the Indians so that they would not be just nomads, but farmers—he therefore educated them in the use of farm implements, way ahead of his time. He wanted to give white boys manual training, which was a foreshadowing of the laboratories and other forms of objective-type training that would come much later. And he was, of course, interested in the moral training of all: whites and Indians. Pargellis points out that "more than half of those things which he did . . . had to do with the instruction of both young and old," and that

he imported a printed press, machines for teaching useful arts, an air-pump, an organ, a set of Napier's bones [ancestor of the slide rule], a surveying compass, an optical machine, encyclopedias, globes and maps, and so committed himself to expenditures which he could not possibly meet without continued Federal support.[88]

Richard gave thirty-four years to Detroit, during which—in the words of a former Presbyterian governor of the state—"perhaps [his] chieftes contribution . . . was education, education, education."[89]

Although there is a recorded account in the St. Anne Church register of one Jean-Bapiste Roucout as the "master of the Christian schools in this town, and choirmaster of this parish,"[90] and although we have already remarked that before 1796 there were several schools in Detroit, especially for the children of the English-speaking residents, Paré claims that it is vain to search for any evidence of a school conducted under church auspices from 1791 to 1804. At that latter date, Richard was to make his educational influence felt. Richard's first educational project was a seminary; in October 1804, he and Dilhet opened their "clergy school" in some rooms of the rectory, and the student enrollment was nine. The course of study included Latin, geography, history, sacred music, and mental prayer.[91] The school was shortly abandoned because of "the scarcity of scholars."[92]

Richard was concerned also for the education of girls, but where would he find trained teachers? He set to work, with Dilhet's help, to train his own. He gathered together four young women from Detroit's best families—Angelique Campau, Monique Labadie, Elisabeth Williams, and Elizabeth Lyons—who were to lay the foundation of the Catholic School System of Detroit. After two years of preparation, the earliest instance of teacher training in the Northwest Territory, the ladies opened an academy in 1804. Richard believed in specialization, so "each of the teachers was prepared for a particular department of school work."[93] Richard had, no doubt, the idea of founding a religious community of sisters, but this was not to be, although Richard referred to their house as the Monastery of St. Mary's, and addressed the teachers as "Sisters."

Fire destroyed Detroit in 1805, and its smoldering ashes sparked in

Richard a determination to build schools. His first thoughts were for a public education for all. To obtain support, he petitioned the legislature for assistance. His language is, here as elsewhere, redolent of his French accent (not surprisingly, at a time when three-fourths of the people of the Northwest Territory liable to taxation did not understand English):

Gabriel Richard prays that for the purpose of erecting a college in which will be taught the languages ancient and modern, and several sciences and enabling him to render the education partly Gratuitous, the corner lot on the military square of the section number 3 and the whole section or a part thereof according to the will and benevolence of the Legislature be given.[94]

Another plea to the same legislative body was presented in the name of Angelique Campau and Elisabeth Williams:

Angelique Campau & Elisabeth Williams pray that the corner's lot on the military Square of the section number 2 and some of the adjacent Lots of the same section, as many as the Legislature shall think proper, be given for the purpose of erecting a young ladies school, together with a lot in the old shipyard on which stand the Barracks.[95]

The fact that the petitions met with no response did not daunt Richard. His was a comprehensive plan for Detroit, and he laid it before the legislature on October 18, 1808. He stated simply his accomplishments and his plans:

Our neighbors on the British side are now erecting a large stone building for an Academy. The undersigned being sensible that it would be shameful for the American Citizens of Detroit, if nothing should be done in their territory for a similar and so valuable Establishment, begs leave to call the attention of the Legislature of Michigan to an object the most important to the welfare of the rising Generation which cannot be but of little advantage, if it is not highly patronized by the Government.

The Honourable Legislature partly knows what has been done by the subscriber for the establishment of schools, and for the Encouragement of literature, scientific knowledge and Useful Arts in this part of the Union. Besides two English schools in the Town of Detroit, there are four other Primary schools for boys and two for young ladies, either in Town, or at Spring Hill, at Grand Marais, even at River Hurons. Three of these schools are kept by three Natives of this Country who had received their first Education by the Reverend Mr. J. Dilhet and of whom two under the direction of the subscriber have learned the first Rudiments of English and Latin Languages, and some principles of Algebra and Geometry so far as to the immortal Archimedes; by necessity they have been forced to stop their studies and to become masters and teachers for others. At Spring Hill under the direction of Angelique Campau and Elizabeth Lyons, as early as the ninth of September last, the number of the scholars has been augmented by four young Indians headed by an old matron their grandmother of the Potowatamies tribe, five or six more are expected to arrive at every moment.

In Detroit in the house lately the property of Captain Elliott, purchased by the subscriber for the very purpose of establishing one Academy for young ladies, under the direction of Miss Elisabeth Williams there are better than thirty young girls who are taught as at Spring Hill, reading, writing, arithmetic, knitting, sewing, spinning, & in these two schools there are already nearly three dozen of spinning wheels, and one loom, on which four pieces of Linen or woollen cloth have been made this last spring or summer.

To encourage the young students by the allurement of pleasure and amusements, the undersigned had these three months past sent orders to New York for a spinning machine of about one hundred spindles, an airpump, an Electrical Apparatus & as they could not be found he is to receive these falls [sic] but an Electrical machine, a number of cards, and few colours for dying the stuff already made or to be made in his Academy.

It would be very necessary to have in Detroit a Public building for a similar Academy in which the high branches of Mathematics, most important languages, Geography, History, Natural and moral Philosophy should be taught to young Gentlemen of our country. . . .

The undersigned acting as Administrator for the said Academies further prays, that, for the Encouragement of Literature and useful Arts to be taught in the said Academies, one of the four Lotteries authorized by the Hon. Leg. on the ninth day of September 1805, may be left to the management of the subscriber as Administrator of the said Academies.[96]

Richard submitted his "Outline of a Scheme of Education for the Territory of Michigan"[97] to the United States Congress in 1809. It holds his ideal of vocational and industrial education to fit youth for afterschool life. He treats at length the problem of Indian education. A new Congress was in Washington, however, and James Madison, not Thomas Jefferson who had believed in Indian education, held the presidency; and so Richard's plans were again ignored. His vision spread too wide. But, says Sister M. Rosalita, "When the War Department sought to formulate a plan of education that would measure up to the needs of the Indian, it took over a system presented by Father Richard to the United States Congress a decade before."[98] Richard deserves the title of Father of Modern Indian Education.

In 1810 Richard was greatly worried by lack of funds to keep the school functioning in Spring Hill. Jefferson had promised him "that some kind of Agreement should take place between the Dept. of the Treasury and the Dept. of War, in order to make the school of Spring Hill enjoy the premises without paying any rent."[99] Now Richard was being pestered for rent. Spring Hill had to go, and Richard started all over again on the Loranger Farm.[100] Here his school and rectory were one.

Richard was also a pioneer in the publication of schoolbooks. While on a visit to the East in 1808-1809, he obtained a printing press. At this time—less than four years after the complete devastation of Detroit by fire—he had this press brought in wagons from Utica, New York, with about 600 pounds of type. By August 1809, he had the press operating, and on August 31 he published Detroit's first newspaper, *The Michigan Essay.*[101] The chief value of the press lay, however, in its output of books

for educational purposes. (Although the press of John McCall had preceded the Richard Press, it never, as far as is known, produced any
books.) [102] The first work to issue from the press was *The Child's Spelling Book* or *Michigan Instructor*. It was actually a twelve-page pamphlet,
and the preface, dated August 1, 1809, stated:

> The great scarcity of School Books in the Territory, is a sufficient apology
> for the appearance of the following pages. This small book is chiefly selected
> from other writers. . . . It is intended to answer the purpose of introducing
> the Youth of this Territory, into the fundamental principles of Education. If it
> gains encouragement it will, perhaps, be succeeded by another Part containing
> Spellings of a maturer kind, intermixed with useful Lessons in Reading: such
> as, Maxims, Proverbs, Fables, Moral Stories, & calculated to inspire the youth-
> ful mind, with a sense of strict propriety and virtue. At the request of several
> Gentlemen and Teachers of this City, it is sent to the Press:—and it is hoped
> that it may meet the approbation and liberal patronage of a generous public.[103]

The press produced "not less than nine books, all but one of which were
intended for use in the schools Father Richard established in Detroit." [104]
None was original, with the possible exception of the speller, and Richard
used at least one of them, *Les Ornemens de la Mémoire*, [105] as a prize for
pupils. After 1816, the press ceased to operate, as far as is known.
Woodford and Hyma observe:

> All told, there was a total of fifty-two known imprints. *The Child's Spelling
> Book* . . . was followed over the years by a succession of such titles as *The
> True Principles of a Catholic*, in 1810; collections of prayers and other re-
> ligious items; school books and reprints of classical works, including a collection
> of La Fontaine's fables. Many of these books reflect the need as well as the
> influence of Richard; they were intended for his pastoral use, for the instruction
> and elevation of the Catholic mind. Most of the published works in the latter
> category bore French titles and were in French text, but some were in English.
> As far as can be determined, Richard wrote nothing original for publication,
> unless it was the spelling book, although, as has been stated, he was the
> translator of some of the press's items.[106]

Richard's long-range plans embraced a Catholic school system set on
firm foundations, and with that end in view he drew up in 1815 a draft
of resolutions for a "Society of the Catholic Schools in the Territory of
Michigan." An examination of the draft shows it to be a plan for the
constitution of a religious order.[107] Religious orders are not so easily
founded, and Richard's plans needed more time than his lifespan to
come to fruition. The first native Michigan sisterhood, the Congregation
of the Sisters, Servants of the Immaculate Heart of Mary, would be
founded November 10, 1845, by the Redemptorist Father Louis Florent
Gillet.

The year 1816 brought Richard a new friend in the person of the
Rev. John Monteith, Michigan's first established Protestant clergyman.
Both men were deeply interested in education and in the idea of a

territorial university. One with them on this matter was Judge Augustus Woodward, a Washington lawyer who had been appointed a judge of the Michigan Territory in 1805. The determination of judge, priest, and minister resulted in the governor and judges passing in 1817 "An Act to establish the Catholepistemiad or University of Michigania." [108] This was, of course, due mostly to the efforts of Richard, and in speaking of it Pargellis once again harkens back to Jefferson, observing that

if Jefferson, in 1819, pushed through the charter for the University of Virginia, in the oldest and proudest state in the Union, Father Richard, two years before, in one of the youngest and most primitive of settlements, had helped push through the act founding the University of Michigan. [109]

By Richard's wish, the office of president of the University was conferred upon Monteith, and Richard was appointed vice president. Richard was also appointed professor of Intellectual Sciences, and of Mathematics and Astronomy. [110] As far as can be determined, however, no courses other than academic were offered. In 1821, control of the Catholepistemiad was taken over by a board of trustees, and on this board Richard served as a member. [111]

A grateful people elected Richard as territorial delegate to the United States Congress in 1823. His appearance in the House of Representatives caused a sensation: he was the first (and only, in the light of subsequent history) Roman Catholic priest to be one of its members. In Washington, his interest in education did not end. He succeeded in getting a grant for the establishment and the maintenance of schools for the Indian tribes that came under his spiritual jurisdiction, and in 1825 set up classes for deaf-mutes, again being ahead of his time and place in using the methods of the Abbé Sicard.

Richard died in 1832 (having been born in 1767), a victim of Asiatic cholera. At his death, his library collection consisted of over 2,000 volumes, covering every field of human interest. It is astounding to see that, in the 38 legal-sized photostat pages of inventory of Richard's estate in the Burton Historical Collection of the Detroit Public Library, 33 pages list books, [112] and it is profitable to peruse the other lists of Richard's books in the same collection: for example, "Manuscript Books Compiled by Father Gabriel Richard"; "Books from the Library of Father Gabriel Richard in the Burton Historical Collection"; "Books from the Library of Father Gabriel Richard to Go to the University of Michigan from Sacred Heart Seminary"; and "Books from the Library of Father Gabriel Richard of Detroit, Each with His Signature on Fly, End Paper or Title Page." Richard had been the perfect embodiment of the words of the Ordinance of 1787 that "religion, morality and knowledge being necessary to good government and the happiness of mankind, schools and the means of education shall ever be encouraged." And Detroit has not forgotten its "second founder." More than one public school is named after him.

The mosaic in the Greyhound bus terminal centers around him, and contains an Indian kneeling before him, two of his schools, and the first building of the University of Michigan. And his is one of the four statues on the facade of Detroit's City Hall. His greatest monument, however, is that he still influences the schools in and around Detroit.


### DIOCESE OF BARDSTOWN, KENTUCKY

Most gratifying during this period is the history of Catholicism and its educational endeavors in Kentucky and the Western territories. This does not pretend anything great by modern standards, but simply indicates that Catholic education maintained, at the very least, the standards of other schools of the time and place. It did not substantially differ, for example, in peripheral conditions, some of which Marcelle points out.[113] The common rate of tuition was 1 pound, 7 shillings per year, paid in such items as tobacco (then legal tender in Kentucky), bear bacon, buffalo steak, jerked venison, furs, young cattle, corn, or whiskey. The teachers were sometimes fit, sometimes not; frequently they were rough, irascible, and addicted to the use of the rod. Often they were travelling Englishmen or wandering Yankees whose major qualification seems to have been the supposition that they had seen a great deal of the world. The buildings were usually "field schools," built on land that could not easily be used for anything else, and there were many orphans because of parents' early death due to hard labor, epidemics, and the new climate.

Before Kentucky was admitted to the Union as the fifteenth state in 1792, there had been colonies of Catholics in the general vicinity of Bardstown. The original Catholic migrants to Kentucky came chiefly from Maryland; dissatisfaction with conditions in the Atlantic states caused them to follow rumors of freedom and unlimited opportunities in the West. Webb reports:

In the year 1785, "a league" of sixty families was formed in Maryland—all Catholics and mostly residents of St. Mary's county—each one of whom was pledged to emigrate to Kentucky within a specified time. Their purpose was to settle together, as well for mutual protection against the Indians, as with the view of securing to themselves, with the least possible delay, the advantages of a pastorate and a church. They were not all to emigrate at once, but as circumstances permitted.[114]

Carroll, first as prefect apostolic and then as bishop after 1790, sought an opportunity to send a priest to the Catholics in Kentucky, and in a letter to the Rev. Stephen Badin, he referred to his many fruitless efforts to secure a priest for the "good Catholics of Nelson County." [115] In 1787, Carroll sent to Kentucky the Rev. Charles Maurice Whelan, an Irish Capuchin, who abandoned his mission three years later.[116] He was succeeded by William de Rohan, "one of those banes of Bishop Carroll's life, a wandering priest," [117] to whom nevertheless must go the honor of having erected Kentucky's first Catholic place of worship—the log chapel of Holy Cross at Pottinger's Creek in 1792. The following year—the year of his ordination to the priesthood—brought Badin to the state, and with his coming the story of Catholicity in Kentucky may be said to enter its first distinct chapter.

Badin, the first priest ordained in the United States, was to earn the title "Apostle of Kentucky." Young and inexperienced, he did not want the Kentucky assignment, but when Carroll insisted, he accepted and spent himself thoroughly in the development of his mission. The Rev. Michael Fournier arrived to assist him in 1797, and the Rev. Anthony Salmon in 1799, but within a few years the hardships of frontier life brought quick death to both. In a letter to Carroll on May 27, 1799, Salmon wrote of the people "in this country [as] backward . . . mean [and] narrowminded." [118] The restless, talented Father John Thayer gave four years of off-and-on service in Kentucky from 1799 to 1803, but proved more of a hindrance than a help to Badin. On the whole, it was Badin who from 1793 until 1805 prepared, as it were, the Catholic soil of Kentucky for the educational plantings of such great men as the Revs. Charles Nerinckx; Edward D. Fenwick (consecrated bishop of Ohio in 1822); Benedict Joseph Flaget, first bishop of Bardstown in 1808; and John B. M. David (made coadjutor to the bishop of Bardstown in 1819), whom Flaget brought to that county for the purpose of opening a seminary.

By 1804, Badin was alone in Kentucky, and the Catholic population had grown. Of that time, he wrote to Bishop Leonard Neale:

After the death of the Rev. Mr. Fournier, . . . I found myself charged alone with the care of 8 or 9 hundred families, amounting at a moderate calculation to at least 6,000 individuals, white and black, occupying 800 miles square, besides the distant congr. of St. Francis, St. Peter, St. Christopher, etc.[119]

In 1805, however, he had the joy of welcoming Nerinckx, who had come from Belgium to Baltimore the year before to offer his services to Carroll. Of less help to Badin was a colony of Trappists who arrived in the fall of 1805. They first took their residence at Pottinger's Creek, then in 1807 moved to Casey's Creek, in 1809 to Florissant, Missouri, and finally to Illinois, but returned to Europe in 1813. Another group of religious was to prove of greater stability, and to make a permanent establishment in Kentucky. They were English Dominicans led by Fenwick, a native of Maryland. Fenwick, having been authorized by Carroll to establish a province of his order in the United States, was directed to go to Kentucky, where he made a preliminary visit in 1805. On June 22 he was appointed provincial. He sent in advance the Revs. Samuel T. Wilson and William R. Tuite and joined them in 1806 when he settled at what is now St. Rose's Farm in Washington County. St. Rose's Priory was formally opened in December, Fenwick having resigned his charge of provincial in September. Carroll's letter of approval, written April 25, 1806, refers to the plan of establishing a Dominican college. The bishop wrote:

The Reverend Mr. Edward Fenwick and other Reverend Clergymen connected with him, having proposed to themselves the establishment of a college or academy in Kentucky, for the education of youth, I not only approve of but greatly rejoice at their having formed such a resolution, which if carried into effect cannot fail of producing the most beneficial effects for improving the minds and morals of the rising generation fortifying their religious principles.[120]

The school opened in 1807, with about a dozen pupils, the institution taking the name of St. Thomas College.[121] Spalding claims that by 1820 the school was closed, for the main work of the Dominicans for many years to come was on the missions.[122]

When in 1810 Flaget was consecrated first bishop of Bardstown (created as a diocese in 1808) he was so poor and the Church in Kentucky so devoid of resources that he had to collect from his friends in Baltimore the means to undertake the long journey to his diocese. It was a vast diocese, comprising the three states of Kentucky, Tennessee, and Ohio, with the territories of Indiana, Illinois, and Michigan. There were ten churches, all but one being log structures, and six more in process of erection. The Catholic population, estimated at 6,000, was attended by two secular priests, Badin and Nerinckx, and three Dominicans: Fenwick, Wilson, and Tuite. Richard was at Detroit, and the Rev. Donatien Olivier was at Kaskaskia.

Amid these pioneer conditions Catholic education in Kentucky made great strides. The establishment of schools was uppermost in Flaget's mind, and he infused his zeal for education into the clergy of his diocese. From the beginning he gave every encouragement to St. Thomas College. He made provision for the development of a native clergy and for that purpose had David initiate seminary studies. In 1819, St. Joseph's College was opened in the basement of David's seminary at Bardstown, and although a separate building for the college was erected the next year, the elementary school continued in the seminary basement. In 1821, St. Mary's College was begun in Marion County, Kentucky.

"THE HOLY LAND"

But the red-letter year in the history of religious life and Catholic education in Kentucky was 1812. In that year, Flaget blessed the foundations of two communities of women religious whose names are inseparably associated with Kentucky: the Sisters of Loretto, Kentucky, and the Sisters of Charity of Nazareth, Kentucky. The *Relatio* which Flaget sent to Rome in 1815 was proof of a diocese on the move and with much work to be done.[123] Before the period under present discussion ended, a third sisterhood entered the scene—the Dominican Sisters in 1822. Because of the great educational work of these three communities which were within a few miles of one another, this territory is to this day called "The Holy Land."

The solution to the problem of providing teachers for Catholic schools in Kentucky seemed to Nerinckx to lie in the organization of a religious community. That was the way it was done in his native Belgium and that was the way he could meet the needs of the times in America. He and Badin considered a teaching sisterhood important even before Flaget came to Bardstown, and he had made an attempt to organize a religious community as early as 1805; but there was a setback when the building erected for the nuns was destroyed by fire. Nerinckx did not give up hope, however, and in 1812 conditions offered another opportunity. Mary Rhodes, convent-educated and recently arrived from Maryland, had opened a little school in an abandoned building in Catholic Hardin's Creek, near St. Charles' Church in Marion County. At the suggestion of Nerinckx, Christine Stuart joined her. The two girls moved into a poor cabin which adjoined their schoolhouse, began to follow a religious routine, and soon admitted a third young lady, Anne Havern. The three begged Nerinckx for direction and advice in forming some sort of religious community, and with Flaget's approval Nerinckx took up the task of guiding them. Thus the first of the communities in Kentucky, the Friends of Mary at the Foot of the Cross (today known as the Sisters of Loretto), was founded at St. Charles, Kentucky. Nerinckx clothed three young ladies in the religious habit on April 25, 1812, and two more on June 29.[124] Their first school, elementary in character and begun in a rude log cabin at St. Charles, was afterwards transferred to the more substantial property of Badin called St. Stephen's Farm at Loretto, Marion County, where the Sisters added Loretto Academy about 1826. At this time the program of study included, besides the primary branches, literature, modern languages, mathematics, astronomy, drawing, painting, and every kind of needlework.[125] No effort was spared to prepare the Sisters for their work as religious teachers; professors from St. Mary's and St. Joseph's College gave them courses in elementary as well as higher branches, and special instructors trained them in art and music. As their number increased they opened other schools, with the result that in 1825 they were conducting five institutions in Kentucky and one in Missouri.[126]

In the same year that the Sisters of Loretto were being organized, a second religious community, the Sisters of Charity of Nazareth, was taking shape under the zealous direction of John B. M. David, head of the diocesan seminary at St. Thomas, near Bardstown. Encouraged by Flaget in his desire to provide further facilities for the education of Catholic youth in Kentucky, David made an appeal for candidates for the proposed foundation during the summer of 1812. In November 1812, Teresa Carico presented herself as a candidate, and in December a second woman, Elizabeth Wells, came with the same intent. In the following January, Catherine Spalding joined them, to be followed several months later by Mary Beaven, Harriet Gardiner, and Mary Gwynn.[127] In June 1813, the sisterhood may be said to have been formally organized, and the nineteen-year-old Catherine Spalding was chosen as the first Superior. David wrote of the event in a letter to Bruté:

We have also started the work of our community of women, upon the foundation of the excellent and inimitable Mr. Nerinckx, whom I can't follow unless from afar. I have assembled 6 women in a house of beams, which is upon our plantation, a half mile from the seminary. It was the dwelling place of a tenant, a house of 18 ft. square on two floors, that is to say, a room below and one above—that's all—adjoining it there is a little log house which serves as kitchen and the loomroom. As soon as there were 6 they assembled in the little chapel of the seminary, after having listened to the Mass of Mgr. at which they were communicants, after a quarter hour of act of grace, they passed one by one into the neighboring room, and gave their votes to Mgr. and to me in the presence of Mr. Chabrat for a Mother, an assistant, and a procuratrix, after which they kissed the hand of their Mother (who by the way, is the youngest of all except one). They received from the mouth of Mgr. the advice which the Holy Spirit evidently dictated, and soon they retired. They have since started their school. They have only two boarders and one or two day students. These are the smallest beginnings, but like I have always desired.[128]

The sisters, not considering themselves competent to teach, spent one year in preparation under the able direction of David before opening their first school for boarders and day scholars near St. Thomas' Church in 1814. The school and teaching reputation of the sisters grew, the enrollment increased, and after four years a larger school building of brick was erected. In 1822, the sisters moved from the first Nazareth to a new site two and a half miles north of Bardstown, and there permanently established the motherhouse. Even before this date, the sisters had founded branch convents and schools. In 1819, they opened the Bethlehem day school in Bardstown; the next year the sisters made an unsuccessful attempt to set up a school at Long Lick, Breckenridge County, where they founded St. Vincent's academy and parochial school; in 1823, Mother Catherine, accompanied by three sisters, opened St. Catherine's School in Scott County; in 1824 the sisters attempted to establish a school at Vincennes, but the absence of a resident priest made their enterprise impossible.[129]

There is no printed copy available of Nazareth's curriculum during this period. *The Catholic Almanac* for 1833-1835, citing the advantages of Nazareth Academy, gave an account of the subjects taught at the time. They included reading, writing, arithmetic, English grammar, geography (with the use of globes), history, rhetoric, botany, natural philosophy including the principles of astronomy, optics, chemistry, plain sewing, marking, needlework, drawing, painting, music, and the French language. The lectures on rhetoric and philosophy (natural and moral) were given by the professors of St. Joseph's College. In point of health, pleasantness, retirement, water, etc., the *Almanac* claimed, Nazareth Academy's situation was inferior to none in the Western country. The school was conducted on principles similar to those of St. Joseph's College, and was under the supervision of the bishops and the inspection of the president and principal professors of the College who quarterly examined the pupils and encouraged their progress. The poor were not forgotten at Nazareth, and a certain number of orphans or destitute children were received upon application. Nazareth Academy's annual vacation extended from the last Thursday of July to the first Monday in September.[130]

The third religious community in Kentucky was founded in 1822, eight years after the Sisters of Charity, when Thomas Wilson, O.P., Superior of the Dominican Order, affiliated nine young ladies with the Order of St. Dominic.[131] Soon they began their first school, the Academy of St. Mary Magdalene, later renamed the Academy of St. Catharine of Sienna, on a farm donated by the father of Mother Angela Sansbury, the first prioress. Despite the usual material obstacles, the school prospered, a fact attested to by their completion of new and larger accomodations in 1825. In 1830 the community, in answer to the request of the Right Rev. Edward Fenwick of Cincinnati, would open their first branch house, a foundation at Somerset, Ohio, to be followed by others in Memphis, Tennessee (1851), and Springfield, Illinois (1873). Webb relates that the school of the Dominican Sisters began with fifteen pupils, and that to raise money for its support and for larger buildings the sisters tramped the country, two by two, begging. To further their own studies they submitted to the direction of the better instructed sisters in the community and to teachers whom they brought from outside.[132]

UNSUCCESSFUL EDUCATIONAL PROJECTS

Nerinckx tried unsuccessfully to found two other religious communities. In 1819, in a letter to his parents, Nerinckx related Flaget's wish for him to establish a religious brotherhood to teach young men and boys.

The object is to have a religious community of men whose aim would be the education of boys, especially those of the middle classes and orphans, whose poverty so often prevents the Church and State from being benefited by their talents.[133]

Nerinckx went to work on this project without delay. He made an appeal to Catholics of all the surrounding counties, requesting a generous contribution. He collected three thousand dollars, and purchased a farm of 311 acres. It was christened Mount Mary's and was intended for a Brotherhood of the Loretto Society. Later in the same year, fire destroyed the main building and four of the smaller ones—a setback not only because of financial loss, but also because several young men had been hoping to join the Brotherhood.

Unceasing in his efforts for the education of all classes, Nerinckx long cherished also a hope of founding, in connection with his Society of the Friends of Mary, an institute of Negro sisters to teach Negro students. With this end in view, he caused a few young Negro children to be adopted in Loretto. In May 1824, he announced that these adopted Negro girls had been admitted to the religious life at Loretto and had a specific religious habit and special rules. Nerinckx's death, however, on August 12, 1824, put an end to this charitable project, as no one made any further effort to promote it.

Flaget still entertained the hope of founding a religious order of men, and actually carried the project into effect in the spring of 1826, when the foundations of the brotherhood were laid at St. Thomas' Seminary. Flaget's plan was to organize a society similar to that of the Brothers of the Christian Schools in France, which would teach catechism to children and servants and prove of assistance to the missionary clergy. The society soon declined and was dissolved at the end of three years. Spalding, seeking a reason for the collapse of the brotherhood, observed:

In this utilitarian age and country, it is difficult to induce men, to whom the world opens so many avenues of industry and of wealth, to leave all things and follow Christ. It requires a healthy Catholic atmosphere to impart to them that heroic vigor of soul, which is an essential condition for the true religious vocation.[134]

### Higher Learning for Boys

The attempts, successful and unsuccessful, to gain teachers and schools for the Catholic children and youth of Kentucky show that Flaget viewed the question of education as among the most important to the interests of religion. He "desired nothing more ardently, than to see schools for children of both sexes rising up under the shadow of the Church in each congregation."[135] Before coming to America he had been a professor of dogma in the Seminary of Nantes, France. After his arrival in this country, he was sent to Vincennes in 1792, where he opened a school and taught the "rudiments of learning, the principles of the catechism and the prayers of the church."[136] In 1796, Flaget came to Baltimore and remained for three years at Georgetown College, "discharging the difficult office of chief disciplinarian, and teaching Geography and French."[137] When Bardstown became his diocese, its progress in education was, to him, a matter of grave concern. We have observed his success in founding schools for girls. Under his guidance there were also established two schools for boys, which attained to the rank of colleges.

St. Joseph's College had its beginnings as a day school in the basement of David's Seminary at Bardstown. It was not until a year later that boarders were admitted, when a separate building was erected for the college. St. Joseph's was placed under the management of the local clergy, with the Rev. George A. M. Elder as president.[138] Flaget, however, always recognized the influence of David on this institution, and he expressed such views in a letter addressed to Archbishop Maréchal of Baltimore in June 1827. Flaget wrote.

It is by him [David] that nearly all the professors of the College have been formed, and this College [St. Joseph's] is the admiration of the western country and the resource of Kentucky. There are now in it one hundred and seven boarders and sixty-five day scholars.[139]

St. Joseph's College prospered, and by 1823 it was "one of the largest and best appointed school structures to be found in the entire western country."[140] On December 27, 1824, the state legislature granted a charter conferring upon it full collegiate powers and privileges. The institution had become, in a few short years, an important factor in the development of higher learning for boys. In 1825, it was necessary to enlarge the building because of an influx of students from the South. Spalding relates:

Among the benefactors of St. Joseph's College, the name of the Rev. N. Martial, the special friend of Bishop Flaget, deserves particular mention. In 1824, he brought up from the South twenty Creole boys for the college; and in the year following, fifty-four accompanied him.[141]

Protestants as well as Catholics were admitted to St. Joseph's College, which, in the words of Flaget, was opened "for those in easy circumstances . . . to give the young men attending the institution, an education as complete as can be obtained in the colleges of France."[142] He continues with information on a school for poor boys connected with the college:

We have also made a trial effort in opening a free school for poor Catholic boys who have not made their First Communion. The half of their time will be employed in work on the farm, to defray the expense of their board, and the other half in learning to read and write, and being instructed in the catechism.[143]

In 1832, a member of the U.S. House of Representatives would praise St. Joseph's College in these words:

In this college are taught all those branches of useful knowledge and of science which qualify man for the duties of life and its rational enjoyments. This college, without the aid of governmental endowment, brought into existence and sustained by individual enterprise, will lose nothing in comparison with any college in the Union. Sir, I believe it is the best west of the mountains: In it are annually instructed about two hundred of the youth of our country upon terms moderate. And we have in its discipline a perfect guaranty for the preservation of the morals of our young men. Its portals are opened to all denominations. Religious bigotry does not extend its unhallowed influence over the consciences of the professors or their pupils. The benevolence of its founder and its conductors is felt in all ranks of society. The orphan and the destitute find ready access to the benefits of this institution, and when there is an inability to pay the moderate charges of board and instruction, none are made.[144]

A second elementary school and college was established in Marion County, Kentucky, in 1821, under the name of St. Mary's Seminary or College. It owed its existence to the encouragment of Flaget and to the self-sacrificing exertions and energy of the Rev. William Byrne. On coming to Kentucky, Byrne was determined to found a school for boys similar to the school for girls established at Loretto. When Nerinckx went to Europe to recruit, Flaget allowed Byrne the use of the farm that Nerinckx had intended for his projected brotherhood. Here he opened a school, St. Mary's Seminary, in an old stone distillery fitted up with rough furniture, partly made by his own hand. Webb draws a graphic picture:

There happened to be on the premises an old stone distillery house of fair dimensions; and having put this in decent repair and filled it up with the roughest of school furniture, he announced from the pulpit of St. Charles' church, that St. Mary's academy would be opened next day for the reception of pupils. The school was quickly filled to overflowing; and after a few years it became necessary to put up other buildings for the accomodation of the ever increasing number of applicants for school privileges.[145]

Tuition at St. Mary's was largely paid in produce, which Byrne partly converted into money and partly exchanged for labor, thus paying "for the farm and for the new buildings." [146]

At first, Byrne was the sole member of the faculty; then he trained his brighter pupils to assist him. For twelve years, he was "president, chief disciplinarian, principal professor, procurator, missionary;—everything at the same time." [147] In 1831, Flaget offered St. Mary's to the Jesuits, but Byrne by Flaget's request continued to fill the office of president until his death on June 5, 1833.[148]

EDUCATIONAL ACCOMPLISHMENTS IN KENTUCKY

Flaget's account of the Catholic educational statistics of Kentucky for the year 1825 show that the diocese of Bardstown had laid secure foundations for Catholic education. Flaget reported:

*Diocesan Seminary at Bardstown.* Seminarians, 19, who also teach in the college. Cost of the building, $6,000.

*Preparatory Seminary at St. Thomas.* Young men, 15; priests, 2; teachers, 5. To this is annexed a *School for Boys,* with 30 students, who pay annually $35 in federal money, mostly in produce. Cost of buildings at St. Thomas, $11,400.

*St. Joseph's College.* Will cost $20,000 when completed.

*St. Mary's Country School.* Cost, $4,000. Charge per session, $6 for tuition, besides board paid in produce. Very popular. Has 120 boys. "Application must be made twelve months in advance to secure admission."

*Sisterhood of Loretto.* Sisters, 100. Convent of Loretto of brick. Cost, $5,000. All their branch-houses made of logs. Five schools in Kentucky. In 1823, sent out a colony to Ste. Geneviève, Mo.

*Sisterhood of Nazareth.* Sisters, 60; 60 boarders in Nazareth Academy. Three other schools in Kentucky, and one at Vincennes, Ind. School at Nazareth becoming popular, and patronized throughout the whole western country.

*Sisterhood of St. Dominic.* Established in 1821. Sisters, 14; boarders, 29.[149]

## DIOCESE OF BOSTON

Puritan New England bitterly opposed the foundation of Catholic schools. When the Rev. John Cheverus became Boston's first bishop in 1810, the diocese embraced New Hampshire, Vermont, and Massachusetts (which then included Maine, Rhode Island, and Connecticut). The scattered Catholics numbered 720, and there were only three Catholic churches—one in Boston, one at Newcastle, and an Indian log chapel in Maine. Catholic education in Boston may be said to have begun in the days of the Rev. Francis Anthony Matignon, with whose arrival on August 20, 1792 "a new era opened in the history of Boston and New England Catholicity." [150] The first known reference to a Catholic school actually functioning in Boston is in connection with a committee meeting held on January 24, 1804, which closed the accounts for a new church building and considered the needs of the parish. The committee discussed provision for a school, and decided that "till a house or room can be provided for a school, and till the Congregation be able to bear the expense, a small compensation be paid to the young gentleman who now keeps a school, to enable him at least to pay a part of his rent, of at least ten dollars a quarter." [151] No known document indicates how long before that date the school began, nor where the rented room was in which the school was held. Items in the church *Account Book* show that the congregation took over the school's upkeep and that it was in continuous existence from January 1804 until November 5, 1807. The same *Account Book* notes that during the year 1805-1806 payments were made for the schooling of poor girls at a Mrs. Sarah Torpey's school.[152]

Matignon believed that a separate fund for a school must be acquired. His parishioners were behind him, and there is proof of an effort to accomplish this purpose in April 1806. Dr. Stephen C. Blyth, a Boston convert to Catholicism, directed a letter to the president of the Massachusetts Senate. Although the plan never materialized, the letter is worth observing. It reads, in part:

Sir,

The Roman Catholics have it in contemplation to establish a charity school in Boston, for the exclusive instruction of poor children of their own communion. For this purpose, a fund will be necessary which they hope to create by a lottery, if the General Court will grant one to their petition . . . . A law has, I understand, been passed that in future no Lotteries shall be permitted, except in support of objects of public utility. It may be alledged that the Establishment in demand cannot plead this advantage, as public schools are numerous & open to youth of all persuasions. I need not affect to furnish a Gentleman of your intelligence with arguments to refute this suggestion—for it is well known to many, whose sphere of information is much more circumscribed than yours, that Catholics have an involuntary & afflicting scruple of sending their children to the common schools, where the integrity of their peculiar faith is apt to be shaken by heedlessness or design. Nor are instances infrequent of Catholics preferring the inconvenience & scantiness of domestic education, & even the want of any, to the hazard of this exposure. The question then is, whether a Legislature should indulge a supposed, but innocent prejudice, productive of much good; or slight & oppose it, to the injury of thousands of a rising generation & in detriment to our national interests.[153]

Matignon kept trying to finance a school, and again the church *Account Book* carries a heading dated September 16, 1806: "Subscription for a Catholic School." Two contributions were entered amounting to $8.05, and then the subscription list was closed.[154] On November 25 of the same year Matignon wrote to his bishop in Baltimore that "our only affliction here is our inability hitherto and perhaps for years hence to finance a Catholic School, which is absolutely indispensable for us." [155] On June 8, 1807, Matignon renewed the subscription list, this time with more success. By November 12, 1807, he was even more successful: he had collected $573.01, but still no school resulted.[156]

The first Catholic school to be established in New England was the Ursuline School opened at Boston in 1820. Its roots, however, go back to the Rev. John Thayer, Boston's first native-born priest, who, despite the fact that his imprudence and high-handedness resulted in a troubled pastorate, held high hopes of establishing a teaching order of women in Boston. All that he could possibly save was put aside for that purpose, and Matignon, assuring Carroll that he had Thayer's collected funds, wrote Carroll that

despite the accusations of cupidity to which [Thayer] had unfortunately given occasion, I continue to believe that he is sincere in declaring that he is eager to use them in pious establishments. . . . It seems to me . . . that an establishment of nuns, destined to the education of girls, such as the Moravians have copied with such success in Bethlehem, would, if once formed by Father Thayer's money, and with picked subjects, accomplish for young ladies what

Father DuBourg is so successfully doing for boys, and would be a blessing for your diocese.[157]

But such a school had to wait until 1820.[158]

Thayer, unable to do successful mission work, retired with Carroll's consent to Ireland in 1811. He did not put aside his great life's object to establish a religious community in Boston. In Limerick, he secured the services of two young women, the Misses Mary and Catherine Ryan, who had been educated by the Ursulines. Thayer wrote Cheverus and Matignon and arranged that the two young ladies should leave for Boston. Before plans for their departure could be completed, Thayer died. The money for the establishment of a convent which he had left to Matignon enabled Cheverus to purchase a plot of land adjoining his church in Franklin Street, where a convent building was erected. Here on June 16, 1820, the Misses Ryan, who had in the meantime completed their religious training at the Ursuline convent at Three Rivers, Canada, opened the first convent school for girls in New England. Before the end of the year more than 100 girls were in attendance as day pupils. The school continued for six years until July 17, 1826, when it was transferred to a more suitable location in Charlestown, Massachusetts, where it served boarders as well as day pupils. In 1834, the Ursuline School and convent would be destroyed by an anti-Catholic mob; the sisters would move to Roxbury, where bigotry would continue to hinder their work; and rather than have a repeat of Charlestown, the Ursulines would leave and move to Canada.[159]

This first real Catholic school of any repute in Boston merits as detailed a description as sources allow. The sisters made their first duty in the diocese that of teaching catechism, and in 1820 their school was devoted to the education of poor Catholic girls. The character of the school, however, changed with the passing years—the branches of study were elevated and extended, and the sisters accepted Protestants as well as Catholics. The latter was not the case in 1822, however, for *The Laity's Directory* of that year made no mention of Protestant students in its announcement. It simply stated:

A religious house whose rule embraces the education of young ladies, being greatly wanted in Boston, the Bishop has lately made choice of the order of Ursulines to superintend that department; and accordingly has invited into his diocese several ladies of the above mentioned order, and established them near his Cathedral: [160]

It continued with brief observations on the methods employed in the school:

The system of education embraced by these pious ladies is in every way calculated to suit this country. In addition to the useful branches of literature they instruct those committed to their charge, in every polite accomplishment.[161]

When the sisters moved to Charlestown, they occupied a farmhouse at the foot of Mount Benedict until the main building on its summit was built in 1827, and on occupancy the character of their curriculum took a decided change. In the spring of 1827, they issued a new prospectus, and opened their school to girls of all denominations. The enrollment increased, so that in 1829 it was necessary to add two large wings.[162] Lord observes:

> From the time of the removal to Mt. Benedict, the Sisters' school changed its character. Previously a day school, it now became a boarding school, and a rather expensive one ($125 a year, plus some extras!). Catholic patronage inevitably fell off; but, on the other hand, the children of the Unitarian aristocracy of Boston swarmed in, drawn by the reputation of the gentle daughters of St. Ursula both as accomplished teachers and as specially proficient in imparting the courtly manners and elegant accomplishments so necessary to young females at that time. The number of pupils usually ranged from 40 to 60. On the night of the catastrophe (just before the end of a summer vacation) there were forty-four of them in the house of whom five came from remote spots as New Orleans and Savannah, and three from Puerto Rico.[163]

A prospectus of this Ursuline School published in 1828 showed that the plan of education was superior, "comprehending all those attainments which may be found necessary, useful, and ornamental in society," and that the teachers were expected "to adorn the minds of their pupils with useful knowledge and to form their hearts to virtue." [164] The academy was divided into two departments—an upper division and a lower division. The Junior Department students were taught the elementary branches, such as reading, writing, grammar, arithmetic, geography, and ancient and modern history. Special attention was paid to orthography, and there was instruction in needlework. Competency in these courses meant promotion to the Senior Department. The girls in the upper classes were taught Latin, French, Spanish, Italian, ancient and modern history, chronology, geometry, logic, moral philosophy, needlework, painting, music, and dancing.[165]

The daily life of the boarders was strictly scheduled. Of this time a former student of the academy would write in 1843:

> The hour of rising in the winter was six and in summer five o'clock . . . . After prayers there was half an hour of silence—that is we were not allowed to turn about or to talk but studied the lessons for the day. Then came breakfast—after that half an hour's recreation usually passed out of doors in the garden or walking in front of the Establishment. When we returned to the house we entered upon the regular school exercises for the day. Each lesson had its appointed hour for recitation. The music lessons and hours for practice being so arranged as not to interfere with any of the lessons. Eleven o'clock was the dinner hour. Then followed an hour's recreation. Sometimes as an indulgence

lengthened into two. Then school again until five when we went to tea. After tea recreation again for a hour or so. Then evening prayers. At seven in winter and at dusk in summer we retired to rest. Wednesday and Saturday afternoons were given us for recreation.[166]

The same student showed her high regard for the religious tolerance at the Academy of Mt. Benedict, when she continued:

> In religious matters we were never interfered with. I never knew of the least attempt to influence in these respects, the minds of any of the Protestant pupils. All allusion to the peculiar tenets of any sect was avoided. At Mass and vespers, the Protestant pupils were required to take their own Bible or prayer books into the Chapel and to read them during the services. The prayers in daily use among us were very simple and such as no one of any denomination could object to. No difference was ever observed in the conduct of the community towards their Catholic and Protestant pupils. All shared alike in their care and kindness.[167]

The Protestant majority feared and hated the nuns and their school, however, and in 1834 destroyed it.[168]

In 1825, Benedict Joseph Fenwick was named second bishop of the diocese of Boston and immediately made his influence felt as a leader of Catholic education in Massachusetts. After he had secured the removal of the Ursulines to Charlestown, he established a day school for boys and girls. The same year he set up a seminary in his own house, where he himself did most of the teaching. The cathedral was enlarged and its basement remodeled for educational purposes; here, in 1829, Fenwick would open a classical school for boys. Shea sums up the educational achievements by that year of 1829:

> There were two schools in Boston, a classical one for boys and an academy for girls, two in Charlestown, one at Lechmere Point, one at Lowell, a classical seminary at Hartford, and some smaller ones, and the Indian school at Bangor, under Father Virgil H. Barber, while the Ursulines afforded the highest education for young ladies.[169]

Thayer, Matignon, and Cheverus made the first steps in bringing Catholic education to Boston; Fenwick set the Catholic Church and education on a solid foundation, and was their true organizer. He was a scholar, but a practical man of affairs as well, and a man of intense activity, initiative, and optimism, and nowhere more so than in the furtherance of Catholic education. Orestes Brownson wrote of Fenwick:

> He seemed to have read everything, and to have retained all that he had read. We never, in our intercourse with him, knew a subject to be broached of which he was ignorant . . . . Upon the whole, he left on us the impression of a man of great natural powers, of varied and profound learning, and of being the best informed man we have ever had the honor of meeting.[170]

Also worthy of special mention in Massachusetts is the city of Lowell.

The first Catholic school there probably came into existence in 1823 or 1824, after a considerable number of Irish immigrants had come to settle.[171] A room was rented for school purposes and an Irish schoolmaster placed in charge. The pupils were charged six cents a week, a not uncommon charge in those days. Since there was no permanent Catholic pastor or parish, the school made little progress. At the annual town meeting of 1830, a committee would be appointed to consider the expedience of establishing a separate school for the Irish. It would be agreed to appropriate $50 annually for the support of this school. At this time Church and State were still united in Massachusetts, and the state-supported schools were controlled by the various religious denominations; Catholics were given the same rights as those of other denominations. This school would not be very successful, however, owing to the scarcity and poverty of Catholics. In the meantime a church would be built and a pastor appointed. This, together with the increased immigration from Ireland, would result in the establishment of two parish schools before 1835, one in the basement of St. Patrick's Church and another at a place called Chapel Hill.[172]

### DIOCESE OF NEW YORK

On the statute books in the colony of New York there remained, until repealed in 1784, the law of 1700 against "Popish Priests and Jesuits," condemning them to perpetual imprisonment. Furtively, the Rev. Ferdinand Farmer came whenever he could from his mission in Lancaster, Pennsylvania, to attend Catholics in New York. Under these conditions it is obvious that at the beginning of the period 1784-1828 the Catholic religion was not flourishing in New York. Carroll sent the Rev. Charles Whelan to the state in 1784, and in the following year Carroll's *Relation of the State of Religion in the United States* cited the number of Catholics in New York as fifteen hundred.[173] The first Roman Catholic Church —St. Peter's on Barclay Street—made its appearance in 1785; here a "free school" was established in 1800.[174] St. Peter's "free school" therefore marks the beginning of Catholic education in New York. Accompanied by religious "Charity Schools" of the Dutch Reformed, Episcopalian, and Presbyterian Churches, it antedated the first school of the Free School Society by six years.

St. Peter's Board of Trustees had to hire rooms for the free school until its building was completed in 1805. By 1806 it had become the largest of the denominational schools in New York, with 220 pupils and a second schoolhouse. In that year a petition signed by 3,000 persons was presented to the state legislature, requesting that a portion of the funds set aside by the state for educational purposes be given to St. Peter's Free School. The petition was granted. During the period from 1795 to 1825, the state was habitually giving financial aid to educational institutions, most of which were Protestant, and in 1806 the Catholics at last received their share of the appropriations. For those children outside the sects conducting schools (Catholics, Episcopalians, Dutch Reformed, and Presbyterians), a group of citizens (among them DeWitt Clinton, then mayor of the city) in 1805 secured the incorporation of the Free School Society. They proposed to establish "a free school in the city of New York for the education of persons in indigent circumstances, who do not belong to or are not provided for by any religious society." [175] This free school, which eventually led to the formation of the public school system in New York, did not neglect religion. Tuesday afternoons were devoted to religious instruction, and on Sunday mornings the pupils assembled in the school, whence they proceeded to attend their respective churches.[176] Religious instruction and the schools were still one in men's minds in the early days of the Republic, as they had been in Colonial times. Secularization of the schools in New York began in 1825, and the Free School Society (which by an act of legislature in 1826 had an authorized change of title to "Public School Society of New York") [177] became the leading educational organization, obtaining a monopoly over the common school funds.

When New York was made a diocese in 1808, it comprised the state of New York and the eastern part of New Jersey. The Rt. Rev. Luke Concanen, selected to rule this see, never took possession of it (see note 17), and Carroll sent Kohlmann, a Jesuit, to New York as administrator. On his arrival he found the congregation of St. Peter's estimated at 14,000, and New York boasted but one Catholic church and one parochial school. Under Kohlmann's able administration from 1808 to 1815, Catholic education in New York began a forward move. In 1809, Kohlmann, aided by Benedict Fenwick, S.J., and four Jesuit scholastics, founded The New York Literary Institute, a classical college. This college began in a rented house on Mulberry Street. From the beginning the college prospered and in July of that year had thirty-five students, four of whom were boarders.[178] In September the school was moved to Broadway, and in the following spring to the site where St. Patrick's Cathedral is now located. Fenwick was made head of the college, which by 1813 had seventy-four boarders. In that year, however, the teaching in the college was turned over to the Trappists, and in 1821 the Jesuits finally sold the institution—the chief reason apparently being the difficulty of supplying teachers.[179]

Kohlmann was concerned also for the education of girls. He secured Ursuline nuns from the Blackrock Convent of Cork in Ireland, three of whom arrived in New York on April 7, 1812, and opened an academy for girls and an orphan asylum. The state granted incorporation to the convent on March 20, 1814. The sisters' convent and the school were greatly aided financially by Mr. Stephen Jumel, and at first the Ursulines supposed the establishment to be his gift, but found that he demanded payment of two-thirds of its value. As no novices joined them and the community was unable to raise the $2,000 required to pay for their home and school, the Sisters returned to Ireland.

Old St. Patrick's Cathedral (Mulberry St.) was erected and dedicated before Bishop John Connolly arrived in New York in 1815. Here, in the basement of this cathedral, New York's second permanent parish school began. The school, taught at first by lay teachers and no religious, accommodated both boys and girls; its population soon soared to 500, and in 1825 a separate school building was erected on Mulberry Street.[180]

Connolly also brought the Sisters of Charity of Emmitsburg to New York to take care of the orphan asylum. Four sisters came in August 1817, with Sister Rose White as their Superior. They occupied a small wooden building on Prince Street, near the cathedral. Five orphans were their first charges, but in a year the number increased to twenty-eight. As was the custom of the time, in order to support themselves and the orphans the Sisters opened a pay school. When in 1820 the Sisters received the help of an extra sister, they established a free school.[181] When the Very Rev. John Power was made administrator of the New York diocese from 1825-1826, he showed special interest in the work of the Sisters of Charity. He erected a three-story brick building that would house 160 orphans, which was completed and dedicated on November 23, 1826, and was almost immediately filled by the 150 orphans the sisters had charitably and quickly gathered for the new asylum.

The first Catholic school in Brooklyn was opened in 1823, in the basement of St. James' Church on Jay Street,[182] and when Bishop John Dubois became third bishop of New York in 1826, educational development continued. The foundation of a teaching brotherhood was attempted in September 1828. Brother James D. Boylan came from Ireland with some assistants, and the community took the name of "The Brothers of Charity in the City of New York for the Education of the Poor." Boylan and his friends took temporary charge of two schools— one at 208 William Street, and the other at 262 Mulberry Street. Opposition arose, mainly because of doubts cast on the motives, credentials, and character of Boylan; he resigned in 1829, and the whole project was abandoned.[183]

### DIOCESE OF PHILADELPHIA

Colonial Philadelphia had shown great promise for Catholic education; it was not to be quickly fulfilled. Shea say that

by the unholy war waged by the trustees of a single church against two successive bishops it was in 1829 without a seminary, a college, a convent academy for the education of young ladies, with but a single asylum, few schools, and a disheartened people.[184]

Carroll had not been able to foresee such sad results when the trustee system was introduced. Before the Revolution, Church holdings had had to be kept in the name of individual priests. After the Revolution, because of a complicated variety of factors, Carroll had to permit each congregation to incorporate under the laws of their respective states and to elect lay trustees who would manage their property and funds. To Carroll, this "trustee system" meant the protection of Church property, and he had always insisted that the lay trustees be subject to ecclesiastical authority. To his dismay, he found the trustees often ambitious and interfering, motivated by power and/or profit; sadly enough, some priests were not exempt from the same failings, and frequently joined with or activated the undermining activities of lay trustees. While trusteeism hindered the progress of Catholic education throughout the country during this period, its effects were particularly strong in Philadelphia. Up to the opening of the Erie Canal in 1825, this city was a leading center open to Europe, and so was quicker prey than others, perhaps, to a Voltairean concept of individual freedom in all areas, including the Church. But this was not the only factor militating against Catholic education in Philadelphia: the War of 1812 hit the people particularly hard, bankrupting the leading laity whose money came from river commerce, which was embargoed during the war, and putting them in a position of not being able to redeem financial promises they had made to the Church.

We have observed that the education of Catholic children in Philadelphia claimed the attention and energies of such committed priests as Molyneux and Farmer. The latter labored in that city until death called him in 1786, while the former spent himself completely until forced to write Carroll to plead for removal elsewhere because of activities pressing too heavily upon him. Nevils' praise of Molyneux is justified:

It was the initiative of Father Molyneux, whose pastorate at St. Mary's and St. Joseph's extended through the Revolution and the anxious years of reconstruction, who in 1781, purchased a house from the Quakers, two stories high, near that hidden shrine today, dear Old St. Joseph's, and inaugurated the first parochial school in the United States. . . . Had Robert Molyneux done nothing else, this would entitle him to the everlasting gratitude of the United States.[185]

This school was called a "free school," in that in 1783 the administrators resolved that each teacher would give free instruction to six poor pupils every year.[186] Pupils who could afford to pay some tuition fee were expected to do so, but this plan appears never to have materialized as the teachers were paid a fixed salary from the parish treasury, and donations and bequests were received for the school's support. Gifts came in the form of land, houses, cash, or bonds. There is an example of a bequest in the 1793 will of James Costelloe, who bequeathed 20 acres of land on Boon Island, Kingsessing, "the rents, issues and profits to be divided into equal parts, one moiety or half to be forever appropriated toward the maintenance and support of the Free School of St. Mary's." [187] Another benefactor of the school was Commodore John Barry, "the Father of the American Navy," who left an annuity of 20 pounds, the principal of which, on the death of his Negro servant, was to be given to St. Mary's and the poor school there. The principal of his annuity when turned over to the trustees amounted to $900.

New parishes arose in Philadelphia. The Germans broke off from St. Mary's in 1788, and erected Holy Trinity church. In the basement of the church they set up a parish school. By a successful lottery in 1806, Holy Trinity was enabled to build a parsonage and St. Joseph's Orphan Asylum, the first institution of its kind established by Catholics in the United States. A third parish was organized in 1796 by members of the Augustinian Order, and was known as St. Augustine's. In 1811, the Augustinians organized St. Augustine's Academy, Crown Street, Philadelphia. St. Augustine's Church preserved a register of the pew-holders of the parish, and that same register recorded the Academy accounts. From it we learn that the school opened on December 9, 1811, and closed June 19, 1815; that thirty-nine students in all were accounted for during that time; that the tuition fee per quarter ranged from $12.00 to $16.00; that among the subjects taught were Latin, Greek, French, Spanish, bookkeeping and mathematics; and that a writing-master was paid the sum of $116.00 for six months and two weeks instruction.[188]

On the whole, when the See of Philadelphia was established in 1808, and the Rt. Rev. Michael Egan took up his duties as its formally installed bishop in 1810, Catholic education was on the upgrade. But factional troubles in St. Mary's Parish would soon make impossible very much educational activity in the diocese for twenty years. In 1814, the Sisters of Charity from Emmitsburg, Maryland, sent three sisters to care for St. Joseph's Orphan Asylum in Philadelphia, and in 1818 they opened a free school for German Catholics.[189] A Catholic Sunday School was organized in 1816 for children who worked during the week—an interesting commentary on the times. The Sunday School curriculum included secular as well as religious subjects, and the school was in session from 8:00 A.M. to 10:00 A.M. and from 2:00 P.M. to 3:00 P.M.[190] At the old Colonial mission centers—Goshenhoppen, Conewago, Lancaster, and Haycock—schools were continued. About 1787, a number of Catholic families from Goshenhoppen crossed the Alleghenies, settled at Sportsman's Hall in Westmoreland County, and erected a little schoolhouse. Conewago in 1795 welcomed the Rev. Demetrius Gallitzin, the famous Russian priest and prince, who settled at Clairfield in 1799, where he completed, on Christmas Eve, a log chapel dedicated to St. Michael. In 1800, he opened a school at Loretto—"a small log building, daubed with mud, and heated by means of a large stone fireplace." [191] He also opened other small schools, but found it difficult to recruit teachers. He planned, therefore, to found a community of teaching sisters, but for lack of candidates his project failed. [192] The diocese of Philadelphia, which had begun with such promise, was in 1828 in an unsatisfactory condition educationally as well as in many other ways, since the aged Bishop Henry Conwell had been called to Rome and told to remain there because of maladministration.

## DIOCESE OF NEW ORLEANS

Carroll appointed the Rev. William DuBourg as administrator apostolic of the diocese of New Orleans in 1812. The diocese comprised Mississippi, Alabama, and the whole of the vast territory west of the Mississippi River, including the old French province of Louisiana. Churches and priests were scarce, and the clergy at New Orleans were led by the independent Father Anthony Sedella. Probably the only permanent Catholic school in the entire area was the Ursuline establishment in New Orleans. Interestingly, after the United States purchased Louisiana from France in 1803 the Ursulines thought of themselves as anything but permanent. The next year, because of their misgivings concerning their fate, they wrote to President Thomas Jefferson two almost identical letters (probably because of uncertainty about mail delivery) asking for an Act of Congress guaranteeing their rights. Jefferson concluded his friendly and respectful reply by writing:

Whatever diversity of shade may appear in the religious opinions of our fellow citizens, the charitable objects of your institution cannot be indifferent to any; and its furtherance of the wholesome purposes of society, by training up its younger members in the way they should go, cannot fail to ensure it the patronage of the government it is under.[193]

DuBourg, education-minded, believed that growth and progress could be brought about only through instruction. He went to Rome to represent the diocese of New Orleans; on the same trip he travelled through Europe to secure priests and teachers. When he embarked for home from Bordeaux on June 28, 1817, he had succeeded in getting some fifty-three persons for work in his diocese—priests, seminarians, brothers and sisters, and other volunteers. Four religious teaching orders were represented in this group: the Congregation of the Mission, or "Vincentians," founded by St. Vincent de Paul (then also called "Lazarists" by the French); the Brothers of the Christian Schools; the Religious of the Sacred Heart; and the Ursulines. St. Louis was to be his center of spiritual renewal,[194] and was officially made a separate diocese in 1826.

For the site of a seminary under the direction of the Vincentians DuBourg selected Boise Brulé, or the Barrens, a settlement of Catholics (from Kentucky) about eighty miles southeast of St. Louis, where the people showed interest and faith, having already built a log church and priest's house under the guidance of the Trappist Father Joseph Dunand. The Rev. Joseph Rosati, C.M., was placed in charge of St. Mary's, as the institution came to be called, which had been erected in 1818 through parishioners' donations and free labor, and opened to students in 1819. Shea describes the completed building as being

sixty feet long by thirty-five wide and four stories high. The study hall was on the ground floor, on the second the chapel, library, and infirmary, while the upper floors were laid off in rooms and dormitories.[195]

The school was a combination secondary school and seminary. In a letter home, dated May 24, 1823, Rosati spoke of their work there. He wrote:

Our seminary is doing very well, every year it furnishes a few priests to the diocese. True, up to the present time we have received students from Europe, nevertheless, we have some belonging to this country also, who give us great hopes. Time was needed to form them. We have at present four priests, sixteen ecclesiastics, twelve secular boarders, and twenty-five day scholars. We have nine brothers of our Congregation of St. Lazarus who work, partly in the fields and partly in the house. Great good might be accomplished, could we send out missionaries among the Protestants and Catholics scattered over a vast extent of territory; but we are hard pressed with all we have to do at home. For besides the Seminary in which we are obliged to conduct a great many classes, we have a very large parish, composed of excellent Catholics who approach the Sacraments, frequently [sic] and who give us work which is not without fatigue, but which is not without pleasure either.[196]

St. Mary's College would continue at the Barrens until 1842, when it would be transferred to Cape Girardeau, Missouri (as St. Vincent's College), and when also the theological seminary would be transferred to St. Louis.[197] After 1842, the institution at the Barrens would become a preparatory seminary.[198]

The erection of St. Louis College on the site of the old Spanish Catholic Church took place in 1819, almost coincidentally with the building of DuBourg's cathedral.[199] The moving spirit in this undertaking was the young curate of the cathedral, Francis Niel, who became the college's first president. The building was two-storied and housed sixty to seventy students. In its early years the secular priests of St. Louis Cathedral made up the faculty.[200] On May 11, 1826, DuBourg advised the closing of the school because there were not enough priests available as professors, but even before that time DuBourg was anxious to entrust the college to the Jesuits, as his letter of November 27, 1823, to the Rev. Francis Neale, the Maryland Superior of the Jesuits, proves:

I would feel disposed to give your society two beautiful squares of ground in the City of St. Louis and to help in the erection of a home for an academy as a preparation for college, if you thought you could spare a couple of your brethren, even scholastics, to commence the establishment; in which case I will shut up the one that is now kept by some of my priests on the Bishop's premises.[201]

In 1829, the Jesuits took over the college, at a new site at the edge of town about twelve blocks away, and when classes began there was a faculty of five Jesuits and a total registration of ten boarders and thirty externs, which would quickly grow to a total of one hundred and fifty pupils.[202] On December 28, 1832, the college was raised to the rank of a university under the title of Saint Louis University. According to the *Catholic Almanac* of 1833, at that time it included in its curriculum Latin, Greek, French, English, Writing, Arithmetic, Mathematics, Geography, and Natural Philosophy.[203]

The first members of the Religious of the Sacred Heart, founded at Paris in 1800 by St. Madeleine Sophie Barat, came to the United States with Madame Philippine Duchesne as Superior in 1818, beginning their work at St. Charles, Missouri, with an academy and parochial school.[204] A year later they moved to Florissant, a village fifteen miles north of St. Louis, where in 1821 they had "a novitiate, with five novices and several postulants, a thriving seminary for the daughters of the wealthy of this and the neighboring States, and a day-school for girls of the poorer class."[205] It was in part their attention to the education of the wealthy that caused their being misnamed the "Madames of the Sacred Heart." Actually, the term had begun during the French Revolution when, to elude detection, the religious wore widows' garb and were called "mesdames." When they came to the United States, the local inhabitants, seeing that they educated girls from the upper classes, and not being overly familiar with French terminology, anglicized it. The Sisters did not educate only the upper classes, however. As we just mentioned, they also conducted a parochial school for the poor, and conducted the first school for Negroes in the area as well. As to the Young Ladies Academy at the Convent of the Sacred Heart, St. Louis, the information available marks it as on the secondary level. The following courses were offered:

English and French-Reading, Writing, Grammar, Arithmetic, Sacred and Profane History, Geography, use of the Globes, projection of Maps, Mythology, Poetry, Rhetoric, Natural Philosophy and domestic Economy, Sewing, Marking, Lace, Muslin, Tapestry and Bead Work; Painting on Velvet and Satin, Drawing, Painting in water colors and crayons; Shell work, and chrystalized Parlor Ornaments; Music, vocal and instrumental.[206]

The Institute was now ready to send colonies into other parts of the diocese, and established the first branch house in 1821 at the little Acadian town of Grand Coteau, in lower Louisiana. There they established another secondary school, which today prides itself on having the longest continuous existence of any Sacred Heart school in either North or South America, and also on the fact that Blessed Philippine Duchesne visited there in 1822 and 1829.[207] From 1838 to 1842, Cornelia Connelly —convert and foundress of the Society of the Holy Child Jesus, whose interesting life was dramatized in the off-Broadway play *Connelly vs. Connelly*—lived in a cottage on the property and taught in the school.[208]

In 1822, DuBourg wrote to Nerinckx in Kentucky, requesting a colony of Lorettines for his diocese in St. Louis. Nerinckx agreed, for he was pleased that Rosati, Superior of the Seminary of St. Mary at the Barrens, was to be their spiritual director. Thirteen sisters were sent to St. Louis for the purpose of establishing an academy and school for girls. Actually, they began a school and an orphanage in their log house. Their institution was called Bethlehem; it was transferred to Cape Girardeau in 1838.[209]

In November 1828 the Sisters of Charity of Emmitsburg, Maryland, sent four members of their community to take charge of a hospital in St. Louis—the first hospital west of the Mississsppi River. In 1834, when Rosati gave them a small house on Third and Walnut streets to be used as an orphan asylum and day school, the sisters would take on educational work. DuBourg had hoped, too, for the establishment of a teaching brotherhood in his diocese, but the plan fell through. Three Brothers of the Christian Schools came from France in 1817, and actually began a boys' school at Ste. Geneviève, Missouri. The Bishop, however, separated the brothers and sent them to separate missions, hoping in that way to achieve a widening circle of educational efficiency. Instead the brothers, thus separated, left the order. Nevertheless, the over-all conditions in the diocese of New Orleans during this period indicated that foundations were laid that were formative of the future.

## DIOCESE OF CHARLESTON

The choice of bishop for the newly formed diocese of Charleston, South Carolina, in 1820 fell upon the Rev. John England, onetime professor and president of St. Mary's Diocesan College in Cork, Ireland, and, at the date of his appointment, parish priest of Bandon, a town some sixteen miles from Cork. The See of Charleston in 1820 comprised the states of South Carolina, North Carolina, and Georgia. It was a difficult diocese, with an estimated 3,600 Catholics in a population of 1,482,559—a diocese that took pride in its slave labor and drew its social lines fine. By culture and tradition the Protestant majority was antagonistic to Catholics and, worse still, schismatic priests had weakened the faith of Charleston's Catholics and brought discredit to the Church. England found upon his arrival at Charleston only two priests and two churches in the whole diocese.[210] He would labor here until his death in 1842. His educational efforts must have been a disappointment to him in that they produced unsatisfying results, but we can only marvel that he accomplished anything at all under such unfavorable conditions.

To counteract the ignorance prevailing among the Catholics of his diocese as to the doctrines of their faith and their religious duties, England organized a Book Society. On June 5, 1822, he founded *The United States Catholic Miscellany*, which strictly speaking was the first Catholic newspaper in the United States.[211] His chief educational endeavor, however, during this period was the establishment of the Charleston Seminary, which bore the high-sounding name of "The Philosophical and Classical Seminary of Charleston." The absolute necessity of a native clergy was ever on England's mind. By January 1822, he had, according to Guilday, developed his long-range educational plans. Guilday writes:

These included: the affiliation of all private schools conducted by Catholic schoolmasters in the three States to the Philosophical and Classical Seminary in Charleston; the founding of other schools of an elementary and secondary character wherever Catholics guaranteed their support; the establishment of a college-seminary in the episcopal city for the higher courses and for the priesthood. To these parts of his system he intended to add schools for the education of the free negroes of Charleston.[212]

England saw in the Charleston Seminary the future of Catholic higher education in the South. It became popular almost immediately as there was no similar academy in the city (Charleston College having closed for lack of funds), and upon opening showed an enrollment of twelve Catholic and fifty-one non-Catholic pupils. The difficulties England faced in staffing the literary institution, its failures because of Protestant prejudices, and its perseverance through to success are recounted by Shea in these words:

Bishop England was not only president, but teacher, compelled frequently to attend to almost all the classes, though gradually he was assisted by some candidates for orders. . . . Suddenly the Protestant denominational papers began to attack the institution. . . . The result was disastrous to Bishop England's seminary, which saw its roll of pupils dwindle from one hundred and thirty to thirty. He maintained it, however, and its pupils took high honors in the State College at Columbia.[213]

England himself, in a letter to his friend, the Hon. William Gaston, spoke of the burden the school imposed on him when he wrote:

I had to perform the entire clerical duty of this city during the summer and superintend a large school which I had established. I have had to teach mathematics therein myself during the last two months and to study algebra, of which my knowledge was never extraordinary, so as to be able to teach an advanced class.[214]

A year later, in a letter addressed to Archbishop Maréchal, he referred optimistically to his seminary. "I hope," he said, "to make this school the source of much benefit to our Church in the South." [215]

In spite of Protestant opposition and a shortage of teachers, England would keep the school open until 1836. He was convinced that prejudice and bigotry go hand in hand with ignorance, and that education could effect change. The poverty of the Catholic Church in Charleston hindered his educational attempts, and it must have taken persevering courage to continue the pursuit of his plans in the face of criticism, not only from those not of his faith, but from many from whom he had reason to expect friendliness and assistance.

## Government and Catholic Education

Because "the separation of Church and State in the United States is so secure that for millions of Americans the question arises only in the limited context of education"; [216] because in this period in which the Federal Constitution was written all Church-State controversies over education have their origins; and because in fact many subsequent Supreme Court decisions on Catholic education would harken back to concepts, opinions, climate, and texts from this period, it is necessary to include some remarks here on this subject. First, one must recall that from Colonial times until the 1830's and after, the entire mode of education in the United States was through private schools. To understand the Government's role in such schools, and its relationships with the Church, it is necessary to move back to the colonies that would later become the United States, in which conditions had existed bearing upon all of subsequent history in this matter. Foremost among these was the "establishment" of religion, a brief definition of which is provided by the *Encyclopedia Britannica*:

Establishment implies the existence of some definite and distinctive relation between the state and a religious society (or conceivably more than one) other than that which is shared in by other societies, of the same general character. . . . In a word, establishment is of the nature of a monopoly.[217]

Antieau, Downey, and Roberts present some of its characteristics when they assert that establishment was a shorthand expression which referred to an alliance with the following general characteristics:

1. A state church officially recognized and protected by the sovereign;
2. A state church whose members alone were eligible to vote, to hold public office, and to practice a profession;
3. A state church which compelled religious orthodoxy under penalty of fine and imprisonment;
4. A state church willing to expel dissenters from the commonwealth;
5. A state church financed by taxes upon all members of the community;

6. A state church which alone could freely hold public worship and evangelize;
7. A state church which alone could perform valid marriages, burials, etc.[218]

### FEDERAL LEVEL

It is important to make clear that there never has been an established church on the federal level in the United States. When the delegates to the Constitutional Convention met in Philadelphia in 1787 to draft a Federal Constitution there was, because of their background and colonial experience, a strong sentiment in favor of religious liberty. The lingering bad odor of preferential treatment to established churches and intolerance and persecution of dissenting sects caused a dissatisfaction that the First Congress also tried to right in 1789. Parsons observed:

It is clear that the only possible outcome that political wisdom could dictate was to forbid the Federal Government to establish any church, to treat all churches on a basis of equality, and to allow each State to establish a church of its choice, or not, as it pleased.[219]

The Catholic representatives—Daniel Carroll of Maryland and Thomas Fitzsimmons of Pennsylvania—shared these sentiments. The Constitution, however, made but timid reference to religion; its principle preoccupation with religious liberty concerned test oaths. Such commentators on the Constitution as Story [220] and Corwin [221] agree on the reasons for this almost complete silence, and their conclusions are well summarized in the appellees' brief in the McCollum case:

Religion was not mentioned, first, because it was intended that the Federal Government should have no control over the subject just as the document made no mention of education or intrastate commerce for the same reason: and, second, because the religious beliefs and practices of the people throughout the States, as well as the extent of the control exercised over religion by the States, were so diverse that it was wholly impractical to attempt any uniform system of relationship between religion and government.[222]

It cannot be said that the Convention wished to show "any disinterest in religion or its welfare, but rather spoke eloquently of the anxiety of the Framers to protect it, foster it, and preeminently, to leave it a local rather than a national matter." [223]

The religious clause of the First Amendment—"Congress shall make no law respecting an establishment of religion or prohibiting the free exercise thereof"—legally ended the religious intolerance of Colonial times for the federal government of the country at large, but not for individual states, except gradually in the course of time. The First Amendment would not be applicable to the states until the Fourteenth Amendment made it so in 1868. Congress asked James Madison, who proposed the First Amendment, to give his understanding of the Amendment. His answer appears in the Annals of Congress, which indicate that he apprehended the meaning of the words to be, that Congress should not establish a religion and enforce the legal observance of it by law, nor compel men to worship God in any manner contrary to their conscience.[224]

The First Amendment, then, was framed to bar preferential treatment of any individual religious sect—in other words to ban a national church, but not necessarily to prohibit help to churches; to have the "disestablishment" of religion in the first part of the Amendment serve the freedom of conscience in its second part; and in the context of education to guarantee complete personal fulfillment without hindrance from the government. Antieau, Downey, and Roberts write:

An examination of the early activities of the Federal Government indicates that the people approved and welcomed its aid to church-related activities. Because of the influence of congregationalism and an awareness of the possibility of abuses, the American community probably did not desire any clergy other than chaplains to be paid directly by the Federal Government. On the other hand, church-related activities in behalf of the common good were never considered undesirable merely because they were associated with religion. It was understood that the Federal Government properly held a strong interest in them. For example, Congress provided land for churches on the western frontier, undoubtedly because settlers would thereby be encouraged to move west and develop the land. Furthermore, in order to assimilate and pacify the Indians, the Federal Government financially supported—without preference or favoritism—mission activities of many religious organizations among the Indians. To maintain the proper moral tone in the armed forces, Congress provided military chaplains. These examples of governmental involvement in these so-called "religious" areas indicate that the men in the early Congresses took a pragmatic view of church-state relations. They did not harbor the opinion that the establishment clause required the Federal Government to be antagonistic or even neutral in matters of religion. To the contrary: they believed they had the power to accommodate and encourage the interests concurrent of religion and government.[225]

The Constitution addressed itself therefore to disestablishment and not to separation. "Separation," says Parsons, "as a doctrine or principle did not enter the picture of the First Amendment." [226] The development of the concept of separation of Church and State in the way in which some interpret it in the twentieth century seems unwarranted by the intention, the language, and the context of the authors of the First Amendment to the Constitution. In fact, the phrase "separation of Church and State" does not appear in any Supreme Court decision until 1879—at which time it indicated only that a person's religious beliefs did not excuse him from crime in the practice of polygamy, against which Congress had legislated.

The individual colonies, which with independence became states, presented a different picture. Before the Revolution, ten colonies had had established churches: Calvinist Congregationalism in New England, which included Massachusetts, Connecticut, and New Hampshire; the Church of England in Virgina and the two Carolinas; and changes in establishment in New York, New Jersey, Maryland, and Georgia. There had been no established church in Pennsylvania, Rhode Island, and Delaware, but even in these three colonies some churches had been privileged.[227] The strong determination to attain religious liberty and to guarantee "disestablishment" was a long struggle, not ending with the ratification of the Bill of Rights in 1791. In some states where the practice of religious freedom was stronger and establishment had never gained a foothold, the problem was small; in other states, the process was slow. In Virginia it took ten years—from 1776 to 1786; in Massachusetts more than fifty—1776 to 1833.[228] Billington indicates that in the struggle of the intervening years, although popular leaders received most of the glory, "the real heroes were the rank and file of the Presbyterians, Baptists, Quakers and Catholics." [229]

## SOUTHERN COLONIES

Virginia may be considered to typify the Anglican establishment in the southern colonies. From the very beginning, the established church there had been the Anglican, whose local parishes had carried out not only the affairs of the Church, but functions of local government as well. They had set the tax rules for the relief of the poor, built churches from money gathered by local taxation, and given pieces of land (called glebes) to Anglican parsons. Anglican parishes had kept public records of births, deaths, and marriages, and only their ministers could conduct marriage and funeral services. Children whose parents had not been married in the Church of England had been declared illegitimate. Dissenters had been expelled—for example, Quakers had been considered a "turbulent" sect and quickly expelled from the colony, "popish priests" excluded by law, and Catholics disqualified from holding office. Teachers in Virginia had had to be certified by the archbishop of Canterbury.[230]

Virginia also led all the rest in disestablishing religion after the Revolution, and the sentiments and actions of that colony influenced the rest of the country, including the federal government. Notable were "two historical documents that have been quoted and cited in all discussions of American church-state relationships," [231] Thomas Jefferson's *Bill for Establishing Religious Freedom* and James Madison's *Memorial and Remonstrance Against Religious Assessments*. Jefferson had drafted his document as early as 1777, but the Virginia legislature did not enact it finally until 1786. Opposing tax support of the Anglican church because this "tends . . . to corrupt the principles of that very religion it is meant to encourage, by bribing, with a monopoly of worldly honours and emoluments, those who will externally profess and conform to it," [232] it concluded:

We the General Assembly of Virginia do enact that no man shall be compelled to frequent or support any religious worship, place, or ministry whatsoever, nor shall be enforced, restrained, molested, or burthened in his body or goods, nor shall otherwise suffer, on account of his religious opinions or belief; but that all men shall be free to profess, and by argument to maintain, their opinions in matters of religion, and that the same shall in no wise diminish, enlarge, or affect their civil capacities.

. . . we are free to declare, and do declare, that the rights hereby asserted are of the natural rights of mankind, and that if any act shall be hereafter passed to repeal the present or to narrow its operation, such act will be an infringement of natural right.[233]

In many other aspects of establishment in Virginia—compulsory church attendance, for example, and favored political status for members—Jefferson was also the leader of the opposition.

Jefferson's positions on all of the above have given rise to a much-used metaphor taken from this misquotable gentleman. This is his phrase about the "wall of separation between church and state," which appeared in his letter of January 1, 1802, to the Baptist Association of Danbury, Connecticut, in which he wrote, among other things:

Believing with you that religion is a matter which lies solely between man and his God, that he owes account to none other for his faith or his worship, that the legislative powers of government reach actions only, and not opinions, I contemplate with sovereign reverence that act of the whole American people which declared that their legislature should "make no law respecting an establishment of religion, or prohibiting the free exercise thereof," thus building a wall of separation between Church and State. Adhering to this expression of the supreme will of the nation on behalf of the rights of conscience, I shall see with sincere satisfaction the progress of those sentiments which tend to restore to man all his natural rights, convinced he has no natural right in opposition to his social duties.[234]

Jefferson's figure of speech would give rise much later to slogans and symbols, and even at times, seemingly, to a rule of law.[235] Over-enthusiastic applications of this metaphor would indicate a forgetfulness of many other statements of Jefferson favorable to religion; [236] and its overly ritualistic application would not only result in Jefferson's desired disestablishment and freedom of exercise of religion, but in effect would "establish" secularism.

Although the disestablishment of the Anglican Church was taking place in Virginia, and although Jefferson was—as we have said—leading the movement, this is no indication that the Virginians wanted the state hostile to religion or that they desired a separation that was so complete and absolute that the state could be interpreted as being not in support of religion. As a matter of fact, in 1784 Patrick Henry introduced into the Virginia Legislature "A Bill establishing a provision for Teachers of the Christian Religion," which carried by 47 votes to 32; after some weeks a bill was brought in to effectuate the resolution. The bill had the support of George Washington, who wrote a letter to George Mason to this effect, and of Richard Henry Lee, who on November 26, 1784, wrote to Madison in favor of the bill. When on October 9, 1792, the Quakers sent the Virginia General Assembly a Memorial objecting to the latter's having a chaplain at public expense, the General Assembly rejected it as well as other comparable Memorials. On December 2, 1791, the state authorized the Episcopal Church to conduct a public lottery, a privilege conferred at other times on other religious groups. The state also gave tax exemptions to religious societies and donated land to educational institutions controlled by religious sects.

The second of Virginia's influential documents, Madison's *Memorial and Remonstrance,* came about through interesting circumstances. Patrick Henry's bill, which was just mentioned, provided for religious assessments to support "the Christian Church," without naming any particular denomination. It gave each taxpayer the privilege of designating which church should receive his share of the tax. Madison sent throughout Virginia his *Memorial and Remonstrance,* in which he remonstrated—rightly—against the bill for fifteen reasons:

1. Because we hold it for a fundamental and undeniable truth, "that Religion or the duty which we owe to our Creator and the Manner of discharging it, can be directed only by reason and conviction, not by force or violence." . . .
2. Because if religion be exempt from the authority of the Society at large, still less can it be subject to that of the Legislative Body. . . .
3. Because it is proper to take alarm at the first experiment on our liberties. . . .
4. Because, the bill violates that equality which ought to be the basis of every law, and which is more indispensible, in proportion as the validity or expediency of any law is more liable to be impeached. . . . Whilst we assert for ourselves a freedom to embrace, to profess and to observe the Religion which we believe to be of divine origin, we cannot deny an equal freedom to those whose minds have not yet yielded to the evidence which has convinced us. If this freedom be abused, it is an offence against God, not against man. . . .
5. Because the bill implies either that the Civil Magistrate is a competent Judge of Religious truth; or that he may employ Religion as an engine of Civil policy. . . .
6. Because the establishment proposed by the Bill is not requisite for the support of the Christian Religion. . . .
7. Because experience witnesseth that ecclesiastical establishments, instead of maintaining the purity and efficacy of Religion, have had a contrary operation. . . .

8. Because the establishment in question is not necessary for the support of Civil Government. . . .
9. Because the proposed establishment is a departure from that generous policy, which, offering an asylum to the persecuted and oppressed of every Nation and Religion, promised a lustre to our country, and an accession to the number of its citizens. . . .
10. Because, it will have a like tendency to banish our Citizens. . . .
11. Because, it will destroy that moderation and harmony which the forbearance of our laws to intermeddle with Religion, has produced amongst its several sects. . . .
12. Because, the policy of the bill [is] adverse to the diffusion of the light of Christianity. . . .
13. Because attempts to enforce by legal sanctions, acts obnoxious to so great a proportion of Citizens, tend to enervate the laws in general, and to slacken the bands of Society. . . .
14. Because a measure of such singular magnitude and delicacy ought not to be imposed, without the clearest evidence that it is called for by a majority of citizens. . . .
15. Because, finally, "the equal right of every citizen to the free exercise of his Religion according to the dictates of conscience" is held by the same tenure with all our other rights.[237]

None of the other colonies had the same importance to subsequent history in this matter as Virginia. Although the laws of Maryland's first proprietors, the Roman Catholic Lords Baltimore, had been tolerant, in 1692 the Baltimores had lost control of the colony, for the reason that Puritan power was strong in the government of England. In the same year the Maryland Assembly had made the Church of England the established religion and the persecution of Catholics had begun.[238] The English Acts of Toleration of 1702, which extended to Protestant dissenters in Maryland, had ignored Catholics. It was ironic that this colony, founded by a Catholic with a view to religious freedom, made Catholics the victims of intolerance.[239] North Carolina's history from 1754 to 1765 had been a story of Dissenters' resistance against, and Anglican clergymen's determination in behalf of, an establishment.[240] Although the need for settlers had induced the proprietors of the Carolinas and the trustees of Georgia to try to attract people of any religious faith to their colonies, the Church of England had been the lawfully established church. While North Carolina's constitution guaranteed complete religious freedom, it restricted the holding of public office to Protestants until 1835, when the eligibility requirement was changed to "Christian." Whereas South Carolina's Constitution of 1778 had established "the Christian Protestant religion" in the state, the Constitution of 1790 guaranteed complete freedom of worship. Georgia's Constitution of 1777 had deleted the derogatory term "papist" and extended freedom of worship, but declared the clergy ineligible to hold office, which last restriction was removed by the Constitution of 1789.

## NEW ENGLAND

The Puritans, who had come to Massachusetts Bay in 1628, had brought with them Calvin's principles of theocratic Church-State relationships. Quickly they had established their Bible commonwealth under a civil and ecclesiastical ruling body. The legislative body was the General Court, and the privilege of voting extended only to church members. The Congregationalist Church had been the fundamental institution and had looked upon those outside its ranks as dissenters. Religion had been the supreme concern of the state, and the church had been supported by a tax levied upon all citizens of every town. Expressed theological dissent had meant excommunication and banishment, as in the cases of Anne Hutchison and Roger Williams—the latter because of his spoken beliefs on the separation of Church and State, the former because she had opposed the "covenant of works"—a religion based on obedience to the laws of church and state—and had held instead to an individual's direct intuition of God's grace and love.

In the Massachusetts Bay Colony, Anglicans had been viewed with suspicion and Quakers had had harsh laws adopted against them, the latter having been liable to imprisonment, whippings, and hard labor until banished.[241] Catholics had been looked upon with open hostility. In June, 1700, a law had provided that any Catholic priest or missionary who should be in the colony after September 10, 1700, should be punished with "perpetual imprisonment"; if one so imprisoned should escape and be recaptured, "he shall be punished by death."[242] Connecticut differed little from Massachusetts in its church-state relations.

## MIDDLE COLONIES

In the Middle Colonies, there cannot be said to have been a firmly entrenched establishment. True, the Dutch Reformed Church had enjoyed the privileges of an established church in New Netherland, and pastors had been supported by taxation. This exclusive establishment had been lost when the English took New Amsterdam in 1664, however, and a system of "multiple establishments" had evolved. That is to say, the disestablishment of the Dutch Reformed Church did not mean the separation of Church and State—rather, all *Protestant* churches had been established. In New Jersey, too, Protestantism had been privileged and public office restricted to such believers. On the banks of the Delaware, Penn had created his "holy experiment"—a colony dedicated to the ideals of religious toleration—and this had been the promise in advertisements for settlers. Quaker tolerance had made Penn's colony a refuge for the persecuted of many faiths. On the eve of the Revolution the sects in Pennsylvania included Quaker, German Reformed, Presbyterian, Lutheran, Baptist, Episcopalian, Moravian, Mennonite, Dunker, Catholic, and Dutch Reformed. Even Pennsylvania, however, had given evidence of shades of privilege. Pfeffer writes:

But though the grant of freedom of faith and worship to all who believed in God was theoretically broad enough to encompass not only Catholics but Jews as well, political privileges were limited to Christians, and in practice it appears that neither Catholics nor Jews enjoyed complete freedom of worship, at least in the beginning of the enterprise.[243]

Nevertheless, in educational activities Pennsylvania's tolerant attitude had given schools of all denominations a freedom unheard of in the other colonies.

## Conclusions: Common Denominators

Catholic education in the United States from 1784 through 1828 consisted of attempts at small but worthwhile beginnings in a period when the Church was straitened by poverty and insecurity, teacher shortage, and a scarce and scattered Catholic population. Although one school differed from the other in some particulars, a definite educational pattern was receiving formative foundations in circumstances and conditions, aims, curriculum, texts, teachers, and students. From outside the Church, time and time again prejudice struck out against Catholic priests, convents, and schools. Within, the schools as well as the Church constituted a "melting pot" in which Italians, Germans, Irish, and others had to learn to get along with one another. The added difficulty of trusteeism hindered the progress of education. Catholic poverty was alleviated in education as elsewhere by such European associations as the Association for the Propagation of the Faith at Lyons, France, and the Leopoldine Association for Aiding Missions at Vienna, Austria. It was a step forward that after the American Revolution Catholics were free to build schools, and this they began to do. Their leaders perceived that they were similar to their fellow citizens of other religious persuasions in being inarticulate, with the added difficulties for Catholics of having undergone bitter Colonial legislation against Catholic education. Foremost among the leaders who perceived that the success of the Church in the new republic would depend on the establishment of Catholic educational institutions was the country's first bishop, John Carroll. He saw to it that schools were founded, brought in religious orders, recruited priests, and accepted the designation of the non-Catholics of Baltimore to serve on the board of directors of Baltimore College. This was the beginning of a pattern for this country's bishops of interest in schools, in spite of the many other things clamoring for their attention—a pattern which would come to be taken for granted. When the westward movement due to immigration carried Catholics beyond the Alleghenies, the wilderness did not decrease their educational efforts, and they sacrificed a great deal to provide Catholic schooling. Many Catholic elementary schools of the period were set up in log cabins; church basements, sacristies, and choir lofts; rectory and convent rooms; and abandoned buildings. The purpose, determination, leadership, and perseverance of the Catholics of the time set the Catholic pattern of education on firm formative foundations.

As for their goals, for a minority group lost in a Protestant environment—as Catholics were in those days—of vital importance to the preservation of the Faith was the teaching of religious truths. Catholic education's fundamental aim was therefore essentially uniform—to teach Catholic doctrine; to imbue Catholic youth with the spirit of Christ; and to instill the realization that man is God's—formed in God's image and to be fashioned to Godlikeness to become more worthy of God as his final goal. The schools did not forget that man must live in this world; they sought to equip students to take their place in society, and to present the rudiments of a literary tradition. The emphases must have been considered desirable, judging by the number of requests of well-to-do non-Catholics to enter some Catholic schools.

The curriculum of the Catholic elementary schools—very basic—gave prime importance to religious instruction and also taught the rudiments of reading, writing, and ciphering. Catechetical instruction was a drill "learn by heart" process, a memorization of dry theological formulae with little explanation and discussion; the question-and-answer method was used, as befitted the format of the catechisms in use. Three popular catechisms during this period and for some years afterward were those of Butler and Challoner, and an American translation of *The Catechism of the Council of Trent*.[244] American Catholic authors were a rarity, but the pioneer attempts of the Revs. Robert Molyneux in Philadelphia and Gabriel Richard in Detroit established the beginnings of the notion of Catholic textbooks. As far as is known, Molyneux was the first in the United States to publish textbooks for use in Catholic schools. In 1785, he printed a spelling primer with a catechism appended, and seems to have been actively interested in the publication in the same year of what was probably the first American edition of Challoner's *The Catholic Christian*.[245] Richard, as was observed, published a series of textbooks in French and English for the use of pupils in his Northwest missions. Catholic schools also adapted textbooks from other denominational schools by deleting objectionable parts. Mathew Carey, the celebrated Catholic publisher of Philadelphia, published texts for elementary and secondary Catholic schools.[246]

On the secondary level, Catholic schools followed a classical curriculum—as evidenced by school prospectuses. A too rigid classical curriculum was found inadequate for the demands and needs of life in the new republic, but no great change was obvious in boys' curricula during this period. The curriculum of the girls' academies had more practical elements: since woman's place was considered to be in the home, girls were prepared for duties as wives and mothers. Their education was to be first religious and moral, and then intellectual and cultural. Habits of regularity, neatness, and order were to be developed, with an emphasis on manners and deportment. The physical side was not neglected, every effort being made to preserve the girls' health. The production of the ideal Christian woman was the early Catholic academies' aim, with which the curriculum was in keeping, and many non-Catholic parents enrolled their daughters in such institutions in order to ready them for refined and polite society.

The preparation of teachers, up to at least the time of the Revolution, had been unheard of, and teacher standards were very low. Throughout this period, and into the next, teacher-sexton and teacher-organist combinations were not uncommon; as late as 1862 a Catholic newspaper advertisement sought a teacher-sexton.[247] The first non-Catholic normal school opened at Concord, Vermont, in 1823, and the first American state normal school would not open until 1839, at Lexington, Massachusetts. Catholic educators, however, arrived at the concept of teacher-training earlier. The teaching sisterhoods founded during this period were trained by educated priests, the first groups of Sisters not considering themselves sufficiently competent; thereafter they themselves trained their novices within their congregations. The priest-teachers in the boys' schools of the new republic were often learned men, educated on the Continent, and of unrivalled academic ability. They were, however, few in number, and were hindered by administrative and missionary duties; consequently, they developed a system of student-teaching whereby the better students in the more advanced classes taught those in the lower grades. Such in-service training was remarkably successful, but the teacher shortage continued to be a problem and caused some schools to close. But scarcity of teachers was a problem common to all denominations, and in that respect Catholic schools were not inferior to other schools; indeed, they were more fortunate than most others in having groups of religious—dedicated teachers living in community—who gave themselves without any consideration of financial remuneration. During this period, the pattern of the elementary school teacher's being a nun became more and more accepted. With regard to nuns, there was the beginning of a double stream: those communities who came from abroad, and those originating here. The first in the latter category were the Visitation nuns in 1814.

Concerning students, enrollments were small in comparison with the population. An educational consciousness had not yet awakened, and among the majority there was a lack of interest in education. If a pupil learned to read, write, and cipher (and in the case of Catholics was versed in his religious doctrines), he was considered educated; and not to have grasped those skills brought no reproach. The country was poor economically and culturally, and was busy with the job of finding its economic and cultural feet. All of this applied particularly to the secondary level where, except for free schools for the poor which the Church was anxious to establish in each diocese, and which the sisters, charitable organizations, and church collections supported, education was expensive and for the better class. In many cases, Sisters were able to conduct schools for the poor only because of the payment received from the academy pupils.

As far as admission to Catholic academies and colleges was concerned, the principal requirements for both boys and girls were ability to read and write, moral integrity, and enough money to pay the tuition fee. The monied students who were able to enter were expected to live according to strict rules. Much emphasis was placed on polite deportment, uniform dress, propriety, morality, and—for Catholic students especially—religious observance. Boarders were not allowed to leave overnight, and were even encouraged to remain during the summer vacation. The administration limited visitors, regulated letter writing, and frowned upon excess pocket money. Parents wanted constant watchfulness, but there is evidence that the students of that day, making allowances for the era, did not differ from the students of our day. The Rev. Stephen Dubuisson of Georgetown College, for example, complained in 1827 of "the want of piety among the boys, the love of dressing, the rage of going out, the ruinous habit of visiting confectioners' shops and the great liberty in reading." [248]

## CHAPTER III

# *1829-1884:* Transition

## Social Changes

THE YEARS BETWEEN 1829 and 1884 radically altered the framework of society in the United States. Consider, for example, some random interesting facets characteristic of society at the beginning of this period and for a varying number of years thereafter: there was not a public library in the country; almost all furniture was imported from England; there was only one hat factory, and it made cocked hats; buttons were scarce and expensive, and trousers were fastened with pegs or lace; every gentleman wore a queue and powdered his hair; Virginia contained a fifth of the whole population of the country; a man who jeered at a preacher or criticized a sermon was fined; two stagecoaches bore all the travel between New York and Boston; a whipping post and pillory were still standing in both these cities; and beef, pork, salt fish, potatoes, and hominy were the staple diet all the year around. The factory became part of the American scene, a result of revolution in industry. Craftsmen felt insecure as one after another of the old skilled trades was either mechanized or so simplified that special competence was no longer necessary. Machines were tended by women and children, working hours were long, and wages were low. The importance of communication increased with each decade as the earlier simple manner of living became complicated by commercialized agriculture and mechanized industry. Transportation improved, commerce grew, and the inevitable result was the growth of cities. The nation absorbed a host of immigrants, who thronged into the industrial centers or joined the march of Americans to the West, where frontiers gave way before the growth of railroads, the improvement of farm machinery, and expanding markets.[1]

The American nation was in a stage of transition. In the search for its identity, it made giant strides in finding itself before 1860. Then a Civil War, in which the losses of life and property were staggering, left deep scars. After the war, the conquered Southland was completely occupied with the problems of reconstruction and survival, while the industrial North moved into unprecedented productive capacity. Industry had conquered agriculture. American workers, in confused and fumbling fashion, tried to organize effectively, and to adjust through labor unions. No longer were Americans an agricultural people, "provincial in viewpoint, unaware of the world around them, distrustful of strong government, and culturally immature"; before the nineteenth century closed, they would have become "an industrial people international in viewpoint, imperialistically minded, and culturally awakened." [2]

Industrialization and urbanization stimulated progress in literature and art. At first, American authors looked longingly back to pre-Civil War days, but gradually they took on a realistic tone, and "presented accurate and merciless pictures of a society adjusting to a machine civilization." [3] The image was unlovely—a "gilded age" that needed to be refined and honed. The economic collapse of 1873 caused panic and left three million men unemployed. The industrial world bounced back with stronger force than ever, and widened the gulf between rich and poor. Many Americans, caught in a maze of secular interests, lost their appetite for things religious, and churches worried as to how to combat the growing secular trend. Schlesinger observes:

Perhaps at no time in its American development has the path of Christianity been so sorely beset with pitfalls and perils as in the last quarter of the nineteenth century. The validity of the Bible itself seemed at stake in the light of new pronouncements of science and scholarship. Darwinism, the emerging science of biblical criticism, the increasing knowledge and study of other great religions—such threats to orthodoxy could not be ignored, yet how were they to be met? [4]

## Public Education

Forces were now at work which revolutionized the entire character of public education, and Catholic education could no more be immune to tendencies for change than its secular counterparts. Catholic education, indeed, cannot fairly be considered apart from its contemporaneous public counterpart. The increase of educational opportunities for the masses, adoption of new education theories from Europe, curricula suited to the individual's needs and abilities—these and other changing concepts of education in the public schools had repercussions in Catholic educational circles too. The rise of industrialism, requiring workers to be educated beyond the bare rudiments of reading and writing, and the spirit of humanitarianism, which urged the improvement of the lot of the common man, brought about a cry for free, tax-supported, state-controlled, non-sectarian schools. Leading public advocates were men like James D. Carter and Horace Mann in Massachusetts, and Henry Barnard in Connecticut and Rhode Island; in the old Northwest, Calvin E. Stowe; Samuel Galloway and Samuel Lewis in Ohio; Caleb Mills in Indiana; Ninian W. Edwards in Illinois; Isaac E. Crary and John D. Pierce in Michigan; and in the South Calvin H. Wiley of North Carolina, Charles F. Mercer in Virginia, and Robert Breckenridge in Kentucky. Although tax-supported schooling was not popular at first, the nation was socially, politically, and economically ready. It needed a leader to educate public opinion and it found one in Horace Mann, first secretary of Massachusetts' first State Board of Education. Mann's twelve annual *Reports* influenced every state in the North and convinced the American people that the United States needed a system of public education that was free, universal, and nonsectarian. Social efficiency, civic virtue, and character development were the aims of Mann's educational program. By the end of this period tax-supported free schooling was accepted, and the secularization of these schools well begun. The religious aim in education was on the way to being eliminated.

Public schools of this time experienced far-reaching changes in curriculum. The spirit of utilitarianism which permeated the new industrial America and the needs of frontier living led to an emphasis upon practical subjects. Greek and Latin were replaced gradually with such subjects as science, mathematics, geography, economics, and history. The graded-class organization was established, modeled on the graded school system of Prussia, which received favorable appraisal in Mann's *Seventh Annual Report*.[5] The elementary schools were also influenced by other educational ideas from Europe, especially those of Johann Heinrich Pestalozzi and Friedrich Wilhelm Froebel. Pestalozzian contributions led the elementary public schools to introduce investigation and observation, replacing the mere memorization of facts. Froebel's kindergarten stressed play, learning by doing, motor activity, and the social importance of education. Compulsory school attendance increased the population of the elementary schools. The first law compelling the attendance of every child between the ages of eight and fourteen was passed in Massachusetts in 1852. By 1918, compulsory education would extend to every state. The federal government, too, became concerned about the nation's schools. The United States Department of Education was created in 1867 to provide educational information and to improve school systems throughout the country; it became the present Office of Education in 1869.[6] The study of real objects and the importance of child activity in the classroom now called for better training of elementary school teachers. Although the first American state normal school was established in Lexington, Massachusetts, in 1839, the normal-school idea did not grow rapidly until after the Civil War. Twenty-two states publicly supported normal schools by 1870; by 1900 the number of public schools engaged in the training of teachers would increase to 170 and private normal schools would number 118. Teachers were helped to be professional not only by the increase of normal schools, but by state and national organizations of teachers and superintendents as well. In 1857, ten state teachers' associations issued a call to all teachers of the nation to organize as a National Teachers Association; in 1870 this became the National Education Association.

On the secondary level, the high school evolved from the academy. Considered for the most part as terminal, it was strong in its appeal as the poor man's college. Opposition to tax support for high schools was squelched in 1874 when the Supreme Court of the State of Michigan, in the "Kalamazoo Case," legalized the expenditure of public funds for the high school. Similar legislation followed in other states. Gradually, the high school moved into its own as part of the educational system of each state. A change took place in the character of the high-school curriculum. New subjects were introduced to prepare students for all areas of living—business courses, music, art, agriculture, manual training, physical education, and household arts, as well as the old classical studies of the academy days. Secondary education had responded to the needs of America's social and industrial life.

In higher education it was the era of "multiplication and variation of colleges." [7] By 1860, there were 182 permanent colleges and universities in the United States—in the main denominational colleges financed by tuition fees and donations of the faithful. After the Civil War, new types of higher educational institutions appeared—technological colleges, colleges for women, and coeducational institutes. The Morrill Act of 1862 gave the United States land-grant colleges which had as their major purpose the teaching of agriculture and the mechanical arts.[8] The first women's colleges arose in the South. Wesleyan Female College of Macon, Georgia, in 1836 became the first college to confer higher degrees on women, but it was not until after the Civil War that the movement gathered momentum. Coeducation was an established pattern by the end of this period. Oberlin, the first American coeducational college, opened in Ohio in 1833; forty years later, coeducational colleges and universities outnumbered separate women's institutions twentyfold. Not only did the liberal-arts colleges increase in number, but changes occurred within their curricula too. In 1869, Charles W. Eliot was elected president of Harvard. In his inaugural address, he announced his belief in an elective system, claiming that "the individual traits of different minds have not been sufficiently attended to." [9] This was a radical stand in a time that prided itself on its liberal-arts curriculum. Eliot held his ground, confident that only in the freedom of an elective system would leaders for the new America be produced. Such a system, with "its revolutionary implications, was a logical expression of the spirit of the time." [10]

## Catholic Education

In such a milieu of society and of public education, how did the Roman Catholic Church fare educationally from the First Provincial Council of Baltimore in 1829 through the Third Plenary Council of Baltimore in 1884? The first relevant observation pertains to the Church's growth. From Colonial and early National times when, east of the Mississippi, Catholicism had no home beyond the limits of Maryland and Pennsylvania, except in the old French hamlets, the growth of the Church was not uniform. The greatest signs of vitality were, as we have seen, in Maryland, Kentucky, Louisiana, and Missouri. In New York and Pennsylvania, during the days of the new republic, the bishops had found themselves hampered and thwarted in such a way that it was impossible for them to make even remote plans for any diocesan institutions.[11] Such was the position of the Church in the United States when the First Provincial Council of Baltimore met in 1829. The Catholic population of the United States at that time was estimated at 500,000; that of the whole country was 12,000,000. Estimates of Catholic population are all that we can rely upon for this period when there was no accurate Catholic census. By the time of the Third Plenary Council in 1884, however, Catholics numbered more than 8,000,000.[12] This amazing increase was due, in large part, to immigration from Europe, particularly Ireland and Germany.

The main reasons for the Irish immigration to America were the mercantile policies of the conquering British in their homeland, the foreign Anglican Church there, and the crushing effects of the potato blight of 1821 and the terrible famine of 1845. Wittke, a sound authority, remarks:

The figures for the period of the Irish famine immigration mounted to startling totals: 92,484 in 1846, 196,224 in 1847, 173,174 in 1848, 204,771 in 1849, and 206,041 in 1850. The Census of 1850 reported 961,719 Irish in the United States; by 1860, the total had reached 1,611,304. These were to be found in greatest numbers in New York, Pennsylvania, Massachusetts, Illinois, Ohio, and New Jersey.[13]

Most of the Irish immigrants were Catholics. The Church in the United States was important to them, and they became important to it. Indeed, as early as 1868, Maguire wrote:

There is scarcely an ecclesiastical seminary for English-speaking students, in which the great majority of those now preparing for the service of the sanctuary do not belong, if not by birth, at least by blood, to that historic land.[14]

Inasmuch as the Irish immigrants came from an agricultural country, it seems paradoxical that they huddled together in the slums of the new American cities. Their poverty, however, kept them from moving to the interior, where the purchase of land would have been impossible. Then, too, the Irish were a social people, and the cities attracted them. They were unskilled workers and lacking in education. At first they lived under harsh economic conditions, as common laborers and factory workers, but they adapted rapidly to their new environment, and gradually improved their economic condition. Near the end of the period, immigrants from other countries took up the common labor jobs, and the Irish contractor, superintendent, and foreman became common. There were, of course, Irish who remained in the slums, but overall the group presented a picture of gradual adaptation to and eventual acceptance by American society. And always during this time the Irish Catholic was "the most important element in the Church in this country."[15]

Shiploads of Catholic German immigrants also arrived. Before the Civil War, Germans left their homeland for economic reasons. Land was cheap in America, and the soil was good. But after the Civil War, conditions in Germany sent more immigrants than ever before. The unification of Germany in 1870 brought in its wake political conditions which drove many Germans from their fatherland. Catholics were persecuted under the *Kulturkampf*—a struggle between the Roman Catholic Church and the German government, mainly over the latter's efforts to control educational and ecclesiastical appointments in the interests of the political policy of centralization.[16] Of this period Barry writes:

They [the Germans] totaled around 700,000 in number from 1865 to 1900, and became the largest Catholic immigrant group arriving in the States. Between 1830-1870 Irish immigrants had come in the largest numbers, up to 50 per cent above the German totals. But by 1865 the Germans had equaled the Irish influx and, from 1870-1890, the Germans led the field.[17]

Many Germans settled in American cities,[18] but to a great extent they were farmers who selected agricultural areas, especially in what became known as the "German belt"—beginning between New York and Maryland and spreading westward "through the Ohio river basin to the Great Lakes and out into the prairie states beyond the Mississippi river."[19] The German farmer was thrifty and industrious, irritated by wasteful methods, and annoyed by laziness. To Americans, on the other hand, the German appeared to be "inexcusably frugal, materialistic, and penurious"[20]—a contrast to the Irish immigrant who was "wasteful and generous, helping his neighbor, whoever he was, when in distress, sighing in his soul for the Emerald Isle across the sea, and always willing to help those whom he had left behind."[21] Differences between these two leading immigrant Catholic peoples were to be "resolved in the Catholic climate of the Church [in the United States], through the attainment of a gradual understanding of pluralistic, mutual differences, and a compromise of nonessentials in favor of true Christian unity." [22]

German immigrants did not quickly lay aside the customs and language of their fatherland. They demanded national parishes and schools which gave instruction in the German language. The Church encouraged Americanization of the immigrant, but in the case of the Germans during this period, it proved a prolonged and often painful process. These were a people with "a firm loyalty to their religion, masterly organizational techniques, and a strong community pattern of worship, culture, and social action." [23]

During this era of the Church Councils in the United States, the Church endeavored to keep pace with the needs of her increasing numbers. Protestant America, conscious of a growing Catholic immigrant population, and convinced that the Roman Catholic Church was subversive of true Americanism, caused many states to become hotbeds of Nativism. Hostility to both the immigrants and the Catholic Church motivated the "Native American" parties that sprang up during the late 1840's and early 1850's.[24] Many Protestants were actuated by the fear that the Roman Catholic Church was preparing for the day when the Pope himself might transfer his headquarters to this country.

The foregoing remarks on public education and on Catholic growth must receive some specific application to Catholic education. Protestant acceptance of Horace Mann's nonsectarian religion in the schools marked a significant change in the theretofore traditional view of the school's function. Protestants, making a prudential judgment for that time (given the religious pluralism and their understanding of the need to "Americanize" immigrants through the common school), now began to opt for dual institutions, the public school for the secular realm of education and the Sunday school for the religious. The newly arrived Catholics, seeing the common schools as reflecting the definitely Protestant ethos which permeated American culture at the time, could not accept this solution. They, and their hierarchy, could not in conscience permit their children to attend schools conducted mainly by Protestant teachers, with a Protestant viewpoint, and with religious instruction and religious exercises of a decidedly Protestant (even if nondenominational) character. The growing secularistic nature of instruction in the public schools was no improvement.

The Councils of Baltimore looked seriously at the problem, legislated that parochial schools be increased in number, and urged Catholic parents to contribute to the schools' support. Parochial schools sprang up everywhere. Higher education for boys received a new impulse through the concerted efforts of the hierarchy, diocesan clergy, and teaching brotherhoods. Many academies for girls were established and conducted under the direction of religious orders of women. And all the while there was steady improvement in methods, curricula, training of teachers, and school buildings. As for the story of the foundations and sacrifices of the many teaching orders of brothers and sisters who came to the country during these years, each community warrants a volume in itself. Without taking into consideration the *branches* of the many religious teaching communities which were established in this country from 1829 to 1884, or diocesan groups, the tables on the following pages are presented as key points of relevance to the growth of the Church and to the expansion of Catholic education, which would have been impossible without such teaching communities. Only communities which engaged in educational activities are listed.

TABLE I

NON-DIOCESAN TEACHING COMMUNITIES OF RELIGIOUS WOMEN, 1829-1884 *

| RELIGIOUS COMMUNITY | DATE OF ESTABLISHMENT IN U.S. | PLACE OF FOUNDATION IN U.S. |
|---|---|---|
| 1. *Oblate Sisters of Providence* | 1829 | Baltimore, Md. |
| 2. *Sisters of Our Lady of Mercy* | 1829 | Charleston, S.C. |
| 3. *Les Dames de la Retraite* | 1830 | Philadelphia, Pa. |
| 4. *Sisters of Charity of the Blessed Virgin Mary* | 1833 | Philadelphia, Pa. |
| 5. *Sisters of Our Lady of Mount Carmel* | 1833 | New Orleans, La. |
| 6. *Sisters of St. Joseph* | 1836 | Carondelet, St. Louis, Mo. |
| 7. *Sisters of Providence* | 1840 | St. Mary-of-the-Woods, La. |
| 8. *Sisters of Notre Dame de Namur* | 1840 | Cincinnati, Ohio |
| 9. *The Sisters of the Holy Family* | 1842 | New Orleans, La. |
| 10. *Sisters of the Holy Cross* | 1843 | Bertrand, Mich. |
| 11. *Sisters of Mercy* | 1843 | Pittsburgh, Pa. |
| 12. *Sisters of the Precious Blood* | 1844 | New Riegel, Seneca County, Ohio |
| 13. *Sisters, Servants of the Immaculate Heart of Mary* | 1845 | Monroe, Mich. |
| 14. *School Sisters of Notre Dame* | 1847 | St. Mary's, Pa. (The School Sisters of Notre Dame remained here from Aug. 15, 1847, until Oct. 8, 1847, and then removed to Baltimore.) |
| 15. *Sisters of the Third Order of St. Francis of Assisi* | 1849 | Nojoshing (now known as St. Francis), Wis. |
| 16. *Sisters of Charity of St. Augustine* | 1851 | Cleveland, Ohio |

| RELIGIOUS COMMUNITY | DATE OF ESTABLISHMENT IN U.S. | PLACE OF FOUNDATION IN U.S. |
|---|---|---|
| 17. Benedictine Sisters | 1852 | St. Mary's, Pa. |
| 18. Sisters of the Incarnate Word and Blessed Sacrament | 1853 | Brownsville, Tex. |
| 19. Sisters of the Presentation | 1854 | San Francisco, Calif. |
| 20. Daughters of the Cross | 1855 | Avoyelles Parish, La. |
| 21. Grey Nuns | 1855 | Toledo, Ohio |
| 22. Daughters of Charity, Servants of the Poor | 1856 | Vancouver, Wash. |
| 23. Sisters of St. Agnes | 1858 | Barton, Washington County, Wis. |
| 24. Sisters of the Holy Names of Jesus and Mary | 1859 | Portland, Ore. |
| 25. Sisters of the Congregation of Notre Dame | 1860 | Bourbonnais, Ill. |
| 26. Religious of the Holy Child Jesus | 1862 | Towanda, Bradford County, Pa. |
| 27. Sisters of St. Mary of Namur | 1863 | Lockport, N.Y. |
| 28. Sisters of the Holy Humility of Mary | 1864 | Louisville, Ohio |
| 29. Sisters of Charity of the Incarnate Word | 1866 | Galveston, Tex. |
| 30. Sisters of Divine Providence | 1866 | Austin, Tex. |
| 31. Poor Handmaids of Jesus Christ | 1868 | Hesse Cassel, Ind. |
| 32. Sisters of St. Ann | 1870 | New York, N.Y. |
| 33. Sisters of the Immaculate Heart | 1871 | Gilroy, Calif. |
| 34. Sisters of the Most Holy Sacrament | 1872 | New Orleans, La. |
| 35. Sisters of Providence | 1873 | Holyoke, Mass. |
| 36. Sisters of Christian Charity | 1873 | New Orleans, La. |
| 37. Sisters of the Présentation de Marie | 1873 | Glens Falls, N.Y. |
| 38. Sisters of the Immaculate Conception | 1873 | Labadieville, La. |
| 39. Sisters of Charity of Our Lady, Mother of Mercy | 1873 | Baltic, Conn. |
| 40. Sisters of Notre Dame | 1874 | Cleveland, Ohio |
| 41. Sisters of Divine Providence | 1876 | Pittsburgh, Pa. |
| 42. Religious of the Sacred Heart of Mary | 1877 | Sag Harbor, L.I., N.Y. |
| 43. Religious of Jesus and Mary | 1877 | Fall River, Mass. |
| 44. Sisters of St. Joseph of Peace | 1884 | Jersey City, N.J. |

* This table is compiled from the following sources: Elinor Tong Dehey, *Religious Orders of Women in the United States* (Hammond, Indiana: W. B. Conkey Co., 1930), pp. 180-666; Thomas P. McCarthy, *Guide to the Sisterhoods in the United States* (Washington, D.C.: The Catholic University of America Press, 1964); John O'Kane Murray, *Catholic Education in the United States: A Statistical Review* (New York: E. Steiger Press, 1879), pp. 6-13. Both this and the following table were also checked against *Sadlier's Catholic Almanac and Ordo* for the years 1829-1884.

TABLE II

TEACHING BROTHERHOODS, 1829-1884 *

| RELIGIOUS COMMUNITY | DATE OF ESTABLISHMENT IN U.S. | PLACE OF FOUNDATION IN U.S. |
|---|---|---|
| 1. Brothers of the Congregation of Holy Cross | 1841 | Vincennes, Ind. |
| 2. Presentation Brothers | 1845 | Pittsburgh, Pa. |
| 3. Brothers of the Christian Schools | 1846 [1845] | Baltimore, Md. |
| 4. Brothers of St. Patrick | 1846 | Baltimore, Md. |
| 5. Brothers of the Sacred Heart | 1847 | Mobile, Ala. |
| 6. Franciscan Brothers | 1847 | Pittsburgh, Pa. |
| 7. Brothers of Mary | 1849 | Cincinnati, Ohio |
| 8. Xaverian Brothers | 1854 | Louisville, Ky. |
| 9. Brothers of the Holy Infancy | 1855 | Buffalo, N.Y. |
| 10. Brothers of Charity | 1874 | Boston, Mass. |
| 11. Marist Brothers of the Schools | 1882 | Poughkeepsie, N.Y. |

* This table is compiled from the following sources: John Gilmary Shea, *The History of the Catholic Church in the United States* (New York: John G. Shea, 1888), IV, 34, 71, 75, 485; John H. Lamott, *History of the Archdiocese of Cincinnati, 1821-1921* (New York: Frederick Pustet Co., 1921), pp. 239-242; Charles Warren Currier, *History of Religious Orders* (New York: Murphy & McCarthy, 1894), pp. 455-457, 489, 492-493, 499-501, 502-505, 518-524.

These teaching orders ameliorated, at least in part, the lack of teachers that had previously restricted the growth of Catholic education. They were dedicated men and women who, through their organized communities, gave a definite structure and form to Catholic schooling.

It is impossible within the limits of this study to discuss in detail Catholic educational activities in every diocese or state during this period. Several dioceses have been selected for consideration because they are typical of what went on in others, and point to patterns that were beginning to evolve.

### DIOCESE OF CINCINNATI

Cincinnati was originally part of the diocese of Bardstown, Kentucky. When Cincinnati had been constituted a separate diocese in 1821, it had embraced the entire state of Ohio, and included Michigan and Wisconsin until 1833. The early hero of both Church and education there was Bishop Edward Fenwick, O.P., who died in 1832. Bishop Benedict J. Flaget had consecrated him on January 13, 1822, in St. Rose's Church, in St. Rose, Kentucky.[25] Before leaving St. Rose's on January 25, Fenwick wrote a letter to the cardinal prefect of the Propaganda at Rome in which he expressed gratitude for favors received, and in a postscript related some of the conditions of the Church in Ohio. According to Fenwick, there were 6,000 Catholics scattered throughout the state.[26] Upon Fenwick's arrival, Cincinnati was the poorest of dioceses, but Catholics and non-Catholics alike rejoiced at his coming. *The Liberty Hall and Cincinnati Gazette* reported:

This circumstance [Fenwick's consecration and appointment] interests not only the Catholics, but all the friends of literature and useful knowledge, as we understand that his intention is ultimately to open a school, aided by the members of his order so long distinguished for their piety and learning.[27]

Fenwick, as we observed in the preceding chapter, had already had experience in Kentucky with Catholic education. From the beginning of his episcopal work in Cincinnati, he was "convinced that a college and seminary in, or near, Cincinnati was essential for the good of religion in his diocese." [28] The education of youth and the founding of schools were as important to him as the establishment of churches. On borrowed money he went to Europe, where he interested wealthy Catholics not only in the cause of his pioneer diocese but in that of his educational projects. The Association for the Propagation of the Faith provided incalculable assistance.

While in Europe Fenwick sought to obtain some religious women for his hoped-for Catholic schools. He succeeded in getting only one, Sister Saint Paul of the French Sisters of Mercy. She was the first nun ever in Cincinnati or even in the state of Ohio. In 1825, Sister Saint Paul, in company with Eliza Rose Powell,[29] opened a school. Fenwick wrote of the school to his friend, the Rev. Stephen Badin, in these words:

You will learn with pleasure that I have two religieuses in Cincinnati, Sister Saint Paul and one of my neophytes from Kentucky, who has become associated with her. The two have a school attended by twenty-five girls. They live by charity.[30]

O'Daniel observes that "theirs was the first sisters' and the first Catholic school in Ohio—and probably the state's first free school." [31] Fenwick had made a start. In 1826, he brought two Collettine Poor Clare nuns, Françoise Vindevoghel and Victoire de Seilles, from Bruges, and a Beguine from Ghent, Sister Adolphine Malingie. In 1827, they also established a girls' school and had seventy pupils, besides teaching many poor children on Sundays.[32] These two educational endeavors, however, were of short duration. Sister Saint Paul died in 1827; the two Poor Clares left Cincinnati for Pittsburgh in 1827; and the Beguine Sister returned to her lay status. O'Daniel comments on these educational failures:

These earlier efforts for Catholic education were an augury of other endeavors along the same lines soon to be crowned with success in both Cincinnati and Somerset, and to be a source of unspeakable joy to the good bishop, as well as of incalculable blessings to religion in Ohio.[33]

Success came at last with the opening of St. Francis Xavier's Theological Seminary on May 11, 1829. Work began with ten students—four in theology and six in humanities. In the same year of 1829, on October 27, four Sisters of Charity of Mother Seton at Emmitsburg, Maryland, came to work in Cincinnati: Sisters Francis Xavier Jordan, Victoria Fitzgerald, Beatrice Tyler, and Albina Levy.[34] On February 25, 1830, Fenwick wrote that they already had "one hundred and six children in the school, and five orphans in the asylum." [35] In January 1830, Fenwick succeeded in getting four Sisters of St. Dominic also to come from Kentucky and teach in Cincinnati: Sisters Emily Elder, Agnes Harbin, Catherine Mudd, and Benvin Sansbury. A new three-story convent and school was built for them, and the sisters came to rank so highly in the estimation of all the people that they were employed in 1832 by the school directors of their district to teach in the district school. Fenwick's dream college also became a reality on October 17, 1831. It opened under the name of *Cincinnati Athenaeum Religioni et Artibus Sacrum*, and offered a six-year classical course. Non-Catholics as well as Catholics attended the *Athenaeum*, as it came to be called. The name was changed to St. Xavier College in 1840. Fenwick had labored well in Cincinnati in the cause of Catholic education; on this point O'Daniel comments:

If possible, in building a house of prayer for his people, he also secured ground for a school so that, when the parish should be able to support it, the little ones of Christ might have the blessings of a Catholic education, a circumstance which shows his good judgment and keen foresight.[36]

John Baptist Purcell was installed as Cincinnati's new bishop on November 14, 1833, Fenwick having died on September 26, 1832. The almost fifty years of Purcell's episcopacy (1833–1879) witnessed great educational activity in Cincinnati. These were the Irish and German immigration years and, in the march of the German immigrant to the Midwest, Cincinnati became a little Germany. By the year 1833 the German population there was estimated at five thousand. They were people willing to make any sacrifice in order that their children be educated. And they had to make sacrifices. The anti-Catholic reaction to the immigrants saw the rise of the Native-American and Know-Nothing movements, and the Church's schools became a special target for attack, not only in Cincinnati, but throughout the nation. Although the Nativists used every possible means to impede the progress of Catholic schools, the growth of Catholic education in Cincinnati during the period was phenomenal. The five Provincial Councils of Cincinnati are proof of the concern of that diocese, clergy and laity, to further Catholic education.[37] Guilday says that "the movement toward parochial school education received its greatest impetus from the Provincial Councils of Cincinnati between 1852 and 1866." [38] And Spalding declared that "the question of religious education was, in the minds of the fathers of the Cincinnati

Councils, the test of fidelity or infidelity to God." [39] The keynote of the
Provincial Councils of Cincinnati pertaining to education was struck in
the first pastoral letter, written by the Most Reverend Martin J. Spalding,
bishop of Louisville, Kentucky, and issued on the closing day of the
First Council, May 20, 1855. In part, it said to Catholics under its
jurisdiction:

> Earnestly do we desire to see a parochial school in connection with every
> Catholic Church in this province; and we hope the day is not distant when
> this wish nearest our hearts shall be fully realized. With all the influences con-
> stantly at work to unsettle the faith of our children, and to pervert their tender
> minds from the religion of their fathers, and with all the lamentable results of
> these influences constantly before our eyes, we cannot too strongly exhort you
> to contribute generously of your means to enable your pastor to carry out this
> great work. The erection of Catholic schools is, in many respects, as important
> an object as the building of new churches. The Catholic Church has ever been
> the greatest promoter of education; she erected colleges and universities and
> she covered the earth with free schools, reared under the shadow of her church
> edifices, centuries before the fatal troubles of the sixteenth century came to
> unsettle the faith by severing the unity of Christendom; and she is as great a
> friend of education now as she was then; but she wishes it not to be severed
> from religion, which is its main support and solid foundation.[40]

Purcell himself issued a pastoral letter on the decrees of the First
Provincial Council of Cincinnati, and warmly praised the German
Catholics in his diocese. He remarked:

> Our excellent German congregations leave us nothing to desire on this sub-
> ject. The children attend at Mass every morning, they sing with one accord
> the praises of God, they go from the church to the school. They are accus-
> tomed to cleanliness and neatness of dress, to punctuality and order, to dili-
> gence and affectionate respect for their parents, the Reverend Clergy and their
> teachers. We have nothing more at heart than that the pupils of our English
> schools should imitate these examples. We have convinced an implacable ma-
> jority that they do us an injustice by depriving us of our proportionate share
> of the School Fund.[41]

To discuss Catholic educational activity in Cincinnati from the time of
Fenwick's death in 1832 until the end of this period in 1884 is to linger
on Purcell's education achievements (Purcell died on July 4, 1883.) [42] He
introduced many religious communities, the first being the Sisters of
Notre Dame de Namur, who arrived in 1840 and opened a Young
Ladies' Literary Institute and Boarding School on January 18, 1841. A
month after the school's opening, there were thirty pupils in the day
school, and one boarder, an Episcopalian. They also had a free school in
which, at that time, there were between thirty and forty pupils.[43] The
Sisters of the Most Precious Blood came from Switzerland in 1844 and
opened a girls' school at New Riegel in Seneca County; in 1845, an
Ursuline community of eleven members arrived from France, settled in
Brown County, and opened an academy for young ladies; the Sisters of

Mercy came in 1858 and opened a day school and a night school; in 1869 the Ladies of the Sacred Heart opened a school in Cincinnati on Sixth Street, near Stone; at St. Bernard, Ohio, the Sisters of the Third Order Regular of St. Francis in 1876 began teaching in a school attached to St. Clement's Church, where the Franciscan Fathers ministered; and the Sisters of Christian Charity took charge of a school at Pique, Ohio, in 1881. (Purcell also brought to the diocese other Sisterhoods engaged in charitable and social work—for example, the Sisters of the Good Shepherd in 1857, and the Sisters of the Poor of St. Francis in 1858.)

Year after year the educational growth continued. Orders of men came to work among the Catholic boys. The Jesuits took charge of the *Athenaeum* in 1840 and changed its name to St. Xavier College. The *Catholic Almanac* of 1842 made this reference to St. Xavier's:

This literary establishment was opened on the first Monday of November, 1840, under the direction of the Fathers of the Society of Jesus, and the patronage of the Right Rev. Dr. Purcell, Bishop of Cincinnati. The buildings are spacious, airy, and well adapted for school purposes; the diet is wholesome and abundant. The professors, six in number, are members of the Catholic clergy, exclusively devoted to the education of youth in virtue and science; they will spare no pains to improve the hearts and inform the minds of their pupils. They will be aided in this undertaking by five assistant tutors.[44]

On March 5, 1842, St. Xavier College was incorporated in the state of Ohio, and became empowered to confer degrees in the state. (In 1920, the college would become St. Xavier University.) The Vincentian Fathers attempted to conduct a diocesan seminary in 1842, but they found their location in Brown County to be undesirable and closed the institution in 1845. The year 1849 marked the arrival of the Brothers of the Society of Mary, who one year later opened a school at Dayton—a day and boarding school. On December 26, 1855, all the buildings on the place burned, but by 1857 the Brothers had new buildings in readiness for twenty pupils. This was St. Mary's Institute, which would begin its career as Dayton University in 1920. The Holy Cross Fathers opened St. Joseph's College in Cincinnati in 1871.

Although Catholic education in Cincinnati displayed excellent growth during the period under discussion, it was growth under difficult conditions. "In the great diocese of Cincinnati, as elsewhere," says Shea, "the question of education was agitated; but the dominant majority would neither make the public schools such that Catholics could use them, nor establish a separate system of schools for them."[45] Lamott observes:

From the earliest years of its existence, the diocese of Cincinnati endeavored to erect and maintain parochial schools for the primary education of its children. The first two bishops of the diocese considered the necessity of such schools as a matter of course, so that wherever Catholic churches were built, the Catholic parochial school was sure to follow if indeed it had not even antici-pated the church. It was only after opposition to the parochial schools began to manifest itself in 1853, that the necessity of providing parochial schools be-came a matter of legislation, and then each and every diocesan synod and pro-vincial council held in the archdiocese of Cincinnati concerned themselves with the subject.[46]

Cincinnati had grown so much that in 1850 it was raised to the dignity of an archdiocese, with the dioceses of Louisville, Detroit, Vincennes, and Cleveland as suffragan sees. Lamott, whom we have quoted so often because he derived his information wherever possible from primary sources, traces the corresponding growth of Catholic education when he says:

In 1854, nearly every church in the archdiocese had its school, filled with pu-pils. In 1860, there were 61 schools, and in 1870, 103 schools. In 1908, in the *First Annual Report of the Superintendent of the Parish Schools of the Cin-cinnati Archdiocese,* there were scattered in eighteen of the counties of Ohio subject to the jurisdiction of Cincinnati, 110 parochial schools, frequented by 27,233 pupils, and taught by 602 teachers.[47]

### DIOCESE OF VINCENNES

Pope Gregory XVI created the see of Vincennes in 1834, separating it from the diocese of Bardstown, Kentucky, and giving it as its first bishop the learned Simon William Gabriel Bruté. Vincennes at that time in-cluded not only the state of Indiana but also eastern Illinois. According to Shea, the Catholic population was poor, "generally ignorant, and re-quiring much instruction and rousing." [48] Bruté had to build Catholic education in Vincennes from the very foundation. There was no college, seminary or school outside of the old Indian mission stations. We have seen that there had been a school conducted by Sisters of Charity from Nazareth, Kentucky, in 1824, but they had been recalled to their mother-house before Bruté arrived, owing to the hardships of life at Vincennes. Bruté immediately persuaded them to return. Bruté, on taking up the bishopric at Vincennes, decided to visit his diocese in order to form a definite idea of the number of Catholics. He saw the situation as no less than appalling. He lacked priests and money. As Fenwick had done in Cincinnati, he went to Europe for help, and his visit was not unavailing. On his return he landed in New York on July 20, 1836, with funds and "nineteen priests and seminarians, many of them Bretons, resolute, en-during, full of faith and zeal." [49] With the funds he at once founded two French free schools—one for boys and the other for girls—in which children of all creeds found welcome. Vincennes was in for an educa-tional awakening: Bruté oversaw the establishment of an orphan asylum, an academy for young ladies, a college for secular students, and an ecclesiastical seminary. The aid from Europe also helped to complete the cathedral and erect small churches. The priests were missioned "at the most densely populated posts and the work of spreading Catholicism began to thrive satisfactorily in Indiana."[50]

It is difficult to find sources on Bruté's schools. We do know that the seminary for clerics and the secular college were housed in one building —St. Gabriel's College. The *Catholic Almanac* for 1841 gave the following account of St. Gabriel's:

> The Rev. gentlemen of this institution and of the college attached to it, are members of the Society of Eudists. There are at present nine ecclesiastical students, five of whom are at St. Gabriel's college. . . . This institution was commenced nearly three years ago. . . . It is now permanently established, and confidently solicits the support of an enlightened public. The numerous faculty consists of professors in all the various branches of education, who are permanently connected and identified with the college. . . . The course of instruction is designed to be as extensive as that of any college in the United States. . . . Day Scholars: 1st—Spelling, Writing, third class of Arithmetic. 2nd—Reading, Writing, English Grammar, second class of Arithmetic, Bookkeeping, History and Geography. 3rd—third class of Arithmetic, English Composition, Public Speaking, higher branches of Mathematics, Latin and Greek, or any of those branches. Extra charges—The same as for boarders and fuel for the season.[51]

Bruté had set up a system of schools which made provision for elementary, secondary, and higher education for both sexes.[52]

When Bruté died in 1839 many of his educational hopes were still unfulfilled. His successor, Bishop Célestin de la Hailandière, was sympathetic to Bruté's plans and determined to continue them, but Shea remarks that "his [Hailandière's] mind was one of excessive anxiety, and he sought to do everything himself in his anxiety to accomplish the greatest good."[53] The result was confusion in the diocese, and the bishop, disheartened, resigned his see in 1847.[54] Hailandière had accomplished much in those few years, although it seems that he could see no point of view but his own. As an able financier and builder he was unmatched, but he lacked understanding of the problems of those under his charge, particularly his priests and religious. He brought over from France priests, sisters, and Brothers to work with him. Six Brothers of the Congregation of Holy Cross, for example, accompanied the Rev. Edward Sorin, C.S.C., to Vincennes in 1841—the first of the teaching brotherhoods to be permanently established in this country. At first they taught school at St. Peter's, near Vincennes. Then they moved to the northern part of the state where in 1844 they opened the College of Notre Dame and a Manual Labor School. In the same year of 1844 the state chartered both schools. Notre Dame was from the beginning a university, and Sorin its first president.[55] The *Catholic Almanac* of 1845 said of Notre Dame:

> This institution—under the patronage of the Right Rev. Bishop of Vincennes,

and directed by the Rev. E. Sorin—is open for the reception of young men of
any religious profession, without preference or distinction. The location is on
an eminence, and is one of the most healthy in the state, situated six miles
from the town of Washington, Indiana.[56]

The Sisters of Providence of Ruillé-sur-Loire, France, came to Indiana
in 1840 and established themselves near Terre Haute under the title of
St. Mary-of-the-Woods. Their girls' academy, St. Mary's Institute, was
dedicated on July 5, 1841, and the next day registered four pupils. It was
begun on the same plan as the collegiate institutes of France. Higher
education was its primary object. The charter given in 1846 by the
Indiana legislature granted to St. Mary-of-the-Woods all the rights and
privileges of chartered institutions, and empowered it to confer collegiate degrees whenever students were judged ready to receive them.[57]

Sorin had been instrumental in bringing the Sisters of the Holy Cross
to Vincennes in 1843, in order that they might help the Brothers of the
Holy Cross in the educational work of the diocese. Hailandière had not
encouraged their entrance into his diocese—it had not been his idea.
They came in for their share of trouble under the bishop's displeasure,
as did Sorin, and also Mother Théodore Guérin, Superior of the Sisters of
Providence.[58] The Holy Cross Sisters therefore established themselves at
Bertrand, Michigan, instead. Hailandière's timely resignation gave Vincennes a new bishop in the person of the Right Rev. John Stephen Bazin,
who was destined to rule the diocese for only six months (October,
1847 to April, 1848). The Rt. Rev. James M. Maurice de St. Palais became
Vincennes' fourth bishop, serving until 1877.[59] German immigrants came
and settled throughout the state of Indiana, inhabiting the various
counties of the diocese of Vincennes. Growing parishes made every
effort to supply teachers and schoolhouses. When St. Palais took over the
administration of Vincennes, about one-fourth of the southern parishes
had schools, and during his incumbency seventy-one more schools were
established.[60] Alerding writes:

When the good Bishop's [St. Palais'] eyes closed in death, the Diocese of Vincennes numbered 90,000 souls, 151 churches, and 117 priests. Religious orders,
both male and female, came at his invitation, and exercised their benign influence throughout the length and breadth of his happy diocese. The male orders are the Benedictine Fathers, the Franciscan Fathers at Indianapolis, the
Fathers O.M.C. at Terre Haute, and the Brothers of the Sacred Heart. These
date their advent in the Diocese of Vincennes to Bishop de St. Palais' administration, as do also the following orders: The Sisters of St. Francis, the Nuns of
the Order of the Good Shepherd, the Little Sisters of the Poor, the Ursuline
Sisters, and the Sisters of St. Joseph.[61]

All St. Palais' educational endeavors make for a study in themselves,
but we can mark highlights only. His first work after he undertook the
bishopric was the erection of the Girls' Orphanage at Vincennes. This

institution opened on August 28, 1849, under the care of the Sisters of Providence. Two years later a temporary orphanage for boys opened in the College building at Vincennes, moving after several years to Highland, about three miles from the city. The year 1852 marked the canonical establishment of an order of women whose life work was the promotion of education—the Franciscan Sisters from Vienna, Austria. Two sisters left Vienna for America, but only one, Sister Theresa Hackelmeier, had the courage to persevere with the journey. She established herself at Oldenburg, Ind., received three postulants, and prospered in her educational work. In 1854, St. Palais accepted the Benedictine monks from the famous Abbey of Einsiedeln in Switzerland, and established them permanently at St. Meinrad. Of this remarkable community, Godecker writes:

The Fathers at once entered into the educational field by opening a school to which a college was soon added. The early years for this community, as for all pioneer foundations, were years of trial and suffering. Death claimed some of their most illustrious men, while ill health forced others to return to Europe. In time others became acclimated and ere long the institution began to flourish. By the year 1861 it had become sufficiently spacious to domicile not only the college students but also the diocesan seminarians. Since that year it has been the distinguished privilege of the Benedictine Fathers to educate the seminarians of the diocese.[62]

In 1855, St. Palais had the community of the Sisters of the Holy Cross brought back from Bertrand, Michigan, to St. Mary's, a place two miles from Notre Dame. They immediately accepted the care of schools.

From 1849 to 1857, St. Palais held jurisdiction over the whole state of Indiana. A decree of Pope Pius IX on January 8, 1857, erected the northern half of the state into the diocese of Fort Wayne, granting it forty counties. The diocese of Vincennes continued with fifty-two counties, and was "gradually and steadily built up," says Shea, "mainly by devoted and laborious priests." [63] During his twenty-eight years as bishop, St. Palais directed, encouraged, and entreated his priests, even under their pioneer conditions, to establish schools and to take up the work of Catholic education. Often the basement of the church was the only schoolroom available. This was true, for example, of St. Simon's School, Washington; St. Gabriel's School, Connersville; and St. Lawrence's School, Lawrenceburg. Pastors gave part of their dwellings, rented private homes, and used choir-lofts as places to teach school. It was through the zeal of the pioneer pastor at Oldenburg, the Rev. Francis Joseph Rudolph, for example, that the aforementioned Congregation of the Sisters of St. Francis were brought to the diocese. Rudolph appealed to the Rev. Ambrose Bauhmaier, a Franciscan missionary of New York, to procure Franciscan sisters to help him at Oldenburg. It was through the energy of another such priest in Jasper, Dubois County—the Rev. Joseph

Kundeck—that the Sisters of Providence were introduced to Jasper in 1844, and that the Benedictines of Einsiedeln, Switzerland, sent members to found the above-mentioned St. Meinrad's.

## DIOCESE OF DETROIT

Detroit had had its beginnings in Catholic education with the Rev. Gabriel Richard, whose educational endeavors were sketched in the preceding chapter. His spirit and zeal were caught up in the cause of Catholic education in Detroit by the scholarly Rt. Rev. Frederick Résé, who was consecrated as bishop in 1833, the year following Richard's death, and who took possession of his diocese in January, 1834.[64] Things looked fair to Résé then, for there were Catholic schools not only in the city of Detroit but in the neighboring Catholic settlements. Résé, as vicar-general of the diocese of Cincinnati, had, in 1830, made a visitation to Michigan and knew the schools outside the city—at the old mission of St. Joseph's (later Bertrand) on St. Joseph River, Michigan; at Mt. Clemens, which had been established in 1825 by the Rev. Pierre Dejean with industrial education in mind; and in the larger French settlement of Monroe, where a school had existed since 1820, and where the Rev. Samuel Smith had made an attempt at the formation of a teaching sisterhood. (This attempted religious foundation was dissolved with Smith's removal from Monroe in July, 1831.) [65] Résé had also found a flourishing school existing among the Ottawa Indians at Arbre-Croche (Harbor Springs), some forty miles from Mackinac. This school, too, had been founded by Dejean, who was succeeded at Arbre-Croche in 1831 by the Rev. Frederic Baraga, who had been sent there from Cincinnati by Fenwick, and was destined to work in the Northwest for nearly forty years.[66] Résé was enthusiastic. He even dreamed of Catholic higher education for Detroit.

Résé's St. Philip's College fell far short of his dreams. It was a small structure under the direction of the Oratorian Fathers. To one conscious of evolving patterns of curriculum and discipline, its prospectus, as given in the *Catholic Almanac* of 1837, is worth observation. It reads, in part:

> A good moral and religious education being an inexhaustible source of social and individual happiness, the Right Reverend Bishop Résé, who deeply feels the want of a proper literary and classical establishment in Michigan, has tried to overcome the innumerable obstacles he met with and endeavors now to benefit the country with an institution adapted to the desirable improvement of the education of youth in a thriving and enlightened state. . . . The course of instruction pursued in the College will embrace the Latin, Greek, French and English languages, Poetry, Rhetoric and Oratory, Reading, Writing, Geography, Mathematics and Bookkeeping. A favorable opportunity to become well conversant with the French language will be found in the intercourse with the pupils whose native tongue is French. Strict attention will be paid to the moral conduct of the students, and no infraction of the disciplinary rules of

the College will be connived at; in case of delinquency, the delinquent will first be admonished, and if admonition or if mild and paternal punishment prove ineffectual, he will be sent back to his parents or guardians.

The Regency of the College is Catholic, but the pupils of other denominations are admitted provided they be willing to attend morning and evening prayer, daily and divine worship on Sundays and holydays; good order requiring this compliance; but there shall be no interference or tampering whatever with their religious principles. . . . The price of the scholastic year is fixed at the moderate sum of one hundred dollars, including board and tuition payable quarterly in advance. Washing, mending, medical attendance and medicine at the expense of the parents. No deduction will be made for absence except in cases of protracted sickness, or dismission, either in consequence of a student's leaving the College before the end of the quarter [*sic*]. . . .

Semi-annual reports will be sent to the parents or guardians relative to each student's proficiency, conduct and health.

No leave will be granted to sleep out of the College. The correspondence of the students, except with parents or guardians, is subject to inspection.[67]

The student body never exceeded thirty at any time, but Paré claims that "during the few years of its existence [it] housed several of the future prominent citizens of Detroit." [68] Misfortune pursued the college. It lacked teachers, and appears to have been unoccupied when it burned to the ground in 1842. The diocese had to wait for thirty-five years, and for the coming of the Jesuits, before it had another college.

While awaiting the opportunity to open his college, Résé in 1836 had begun a high school in a building near the rectory—St. Anne's Classical Academy. According to Detroit's historian Richard R. Elliott, who had attended St. Anne's, the courses comprised Geography, Arithmetic, Bookkeeping, Geometry, Ancient and Modern History, Natural and Moral Philosophy, Botany, French, and the Greek and Latin classics— "everything calculated to form the character of the scholar, the gentleman, and the Christian." [69] School life did not run smoothly at the Academy, however: the teacher, William McDonagh, could not deal with the boys, and resigned at the end of the year. Résé's seminarians tried to keep the school functioning, but apparently it was a sorry job, for when Bishop Peter Paul Lefevre came to Detroit in 1841, he closed the Classical Academy. The education of girls in Detroit during Résé's episcopacy was cared for by the Poor Clares. Sr. M. Rosalita discusses at length the "Female Academy of St. Clare's Seminary," quoting from McCabe's *Directory of the City of Detroit* of 1837, which gave an account of the school—its aims and form of government—in the following words:

This Seminary is superintended by the ladies of St. Clare, and embraces all the attainments which are necessary in society. Devoted to the education of female youth, they spare no pains to adorn their minds with useful knowledge, and to form their hearts to virtue. The ordinary branches of education are taught, the terms for which are liberal. The strictest attention is paid to the

cleanliness and health of the pupils; the table plain, but plentiful and wholesome. The government is mild but firm. No pupil is received or continued for
a shorter time than a quarter. The dress of the pupils is uniform, and the articles requisite upon entering merely necessary for comfort and convenience.
The friends of pupils are allowed to visit them at stated times.[70]

The same *Directory* stated that Poor Clares also taught an English and
German Free School in 1837, which had an average attendance of forty-
five pupils. But Résé, scholar though he was, had not the knack of
bringing his educational endeavors to successful continuance. Of his
trouble with the Poor Clares, Sr. M. Rosalita has this to say:

The prosperity of these institutions seemed to augur well for their future but
serious difficulties arose between the Religious and their ecclesiastical superior,
Bishop Résé. Whether the cause of disagreement was property affairs or differences regarding the rule of the Order matters little. The importance of the
trouble, in so far as education was concerned, rests on the fact that before the
close of the decade both educational institutions of the Poor Clares were closed
and they themselves had departed from Detroit.[71]

Résé resigned in 1840, and Paré tries to provide perspective by observing:

The real growth of the Church in Michigan was to come only from European
immigration, and that tide had just begun to flow. No matter how active may
have been the zeal of Bishop Résé and his priests, they were thwarted by dis-
heartening circumstances which only time could change. . . . The educational
projects which he fostered demonstrated how determined he was to build up
a well-rounded Catholic life in his diocese. But of the details of his administration we know scarcely anything.[72]

Detroit had not developed under Résé. As far as Catholic education
was concerned, Peter Paul Lefevre, his successor, was left very little
except problems; but in the twenty-nine years of his administration
"every important center had been established, and subsequent growth
has only filled in the vacant spaces in the original design." [73] Under
Bishop Casper Henry Borgess, who took possession of the see of
Detroit in 1870, the growth of educational activity continued. Accounts
of schools, however, are scarce. We must rely heavily on *Catholic
Almanacs* of the time, and on the histories of religious orders who came
to work in Detroit. The *Catholic Almanac* for 1846, for example, presented the educational scene:

St. Vincent's Select School for girls, conducted by the Sisters of Charity.
Sister Loyola, Sister Servant. This school was opened last May, and numbers
from 50 to 60 pupils. All the branches of a plain and useful education are
taught, and the religious instruction of the scholars is particularly attended to.
Besides, the Sisters have also opened two other schools for poor children, one
for boys under the age of ten years, numbering 75 scholars, and the other for
girls, 87 in number. Catechetical instruction is attended to on every Wednes-

day afternoon, and one hour before high mass on Sundays, and also an hour before vespers.

Trinity Church Male School (English), in Detroit. The school is held in the basement of St. Ann's Church, and numbers 60 pupils.

St. Mary's German School in Detroit. The school is held also in the basement of St. Ann's, and numbers between 40 and 60 pupils, boys and girls.

Besides the above, there are three Sunday Schools and Library. The Library contains 800 volumes, which are issued weekly to the members of the society. . . .

There is a society among the German Catholics in Detroit, that has for its object principally to sustain their Sunday School, Library and Church Music. . . .

Sunday School in Monroe for the English, French and Germans. Number of pupils, 150.[74]

(The Daughters of Charity had arrived in Detroit in 1844.)

Religious orders now began to swell the teaching body in Detroit. The Redemptorist priest, Louis Florent Gillet, founded a local community, the Sisters, Servants of the Immaculate Heart of Mary, in 1845; until 1847 the community bore the title of Sisters of Providence. Four young women—Teresa Maxis and Ann Schaaf, of Baltimore, Maryland; Teresa Renauld of Grosse Pointe, Michigan; and Madame Josette Godfroy Smith, whose brother was the mayor of Monroe, Michigan—volunteered for the new foundation, and Teresa Renauld became the first superior. The first convent of the Sisters, Servants of the Immaculate Heart of Mary, was a log cabin on the banks of the Raisin River at Monroe, Michigan, not far from where St. Mary's convent now stands. The *Catholic Almanac* of 1847 recorded the existence of the Sisters' first academy and said of it:

The plan of education, together with the benefit of Christian instruction, unites every advantage that can be derived from a punctual and conscientious care bestowed on the pupils in every branch of science suitable to their sex, and from the uninterrupted attention which is given to form the manners and principles of the young ladies, and to train them up in the habits of order, neatness and industry. The diet is good, wholesome and abundant. Spacious grounds afford the pupils the facility of pleasant walks, and useful bodily exercises. Their health is the object of constant solicitude; in sickness they are affectionately attended to, and never are they left a moment beyond the reach of inspection. . . .

The branches taught are: Reading, Writing in various styles; Grammar, both French and English; Arithmetic, Chronology, Mythology, Polite Literature, Geography, Elements of Astronomy, Natural Philosophy, Domestic Economy, Book Keeping, by single and double entry; History, sacred and profane, ancient and modern; Plain and Ornamental Needle Work, Bead Work, Tapestry, Lace Work, Marking, Embroidery, with gold and silver; Painting, Worsted Flowers; Music, vocal and instrumental.[75]

The Religious of the Sacred Heart came to Detroit in 1851, and the following year marked the arrival of the School Sisters of Notre Dame. The

Sisters of the Holy Cross were stationed at Bertrand in 1844, as we observed in our study of Vincennes. In 1851, Lefevre's hopes for the education of Detroit's boys were realized by the entrance into the diocese of four Brothers of the Christian Schools who took charge of the school at St. Anne's. A year later four additional brothers were stationed at St. Mary's parish. A third school of the Brothers, St. Peter's Academy, opened in January 1856. Its course of studies was outlined in the *Catholic Almanac* of 1857, whose announcement read, in part:

> The course of instruction comprises English and French Reading, Writing English and French Grammar, Arithmetic, Algebra, ancient and modern History, Geography, Book-keeping, Philosophy, Geometry, Astronomy, use of the globes, drawing and painting in water colors, etc. Number of scholars, 100. Bro. William, first teacher.[76]

Lefevre, it is true, cut less striking a figure in Catholic education in Detroit than did Richard. The many-sidedness of the latter's interests is fascinating, and there is probably no more interesting chapter to be found in the story of Catholic education in the United States than that of Michigan's pioneer priest who without finances, but with determination and perseverance, established the Catholic school system in Detroit. But more than any other, it was Lefevre who set Catholic education there on its feet. "Every phase of diocesan activity," says Paré, "begins with him. The magnificent growth of today rests squarely upon the solid foundations which he left to his successors." [77] Paré, in relating educational activity under Detroit's bishops Résé, Lefevre, and Borgess (in which the author used every available primary source), writes thus about the conclusion of Lefevre's espiscopate:

> At the end of Bishop Lefevre's episcopate . . . there were about twenty schools conducted by the religious communities already mentioned, with a total enrollment of approximately 3500 pupils. This . . . does not tell the whole story. The Sisters were not the pioneers of education in the diocese, particularly outside of Detroit. Almost invariably they came in only to crown the efforts that had been made before them. The pioneers were the little immigrant groups scattered throughout the state, struggling against poverty, but strong in their faith, who managed somehow to procure through primitive buildings and lay teachers the essentials of a Catholic education for their children. In nearly every one of the older parishes the first building erected served for both school and church purposes.[78]

### DIOCESE OF BOSTON

It was difficult, against the odds of anti-Catholic prejudice, scarcity of religious teachers, and limited resources, for Catholic education to show any marked development in the diocese of Boston. But to say there was no progress would be untrue. By 1829, Catholicism's prospects were taking a promising turn for the better. During the period 1829–1884,

Boston became the home of many Catholic immigrants from Ireland and Germany. They brought with them a loyalty to the Catholic faith that sought expression in churches and schools. The Church made strenuous efforts to meet their spiritual and educational needs. Schools grew rapidly. We have space to mark only certain significant milestones that show Boston at one with the other dioceses of the period in its evolving patterns of education, while at the same time retaining its individuality. Its distinctness is witnessed, for example, by the fact that at Benedict Fenwick's installation in 1825, Boston had contained "the most thoroughly English and anti-Catholic portion of the population of the United States," [79] which only gradually lost its Puritan character, as immigrants, particularly the Irish, poured in.

Elementary schools were Fenwick's first concern. In 1827 he had opened two day schools, one for boys, which was the first Catholic school for boys in Boston, and the other for girls, together known as the "Catholic Academy." The boys were taught by priests and seminarians of the cathedral, and the girls by ladies of the parish.[80] In 1831, a school was established in Salem, initiated by the Rev. William Wiley and taught by Miss Elizabeth Sharpe.[81] Fenwick in 1832 brought to Boston the Sisters of Charity from Emmitsburg, Maryland, who established St. Vincent's Orphan Asylum and also opened a free day school. The Catholic schools in the city of Lowell, whose opening we noted in the preceding period, continued to be an encouraging venture. These schools had opened in 1823 or 1824 for the children of Irish immigrants and were adopted into the public school system and supported by public funds. The teachers and textbooks were to be satisfactory to both Catholics and town superiors, and the schoolrooms to be provided by Catholics.[82] The Lowell Plan was a compromise whereby the Church hoped to assert the right of Catholic schools to support from public taxes. It worked well until 1852, when the Rev. John O'Brien invited the Sisters of Notre Dame de Namur to teach in St. Patrick's school there, with the hope that the sisters' school would claim the same public support. (The Sisters of Notre Dame de Namur had arrived in Boston in 1849 at the invitation of the Rev. John McElroy, S.J., to teach in St. Mary's School, Stillman Street, North End.) Not only did the town refuse this aid, but the sisters' request resulted in the town's withdrawal of all financial aid for the Catholic schools of Lowell.

The end of the Lowell experiment was but one incident in the religious bigotry of the Know-Nothing movement. We have already mentioned the burning of the Ursuline convent in Charlestown, just outside Boston, in 1834. In 1855, the Know-Nothing legislature authorized a special committee to invade the privacy of "boarding schools, academies, nunneries, convents, etc.," investigate, and report back. This was just one year after the Sisters of Notre Dame de Namur had staffed the Academy of Notre Dame, Roxbury. Accordingly, twenty-four Know-Nothings drove up to the academy, rushed without permission from attic to cellar snooping into every closet and behind every door, brutally tried to have the children admit that they were cruelly treated by the sisters, acted irreverently in the chapel, and left, only to oblige the sisters to testify later in court.[83] In spite of the anti-Catholic sentiment, however, Catholic elementary educational activity continued. A significant event in the history of the diocese was the establishment of Holy Trinity School in Boston by the Rev. Gerald Plathe in 1844 for the religious education of German Catholic children. Classes were held in the church basement for children of both sexes. It was actually New England's first parochial school; as the number of pupils increased, various buildings on Shawmut Avenue were used, the longest-used site being acquired in 1874.[84] (This school would close in 1961 because of the long-time disappearance of German parishioners, and slum clearance and urban redevelopment.)

The progress of Catholic education, however, left much to be desired until after the Civil War. The diocese was poor and immigrants came too fast.[85] Many children were forced to attend the common schools, which at that time were really Protestant schools. Catholic clergy advised parents to insist that their children attending these schools be excused from Protestant religious exercises. Such pleas usually went unheeded, and Catholic children were punished or expelled for not taking part in Protestant Bible readings and other Protestant exercises. The Eliot School Controversy which occurred in Boston in 1859 is a case in point. A Catholic boy had been whipped for refusing, at his parents' request, to attend the Protestant religious instructions. The Catholic parents brought suit against the teacher, who was acquitted at the trial, and several hundred Catholic boys were suspended from the school until they learned to obey the rules. To add to the injury, the boys' parents were liable to prosecution because the Massachusetts Compulsory Education Law of 1852 demanded school attendance of all children.[86] This controversy caused St. Mary's school for boys to be established in the North End section of Boston in 1859. Because the Rev. Bernardine Wiget, S.J., was the initiator of this project, the school came to be called "Father Wiget's School," and was so designated for many years. Catholic parents were convinced that separate schools for Catholic children were imperative. The American hierarchy strongly expressed their attitude through the Councils of Baltimore, which eventually legislated that schools be established in connection with all Catholic churches. For dioceses with the problems of Boston, compliance was difficult.

To one who is unmindful of the Protestant opposition to Catholics in Boston in those days, the fewness of parochial schools was discouraging. In 1872, there were only 13 Catholic parochial schools in the whole diocese—eleven for girls and two for boys—and less than 6,000 pupils. Schools that had been established in Salem, Lowell, and Lawrence before this date closed for lack of funds. Ten new parish schools were established from 1872 to 1884. On the secondary level, education for girls moved forward with the Sisters of Notre Dame de Namur after the second half of the nineteenth century. They opened the first Catholic parochial secondary school at St. Patrick's, Lowell, in 1854.[87] The same congregation established the first permanent academy for girls in the diocese of Boston when in 1853 they opened St. Mary's Select School for girls on Lancaster Street. The *Catholic Almanac* of 1856 recognized the academy's opening with the following notice:

This school [St. Mary's Female School], under the care of the Sisters of Notre Dame, is attended by about seven hundred children, who receive a good English education, and are moreover exercised in needlework. . . . In the same building a select school has been established under the care of the Sisters, where in addition to the usual branches of education, are taught music, French, etc., on moderate terms.[88]

In 1854 the Sisters of Notre Dame de Namur established their second academy, the Academy of Notre Dame, Roxbury, Mass., as the first boarding school for girls in the diocese of Boston, followed in 1855 by a third academy, the Academy of Notre Dame, in Lowell. One other girls' academy opened during this period—the Academy of Sacré Coeur, established by the Religious of the Sacred Heart in 1880. By the end of 1881 the students numbered forty,[89] and toward the close of the century the school would rank among the "advanced academies" in the diocese.[90] Catholic higher education in Boston traces its origins to the Jesuits and the opening of Boston College, September 5, 1864. The *Catholic Almanac* of 1866 announced collegiate courses in "English, Latin, Greek, Modern Languages, and Mathematics" [91] for day scholars. The enrollment was small at first—only 25 boys—and Murphy gives as a reason the fact that

the people had their public schools, their high schools, both Latin and English, with Harvard College close by for those wishing to follow a professional career. As for the religious training, the Sunday school, was, they thought, quite sufficient. It remained, now, to bring home to the Catholics of Boston the advantages and necessity of higher Christian education.[92]

The College prospered and conferred its first degrees in 1877.

Catholic education in Boston, then, had its own unique pattern of development. The obstacles presented a challenge that the hierarchy, clergy, and laity met with persevering effort and self-sacrifice. We look in vain during this era, however, for any extensive educational development; rather, the growth was slow, for actually the years 1829–1884 were for Boston a formative period in Catholic education. Only after the Third Plenary Council of Baltimore would the Catholic school movement in Boston be given new impetus: twenty-two schools would open between 1884 and 1890. Therefore, "it is customary to take the Third Plenary Council of Baltimore, in 1884, as the starting point of the large development of the Boston parochial system." [93] From then on, the advance of Catholic education in the diocese was phenomenal.

We already noted the unsatisfactory condition of Catholic education in Philadelphia at the beginning of this period, when the unfortunate strife between the clergy and lay trustees stifled educational development. But the Most Rev. Francis Patrick Kenrick, D.D., coadjutor and at the same time administrator of the Philadelphia diocese from 1830 to 1842, and bishop of Philadelphia from 1842 to 1851, changed all that. Nolan writes:

He [Kenrick] arrived in Philadelphia on July 7th, 1830, and within a year (May 28th, 1831, when St. Mary's Church was reopened after an interdict) the courage, the determination, and the zeal displayed by the young Administrator put an end to the outrages of the Trustee System and permanently settled the question of lay interference in Church affairs. [94]

Kenrick decided, for example, that a new church must be erected and that it must be free of any control by a board of trustees. This assignment he passed on to his secretary, the Rev. John Hughes, later bishop of New York. Hughes quickly made his plans, and secured lots on Thirteenth Street where the church was to be erected. Then he "called a meeting of Catholics, at which Mathew Carey presided, and laid before them his project of a church, free school, and refuge for poor girls." [95] A new era opened for the Catholic Church in Philadelphia. Catholic education had many difficulties to surmount, but by the end of the period, Philadelphia fulfilled the promise it had shown in Colonial times. We shall note significant educational activities.

In 1830, Hughes established St. John's Orphan Asylum for boys and girls, conducted by the Sisters of Charity. It was also a free school for day students, who greatly outnumbered the orphans. [96] On March 28, 1832, three Sisters of Charity of Emmitsburg, Maryland, were sent to teach in the Sacred Heart school, a free school for girls at 10 Prune St., near old St. Joseph's Church. Because of its location it came to be called St. Joseph's Church School. [97] On January 29, 1833, the same community of sisters sent three teachers to open St. Mary's School, and just two years later, on January 20, 1835, three more Sisters left the motherhouse for Philadelphia to conduct St. Joseph's Male School. As early as 1834, Kenrick was trying to procure other teaching sisterhoods to help the Sisters of Charity. By 1833, he had Les Dames de la Retraite and the Sisters of Charity of the Blessed Virgin Mary. We know very little of Les Dames de la Retraite, the earliest available record being a notice in the *Catholic Almanac* of 1833 to the effect that Les Dames de la Retraite opened a "Young Ladies' French and English Academy" in the Gothic Mansion on Chestnut Street between 12th and 13th Streets in Philadelphia.[98] The school failed, in part because the tuition was $300 per annum, and in part because of anti-Catholic hostility which culminated in the destruction of St. Michael's, St. Augustine's, and St. Philip's Churches in the 1844 Native American Riots. In the following year those sisters removed to Charleston, S. C., but that venture, too, ended in failure.[99] The Congregation of the Sisters of Charity of the Blessed Virgin Mary, however, was a Philadelphia foundation. The five young women who were the community's first members were from Dublin, Ireland, and had come to America with a desire to teach. The Rev. Terence J. Donaghoe, newly appointed pastor of St. Michael's Church in Philadelphia, was in dire need of teachers when the young women arrived in his parish. With the approbation of Kenrick, Donaghoe drew up a rule of life for the Dublin ladies, and arranged for the establishment of a convent for them in his parish on November 1, 1833. But this congregation, too, left Philadelphia in 1843. They removed to Dubuque, Iowa. Nolan and Kirlin [100] both speak of the hostility of the neighborhood as a cause for the community's closing its school in 1843; recalling the tide of anti-Catholicism that swept Philadelphia at the time, it seems a likely reason. They also had a difference with the bishop.

The nativist-inspired summer riots of 1844, caused in great measure by the question of the Protestant Bible in the common school, wrought great damage to the Catholic Church in Philadelphia. The Nativists had been clamoring that America was a Protestant nation, so that Kenrick, on March 13, 1844, issued in all the city papers a disclaimer of Catholic intention to oust the Bible from the common schools. In part, Kenrick's statement read:

Catholics have not asked that the Bible be excluded from the Public Schools. They have merely desired for their children the liberty of using the Catholic Version in case the reading of the Bible be prescribed by the Controllers or Directors of the Schools. They only desire to enjoy the benefit of the Constitution of the State of Pennsylvania, which guarantees the right of conscience, and precludes any preference of sectarian modes of worship. . . . They desire that the Public Schools be preserved from all sectarian influence and that education be conducted in a way that may enable all citizens equally, to share in its benefits, without any violence being offered to their religious convictions.[101]

But the nativists were not to be cut down by quiet and dignified conduct. Churches and schools were burned, the property destroyed amounting to over $150,000. Kenrick maintained a calm front, and after the frenzy was over took up undauntedly the work of firming up the position of the Catholic Church in Philadelphia.

More religious teachers came to staff the growing free parochial schools. The School Sisters of Notre Dame arrived in Philadelphia on September 21, 1848, to teach the girls of St. Peter's School at Franklin and Fifth Streets which the Redemptorists opened in that year. The Redemptorists themselves taught the boys in the basement of the church.[102] By 1849, the *Catholic Almanac* stated that these schools were educating 160 girls and 120 boys. The Visitation Nuns of Georgetown at Kenrick's persuasion sent a community of sisters to Philadelphia in 1848 to found the Young Ladies Academy of the Visitation at Eleventh and Spruce Streets. By 1851, the Academy had been transferred to a larger building at the corner of Broad and Poplar Streets, the sisters in community numbered nineteen, and forty-five students were registered. The School Sisters of Notre Dame remained in the diocese, but the Visitation Nuns withdrew from Philadelphia in 1853. Two more religious orders of women were brought to Philadelphia by this bishop so concerned for the spiritual and educational welfare of his flock. The Sisters of St. Joseph came in May 1847, and were given charge of St. John's Asylum, attached to St. John's Church on Chestnut Street. On August 28, 1848, they went to teach in the parochial school in Pottsville. The Sisters of the Good Shepherd arrived in 1849, and taught for a year at St. Philip's School in Southwark until they were relieved by the Sisters of St. Joseph, after which the Good Shepherd Nuns began their charitable work of helping unfortunate girls and women.

Kenrick came to Philadelphia convinced that the basic need was good priests, and if that need was supplied the settlement of other issues would follow. He organized a seminary—the Seminary of St. Charles Borromeo—apart from any school for lay students, and in this he veered from the pattern of the day. He encouraged the growth of select academies, but his greatest activity and achievement in the field of Catholic education was his establishment of free schools, established in almost every parish by 1850. Kenrick had tried many times to secure a male teaching order for his free schools for boys. It was not, however, until 1850 that the Christian Brothers, at the invitation of the Rev. Charles Carter, came to teach in the Assumption Parochial School in Philadelphia.[103] Two permanent colleges for men were also established during Kenrick's administration—St. Thomas of Villanova and St. Joseph's. Villanova was founded by the Augustinians in 1843 as a secondary school for boys, as most colleges were in those days. It aimed to give a thorough Catholic education, and the announcement of its existence in the *Catholic Almanac* of 1845 stated that "in accordance with the wishes of parents or guardians, a classical and scientific, or purely mercantile education will be given to their children, or the one will be so blended with the other, as to qualify the pupil to embrace any of the learned professions, or to apply himself to business." [104] Villanova was granted a college charter in 1848. The Society of Jesus opened St. Joseph's College on September 15, 1851, as a classical school, organized and conducted on Jesuit principles of education. St. Joseph's College was regularly chartered in 1854. Kenrick, by slow and painstaking work, set up a system of Catholic schools in Philadelphia. A scholarly man, more at home with his pen [105] than in the midst of active parish duties, he nevertheless proved an efficient administrator. On his appointment to the archbish-opric of Baltimore in 1851 he left Philadelphia a diocese showing marked growth over 1830, and one in which Catholic education was on the move.

Pittsburgh, which was part of the diocese of Philadelphia until 1843,[106] followed the same pattern of growth as other dioceses. Western Pennsylvania's first Catholic school, as we observed, had been opened in 1800 by the Rev. Demetrius Gallitzin, a Russian nobleman, who had established a mission at Loretto.[107] Not until 1828 do we have any rec-ord of a school within the city of Pittsburgh; in that year the Sisters of St. Clare had situated themselves on a knoll, which came to be known as Nunnery Hill, above the old city of Allegheny, and opened an acad-emy. This school closed, however, in 1835, and in 1837 the sisters re-turned to Europe.[108] The first permanent educational establishment in Pittsburgh was made in 1835, and was actually two schools—a day school for boys and girls, and an academy for young ladies. The Sisters of Charity from Emmitsburg, Maryland, staffed both schools, at the invita-tion of the Rev. John O'Reilley, pastor of the parish.[109] The Germans had their own parish at St. Philomena's in 1840, and in 1841 they opened a day school and hired lay teachers to staff it. By the time Pittsburgh be-came a separate diocese in 1843 its Catholic educational picture in-cluded, in the city of Pittsburgh, St. Paul's Day School—Sisters of Char-ity—120 pupils; St. Paul's Academy for girls (Sisters of Charity); and St. Philomena's Day School (lay teachers). Outside the city, there were the elementary school at Loretto, Pennsylvania, and the institution at Sportsman's Hall (now Beatty, Pennsylvania), which would become to-day's St. Vincent's, Latrobe, Pennsylvania.[110]

Pittsburgh's first bishop, the Rt. Rev. Michael O'Connor, encouraged the establishment of Catholic schools wherever possible. The Sisters of Mercy came in 1844 and opened the first free parish school, which was in the basement of old St. Patrick's on Canal Street. For a brief period, the Presentation Brothers were in the city. They opened an academy for boys in 1844 and in 1847 took over the instruction of boys in St. Paul's. But by 1848 they had gone and six Brothers of the Third Order of St. Francis began the erection of a monastery at Loretto. The Brothers pros-pered, and the Academy was incorporated as St. Francis College in 1859, after which the brothers continued to do good service in parochial schools as well. By 1850, the Sisters of Notre Dame had replaced the lay teachers in the German parish school of St. Philomena's.

From 1850 to the end of this period, Catholic educational activity in-creased in Pittsburgh as it did in every diocese in the United States. For the Catholic hierarchy it was a time of grave concern over Catholic edu-cation as the secularization of the public schools became more pro-nounced. The *Thirty-eighth Annual Report of the Catholic Schools in the Diocese of Pittsburgh* (1943) related that, due to the sacrifices of pastors, teachers and people, "from 1850 until 1904, the total number of schools increased to 114." [111] The same *Report* commented on educational conditions in Catholic schools during the period:

There was very little central organization of schools on a diocesan basis during the period. Each school was completely autonomous, and while, generally speaking, the same course of studies was followed throughout the diocese, each community of teachers was answerable only to its own superior and to the pastor of the parish. There were no uniform textbooks and no uniform system of grading. In the secular subjects the parochial schools followed the same course as the public schools of the city and surrounding territory, but each school had its own course in religion.[112]

This was actually the pattern followed in all dioceses.

### DIOCESE OF NEW YORK

In New York, the figure that stands out in bold relief during this period as far as Catholic education is concerned is New York's fourth bishop and first archbishop, John Hughes.[113] In an age when Catholics were few and poor, and when bigotry against them stalked the nation, Hughes labored and fought in New York from 1838 until 1864 as a champion of Catholic educational rights. He has critics today who, perhaps forgetful of the nature and needs of the troubled times in which he lived, question his method of approach. The other side of the picture is that the Church in New York, beset by troubles from within and without, probably needed a leader such as Hughes at that time and in those circumstances, and that a constructive phase of Catholicism in his diocese began with him. Here we deal only with his activities that bear directly on the history of Catholic education in New York, in which his adminisration constituted years of spectacular progress. When Hughes came to New York in 1838, the trustee system was flourishing vigorously. By the following year, he had broken the power of the trustees, and "although from time to time in some churches they gave trouble, they were never able to oppose his authority or resist his orders with success." [114] His people were poor, and the New York diocese was heavily in debt. Hughes, therefore, as was the custom of American bishops of that time, went to Europe to seek help from wealthy Catholics. He sought special aid from the Leopoldine Society in Austria, and received money to further the foundation of a college and seminary that he had in mind. He arrived home on July 18, 1840, and found the Catholics in New York engaged in a determined effort to change the school system. "It was not in his character," wrote Hassard, "to let his people go out to fight, in any good cause, without their bishop at their head." [115] So began Hughes' famous controversy with the Public School Society in New York.

At this time the Public School Society was the dominant educational organization in New York City. It had been founded in 1805, you may remember, to teach children not cared for by religious schools. By 1840 it held a virtual monopoly over the common school funds. It had established nearly one hundred schools, and professed to give a purely secular education and a general religious instruction based on religious principles and morality which all Christians held in common. Catholics could not be satisfied with such schools, for, while the schools professed to be nonsectarian, they were really Protestant, and their textbooks frequently contained distorted material on the Catholic Church.[116] Catholics tried to erect their own schools, but for a poor community this was a difficult task. Hassard, writing in 1866, observed:

So in every parish where a little money could be scraped together, a Catholic free school was opened, either in the church basement, or in some other poor and inconvenient place. But the churches had great ado to provide for the expenses of the altar and the interest on their debts. They were utterly unable to provide fit schoolrooms, nor in many cases could they afford to pay for competent teachers. . . . The number of Catholic children in New York City, of "school age," was, according to the bishop's estimate, from nine to twelve thousand. The church schools, crowded to their utmost capacity provided for four or five thousand; a very few—perhaps two or three hundred—attended public schools; the rest—that is, about half—received no education whatever.[117]

The free school attached to St. Patrick's Cathedral was one of the eight parochial schools of New York for which Hughes entered the school controversy. In 1840, he addressed a large gathering of Catholics in the schoolroom of St. Patrick's to explain the issues. He pointed out that as a consequence of the unjust treatmeat accorded Catholic children in the professedly nonsectarian schools, it had become imperative to establish and support parochial schools. Hughes claimed that in all justice those poor parish schools should have a share of the common school fund, which was raised by the taxation of Catholics as well as Protestants, or that Catholics should at least be exempt from the taxes they were then pouring into the common school fund. He was to go further: on August 10, he held another meeting of the Catholic body, at which he read "An Address of the Roman Catholics to their Fellow Citizens of the City and State of New York"—a strongly worded document that left no question as to the objections of Catholics to the schools of the Public School Society. The Address objected to taxpaying on the part of Catholics "for the purpose of destroying our religion in the minds of our children," and objected to

the cold indifference . . . in those schools—the Scriptures without note or comment—the selection of passages, as reading lessons, from Protestant and prejudiced authors . . . the comments of the teachers, of which the Commissioners cannot be cognizant—the school libraries, stuffed with sectarian works against us . . . a combination of influences prejudicial to our religion, and to whose action it would be criminal in us to expose our children at such an age.[118]

The Public School Society retaliated with a remonstrance to the Common Council of the city, denying the right of Catholics to any portion of the school fund, to which were appended the added protests of Protestant sects who opposed the claims of Hughes. Hughes personally argued the Catholic case, but was turned down. He sought redress in the state legislature, where prolonged discussion of the question resulted in a postponement of a decision for several months. In the meantime, the elections of 1842 intervened. The strength of the independent Catholic ticket in the local elections of 1841 had shown that some change in the existing school system was bound to occur. Under the influence of Governor William H. Seward, the legislature on April 9, 1842 (just three days before the election) passed an act—the Maclay Bill—which extended the common school system of the state to New York City.[119] No school teaching any religious sectarian doctrine was to receive any money from the common school fund. The bill also provided for Board of Education members to be elected by wards. "The ward schools," wrote Hassard, "established under the provisions of the new act took the place of those formerly controlled by the Public School Society; and the Society itself, a few years afterward, having made over its effects to the city authorities, quietly went out of existence." [120] The parochial schools were as poor as ever, but it was a partial victory in that a society hostile to Catholic education had been removed. Hughes knew that further controversy would be useless and directed his energies toward establishing a system of Catholic education in the diocese.

For this plan, no need was greater than that of good teachers. He tried to get various religious orders, and at his request, Mother Madeleine Sophie Barat was persuaded to found a convent of the Sacred Heart in New York City in 1841.[121] In that year, Mother Elizabeth Gallitzin, accompanied by Mothers Catherine Thiefry and Johanna Shannon, arrived to form the nucleus of the foundation community. They occupied a house on the corner of Houston and Mulberry Streets, not far from the cathedral, and opened an academy which, in 1843, numbered sixty pupils, nearly half of whom were boarders. By 1844, the growth of the student body at the academy made larger quarters necessary, and they secured a spacious colonial dwelling in Astoria, Long Island, to which they transferred the boarding school. A small, free day school remained in existence for a while at the old site on Houston Street, with about forty children registered. This was abandoned, as was also the Long Island school, when in 1847 the Religious of the Sacred Heart moved to a permanent establishment at Manhattanville. Toward the close of 1845, Hughes applied in person to the parent house of the Institute of Mercy in Dublin for sisters. In response, Mother Mary Agnes O'Connor and seven Sisters of Mercy sailed from Liverpool on April 13, 1846. At first they lived in cramped and poor quarters in West Washington Place. In May 1848, they removed to the Houston Street property vacated by the Religious of the Sacred Heart, where they opened the Academy of Our Lady of Mercy, a select school for girls. A House of Mercy was built adjoining their convent, where the sisters carried out the work of their holy foundress, Catherine McAuley—the care of destitute and friendless girls.

The Sisters of Charity in the diocese of New York were at first a branch house of the Emmitsburg community. In 1846, New York was threatened with their loss when the superior at Emmitsburg ordered them to return to the observance of their rule and forsake the management of schools and orphanages for boys. Hughes protested, and after lengthy correspondence both sides finally agreed that such of the sisters as chose to remain in New York as a separate community under the control of the bishop could do so. Thirty-one out of fifty sisters joined the new independent congregation under the title of Sisters of Charity of St. Vincent of Paul. They continued their work of education and the care of orphans. Other religious orders came in answer to Hughes' pleas. The Christian Brothers arrived from France in 1846, the Ursulines from St. Louis in 1855, and the School Sisters of Notre Dame from Milwaukee, Wis., in 1857. Numerous parochial schools were founded. Sadlier's *Catholic Almanac and Ordo* for 1864 listed twelve select schools and thirty-one free schools in the New York diocese.[122] The recently established dioceses of Albany, Brooklyn, and Buffalo, which had been part of the New York See, had twenty-six, twenty-eight, and thirteen schools respectively. This, of course, represented tremendous educational growth. Shea wrote that "he [Hughes] found the diocese divided, timid, apathetic; he infused into priests and people a spirit of energy, courage, and self-sacrifice."[123] For him, the question of education was the question of the Church; indeed, he believed that in his time the school was more necessary than the church.

Catholic secondary education for boys had its beginning in New York with the founding of St. John's College, Fordham. Other attempts had been made [124] before Hughes' episcopacy, but had not been successful. Such failures did not discourage Hughes. Already on September 30, 1838, while coadjutor bishop, he "had set about founding a theological seminary at Lafargeville, Jefferson County, in the extreme north-western part of the State of New York, near the Thousand Isles in the St. Lawrence river." [125] It was more Dubois' idea than it was Hughes' that the seminary of St. Vincent de Paul should be placed as far as possible from the distractions and temptations of cities. Hughes removed the seminary from Lafargeville to Fordham in 1840, and Fordham College opened in June 1841.[126] Its first president was the Rev. John McCloskey, afterwards cardinal archbishop of New York. At the 1846 commencement exercises of the college, Hughes announced that he had transferred the college to the Jesuits from Marion County, Kentucky. Fordham by that time was an institution incorporated by the state with power to confer degrees in theology, law, medicine, and the arts.[127]

The New York diocese during this period cannot be considered apart from the dynamic Hughes. James Cardinal Gibbons called him the "fearless champion of Christian education," and stated further that "if today, our Christian schools are so thoroughly established and developed throughout the land, this result is due in no small measure to the bold and timely initiation of the Archbishop of New York." [128]

SLOWER DIOCESES

Other dioceses showed the same potential for educational growth. The Catholic population had increased so rapidly, however, that it was difficult to keep the establishment of Catholic schools commensurate. Guilday noted that from 1834 to 1844 "the personal and material force of the Church of the United States increased at the rate of about 100 per cent; the number of dioceses, bishops, priests, churches, seminaries, colleges, and female academies, having been doubled during that period." [129] Guilday thereupon presents a tabular statement set forth in the *Catholic Almanac* of 1854 under the title "State of Catholicity in the United States in 1808, and Its Progress from That Time to the Present." [130] It showed, among other things, that from 1830 to 1854 the number of Catholic dioceses grew from 11 to 41, colleges from 6 to 20, and female academies from 20 to 112. Some dioceses, such as St. Louis which had been officially split from the diocese of New Orleans in 1826,[131] continued their patterns of transitional growth.

Other areas such as Kentucky, where most of the laborers on the Louisville and Portland Canal and other canals and railroads, and in the development of manufacturing, were Irish and German Catholics, arrived at a turning point starting in the 1830's. Of educational significance is the fact that in 1842 the Sisters of the Good Shepherd came from Angers, France, to Louisville, Kentucky, for the re-education and rehabilitation of socially maladjusted girls, centering their initial programs on vocational training. They were the first religious order to be involved in this apostolate. By the mid-1850's, the Sisters had foundations in Montreal and Philadelphia as well, and in 1857 they arrived in New York City with a few mattresses and blankets, a frying pan, and two or three other utensils, to begin the same work in a rented house on 14th Street.

Because this growth pattern was generally slower in the South, however, we shall now look briefly at two southern dioceses. Bishop John England of Charleston, South Carolina, like other Catholic bishops in the United States during his time, realized that if he were to have teachers for Catholic schools, he would need religious communities. In 1830, three pious ladies, natives of Cork, Ireland, but residing in Baltimore, Maryland, proposed to devote themselves to charitable and educational work in Charleston. They were the Misses Mary and Honora O'Gorman and their niece, Teresa Barry. With the material help of Miss Julia Datty, a native of Santo Domingo, England formed them into an independent community, gave them the rules of the Presentation Order,[132] and the title of Sisters of Our Lady of Mercy. The sisters opened an orphan asylum and an academy and school for girls shortly before 1840.[133] At about the same time, Les Dames de la Retraite came to Charleston from Philadelphia. Their stay was temporary as it had been in Philadelphia, and one can only surmise that, since the sisters were French, their lack of English proved an obstacle. The exact time of their leaving Charleston is not definitely known. In 1834, England brought a third sisterhood to Charleston, the Ursulines, from Blackrock Convent, Cork. The Leopoldine Association in Vienna paid their passage money and part of the cost of their convent in Charleston, which adjoined the cathedral on Broad Street; here they opened an academy.

The slaves in Charleston were a prime concern of England. O'Connell relates that "he [England] began to teach them and founded schools, one under a priest for the males, and the other for girls under the care of the Sisters of Mercy." [134] His efforts in this direction were blocked, however, by severe legislation prohibiting teaching Negroes to read and write, and the Bishop had to close the school.[135] England was also very much concerned over the Catholic education of boys. He hoped to secure a teaching brotherhood for this purpose, but was unable to see the realization of that dream.[136] His own words give us an idea of the scope of his educational plans. In an address to the Fifteenth Convention of the Church in South Carolina on November 25, 1838, England said:

In order to effect the religious education of the children properly, nothing could be more useful than to have schools in which the sciences may be taught and the lower branches of education attended to, at the same time that the children belonging to our congregations could therein receive the proper religious instruction. I have made efforts for this purpose at different times, hitherto with but little success as regards the male department. You will not need any reasoning from me to convince you of its necessity. The only question is, respecting its practicability, and every day more urgently presses upon us the necessity of its consideration.[137]

England's real influence upon Catholic education seems rather minimal. Of all the educational establishments which England set up, none has lasted to the present. The Sisters of Our Lady of Mercy, however, whom he founded, still devote their energies to the education of Catholic youth in Charleston. Of the time immediately following England in Charleston, Guilday observes:

One by one during Bishop Reynold's administration, his [England's] projects were abandoned and the unity of spirit he had given to the church in the three parishes constituting his diocese of Charleston began quickly to wane.[138]

Georgia had remained a part of the archdiocese of Baltimore until 1820, when the diocese of Charleston, South Carolina, had been founded, at which time it had become a part of the Charleston diocese. In 1832, Bishop John England estimated the Catholic congregation in Savannah at five hundred. Of the progress made by 1850 in the area comprising the state of Georgia and eastern Florida, and extending from the Atlantic Ocean to the Appalachicola River, Shea wrote that it

contained twelve churches, or rather chapels, at Savannah, Augusta, Locust Grove, Washington, Macon, Atlanta, Columbus, and St. Mary's in Georgia; three in Florida, at St. Augustine, Key West, and Tallahassee. The institutions were an academy and an orphan asylum at Savannah under the Sisters of Mercy; day-school and asylum at Augusta under Very Rev. John Barry.[139]

Rome therefore established Savannah as a separate diocese on July 19, 1850.

Despite the ecclesiastical growth, the Right Rev. Francis Xavier Gartland, Savannah's first bishop, found in his newly organized diocese only one Catholic school. The school had been established by the Sisters of Our Lady of Mercy of Charleston, who at the request of the Very Rev. Jeremiah F. O'Neil had sent six sisters to Savannah on June 23, 1845, to open a boarding school, an orphanage, and also a parish school for day students. This Academy was incorporated by the State Legislature in 1849,[140] and in 1850, it had 8 Sisters of Mercy, 17 boarders, 15 orphans, 70 day pupils, and 60 children in the free school.[141] Gartland worked hard to extend Catholic educational facilities. He visited Europe to obtain priests and means, and obtained help from the Leopoldine Association. On his return he established the Sisters of Mercy in Augusta in 1853, where they opened St. Mary's Academy and an orphanage and free school. When Gartland died, however, in 1854, a victim of yellow fever, educational activity in the diocese came to a standstill. Georgia's second bishop, the Right Rev. John Barry, was broken in health even at the time of his consecration in 1857; he gave only two further years of service, in which time no new educational facilities were developed. Florida was made a vicariate in 1857, after which the diocese of Savannah embraced only Georgia.

The Civil War had already begun when the Right Rev. Augustine Verot, S.S., was made Savannah's bishop in 1861. Catholicism in Georgia shared the general desolation of the South. A long period of disorganization followed the war. The South was prostrate, and the Church labored to retain some order and life among her distracted people. O'Connell observes that the "preservation of Catholicity in the Carolinas and Georgia is among the greatest triumphs of the Church in America." [142] Verot worked zealously to meet the new tragic state of affairs. The Sisters of Mercy began St. Joseph's Academy at Columbus in 1862, Immaculate Conception Academy at Atlanta, and Sacred Heart School at Macon in 1866. Growth was slow, but the same trends that prevailed in other dioceses were here discernible as at least incipient: e.g., the desire of diocesan administrators to have religious teachers in their schools, and their visits to Europe to secure priests, teachers, and financial help. Savannah, however, was unique in two ways. First, because of the scarcity of priests and sisters, the burden of Catholic education was carried mainly by Catholic lay teachers; and second, a scheme of cooperation between officials of the Catholic schools and those of the public schools worked successfully in Savannah. Of this last arrangement, made in 1870, Ellis observes that "the board was given the powers and responsibility for the repair of the buildings, and hiring and testing of teachers, and the selection of textbooks, except in history, reading, and geography." [143] The Catholic schools were added to the Savannah public school system in 1871, and the compromise would work to the advantage of both sides for forty-five years. [144]

To the Irish immigrants who began to move into Georgia in the 1830's must go the credit for establishing the first permanent Catholic schools in the diocese. The Sisters of Mercy did not arrive until 1845 and Savannah already had six schools at that time. These schools were poor, of course, and laymen went from door to door collecting funds for their upkeep. [145] The growth of Catholic education in the diocese was certainly not phenomenal, but viewed in the light of the obstacles and distressing conditions, both what growth there was and the compromise plan were remarkable.

It might also be of interest to note here that Catholic education was at this time having a unique pattern of development in what would become our fiftieth state, Hawaii. By the time French Catholic missioners (the Fathers of the Sacred Hearts) arrived in 1827, Congregational Presbyterians who had arrived from Boston in 1819 had already gained the ruling class and established themselves throughout the Islands—an achievement of, above all, their schools. [146] By 1840, when the early vigor of the Protestant schools had waned, the Protestant missionary groups, fearful of the spread of Catholicism and its schools, impelled the government to enact school legislation setting up Protestant schools at which attendance was obligatory. The Rev. Louis Maigret, SS.CC., objected strenuously to the clause placing teacher certification in the hands of Protestant ministers, resulting in a revision of the law to state that "no person is by this law considered a teacher unless he have a teacher's certificate from the general school agent." [147] On Nov. 10, 1845, King Kamehameha III granted Maigret's Catholic mission at Kaneohe a grant of land for a school; attendance, never stable, declined after 1865, and in 1882 the school administration decided to close and to move to the more inhabited side of the island. When in 1854 the Mormons bid for separate schools, the legislature changed the school organization from a sectarian to a territorial plan—continuing to provide tax exemption, however, to those who preferred to establish schools of their own. In 1880, one Father William J. Larkin, a secular priest, founded the "College of St. Louis, an Hawaiian Commercial and Business Academy," on Bretania St., Honolulu; the next year, because of a tragic fire which killed a young boy, the school was closed; Larkin, imprisoned at first, left the Islands, and seems to have died in San Francisco in 1906.[148] As the public school pattern expanded, a greater measure of control over private institutions was added to non-support, and the Hawaiian government, desiring annexation to the U. S. even then, imitated mainland U. S. procedures more and more.

## Church Legislation: The Councils of Baltimore

Only an appreciation of the foregoing account of difficulties encountered, and of the concern of clergy and laity for Catholic children in the common schools, can make understandable the legislation of the Church during this period affecting education. By 1885, the educational decrees of the plenary and provincial councils of the Catholic Church in the United States, the rulings of diocesan synods, and the statements of bishops in their pastoral letters, made clear the need, concept, and function of separate Catholic schools. In 1829, the date of the First Provincial Council of Baltimore, despite the number of Catholic schools in existence, many Catholic children were still being exposed to the danger of losing their Faith in the common schools. Recognizing this danger to Catholic youth, and in the hope of spurring Catholic efforts to even greater heights of educational achievement, the First Provincial Council of Baltimore passed the first formal Catholic educational legislation affecting the country at large. It decreed, for example:

Since it is evident that very many children of Catholic parents, especially the poor, have been exposed and are still exposed, in many places of this Province, to great danger of the loss of faith or the corruption of morals, on account of the lack of such teachers as could safely be entrusted with so great an office, we judge it absolutely necessary that schools should be established, in which the young may be taught the principles of faith and morality, while being instructed in letters.[149]

The First Provincial Council also showed concern over textbooks. The bishops stated:

Since not infrequently, in the books generally used in the schools, much is found by which the principles of our faith are impugned, our dogmas falsely expounded, and history perverted, by reason of which the minds of children are imbued with errors to the most grievous peril of their souls, the application of some remedy for this great evil is demanded not only by our zeal for religion, and the right education of youth, but even by the very honor of these United States.[150]

The bishops decreed that the books used in the schools should be examined and purged of any errors about the Catholic religion.

The Fathers of the Council also signed two pastoral letters, both composed by Bishop John England—one to the clergy and one to the laity. In the "Pastoral Letter to the Laity," England's gifted pen exhorted parents in these words:

God has made you the guardians of those children (the dear pledges of your elevated and sanctified affection) to lead them to His service upon earth, that they might become saints in Heaven. "What will it avail them to gain the whole world if they lost their souls?" . . . attend to the education of your child; teaching him first to seek the kingdom of God and His justice, and having food and raiment to be therewith content. Teach him to be industrious, to be frugal, to be humble and fully resigned to the will of . . . God.[151]

Continuing, England maintained that the only way to insure the proper religious education of youth is to train them in filial piety and the practice of virtue, beginning in early childhood. Their education, which England called "their unfolding perceptions," should "be imbued with the mild and lovely tints of religious truth and pure devotion," and as their reasoning powers develop they should be nourished by those truths "which our holy religion so abundantly affords." Again and again the Pastoral insisted that the great duty of parents is to watch over the spiritual concerns of their children. Their duty can be best fulfilled in the home, but, because it is often necessary to entrust the child to another, parents should "seek for those teachers who will cultivate the seed which you [parents] have sown," for teachers "of tried virtue, and surrounded by favorable circumstances." The Pastoral declared that

the mind of the very infant is predisposed against us by the recitals of the nursery; and the school-boy can scarcely find a book in which some one or more of our institutions or practices is not exhibited far otherwise than it really is, and greatly to our disadvantage.[152]

In the "Pastoral Letter to the Clergy," England reminded priests of their duty to instruct the young in the truths of the Faith. He praised the efforts already made in the establishment of Catholic educational institutions, and begged the clergy to "encourage and cherish those pious souls that so meritoriously devote themselves to the instruction of children in the way of the God of truth."

The Second Provincial Council convened on August 20, 1833. The bishops legislated for the creation of a more efficient Catholic parochial school system and appointed a committee to examine the textbooks used in public schools. The presidents of three principal Catholic educational institutions—Georgetown University, St. Mary's College, Baltimore, and Mount St. Mary's, Emmitsburg—were appointed as the committee to supervise the preparation of suitable textbooks.[153] Again England wrote the pastoral letter of the Council and treated Catholic education as of utmost importance. The pastoral stated:

We have . . . at all times, used our best efforts to provide, as far as our means would permit . . . colleges and schools in which your children, whether male or female, might have the best opportunities of literature and science, united to a strict protection of their morals and the best safeguards of their faith.[154]

The Third Provincial Council of Baltimore met in 1837, and although the topic of education was not treated at the Council it was considered in the pastoral letter which was issued at the Council's close and which again was England's composition. Speaking in the name of the Council Fathers he begged Catholics to support the Catholic schools already established. He praised those schools, declaring that

we are persuaded, that amongst those under our superintendence, are to be found, some of the most scientific and literary houses of education which our nation possesses; some establishments for the instruction of youth, male and female, in which there are successfully taught those speculative and practical lessons which inform the understanding, regulate the imagination, cultivate the taste, ameliorate the heart, improve the disposition, impress the importance and obligation of fulfilling every social, civic, domestic and religious duty, and teach the best mode of their performance.[155]

It is interesting that, in spite of the urgency of the First, Second, and Third Provincial Councils of Baltimore on education, a lethargy and apathy seemed to characterize the Catholic masses; this may require further research.

By 1840, when the Fourth Provincial Council was held, Catholic immigrants were pouring in and funds were not available to provide schools quickly enough to keep up with the growing population; consequently, many children of Catholic immigrant parents found their way into the anti-Catholic public schools. The Fourth Provincial Council considered this matter, and advised clergy and parents alike to assert their civil rights. In the pastoral letter that followed the Fifth Provincial Council of Baltimore in 1843, the bishops repeated warnings against public schools—saying, for example:

We have seen with serious alarm, efforts made to poison the fountains of public education, by giving it a sectarian hue, and accustoming children to the use of a version of the Bible made under sectarian bias, and placing in their hands books of various kinds replete with offensive and dangerous matter. This is plainly opposed to the free genius of our civil institutions. We admonish parents of the awful account they must give at the divine tribunal, should their children, by their neglect or connivance, be imbued with false principles, and led away from the path of salvation. . . . Let them, therefore, avail themselves of their natural rights.[156]

In the Sixth and Seventh Provincial Councils, held respectively in 1846 and 1849, a time of persecution for Catholics, we read nothing of Catholic education. Educational legislation for Catholic schools came next through the First Plenary Council of Baltimore in 1852. By this time the hierarchy realized that it was useless to think of coming to terms with the public schools, and the Council exhorted bishops to establish parochial schools in their dioceses whenever possible.[157] And the bishops in the pastoral letter following the First Plenary Council wrote:

Encourage the establishment and support of Catholic schools, make every sacrifice which may be necessary for this object; spare our hearts the pain of beholding the youth whom, after the example of our Master, we so much love, involved in all the evils of an uncatholic education, evils too multiplied and too obvious to require that we should do more than raise our voices in solemn protest against the system from which they spring.[158]

Detailed preparations were made for the Second Plenary Council, convoked in 1866. It was attended by seven archbishops, thirty-eight bishops, three abbots, and over one hundred twenty theologians—the largest ecclesiastical gathering held up to that time in the United States.[159] New problems had arisen in American society—the aftermath of the Civil War, and the conditions concomitant with rising industrialism. Title IX of the Council Decrees was devoted to "The Instruction and Pious Education of Youth." [160] It stressed the Church's right to teach and to establish schools, and also the great need of Catholic youth to receive a Catholic education, declaring:

The best, nay the only remedy that remains, in order to meet these very grave evils seems to lie in this, that in every diocese schools—each close to the Church—should be erected, in which the Catholic youth may be instructed in letters and the noble arts as well as in religion and sound morals.[161]

The Council Fathers were concerned about the children of the poor, urging pastors to support the schools from the revenues of the parish. Every precaution was to be taken to render as slight as possible the harm to those children who had to attend public schools, and they were to be assembled on Sundays and feast days, and even oftener, for religious instruction. The multiplication of religious communities and the employment of religious teachers in the schools was highly commended, and where religious teachers could not be had, the selection of lay teachers was to be made with care. Archbishop Martin J. Spalding, who had convoked the Council, was concerned with the creation of a national Catholic university and he had the question ready for the Council Fathers. Guilday writes:

The question as submitted to the Fathers of the Second Plenary Council was this: Whether the time had not come for founding a university which would give the Church here ampler means for bringing the truths of our Faith before the more intelligent class of Americans in a manner that could not but arrest their attention.[162]

But the time "had not yet come," says the archbishop's biographer, "though the Fathers of the Second Plenary Council of Baltimore express their most ardent desire to see such an institution established here; and their words concerning the plan of studies which should be pursued in higher ecclesiastical seminaries plainly show the urgent want of a Catholic University in this country." [163]

Finally, the emancipation of slaves gave the bishops concern about the education of colored children. When the mass immigration of Catholics had begun during the 1840's, most Negroes had been living in the rural sections of the South. Catholics had settled mostly in the big cities of the North and West, so there had been little actual contact. The little contact in the North had tended to be abrasive, because the Irish settlers were often competing against the Negroes for the only kinds of job of which both were capable. Catholics had usually accepted the color line which they found where they settled and had not proposed the luminous love and service counseled in the gospels. In consequence, few Negroes became Catholic. Now, Spalding spoke of the responsibility of the clergy

to see that this portion of their flocks be not only not neglected, but even more tenderly cared for. Hence we admonish them, in the name of the Prince of Pastors, to put forth every effort of enlightened zeal for the Christian instruction of the colored people under their charge, especially of the young. And we therefore exhort them to establish in their respective parishes or districts, as soon as may be at all practicable, schools for the colored, as experience proves how difficult it is to impart religious instruction to those that cannot read.[164]

That the Church had been taking the education of the colored seriously, and continued to do so, is witnessed in at least one location by an extremely interesting document entitled "A Special Report of the Commissioner of Education, District of Columbia, 1868." It mentions a free school for the colored which was established in 1868 by the St. Vincent de Paul Society in connection with St. Matthew's church, and five Catholic colored schools in the District exclusively for girls. One girls' school, with an average of 80 pupils, free to all who were unable to pay, and under the auspices of St. Aloysius church (the last built before the Civil War), was under the care of Mrs. Ellen B. Wood, a Haitian who had received her education with white children in Philadelphia and taught for many years in that city and in Camden, N.J. Her assistant was Elizabeth Brown, a native of Philadelphia, who had been educated at St. Frances Academy, Baltimore.[165] St. Martin's church was conducting several schools for the colored. The parochial school for girls, with 45 pupils, had two teachers from Baltimore: the principal, Mary S. Noel, was an ex-nun, and her assistant, Miss Julia Smith, had been educated at St. Frances Academy, Baltimore. St. Martin's "female academy," with more than 40 pupils, was being conducted in connection with the parochial girls' school because of lack of other accommodations, with a plan to separate them. St. Martin's also had an academy and a parochial school for boys, each with about 30 pupils, the principal of which was John McCosker, who had been educated at Georgetown College. The parish also conducted a small night school for adult men, with fifteen students. The Sisters of Georgetown Visitation convent had also "trained many colored girls in the refined and solid attainments of a good education."

The report declares that "no religious sect has, from the earliest history of this District, exhibited so true a Christian spirit towards the colored people as the Catholic."[166] Among those who "established schools and gathered to them the ignorant and poor, both white and colored," were the Rev. Leonard Neale, the archbishop; his brother, the Rev. Francis Neale, founder of Holy Trinity church; a Father Van Lommel, who "himself taught a school in which the white and colored children were instructed together and gratuitously"; and a Father McElroy, who in 1818 established a Sunday school for colored children, "labored with the utmost devotion to gather the poor and despised children under his instruction," and in whose school for two hours each Sunday afternoon "the children were taught spelling, reading, writing and christian doctrine." Of the last-named school, the report indicates that "there are many colored men and women still living in this District, now furrowed and gray with age, who learned to read and write in that school, including some who were slaves at the time," and observes in the same place that

in the years of the mobs, . . . when the Sabbath schools for colored children were broken up in every Protestant church in the District, every Catholic church steadily retained its colored children under the usual Sunday instruction, and these schools embraced all ages, from the mere child to the hoary head.[167]

The decrees of the Third Plenary Council of Baltimore held in 1884 completed the educational legislation for Catholic schools in the United States. Cassidy observed:

The educational decrees of the Third Plenary Council were the culmination of legislation that was initiated in the Synod of 1791, continued through the seven provincial councils (1829–1849), and expressed more forcibly in the First (1852) and Second (1866) Plenary Councils. The laws enacted regarding seminaries, from the synodal legislation of 1791 through the succeeding years down to 1884, were naturally based on similar regulations laid down by the Council of Trent.[168]

There had been more immediate preparations as well. For about ten years prior to the Council, there had been, for example, the propagandizing in behalf of Catholic schools by such as James A. McMaster, who for about forty years beginning in 1848 was the aggressive and volatile editor of *The New York Freeman's Journal and Catholic Register*. His zeal even reached Rome, through Miss Ella B. Edes, a secretary to ecclesiastical officials there, Roman correspondent on ecclesiastical news for several newspapers, writer, guide to Rome for many visiting Americans, and *factotum* for many American prelates. Together, McMaster and Edes are considered by some to be responsible for a decree of the Holy Office to the American archbishops on the subject of Catholic education in 1875 and a decree of the Sacred Congregation of the Inquisition in the following year.[169]

Immediately prior to the Council, therefore, the American bishops held a meeting on November 24, 1883, in Rome with the cardinal prefect of the Sacred Congregation for the Propagation of the Faith. The minutes of the sixth session reveal several interesting facts:

The Most Rev. Bishop of Oregon said some Bishops were of the opinion that the Council should enact a Decree which would require, under a given penalty, that missioners should build parochial schools within a brief interval of time to be specified by the Holy See.

Their Eminences said that it was not expedient that such a decree be enacted in view of the difficulties in which many missioners are involved but that Bishops should insist on the building of schools with appropriate attention to missioners who prove themselves culpably negligent.[170]

The same minutes later indicate that

the same Most Rev. Archbishop [of Milwaukee] asked whether Bishops could prohibit attendance at the public schools in order to prevent harm from coming to the parochial schools.

Their Eminences said that if this was the sole reason involved Bishops could not attach a penalty to their prohibition.[171]

With all this in mind, the Council drew up the following definitive and conclusive legislation regarding Catholic parochial schools:

1. Near every church, when it does not already exist, a parochial school is to be erected within two years from the promulgation of this Council, and to be kept up in the future, unless in the judgment of the Bishop the erection and maintenance of the school is impossible.
2. A priest who is gravely negligent in erecting the school within this time or is gravely negligent in its maintenance after it is erected can and must be removed from that church.
3. The mission or parish which so neglects to aid the priest in erecting or maintaining the school, that on account of this supine negligence the school cannot exist, is to be reprimanded by the Bishop, and if it shall have been contumacious, it is to be given spiritual punishments.
4. All Catholic parents are bound to send their children to parochial schools, unless at home or in other Catholic schools they provide sufficiently and fully for their Christian education, or on account of a good reason approved by the Bishop, using meanwhile the necessary precautions and remedies, they are permitted to send them to other schools.[172]

The laity were to regard the parish schools "as an essential of the Parish, without which the very existence of the Parish in future will be imperilled." Not only the Catholic parents whose children attend the parish schools should give to the schools' support. On this point, the Council declared:

Let the clergy show, as they easily may, that the benefits to faith and morals flowing from the Parish Schools, redound to the good of the whole community. After the Church, then, let the faithful assign the place of honor to the school as a most powerful factor in the preservation of faith and morals, and as the nursery of youth, destined to prove later to us all a source of joy and consolation.[173]

The Third Plenary Council of Baltimore determined to raise the standards of schools as well. Guilday comments thus on the Council's treatment of Title XI, *Education of Catholic Youth:*

Nothing is overlooked or forgotten in this section that would tend to create a more perfect system of Catholic education. Teachers and studies, schools and administration, and methods are all dealt with in detail. High schools, as we now understand the term, were in their infancy in 1884; but the Council recognized the necessity of multiplying Catholic high schools, academies, and colleges, and legislated to the effect that every effort should be put forward by priests and people to create a complete system of Catholic training which would protect the Catholic youth of the land at every stage of its education.[174]

The Council devoted a special section of the decrees to the means of perfecting Catholic schools. Bishops were to appoint a diocesan Board of Examiners. Teachers must acquire a teaching diploma by passing an examination, and this rule was intended to bind all diocesan teachers, whether secular or religious. These diplomas were to be good for five years and to be recognized in every diocese. At the end of the first five years a second and final examination was to be required. The sum of the Council's debatings on this matter was that no one was to teach in a parochial school without having first passed an examination to prove his competence. School committees were also to be named in each diocese; once or twice a year they were to visit every school of their district to examine the pupils, after which they were to send an accurate account of the results to the chairman of the diocesan board.

The Third Plenary Council was concerned also with higher education. It advocated Catholic colleges and encouraged wealthy Catholics to give generously to college foundations and endowments. The Fathers also arrived at the decision that the time was ripe for the erection of The Catholic University of America, at Washington, D.C. The Council considered the education of Negroes and Indians too—Title VII stressing the Christian duty of providing for their education, and urging the bishops to provide churches, schools, orphanages, and asylums to care for

the needs of these forgotten people. Religious instruction received special consideration, and committees were commissioned to prepare what
became the Baltimore Catechism, which after 1885 would become the
standard book for teaching religion in the Catholic elementary schools
of the United States. Later chapters will deal with its nature and use.

## The Government's Role

In the relationship of the Church with the government during this
period in the field of education, the one word that could perhaps best
summarize is "conflict," a conflict that resulted from the secularization
of the public schools in the United States and the concomitant exclusion
of church-related schools from state support. Civil educational legislation became detailed, and focused on three areas: religious tests for full
rights of citizenship, the teaching of sectarian doctrine, and public funds
for private and church schools. As for the first, religious tests,[175] legislation was prohibitive or proscriptive, and therefore the controversies centered mainly around sectarian teaching and state aid for denominational
schools. We have already seen that in New York in the 1840's, Archbishop John Hughes took a stand for a proportionate share of the school
funds and made it very clear that the Protestant version of the Scriptures, Protestant prayers, and Protestant hymns were not to be forced
on the children of Catholics. The controversy became a matter of national as well as local interest, and was one of the liveliest issues in the
election of November, 1841.[176] Catholics censured the public schools
as "godless," "infidel," and "incompetent." Protestants believed "that if
they agreed to papal demands, they would be taxed to support popish
schools whose sole purpose was to win converts against the day when
the Pope was ready for his American conquest." [177]

Long after the election, the pens of Catholic intellectuals picked up
the on-going quarrel. Orestes A. Brownson, a convert to Catholicism in
1844, devoted his energies to the study of the Catholic Church and her
doctrine, and made the Church's problems in America his own. Education in particular interested him. He believed that "education should
instruct, prepare, and fortify the student for the prompt and faithful
discharge of all the duties which pertain to his state in life." [178] He believed in Catholic education, but he considered most criticisms of public
schools by the Catholic press unjust and imprudent. He wrote that

common school education is the order of the day, one of the pets of the times
and Catholics have enough . . . to weigh them down in our non-Catholic society without the additional burden of being thought to oppose it.[179]

But Brownson held that:

Every Catholic . . . every man who loves truth and wishes to conform to it, must be in favor of Catholic schools and Catholic education, if they are Catholic in reality as well as in name.[180]

He had no quarrel with the founding or supporting of Catholic schools or colleges. He agreed that parents "are bound by the law of God to give their children, as far as is in their power, a truly Catholic education," but he did question the effectiveness of the Catholic schools of his day and their "failure to live up to the ideal standard of Catholic education." Fearlessly, he wrote of the Catholic schools of his time:

They do not educate their pupils to be at home and at their ease in their own age and country, or train them to be living, thinking, and energetic men, prepared for the work which actually awaits them in either church or state. As far as we are able to trace the effect of the most approved Catholic education of our days, whether at home or abroad, it tends to repress rather than to quicken the life of the pupil, to unfit rather than to prepare him for the active and zealous discharge either of his religious or his social duties. They who are educated in our schools seem misplaced and mistimed in the world, as if born and educated for a world that has ceased to exist. They come out ignorant of contemporary ideas, contemporary habits of mind, contemporary intelligence and tendencies, and large numbers of them sink into obscurity, and do nothing for their religion or their country.[181]

The same fearlessness, but wholeheartedly in behalf of existing Catholic education, is observed in the words of the Rev. Isaac Hecker:

The [Catholics] are prepared, if their rights be respected, to give their children all the elementary, scientific, and moral education of which they are capable, and even more than the state will ever ask. As an evidence of their spirit and devotion to education witness their schools, academies, and colleges dotted all over the land. No denomination of Christians, no class of American citizens, can stand alongside of Catholics when it is a question of earnestness and self-sacrifice for education. But "No," say the votaries of the Common-school system to Catholics; "we insist that you shall educate your children according to our specially-devised state system, and that, too, under compulsory force; and, what is more, you shall be taxed by the state for its support." [182]

Hecker lashed out, in spite of Brownson's plea for prudence in the school issue, with scathing words that match Brownson's own:

The so-called American public-school system is a cunningly-devised scheme, under the show of zeal for popular education, for forcing the state, in violation of American principles of liberty, to impose an unjust and heavy tax on its citizens, with the intent of injuring the Catholic Church, while in the meantime it is sapping in the minds of the American youth the foundations of all religion and driving them into infidelity.[183]

Misunderstandings, which had already been reaching the courts, grew. The *Donahoe* v. *Richards* case [184] of 1854 in Maine on Bible reading in schools is an example. School authorities forced the reading of the King James Version of the Bible, and the Supreme Court of the State of Maine backed them. This case remained the leading voice on the subject for many years, in spite of Catholic objections. It would not be until 1890 "that the Egerton Bible Case, tried in the Wisconsin courts, reversed the decision in *Donahoe* v. *Richards* and made it possible for Catholic children to attend public school without having their religious beliefs interfered with." [185] The federal government had a close relationship to education during this period. We already noted that by the Morrill Act of 1862, it favored certain specified types of education, and by the creation of the Department of Education in 1867 it extended its influence over the nation's schools, at least indirectly. Federal aid was given to private and religious endeavors in the direction of Negroes and Indians. The federal government, for example, made annual grants to the semi-private Negro institution, Howard University, of amounts that would increase from $10,000 in 1879 to $1,249,000 in 1931.[186] Congress in 1865 established the Freedmen's Bureau, "the first federal agency to take a serious interest in the higher education of negroes." [187] The general work of the Bureau ceased in 1869, but its educational work continued until 1872. The federal government also extended financial aid to denominational schools for Indian children, and Indian agents were appointed (from 1870 to 1880) upon the recommendation of their religious denominations. The Catholic Church was assigned eight agencies, and thirty agencies were given to other denominations.[188]

A very important piece of federal legislation applying to education was the Fourteenth Amendment, passed in 1868. Originally addressed to the Negro, it pertained to the due process of law that must protect a person's life, liberty, and property. It was directed specifically at the states, and part of its Section 1 read:

No State shall make or enforce any law which shall abridge the privileges or immunities of citizens of the United States; nor shall any State deprive any person of life, liberty, or property, without due process of law; nor deny to any person within its jurisdiction the equal protection of the laws.[189]

There is no legal concept of greater significance, no richer idea in balancing the claims of individual persons against the claims of government. Flack, in his comprehensive analysis of the Fourteenth Amendment, claims that

Congress, the House and the Senate, had the following objects and motives in view for submitting the first section of the Fourteenth Amendment to the States for ratification:
  1. To make the Bill of Rights (the first eight [sic] Amendments) binding upon, or applicable to, the States.
  2. To give validity to the Civil Rights Bill.
  3. To declare who were citizens of the United States.[190]

The framers of the Fourteenth Amendment intended its "privileges and immunities" clause to be the vehicle for prohibition of state impairment of the liberties secured by the First Amendment. Not until 1923 would the Amendment begin to fashion the thinking of the Supreme Court on school cases.[191]

This was also the period of the Blaine Amendment—a resolution which was proposed to the House of Representatives by James G. Blaine on December 14, 1865, in response to President Ulysses S. Grant's request for an amendment prohibiting federal aid to any sectarian institution. Grant, in his speech to the Army of the Tennessee at Des Moines, Iowa, on September 29, 1875, said:

Encourage free schools and resolve that not one dollar appropriated for their support shall be appropriated to the support of any sectarian schools. Resolve that neither the state nor the nation, nor both combined, shall support institutions of learning other than those sufficient to afford every child growing up in the land of opportunity of a good common school education, unmixed with sectarian, pagan, or atheistical dogmas. Leave the matter of religion to the family altar, the church, and the private school, supported entirely by private contributions. Keep the church and state forever separate.[192]

On December 7 of the same year, in his annual message to Congress, Grant persevered in his determination to eliminate all state and federal aid to denominational schools and institutions. Again he asked that

a constitutional amendment be submitted to the Legislatures of the several States for ratification making it the duty of each of the several States to establish and forever maintain free public schools . . . ; forbidding the teaching in said schools of religious, atheistic, or pagan tenets; and prohibiting the granting of any school funds, or school taxes, or any part thereof, either by legislative, municipal or other authority, for the benefit or in aid, directly or indirectly, of any religious sect or denomination, or in aid or for the benefit of any other object of any nature or kind whatever.[193]

Blaine, United States Representative from Maine, picked up the challenge. He proposed an amendment to the Constitution, which in Senate discussions was referred to as the School Amendment. In part it stated that

no State shall make any law respecting an establishment of religion or prohibiting the free exercise thereof; and no money raised by taxation in any State for the support of public schools, or derived from any public fund therefor, nor any public lands devoted thereto, shall ever be made under the control of any religious sect or denomination; nor shall any money so raised or lands so devoted be divided between religious sects or denominations.[194]

Religious prejudices flared again in American society. An unsigned article entitled "The President's Speech at Des Moines" appeared in the January 1876 issue of *The Catholic World*. The article's sharp and subtle style marked it the work of Hecker, the periodical's editor. In the same manner that Grant had taken his stand against denominational schools, *The Catholic World* presented the following resolutions:

1. No "Sectarianism" in our common schools; and therefore, "not one dollar" to our present system of schools, because they are sectarian.
2. "Not one dollar" to "pagan" schools, in which God is ignored.
3. "Not one dollar" to "atheistic" schools, in which God is denied in the name of "science falsely so-called." [195]

The conflict continued. On August 15, 1876, the Blaine Amendment was passed by the House, but failed to obtain the necessary two-thirds vote in the Senate.[196] The bill was also defeated the many times it was re-introduced. It was not, however, without success: between 1877 and 1917, its philosophy would be incorporated into amendments of twenty-nine state constitutions; [197] also, Congress compelled every state admitted into the union after 1876 to write into its constitution that it maintained a school system free from sectarian control.

But not all was conflict—there was compromise as well, and under compromise plans some Catholic schools existed within the public school system. We have discussed such a plan as it developed and worked successfully in Savannah, Georgia. The plan was also tried twice in Connecticut. The first attempt was at St. Peter's School in Hartford, which became part of the public school system in 1860. The Rev. Peter Kelly, pastor of St. Peter's, made an arrangement with the public school board by which the parish furnished the school buildings and the teachers were paid by public expense. The arrangement worked for only five years. Whenever vacancies occurred in the teaching staff, they were filled by Protestant teachers, and one of these began the morning exercises with the reading of the Protestant version of the Bible; consequently, the experiment ended.[198] When the school visitors met to make their yearly report in 1866, the Catholic Church was voted guilty of being opposed to religious instruction in the school. Their attitude may be observed in their 1866 report:

Serious difficulty has arisen during the year in the South District in connection with the Main Street branch (Roman Catholic School). While anything like sectarian or partisan instruction is to be avoided, no greater disaster could fall upon our system than to divorce it from all religious influences; and the most unobjectionable form in which those influences can be brought to bear is by the simple and appropriate use of the Bible. . . . And inasmuch as the great mass of the community have accepted the propriety and the right and safety of these principles . . . to remove the Bible from our common schools would be a blow at the foundations of our whole system.[199]

Connecticut made the attempt again in 1868, this time with St. Patrick's School (later called The Hamilton School) in New Haven and, as in the case of St. Peter's, the school building belonged to the Catholic parish and the Catholic teachers were paid yearly salaries. The school was under the Sisters of Mercy. The first years were marked by success and an amazing absence of bigotry. *The New Haven Board of Education Report* for 1869 stated that "in no school is there stronger desire manifested by the teachers to know the best methods of instruction and government; and their success in both is worthy of commendation." [200] In 1878, however, the question of religious exercises in the school again brought the arrangement to a close, with the New Haven Board of Education also objecting to the sisters' wearing religious habits.

The Lowell and Poughkeepsie plans were the most famous compromise systems of the period. In our study of the Boston diocese we noted the reasons for the opening and closing of the experimental school system in Lowell, Massachusetts, from 1831 to 1852. The public school officials had agreed to absorb the Catholic schools on the following terms:

1. The instructors must be examined as to their qualifications by the committee, and receive their appointments from them.
2. The books, exercises, and studies must all be prescribed and regulated by the Committee, and no other whatever must be taught or allowed.
3. These schools must be placed, as respects the examination, inspection, and general supervision of the committee, on precisely the same footing with the other schools of the town.[201]

Gradually, the school lost its Catholic teachers, and the pastor, as we observed, dissatisfied with the religious instruction given in the schools, brought the Sisters of Notre Dame to the parish in 1852. But when the request was made and refused that the arrangement of the schools at Lowell extend to the sisters' school, the Lowell Plan, one of the earliest compromise plans between state and Church officials, was abandoned. The Poughkeepsie Plan was introduced into the archdiocese of New York in 1873 as a means by which the Rev. Patrick F. McSweeny, pastor of St. Peter's Church in Poughkeepsie, New York, hoped to meet the exigencies of the financial problems in his schools. McSweeny offered

1. The school house in Clover Street and in Mill Street to be let to the Board at the annual rent of one dollar each.
2. The male teachers to be subjected to oral or written examinations, or to both, by the Board and the female teachers to a written examination, if such examination of the teachers should be desired by the Board as proof of competency.
3. No religious exercises to be held, nor religious instruction given during the school hours.
4. The school to be thrown open to all denominations and no interference made with any Religion.

5. The Board to be entitled to inspect the school and to examine the children.

And in return, he requested

1. The Board to pay teachers, buy houses and furniture in repair and pay heating expenses, etc.
2. The teachers to be nominated by the Pastor.
3. The Female Teachers to be exempted from oral examinations.
4. The Pastor to retain the right of using the school houses at hours other than those devoted to school exercises.[202]

On July 9, 1873, a committee of five school board members adopted McSweeny's plan substantially. It refused, however, permission to the pastor to nominate teachers for the schools. It recommended that "the teachers . . . be selected, employed, paid, and subject to dismissal by the board . . . and such teachers and the pupils attending such schools shall at all times during school hours be subject to the control and authority of the board." [203] The Board of Education adopted the recommendations. Archbishop John McCloskey of New York gave his approval and the Poughkeepsie Plan was off to a satisfactory start. The Catholic school buildings on Mill and Clover Streets thereafter constituted a public school, and the school board paid St. Peter's Church $1.00 per year for each of the buildings and their furniture. Schools No. 11 and No. 12 admitted no religious exercises during class hours. McSweeny planned for religious instruction to be given in the afternoon recess before secular courses resumed in the afternoon. On this matter, he wrote:

Let the state appoint Catholic teachers for Catholic children, and Protestant teachers for Protestant children, prescribing the present neutral system of education for certain hours of the school-day, and giving also a fixed hour or hours for daily religious instruction. According to the plan in use in Poughkeepsie, N. Y., the teachers are Catholics in public schools No. 11 and 12, just as they are Protestants in the other schools under the same board. The following is the order of daily exercises:

8.45—Morning prayers.
9 to 12—Regular secular course as in other schools.
12—Short prayer; then recess.
1. P.M.—Religious instruction.
1.30—Regular secular course.
3—Closing religious exercises.

The state school-hours are from 9 to 12 and 1.30 to 3, and no child is *compelled* to be at the religious exercises unless by *its own parents'* desire. If a Protestant wishes to send his child to the Catholic public school he may do so, and it is taught in precisely the same way as it is now in the ordinary public school.[204]

The Poughkeepsie Plan worked successfully until 1895.[205] It was legally terminated on December 23, 1898, when the State Superintendent of Public Instruction, Charles R. Skinner, ruled the plan illegal because it permitted the wearing of religious garb by public school teachers and the permanent leasing of public school buildings.[206]

## Conclusions

Social conditions at the beginning of this period were such that the country did not have the right to expect much of Catholic education, any more than of any other cultural effort. Nevertheless Catholic education continued to contribute, and as industrialization, the Civil War, and other influences wrought changes, Catholic education as well as public accommodated itself to the transition. For the Catholic Church at large, the growth observed in Chapter II continued through this period (and, indeed, will continue into Chapter IV). This growth was especially observable in the North, particularly in urban areas; it was slower in the South because of such complex problems as slavery and the devastation of the Civil War. The fact that most of the growth took place through immigration eliminated the possibility of the Church's becoming aristocratic, and the Church did its best to keep pace with all the needs, including education, of her increasing numbers.

As the period wore on, it became increasingly obvious that all youth, Catholic included, needed more education. The formerly considerable influence of the "Enlightenment" (on the non-Catholic milieu), with its dichotomy between education and manual labor, its opposition to the principle of education for the masses, and its consequent disinclination for the lower classes to attend school, began to wane. The needs of an ever more industrial society for trained personnel increased. Catholic education was slower than its public counterpart to make necessary curricular changes to accommodate it. When the public school took positions against religious instruction, however, and it became increasingly obvious that for the first time in history an educational pattern was to be attempted without religion, it became equally clear that the Church was going to have to step up its efforts to educate. The Church's elementary schools would have to grow, in order to accommodate the immigrants and to adapt to an awakening desire for education. On the middle level, the original strain of academies now proliferated as Catholics and others attempted to supply the educational desires of the upper classes. The teaching communities of Sisters and Brothers continued to increase, each community warranting—and usually receiving—a volume in itself. Throughout the pattern, the emphasis seemed to be less and less on personal formation and fulfillment and more and more on the transmission of culture. Nativist opposition to Catholic culture as "alien" solidified Catholic interpretation of this emphasis as a need, and polarization took place. In other terms, Catholic education changed from a leaven mentality to one of siege. Help from abroad supplemented both money and personnel generously supplied at home.

The official Church expressed itself first at the Provincial Councils of Cincinnati, conducted for the most part by and for Germans, who from the beginning, for a variety of reasons, constantly demonstrated their favor of Catholic schools. The entire United States hierarchy at the Councils of Baltimore then backed legislatively the position of encouragement and support which they would continue to reiterate to the present. Discussions of the philosophy and theory of Catholic education were begun by such great lights as James Cardinal Gibbons and bishops John Hughes, John England, Francis Kenrick, Benedict Fenwick, and Martin J. and John L. Spalding; among the clergy, by the Rev. Isaac Hecker of the *Catholic World*, Peter Kelly of Hartford, Connecticut, and Patrick McSweeny of Poughkeepsie, New York; and among the laity, by Orestes A. Brownson and Mathew Carey. Although the laity were helping the religious to teach in some Catholic schools and in others were the sole teachers for many years (e.g., Savannah, Georgia), and Catholic parents were beginning to bring legal suits against prejudice (e.g., *Donahoe* v. *Richards*), no one could make any mistake about the fact that the "official" position of the Roman Catholic Church in the United States at that time—again for a variety of reasons—was expressed by the hierarchy, with a loyal clergy and laity behind them.

One of the reasons was the recognition that the Church needed a strong leadership, for the road was not easy. The needs of the Catholic people, as of most of the population, made them bread-and-butter oriented; they were divided, timid, and apathetic; and in educational matters there was the ever-present opposition of some of their own. Then, too, they were suffering under the bigotry of some fellow-citizens, demonstrated by the nativist-inspired summer riots in Philadelphia, the burning of the Ursuline convent in Charlestown, Massachusetts, the cruel and unjust (though not illegal) inspection of the Notre Dame Academy in Roxbury, Massachusetts, and prejudiced public-school textbooks. It went even higher, however, with a speech of a President of the United States, Ulysses S. Grant, in 1875, and the many proposals for a hostile Blaine Amendment to the Federal Constitution beginning in 1876 (the centennial of the Declaration of Independence!). The last-named succeeded in many state constitutions. Official government, however, was usually much more fair. On the federal level, the Fourteenth Amendment of 1868 provided all citizens with due process of law to protect their life, liberty, and property. On lower levels, compromise plans to help Catholic education as well as local communities were established in such cities as Savannah, Georgia; Hartford, Connecticut; Lowell, Massachusetts; and Poughkeepsie, New York. Catholic education emerged from this period of transition larger, more solidly founded, and more perfectly formed, than when it entered.

## CHAPTER IV

# 1885-1917: Further Growth

## Social Changes

IN THE LATE NINETEENTH CENTURY, the United States was still in the process of transformation from an agrarian and rural nation into an urban and industrial one. Scientific and technological developments were moving Americans from farms to factories. Population showed a marked increase as a great flood of immigrants poured in. The Far West, opened for settlement in the previous generation, expanded and prospered. The period was, in the main, one of prosperity, but unemployment, poverty, slums, disease, child labor, excessive working hours, and low wages clamored for attention. The rising materialism of the nation embraced the philosophies of naturalism and pragmatism, the concept of individualism, and the cult of success. Darwinism engendered questioning of the validity of the Bible. Despite religion's critical period, however, the turn of the century found it gaining in strength. In fact, the first decade of the twentieth century—years of innocence, exuberance, and big beginnings—began with warnings that the end of the world was at hand and that people had better repent. In 1900, there were 8,000 autos in the country, with fewer than ten miles of concrete road and knickered boys shouting, "Get a horse!" at stuck horseless carriages. Gaslights lit the streets, and there were no electric refrigerators, few gas ranges, no airplanes or radios, and few telephones. For an unskilled laborer, a wage of $1.50 a day was typical, and labor unions were small and fierce, but impotent. The average annual income for a family was $650, but sugar was only 4¢ a pound and butter 24¢. In the world of women, there was no right to vote, and a "lady cashier" could earn $8 per week, while a girl "over 14, to label samples" was offered $2.50 per week. In the children's world, diphtheria and croup were dread diseases, and children worked in mines on a 12-hour day for 35¢. It was a decade of industrial tycoons and no income tax. There were only 45 stars in the United States flag, and American soldiers were occupying territory in the Caribbean and in the Pacific. But the people had roots and stability: they knew the people in their own town, and their children attended the same school they had. In 1903, the Wright brothers flew across 120 feet of sand dune in a mechanical heavier-than-air machine, and in the next decade people cheered when a plane first flew cross-country—in 49 days! The Panama Canal opened, and Barney Oldfield drove a car at 131.7 miles per hour. Coming off the presses were the first Tarzan books, Robert Frost's first poems, and *Riders of the Purple Sage*. At the soundless movies, people were chuckling at Charlie Chaplin and were vamped by Theda Bara. By 1917, the United States led the world in the production of manufactured goods. This was the time of the militant suffragette, and the time not to be a slacker in the "war to end war," the war to make the world safe for democracy.

## Public Education

Growth and maturation was characteristic not only of United States society but of American education as well. The public sector of education witnessed its greatest changes. Such far-seeing and energetic educators as Charles William Eliot, for forty years president of Harvard, and William Torrey Harris, the United States Commissioner of Education from 1889 to 1906, furthered educational reforms. Harris fought for persons of every social stratum to have the right to an education, introduced scientific and manual arts into the curriculum, and advocated high schools at a time when they were not universally accepted. By bringing Susan E. Blow to St. Louis, he initiated a movement to make the kindergarten a part of public education. Eliot, who in 1893 was chairman of the Committee of Ten on Secondary School Studies, gave vogue to the elective principle in higher education and sowed the seed of the junior high school. An address he gave before the National Education Association in 1892 on "Undesirable and Desirable Uniformity in Schools" was among the beginnings of a realization of the need to meet individual differences in the classrooms.[1]

As cities grew in number and size, secondary education had quantitative triumphs. State systems of education were established, and also state and regional accreditation associations. The New England Association of Colleges and Secondary Schools was founded in 1886, the Middle States Association in 1887, the North Central Association in 1894, and the Southern Association in 1895. The Northwestern Association of Secondary and Higher Schools would be established in 1918, and the Western Association of Schools and Colleges in 1927.[2] By 1910 every state had normal schools for the training of its teachers, but the shortage of good teachers, especially in elementary schools, was cause for concern. President John W. Cook of the State Normal School at De Kalb, Illinois, speaking before the National Education Association in 1914 remarked that 550 thousand public school teachers in the United States had charge of eighteen million children, and that sixty thousand of those teachers had no professional training.[3]

Elementary public school populations zoomed as compulsory attendance and child labor laws tended to improve. The child was given new consideration. G. Stanley Hall's *The Contents of Children's Minds on Entering School*[4] in 1893 and his scientific studies of child nature influenced the methods and curricula of the schools. There was a marked increase in the quantity of written works on education, and a general interest in educational theory. For most of the nineteenth century, and in the opening years of the twentieth, United States educators turned to Europe, and American schools embraced Pestalozzian, Froebelian, and Herbartian concepts. As the twentieth century moved into its second decade, however, a definite native pedagogy was born. Fathered by Francis W. Parker at Quincy, Massachusetts, with an attack on the traditional methods of the schools, and nurtured by John Dewey, it would mature in the form of progressive education in the free public schools of America. Then it was declared that the public school was the chief means of social betterment. The aim of education became social efficiency, and the virtues of responsibility and social insight came to be cultivated over those of obedience and submission. Public schools had become a fixed part of the American way of life, having evolved from Protestant-tinged beginnings into an educational system on a secularistic base. They were tax-supported, free to the public, nonsectarian, and integrated into state systems.

## The New Immigration and the Catholic Church

From 1885 to 1917, the Catholic Church in the United States rose from a position of subjugation to one of relative power and prestige, sharing in the changes of the nation and growing with its growth. These were years when the tide of immigration ran high, and with the immigrant influx the Catholic Church in America gained strength. The newcomers were not a mere numerical addition—they were the Church. At the Declaration of Independence, the Catholic Church in this country had been practically nonexistent, and the early immigrants did not find a Church ready to function competently in assimilating them and meeting their needs. In many instances, church, pastors, and even the hierarchy had had to be provided by the immigrants.[5] The years 1885 to 1917 saw the Catholic Church lay sturdy foundations on which this "most disliked suspect of all the American churches" would build and develop into the "strongest single denomination in the land."[6] It is difficult, however, to determine the number of Catholic immigrants to the United States. The Church enumerated its members by statistical returns of pastors and bishops which were not consistently accurate, and the government in its census records did not classify people according to religious affiliation. In 1890, 1906, and 1916, the government did compile data on the religious organization and affiliation of its population, but these findings too were based on parish reports.[7] The *Official Catholic Directory* of the year 1890 registered 7,855,000 Catholics;[8] by 1920, the figure would stand at 17,735,553.[9] Current corrected figures claim that 9 million would be a better estimate for the opening decade of the nineties, and that the Catholic population was 20 million in 1920. In either case, the overall growth is clear.

During this period the number of immigrants from Germany, Ireland, and Great Britain decreased. The new arrivals, for the most part semi-skilled workers or peasants, came from central and southern Europe, especially Austria-Hungary, Italy, and Russia. How the Church ever succeeded in caring for her enormous influx of new members defies depiction. Catholic immigrants of the 1890's and early 1900's brought with them difficulties and dangers, first of all, for themselves, because they were strikingly different from the natives in language, customs, culture, and personal standards of living, and spoke in tongues that grated sharply on American ears. They were unwanted "strangers in the land"; poverty caused them to live in the worst quarters of the industrial towns, where they were slow to join labor movements and appeared to take little interest in the political and economic questions discussed by their fellow workers. They wanted to make quick money in this industrial new world and return to their homeland. But America held them and, with a fecundity that was another cause for alarm to their neighbors, they quickly overpopulated the foreign quarters that sprang up in urban areas.[10]

The immigrants brought problems for the Church, too, resulting in trouble both from within and from without. Within, the immigrants clashed among themselves: the Irish and Germans had not yet learned to live peaceably together. The Church, depending upon the insights of each bishop, labored to integrate them and, through foreign-language schools, to equip the immigrant child to become a respected American citizen versed in the language, manners, and customs of the nation. Outside the Church, powerful Protestant groups feared what they considered these "unchanged masses of foreigners, entrenched in America and yet not of it,"[11] and refused to accept them. Those who by now considered themselves native Americans resented a Church which seemed to give its major allegiance to Rome and sponsored a separate school system.

Alarmed by the influx of Catholic immigrants and by reports that a papal representative was to take up residence at Washington, nativism revived. There were mutterings about Roman encroachments in public affairs. In 1887 Henry Bowers founded the American Protective Association—the notorious "A.P.A."—in Clinton, Iowa, with the express purpose of defending American institutions against foreign aggression.[12] The organization had a lingering existence until 1892, when it acquired a new president in William J. H. Traynor and began its boom years. Though its influence was stronger in the Middle West, the organization had national influence through such publications as the *A.P.A. Maga zine*[13] and Traynor's *Patriotic American*.[14] The Detroit organ of the A.P.A. even went so far as to publish a fake encyclical ascribed to Leo XIII in which the date was provided for Catholics of the United States to engage in a holy massacre of all Protestants.[15] The success of the A.P.A. from 1892 until 1896 may be attributed in no small measure to the astute and practical leadership of Traynor, but the underlying source of its strength undoubtedly rested in Protestant attitudes and unfounded fears. According to Desmond, three constant factors gave the A.P.A. the huge following it possessed during Traynor's presidency. They were: (1) the hereditary Protestant antagonism and suspicion of the Catholic Church; (2) the prejudice, frequently engendered by the conduct of Irish-American politicians; (3) the occasional Catholic society parade or demonstration which was calculated to alarm the Protestants who witnessed it.[16]

But more germane to our study was the school question. The facts that, after the Third Plenary Council of Baltimore in 1884, there was an expansion of parochial schools, and that the Catholic Church felt entitled to financial aid from the state for school support, made the A.P.A. determined to cut the ground from under Catholic education. It exerted itself to oppose, for example, federal grants to the Bureau of Catholic Indian Missions. Mixing in presidential politics claimed much of the energies of the A.P.A. after 1896, but failures in this field brought loss of prestige. By 1900, the A.P.A.'s history may be said for all purposes to have closed, although it remained in existence until 1911, when nativism showed itself under a different guise.[17]

## *Catholic Hesitation over New Influences Shaping U. S. Education*

From the turn of the century a sophisticated intellectual racism was obvious in American society. Those with nativist proclivities adapted social Darwinism to relegate the immigrant to the role of the most unfit. An intellectual elite sprang up, and literature and the arts flourished.

Catholic leaders, caught up in the problem of providing schools and direction for the stream of foreign-language-speaking immigrants, found no time to contribute to this cultural drive, and their contributions to American thought were meager. Catholic philosophy and doctrine found much of the prevailing intellectual climate in the United States stifling for some of the fundamental truths in which they believed. In the realm of education, there were wide differences between the public and Catholic viewpoints. In the late 1800's, for example, three young men—Charles De Garmo, and Frank M. and Charles A. McMurray—studied at Jena, Germany, and brought back to the United States the views of Johann Friedrich Herbart and, with emphasis on education as a cultural asset, saw their implementation in the public schools. The National Herbartian Society was founded in 1892, having as its first president De Garmo, who zealously brought Herbartian principles to American educators. State normal schools and teachers' colleges accepted Herbartianism. To Catholics, however, Herbart's theory of apperception left little place for free will. His ethical aim of education underemphasized the importance of virtue, a product of free will. The stress that Herbartians laid upon the accumulation of knowledge alone did not produce for Catholics the moral man, and Catholics were of the opinion that the Herbartian efforts to make interest the key to learning overlooked the disciplinary benefit of effort.[18] Perhaps more fundamentally, Catholic educators differed with the Herbartians on the aims of education—the latter aspiring to prepare a man of culture, good moral character, and many-sidedness of interest, the former concentrating at that time on man's eternal destiny.

Also shaping American education were the contributions of Francis Wayland Parker who, between 1883 and 1889, was principal of the Cook County Normal School in Chicago, Illinois. Following Pestalozzian theories, Parker asserted the primacy of method over content, ascribed to the teacher the function of the organization of sound community life, and described the school as a model home, a complete community, an embryonic democracy. When children grow up in freedom, Parker taught, their originally good natures will assure a democratic society; [19] to contemporaneous Catholics, this philosophy was a reflection of Jean-Jacques Rousseau. Catholic educators rejected also Parker's faith in inevitable progress and the role of divinity in man's life, as emanating from German Idealism. The views of Harvard's Charles W. Eliot on the free election of curriculum subjects and his criticism of Jesuit education caused a stir in Catholic circles. William Torrey Harris, then the nation's Commissioner of Education, held the belief that secular studies could not be pursued under the same roof as religious doctrines. His public school must be a purely secular institution. Harris' Hegelian philosophy led him to stress man's cultural heritage and to consider its transmission the chief concern of the schools.[20]

The year 1910 ushered in a new era of scientific interest in education, one of definite utilitarian emphasis. The publication of the Thorndike handwriting scale at that time was a beginning of the contemporary movement for measuring educational products scientifically. The child became the exclusive center of education, and psychologists of the early twentieth century posited the quantitative measurability of all areas of a child's development. A new education was in the making, but it was not a system in which Catholic educators were desirous of taking a part. John Dewey was urging that the aim of education be social efficiency. His proposed curriculum and methods were, in his words, "as much a product of the changed social situation and as much an effort to meet the needs of the new society that is forming, as are changes in modes of industry and commerce." [21] This progressive movement in education had overtones unacceptable to Catholic educators; its principles and Catholic philosophy were poles apart. Catholics saw in all these new educational movements an intellectual and social development with religion banished from the schools. Besides, religious practices in the public schools could not keep both Catholics and Protestants happy. The compulsory reading of the King James Version of the Bible, the singing of Protestant hymns, and a definite pervasion of secularistic philosophy and anti-Catholic bigotry caused a defensive reaction among Catholics. The latter at times tended to condemn the public school in one fell swoop, as if these institutions had no merit at all.

## Tumult in the Church

### THE SCHOOL CONTROVERSY

Despite the hopes of the Third Plenary Council of Baltimore (1884) for rapidly increasing the number of parochial schools, progress in that respect came slowly "within the next decade, for the percentage of parishes with schools moved up from only forty to forty-four." [22] Obviously, not all Catholic children were in Catholic schools. Marked as disloyal to the Catholic faith were those parents who, sometimes out of financial necessity and sometimes for less worthy reasons, sent their children to public schools. Some outstanding Catholic churchmen, however, saw in this attitude possibly more harm than good for the Church and education. James Cardinal Gibbons, when archbishop of Baltimore, had on March 7, 1883, issued a pastoral letter *On Christian Education* in which there was insistence on the erection of Catholic parochial schools, but no violent disapproval of the state school system. This, too, had been the mood and tone of the Third Plenary Council of Baltimore. Controversy flamed high with an address of Archbishop John Ireland to the National Education Association at St. Paul, Minnesota, in 1890.

No member of the Roman Catholic hierarchy in this country had ever uttered a speech like it on Catholic and state schools. Ireland granted the state the right to establish schools, and favored compulsory education. He praised the state's generosity in offering free education, but objected to the public school because it made no provision for religious instruction. For this reason, the parish schools, which at this time enrolled seven hundred and fifty thousand pupils, had become a necessity. The archbishop made two proposals to lighten the load of double taxation on Catholics and to facilitate the teaching of religion with the public schools. First, Ireland suggested a denominational system, by which each religion would have its own schools, state-regulated and state-supported. His second proposal, if the first should prove impossible, was a compromise, in which he indicated his favor of the Poughkeepsie Plan which had been in effect in New York since 1873 [23] and was in operation elsewhere in the nation as well.[24]

Catholic criticism came hard and fast upon Ireland's speech. Some of his expressions seemed to presage the abandonment of the parochial school system. The archbishop followed up his statements by action, and he authorized the pastors of Faribault and Stillwater in his archdiocese to put the Poughkeepsie Plan to work in their schools. A war of words ensued, carried into the public press by prelates, priests, and laymen of Catholic as well as Protestant persuasion. It was not the Faribault and Stillwater adoptions of the Poughkeepsie Plan that sparked the heated controversy, however. It was Ireland's speech, with its lavish praise of public schools and its words of regret over the need for parochial schools to exist. Ireland's sharpest critics were several of his fellow bishops, most notably Bernard J. McQuaid of Rochester and Michael A. Corrigan of New York.[25] Along with Archbishop Francis Katzer of Milwaukee and priests of German extraction, they represented the conservative leadership of the American Church. Gibbons, however, gave Ireland his quiet but staunch support. Bishop John Keane, rector of The Catholic University of America, also enthusiastically upheld Ireland's cause. It was, indeed, an issue in which personalities as well as principles clashed.

To make matters worse, in December 1891, the Rev. Thomas Bouquillon, D.D., professor of moral theology at The Catholic University of America, published a thirty-two-page pamphlet, *Education: To Whom Does It Belong?*, challenging the traditional thought of the Church that the state has only a substitutional right in education. This was a new viewpoint, Bouquillon granting the state far greater rights over education than Catholics had previously. Although the preface to the pamphlet declared that "theoretical principles only are dealt with," [26] the author's argument throughout clearly substantiated the position of Ireland. Bouquillon wrote that education "belongs to the individual, physical or moral, to the family, to the state, to the Church, to none of these solely and exclusively, but to all four combined in harmonious working." [27] He further maintained that "the state has been endowed by God with the right of founding schools that contribute to its welfare." [28] Although Bouquillon's basic premise, that the state has a special right to educate, would become accepted Catholic teaching, in 1890 it was unheard of. His pamphlet held that every man has the right to communicate truth to those wishing to receive it. While this is true of the individual in society, this right must be subordinated to the common good. Parents have the first and basic special right to educate, again subject to religious and civil control based on the idea of the primacy of the common good. Civil authority also has a special right to educate based on the idea of the promotion of the common good; it even has the duty to do so should the parents neglect this function which is so important to society. The state cannot, however, determine the particular school beyond establishing basic requirements in line with the common good of the state. The Church has the obligation of teaching religious and moral truths and, indirectly as necessity indicates, the obligation of teaching secular subjects.

Within a week of the publication of *Education: To Whom Does It Belong?* the Reverend René I. Holaind, S.J., professor of ethics at the Jesuit Seminary at Woodstock College, Maryland, published an answering brochure, entitled *The Parent First.* He claimed that education is essentially the right and duty of the Church and the parents. The state enters the field at the bidding of either or both of these. Although granting that when individuals are deficient the state may supply schools, Holaind allowed this only when schools were absolutely necessary. Since the right to control non-state schools would abrogate the rights and duties of parents and the Church, the state has no right to such control, argued Holaind.[29] The two pamphlets promoted intense and bitter public discussion, which came to be called the "Bouquillon controversy." Many critics viewed Bouquillon's pamphlet as having been inspired by Ireland to give a doctrinal basis to the Faribault-Stillwater school plan. In his *Memorial,* Ireland denied any knowledge of Bouquillon's pamphlet before he had seen it in print.[30] He defended his action in the Faribault-Stillwater case as a sound administrative decision based on the situation of the two towns involved: the local Catholics could not afford to support their schools, and through this plan Ireland hoped to assure a sound education in the various secular disciplines united with a religious formation program very similar to that of the ordinary parochial school. To say that he was against parochial education was to fly in the face of the evidence of his administration: his record was one of the finest in parochial school construction and development. His 1890 talk, contrary to what his enemies said in Rome, favored the state schools as much as possible "in order to gain their co-operation afterwards for the schools of the Church." [31] Further, in that same NEA address, he had clearly pointed out the demands of Catholics and the unjust burden of the existing tax situation. In brief, Ireland pleaded for the Faribault Plan as a particular decision of a prudent administrator faced with a difficult situation: he insisted that such a decision did not necessarily represent a general statement of policy either for the United States as a whole or for the diocese as such.

Ireland's defense was brilliant: his enemies argued that he contradicted the Third Plenary Council of Baltimore, and Ireland cited the Third Plenary Council clearly, directly, and at length as his charter for action; his enemies argued that he was an opponent of parochial schools, and he proved his plan as the only way to maintain a viable program of Christian education in the particular situations of the two towns involved; his enemies accused him of innovating, and Ireland cited a list of schools in various dioceses with long traditions of similar programs. He then convincingly concluded that in reality it was not the school situation, but such other factors as Protestant prejudice, which caused his enemies to speak out—reasons "which anyone acquainted with the position of affairs in the United States for the past few years will readily understand." [32] One final objection to Ireland's position and his defense merits mention—not only because the objection was central to his opponents' attack, but also because Ireland's answer is as modern as today. The objection was that Ireland's action in Faribault and Stillwater would, if approved, have the effect of weakening Catholic commitment to parochial schools at a time when they were increasing in strength and favor. In his answer, Ireland noted several interesting facts: (1) in spite of all that had been done, less than one half of Catholic children were in parochial schools; (2) pastors repeatedly told him of the heavy financial burden which parochial schools entailed; and (3) financial limitations made it difficult to maintain the parochial schools on a par with the public schools. Ireland stated his quandary in the closing words of the *Memorial*:

In view of the fact that on account of the poverty of our people the decrees of the Council of Baltimore regarding parochial schools can not for the moment be executed in several parts of the United States, what plan of action can a bishop use meanwhile to procure instruction for those children who cannot in consequence for the present, be provided with parochial schools, and for which condition that Council has not provided? [33]

Meanwhile the "Bouquillon controversy" raged with intense and bitter public discussion. Both sides appealed to Rome for a solution, and in November 1892, Archbishop Francesco Satolli, then a special representative of Rome to the United States, presented his Fourteen Propositions with the hope of solving the question. These points, proposed by Satolli with papal approval, express rather fully Ireland's own views and, at least implicitly, vindicate Bouquillon's position on the state's right as an educational agency.[34] The fourteen points in summary form, particularly points five through eleven, show this: (1) Catholic schools should continue to be erected and improved and made equal to the public schools; (2) where Catholic school maintenance is impossible and the dangers of perversion are removed, Catholic children may attend public schools; (3) Catholic school teachers must be adequate and must pass diocesan examinations; (4) normal schools should be established; (5) it is strictly forbidden for priests to excommunicate parents who wish to send their children to public schools; (6) since the Church is established to teach faith and morals, "absolutely and universally speaking, there is no repugnance in their learning the first elements, and the higher branches of arts and the natural sciences in public schools, controlled by the State, whose office is to provide, maintain, and protect everything by which its citizens are formed to moral fitness, while they live peaceably together, with a sufficiency of temporal goods, under laws promulgated by civil authorities";[35] (7) regarding public schools, "the Church and the Holy See neither condemn nor treat public schools with indifference, but desire that there should be public schools in every state as the number and circumstances of the people require for the cultivation of the useful arts and natural sciences";[36] (8) if the dangers are removed, children may be permitted to attend public schools, though pastors and parents must cooperate to see that they receive adequate religious instruction; (9) regarding the feasibility of establishing parochial schools, ordinaries are to decide based on local circumstances; (10) no reproach is to be directed to Catholic parents who secure private education for their children, provided they see to their religous education as well; (11) it is greatly to be desired that ordinaries and members of local school boards work together to form schools agreeable to both Church and State; (12) for Catholic students in public schools, the best possible religious education should be provided; (13) it is strongly recommended that Catholic school teachers have degrees recognized by the state; and (14) teachers trained in normal schools should receive state degrees.[37]

Satolli's propositions did not satisfy, for some of the American bishops saw in them a danger to parochial schools. Pope Leo XIII therefore asked the bishops to submit their points of view to the Holy See. They held divergent views, and did not write a joint letter. Bishop William J. McCloskey of Louisville, Kentucky, thought that Satolli's propositions would be "the death blow, to a certain extent, of our Catholic schools."[38] Bishop Bernard J. McQuaid of Rochester, N. Y., bitterly opposed Satolli's propositions; writing to Archbishop Michael A. Corrigan of New York City on Dec. 13, 1892, he remarked that "we are all in a nice pickle thanks to Leo XIII and his delegate."[39] Bishop John J. Kain of Wheeling, West Virginia, wrote to the Pope praising the propositions for their great service to the Catholic Church in the United States. On May 31, 1893, Leo XIII addressed a letter on the subject to Gibbons. The Pope supported the decrees of the Third Plenary Council of Baltimore, and encouraged the building of Catholic schools, but gave local ordinaries the right to decide the conditions under which Catholic students might attend public schools. He pleaded for an end to the controversy and begged that harmony be restored among the prelates of the Church in the United States.[40]

AMERICANISM

Although the injunction of Pope Leo XIII terminated the school controversy, the Catholic Church in America did not know peace. Once more during this period, in 1899 to be exact, when Catholics in the United States were experiencing a questioning of their doctrinal ortho-doxy, Rome was forced to intervene. The broad approach of Gibbons, Ireland, and Keane to the school question, to labor organization, and to Catholic participation in the World's Parliament of Religions at Chicago in 1893, caused conservative Catholics to fear for the integrity of the Faith in the United States. The thriving state of American Catholi-cism attracted the attention of European observers and, in France in particular, this fostered debate among liberals and conservatives. The dispute came to a head with the free French translation of Walter Eliott's *Life of Father Hecker.*[41] The work was attacked as heretical, and the heresy was termed "Americanism." The same Supreme Pontiff, Leo XIII, felt obliged to intervene, and on January 22, 1899, he ad-dressed to Gibbons an apostolic letter *Testem benevolentiae*[42] outlining possible errors on the part of American Catholics. The Pope wrote that underlying these errors were some erroneous broad principles that he claimed "may be reduced to this: that, in order the more easily to bring over to Catholic doctrine those who dissent from it, the Church ought to adapt herself somewhat to our advanced civilization, and, relaxing her ancient rigor, show some indulgence to modern popular theories and methods."[43] The Pope cited instances of errors consequent upon these principles: e.g., the claim that the Holy Spirit's direct action on in-dividual souls was to be preferred to any kind of external spiritual guidance, that natural virtues should be emphasized as more suitable for modern times, and that active virtues were to be stressed. In part, the Holy Father rebuked:

In point of fact, it is especially in the cultivation of virtue that the assistance of the Holy Spirit is indispensable. . . . It is hard to understand how those who are imbued with Christian principles can place the natural ahead of the super-natural virtues, and attribute to them greater power and fecundity.[44]

In Gibbons' reply to the Pope, the Cardinal said that "this doctrine, which I deliberately call extravagant and absurd, this Americanism, as it has been called, has nothing in common with the views, aspirations, doctrine and conduct of Americans."[45]

These were trying years for the Catholic Church in America. Beset from without by the forces of nativism which labeled Catholics as un-American, and "subject within to feuds among the bishops by reason of their conflicting interpretations on the role of the Church in public affairs," [46] it was a time of tension and disunity. By the twentieth century, however, the "growing pains" of the Church in the United States had subsided—maturity came, and she stood firmly on her own feet.[47] On June 29, 1908, Pope Pius X removed American Catholics from the jurisdiction of the Congregation "De Propaganda Fide," which had charge over missionary areas of the Church—the Holy See no longer considered this a mission country. In spite of friction from within and persecution from without, it had gained in strength.

## The Government and Catholic Education

Bible reading, Protestant hymn singing, and the question of religious sisters in state schools were the main issues of contention in the courts at this time. Religious practices in public schools resulted in lawsuits, and many of these were brought by parents of Catholic children. Concerning the propriety of Bible reading in public schools, there were conflicting results. The 1910 Illinois case of *People* v. *Board of Education* prohibited the Bible completely,[48] and Louisiana's *Herold* v. *Parish Board of Education* in 1915 decided that the reading of the Bible, even if not compulsory, was unconstitutional, as giving preference to Christians over Jews.[49] Court cases in twelve other states, however, allowed Bible reading in public schools.[50] On the legality of holding religious services and Sunday schools in public school buildings, the courts manifested similar confusion.

Another matter placed before the courts was the employment of Roman Catholic nuns to teach in public schools. Both Pennsylvania (in the 1910 case of *Commonwealth* v. *Herr*)[51] and New York (in the 1906 case of *O'Connor* v. *Hendrick*) [52] upheld statutes forbidding teachers to wear religious garb. This would be the public policy of the majority of the states, even where the contributions of teaching religious sisters were manifestly great. For example, in Albuquerque, N.M., after the Sisters of Charity of Cincinnati had opened Our Lady of the Angels School in 1883, they responded to public need by converting their establishment into "Public School No. 12," which formally opened on February 22, 1884. In 1891 (almost immediately after the city of Albuquerque acquired its first public school property in 1890), the Board of Education made the requirement that all public school teachers must wear secular garb, and the Sisters refused to comply. The Board therefore in the fall of 1891 opened a public school with secular teachers in charge, and the Sisters renamed their school St. Vincent Academy, in honor of St.

Vincent de Paul, the patron saint of their order. (It held its last Commencement Exercises—for a graduating class of 35 girls—in May 1969.) A different decision was reached by the Supreme Court of Pennsylvania in 1894 in the case of *Hysong* v. *Gallitzin*,[53] "where it was held that school districts might employ as teachers sisters of a religious order of the Roman Catholic Church, and permit them while teaching to wear the garb of their order, provided no religious sectarian instruction should be given, nor any religious sectarian exercises engaged in." [54] Also, in Michigan, in 1878 the new pastor of the Catholic parish on Beaver Island in Lake Michigan, 33 miles off the mainland, requested Dominican Sisters for Holy Cross school. Because the local County of Charlevoix had had to give up its little village school there due to the impossibility of getting teachers from the mainland, the Sisters also complied with an official public request to take it over as well. Ultimately, both schools were consolidated, and the Sisters contracted with the Charlevoix County school system. At this writing, this plan still exists, with four Sisters teaching there in accord with the requirements of the State of Michigan.

As a result of restrictive legislation, religious and educational leaders who were interested in imparting moral and spiritual values attempted a variety of circuitous means. The Poughkeepsie and Faribault plans already mentioned were examples of such efforts. Another attempt was the "released-time" programs, the practice of releasing students from public schools for attendance at religious classes under Church auspices during school time. At first a Protestant concept, this kind of program was suggested in 1905 by George U. Wenner to an interchurch conference at Carnegie Hall in New York City. The Conference passed a resolution to the same effect, which was debated at the annual meeting of the Federation of Churches of New York on January 30, 1906. At the next meeting, April 30, several Protestant ministers, a rabbi, and a Catholic priest endorsed the resolution.[55]

The types of released-time programs varied greatly as time went on, often consisting in a Protestant community-type interdenominational program. All programs, however, had several common characteristics: in an effort to place religion in the curriculum, instruction was given during school time; attendance was voluntary, with the written consent of parents required; religious denominations were not forced to take part; cooperating churches assumed full responsibility for staff, curriculum, and costs; students not participating remained in the classroom; and the religious denomination usually kept attendance records and reported them to school officials.[56] There were obvious difficulties involved: the scheduling of a proper time, for example, and busy and unprepared clergymen and instructors. From the very beginning, released time was largely an urban movement. Although it embraced all elementary and secondary grades, it most frequently concentrated on grades four through six. (The cooperation of the state in released-time programs even on a nondiscriminatory basis would be questioned by the courts in 1948, in the case of *McCollum* v. *Board of Education*.[57] This decision would outlaw the released-time program for religious instruction on public school premises in thirty-seven states.[58] There was a national Catholic reaction of dismay, and the decision in *Zorach* v. *Clauson* [59] in 1952 would allow released-time programs, if the students desirous of religious instruction would leave the public school grounds to go to religious centers for religious instruction or denominational exercises.)

Released-time programs did not, however—even under optimum conditions—satisfactorily supply the need for religion in public schools. Ireland put his finger on the Church's source of dissatisfaction, in his criticism in another connection that "the state school tends to eliminate religion from the minds and hearts of the youth of the country." [60] Ireland did not agree that an hour of Sunday School every week was satisfactory religious instruction. He argued:

An hour in the week to study religion is as nothing, and during that hour the small number only [*sic*] will be present. The churches are open and the teachers are at hand, but the non-religious school has engrossed the attention and the energies of the child during five days of the week; he is unwilling to submit to the drudgery of a further hour's work on Sunday. . . .The teaching of religion is not a function of the state; but the State should, for the sake of the people, and for its own sake, permit and facilitate the teaching of religion by the Church. This the State does not do; rather, it hinders and prevents the work of the Church.[61]

But Catholic education during this period aimed, as it still does, at the complete education of its students and not merely at the teaching of religious truths. Leo XIII spoke to this point:

An education cannot be deemed complete which takes no notice of modern sciences. It is obvious that in the existing keen competition of talents, and the widespread and, in itself, noble and praiseworthy passion for knowledge, Catholics ought to be not followers but leaders. It is necessary, therefore, that they should cultivate every refinement of learning, and zealously train their minds to the discovery of truth and the investigation, so far as it is possible, of the entire domain of nature.[62]

## Growth and Expansion of Catholic Education

### ELEMENTARY EDUCATION

In Catholic education during this period the most conspicuous growth took place in the parochial elementary schools, motivated somewhat by the insistence of the Third Plenary Council in Baltimore. How much of the progress was due to Baltimore III, and how much to such extrinsic factors as greater Catholic affluence, will probably never be known. Reliable statistics of growth are difficult to secure, but Table I helps to show the steady increase in school buildings and pupil enrollment. The growth is not only an objective one, but also proportionate to the Catholic population. The figures are not exact; Wolff wrote in December 1892:

According to the last Catholic Directory the number of children in Catholic parochial schools in the year 1891, so far as could be ascertained was 700,753. To this must be added at the very least, 50,000 children attending Catholic parochial schools from which no reports were received. There are upwards of 25,000 children in Catholic orphan asylums to which schools are attached (the exact number reported is 24,572 and fourteen dioceses are not reported). Moreover, there are other Catholic elementary institutions in which Catholic children are educated. Taking these facts into consideration we feel fully justified in saying that the number of Catholic children in parochial or other like schools of from seven to fourteen years of age is at least 800,000 and probably 850,000.[63]

TABLE I

CATHOLIC PAROCHIAL SCHOOL GROWTH IN THE U.S., 1880–1920 *

| YEAR | CATHOLIC POPULATION | PAROCHIAL SCHOOLS | PUPIL ENROLLMENT |
|------|---------------------|-------------------|------------------|
| 1880 | 6,143,222 | 2,246 | 405,234 |
| 1890 | 8,277,039 | 3,194 | 633,238 |
| 1900 | 10,129,677 | 3,811 | 854,523 |
| 1910 | 14,347,027 | 4,845 | 1,237,251 |
| 1920 | 17,735,553 | 5,852 | 1,701,219 |

* This table is compiled from the following sources: *Sadlier's Catholic Directory, Almanac and Ordo* (New York: D. & J. Sadlier & Co., 1880), p. xxxii; *ibid.*, 1890, p. 407; *The Catholic Directory, Almanac 1900* (Milwaukee: M. H. Wiltzius & Co., 1900), p. 822; *ibid.*, 1910, p. 1029; *The Official Catholic Directory 1920* (New York: P. J. Kenedy & Sons, 1920), p. 1011.

The Third Plenary Council was, of course, aware that there was no *system* of Catholic elementary education in the United States. The hierarchy had been concerned with establishing schools, and attention to this basic need left no time or resources for a consideration of uniting schools into some organization. Parochial schools were for the most part independent units, having little or no relation to others. The teaching sisterhoods, and to a lesser extent the teaching brotherhoods, furnished their faculties. These religious teachers operated their schools according to the directions in their individual Rules and Constitutions, and the local superior was usually the principal of the school. The number of lay teachers was negligible. Thus, a diocesan *pattern* resulted. McCluskey sums up the administrative setup which has remained essentially the same from that day to this:

Each parish, like the local school district in the public school system, bears the responsibility for building and operating its own school. A diocesan superintendent appointed by the bishop has general supervision over all parochial schools, but the local pastor functions as the agent for the diocese in managing his own school. The pastor engages the faculty, collects parish funds for operational expenses, supervises maintenance, plans expansion, and supplies moral support. He does not, however, enter directly into the academic administration, though by reason of his pastoral title he is the head of the school.[64]

Aware of the need to establish a uniform curriculum and system of grading, of the need for unity to bring about diocesan patterns, and of the suggestions of the Third Plenary Council of Baltimore, the Fifth Synod of the New York Archdiocese in 1886 established the first diocesan school board. (This group in 1887 issued a *Directory and Course of Instruction* which detailed the material to be treated in each subject at each level, and in 1888 became perhaps the first to appoint a diocesan school superintendent, the Reverend William J. Degnam.[65]) The spur to parochial school expansion was the "aim of educating citizens in matters of both body and soul." [66] Catholic educators were concerned that the efficiency of the Catholic elementary schools achieve public recognition. In 1901, the Rev. Louis S. Walsh wrote:

Let our standard and products be known; for it is impossible under modern conditions to make headway on any other lines. This is one and a very strong reason why the formulated State system ought to be a guide for all secular branches in every school, in this sense, that the ground covered in all elementary studies, the time and importance given to each branch, and the civic ideas that make a State or Nation, should be closely followed, through Catholic books and with Catholic teachers.[67]

The Catholic elementary schools of the late nineteenth and early twentieth centuries mirrored the ethnic character of their immigrant neighborhoods. Parochial pupils of that time "might perhaps have been more safely classified as the children of the poor than would their counterparts of the parish schools of today." [68]

Educational advance and expansion brought problems, one solution for which seemed to lie in bringing Catholic educators together in order that, by a comparison of opinions and experiences, and by a pooling of ideas, common problems might be resolved and future progress planned. The National Education Association formed by public school teachers and administrators in 1870 exemplified the advantages of unification. Catholic leadership was supplied by the Most Rev. Thomas J. Conaty, rector of The Catholic University of America, whose efforts were instrumental in starting three organizations: the Educational Conference of Seminary Faculties (1897), the Association of Catholic Colleges (1898),

and the Parish School Conference (1902).[69] At a national convention in
St. Louis in 1904, the three separate organizations fused to form the
Catholic Educational Association. (In 1927 this organization changed its
name to the National Catholic Educational Association.[70] The CEA was
launched as a voluntary association whose function was neither legislative nor executive, but deliberative and informative.)[71] The *Report* of
the Association's first meeting stated:

> The advantages of association have not heretofore been so apparent in the
> conditions of our development. Each school and institution developed to suit
> particular conditions, and there was no special reason for co-operation or
> association among the various Catholic educational interests of the country. . . .
> We are now passing through new conditions . . . the time is ripe for greater
> unity of action and sympathetic co-operation.[72]

The *Report* pointed out the advantages expected:

> It will bring together at stated intervals the leading Catholic educators of
> the country, and give an opportunity of exchanging views and of discussing
> educational problems. It will stimulate, support, and extend Catholic educa-
> tional activity, and afford encouragement to all engaged in the work. It will
> make us aware of the defects of our system, and through it the experience of
> one may become the profit of all. It will make us conscious of our power, and
> help us to direct our energy, and to make the most effective use of our re-
> sources. It will help in the work of organizing parish schools into unified
> diocesan systems. It should help to promote harmony and coordination of all
> Catholic educational interests.[73]

During this period the Association had several separate departments,
resulting from the amalgamation that went into its creation: the
Catholic Seminary Department, the Catholic College and University De-
partment, and the Catholic School Department. The constitution made it
clear that "other departments may be added with the approval of the
Executive Board of the Association," [74] and left the organization open
to change. It would extend its departments to seven: Major Seminary,
Minor Seminary, College and University, Superintendents, Secondary
School, Elementary School, and Special Education for the Physically and
Mentally Handicapped. Two autonomous sections would be added—the
Vocation Section and the Sister-Formation Section—and later a commission for Adult Education. Through its meetings and publications the
Association interprets Catholic education to the public at large.[75] It grew
in size [76] and influence and accomplished its goals of cooperation and
professionalization as the Catholic Church moved from the status of
immigrant to full participant in the affairs of the nation.

## MIDDLE-LEVEL EDUCATION

After 1890, the growth of the middle-level school was one of the most
striking educational developments in the United States. Although

the first high school in the United States had been established in
Boston in 1821,[77] the development of public secondary education was
slow. The academy had remained the dominant institution. Due to the
greater educational needs of an increasingly complex industrial society
after the Civil War, however, and the already-mentioned Kalamazoo
Case of 1874, during the period 1885 to 1917 the public high schools
expanded their programs of studies, and tried to accommodate pupils
for whom the high school course was terminal as well as those for whom
it was a preparation for college. In 1893, the NEA's Committee of Ten
on Secondary School Studies wanted the high schools to be integrated
into the American educational system. The Committee stressed the need
for standardization of requirements and uniformity of content for college-
bound students and proposed a program of courses as a standard college-
preparatory curriculum for all high schools.[78] The high school course,
then, remained principally of a college-preparatory nature. At the end
of the period, in 1917, the Smith-Hughes Act was passed to foster vocational education in high schools, but by that time public secondary
education had a sure footing.

Catholics were unable at first to set up a parallel. They lacked the
funds, and the individual parish schools, as already remarked, had not
been organized into a system. An even greater obstacle, according to
Burns, was the fact that "pastors who are zealous enough in the cause of
the parochial school disavow belief in the necessity or possibility of
Catholic high schools" [79]—an observation that was true of the laity as
well. But this idea slowly gave way before the pressures of an industrial
society and the accelerated public high school movement. A great impetus was given to the Catholic high school movement when the Catholic
High School of Philadelphia was founded in 1890, through a generous
gift of Thomas E. Cahill of that city. Cahill had died on August 9, 1878,
and Kirlin writes that

the bequests of his [Cahill's] will were $1,000 annually for the relief of the
poor of St. Patrick's, St. Francis's, and St. Charles's parishes, and $1,000
annually for the support of St. Patrick's Parish School. The remainder of his
estate, amounting to about a million dollars, he devised for the erection of the
Roman Catholic High School of Philadelphia, for the free education of boys.
On 5 September, 1890, this magnificent High School, at Broad and Vine Streets,
was dedicated by Archbishop [Patrick John] Ryan, to the purpose designed
by its founder.[80]

The Catholic High School of Philadelphia held the position of a central
high school, but remained a part of the parish school system under the
control of the head of the diocese. Its faculty comprised a president and
vice-president, both priests, and eighteen lay instructors.[81]

The Catholic Educational Association at its first general meeting in
1904 drew the attention of Catholic educators to the Catholic high-school
movement. In October of the preceding year, a committee on high

schools had been appointed consisting of two members each from the Catholic College Conference and the Conference of Parochial School Superintendents, for the purpose of investigating the condition of Catholic secondary schools and suggesting means for the establishment of Catholic high schools.[82] The Committee submitted to the CEA in 1904 a series of nine resolutions which were unanimously adopted. These resolutions stated that religious training is as important to the high-school age as to the younger student; Catholic high schools for boys as well as for girls should be set up; the time was ripe; in cities there should be central Catholic high schools for several parishes; under this concept a Catholic high school is feasible in almost every city; the Catholic high schools should be included in the diocesan school system; curricula should provide for both terminal education and preparation for college; the latter curriculum should be at least equal to the entrance requirements of the Catholic college; and it is generally desirable that these schools be under religious communities, and especially desirable that religious communities of men undertake these schools for boys.[83] The CEA appointed another Committee on High Schools in 1908. Its assignment was to prepare a report

which would exhibit the number, location and character of the existing Catholic high schools for boys, together with as much information as might be obtainable about the curriculum and the teaching, the whole to be accompanied by a statement which, while summarizing the statistics obtained, would at the same time, present the conclusions arrived at by the Committee in regard to the entire subject of Catholic high schools.[84]

The Committee initiated the study by checking the *Catholic Directory* of 1910 to locate all parish schools which had six teachers or more (thus being likely to have more than eight elementary grades). The list included 1,474 schools. The Committee then sent each school a letter of inquiry, with the purpose of discovering the number involved in secondary school work. It concluded that one-third of the large parish schools had high-school grades, and that the number of Catholic parish high schools actually in existence was between four and five hundred, "representing every section of the country and almost every diocese." [85] The Committee lamented the lack of teachers, and in this connection made the following recommendation:

There seems to be no good reason why, in central Catholic high schools in the larger cities, several religious communities may not cooperate in the formation of the teaching staff. This is the plan that is contemplated in the case of the Central Girls' Catholic High School that is now rising in Philadelphia.[86]

It assumed that a typical popular high school, with four regular grades and two commercial grades, required a minimum of seven teachers, and it cited the Boys' Catholic Central High School at Grand Rapids, Michigan, as an example. Diocesan high schools were preferred. The

*Report* stated that if the Catholic high school "is to be a central and common superior school, coordinated with the parish schools surrounding it, [it] must be established by or adopted by the Bishop and be directly under diocesan control," [87] and that where possible it should be parish contributions rather than individual tuition fees that should support Catholic high schools. The Committee *Report* was presented to the meeting of the Association in Chicago in June 1911.

Although the real turning point in the thinking of Roman Catholics, clergy and laity alike, on the desirability of secondary schools came with the presentation of this *Report* of 1911, it was a disappointing report in some respects. In the matter of curriculum, for example, the Committee held to a full four-year curriculum to satisfy the demands of the colleges —articulated with the Catholic elementary school curriculum below it and the Catholic college curriculum above it. No case was made for a course of study answering the needs of those for whom high school would be terminal. It frowned on manual training courses, claiming that "the high school being what it is, a school mainly for the education of the children of the middle classes, its purpose and function must necessarily exclude industrial training." [88] The Catholic Educational Association was not satisfied that all areas of the Catholic high-school problem had been probed; its Advisory Board engaged in further study of certain problems relating to the Catholic high school, and reported to the Executive Board in 1915. Thinking had changed on high-school curriculum, and the Advisory Board stated that it "must be adjusted so as to meet better the needs of its pupils, in face of the ever-increasing complexity of our industrial and economic life." [89] The form that this readjustment should take was not yet clear. The Advisory Board, however, referred to a plan which it had presented and which had been adopted by the Executive Board in November 1914. The plan had in mind only the education of boys, embodied broad principles for solving the curriculum problem, and showed the trend toward "more differentiation of work in our secondary schools." [90] By the end of the period, Catholic secondary schools showed progress. It was not until after World War I, however, that both the nation as a whole and Catholic education specifically would take greater interest in the proliferation of high-school education.

## HIGHER EDUCATION

### GENERAL DEVELOPMENTS

On the level of higher education, certain developments during this period pertained to both Catholic and non-Catholic institutions. Standardization, to bridge the widening gap between secondary school and higher education, and also to articulate between the two levels, became a fact through such means as accrediting associations, standardized regional examinations (first introduced by the Board of Regents of the State of New York in 1878),[91] and the supervision of uniform college entrance examinations (proposed in the 1890's by Nicholas Murray Butler), which evolved into the College Entrance Examination Board.[92] The period witnessed the advent of the junior college, a new rung on the educational ladder, which added the thirteenth and fourteenth years of instruction to the public school system. Its curriculum was geared to the people's needs, and it became "in reality what the high school pretended to be in name, a people's college." [93] Roman Catholic efforts were, here as elsewhere, as vigorous and extensive as paucity of funds, lack of teaching personnel, and religious prejudice allowed. By 1860, there had been 14 permanent Catholic colleges, and this number reached 63 by the turn of the century. By 1930, there would be 126—including 49 colleges for women—the majority controlled by various religious orders.

## THE CATHOLIC UNIVERSITY OF AMERICA

The apex of Catholic higher education in the United States came with the establishment of The Catholic University of America at Washington, D.C., in 1889. We have already noted that at the Second Plenary Council of Baltimore in 1866, Bishop Martin J. Spalding had tried to initiate a move for the establishment of the University,[94] but financially the Church had not been prepared. At the Third Plenary Council in 1884, Spalding's nephew John Lancaster Spalding had pleaded for a university to fulfil the need for a better education for the clergy.[95] Spalding, concerned about intellectual weakness among Catholics in the United States, had observed that

if we are to be intellectually the equals of others, we must have with them equal advantages of education; and so long as we look rather to the multiplying of schools and seminaries than to the creation of a real university, our progress will be slow and uncertain, because a university is the great ordinary means to the best cultivation of mind.[96]

The Fathers of the Third Plenary Council considered the time ripe, especially since the financial strain was eased by an endowment of $300,000 from Mary Gwendolyn Caldwell, a convert to Catholicism.[97] Gibbons appointed a committee to resolve plans for the new university. In 1885 Pope Leo XIII sent his personal approval, which he further endorsed in 1887 in a letter addressed to Gibbons and the other United States bishops. On April 19, 1887, the University was incorporated under the laws of the District of Columbia.[98] Bishop John J. Keane of Richmond had been chosen as the first rector the previous year, in October 1886, after Spalding had declined the offer.[99] Spalding laid the cornerstone of Caldwell Hall, the original building, on May 24, 1888, and "in the presence of President Grover Cleveland and a large assembly of distinguished guests," [100] he delivered the principal address. His words set forth the aims of this University:

Certainly a true university will be the home both of ancient wisdom and of new learning; it will teach the best that is known, and encourage research; it will stimulate thought, refine taste, and awaken the love of excellence; it will be at once a scientific institute, a school of culture, and a training ground for the business of life; it will educate the minds that give direction to the age; it will be a nursery of ideas, a center of influence. The good we do men is quickly lost, the truth we leave them remains forever; and therefore, the aim of the best education is to enable students to see what is true, and to inspire them with the love of all truth . . . the university will make culture its first aim, and its scope will widen as the thoughts and attainments of men are enlarged and multiplied. Here if anywhere shall be found teachers whose one passion is the love of truth, which is the love of God and of man.[101]

On March 7, 1889, Leo XIII's apostolic letter *Magni Nobis Gaudii* [102] formally approved the statutes of the University, and granted it pontifical status—the first university of its kind in the United States. The University formally opened on November 13, 1889, with a ceremony at which President Benjamin Harrison was among those in attendance. In addition to Keane, the rector, and the Rev. Philip J. Garrigan, the vice-rector, the faculty numbered ten, of whom two were Sulpician priests, two Paulist priests, five diocesan priests, and one layman (Charles W. Stoddard, a lecturer in English). The students numbered 46, of whom 36 came from 21 dioceses (Baltimore being in the lead with four). (Women were not admitted until 1928.) The University opened as a graduate school of theology for the clergy only, but in October 1895, the School of Philosophy and the School of Social Sciences were added. Because of the University's financial difficulties, at the suggestion of the third rector, Denis J. O'Connell, Pope Pius X in September of 1903 authorized an annual collection to be taken up in all the dioceses of the country for its support. The introduction of undergraduate lay students in the fall of 1905 was a step hastened by financial troubles. In 1911 a summer session began in Washington.[103] To treat the emotional problems of children, the Child Center was established in 1916.

The founding fathers of Catholic University looked upon it not only as the apex of the Catholic educational system in the United States, but also as an agent that would unify and guide it. Thus the original 1889 constitution of the University, approved by the Congregation of Seminaries and Universities in Rome, authorized a program of affiliation of Catholic educational institutions in this country to the University.[104] In addition, Pope Leo XIII in *Magni Nobis Gaudii* said:

We exhort you all that you shall take care to affiliate with your university, your seminaries, colleges, and other Catholic institutions according to the plan suggested in the Constitutions, in such a manner as not to destroy their autonomy.[105]

Both the University's constitution and the apostolic letter envisioned a voluntary program whereby the University would set high academic standards which would have to be met by the independently-operated affiliates. Catholic educational leaders realized that the service which the University was capable of rendering to the Catholic high schools and colleges must remain limited unless some plan of affiliation or unification could be devised whereby from this central institution a strong directive influence might be exercised. There were difficulties: the University naturally demanded some proof of efficiency on the part of the schools seeking affiliation; the high schools and colleges were under a corps of teachers whose opportunities for effective teacher-training were very diverse; zeal had not been lacking on the part of religious teaching communities, but conditions were not such as to warrant complete satisfaction. The Summer School for Sisters in 1911 hastened the day of affiliation, for it meant that the sisterhoods had the intention of attaining, at least for their better qualified members, academic degrees and professional training. The Rev. Thomas Edward Shields, then dean of the University's Catholic Sisters College, and the Rt. Rev. Edward A. Pace, University Director of Studies, stood strongly behind the affiliation movement. On April 17, 1912, therefore, the fourth rector of the University, the Most Rev. Thomas J. Shahan, submitted to the board of trustees a detailed practical plan prepared by Shields. The approval of the trustees gave birth to the first comprehensive plan of affiliation [106] under Catholic auspices in this country. Among the methods included in the 1912 plan to maintain high quantitative and qualitative standards for affiliates were such usual techniques of the day as inspections, reports, testing, and scholarship ratings. Shields added a broader vision, however, viewing affiliation as one part of a master plan to upgrade curricula, to improve instructional outcome, and to supplement university efforts in teacher training. He introduced Catholic educational literature. He emphasized the high school as the middle school of the entire system, developed its curriculum as well as psychologically sound teaching methodology, and through affiliation was thus able to contribute substantially to the quality and articulation of the entire Catholic system.

## TEACHER EDUCATION

At the turn of the century, whether under state or private auspices, schools established for the purpose of teacher education were mostly independent of academic institutions, and thus inherited the weaknesses of other professional schools of the time, e.g., schools of law and medicine. As chairs and departments of education became established in universities, private institutions sought to affiliate. Thus, for example, the New York College for Teachers, chartered as a private institution in 1889, was affiliated as Teachers College, Columbia University, in 1898. By 1903, eighteen New York private colleges had chairs of pedagogy.[107]

By the turn of the century such other universities as Michigan, New York, Cornell, and Chicago had established departments or schools of education. Harvard's Department of Education, reluctantly established in 1891, would become the Graduate School of Education in 1921. In the Catholic area, once again, growth was much slower. Although Archbishop Francesco Satolli on his visit to the United States from the Vatican in 1892 presented definite views on the education of Catholic teachers, his suggestions were at first not enthusiastically received. Encouraging Catholic teachers to qualify for state certification, Satolli said:

Care should be taken that the teachers prove themselves qualified, not only by previous examination before the diocesan board and by certificate or diploma received from it, but also by having a teacher's diploma from the school board of the State, awarded after successful examination. This is urged, first so as not to appear indifferent, without reason, to what public authority requires for teaching. Secondly, a better opinion of the Catholic schools will be created. Thirdly, greater assurance will be given to parents that Catholic schools are not inferior to public schools. Fourthly, and lastly, we think that this plan will prepare the way for the State to see . . . that the laws are observed.[108]

And he continued:

For the sake of the Catholic cause, let there be among laymen a growing rivalry to take the diploma and doctorate, so that possessed of the knowledge and qualifications requisite for teaching, they may compete for and honorably obtain positions in the public gymnasia, lyceums, and scientific institutions.[109]

As has already been observed, the whole tone of the School Decrees of the Third Plenary Council had been of a very progressive character with respect to teacher training and certification. Stating that the school's success depended on the fitness of the teachers—*"maxime ab idoneitate magistrorum dependet"* [110]—the Council had decreed that teachers must prove themselves qualified by examination. Burns too readily took an optimistic view of the Catholic teacher situation in the years between the Council and his writing in 1912, claiming that "in a general way it may be said that the decree of the Council has had the hoped-for effect so far as regards the establishment of normal schools by the communities, and the length of their course." [111] Spalding was of a different mind. He held the view in 1890 that "in the larger communities of teaching women, a certain amount of Normal School instruction and training may be, and no doubt is, given during the novitiate; but for obvious reasons, in their way comparatively little can be accomplished." [112] He recommended at the same time that a "central Normal School, a sort of Educational University," be established for the purpose of teacher education. His plans were practical. He suggested that

the most competent professors, whether men or women, lay or cleric, should be called to fill the different chairs. The history of education, the theories of education, physiology, and psychology in their bearings upon education, the methods of education, should, of course, form part of the curriculum. Philosophy and literature, and possibly the classical languages and physics, should also have chairs; for the aim of a true Normal School is not merely to impart professional and technical knowledge and skill, but to give culture of mind, without which the teacher always works at a disadvantage.[113]

In founding The Catholic University of America and defining its scope, Pope Leo XIII had made the provision that the University admit to its faculty and student body members of the various religious communities and teaching orders, the secular clergy, and the laity, and that the influence of the new seat of learning was to extend to all other Catholic institutions in the country.[114] Keane, the first rector, in an article published in 1888, had strongly recommended that the religious orders and congregations should be prepared for their important task by a training that would enable them to impart knowledge successfully.[115] From the beginning, then, it was understood that the work of preparing teachers and superintendents should be one of the main objectives of this pontifical institution. Financial limitations, however, at first hindered the realization of this end—or perhaps the delay was due to the absence of an enthusiastic leader ready to do more than theorize on the advantages of teacher education within the University. At any rate, in 1898 Pace, then dean of the Faculty of Philosophy, stated his views on a Department of Education within the University in these words:

A Department of Pedagogy would meet a need that is felt in all the Schools. The training of teachers is an important function of the University and the most valuable service that it can render to the colleges. The essentials of this training are gotten by specialized study and research in the branch for which the teacher is preparing. But he should also be familiar with the history of education, its methods, and its progress in our own country and in foreign countries. Such a pedagogical formation is one of the best means of improving our educational custom in all its grades.[116]

The next year the same dean again gave evidence of his awareness of the great need:

The want of a Department of Pedagogy has been felt ever since the Faculty was organized; it is now more pressing in view of recent movements in Catholic secondary education. The main problem with which the college association has to deal is that of providing better opportunities for the preparation of those who are to teach either in the college or in the preparatory school. It would be a great advantage both to the University and to our whole educational system, if such preparation were given here. In the principal universities of the country numerous courses are offered on the principles of education, the history of education, child study, school hygiene, school organization, and the methods of teaching the various subjects included in the school curriculum. Instruction on these lines is essential to our Catholic teachers, if their schools are to compete successfully with rival institutions. The work might be organized by three or four instructors, and the department would profit by the courses given in the other schools under this Faculty.[117]

Plans for a Department of Education began to move ahead more rapidly with the coming of the Rev. Dr. Thomas Edward Shields to the University faculty in 1902. At first, he served as an instructor in physiological psychology. In 1904, however, he set about preparing the way for the development of the Department of Education by offering, in conjunction with Dean Pace, courses in the philosophy, psychology, and history of education. When Dr. William Turner joined the University in 1906, his aid was enlisted. The Department of Education became a reality in 1908—under the School of Philosophy.[118] Under its aegis a ten-monthly journal of education, *The Catholic Educational Review*, published its first issue in January 1911. The same year saw the estabilshment at Catholic University of "Teacher's College" for the teaching sisterhoods, which was approved by Pope St. Pius X on January 5, 1912, and incorporated as a separate institution under the title of "The Catholic Sisters College" on April 22, 1914.[119] Supported by Pace and the rector, Bishop Thomas J. Shahan, Shields had, by his success in founding The Catholic Sisters College, brought into actuality the hopes and visions of another great Catholic American educator, John L. Spalding. For Catholic University's Education Department, Spalding envisioned the lecture halls and classrooms in a central building around which would be grouped houses of the various teaching communities of women.[120]

We have seen that Catholic education was from its earliest beginnings dependent upon the teaching activities of religious orders. The individual teaching congregations had tried to give some professional training to their members, but this usually consisted in older members of the community teaching the younger sisters.[121] Sister Maria Concepta McDermott in her study of the Congregation of the Sisters of the Holy Cross reviewed "more than a hundred years of patient effort to meet demands for classroom instructors—demands that came from bishops, pastors, and parents." [122] Revealing "the ordinary means by which the teacher in the era 1855 to 1900 was prepared in Holy Cross," she observed:

The training ran a gamut of practices: individual instruction; the opening of a scholasticate for formal study; apprenticeship under a master teacher; lecture series on pertinent subjects, emerging in the seventies and eighties into more formalized programs; and by the end of the century the summer school and the institute.[123]

While there was no so-called professional training, a tradition of teaching methods was handed down from one generation to the next in religious communities.[124] This was not always satisfactory. Cross quotes Ireland to the effect that, although the sisters were considered generally satisfactory for the youngest children, parents often complained that they graduated the older ones less fit for the battle of life than those from public schools. Cross cites also a priest of the last decade of the nineteenth century who attributed to laymen a criticism of Catholic teachers in their teaching of the sciences and literature.[125]

The public schools had similar teacher problems. A democratic school system that proclaimed the responsibility of educating every child in public schools at public expense must train teachers in great numbers. With nineteenth-century American public-school teachers, quality was sacrificed to quantity. It was "a century of exploration, experimentation, and change in teacher training." [126] By the end of the century, teaching had certainly not reached the status of a profession, in spite of the life-long struggle of Horace Mann in the earlier third of the century to further that end. Meyers observed:

Little or no preparation was demanded of teachers in the public school system, and although state normals began in 1839, most of the teachers up to 1900 were admitted to the teaching field through county or state examinations in which political influence often counted for more than intellectual endowment.[127]

So, before 1900, Roman Catholic religious teachers were on the whole as well prepared as, and in many cases better prepared than, public school teachers. This is not to say that in either case the preparation was adequate. The raising of educational standards has been a slow process. The rating of teachers is a delicate business, however, and evades the measuring techniques even of a century as scientific as our own. Henry D. Hervey, in an address delivered at the National Education Association in 1921, stressed the difficulty of teacher rating and claimed that it was an attempt

to measure the immaterial in terms of the material. How can such things as influence, stimulus, inspiration, professional zeal, character, in short all of those subtle spiritual forces that are vaguely grouped together under the term "personality"—how can these elusive, imponderable, and intangible things be measured? We may measure scholarship, but scholarship does not make a teacher. . . . Furthermore, our immediate and superficial judgment might be completely reversed if we could read the future and could know what permanent impress upon the lives of the children the influence of teachers may make.[128]

What Hervey said of this time and earlier is still true: "We do not yet possess an instrument delicate enough for the measuring of a teacher's worth." [129]

As for religious teaching congregations, "the standards proposed were suggested not by state legislature but by the vocational objectives of the sisters themselves." [130] The teaching community had its Teacher's Guide or School Manual which gave a clear picture of the methods employed. Of this genre, the *School Manual for the Use of the Sisters of St. Joseph of Carondelet* published in 1883–84 went into effect during the period now under discussion, and is an example of the openness of religious teaching orders to suggestions of new educational ideas. The Introduction reads:

It was considered, that to restrict the teachers to particular ways of conducting the different studies, would be to close the door to future improvements, as
new ideas and suggestions on these subjects are constantly appearing. . . . In
this Manual, then, will be given principally, what relates to the teacher's work.
Classification, school regulations, study, records, government, etc., features,
which it is desirable should be as much alike in all our schools as possible
[*sic*]. . . . These suggestions are not intended to trammel the teacher in the
exercise of a wise discretion, but are given simply as aids to those who may
need them.[131]

This *Manual*, which is a gem, presents a strong indication that Catholic
schoolteachers of the time were concerned with new methods. Herbart
had not yet secured a firm footing in the American schools when the
*Manual* suggested:

Explain each new lesson assigned, if necessary, by familiar remarks and illustrations, that each pupil may know before she is sent to her seat *what* she is
expected to do at the next recitation, and *how* it is to be done, that she may
study understandingly and successfully. Where the text-book routine—assigning
pages and hearing recitations—belongs to a past age, *you must teach.* . . .
Assign many questions of your own preparing or selected from kindred textbooks, involving an application of what the pupils have learned, to the business
of life. . . . Each lesson should be to some extent a review of the previous
lesson.[132]

In the same modern tone, the *Manual* proceeded to outline methods
of teaching various subjects. Today's reader must constantly refer back
to the date of publication of the *Manual*, or he forgets that this is not a
handbook of method for teaching in the elementary schools today. Such
statements as the following are random examples:

Teaching chronological tables is not teaching history. . . . Encouragement
inspires confidence, and children, more than others, need it. . . . Begin each
new lesson with conversation on objects or pictures illustrative of the reading
lesson, to awaken interest and develop the idea: then, the printed word, the
sound character, and the sounds. . . . The mastery of our language should be
the end aimed at in this study [of grammar]. Teaching mere rules and con-
structions will not accomplish this. The correct *use* of language is the only, or
chief means to acquire this mastery.[133]

Perhaps most surprising of all is the fact that it recommended in 1884
inter-classroom visitation by the teaching sisters! The *Manual* stated
that "each teacher is allowed one day in the term to visit one of the
other sisters' rooms." [134] A sister-directress supervised the teachers and
made to the Superioress-General or Provincial a yearly report on each
teacher's abilities and qualifications.[135] This custom prevailed in most
religious communities of the period.

The above detail is not presented as a case for the efficiency of Catholic teachers during this period. We have already observed that their
professional training as well as that of the public school teachers was

limited. It does, however, provide evidence that many Catholic teachers were open to suggestion and anxious to give their best. They may not have achieved efficiency of a high standard, but they did have efficiency as a goal; and when in 1911 the Catholic summer school movement was inaugurated, their patronage gave evidence of their anxiety to prepare themselves better for their work. Indeed, from 1902 onward, professors of Catholic University gave lectures during vacations at convents and at diocesan institutions at the invitation of teaching communities; and in 1905 an extensive correspondence course in several fields was organized.[136] In connection with the latter, Shields wrote:

The teachers in parochial schools, high schools, academies, colleges, and the teachers and pupils of the novitiate training schools in all parts of the country are taking this course. Much of the work done by these classes is of a very high order. . . . It is, indeed, a matter of encouragement to all who are interested in our Catholic schools to find our teaching communities so eager to improve their methods, and so ready to accept suggestions. While these communities have their own traditions, growing out of successful work in the past, and their own methods, which have the sanction of long experience, they are not on this account unwilling to move forward.[137]

The number of teaching nuns who in some instances were endeavoring to improve by seeking affiliation with non-Catholic institutions was a sign to Shields of the need for help from Catholic University. Of these he wrote:

The willingness of our Catholic teachers to look for help beyond their own order, or even outside the Catholic Church and her institutions, must not be taken as evidence of the surrender of principle, nor must it be taken to mean an abandonment of anything which these teachers consider essential; nor does it mean an express desire on the part of our schools or of our teaching communities to coalesce with non-Catholic systems of education. What it does prove is the earnest desire of our teachers to do their own work better; the desire that their graduates shall be worthy competitors in every sphere of life with the graduates of other institutions. It also proves their broad-mindedness and their eagerness to avail themselves of whatever is best in the recent developments of science.[138]

### CURRICULUM

In curriculum, there were certain developments in the public school area that had some influence on the Catholic schools. As we observed in connection with middle-level schools, the National Education Association in 1892 appointed the Committee of Ten on Secondary School Studies, to clarify the then-confused role of the American high school and to suggest possible standardization of certain curriculum areas. Nor was the elementary school overlooked: in 1893 the same Association appointed the Committee of Fifteen on Elementary Education. That committee, composed of college personnel and school superintendents, appointed subcommittees to study each of three critical areas of public education: teacher training, study correlation in the elementary school, and administration and organization of public school systems. The subcommittees reported in 1895.

The report of the subcommittee on the training of teachers had a far-reaching influence on teacher-training institutions. It crystallized and prolonged the conflict between the liberal-arts camp and the camp opting for simple professional education. More constructively, it recognized recent developments, increased the recognition of psychology in the training of the teacher, and gave the nod to the teacher's need for laboratory experience. The report stated succinctly:

> Professional training comprises two parts: (a) The science of teaching, and (b) the art of teaching.
>
> In the *science of teaching* are included: (1) Psychology as a basis for principles and methods; (2) methodology as a guide to instruction; (3) school economy, which adjusts the conditions of work; and (4) history of education, which gives breadth of view.
>
> The *art of teaching* is best gained: (1) by observation of good teaching; (2) by practice teaching under criticism.[139]

The subcommittee on the correlation of studies revealed basic differences of approach. There was general agreement that students' experiences were necessary foundations for education, that the correlation of studies had to be based on psychological research, and that further study was needed on the essential elements of elementary education. What those essential elements were, however, led to a widespread debate over the child-centered versus the subject-centered curriculum. Dr. William T. Harris, United States Commissioner of Education, presented the "Report of the Sub-Committee on the Correlation of Studies in Elementary Education," and struck the keynote of the report in the following passage:

> Your committee is of the opinion that psychology of both kinds, physiological and introspective, can hold only a subordinate place in the settlement of questions relating to the correlation of studies. The branches to be studied, and the extent to which they are studied, will be determined mainly by the demands of one's civilization.[140]

The most immediate results were procured by the subcommittee on school administration. It succeeded in its aim of separating the administration of the school from direct political influence and in defining for many years to come the differing roles of business and instructional administration. The report implied that governors' appointments of state superintendents had been motivated by political patronage. The report on the "Powers and Duties of State Superintendents" concluded with the suggestion that this position in particular and education in general be separated from politics:

The board of regents in New York, the board of education in Massachusetts, the supreme bench in Pennsylvania are sufficiently removed from the mishaps of politics to insure the selection of a suitable man. Where the method of selection by popular election or gubernatorial appointment prevails, a term of four years is better than a term of two years; but the experience of Massachusetts has shown that appointment by a state board for a term of one year is not incompatible with long tenure of office. Whatever be the method of selection adopted, the farther it is removed from the accidents and mishaps of politics and popular elections the better it will be for the school system and the children, for whose sole benefit schools are established and conducted.[141]

The influence of these committee reports on private school systems is difficult to assess. In Catholic education, a unified philosophy of man and of the nature of learning determined—then and now—a very evident academic organization of the curriculum. In organization and administration, the more autonomous units of the Catholic system did not yield to the setting up of junior high schools and junior colleges to the same degree as did publicly supported institutions, a major part of the reason probably being financial. The Catholic school system did, however, profit from the research of these committees in the field of educational administration.

SOME TEXTS

The more unified Catholic philosophy of which we spoke still looked upon the goal of its educational system as complete personal formation. Some of this entailed a high concentration on man's eternal destiny rather than on his life on earth, to the extent that it sometimes resulted in a lag in keeping up with educational findings. This was particularly evident in some textbooks. This was a time when the influences of such innovators as, for example, Johann Pestalozzi and Johann F. Herbart were being brought to the United States. It is interesting to compare the readers for public school use—obviously influenced by the psychological innovators—with those published for Catholic school use. Considering the serious injunction of the Third Plenary Council of Baltimore to publish Catholic textbooks, one would expect that the Catholic educators of the time would have come up with something worthwhile. One is disappointed to learn that, in the area of readers at least, textbooks for public schools were far superior when judged by such psychological criteria, innovative then, as the presence of nursery rhymes, fairy stories, and fables in readers for the primary grades; well-represented Bible selections in the middle grades, moving on to the study of history; for the more advanced, tales of famous world heroes and great American authors; openness to the possibility of correlation with such other areas as music, drawing, and singing; content allowing for free class discussion by the teacher upon questions of right and wrong; nature study stories and observations; subject matter so selected, arranged, and presented as to evidence awareness of the processes of children's minds and to interest them; content to assist the child in his social and economic environment; and material allowing for the use of the five formal Herbartian steps.

According to the above criteria, of eight series of public school readers of the time, two revealed strong progressive influences: the 1899 publication *Stepping Stones to Literature* [142] and one of the 1913 *Story Hour Readers*.[143] Three more showed definite but weaker influence: *The Graded Literature Readers*, published in 1899; [144] *The Reading Literature Series* of 1910; [145] and *The Riverside Readers* of 1913.[146] Showing less Herbartian or other modern influences were *The Rational Method in Reading* of 1894,[147] and *The Aldine Readers* of 1907.[148] With no perceptible modern influences were *The Beacon Readers* of 1912.[149] Catholic readers showing some evidence of psychological understanding commensurate with the times are Benziger Brothers' *The New Century Catholic Series*, published in 1905; [150] *The De La Salle Series* of the Brothers of the Christian Schools, published in 1906; [151] and *The Catholic Education Series* of 1915.[152] In the Preface to their Second Reader, the Brothers of the Christian Schools stated:

These readers have been specially designed to elicit thought and facilitate literary composition. The lessons have been written or selected with a view to interest as well as to instruct; to cultivate a taste for the best literature and to build up a strong moral character and to imbue our children with an intelligent love of Faith and country.[153]

Thomas Edward Shields, the great Catholic educational psychologist, was strongly in favor of the principle of correlation, in religion and in other areas:

The principle of correlation as it is now currently accepted in the field of education demands that each new thought element be related to the previous content of the mind, not along structural lines alone, but in a relationship of reciprocal activity. In the name of this principle, the teacher insists that each new thought element taken into the mind shall be so related to the previous mental content as to shed its light upon every item of previously assimilated knowledge, and that in turn it shall be illumined and rendered intelligible by the light that falls upon it from each truth that holds a place in the structure of the growing mind. . . . This principle of correlation should find a threefold application in every school. It should enter into the structure of the curriculum; it should govern the organization of the materials in each subject; and it should find a clear embodiment in the textbooks used.[154]

Shields seems to have been the first who, while giving religion a central place, successfully utilized in his readers the best to be taken from the new psychologies prevalent in his time.

*The Catholic National Series* of Richard Gilmour, bishop of Cleveland, gave less evidence of awareness of prevailing psychological trends when he published it in 1899.[155] Seeming to have no awareness at all, however, were the *Metropolitan Readers* of 1871,[156] *The Graded Catholic Education Series* of 1881,[157] and the *McBride Readers* of 1898.[158] The *Metropolitan Readers* were still in use toward the end of the century, gave no evidence of attempted revision over that period, and were rather typical of many other Catholic books of the time. Mother Angela, their author, claimed in the preface to the Second Reader that "the engravings have been carefully designed to interest and awaken thoughts of piety in little children," and that the lessons were "taken from Canon Schmidt, Faber and other Catholic authors." [159] This is especially interesting when one remembers that this was a reader for only the second level! One finds stories of angels and saints, Adam and Eve, Noah and the Ark, etc., and, in the Second Reader mentioned above, a lengthy selection entitled "The Virtuous Queen, Catherine of Aragon." Mother Angela's emphasis was definitely religious, with no movement toward a broader reading program which might aim at developing an appreciation of literature. The preface of the Fourth Reader of *The Graded Catholic Education Series* presented the author's aim as being to "convey such instruction as is best fitted to form virtue and usefulness in the hearts and minds of the young." [160] On every fifth or sixth page of the *McBride Readers* appeared the type of fundamental religion lesson that one finds in the early catechisms of the time. Prayers at the end of these readers were set out in small print, and the introduction to both texts suggested that they be read to the pupils until memorized. During this period, however, many public school texts were used in Catholic schools. In the *Report of the Proceedings and Addresses of the Second Annual Meeting* of the Catholic Educational Association in 1905, the Rev. Thomas J. O'Brien, inspector of Catholic schools for the diocese of Brooklyn, New York, had this to say:

For what reason then are non-Catholic authors received favorably in some, shall I say many, Catholic schools? Public examinations, on public school lines, have led to the use of public books. The questions largely were based on these books used in the public schools and teachers felt that their pupils would do better if these were the textbooks used in the Catholic schools also. There was less objection to their use as the publishers, seeing the Catholic schools opening up to them a large trade, were willing to expurgate whatever was objectionable from a Catholic standpoint. . . . Many of our religious teachers say that our Catholic school books are inferior in scholarship and in pedagogic arrangement to the non-Catholic textbooks. But that, if it is true, is a reflection on their own scholarship and pedagogy, a confession of inability to produce for their own schools standard textbooks.[161]

CATECHETICS

Unfortunately the same lack of awareness of modern psychological findings on youth was evident in the area most responsible for personal religious formation: catechetics. The catechism of the Third Plenary Council of Baltimore, like most other catechisms of the time, was more abstract than the mind of the child could grasp, purposefully defensive of the Church, and expressed in technical theological terms, purporting to contain a complete summation of the teaching of theology.[162] The method of teaching it was as defective as the content: the teacher analyzed the lesson and then expected parrot memorization before giving an explanation.

Attempts to discover the basic source(s) from which the Baltimore Catechism (published in 1886) was derived, and the actual author(s), seem fruitless. It was the recollection of the Most Rev. Sebastian G. Mesmer, archbishop of Milwaukee, that the Council had put great stress on having a catechism that was uniform: "To several objections raised at the last meeting that the proposed Catechism was very imperfect, in fact inferior, answer was made that uniformity was more important." [163] He and others were of the opinion that it was the Rt. Rev. Jannarius de Concilio, theologian to Bishop O'Connor of Nebraska, to whom the major responsibility of formulating the catechism had fallen. If this were the case, Mesmer was of the further opinion that "it is just possible that, being a born Italian, he followed Bellarmine's Catechism used in his native land." [164] The Rev. F. J. O'Reilly, however, who lived with Spalding for fourteen years, had the impression that, in the formulation of the Baltimore Catechism, "Butler's Catechism was bent to suit United States needs, [and that] Bishop Spalding did most of the work." [165] The Rt. Rev. John K. Sharp, in preparing to write on the subject, learned from a conversation with the Very Rev. Thomas McMillan, C.S.P., "joint editor with the Rev. Dr. Fox of the revised Deharbe's Catechism," that

from the termination of the Council in early December, 1884, until at least as late as 25 January, 1885, Bishop Spalding remained in New York City as the guest of the Paulist Fathers. . . . During this period the Bishop and Mons. de Concilio worked upon the Catechism.[166]

Correspondence in the Baltimore Cathedral Archives would seem to substantiate that Spalding was responsible for getting the catechism together. In a letter of Feb. 23, 1885, to Gibbons, for example, Spalding states that "I have received suggestions from all the abps [*sic*, for *archbishops*] concerning catechism, and have made such changes as seemed desirable." [167] He mentions at the same time that "the corrected proof is now in the hands of Mr. Kehoe" (Lawrence Kehoe of the Catholic Publication Society in New York City). The same Archives contain letters from Kehoe to Gibbons on the subject, one on March 2, 1885, stating that "Bishop Spalding sends me today the last of the corrections for Catechism, and says it must have your *Imprimatur*." [168] On June 4,

1888, Kehoe wrote Gibbons that "Bishop Spalding suggested that I write to you and ask you if you thought it best to make a smaller Catechism out of the one now made." [169] Sharp expresses the opinion that it is possible for the Baltimore Catechism to have gone back as far as "the Catechism of Laurence Vaux of Manchester [England], 1597, and . . . the Abstract of the Douai Catechism written in 1649 by Henry Turberville." [170] Also to be considered was "the English Bishop Challoner's *Abridgment of Christian Doctrine,* produced at St. Omer," which had in turn been approved by Bishop Carroll in the United States, where the fourteenth edition was printed at Baltimore in 1798, and which had had a long history of use and approval since that time. A possible further source of the Baltimore Catechism was Bishop Hay's *An Abridgment of the Christian Doctrine,* published in Philadelphia in 1803.[171]

The Baltimore Catechism, although never intended as a classroom text, became one. In the classroom, the Bible was presented in "Bible History" [172] texts unrelated to the catechism. Liturgy, when it had any meaning at all, referred to the ceremonies and the rubrics and to the Church year of feasts and seasons. Attempts were made, however, during this time to make the Catechism more interesting and understandable to the student.

The Rev. Thomas L. Kinkead's *An Explanation of the Baltimore Catechism,* for the use of Sunday school teachers and advanced classes, was published in 1891. It held the approbations of Gibbons and twenty-six other members of the American hierarchy. According to Kinkead, the purpose of the work was "to be practical, and to teach Catholics what they should know, and how these truths of their catechism are constantly coming up in the performance of their every-day duties." [173] The Rev. Peter C. Yorke's *Textbooks of Religion for Parochial and Sunday Schools* of 1898 was one initial effort to present the entire contents of Christian Doctrine over a period of the elementary school span of eight years, with a gradual development of the material adapted to the mind of the growing child. In the Preface to the Readers, the author made it clear that "the foundation of the series is the Baltimore Catechism. As this is the official catechism of the Church in America, the compilers have not considered themselves at liberty to depart from it, except in some minor verbal details." [174] This text, however, in spite of its attempt at graded content, upheld the memorization method of study.

Pierre Ranwez, S.J., claims that at the end of this period "a good number of Catholics became aware of a crisis in religious instruction," and continues that

the realization came early that catechism lessons often sinned in three ways in particular: (1) They were deductive and abstract. Only the concrete, it was seen, interests a child. The learner can be introduced to general concepts in a gradual way only by starting with tangible realities and having experience out of which concepts may grow. (2) They were chiefly expository, and the participation of the pupil was limited. (3) They took little account of the diversity among groups of learners, and of the temperament and intellectual or emotional capacities of individual pupils. In short, they were characterized by a lack of adaptability.[175]

At the Fifth Annual Convention of the Catholic Educational Association in 1908, the subject provoked much discussion. Shields, in a paper entitled "The Method of Teaching Religion," quoted the views of two Roman Catholic superintendents of schools on the method of teaching religion then in vogue. According to Shields, the Rev. Thomas Devlin, superintendent of schools in the diocese of Pittsburgh, believed that

the memorizing of the text of the catechism, or Bible or Church history, is not sufficient for a religious education. Without explanation such an exercise is not even worthy of the name of instruction, which, though better than mere recitation, is also insufficient. Instruction enlightens the understanding; of itself it does not reach the heart. To be effective, the knowledge imparted must form the character. It must direct the conscience, influence the will, govern the conduct. To teach children their duties is important, but to teach them to love their duties and to find happiness in fulfilling them is the aim and purpose of Christian education. . . . In this, as in all other branches, sound principles of teaching should not be ignored, and the value of illustrations, examples, object lessons and of natural methods in accordance with the philosophy of mind and its laws of development should receive due attention. . . . The fault of exercising the memory chiefly has not been confined to the teaching of catechism.[176]

And Shields claimed that the Rev. James F. Nolan, superintendent of parish schools in the archdiocese of Baltimore, held similar views:

We are . . . apt to rest content and feel gratified when the words of the text have been thoroughly committed to memory, forgetting that to teach children their religion means far more than merely to teach them their catechism. . . . Of late years wonderful improvements have been made in the method of imparting secular knowledge, in making abstract ideas concrete. Pictures, charts, maps, sandboards and objects from nature have been called into requisition with splendid results. Is there any reason why this same method should not be employed in teaching catechism? [177]

These superintendents did not stand alone in their view. Shields himself, great Catholic psychologist and educator that he was, had clear, practical views on the subject. He stated:

While we must begin by presenting to the young child the great fundamental truths of religion in a form suited to his capacity, we must not content ourselves with this. As he grows from childhood into manhood under our guidance, these self-same truths must be presented to him over and over again, and on each repetition the setting and the manner of presentation must be suited to the phase of mental development which he shall have attained. Mere repetition will not do. Each time the truth is presented it must be clothed in a new interest and put in a new setting. Mere expansion will not do, nor will the addition of a multitude of details suffice. Definitions of terms, fuller explanations and more numerous illustrations, however suitable or well chosen, are of no avail if the matter shall have grown stale to the mind of the pupil.[178]

Not all educators of the Catholic Educational Association meeting in 1908 agreed with Shields. Yorke (whose catechism has been mentioned above) declared that he did not agree with Shields that a child should learn by rote only the things that he understood. He edged away from the new psychological thinkings of the time, and contended:

> Prayers, catechism, the Bible, pictures, hymns, the saints, the liturgy, devotions, Church history and the like are the old traditional means for the inculcation of Christian Doctrine. No doubt there is in them much that is waste, much that is mere memory-load, much that is unscientific, but that is only saying that they are natural. They are the food on which the Christian people have fed from time immemorial and on them twice thirty generations of the Saints have been built up to the full measure of the stature of Christ. . . . Since the time St. Paul exhorted Timothy to hold the form of sound words, the Church has been careful to formulate her doctrine in clear and precise statements. While there is need of much preliminary training and the catechism itself should be the flowering of the previous instruction, a formulated answer is necessary and such a formulated answer is best provided for by the catechism method.[179]

Pace, also of Catholic University, hurried to Shields' defense, at the same time exposing his own views on the method of teaching religion. Addressing Yorke, he said that

> Dr. Shields does not object to the cultivation of memory; what he does object to is the use of memory in such a way as to make the mind a mere record of answers which may or may not be understood. What is the value of such memorizing? The phonograph remembers; it is a better preserver than any human mind; but what good does all that do to the phonograph? . . . Such a retention of words without meaning for the learner may often be found in grown-up children who have abandoned the practice of their religion after leaving an otherwise excellent Christian school.[180]

These views of leading Catholic educators bear witness that a movement for change in the method of catechetical instruction and in the content of catechism texts was beginning during the period 1885–1917, even as the Baltimore Catechism was getting under way.

## Students

### THE IMMIGRANT

The majority of students in Catholic schools during this period may be categorized into two main groups—the second-generation children of the "old immigrant" movement and the "newer immigrants" who came in large numbers from central and southern Europe during the years 1880–1917. The Irish had come to feel more "American" than other immigrant groups. Among the Germans the trend toward "Amercanism" was also clear, but the new immigrants "because of the lateness of their immigration or for other special reasons stuck at the first generation stage of assimilation through the early decades of the twentieth century." [181] Gleason, author of that observation, would observe also (as late as 1967) that "the full assimilation of the Catholic population considered as a whole was held back by these groups until very recent times." [182] In appearance, language, and customs the "new immigrants" differed radically from the now settled Irish and German immigrants, and consequently they faced a hostile environment. A considerable number of the children of the new immigrants were placed in Roman Catholic schools.

Even famous public educators showed prejudiced attitudes toward the immigrant. Charles W. Eliot, for example, made these observations in an address before the Connecticut State Teachers' Association:

> That labor strikes should occur more and more frequently and be more and more widespread has been another serious disappointment in regard to the outcome of popular education. . . . It should be observed, however, concerning this disappointment, that it results in large measure from a difficulty which accounts for a good many troubles in the U. S., namely, the difficulty of assimilating year after year large numbers of foreigners.[183]

William Torrey Harris recognized the prevalence of political corruption, for which he did not blame the "robber barons" or the unregulated activities of railroads and corporations, but rather the large numbers of unlettered immigrants. Curti observed:

> As the immigrant hoards multiplied, there was an increasing tendency to blame the newcomers for the gravest abuses of political corruption; and the Americanization movement, which the schools adopted, was welcomed with naive faith.[184]

The public school held that it was its special mission to assimilate the immigrant—to form the foreign-born, to instill into him American conceptions of law and order and government.[185] On this point, public school educators manifested bitterness toward the Catholic Church. In 1894, for example, a text of the public school system in Massachusetts stated:

> While the isolation of even this portion [10.6% in 1894 in Catholic schools] of the school population is to be regretted for their own sakes—separated thus from those early associations in work and play by which the individuals of each generation become affiliated with one another in youth, prevented thus from growing into the possession of those common thoughts and purposes which mark interests common and imply one people, born, and reared and molded into a sect, rather than into a nation—while this is a misfortune for those who are subjected to it, we have profound reason for congratulation and thankfulness that this divisive spirit has gained so slight a hold upon the people of our State.[186]

For Catholics, then and now, the local unit was the parish. The parish in turn was dependent in many ways on the school. As Wolff put it:

"It is from *them* [children educated in the parish schools] and not from the Catholic children educated in the public school, that the Sodalities and Confraternities of the parish are chiefly recruited and receive their most exemplary members." [187]

For the immigrant the parish presented something familiar, something of the culture he had left behind. Many parishes, in order to accommodate the immigrant better, were national, based on country of origin. Of such parish systems, Thomas C. Harte wrote:

The administrative personnel of the parish and its institutions is often selected with a view to the ethnic composition of its population, so that priests and Sisters of Irish descent are assigned to an Irish parish, Italians to an Italian parish, and so on. The national origin of the pastor particularly is often a matter of grave concern to the parishioners, and the extent of their cooperation with him may depend ultimately on whether or not he is "one of our own kind." [188]

It was not the policy of the Church to preserve such a system. Commenting on the foreign-language parishes of the period, Harbrecht remarks that "the general tendency is to keep the foreign language as long as the foreign born are in the majority." [189]

The Church saw the process of Americanizing as gradual and not forced. The Church's aim for the immigrant was twofold: to have him hold on to his Roman Catholic faith, and at the same time to prepare him to be a good American citizen. Gibbons believed that the foreign-language parish schools for immigrant children made easy agencies of transition into the American way of life. Convincingly, he said:

Our Catholic schools afford a much easier pathway for the foreigner to enter the American life than is the case in the public school. There the child must enter at once upon the use of the English language—perhaps under the guidance of one who does not know the habits and customs of the immigrant child, and hence cannot enter into complete sympathy with his work. . . . In the Catholic school they come under the instruction of those who know the respective languages and can understand their peculiar idioms of thought and speech. With the English language as a constantly enlarging part of their course, they are gradually, almost unconsciously, brought into complete sympathy with American ideals, and readily adapt themselves to American manners and customs.[190]

There were indeed, however, some of those operating the Church's educational establishments who were not in favor of Americanization for the immigrant. They held the opinion that the faith of the immigrant could be protected only by protecting his culture, nationality, and language from the influence of "WASP" America—White, Anglo-Saxon, and Protestant. The Catholic schools in such cases retarded assimilation and fortified a "ghetto mentality" in the immigrants. In view of the violent anti-Catholicism of the times and the rise of such groups as the American Protective Association, there was at least a modicum of correct thinking in their position. Among those "suspicious of undue accommodation to American ideas" [191] were Archbishop Michael A. Corrigan of New York, Bishop Bernard McQuaid of Rochester, New York, and the German bishops of the United States. Many a German pastor refused to introduce English into his church. Many of the immigrants themselves even went so far as to petition Pope Leo XIII on April 16, 1891, for "their priests, their parishes, their schools, their societies, [and] their language." [192]

The making of an American out of an immigrant child was a difficult job for Catholic and public schools alike. The child was torn between loyalties to his school and to his home. Angelo Patri, a public schoolmaster in one of New York's immigrant sections during the period, wrote of his students:

Most of our children came from little two, three and four room flats, strung along block upon block. In such homes there was little time or room for play, work or fun. . . . There was a mixture of races. There were people who had come from various countries of Europe and they differed in their attitude towards ethics, society, religion, education, and cleanliness. These differences isolated the various groups, the families, and the blocks.[193]

Patri claimed that the parents of his students did not understand the newer conditions of life in America. They did not understand the American school, and of immigrant parents and of their difficulties and differences with their children he wrote:

In their turn they [the parents] were misunderstood even by their own children. The child saw in the rush of the school life the idea of getting on. In school he saw life in a white collar, fine clothes, and an easy job. Home was not like this.[194]

And Patri, teaching in the public schools, concluded:

I have been a part of many movements to Americanize the foreigner, but I see that the child is the only one who can carry the message of democracy if the message is to be carried at all. If the child fails to make the connection between the ideals of the school and the fundamental beliefs of the people, there is none other to do it. The children are the chain that must bind people together.[195]

Such a statement may perhaps help to build a case for the Catholic foreign-language school of the period, where the *gradual* process of assimilation sought to prevent a wide rift between home and school.

Many children of the immigrants, however, were growing up without any educational opportunities whatsoever. America's Industrial Revolution brought with it the widespread evil of child labor. Raymond G. Fuller observed:

Statistically—that is, according to the federal census of occupations—child labor in the United States reached its highest point in 1910. In 1880 there were 1,118,356 children from ten to fifteen years of age (16.8 per cent of all in that age group) engaged in gainful occupations. In 1900 there were 1,750,178, or 18.2 per cent of the same age group. In 1910 there were 1,990,225, or 18.4 per cent.[196]

Fuller was quick to add that "there is much child labor not covered by the census figures," and in startling statistics related that "in 1918 nearly 5,000,000 children from six to eighteen in the United States were not enrolled in any school, public, private, or parochial—one sixth of the total number!"[197] Obviously, many Catholic children were among them. The period made great progress, however, in child-labor reform and in the extension of educational opportunity. The factory system, which employed "children at the youngest possible age for the longest durable hours,"[198] fiinally aroused the social conscience of America. Reformers envisioned the school as one agency of social reform, and advocated compulsory education. By 1918, the compulsory school attendance law would gain nationwide application in all states.[199] An awareness of child needs in an industrialized society caused the school to change its traditional educational patterns and to introduce more practical curricula. The picture in the Catholic immigrant schools of the period, however, was not a pretty one. Browne faces the truth squarely, and sums up the situation neatly, in these words:

The poorer children were at times subjected to a harsh though recognized evil in being crowded into rooms with up to a hundred occupants. It must be recalled, too, that in the larger schools many of these children before the days of our restrictive immigration laws were either of foreign birth or came from homes where at best only halting English was spoken. Probably a fourth of these students ever finished the eighth grade and then, even as late as 1915, about ninety per cent of them joined the pool of half-employed industrial workers. About three out of a hundred ever went to college and by 1916 the lack of encouragement toward further schooling for talented Catholic children was noted by educators.[200]

### THE NEGRO

A special type of student in Catholic schools during the period was the American Negro. The Negro Catholic population was not large. In June 1883, an unsigned article in *The Catholic World* stated:

The census of 1880 tells us of nearly seven million of colored people in the United States, nine-tenths of them living in the former slave States. Only about one hundred thousand of them are Catholics.[201]

According to Gibbons in 1892, there were eight million black people of which only two per cent were Catholic. Why so few Catholic Negroes? John T. Gillard, S.S.J., had a very likely answer in his claim that "there were few points of contact between the Catholic Church and the Negroes" [202] before this period. Gillard amplified:

[The Church] had her hands full trying to provide anything like adequate care for the millions of immigrants from Catholic sections of Europe who settled largely in the expanding industrial centers. . . . The concentration of so many millions of immigrants and their children in the thickly populated industrial centers of the country made the Catholic Church almost completely an urban Church . . . The Negro on the contrary, until just recently, has always been rural. . . . With the Negro predominantly rural, and the Catholic Church just as predominantly urban, it was altogether unlikely that many Negroes would come within the sphere of influence of the Catholic Church even had they not been concentrated in the Protestant South.[203]

When the Church did have contacts with the Negro, her work in their behalf was seriously hindered by lack of priests and Catholic teachers, by bigotry, and by prejudice even on the part of some of her own.

We observed in the preceding chapter that the Second Plenary Council of Baltimore had made a study of the situation of the Negro in the United States. One of the principal motives for calling that Council had been, in the words of Archbishop John Spalding, the "urgent duty to discuss the future status of the Negro." He elaborated:

Four million of these unfortunate beings are thrown on our charity, and they silently but eloquently appeal to us for help. We have a golden opportunity to reap a harvest of souls, which neglected, may not return.[204]

The Council had devoted a chapter to the Negro, in which the Council Fathers had begged priests "to devote to this work their efforts, their time, and finally, if it be possible, their entire life," and urged religious communities of both sexes to open schools for the black people. [205] The Third Plenary Council of 1884 is of greater importance, however, for a consideration of the Negro during this period which immediately followed it. Strongly the Council stated: "It is our will that bishops exert every effort to provide the Negro, wherever possible, with churches, schools, orphanages, and homes for the poor." [206] Realizing the lack of priests, the Council suggested that lay helpers teach the catechism and hymns; conscious, too, of the need for funds, the Council Fathers made mandatory an annual collection in all the churches of the United States and the appointment of a special commission to handle the money so collected for the benefit of both Negroes and Indians.[207]

The Church's first organized effort on behalf of Negro Catholics after the Civil War had been made by the Josephite Fathers, who began their work in this country in 1871. They came from Mill Hill, near London,

England, where they had been founded in 1866 by the Reverend, later Cardinal, Herbert Vaughan. In 1872, the Fathers of the Holy Ghost, a French Society, had come to the United States to work among the Negro people.[208] Gillard observes:

With the Josephites, the Fathers of the Holy Ghost were the backbone of the Colored Missions until they were joined by the Fathers of the Divine Word in 1906 and the African Mission Fathers in 1907. Other missionary organizations in the course of time took over assignments in behalf of the Negroes, but until very recently [1940] the bulk of the work was done by members of these four organizations.[209]

A number of religious orders of women, too, dedicated themselves to the service of the Negro. In 1881, the Franciscan Sisters had come to Baltimore, Maryland, from their motherhouse at Mill Hill, London, England—the only white sisterhood at that time "devoting themselves exclusively to work for the colored race." [210] A small house on St. Paul Street in Baltimore became the first St. Elizabeth's Home for Colored Children. In 1889, a residence on Maryland and Twenty-third Streets, Baltimore, was given to the community, and here they established a United States novitiate. The Mission Helpers, Servants of the Sacred Heart, began work in Baltimore in 1890, when they were founded in this country with the approbation and encouragement of James Cardinal Gibbons. At first they taught only Negro children under the direction of the Josephite Fathers. Their missionary activities included catechism classes and social service work. Mrs. Margaret Murphy of San Antonio, Texas, established St. Peter Claver's School in 1888 for the education of Negro children, and in 1893 brought about the foundation, for the same purpose, of the Sister Servants of the Holy Ghost and Mary Immaculate.[211]

A community of white sisters which especially gave an impetus to the educational work of Negroes in the United States was the Sisters of the Blessed Sacrament, founded in 1891 by Mother Katharine Drexel. Joseph Butsch, S.S.J., writing in 1917 of the work of this community, remarked:

The Sisters of the Blessed Sacrament have had a remarkable growth, having now [1917] about two hundred sisters. Within a few years they have established convents and schools for Negro children in a number of cities, including Philadelphia, New York, Boston, St. Louis, Chicago, New Orleans, Cincinnati, Columbus, Ohio; Nashville, Tenn.; Atlanta, Savannah; and Rock Castle, Va.[212]

There were also two congregations of Negro nuns laboring among their own during the period: The Oblate Sisters of Providence and The Sisters of the Holy Family. The Oblate Sisters were a United States foundation, established in Baltimore in 1829. The Sisters of the Holy Family had had their beginnings in New Orleans, Louisiana, on November 21,

1842; at that time "four zealous colored women in the interests of the
education of youth and the care of the needy of their own race," [213]
under the direction of the Rev. Etienne Rousselon, vicar-general of the
diocese of New Orleans, united in a religious community. Before the
period ended, another Negro congregation of sisters was established:
The Congregation of the Handmaids of the Most Pure Heart of Mary,
founded in 1917 at Savannah, Georgia, through the efforts of the Rev.
Ignatius Lisner, S.M.A., in behalf of Negro Catholics. Of the activities
of this community, Dehey wrote that "settlement work of every description is within the scope of the Constitutions of the Congregation." [214]

The history of the Catholic Negro's "progress in education and religion
is a record of persistent strivings, a long drawn out effort and struggle
on the part of members of the race itself as also on the part of their
friends." [215] It was only after the Civil War that the Catholic Church
had dared take any determined stand to promote the conversion and
further the progress of the black race. Gibbons, "the leader of the
American Church" and "the occupant of the premier see of the United
States" during the period, was concerned for the Negroes, and believed
that they should be taught useful trades "if they were to become a
factor in their country's prosperity, to make their presence felt, and to
exercise any influence in bettering their status." [216]

Amidst the two great obstacles of prejudice and opposition from
whites of all faiths, therefore, the Catholic Church slowly but steadily
advanced in its missionary work for the emancipated slaves. This
progress would be imperceptible at times: for example, around 1910
St. Francis Xavier Church in Newtown, Maryland (below the Mason-
Dixon Line and established, you will remember, in 1640), installed a
stained-glass window with the inscription, "Gift of Our Colored Congregation." One still reads the inscription and still sees above it the
image of the suffering Christ on Veronica's veil—to be interpreted as
either sympathy with the sufferings of the Negro, or a recognition that
Christ's image is in the Negro as well as in the white. Butsch shows the
Negro advance statistically in a computation of Catholic work for
Negroes in this country,[217] based on the *Annual Reports* of the Commissioners of the Negro and Indian Mission Fund (Table II):

TABLE II

CATHOLIC CHURCH AMONG U. S. NEGROES

| YEAR | 1890 | 1900 | 1910 | 1917 |
|---|---|---|---|---|
| *Priests* | 30 | 45 | 59 | 105 |
| *Churches* | 25 | 40 | 75 | 101 |
| *Schools* | 98 | 81 | 134 | 141 |
| *Pupils* | 6,093 | 6,201 | 9,060 | 14,997 |
| *Children Baptized* | 4,907 | 5,198 | 4,735 | 6,110 |
| *Adult Converts* | 853 | 797 | 1,079 | 1,640 |

## THE AMERICAN INDIAN

The American Indian may be considered as another special type of student in Roman Catholic schools during this period. We have already seen that the Bureau of Catholic Indian Missions had been created in 1879 and that its effectiveness had led the Third Plenary Council of Baltimore in 1884 to make it a permanent institution. We noted the unfairness of the federal government's distribution of agencies—the off-shoot of President Ulysses S. Grant's Peace Policy—when of the seventy-two agencies among which the Indians were distributed, Catholics had been first established in thirty-eight and now were assigned to only eight.[218] But the Bureau, under its first capable director—Jean-Baptiste Abraham Brouillet—prospered. Its objectives were only four—brief and practical:

1. To direct the administration of such agencies as were specially assigned to the care of Catholic missionaries.
2. To secure, if possible, the remainder of those agencies to which Catholic missionaries were justly entitled under the terms of the Peace Policy.
3. To protect the religious faith and material interests of all Catholic Indians.
4. To secure the establishment of suitable schools for Indian boys and girls; to procure for the Indians moral and practical Christian teachers, with adequate compensation for their services; to develop a general interest in Indian education; and to secure means with which to erect school buildings in all cases possible.[219]

In 1894, the Bureau of Catholic Indian Missions was superseded by a new corporation, the Commission for the Catholic Missions among the Negroes and Indians, chartered in perpetuity by an act of the General Assembly of Maryland, with the archbishops of Baltimore, New York, and Philadelphia as incorporators. According to the Rev. Charles Warren Currier, the objects of this corporation were

to educate the American Indian and colored races throughout the State of Maryland, and beyond its borders in any of the states or territories of the United States, directly, and also indirectly, by the training of their teachers and others, especially to train their youth to become self-sustaining men and women, using such methods of instruction in the principles of religion and human knowledge as may be best adapted to their purposes; also to visit the sick and the poor of these races, and to act as the guardian of such of their orphans and minor children as may be committed to their care.[220]

The Act of Incorporation presupposed that the activities of the Bureau were to extend to colored peoples, but, true to its original spirit, it devoted itself exclusively to the Indian.

In 1877, the Bureau of Catholic Indian Missions had persuaded the federal government to inaugurate the "Contract School System," in order that its educational work be extended. Currier related that the Bureau entered into negotiations with the Commissioner of Indian Affairs, offering to provide buildings, furniture, etc., and to furnish board, lodging, tuition, clothing, etc. to the pupils if, in exchange, the government would allow a fixed annual per capita compensation. The proposition was accepted, and several contracts were entered into, the government allowing from $100 to $150 for boarding schools and $30 for day schools.[221]

*Sadlier's Catholic Directory* for 1890, writing of this "Contract School System" for the benefit of Indian students, stated:

The principal work of the Bureau is the establishment of Boarding and Day schools among the Indian tribes, and the procurement from the government of funds for their support and maintenance, which is done by means of contracts entered into between the Commissioner of Indian Affairs and the Bureau.

For the fiscal year beginning July 1, 1889, and ending June 30, 1890, the Bureau has secured contracts for carrying 48 Boarding and 17 Day Schools, providing for the support and tuition of 3,110 boarding pupils and the tuition of 680 day pupils, with an aggregate compensation of $356,606.[222]

The success of the Catholic Indian schools aroused a bigoted opposition from many who felt that the Catholic missions were receiving an unduly large share of government contracts. The American Protective Association, the House of Bishops of the Protestant Episcopal Church, and various other sectarian groups conducted a powerful lobby in Congress; the *Journal of the Senate* carried petitions which averaged ten daily in the year 1893-94.[223] Consequently appropriations were cut in 1895, and ceased altogether in 1900. After Theodore Roosevelt became President in 1901, the Rev. William H. Ketcham, then director of the Catholic Indian Bureau, requested that he give Indian parents the right to use their share of the Indian Education Fund to support their children attending mission schools. The understanding President had the director instruct the Indians to make their desire known by means of a petition. Francis E. Leupp, Commissioner of Indian Affairs, then agreed to contract with the Catholic Indian Bureau for a number of Indian children, but the Indian Rights Assocation incited Reuben Quick Bear and other Indians to apply for an injunction to restrain the contract. The case finally went to the Supreme Court, where the decision was rendered in 1908 that Indians could use Indian Tribal Funds for the education of their children in Catholic mission schools if they so chose.[224]

In 1902, when appropriations were cut from Catholic Indian schools, the Commission for the Catholic Missions among the Negroes and Indians, headed by Gibbons, made a strong appeal for generosity on the part of the Catholic people in the coming regular annual collection. The "Appeal in Behalf of the Negro and Indian Missions in the United States" read in part:

On account of the dreadful crisis through which our Indian Missions are passing, they should appeal to us in tones of thunder. Deprived of Government help, which they have a right to expect, the numerous schools, nurseries of Catholicity and civilization, which were flourishing among the different tribes, are on the verge of destruction . . . . Since the school is the life of the Indian mission, the Prelates are for the present directing their united energies toward maintaining this most necessary auxiliary and missionary work.[225]

Mother Katherine Drexel, foundress of the Sisters of the Blessed Sacrament, came to the aid of the Bureau. In the Indian schools, the students were provided with tuition, board, and clothing. They were given an elementary English education up to the fifth grade. Manual training was stressed. The boys were taught agriculture, shoemaking, carpentry, and other trades. The girls learned gardening and dairy work, sewing, lacemaking, and domestic science.

Finally, in tribute to both the Indians and those who have sacrificed to teach them, excerpts from the diary of Sister Mary Meinrada, O.F.M., now old and retired, are revealing. The diary began on September 1, 1901, when with two other sisters she headed by train from her motherhouse in Philadelphia for an Indian reservation in Pawhuska, Oklahoma. On the trip, they once had to sit up all night; the old man sitting across from them was robbed; and they had to wait all day at the station in Independence, Kansas, for another train connection. For a description of their late arrival, Sister Meinrada's unpolished words on her unnumbered pages are best:

A gentleman was going our way, but he had only an open spring wagon, so we decided that was the best we could do, so the three Nuns started out on the dark dusty road, up hill and down, across the creeks through the darkness, about from four to five hours ride, we arrived safe about mid-night, tired and our backs felt almost broken.[226]

At the Osage Indian School for girls, the children were white, Indian, and mixed breed. The diary tells of the sisters' having to ford Hominy Creek to visit Indians; of pupils of whom Sister was especially proud; of her teaching simultaneously sixty pupils from the sixth to the eleventh grades; of being accepted to witness a "Medicine Camp" at prayer because, though "white people" were excluded, "they looked upon us as belonging to them"; and even of a cyclone. For her pupils, she showed an evident affection when she wrote:

Many of our Indian girl students had great talent in Music, one graduating from the Conservatory of Music in Boston. . . . The Indians, as a rule, are on a par with white children, in their studies, during the various work assigned to each grade. They far surpass them in art and athletics. Many won prizes from State and even Foreign sources for their art work. It is noted that in paintings, no matter how bright their colors, [they] are so blended that they never clash.

Although it is usually the famous about whom history is written, it is this type of person who makes history.

## Aims

Through all their activities, Catholic educators were speculating on the goals and purposes of education. Some of the more profound thinkers, such as Spalding, even went back as far as Pythagoras to come up with a definition of education as "the training of a human being with a view to make him all he may become." He also voiced the perennial aims of Catholic education when he said that "the end of education is to fit him [man] for completeness of life, to train all his faculties, to call all his endowments into play, to make him symmetrical and whole in body and soul." He was also realistic enough to add that "this, of course, is the ideal, and consequently the unattainable; but in the light of ideals alone do we see rightly and judge truly; and to take a lower view of the aim and end of education is to take a partial view." [227] In all of the process, he perceived the importance of religion, observing that "science and art and progress, all conspire with religion to upbuild man's being and to mould him into ever-increasing likeness to God." [228] In this he was joined by all Catholic educators, who saw in religion's role in education their very *raison d'être*. Archbishop Michael Curley put it succinctly when he said in words reminiscent of George Washington's farewell address that "morality and religion are essential factors in the formation of true character [and that] no morality worthy of the name can be imparted or practiced that does not rest on religion as a foundation." [229]

The goals Spalding perceived were also practical, for he said that "the school which awakens a desire of knowledge is better than the school which only imparts knowledge; for the young do not know, but only seem to know, and unless they carry into life the love of study they will never become really educated." [230] Shields put it another way, when he wrote that

the unchanging aim of Christian education is, and always has been, to put the pupil into possession of a body of truth derived from nature and from divine revelation, from the concrete work of man's hand, and from the content of human speech, in order to bring his conduct into conformity with Christian ideals and with the standards of the civilization of his day.[231]

Shields also advised that

the teacher should attempt to formulate for himself a series of concrete and definite secondary aims which in their turn may be regarded as means to the attainment of the ultimate aim.[232]

Among those secondary aims of Catholic education that had to do with religion as such during this period, one finds listed such goals as attendance at Sunday Mass, monthly communion, frequent confession, generous financial contributions to the Church, acknowledgement of papal and hierarchical authority, informality with the clergy, strict sexual morality, and more detailed knowledge of the Catholic religion.

## Outcomes

In the latter aims at least, Catholic education has been reasonably successful. In spite of this, and also despite Catholic education's growth, both qualitative and quantitative, during this period, there was no more unanimity of Catholic thought about its necessity or desirability at the period's conclusion than there has been at any other time in United States Catholic history. The Irish-American who wanted to escape from the ghetto frequently looked upon the public school as his passport. Many of the Catholic middle class perceived that the public school texts had removed their more gross anti-Catholic sentiments. Many Catholics who wanted to step up from traditional immigrant occupations became teachers, and were eagerly employed by public schools. Many district school boards had as members good Catholics, and at times even priests. Pastors took contradictory attitudes towards both public and parochial schools. One pastor might see in the building of a school an ideal method of developing unity and loyalty in his parishioners, and do all in his power to get parents to send their children to the school when built, including denouncing recalcitrants by name from the pulpit and refusing them absolution in the confessional. His neighboring pastor, on the other hand, might be disinclined to have a parish school for any number of such reasons as a feeling for his parishioners' poverty, respect for the local public schools, fear that an increase in the number of parish schools might reawaken latent anti-Catholicism, or just plain unwillingness to take the time and trouble that the effort would cost. One priest, the Rev. Edward McGlynn of New York City, "believed that the problems of social welfare were so overwhelming that neither priest nor people had time or money to spare to devote to education." [233]

Perhaps a quintessential presentation of some of the paradox may have issued from the pen of one man, the Rev. Philip R. McDevitt, superintendent of schools in the diocese of Philadelphia in the beginning of the century, later bishop of the diocese of Harrisburg, Pennsylvania, and always interested in education. To a request of June 6, 1910, for information by one S. Edwin Megargee, Esq., McDevitt wrote:

Perhaps this fact may be of interest to you to know that there are only about ten cities, perhaps twelve cities, in the United States that are caring for more children in the public schools than the Catholics of Philadelphia care for in the parish schools. . . .

May I suggest that in any statement on this subject emphasis should be placed not upon . . . the scandalous fact that the city of Philadelphia does not, and perhaps never did in its history, provide adequately for the education of its children, and, moreover, would be bankrupt to-morrow if the Catholics of Philadelphia closed their schools and demanded a free education from the city.[234]

In a letter to "Brother Edward" on Jan. 27, 1914, on the other hand, he wrote:

Doctor Howard seems to believe that the principal, if not the only cause of the poor work of the present [Catholic] school system, is the curriculum. I presume to say that the curriculum is but one and a secondary cause of present day inefficiency in the schools. . . .

Other and far greater causes of the inefficiency are (a) poorly trained teachers; (b) crowded classes; (c) short school term; (d) inadequate equipment.[235]

## Conclusions

This period was a critical one for organized religion in the United States: materialism, and its cult of success, pragmatism, naturalism, and Darwinism permeated the country. Specifically directed against Catholics was a renewal of prejudice to which the American Protective Association and a sophisticated intellectual racism bore witness. Nevertheless, the Catholic Church grew in power and prestige, relatively speaking, from her former position of subjugation—due in no small measure to immigrants and their fecundity. In education, Catholics—following the lead of the public sector—were beginning a notion of cooperation through organizations to bring their educators together for discussions of problems and possible solutions. The Catholic Educational Association (later to add the adjective "National") was formed in 1904 from previously existing smaller groups, and other Catholic educational associations formed at around the same time.

Because child labor had finally come to an end and states were legislating compulsory education laws with teeth, the school population in both the public and private sectors zoomed. In Catholic elementary schools, this factor combined with the legislation of the Third Plenary Council of Baltimore of 1884 to bring about crowded classrooms and inadequate equipment. How much of this growth was due specifically to the Council will probably never be accurately determined. On the middle level of Catholic education, as of its public counterpart, there were striking developments. The Committee on High Schools made a report to the Catholic Educational Association in 1911 that was a turning point, but because of some inadequacies the CEA authorized further study, the report on which was made in 1915. This period also witnessed the founding of the first Central Catholic High School. Nevertheless, Catholics as well as the nation at large would have to wait until after World War I for meaningful interest in this level of education.

In higher education, in the midst of general developments in areas such as standardization and supervision, Catholic University came into being in 1889, after having been talked about and fought over for many years. It was conceived as not only the apex of Catholic education in the United States, but also as the agent to unify and guide it, to raise its standards through a program of affiliation, and to prepare its teachers.

Pertaining to teachers, this period witnessed the growth of teacher-training institutions under public auspices, which faced difficulties in such areas as experimentation and the problem of quantity versus quality. Among Catholics, the growth of this concept was slower—despite the 1892 plea of Apostolic Delegate Francesco Satolli for Catholic teachers to acquire state certification, the Third Plenary Council of Baltimore's legislation on proper teacher training, and the public statements of Bishop John L. Spalding. On the other hand, there was among Catholics as among others the inception of professionalism among teachers, and surprisingly, before 1900 when teachers in all schools were limited in their preparation and horizons, there were evidences that Catholic teachers were sometimes better prepared than their counterparts elsewhere. Teaching religious communities attempted teacher preparation through such practices as individual instruction, scholasticates, apprenticeships, lectures, summer schools, and institutes. There was, however, evidence that they were less prepared for teaching older children and in the sciences. Girls' liberal arts colleges, whose graduates were likely to teach, started now.

As for their students, there were developments in both theory and practice. With regard to the former, the ideas of Pestalozzi, Herbart, and Froebel were further introduced into United States education from abroad, one factor that would later lead into progressive education. There was scientific interest in education on the part of workers such as Edward L. Thorndike, with his principle that everything that exists, exists in quantity, and can be measured. Education's "Procrustean Bed" began its demise with the perception of individual differences by such leaders as William T. Harris, Charles W. Eliot, and John Dewey. Most of these developments, however, left Catholic educationists in an intellectual ferment. They could not accept Pestalozzi because of his naturalism, Herbart because of his determinism, Froebel because of his pantheism, progressive education because of what they considered undue freedom for the child and a forgetfulness of Original Sin; or Thorndike because of his mechanism. Within, there was further ferment because of the Bouquillon controversy on the state's right to educate, in which there was public and vociferous involvement of such famous bishops as John Ireland of St. Paul, Minnesota, on one side, and Bernard McQuaid of Rochester, New York, and Michael Corrigan of New York City on the other. An official statement of Apostolic Delegate Satolli seemed to settle nothing, for subsequent charges of a heresy called "Americanism," and Pope Leo XIII's *Testem benevolentiae,* all independent of this situation, did not assuage the resultant acrimony.

With regard to practice, Catholic-school students comprised, in addition to the "average" United States Catholic, several minority groups. First were the immigrants and their children, who were blamed for many of society's problems and ills, even by public educators. Catholic educators tried to meet this renewed prejudice by making their students not only Catholic, but also American. For the Catholics among the immigrants, the parish was the unit that was familiar from their place of origin; an integral part of this, especially among the Germans, was the parish school. This last, like its public counterpart, could not help but divide the immigrant child's loyalties and separate him to a certain extent from his foreign-sounding and foreign-looking parents; but it made the transition slower and therefore probably softer, easier, and psychologically more sound. In this time of mere beginnings of perception into the evils of child labor and the extremely slow process of eliminating it, however, a higher percentage of immigrant children and immigrants' children than among the total population were working; for them, extensive schooling was out of the question. Another minority group, the Negro, did not contain very many Catholics, for many and complex reasons. Nevertheless, during this period religious communities were started both for and of Negroes. Also, the Second and Third Plenary Councils of Baltimore had urged attention to the religion and education of the Negro. The effects of Baltimore III were more lasting, because it urged the laity to participate in this work, established a mandatory nationwide annual collection for the Negro and the American Indian, and established a special commission for both. With regard to the Indian, the success of Catholic agencies among them created some envy and resulted in an unfairness, *vis-à-vis* the Indian education program of the Catholic Church, from the federal government.

The federal government, especially its judicial branch, was no less confused during this period, however, in other relations with Catholic education. Many Catholic parents now took the step, unprecedented for them, of bringing cases all the way to the United States Supreme Court. The subject matter covered such activities in public schools as Protestant Bible reading, Protestant hymn singing, and Protestant religious services; others brought suit about such items as Catholic nuns' teaching in religious garb in public schools. The federal courts manifested confusion with regard to Protestant hymns and services, and the state courts equal confusion and contradiction among one another with regard to nuns' teaching in religious habits in public schools. Continued Catholic interest in the roughly 50 per cent of Catholic children not provided for by Catholic education brought about the adoption of such circuitous means of instilling religion as "released time" programs, which had originated among Protestants and would in turn engender more court cases.

The curriculum was related to goals, about which many Catholic educators theorized, coming up with new and practical phrasings for what was perennial. Out of the controversies came a more sophisticated philosophy of Catholic education. But because of initial Catholic rejection of such innovators as Pestalozzi and Herbart, improvements in Catholic textbooks that could have resulted from accepting what was worthwhile did not come, by and large. As a result, some Catholic texts wound up academically inferior to many in public school use, in spite of the added motivation of Baltimore III's legislation to produce good Catholic textbooks. Unfortunately, this same predisposition to reject change and improvements from outside also frequently resulted in poor quality in that area in which Catholic education found a prime reason for its existence—catechetics, the imparting of religious truths. Rote memorization (not uncommon in education of the time) of the Catechism of Baltimore III (the origins of which catechism were deep-rooted in Catholic history) was too frequent. Before the end of this period, however, an awareness of the inadequacy of the procedure grew, and such leaders as the Revs. Thomas E. Shields and Edward A. Pace of Catholic University initiated improvement.

At the end of this period, despite the many reasons for optimism, there was no more unanimity among Catholics *vis-à-vis* the desirability of maintaining their educational system than before (or since!): the Irish-American wanting a way out of the ghetto often tried the public school as his passport, many middle-class Catholics rationalized, many upwardly mobile Catholic immigrants became public-school teachers, many good Catholics served on public-school boards of education, and even some priests disagreed as to the desirability of Catholic schools. (The most famous was, perhaps, the Rev. Edward McGlynn of New York City.)

## CHAPTER V

# 1918-1957: Maturing Process

## Social Conditions

IN ORDER TO UNDERSTAND more easily our subject during this period, it is necessary to mention at least some of the social and cultural trends in whose midst Catholic educational history was made. In 1918 America was weary of war. It wanted neutrality, isolation, withdrawal from world commitments, peace, and a "return to normalcy." [1] There were serious economic and social problems to be solved at home. American business plunged up and down with recurring unsteadiness and then took a definite upswing which marked the 1920's as a decade of high prosperity. The country was gripped in a "Red scare": it suspected that the Communist rulers in Russia planned a world uprising of the proletariat, and a bomb explosion in Wall Street on September 16, 1920, which killed more than thirty people, caused a nervous wave of fear.[2] Aliens whose views were regarded as radical were deported; because fear breeds intolerance and hysteria, a resurgence of nativism occurred. A revived Ku Klux Klan lashed out at Jews, Negroes, Catholics, and all foreign born.[3] There were insistent demands for curbs on immigration and a reversal of America's traditional immigrant policy. Congress caught the spirit of hostility toward the immigrant, and Wittke writes that

an analysis of the debates in Congress will show that there was a general feeling of dissatisfaction with the newer immigrants as contrasted with the old, a belief that immigration would increase unemployment in the United States and depress labor standards, and a growing feeling that American social and political institutions must be protected against "reds," "hyphenates," and others who were likely to criticize the established order.[4]

The nation's gates closed to outsiders. "The United States was through with Europe," says Wittke, "and had no interest in the radical experiments that broke out in Russia and elsewhere." [5]

From those serious problems and from postwar disillusionment, Americans sought relief in a search for recreational excitement. The tempo of life quickened, and the 1920's earned the title of the "Jazz Age." The decade witnessed a revolution in morals and customs. Silent motion pictures—and the "talking pictures" which became possible in 1927—set styles in manners and fashions. "For the rising generation," opines Hicks, "the lessons they [the movies] taught were doubtless more effective than the precepts of the schoolroom." [6] The radio, another new influence upon American life, blared forth the jazz music that gave the age its name. Young people danced to unconventional rhythms. Women smoked cigarettes, raised hemlines, bobbed their hair, wore heavy make-up, and asserted their right to drink with men. City habits reached out to engulf the whole country. Motor cars raced through city and countryside. In 1926, Charles A. Lindbergh opened the way to transatlantic flight. A highly mechanized age set in. In the nation's celebration of "boom times," for most Americans the rest of the world, uninvited, slipped by.

American complacency was shattered, however, in the 1930's. The party was over. The stock market crash of October 1929 marked the beginning of the worst economic depression that the United States has ever known. Literally millions of people were on relief. Morale deteriorated as a result of soup kitchens and breadlines. Crime increased. "Home" for many families was the street. "Particularly shocking," observes Blake, "was the report that 200,000 homeless children were wandering through the country." [7] This economic crisis, in the words of Curti, "made educators of every shade of opinion more socially conscious and more willing to assume new responsibilities for building a better and more truly democratic order." [8] President Franklin D. Roosevelt initiated the New Deal—a pragmatic approach to the economic disaster, a series of experiments and reforms to oust hunger and homelessness from the nation.

While the Americans played through the prosperous Twenties and suffered during the adverse Thirties, European and Asiatic governments pursued policies that could lead only to war. On Dec. 7, 1941, Japan's attack on Pearl Harbor brought the United States into the Second World War. Dubious peace came with United States' atomic bombings of Hiroshima and Nagasaki. The American nation, no longer able to cut itself off, "accepted the role of champion of democracy throughout the world," and when it did so, "every divergence from democracy at home became a dangerously weak point in its armor." [9] Roosevelt's proposed Four Freedoms for the world (freedom of speech, freedom to worship God in one's own way, freedom from want, and

freedom from fear)[10] highlighted the evils of discrimination in education, employment, and housing that plagued many Negro Americans,
whose drive toward equality had begun. Prosperity returned. The individualism of the 1920's was rejected, and groupism was the order
of the day. Ernest Hemingway set the tone of the Forties—no man is
an island—in his 1940 book *For Whom the Bell Tolls.*[11] When the decade
of the 1940's ended, there were nineteen million more Americans than
when it had begun.[12] The scars of the Great Depression and of World
War II left bitter memories and engendered fear in the midst of prosperity. Juvenile delinquency menaced the nation. Alcoholism and drug
addiction increased, especially among the young, and suggested a
dangerously maladjusted generation.[13] Yet in the midst of rebelliousness
the nation made a return to religion, and church membership expanded.
The schools were held responsible to a great extent for America's restless
youth. Progressive education came under fire. As early as 1940, Walter
Lippmann downed the progressive schools. In the system, he declared,

there is no common faith, no common body of principle, no common body of
knowledge, no common moral and intellectual discipline. Yet the graduates of
these modern schools are expected to form a civilized community. They are
expected to govern themselves.[14]

America was shamed when many servicemen showed reading disabilities
in World War II. The race for literacy intensified. Americans became a
reading people, but the reading taste held immature elements: popular
magazines and comic books sold by the hundreds of thousands. Near
the end of the decade, in 1947, twelve televsion stations, which were
telecasting programs in nine American cities, marked the beginnings of
the television industry.[15]

In the 1950's, the technological revolution that had brought high
promise and optimism to the 1920's came to full flowering. It was an
"appliance age." Suddenly, as Link and Catton observe, American
homes needed "air conditioners, electric blankets, dehumidifiers, electric
and gas clothes dryers and automatic washing machines, home freezers,
electric dishwashers and garbage disposal units, power lawn mowers,
and a hundred other such gadgets." [16] Automobiles multiplied, and air
travel was commonplace. Advances in the fields of medicine and surgery
lengthened American lives. Peril kept pace with prosperity. America was
jealous of its atomic monopoly, and Russia was its greatest rival. The
feverish arms race began. Fear of extermination—unvoiced but almost
tangible—depressed many Americans. For comfort they read Bishop
Fulton J. Sheen's *Peace of Soul* [17] and Norman Vincent Peale's *The
Power of Positive Thinking.*[18] Then, in October of 1957, the American
public was stunned by the launching of Russia's Sputnik I satellite. The
event triggered off an outpouring of criticism of the existing educational
system. "A shocked and humiliated nation," says Cremin, "embarked on

a bitter orgy of pedagogical soul-searching." [19] Link and Catton recount that the substance of the criticism was that

modern progressivism, by emasculating scholarship and subject matter in the interests of pedagogic techniques and "life adjustment," had sapped much intellectual vitality, rigor, focus, and discipline from the school system—and hence from many young American minds. What was needed, the critics felt, was a fundamental shift in emphasis that would concentrate upon more rigorous intellectual training in the basic academic disciplines—English, history, mathematics, science, languages—and a clearer definition of the schools' primary responsibilities, which involved, at bottom, teaching pupils how to think. [20]

## Public Education

In a speech at the beginning of this period, the Rt. Rev. Philip Mc-Devitt of Philadelphia presented information from the *Research Bulletin* of the National Education Association of September 1923 on the public school. [21] He cited it as pointing to five weak spots in the public school system of the time. First was the allegation that the state compulsory school laws were not yet being enforced. According to the 1920 census, 1,438,000 children over seven years of age and under fourteen did not attend school a single day between September 1, 1919, and January 1, 1920: these figures did not tell the whole story, either, because thousands were falsely reported as attending school. Massachusetts, with 3.9 per cent absent, had the best record, while Louisiana, with 24.1 per cent, had the worst. Secondly, the one-room school still existed in great numbers: it was estimated that in 1920 there were 189,227 one-room schools, involving approximately four million of the twenty-three million public school children. Thirdly, untrained, inexperienced, and incompetent teachers were found in many of the nation's classrooms. Thousands of them, eighteen and nineteen years of age, were being given each year a far greater responsibility—the training of the citizens of tomorrow—than that of the ballot, for which the age of twenty-one was required. At least 54 per cent of the nation's teachers had less training than normal school graduation or the equivalent. Nearly one teacher of every four in the rural schools had less than two years' training beyond elementary school graduation. As for lack of experience and maturity, 36 per cent of the rural teachers had less than two years' experience, and 25 per cent were less than twenty-one years of age. Fourthly, the salaries paid in many states were too low to attract competent teachers. Fifthly and finally, the children of the United States did not have equal opportunity to obtain an education. Eight states were providing over $100 annually per pupil in financial support, and seven states less than $25. There were also variations within the states: e.g., in Minnesota, the average expenditure per child in 1921 varied from $829 in some districts to $49 in others. There were also variations in the length of the school term: in New Jersey, the average length of the school term in 1920 was 189 days, in South Carolina only 109.6 days, and in parts of Arkansas as low as 77 days.

The second question which the *Research Bulletin* asked was, "What national defects result?" It gave five answers. First, child labor was denying thousands of children an educational opportunity. In 1920, the census revealed over 1 million child laborers from ten to fifteen years of age, not including those under ten, in which category some scholars believed there were again as many in some communities. Secondly, there were millions of native-born people who were illiterate. Thirdly, millions of citizens lacked the education necessary for intelligent citizenship in a democracy. The 1920 census indicated that over 2.5 million native-born adults were illiterate. Among the native-born who were twenty-one years of age and over, Mississippi had 20.8 per cent illiterate, the highest, and Washington State had 0.36 per cent, the lowest. Fourthly, all of this was resulting in preventable deficiencies that were costing the nation millions of dollars each year: in time of war, such persons were unfit for military service, and in peace they were a waste for industry. Finally, the retardation rates among school children were making the United States a nation of sixth-graders.

More importantly, as the United States was entering its technological age public schools were forced into a reinterpretation and reappraisal of their educational goals. The period witnessed a number of studies which purported to discover how public education could best serve individual and social needs. The Seven Cardinal Principles of Secondary Education, drawn up in 1918 by the Commission on the Reorganization of Secondary Education of the National Education Association,[22] and based on Herbert Spencer's *Education: Intellectual, Moral and Physical*,[23] was the first statement of goals by public educators. Education should aim to achieve health, command of fundamental processes (such as reading, writing, arithmetical computations, and oral and written expression), worthy home membership, vocation (equipping an individual to secure a livelihood), civic education, worthy use of leisure, and ethical character.[24] During the depression years one of the most active study groups was the NEA Committee on Social-Economic Goals.[25] In its 1934 report, the Committee listed ten desirable social-economic goals of Americans. According to the Committee, every individual is entitled to hereditary strength, physical security, participation in an evolving culture, an active and flexible personality, suitable occupation, economic and mental security, equality of opportunity, freedom, and fair play.[26] "Let every teacher," said the Committee, "make himself a student of these social-economic goals and interpret them to the people." [27]

Near the end of the period, in 1955, the White House Conference on

Education presented a list of fourteen aims for elementary and secondary public schools. In scope and specificity these aims differed from NEA's social-economic goals and showed society's changed vision of education. The White House Conference on Education stated that the public school should develop the fundamental skills of communication; appreciation of our democratic heritage; knowledge of American institutions, civil rights, and responsibilities; respect and appreciation for human values and for the beliefs of others; ability to think and evaluate constructively and creatively; effective work habits and self-discipline; social competence as a contributing member of family and community; ethical behavior based on a sense of moral and spiritual values; intellectual curiosity and eagerness for lifelong learning; aesthetic appreciation and self-expression in the arts; physical and mental health; wise use of time, including constructive leisure activities; understanding of the physical world and man's relation to it as represented through a basic knowledge of the sciences; and an awareness of our relationships with the world community.[28] Public school educators of the period insisted that their aims include the inculcation of moral and spiritual values. Willard E. Givens, Executive Secretary of the NEA, observed in 1948:

One of the important objectives of public education has been, and always will be, to inspire in youth a deep appreciation for the basic spiritual and religious values which give meaning to existence, provide the foundation of good character, and are guides to a high order of human conduct.[29]

The aims, however, that for the most part were implemented in the public schools during the period between the two world wars were those of progressive education: the child must have freedom to develop naturally; interest should be the motive of all work; the teacher should be a guide, not a taskmaster; teachers should encourage use of all the senses and the study of real life activities as well as books; teachers should promote the use of information to draw correct conclusions and to express them logically; the scientific study of child development must be stressed and efforts made to link learning activities with community life and problems; and the school was to be a laboratory where worthy ideas were to be tried out.[30] An attempt to apply the ideas of John Dewey to the classrooms of America wrought radical changes in curricula and school plants. The curriculum was expanded and reorganized, with increased attention to "opportunities for work in trades, agriculture, home economics, physical education, and the arts." [31] Students were grouped on the basis of intelligence and achievement tests. Projects competed with recitations. A new informality crept into the classroom. Fresher and more attractive textbooks caught the children's attention, and lessons were taught with such supplementary aids as flash cards, slides, filmstrips, and phonograph records. Improved facilities—better lighting, gymnasiums, shops, miniature tables and chairs, cafeterias, laboratories, and movable furniture and partitions—"all testified," according to Cremin, "to the changing program and commitment of the school." [32] But progressive education came under fire after World War II. In the words of Cremin, "a movement that had for half a century enlisted the enthusiasm, the loyalty, the imagination, and the energy of large segments of the American public and the teaching profession became, in the decade following World War II, anathema." [33] Link and Catton give reasons for the movement's decline:

Its weaknesses were many. Its intellectual vitality was largely gone. It lacked a clear and consistent program or philosophical base. It was torn by internal schisms and arid factional disputes, badly overprofessionalized, and inbred. Finally, it was too much addicted to jargon and slogans as a substitute for constructive thought and increasingly out of touch with the changes that had transformed American society since 1929.[34]

The activity method and the activity curriculum were a protest against the passive learning of the traditional schools, but the pendulum had swung too far in the opposite direction. The essentialists, of whom William C. Bagley was the outstanding leader, criticized the extreme views of progressive educationalists and claimed that the chief function of education is to transmit the cultural heritage. Remarks educational historian H. G. Good:

The general public became concerned about the teaching of the fundamentals of reading, writing, and arithmetic, which they considered insufficient. They thought there should be more drill. They wanted a stricter, more evident, discipline.[35]

A reappraisal of public education began and Americans wanted an educational reform that was nonprogressive.

Aims, and their realization through curricula and teaching methods, have deliberately been focal points in our consideration of public education, for therein one finds cause for contrast with Catholic education. Milestones we might have marked with ease, but if a study of Catholic education is to receive some light from public education it must investigate its framework of philosophy and its concepts of the psychology of learning. Were Catholic educators for the most part imitators rather than innovators, and if so how far did such imitation go? What had Catholic education to do with progressive education, which took over the public schools of this period, and which had its remote ancestry in such as Jean-Jacques Rousseau, and its more immediate parentage in such as Pestalozzi, Herbart, Froebel, and Dewey? The Rev. Gerard Sloyan supplied an answer:

The forgotten truth that the child as learner is a being more important than all teachers, methods, and instruments in the precise matter of learning was the cornerstone of Dewey's successful edifice. Johnson [Monsignor George Johnson] saw clearly in Dewey's doctrine its theological heresy, its philosophical errors, and the pedagogical flaw whereby it shrinks from scientific evaluation and flies in the face of experience and common sense. Nonetheless, he was insistent in admitting that organized education in its smugness, its zeal for routine and standardization, its failure to take account of social changes or to profit by the findings of educational science too frequently lost sight of the child and his needs.[36]

And more than thirty years before—in 1921—Dr. Thomas Shields of The Catholic University of America had declared that "pragmatism and the Gospel unite in establishing a test for the value of educational doctrines." [37] One thing, however, is certain: progressive public school education forced Catholics to investigate more deeply and more precisely their educational philosophy, particularly in the areas of the origin, nature, and destiny of the child. It also forced them to a curriculum-revision program—a vital, effective curriculum built on the personal and social needs of Catholic youth.

## Catholic Education

### STATISTICS

For Catholic education the years from 1918 to 1957 were, in the words of the Rev. Henry J. Browne, "a half-century of progress." [38] The statistics for those times show remarkable growth. *The Official Catholic Directory* for 1917 gives the following information regarding the general status of Catholic education in that year in the United States: 102 seminaries with a student enrollment of 6,898; 216 colleges for boys; 676 academies for girls; 5,687 parishes with schools; and a Catholic school population of 1,537,644, out of a total Catholic population of 17,022,879.[39] At the end of the period (1957), *The Official Catholic Directory* listed the Catholic population as 34,563,851, and presented the following breakdown of educational statistics: 259 colleges and universities with a student enrollment of 259,277; 1,539 high schools, diocesan and parochial, with 448,408 students; 846 private high schools with 274,355 students; 9,274 elementary schools, parochial and institutional, with an enrollment of 3,616,455; and 498 private elementary schools, with 92,565 students.[40] Catholic education had weathered the depression well, and statistics for 1936 were encouraging, as will be seen in Table I on the next page.

TABLE I

NATIONAL SUMMARY OF ALL CLASSES OF CATHOLIC EDUCATIONAL INSTITUTIONS FOR 1936 *

| | NO. OF SCHOOLS | INSTRUCTORS | | | STUDENTS | | |
| --- | --- | --- | --- | --- | --- | --- | --- |
| | | RELIGIOUS | LAY | TOTAL | MEN | WOMEN | TOTAL |
| SEMINARIES | | | | | | | |
| Major | 93 | 921 | 32 | 953 | 8,019 | . . . . | 8,019 |
| Preparatory | 79 | 993 | 85 | 1,078 | 9,427 | . . . . | 9,427 |
| UNIVERSITIES AND COLLEGES | | | | | | | |
| Universities | 23 | 1,141 | 4,106 | 5,247 | 44,303 | 23,552 | 67,855 |
| Men's colleges | 56 | 1,215 | 570 | 1,785 | 18,052 | 5,772 | 23,824 |
| Women's colleges | 105 | 2,703 | 1,057 | 3,760 | 316 | 36,428 | 36,744 |
| DIOCESAN TEACHERS' COLLEGES | 6 | 170 | 23 | 193 | 23 | 1,992 | 2,015 |
| NORMAL SCHOOLS | 34 | 697 | 113 | 810 | 315 | 6,821 | 7,136 |
| SECONDARY SCHOOLS | 1,945 | 14,121 | 2,663 | 16,784 | 124,265 | 160,471 | 284,736 |
| ELEMENTARY SCHOOLS | 7,929 | 55,467 | 3,436 | 58,903 | 1,056,017 | 1,046,872 | 2,102,889 |
| TOTAL | 10,270 | 77,428 | 12,085 | 89,513 | 1,260,737 | 1,281,908 | 2,542,645 |

* National Catholic Welfare Conference, *Summary of Catholic Education 1935-1936* (Washington, D.C., 1938), p. 21.

Prosperity followed World War II, and the "baby boom" of the 1940's caused enrollment to soar in elementary schools by the end of that decade.

### GOALS

We have seen that public education during the period came up with a multiplicity of educational goals which to Catholic scrutiny failed to distinguish between the ultimate and the proximate. The goal of education for John Dewey was the development of the social being in social efficiency. For him this was a moral goal, and he had said that "apart from participation in social life, the school has no moral end or aim." [41] Thus he established social efficiency as the ultimate standard of morality and as the ultimate goal of education. Catholics opposed such a philosophy because it ignored fundamental aspects of man's nature and of his final end. Educational objectives, as far as Catholics were concerned, were twofold: ultimate and immediate—changeless and changing. The ultimate aim remained ever the same—knowledge of God in view of man's eternal destiny. The immediate aims, necessary to further the ultimate aim, took cognizance of man as a member of society in which he has a duty to work for his own well-being and for the common good. Immediate goals change with society's changing needs and demands.

Thus two divergent philosophical views—the social experimentalism of Dewey's progressive education and the social traditionalism of Bagley's essentialism—were holding the ultimate aim of education to be *social*. Bagley, it is true, opposed what he considered to be the errors of progressive education. He wrote:

Generally speaking, the recognized essentials should be taught as such through a systematic program of studies and activities for the carrying out of which the teachers should be responsible. [42]

Bagley was set against minimizing the effort in learning. He believed that the progressive theories were an enfeebling lot, for he recognized certain "emergents," such as mind, will, and the "capacity for sustaining effort in the face of desire." [43] Catholics favored Bagley for his defense of systematic instruction in the fundamental subjects as opposed to incidental learning, but they could not agree with his naturalism, his belief in the perfectibility of man through "emergent evolution" due to man alone, and his materialistic monism, which failed to recognize any distinction between God and the world and between spiritual and material principles in man. Bagley and the progressives actually hoped to arrive at the same social goal through different proximate aims. The main significant differences between them and Catholic educators was that the proximate aims of education for the latter had to be chosen in reference to an eternal and supernatural aim and set of values. [44]

The Bishops of the United States were not slow to enunciate the aims of Catholic education. In 1919, for example, the entire Section XIII of the Pastoral Letter of the Archbishops and Bishops of the United States pertained to education.[45] Guilday described this pastoral as one which

reaches out into realms that were not trodden by the prelates of former days; it has been justly praised by Catholics and non-Catholics of this and other lands; and it must always be reckoned among the greatest documents of the reconstruction crisis which followed the World War.[46]

Introductory expressions of the Pastoral touched upon the need for sound education and stressed the educational problem which existed in a changing industrial society confused by conflicting theories of education. Included were the following observations:

It is necessary to provide for the future by shaping the thought and guiding the purpose of our children and youth toward a complete understanding and discharge of their duties. Herein lies the importance of education and the responsibility of those to whom it is entrusted. Serious at all times, the educational problem is now graver and more complex by reason of the manifold demands that are made on the school, the changes in our industrial conditions, and above all, by reason of the confusion and error which obscure the purpose of life and therefore of true education.

The Pastoral emphasized the necessity for education to move in the right direction—to have the correct goals. It stated:

While, therefore, it is useful to improve education by organizing the work of the schools, enriching the content of knowledge and refining the methods of teaching, it is still more necessary to insure that all educational activity shall be guided by sound principles toward the attainment of its true purpose.

The Pastoral restated the basic principles of Catholic education. As the first of these it indicated that "education is a cooperation by human agencies with the Creator for the attainment of His purpose in regard to the individual who is to be educated, and in regard to the social order of which he is a member." As a second principle it pointed out that "since the child is endowed with physical, intellectual, and moral capacities, all these must be developed harmoniously." Thirdly, it stated that "the performance, sincere and complete, of religious duties, ensures the fulfillment of other obligations." Fourthly, it asserted that religious training should so permeate instruction in other kinds of knowledge that "its influence will be felt in every circumstance of life." The fifth basic principle was that "an education that unites intellectual, moral and religious elements, is the best training for citizenship."

The National Catholic Educational Association (then the Catholic Educatonal Association) advocated and strongly insisted upon these principles of Catholic education. Before the Pastoral Letter was issued, at the 1917 meeting held at Buffalo, New York, the Rev. Patrick J. McCormack had said:

We justify the existence of our separate system by our needs as Catholics to supply in education what is the better part. Our standard must in consequence represent our aim; and the institutions which are governed by it, live by it, no matter what they teach, be it of advanced or elementary grade, be it cultural or vocational, must in very truth be Catholic; their standardization should therefore first be determined by what they do for the moral and religious training of our youth before being considered in relation to any other aim or measure of efficiency.[47]

During the 1920's the aim of Catholic education was a recurring theme at the NCEA meetings, as a few further examples will show. At the 1920 meeting, Brother Albert L. Hollinger, S.M., read a paper entitled, "Getting Full Value Out of Catholic Education," in which he stated that the Catholic system of education aimed to fit youth "spiritually, intellectually, and socially, to take their places in the councils of men and women of the nation."[48] At the 1921 meeting, the Rev. Joseph Wehrle declared that Catholic education "seeks to develop the individual for complete living by the standards of man's eternal destiny"; for, he continued, "the individual has not only the right to enjoy the inheritance of science, literature, art, and social institutions, but of religion as well."[49] In 1929, the Rev. Daniel Feeney made a clear distinction between secular and Catholic education. The distinction lay in the realm of aims. Feeney said:

All Catholic educators agree that Catholic Education does not mean secular education plus the recitation of prayers and a knowledge of the Catechism. We maintain that the child is a moral agent endowed with an immortal soul, answerable to God; we further maintain that religious training is the only effective training in the complete development of this moral agent; we have accepted man's real valuation at the price quoted by Our Lord, that not even the possession of the whole world can compensate for the failure of the realization of that soul's eternal destiny. With these convictions Catholic Education aims to inform the entire curriculum and permeate the whole child every minute of every day.[50]

The NCEA continued its concern for awareness of Catholic educational goals throughout the period. After 1929, however, no doubt could exist in the minds of Catholic educators as to their pursuance of aims: on December 31 of that year, Pope Pius XI spoke authoritatively on the subject in *The Christian Education of Youth*.[51] After 1938, the goals of Catholic education were strengthened by the institution of the Commission on American Citizenship, which was founded at Catholic University, and which will be discussed further on in this chapter. The NCEA reaffirmed the teachings of Pius XI on educational aims, and emphasized the practical doings of the Commission in the realization of these aims. The Very Reverend Paul C. Reinert, S.J., for example, speaking at the forty-ninth NCEA meeting in 1952, observed:

Even though . . . our schools have more than purely secular educational aims, even though we have unique spiritual and supernatural objectives in our Catholic education, these cannot be substituted for the additional basic goal we must have of providing our students with a sound thorough-going education. This is not an "either-or" but a "both-and" responsibility.[52]

The encyclical of Pius XI on *The Christian Education of Youth* remains to this day the most authoritative papal expression on the subject, but it must be understood in its historical setting. Pius XI spoke in a time of totalitarian governments whose philosophy in education was to subjugate the whole life of the child to themselves. The encyclical opposed such a policy, particularly as it was applied by fascism in Italy. The historical circumstances of such concomitant phenomena as fascism and national socialism make it understandable that the encyclical emphasized moral and religious education with the express purpose of showing that the state cannot of itself adequately fulfill this role. "The proper and immediate end of Christian education," declared the encyclical, "is to cooperate with divine grace in forming the true and perfect Christian, that is, to form Christ Himself in those regenerated by baptism." In this connection, the Rev. Raymond A. Lucker called the period from 1930 to 1955 a period of shift in emphasis of Catholic religious educational goals from information to Christian formation; the goal of the period after that he labelled "initiation" into the life of Christ through the liturgy.[53] The encyclical pointed out that

Christian education takes in the whole aggregate of human life, physical and spiritual, intellectual and moral, individual, domestic and social, not with a view of reducing it in any way, but in order to elevate, regulate and perfect it, in accordance with the example and teaching of Christ.[54]

Pius XI went on to say, "The true Christian does not renounce the activities of this life, he does not stunt his natural faculties; but he develops and protects them, by coordinating them with the supernatural." The encyclical declared Christian education to be the only perfect and true education:

Since education consists essentially in preparing man for what he must be and for what he must do here below in order to attain the sublime end for which he was created, it is clear that there can be no true education which is not wholly directed to man's last end.[55]

With respect to this ultimate aim of Catholic education, from kindergarten through graduate school there never has been substantial change. For American Catholic educators of the 1930's, there was no question of the *ultimate* aim. The question was to what extent the school should emphasize *immediate* aims: what were to be the immediate goals of Christian education in American *democratic* society? As early as 1919, Monsignor George Johnson had asserted that "Catholic education must work out a practical social philosophy of its own, and not be satisfied to follow where blind guides may lead." [56] The same author wrote in 1925 that

the aim of the Catholic elementary school is to provide the child with those experiences which are calculated to develop in him such knowledge, apprecia- tions, and habits, as will yield a character equal to the contingencies of funda- mental Christian living in American democratic society.[57]

Pope Pius XI in September 1938 instructed the bishops of the United States to draw up for Catholic Americans "a constructive social program of education based on Christian principles." [58] In compliance with that request, the United States bishops met in Washington, D.C., in October 1938, and set up the Commission on American Citizenship. Johnson had his chance now to direct the fashioning of proximate educational goals whereby Catholics would become "better men for better times." [59] He did a superb job. In any consideration of educational aims between 1918 and 1957, space must be given to the five major proximate goals of Christian education established by the Commission under his direc- tion. In Johnson's own words:

The goals of Christian education in American democratic society might be summed up as follows:

*Physical fitness,* or the habits of healthful living based on an understanding of the body and its needs, and right attitudes toward everything that contrib- utes to good health.

*Economic literacy,* or an understanding of the workings of modern industrial civilization, with all that it involves of interdependence, adequate to yield an appreciation of the value of work and a zeal for social justice.

*Social virtue,* based on an understanding of American life and the workings of democracy, making the individual ready to make those sacrifices of self- interest that are necessary if he is to live with his fellow man in peace and unity.

*Cultural development,* rooted in a familiarity with the beauty the human mind has created and enshrined in its literature, its music, and its art, and flowering in a taste for finer things that will banish the low, the lewd, the vulgar, and the decadent.

*Moral perfection,* or saintliness, the crown of all the rest, achieved in and through all the rest, fulfilling the purpose of man's existence, because it purifies him and unites him with his God.

In the measure that Catholic education reaches these goals, it justifies its existence and enriches our national life. At the same time, it increases the mea- sure of human happiness, for it produces people who have grown up unto the measure of the age and the stature of Christ, and who, functioning for Him, "go about doing good." They are the better men and women whose coming better times await.[60]

Before the Commission on American Citizenship presented the above plan of Christian social living in 1944, the Secondary School Department of the Catholic Educational Association had come up in 1939 with seven broad objectives of Catholic secondary education. (The statement listed 68 specific outcomes to be sought in the fulfillment of these objectives!) The objectives took the form of seven qualities to be brought out, i.e., to develop Catholics who were intelligent, spiritually vigorous, cultured, healthy, vocationally prepared, social-minded, and truly American.[61]

The encyclical of Pius XI had set American Catholic educators to thinking through their proximate aims of Catholic education. After the Holy Father had presented the principles, educators were eager to apply them. The encyclical missed no point of importance. It stressed education's ultimate aim—"preparing man . . . to attain the sublime end for which he was created"; the proximate objective—"to cooperate with Divine Grace in forming the true and perfect Christian"; the subject of Catholic education—"man whole and entire, soul united to body in unity of nature, with all his faculties natural and supernatural, such as right reason and Revelation show him to be; man, therefore, fallen from his original estate, but redeemed by Christ"; the means—"above all, the mind must be enlightened and the will strengthened by supernatural truth and by the means of grace"; the scope—"the whole aggregate of human life"; and the product of such education—"the supernatural man who thinks, judges, and acts constantly and consistently in accordance with right reason illumined by the supernatural light of the example and teaching of Christ." [62] It remained for Catholic educators to translate these principles into specific objectives, and we have observed their worthy attempts to do so. If the implementation of the proximate objectives sometimes proved a disappointment, it must be remembered that proximate goals in themselves are never fully attained. They are but stepping-stones to the ultimate end.

For American Catholics, educational aims had been clarified. Once more, however, during this period, on November 17, 1950, the United States Bishops published another important statement on the subject— "The Child: Citizen of Two Worlds." The ultimate aim of education was their particular concern. They said:

In recent decades, striking advances have been made in meeting the child's physical, emotional, and social needs; but his moral and religious needs have not been met with the same solicitude and understanding. As a result, many of our children today betray confusion and insecurity because these unmet needs are fundamental to the harmonious development of their whole nature. The child must be seen whole and entire. He must be seen as a citizen of two worlds. He belongs to this world surely, but his first and highest allegiance is to the kingdom of God. From his earliest years he must be taught that his chief significance comes from the fact that he is created by God and is destined for life with God in eternity.[63]

The Bishops contended that the person with allegiance to the Kingdom of God as well as to this world "will urgently need the integrating force of religion as taught by Christ." This will have four consequences. The first of these is a sense of God, a good thing for the child, to whom two courses are open: either to be God-centered or self-centered. The second consequence, said the Bishops, is a sense of direction for continuing purpose in life, for "it will teach him that he was made to know, love, and serve God in this world as the condition for meriting eternal happiness." Thirdly, the integrating force of religion in education will result in a sense of responsibility, because religion insists upon "that sense of accountability to God." Lastly, "religion will challenge him to sanctify whatever walk of life he chooses," and will thus result in a sense of mission. The basis of education for Catholics is to be found in the Bishops' summary of the philosophy of Christian education.[64]

The years 1918 to 1957 were marked, as we have observed, by social shocks and bewildering change. Varying philosophies abounded, and for Catholic parents and educators guidelines were needed. Aims had to be spelled out, and they were spelled out—"Whole man, Christian, Catholic." "To the production of Christian humanists," said John Courtney Murray, S.J., in 1941, "the whole of Christian education is directed." But Murray held that this aim, "simple in itself," is "enormously complex in its achievement." A union of grace and nature is "a synthesis infinitely delicate," but in that lies the Catholic educator's aim for the formation of the person. Murray ascribed to Catholic educators the belief that to be a whole man is to be Catholic; he and they both knew that they would be judged by their products in American society. Murray knew that this nation has a genius for the practical. He wrote:

We cannot, then, resent it when the secularist proposes to test the truth of our premise by the product we turn out. He is not being unfair when he says to our product: "I shall judge the validity of your Christianity by the type of manhood it has wrought in you. Let us see. Are you at peace with yourself? Have you resolved in yourself the interior conflict that tears me apart? Are you able to resist the attraction of matter, and to save yourself from immersion in it? Do you understand this world? Are you able to see a meaning in its history? Do you love it, and all of us who live in it, enough to be willing to die for its salvation? Does the salvation of humanity mean anything to you, or are you only interested in saving yourself? You say you are a whole man—are you?" [65]

Murray had no answer to such questions. He posed instead another question for the consideration of Catholic educators in the 1940's: "We want to make whole men: well, then, are we making Christians and Catholics?"

### CURRICULUM

It is in the light of a school's philosophy of education—its aims and objectives—that the educational program is worked out. The school's activities, particularly its curriculum, take much of their color from the particular times as well. The curriculum may therefore be said to reflect life (except for a certain lamentable lag) as well as the school's philosophy. Curriculum was a big issue in education from 1918 to 1957. In Colonial times life had been simple and the elementary curriculum, for example, had been a simple matter of the three R's—religion, reading, and writing. Commercial activity in the new republic had added new emphasis to arithmetic. The War of 1812 had brought the beginnings of industrialization, and for the remainder of the nineteenth century, further curricular changes—cautious at first and then accelerated —had been made. Social forces had beat upon the schools and, as we have seen, new types of studies and even special schools at all levels of education had appeared, which had catered to the needs of an industrialized society. But tremendous change in the curricula of both public and private schools came during the years from 1918 to 1957. One word may best characterize the curriculum of the period—*social*. How did this differ in Catholic and public schools? What curriculum did Catholic educational circles adopt for the swift-changing twentieth century? What constructive measures did Catholics take to design a curriculum fitted to the century and at the same time in keeping with the aims of Catholic education?

The twentieth century ushered in the scientific study of education. Edward Lee Thorndike of Teachers College, Columbia University, built upon the work of G. Stanley Hall, William James, and J. McKeen Cattell, and now "took the lead in developing the modern fields of educational psychology and measurement.[66] An age of testing and experimentation began. Instruments and techniques for mental measurement affected curriculum designs. Not only *what* the child should learn became a matter of question, but more importantly *how* he learns, and how the learning can be measured. "Learning is connecting," proclaimed Thorndike. "The mind is man's connection-system." [67] On the basis of results obtained from his study of the associative processes in chickens, Thorndike constructed his S-R bond theory of learning. For him, successful teaching turned upon a careful manipulation of the learner. Man's mental faculty consists of a relatively large number of high-quality neurons which form S-R bonds by repetition (exercise), in accordance with criteria of satisfyingness (effect). Catholic philosophy would have none of this concept, claiming that it was excessively physiologically based. Catholics hold that man is a composite of body and soul joined in substantial union to form one complete substance, and that cognition, like any other human activity, is the function neither of the soul alone nor of the body alone, but of the animated whole. Human learning is distinguished from animal learning; animals have sense knowledge and the ability to discriminate between one object and another, but lack the power of abstraction and cannot form general concepts. The difference between human and animal learning is not a simple quantitative difference in neurons, but a difference in kind. To Thorndike, however, man was not only a part but also a product of nature, to be studied as any other phenomenon in nature, that is, by the methods of natural science alone.[68] His concept of human nature was a mechanistic and deterministic one, and it shaped his laws of learning. Catholics agreed that these laws existed, but strongly opposed Thorndike's interpretation of them.

Thorndike's principles moved into the American public school. The use of standard tests and measurements of mental abilities and of educational achievement widened greatly during the 1930's and 1940's, until it became one of the most significant movements in American education. Attempts were made to measure not only academic achievement, but also differences in native abilities, character, and conduct. In the preface of a Catholic book on education by McGucken in 1934, Dr. Joseph Husslein bitterly attacked the "robot theory of education . . . which makes of a man a mere mechanism without a soul; the materialistic philosophy that sees in his every action the inevitable resultant of purely chemical and physical reaction; the consequent rejection of all true freedom of the will, and so of the very possibility of morality itself." [69] An author whose presentation of the measurement movement was satisfactorily received in public schools was Mybert E. Broom; he considered measurement a vital, functioning part of the school programs, since findings from achievement tests influenced the adjustment of the school organization, curriculum, and methods of instruction to the varying needs and abilities of the pupils. "It is obvious," wrote Broom, "that modern education cannot function effectively without the use of a great deal of measurement," and he sounded a note of warning:

There is no doubt that educators with a limited knowledge of measurement have misused materials heretofore, and there is equally little doubt that the educator who casually accepts and uses carelessly standardized tests will encounter difficulties. Measuring is a scientific process, and it should be reserved to those adequately trained to use tests and examinations properly and to interpret results that they yield.[70]

Gradually, Catholic schools came to see that the testing movement had its merits. Lifted from its naturalistic philosophical base and purged in a Catholic philosophy of education, it could be an aid to individual student progress. Certain Catholic educators made such views public, particularly at the annual meetings of the Catholic Educational Association. At its twenty-first meeting, Thomas G. Foran of Catholic University spoke forcefully on "The Usefulness of Educational Tests." He said:

There is a very real place for educational measurements in Catholic schools. It is hoped that in the near future tests designed specifically for Catholic schools will be available. The limitation of tests should not be omitted from consideration nor should tautology obscure their value. They are *not* omnipotent, they *are* useful.[71]

From the same university in 1929, two other voices were raised in support of the testing movement: the Rev. Maurice S. Sheehy upheld "The Use of Personality Rating Scales in Educational Guidance," [72] and the Rev. John M. Cooper thought that advantage should be taken of the vast amount of study and research that had gone into the "Diagnosis and Treatment of the Factors in Moral Conduct," and wrote:

Modern intensive study of the factors underlying behavior has laid at our feet a wealth of new information on these factors as they work in our contemporary life and on natural methods of treating them. We should avail ourselves to the utmost of this newer knowledge. In doing so, however, while we should make every reasonable use of the natural means and motives in treatment, we should particularly build up the supreme subjective factors of *ideals* and of *grace* by intensive appeal to the supernatural motives and by generous use of the supernatural means provided through prayer and the Sacraments.[73]

Sheehy, concerned for the future of Catholic education as well as for the students of his time, concluded:

A proper study and evaluation of personality traits is a first step towards rendering efficient educational service. I hope that the day will soon come when the teachers in the parochial school, the high school, and the college will realize that their task lies with unit personalities, and that educational guidance in Catholic schools will then be a continuous process with this major objective, enrichment of life of the individual student.[74]

On the whole, however, the measurement movement found an unsteady footing in Catholic schools at this time. Not until the end of the period did Catholic education cease to be chagrined over analytic theories involving the irrationality of man, the sexuality of children, the role of the unconscious, and determinism, all having overtones of psychoanalytic thought, opposed somewhat to free will, and presenting a threat to Catholic concern over the dignity and non-materiality of man. As the period ended, Catholic theorists lessened their objections to the objective methodology, and introduced into Catholic schools such objective methods of observation as group testing and individual measurement. The rigidities of both schools of thought which had caused such a polarization of views relaxed, and both public and private schools worked overtime to fit their curricula into their philosophies and to keep such curricula geared to the swiftly-changing times.

Thorndike's psychology influenced greatly the curriculum of the public schools. Curti, who examined Thorndike's writings to discover their educational and social implications, made the following inference:

If there is no necessary transfer of learning and improvement, then there must be special training for special ends; obviously, the curriculum must be widened. If in training the intellect no subject is preferable to another, then a pragmatic or utilitarian value will determine which subjects shall make up the curriculum.

This, in effect, means more science, greater attention to the social studies, and support for technical, industrial, and household subjects.[75]

Indeed, continued Curti, the elementary and secondary school curricula took on a "utilitarian flavor." In this flavor the public school was more intensely saturated, because of the writings of Franklin Bobbitt, who from 1909 to his death in 1957 taught at the University of Chicago. His major books—*What Schools Teach and Might Teach* (1916), *The Curriculum* (1918), *How to Make a Curriculum* (1924), and *The Curriculum of Modern Education* (1941)[76]—influenced public school curriculum designers across the nation. For Bobbitt, "the good life is both the objective and the process" of education; moral education is training in group consciousness; and formal religion is approved only to the extent that it promotes "humanitarian vision." Obviously such an influence could not penetrate very deeply into the Catholic school pattern.

The curriculum of the public school of the period, so often referred to as the "activity program," was a logical outcome of the philosophies of William James and John Dewey, garnished with the psychology of Thorndike. James had asked American teachers to adopt with him the biological concept of man and to stress "the fact that man, whatever else he may be, is primarily a practical being, whose mind is given him to aid in adapting him to this world's life." Education became therefore "the organization of acquired habits of conduct and tendencies to behavior" [77] Thorndike, as we have seen, overemphasized the behavioristic view of man. Dewey gave a positivistic sociological turn to educational naturalism. He believed that the student "lives in, for, and by society." [78] The school must become a social institution, the classroom must be an active place, and learning must be by doing. Catholic educators saw the theological heresy in Dewey's theory—a denial of the whole concept of the supernatural—but they realized, too, that "every heresy is the revenge of a forgotten truth." [79]

Truth about the educative process lurked in the new activity curriculum. Leaders of Catholic educational thought prepared to seek that truth. Early in the period, Shields wrote of the school curriculum:

More and more educators are coming to realize that real education must be interpreted in terms of experience. The business of the curriculum, therefore, is chiefly to supply to the children the right kind of experience. . . . Education is not a mere knowing or remembering; it is preeminently a matter of doing.[80]

But the same author firmly declared that Catholics "cannot take over the curriculum or methods or ideals of the state schools into Catholic schools, for the simple reason that the ultimate aim of Catholic education is higher than that of the state schools." [81] To carry out an activity program in Catholic schools, to design a curriculum that would lend itself to doing, it was necessary to set up certain Catholic principles and guide-

lines. This task fell to Johnson of Catholic University. We have already
stated his five proximate goals of Christian education. These were fundamental for the activity curriculum he had in mind. Johnson realized that
many progressive educationists had gone too far in the name of activity,
exalting activity for activity's sake, but he looked at the organized curriculum of conservative schools and saw a dismal picture:

The daily program never changed, the curriculum consisted of formal subject
matter, logically arranged and determined by convention. In the offing loomed
the examination which all the children, regardless of individual differences had
to take, success in which depended on giving back to the teacher, as intact as
possible, the information which she and the textbook had conveyed.[82]

There was an evident tendency to neglect the social aspect of Catholic
education. The curricula had become crystallized and static, resisting
change. Child-nature was not recognized. Something had to be done to
provide Catholic schools with a balanced curriculum, adaptable to circumstances and times.

The Commission on American Citizenship in which Johnson played
an outstanding role as curriculum director was, as we have seen, set in
motion in 1938. But for more than twenty years before that time, Johnson
had made his own the problem of the Catholic school curriculum. The
elementary school curriculum, he had said in his doctoral dissertation,

should present such information concerning God, man and nature, and cultivate such knowledge, build up such habits, foster such attitudes, interests and
ideals, as will enable the child at the completion of his course to take his place
in life, a thorough Catholic and an efficient member of society, truly Christian
in his own individual character, able to maintain himself economically, realizing
his duties as a good citizen, prepared to make the proper use of the goods of
life.[83]

Johnson's influence on the Catholic elementary school curricula in the
United States since 1943 is incalculable. In that year his *Better Men for
Better Times* [84] was published, and it contained the principles for de-
signing the curriculum of a needed activity program in Catholic schools.
The child's basic relationships were to be kept in mind—with God and
the Church; toward his fellowman; with nature, an understanding of
which would help in the formation of a conscience concerning the
proper use of material things; and to self, which is actually an outcome
of his other relationships.[85] Starting from this base, the Commission on
American Citizenship set up a curriculum for Catholic elementary
schools. The objective of the curriculum was the direction of the school
program toward the growth of each child and was named *Guiding
Growth in Christian Social Living*.[86] It was organized into three volumes
—for the primary, intermediate, and upper grades respectively. It was
not intended to be a course of study but a directive, broad enough to
be a source from which detailed study courses might be drawn. It was

written for the teacher, for Johnson realized that a curriculum must come to life in a teacher's hand and bear fruit in the student's learning experiences. No hard and fast rules were set down, but helpful suggestions and hints to the teacher helped her function more efficiently in the classroom. Johnson valued the teacher over the curriculum. In 1924, he wrote:

The good teacher inspires while she instructs . . . practices virtue in meeting situations, solves the problem of classroom living. . . . By her preparation of material, by her encouragement and patience, by her reliance upon Divine help she will make the curriculum a true course of action by which the child may pursue the knowledge of truth and the practice of virtue in Christian social living.[87]

No subject in the elementary school has undergone more experimentation and aroused more debate than has reading. To evaluate the curriculum which the Commission established for Christian social living, therefore, it may be well to evaluate one of its effects—the *Faith and Freedom Series* readers.[88] Before their appearance in 1941, the authors of Catholic reading texts had made attempts to implement in the schools such teachings as the *Faith and Freedom Series* purposed to convey. Proof lies in a sampling of readers from each decade of the period. In 1917 and the early Twenties, Shields' *Catholic Education Series* [89] gave evidence that, for the author, reading was considered as an excellent way of deepening an understanding of Christ-like living, forming correct attitudes, strengthening the pupils' relationships with their fellow-men, molding citizens to live in a Christian democracy, and perfecting pupils' relationships with their Creator. The *De La Salle Fifth Reader* in 1929 declared that its purpose was to "inculcate Christian and Patriotic virtues." [90] In 1931, the *Cathedral Basic Readers* [91] first appeared. The *Teacher's Guide Book* for those readers stated that the "selections are grouped according to specific fields of interest such as Nature, Catholic Action, Citizenship, World Friendship and Industry." [92] In the 1940's and 1950's the *Faith and Freedom Series* readers swept the country. They claimed to present simultaneously the elements of Christian social living and all skills essential to successful reading instruction. The author of the primary readers in the series—Sister M. Marguerite, S.N.D. —said that the aim of all readers is "to bridge the gap which has existed for so long a time between the teaching of religious truths and their translation into life situations," and continued by explaining how the readers were compiled in order to attain their purpose:

The *Faith and Freedom Readers* are basic books set down in regular textbook form. The content of each book in the series has the common base of the love of God expressed through love of one's fellow men. The books are intended to instruct as well as to entertain, and each book in the series presents a new progression in the development of the social virtues motivated by faith and the imitation of Christ. The material of all the books centers around the social-religious life of the child in the home, the neighborhood, the local community, and the nation. It provides him not alone with interesting story situations similar to those which he meets in his own everyday experiences, but also with types of conduct most in harmony with the teaching of Faith and the ideals of Christian life.[93]

The idea of readers with religious and moral content was obviously not new, but these were the first readers to be such complete exponents of a social message based on religion, and this was the first time, too, that any series was so wholly absorbed into the elementary Catholic curricula of the United States.

Not only conservative policies, but financial strains, too, caused Catholic schools to lag behind public schools in their efforts to provide adequate curricula for the changing times. This was particularly true of the secondary schools, which were considerably slower in breaking away from traditional college-preparatory courses and in introducing courses intended for vocational training. By the 1930's, the need for change and broader curricular provisions in Catholic high schools was evident. Curriculum studies of that time in Catholic secondary education are revealing. Brother Francis de Sales O'Neil, F.S.C., made such a study in 1930 for the purpose of determining the practices which prevailed in 42 states with respect to the differentiation of curricula, the basic courses common to all curricula, and the specific courses most frequently offered in the Catholic high schools. He concluded that the "private schools are still purely academic in curricular offerings, and very conservative in introducing vocational subjects." [94] In 1931, John R. Rooney made a survey of Catholic high schools, drawing his conclusions from the data analyzed from 283 questionnaires representing schools in almost every state. He, too, claimed that "the greater part of our education continues to center upon the subjects generally referred to as cultural or disciplinary." [95] Twenty years later, in 1951, Edward F. Spiers researched the central Catholic high schools of the nation to determine their status. He gave schools the opportunity to identify their educational programs under one of the following titles: Comprehensive, Academic, Commercial, Technical, Agricultural, or Vocational. The label *Academic* was reserved for those schools which granted credit for only the so-called academic subjects. The term *Comprehensive* represented the schools which offered a choice to an unselected student body. Of 97 schools which classified their educational program, 71 offered a comprehensive curriculum. None of the schools classed themselves as Agricultural, Technical, Vocational, or Commercial. Some specialized training, however, was being offered by all the schools, except thirteen, in all or some of the following fields: business, home economics, fine arts, mechanical arts, woodwork, printing, electricity, and radio.[96]

In the field of business education, the textbooks used in Catholic schools were the same as those used in public schools. Sister Alexius Wagner, O.P., published a research study in 1949 in which she reviewed 150 business education textbooks on the market from 1918 to 1948. She noted a marked improvement from year to year in the general format of the books, type of material, objectives, and aids provided for teachers. She attributed the improvements to various factors: principally, she observed that book publishers were now willing to provide what teachers and administrators wanted, maintain educational research divisions, conduct surveys, and serve education through accurate, modern textbooks. She found the material relevant, timely, and updated.[97] In 1953, however, a text for business education was published for Catholic schools— *Encyclical Dictation* [98]—in which the author, Sister M. Therese, O.S.F., integrated shorthand with the study of the papal encyclicals *Divini Redemptoris* and *Quadragesimo Anno.* The objective of the text was excellence in shorthand, but it also presented one opportunity to penetrate the students' thinking with the mind of the Church in social matters.

Catholic high school educators, alerted by Johnson's achievements in the elementary field, kept pushing for a secondary curriculum keyed to social and individual needs. Brother Louis J. Faerber, S.M., of the University of Dayton, Ohio, spoke out fearlessly on the subject at the meeting of the NCEA in 1951. Some of his pointed questions were:

Are we guilty of catering too much to a program of instruction which prepared merely for college entrance regardless of the fact that "Christian foundation learnings" have values that far transcend college preparation?

Pupils have the right to gain that kind of education which best fits their needs. Do we provide for these rights? They have a right to preparation for marriage and family living. They have a right to an education which equips them with a degree of initial employability. They have a right to adequate guidance. Do we accord them these rights in the construction of the curriculum?

Do we show undue partiality to the white-collar aspects of education at the expense of the dignity of other forms of work, particularly the manual skills?

Are our marking system and policy of promotions within the curriculum geared to fair practices on the basis of the native capacities of our pupils? [99]

Catholic educators were realizing that the secondary level curriculum must, like the elementary program, emphasize man's "personal dignity, his immortal destiny, his relation to God, to his fellow man, and to material nature.[100]

The main purpose of Catholic education, however, has always been the complete formation of the entire individual. For more directly accomplishing this goal, in the area of catechetics from 1918 to 1957 there was reform, renewal, and improvement in content, method, and texts. The period opened, as we observed in the preceding chapter, with Pace and Shields of Catholic University attempting to bring the influence of modern psychological insights to catechetical instruction. The activity programs in the public schools, the emphasis on interest, and the learning-by-doing which affected the Catholic school curriculum left their influence, too, on the teaching of religion. In the last century, religious instruction had consisted primarily in impressing the truths of Christianity on the memory, after which the truths were explained. In the light of the new science of psychology, the teaching of religion was to be accomplished in terms of both the psychological and the academic—but this was a hard pull away from the past. Religious educators from 1918 to 1957 tried new and various ways to make the catechism interesting to the child. As the Rev. Stephen Aylward said in his *Cathechism Comes to Life:*

We have to pack our truth with interest to make the class *want* to dig in and understand it. We can explain it till *our* teeth drop out and *their* wisdom teeth come in, but if the children are not first interested they want no part of it. They may babble the facts and rattle off the correct answers but . . . it has no personal meaning to them and no spiritual application to the approaching battle of life, nor even to their daily lives.[101]

Aylward tried to practice what he preached in his book, which was "a practical method of vitalizing Catechism"[102] for teachers. Of other Catholic efforts to update catechetical instruction during the period, only examples can be cited; a detailed study of the topic would fill a volume in itself.

In 1929, the Rev. Rudolph G. Bandas, then professor of dogmatic theology, St. Paul Seminary, and of catechetics, Diocesan Normal School, both of St. Paul, Minnesota, attacked the defects in current methods of teaching religion. He emphasized the need of vital catechetical instruction. Using a historical approach, he showed that in century after century new methods had been adapted to meet new conditions, while the aim—the teaching of the most vital and most basic truths of the Catholic faith—remained the same. He insisted that the catechism, the Bible, Church history, and liturgy be closely correlated. Overemphasis on memory was to be discarded:

The abstract statements of the Catechism are the conclusions of a whole reasoning process, formulas deduced from a host of concrete facts. To attempt to teach them to the child, without supplying the concrete facts on which they are based, is to go counter to all laws of psychology.[103]

Bandas was heard from again on the same subject. In 1935, he wrote *Catechetics in the New Testament;* in 1937, *Modern Problems in the Light of Christian Principles: A Manual for Classes, Study Clubs, and Open Forums of College and University Students;* and in 1957, *Catechetical and Confraternity Methods.*[104]

In the late 1920's, the liturgical movement came to America from Europe, largely under the influence of Virgil Michel, O.S.B., of St. John's Abbey, Collegeville, Minnesota, who was nationally recognized as a "leader in social-liturgical thought." [105] He tried to give a knowledge of the liturgy to teachers, who in turn could train children to be open to the liturgy in their religious formation. He implemented his teachings with a series of texts graded for elementary schools—*The Christ Life Series*.[106] The series focused on Christ as their center and were founded on the Bible. From this series evolved *The Christian Religion Series*,[107] to be used in high school and colleges.

The Rev. Joseph J. Baierl of St. Bernard's Seminary, Rochester, New York, brought the Munich Method to the United States, explaining it first in 1919 in *The Creed Explained*.[108] The book embodied an explanation of the Creed according to the Munich Method. Baierl followed this volume by another in 1922, *The Sacraments Explained*, and yet another, *The Commandments Explained*,[109] in 1934—all based on the Munich Method. This method—a psychological one—had originated in Germany at the beginning of the present century with the Society of Catechists of Munich. Actually, it applied to the teaching of religion the principles developed by Johann Friedrich Herbart and developed by Tuiskon Ziller at Leipzig.[110] Baierl wrote:

It [the Munich Method] demands in the first place, that each lesson shall constitute a *catechetical unit*, namely coordination of the essentially related questions and answers, and such as can be brought under the light of a single story or illustration. In the second place, that the several stages of the learning process be pursued. There are three: presentation, explanation, application. In the third place, that the three adjunct, though non-essential, stages be utilized; namely, preparation, aim, synthesis. The children are first *prepared* by connecting the question with the actual contents of their minds (apperception). In the second place, the teacher announces the *aim* he has in view. This in the third place, is illustrated by a story. The various points of the story in their bearing on the aim are then *explained*. These several points are next summed up in a *synthesis*. Lastly, the application is made to the child's actual life and conduct. Such is the method in a nutshell.[111]

But the Munich Method did not satisfy. Religious educators felt that religious instruction in the schools and colleges still lacked vitality and was far from fulfilling its real function as the heart of the curriculum. The Rev. Gerard S. Sloyan in *Speaking of Religious Education* observed in 1968:

It is instructive to read the treatment of the teaching of religion . . . between 1900 and 1950. Considerable attention was paid to it in National Catholic Education Association *Proceedings*, the *Journal of Religious Instruction* (later *The Christian*), and *The Catholic School Journal*. The literature was largely given to deploring the situation, but it did not have many solid proposals to offer.[112]

Then Sloyan recorded a turning point. A new era in catechetics began. Sloyan wrote:

When Johannes Hofinger of Manila began to appear in . . . [*The Catholic School Journal*] and in *Worship* in the mid-fifties, even the most casual reader could tell that this was something new. The introduction of the notion of the primitive *kerygma* as central, basically the work of Bultmann, Barth, and Dodd though popularized in German-language Catholic circles by Jungmann and others, came as a fresh breeze. The entire project of religious education entered upon a decade of biblical and theological concern after years of attempted, impossible marriage between the religion of standard catechisms and the "Munich Method" with its Herbartian steps.[113]

Sloyan elsewhere named those with whom catechetics moved forward in the United States during this period:

U. S. catechetical progress between 1930 and 1950 is associated chiefly with the names of R. G. Bandas, J. B. Collins, Sr. M. Rosalia Walsh, M. I. Schumacher, W. H. Russell, W. Farrell and Abp. E. V. O'Hara of Kansas City, Mo. (protagonist of the Confraternity of Christian Doctrine and religious vacation school movement).[114]

Sloyan's statement, however, that Catholic literature of the period "was largely given to deploring the situation, but [that] it did not have many solid proposals to offer"[115] can be argued. Proposals were made which were considered solid at the time. In this regard the attempts at revision of the Baltimore Catechism, to fashion it to the learning capacities of the elementary-level child, should not be overlooked. In 1935, definite action toward the preparation of a revision of the Catechism was taken by the hierarchy through an Episcopal Committee on Confraternity of Christian Doctrine. The Rev. Francis J. Connell, C.SS.R., explained the revision plans in detail at the Thirty-seventh Annual Meeting of the NCEA when he said:

From the very beginning every effort was made to secure the collaboration of as many competent persons as possible. Every bishop and every major religious superior, and also certain other individuals of recognized abilities, received a set of thirty-seven large work-sheets; one for each lesson of the Catechism. . . . Only Catechism number 2 was considered, the plan being to put off until later the work of preparing a shorter text for younger children and a more extended text for older boys and girls.[116]

Connell told of the grounds of complaint against the Baltimore Catechism: it contained some theological inaccuracies, had a too difficult phraseology for an elementary school child, and omitted some important truths. He concluded with an observation that is important for all times: it is the *teacher* rather than any catechism text that is the main factor in the religious instruction of children. "The catechism," said Connell, "is intended to provide only a framework of religious training; the building up must be done by those appointed to impart Christian doctrine to Christ's little ones."

In 1941, *A Catechism of Christian Doctrine, Revised Edition of the Baltimore Catechism No. 2* was published under the auspices of the Confraternity of Christian Doctrine.[117] In 1942, the Rev. Michael Mc-

Guire issued *The New Baltimore Catechism No. 1* for younger children.[118] The following year, 1943, saw the publication of Connell's *The New Baltimore Catechism No. 3*, which was "intended primarily for Catholic children in the upper grades of elementary schools and the first two grades of high schools." The author tried to fit the learnings of the text to life situations. He wrote in the Preface:

Above all, both in the text and in the exercises, the special needs of the times in which we live have been taken into account. The objections read in modern literature or heard in modern secular classrooms are answered; the moral problems that confront the people of today are given express and detailed treatment.[119]

In the mid-Forties the teaching of religion turned more and more to the early Christian catechetical narrative-historical approach, and made religion for both adults and children Christ-centered. Religious leaders were concerned that students be inspired towards an encounter with Christ and to commitment resulting in apostolic action. Texts developed a new format, an example of which was the *Our Quest for Happiness*[120] series. These high school texts sought a harmonious unity of doctrine and precept instead of the traditional division between dogma and morals, were centered in Christ, and were saturated with the Bible and the liturgy. They contained eye-catching illustrations, suggested uses for supplementary audio-visual materials, and presented questions for discussion and thought. Their kerygmatic principles led them to return to the core of the Christian message as proclaimed by the Apostles, so that in revealed doctrine they descended from God through Christ and His Church to divine life through the Sacraments; then they attempted to lead the students to an ascent to God through love. The aim of these texts was not solely knowledge of religion, but the formation of Catholic youth to live personally close to Christ in all their relations at home, in school, and with their neighbors. The central theme running through the four volumes was "God is Love,"[121] and it attempted to show the students that their happiness lay in the spreading of that love to others. All four texts gave particular treatment to human rights in both their individual and social aspects; this treatment culminated in the final year, when all of the implications of human rights were considered under the virtue which binds them all together—viz., justice.[122]

On the college level, Monsignor John M. Cooper of Catholic University, founder of that university's Department of Religious Education in 1936, made a major contribution to updating the teaching of religion. Cooper wrote *Religious Outlines for Colleges*,[123] texts which attempted to make theology intelligible to the college mentality, and were as Sloyan says "a challenge to the 19th century type of Manuals in use."[124] In 1924 Cooper published a slim volume entitled *The Content of the Ad-*

*vanced Religion Course*,[125] the five chapters of which had been published originally in *The Catholic Educational Review* in 1923.[126] The chapters dealt with the moral, dogmatic, historical, apologetic, and ascetic content of the advanced religion course, and each chapter suggested needed reform in textbooks. The ideas contained in this work fit the sixth decade of the twentieth century as well as the second, so far was Cooper ahead of his time. Of moral content in texts, for example, he wrote:

Ninety-five to ninety-nine per cent of the student body in Catholic high schools and colleges for boys and one hundred per cent in those for girls will never become confessors or sacerdotal spiritual advisers. They will live their span of life as laymen and lay women in the world. Obviously our moral education and moral textbooks should aim at equipping them, not for hearing confessions, but for living in the world.[127]

For the teaching of historical content, Cooper suggested what was at that time a novel idea, namely that of treating "each topic in reverse chronological order," feeling strongly that it is "better to begin with the present and work back [and to] begin also with the near-at-hand and work out." Such leaders as Cooper and the others mentioned above testify that the period gave an impetus to a reform movement in the teaching of religion that has grown and not yet ended.

### TEACHERS

The training of the lay and the religious teacher in the Catholic school of any given time must be judged in the light of the general training of teachers of that same time. In 1899 it had been reported in the NEA *Journal* that 75 per cent of the teachers in this country had been entering upon their work without any special training whatsoever and that the training of much of the remainder had been much less extensive and less satisfactory than that required for any other profession.[128] Of this lack of professionalization, Sister Maria Concepta McDermott in *The Making of a Sister-Teacher* remarked:

In the year 1903 to 1904, 499 private high schools and 272 public high schools offered some course of instruction for future teachers. Actually the number of trained teachers in the state was very small because it was easy to enter teaching, and in most states to do so without the necessity of any training. If we average all the states of the union, we find 15 to 20% of teachers in the public school had received some training. The remaining 80 to 85% had been prepared by private study, tested wholly by examination and experience, and had no professional preparation at the time.[129]

Sister Bertrande Meyers in *The Education of Sisters* also commented on this low status of teacher preparation before World War I. She observed that

although state normals began in 1839, most of the teachers up to 1900 were admitted to the teaching field through county or state examinations in which political influence often counted for more than intellectual endowment.[130]

The public school teacher had been poorly paid—the work had neither offered the opportunity nor provided the conditions of a real career.[131] The training of the religious teachers in the Catholic schools had consisted for the most part of an in-service training, as we observed in the preceding chapter, under the guidance of the more advanced members of the religious community. On the whole, before World War I the professional preparation of Catholic school teachers had compared not unfavorably with that of public school teachers. Indeed, it may well be argued that the religious had held the favored position. Community living offered daily opportunities for exchanges of classroom experiences, advice on educational matters, and the total enrichment of a teacher's general fund of knowledge.

After World War I, a new era in teacher education began in the United States. The economic boom meant higher teacher salaries. Higher salaries meant a rise in the standards of admission to the teaching profession. Compulsory education laws sent more children into the classrooms. Better teachers were needed. Meyers noted the states' awakening to the situation when she observed that "the creation of state departments of education to judge and pass on teacher-efficiency, new emphasis on inspection of schools and supervision of instruction, combined to strengthen the forces at work for the improvement and elevation of standards." [132] Religious communities, with little funds to pay for normal school or college courses, set out on an uphill struggle to obtain certification for as many of their members as possible, and to secure accreditation for their high schools.

In 1925, the Rev. Edward Jordan of Catholic University, speaking at the Annual Meeting of the NCEA, gave an over-all view of teacher requirements at that time:

We are apparently all agreed that the minimum requirement for a teacher in the elementary school should be the completion of a good normal course after graduation from an accredited high school. For secondary teachers we consider graduation from a standard college essential; and for a college teacher at least a year of university is desirable.[133]

Two years later, in 1927, Sylvester Schmitz, A.M., under the direction of George Johnson of the same university, completed a study of the professional standing of Catholic sister-teachers and public school teachers in the United States. Schmitz used two years of advanced training beyond the secondary school stage as a criterion of adequate preparation for teaching in the elementary school (the commonly accepted standard at that time). His findings showed that 57.2 per cent of the sisters as compared with 50.6 per cent of the public school teachers measured up to the standard of minimal preparation. Statistically, Schmitz showed that if all the advanced training which the sisters had had were evenly distributed among all the sisters employed in the Catholic schools, this amount would be expressed by a single index number of 1.6 years of advanced training per sister. The corresponding number for public school teachers was 1.3 years of advanced training per teacher. The sister-teachers in the high schools made an even better showing. The findings revealed that 75 per cent of the sisters, as compared with only 66 per cent of the teachers in the public high schools, had had four years of college training. Schmitz took time in this highly statistical study to make the following significant comment:

It should be remembered that this statistical procedure does not do justice to many Religious teachers when attempting to estimate their professional standing. Many of these teachers in service for a quarter of a century received their training before the credit system of estimating amounts of work was extensively employed in Catholic institutions. . . . Furthermore, it should not be forgotten that teaching is not a stepping stone to a life career in the case of a Religious teacher. Teaching is her life work. Not financial remuneration, but the most noble and sublime of ideals and spiritual values are the dynamic, motivating principle underlying her professional work. Her study, reading and experience, continually improve her professional preparedness for the job of teaching. The amount of this improvement cannot be measured by any educational yardstick.[134]

Schmitz recommended pre-service training of religious teachers, although he realized that the Catholic teacher shortage would still demand in-service training. In the twentieth century many summer schools, Saturday classes, and extension courses of various kinds had been initiated to improve the professional status of Catholic-school teachers, and they had done much. The first evidences of in-service training had been in 1905 at such places as Cathedral College, New York City, where late afternoon classes were held for teaching communities serving the New York schools, and summer institutes held in Portland, Oregon, which had begun about the same time.[135] The movement grew. By 1921 the National Catholic Welfare Conference listed summer schools in Little Rock, Arkansas; San Francisco; Sisters College at Catholic University; three schools in Chicago; Notre Dame; Columbia College, Dubuque, Iowa; St. Benedict's in Atchison, Kansas; Loyola of New Orleans; Boston College; St. Louis University; Creighton University in Omaha, Nebraska; St. John's, Fordham, and Canisius in New York; Marquette, Villanova, and Duquesne in Pennsylvania; and in Ohio, St. Xavier's College in Cincinnati, St. John's University in Toledo, and the University of Dayton.[136] These colleges and universities opened their courses to teaching sisters, offering credits towards degrees.

The 1920's saw the steady development of Catholic teacher training under diocesan auspices. The Rev. Francis J. Macelwane, diocesan superintendent of schools of Toledo, Ohio, read a paper entitled "A

Diocesan Normal School" at the Meeting of the Catholic Educational Association in 1924.[137] Macelwane had organized Teachers' College of St. John's University, diocesan normal school of the diocese of Toledo, just two years before. Shortly after this, in 1928, his state of Ohio took the lead in this area. The files of the Athenaeum of Ohio, now located in the office of the superintendent of schools in Cincinnati, contain the following information:

In the winter of 1928 new requirements for certification of teachers were put into effect by the State Department of Education of Ohio, effective in September of the same year. The nature of these requirements made it advisable to coordinate all teacher training needs of the diocesan elementary and high schools under the policy of expansion inaugurated.

The state of Ohio made the unique proposition that, if in each of the four dioceses then in the state the small teacher-training schools would consolidate into one institution, the state would recognize this as the official teacher-training institution for that diocese, thus also entitling graduates to state certification. For the diocese of Toledo, the institution so designated was De Sales College; for the diocese of Columbus, St. Mary of the Springs; for the diocese of Cleveland, Sisters' College; and for the archdiocese of Cincinnati, Teachers' College under the supervision of the Athenaeum, whose purpose was "the final control, direction and supervision of all colleges, seminaries, academies, and institutions of higher learning in the Archdiocese of Cincinnati." At about the same time, the diocese of Brooklyn, N.Y., under the direction of Rt. Rev. Msgr. Joseph V. S. McClancy, inaugurated a program of diocesan normal training for its Catholic teachers.[138] When the diocesan superintendent of schools at Wichita, Kansas, addressed the NCEA in 1930 on "The Diocesan Normal School," he spoke of the definite steps taken to provide facilities for such training in many dioceses, and he mentioned that

school authorities . . . assumed varying degrees of control over Catholic teacher training, and endeavored to make available for the teachers of their respective systems the most liberal educational facilities possible under the circumstances.[139]

By 1930 most religious communities were anxiously seeking degrees for their teachers through secular colleges, Catholic colleges, diocesan institutions, extension courses, Saturday classes, and summer school sessions. The credit craze had begun.[140] The Catholic teachers' level of preparation moved upward.[141] They were well on their way from evangelism to professionalism.

After 1920, the year of the first biennial survey of the National Catholic Welfare Conference Department of Education, teachers in Catholic schools in the United States had increased in midcentury by 61,778 in number, or 113.8 per cent. Lay Catholic school teachers in 1950 numbered 20,075 out of a faculty total of 116,043,[142] and were definitely on

the increase: NCWC's school survey at the end of this period showed
49,648 lay teachers out of a total of 171,181 teachers in all classes
of Catholic educational institutions.[143] The lay teacher's role in Catholic education improved. Before World War II, he/she was relegated to
the position of a substitute, accepted only because there were not
enough religious teaching. As soon as it was at all possible such teachers
were replaced by sisters or brothers. This situation was due mainly to
financial reasons. Catholics, forced to build and maintain their own
schools, and at the same time pay taxes for the support of the public
school system, were unable to pay sufficient salaries to lay teachers. But
because of zeal for the cause of Catholic education, lay teachers continued to move into Catholic schools during this period. Sister Marie
Theresa, S.C., supervisor of schools for the Sisters of Charity, Mt. St.
Vincent, New York, in 1953 commented on the lay teacher situation in
Catholic schools from 1920 to 1940. "We offered them," she said, "a
bare pittance for salary, no tenure, no advancement, and no security.
Fabulous salaries of some fifty or sixty dollars a month were their
compensation!" [144] By this time (1953), lay teacher participation was
recognized as a necessary factor in Catholic education in the United
States. Salaries were still a problem, and Sister Marie Theresa, speaking
of the current situation, said:

It would seem, however, that our salary scale has not grown apace with our
professional requirements. Many young teachers today are forced to seek employment of a non-professional or a semi-professional nature after school hours
and on Saturdays to implement the meager salaries we offer them for teaching
services in our schools. If we expect professional status in our lay teachers, we
must, in justice, pay them a living wage. Five or seven dollars a day, which is
considered in some, if not in most, areas a good salary for the lay teacher, is
not a fair, much less a living, wage.[145]

By the end of the period, the lay teacher's religious coworkers felt that
he should have social security and "also the security which comes from
wholehearted acceptance by every member of the staff." [146] In 1948,
Monsignor Carl J. Ryan, then superintendent of schools in the archdiocese of Cincinnati, made a case for the lay teacher in *The Homiletic
and Pastoral Review*. He stressed the many contributions made by such
teachers to Catholic education. Lay teachers, he claimed, "bridge the
gap between life in the community at large and what goes on in the
school"; in high school, they are "prepared to present adequately the
problems of the work-a-day world"; and since they live among the school
graduates they are "in an advantageous position to measure the results
of Catholic education." [147] Ryan emphasized the fact that the good
Catholic lay teacher made a tremendous contribution to the character
formation of pupils in Catholic schools. He observed that "pupils take
for granted moral goodness and practical Catholic living on the part of
their Religious teachers. But when they see this in the lay teacher, it

strikes them just a bit differently." [148] Ryan believed that the lay teacher had a definite place in the field of Catholic education and made his own special contribution. He wrote:

I am quite convinced that our Catholic schools will never attain their goal of turning out Catholic men and women fully equipped to meet their religious, social, and civic obligations in these United States until we have a liberal supply of lay teachers on all levels of Catholic education from the elementary school to the university.[149]

It may well be said that during the period from 1918 to 1957 the Catholic lay teacher came into his own. Pius XI reflected the mind of the Church on the matter when he said:

Indeed it fills Our soul with consolation and gratitude towards the divine Goodness to see, side by side with Religious men and women engaged in teaching, such a large number of excellent lay teachers, who, for their greater spiritual advancement, are often grouped in special sodalities and associations, which are worthy of praise and encouragement as most excellent and powerful auxiliaries of "Catholic Action." [150]

Assisting specifically teaching religious women in preparing themselves better for their role of teaching was the Sister-Formation Movement. The expression "sister-formation" means, according to Sister Mary Emil I.H.M., first chairman of the National Sister-Formation Committee, writing in 1954, "the integral and integrated training of the Sister-teacher, nurse, or social worker." [151] Better religious and better professional people are its aim—a combination of spiritual and intellectual training. At the Annual Meeting of the NCEA in 1956, Sister Mary Emil explained further that the expression "was chosen to stand not only for the education of the Sister in a formal and academic sense, but for all the influences, spiritual and intellectual, formal and informal, preservice and inservice, which go to make her [the Sister] a better religious and a better professional person." [152] It is a matter of a climate of opinion of religious communities contributing all they can to the cause—of generous collaboration on the part of all those engaged in sister-formation—by which help the sister-teacher strives to satisfy her obligations in justice to her students and to do credit to Catholic education.

Sister-formation was initiated as a movement, although not under that name, at the NCEA Convention in Kansas City in 1952. It began with a panel in the Teacher Education Section on the advice of Pope Pius XII to teaching sisters.[154] In 1951, the Holy Father, speaking to school sisters, declared:

Many of your schools are being described and praised to Us as being very good. But not all. It is Our fervent wish that all endeavor to become excellent. This presupposes that your teaching Sisters are masters of the subjects they expound. See to it, therefore, that they are well trained and that their education corresponds in quality and academic degrees to that demanded by the State.[155]

The NCEA, concerned with implementation of the Holy Father's advice, made a survey of sister education, completed in 1952 and discussed through 1953. As a response to the problems pointed up in this survey, there were organized the Sister-Formation Conferences. These Conferences—two-day gatherings—were to be held in each of the six NCEA geographical regions where higher superiors, representing the administration and formation staff, met to exchange ideas.[156] The first Conferences were held in 1954-1955. "In the first year," said Sister Mary Emil, "some 246 religious communities participated, and some 170 general and provincial superiors." [157] On these first meetings, Sister Mary Emil summarized:

Speakers and Sister participants were pretty much of a mind that loyalty to the Holy Father and response to the needs of our times required that every community, in its own way and at best rate consistent with its own situation and problems, should strive for the bachelor's degree as a minimum educational training for a Sister, and for a juniorate to provide for spiritual formation continued after the novitiate.[158]

And Sister Mary Emil continued to bring the doings of the SFC (Sister-Formation Conference) up to date:

[The] SFC for next year [1957] will concern itself with an actual curriculum, or a series of curricular patterns, in an attempt to translate the ideals of integration at least into a program of studies. In order to do this, we have obtained a grant of $50,000 from the Fund for the Advancement of Education, which has enabled three of us to study best practices and felt needs in the Sister education programs of the United States and Europe. This research will be followed, next summer, by a workshop in which a group of fifteen Sisters from various communities and regions, and with eminence in their academic fields, will spend three months in planning curricular objectives and specifics for the education of sisters, as sisters.[159]

The fifteen Sister-educators took part in the SFC curriculum-construction project during a three-month workshop in Everett, Wash., from June 1 to August 31, 1956. A report of the workshop was distributed to motherhouses in October. Immediately it became the educational Bible in sister education, not only in the United States, but in many foreign countries as well. Among the important features of an ideal sister-education proposed at Everett were special sequences in philosophy and theology; a substantial base of liberal education comprising courses in the humanities, the social sciences, and the natural sciences; professional education built on this liberal block; provision for some specialization or concentration in one or more fields; a co-curricular program of planned and directed experiences strengthening art, music, speech and drama, literature, foreign languages, and physical education; contemporaneity (the need for sisters to be informed about today's world); and planning through the fifth year and thereafter, since the education of sisters continues throughout life.[160]

Roman Catholic teachers of the period were motivated to seek a higher level of professional training and experience, not only because of the improvements in public teacher-education and the standards set up by accrediting agencies and city and state educational authorities, but particularly by the exhortations of Popes Pius XI and Pius XII on that subject. Pius XI stressed the importance of the qualified teacher when he said that "perfect schools are the result not so much of good methods as of good teachers, teachers who are thoroughly prepared and well-grounded in the matter they have to teach." [161] Pius XII, as we have seen, gave the spur to the Sister-Formation Movement by his demand that the education of the sister-teacher correspond "in quality and academic degrees to that demanded by the State." [162] Assisting in the work were the Revs. Michael J. McKeough, O.Praem., and Joseph A. Gorham, both of whom joined Catholic University's staff in 1945. McKeough was a very powerful force on the secondary level, highly respected, and a strong advocate of regional accreditation. Gorham, to his untimely death in 1967, helped train many superintendents and other administrators, was instrumental in bringing school administration into the realm of the respected professional, and was highly regarded by his countless students from all over the country.

As with most areas of Catholic education, not everyone was in agreement with the current attempts at upgrading teachers. Many of the larger communities which attempted to implement Sister-formation wound up in heartache. Many other religious communities rejected it entirely—encouraged in this by John Cardinal O'Hara of Philadelphia. O'Hara was rather unique in some of his educational concepts: his lectures on the subject often emphasized quantity over quality; in a laudable attempt to have every child in his diocese in a Catholic school, he was responsible for some elementary school classes that ran as high as 100 or more children; he built many coinstitutional high schools; and his massive school building programs (at times without plans for staffing) caused severe strain to the two dioceses in which he served as bishop, Buffalo and Philadelphia. On the more positive side, he was the first to open to the public his usage of funds. In the present connection, he feuded with NCEA over Sister-formation, genuinely believing—not without reason—that one did not require a college training to be a good teacher. Indeed, research points to the difficulty of defining just what constitutes a good teacher.

## STUDENTS

The public schools of the time interpreted child nature in the light of Rousseau's naturalism, and utilized psychologies of childhood which either neglected or denied the spiritual aspect of man's nature. Pius XI firmly declared that the student—"the subject of Christian education" —is to be considered as "man whole and entire, soul united to body in unity of nature," [163] and that all education must be directed to the development of that dual nature in the educand. The Holy Father forcefully condemned the philosophy of naturalism applied to education, stating that "every form of pedagogic naturalism which in any way excludes or overlooks supernatural Christian formation in the teaching of youth is false." [164] He pointed out the Catholic school's obligation to guide the child and not to allow him to flounder in the morass of his own interests, and warned all concerned with the Christian education of the student against false educational theories which

appeal to a pretended self-government and unrestrained freedom on the part of the child, and which diminish or even suppress the teacher's authority and action, attributing to the child an exclusive primacy of initiative, and an activity independent of any higher law, natural or divine, in the work of his education.[165]

Psychology—child psychology, educational psychology, and social psychology—dominated the field of American education during this period. The child was given new consideration. As early as 1895, the NEA's Committee of Fifteen had reported that "modern education emphasizes the opinion that the child, not the subject of study, is the guide to the teacher's efforts. To know the child is of paramount importance." [166] No longer was the child to be fitted to the school, but in accordance with the views of G. Stanley Hall the school was to be fitted to the child. "Thus," says Cremin, "did Hall build upon the laissez-faire pedagogy first advanced in *Emile* the idea of a child-centered school whose curriculum would be tailored to a larger view of the nature, growth, and development of children." [167] The science of child psychology was enabled to reach a high point of development during the years 1918-1957 because the spadework had been done in the eighteenth, nineteenth, and early twentieth centuries. Rousseau in 1762 had advocated that free expression be given to the child's native abilities and interests; [168] Pestalozzi in the eighteenth century had kept the first scientific record of child development; [169] and Froebel had written of early child training in his *Education of Man* in 1826.[170] The credit for introducing the experimental approach to child study, however, goes to G. Stanley Hall of Clark University at Worcester, Massachusetts.[171] Hall's publications of *Contents of Children's Minds on Entering School* [172] in 1893, and the two huge volumes called *Adolescence: Its Psychology, and Its Relations to Physiology, Anthropology, Sociology, Sex, Crime, Religion, and Education* [173] of 1904 had a tremendous vogue.

Child-study organizations and periodicals multiplied. The child had to be observed, studied, and reported. At Hall's suggestion, for example, the Worcester State Normal School collected 35,000 records of observations on school children, all taken under carefully prescribed conditions. "James and Dewey," says Edwin G. Boring, "gave educational psychology [in America] its philosophical sanction, but Hall's compelling dynamism was what got it started." [174] In a study of the student of the twentieth century one cannot disregard Hall's influence. Dewey, whose name must be forever linked with use, experiment, and innovation, by this very pragmatism gave America a system of functional psychology. For Dewey's vision of American education such a system formed the right background for educational psychology, since it freed "the psychologist to study both what is useful to society and what is useful to the individual organism." [175]

The student must be measured and assessed—his memory, imagination, motor skill, personality, intelligence, attention, comprehension, esthetic appreciation, achievement in school subjects, and, indeed, all his human faculties. For students of the period it was a testing time, and the laboratory was a going concern. The new psychological movement had some very bright spots to recommend it. Before the twentieth century, education had been something that was "done" to the student. No one had bothered much about him in himself. There had been talk about teachers, courses of studies, textbooks, and school buildings—but hardly any about the student, unless he proved a stumbling block to the smooth operation of the school and was considered in that phase of education called discipline. Suddenly, educators were very much concerned about the student's patterns of development. Behaviorists believed that they could fashion the young animal into anything they wished. Even as late as 1952, the editor of *The Catholic School Journal* wrote that the student was the "forgotten man" in education, and that it was "imperative to examine anew the whole educational process from the standpoint of the student." [176] Nevertheless, the psychological movement was focusing on youth, and it showed up both the public and private schools' neglect and regimentation of their students. In 1921, Shields of Catholic University wrote of the good that pupils would derive from the "growing knowledge of genetic psychology." Happy in the new understanding gained in the area of child nature, Shields continued:

From the advances in this field thus far made, the conviction is reached that education does not consist in loading the memory with details nor in forcing the pupils to learn things that are devoid of interest. On the side of affective consciousness, the conviction is gaining ground that moral training should not be given by prohibitions that, too infrequently, suggest wrongdoing so much as by the positive teaching of what is right, reinforced by attractive concrete examples.[177]

Shields was quick to mark Hall's philosophy "in sharp contrast to that maintained by the Catholic Church," but he was just as quick to note the agreements which they held regarding the student: "It is the business of education to adjust the child to earthly environments, to the social institutions in which he must act his part." [178] Then, according to Shields, the student would be more worthy of membership in the Church.

But shadows lurked in the picture. The new psychology saw masses of students—statistics denied the individual case. Fatal to cultural studies, the new movement pushed history from the classroom. Students lost respect for the true values of life (and perhaps some present campus conflicts may stem from neglect of the teaching of such values). Some public educators, too, such as Willard S. Elsbree, professor of education at Teachers College, Columbia University, wrote of the "need for consideration of the whole child"; [179] for him, physical, mental, emotional, and social growth were essential to wholesome development. In the formation of his "whole child," spiritual growth was ignored. The student's aim was social efficiency and, in the final analysis, the student himself did not count for much. Society mattered. He must contribute to its well-being. He must be civic-minded. Life-adjustment programs were part of the student's course of studies. Vocational and education-for-life information was presented to the pupils through clubs, interviews, group conferences, civic organizations, classes in occupation, visits to industries, school publications, and classroom radio programs. An "activities period" was part of the regular daily schedule of the school. The words of three public educators of the period gave a rationale for the emphasis on student activity:

It is in this participation that a pupil matures his attitudes toward people and things, develops his ability to solve interesting problems and to make many adjustments, social and otherwise. In this laboratory of "play" a pupil learns to face many realities of life the significance of which he does not catch in formal courses of study. . . . There is virtue in activity. Civilized society aspires to constructive activity. . . . Initiative is encouraged on every hand so long as it seems to contribute to the recognized objectives of the group.[180]

Catholic students, too, were activity-students. It was the trend of the times. Great Catholic educators like Johnson, as we observed above, succeeded in channeling activity programs into Christian sources, and the Catholic student was to make the school "a training ground for virtue." [181]

The core of a Catholic philosophy of education is the dignity and worth of the individual person. The Catholic educator sees the child as a creature of God, made in His image and likeness; therefore, no student may be overlooked. For the exceptional child, the Rev. Stephen J. Landherr, C.SS.R., bespoke Catholic interest in 1942. He mentioned eleven Catholic schools for the deaf out of a total of 206 in the country. Optimistically, he mentioned that it had been a French priest, Abbé Charles Michel de L'Epée (1712-98), who standardized the sign language, and he wrote "I know of no other religious denomination that has even half a dozen schools in this country"; [182] but he realistically added that there was much more to be done. He indicated that the same could be said, *mutatis mutandis*, about the blind. A Catholic, Valentin Hauy (1745-1822), had begun the movement establishing educational institutions and industrial training schools for the blind, and another Catholic, Louis Braille (1809-52), had originated the raised printing for the blind that still bears his name—but much remained undone. The Rev. William F. Jenks, C.SS.R., assistant secretary of the Special Education Department of the NCEA, spoke, at that organization's Annual Meeting in 1955, on the implementation of Catholic philosophy in the area of special education:

Every child has a democratic and Christian right to an education commensurate with his ability to learn. The principle of equal educational opportunity is violated when we proceed upon the theory that we need not worry about the bright child and cannot do anything for the mentally retarded child.[183]

Catholic educators had attempted to help the exceptional child in the past. Pioneering attempts had been small due to lack of financial resources and trained personnel, but by mid-century the movement gained momentum. In 1954, the NCEA established a Department of Special Education. Whereas before that date certain sections of NCEA were concerned with the education of the deaf and blind, after that time all areas were coordinated into one department. Individual differences had been highlighted with the advent of psychology as a science, and exceptional children received more attention from public and Catholic school educators than ever before.

The Rev. Elmer H. Behrmann, director of special education of the archdiocese of St. Louis, Missouri, read statistics concerning exceptional children before the NCEA in 1954:

National statistics show that an estimated 12.4% of all children between the ages of 5 and 19 are atypical, or approximately 4,166,896. Of this estimated total there are only about 11.0% or 441,820 exceptional children under training in day or residential special schools or classes in the United States.

Applying these statistics to the number of Catholic children in private and parochial elementary and high schools in 1953 amounting to 3,501,500, we reach the rather startling total of 434,186 Catholic children needing special education, if they are to have opportunities of training and educational growth commensurate with their native abilities or levels of achievement.[184]

This 1951 survey provided statistics relative to Catholic facilities for such children, showing that there were then only fifteen schools for the mentally handicapped, four schools for the blind, ten schools for the deaf, and five schools for crippled children. But even in the short span of three years much had been accomplished, and Behrmann could add that

since 1951 additional Catholic facilities for handicapped children, both private and diocesan, have come into being, including special day and residential classes for mentally retarded children, special classes for partially sighted children, classes for the cerebral palsied child, remedial reading clinics, and child guidance centers.[185]

The Special Education Movement in Catholic educational circles received an uplift and the encouragement to move forward at the first Workshop on Special Education of the Exceptional Child sponsored by Catholic University in June 1952. The workshop aimed to show the great need for special classes in Catholic schools; to provide specialized training in a Catholic atmosphere for Catholic educators, and a religious training in special classes for atypical children; to explain and demonstrate the latest methods of educating the exceptional child; and to urge Catholic educators to start now and obtain normal results in educating the exceptional child, as they had obtained exceptional results in educating the normal child.[186]

As regards Negroes, they continued to constitute but a small percentage of the United States Catholic population. The 1940's saw about 45,000 Negro students in Catholic schools.[187] Especially through the work of the Josephite Fathers and Mother Katherine Drexel's Sisters of the Blessed Sacrament, the Negro was assimilated into the Catholic educational system. The majority of the elementary and high schools were, as might be expected, in the South. In the North, except for large centers of Negro population, there was no need for schools for black students, as they were beginning to be enrolled without discrimination in the diocesan school system.[188]

Immediately after World War I there were many reasons for concern over the type of education the Negro was receiving, especially in the South: Negro performance in Army examinations, the rejection rate of Negroes for military service, the demands of Negroes returning from the Army for greater equality, Negro participation in the nation's new industrialization, and his migration—a part of the current phenomenon of urbanization. Although the general trend in education for the Negro might be said to have included expanding school enrollments, improved school facilities, and better finances, the southern states dragged their feet, refusing Negroes admission to state colleges and initiating plans for tuition grants to Negro residents to pursue graduate and professional education in private colleges for Negroes outside their own state.

For a breakthrough the Negro had recourse to the court system. The first cases involved higher education. In 1936, the *Pearson* v. *Murray* decision in Maryland opened state graduate and professional schools to Negroes in all southern states except Alabama, Florida, Georgia, Mississippi, and South Carolina. In 1938, The U.S. Supreme Court decision in *State of Missouri ex. rel. Gaines* v. *Canada* presented a new interpretation of "separate but equal" in requiring the same educational opportunities for all residents of any state. Most southern states, however, rather than admit Negroes to state universities for whites, established separate graduate and professional schools for Negroes to abide by the Gaines decision. In 1947, in *Sipuel* v. *Board of Regents*, the United States Supreme Court declared that each state must provide opportunity for education that was truly equal within its borders, and in two Supreme Court decisions in 1949—*Sweatt* v. *Painter* and *Mc-Laurin* v. *Oklahoma State Regents*—the test of equality was made to be segregation *within the school.* Thereupon twelve southern states accepted Negro students in graduate and professional schools under court order, and two states complied freely. On May 17, 1954, the "separate but equal" concept was thrown out by the Supreme Court—in the case of *Brown* v. *Board of Education.*[189] Although continuous litigation followed that decision, the integration of the Negro student proceeded more rapidly after it.

In general, Catholic attitudes here were not unlike those of their neighbors. This pattern, especially in the South and some "inner city" sections in the North, may be criticized as not measuring up to the principles of Jesus Christ. When, however, one witnesses, as has this author, burned-out schools, churches, convents, and rectories in those areas of the South in which Catholic leaders moved too fast for the local population, one is brought to the sobering realization that practical decisions must be made on the basis of prudence and maturity. On the other hand, even before the *Brown* desegregation decision of 1954 there were many Catholic attitudes that were exceptions to local prejudices. Some were on the national level. In July 1918, for example, the Catholic Student Mission Crusade was founded at Techny, Illinois, to interest Catholic students in the missions, a large part of which, in this instance, were Negro. In 1920 the Society of the Divine Word established St. Augustine's Seminary in Bay St. Louis, Mississippi, to train Negro candidates for their religious community; their first candidate to become a priest was Maurice Rousseve, ordained May 23, 1934. The Catholic Interracial Council, formed under the Rev. John LaFarge, S.J., on May 20, 1934, in New York City, had its ultimate origins early in 1917, when Dr. Thomas W. Turner, a Catholic Negro educator at Hampton Institute, Hampton, Virginia, had organized the Committee Against the Extension of Race Prejudice in the Church. From the Northeast Clergy Conference, formed for Negro welfare under LaFarge and other priests in Newark, New Jersey, on Nov. 12, 1933, other Clergy Conferences developed with essentially the same purposes. Also helpful were Baroness Catherine De Hueck's Friendship Houses, founded in 1938 at first in Harlem and then in other cities; Fides House, established in 1940 at Washington, D.C.; and the Catholic Worker Houses of Hospitality, formed by Dorothy Day to supply food and shelter to all the needy. In 1943, the annual statement of the Bishops of the country dealt with the race question and the need for equality. In 1946, Mrs. Roger L. Putnam, under the patronage of Richard Cardinal Cushing of Boston, founded a group called Catholic Scholarships for Negroes; its primary purpose was not only to help young Negroes receive a good training in the arts and sciences, but also to enable them to return to help their own people. Catholic college administrators often supplemented the small grants of this group by waiving all tuition costs and other fees. The group, despite its title, does not limit its grants to Catholics.

On local levels, precise activities for Catholics as well as others were determined by sectional differences. Catholics are justifiably proud of all activities in the direction of Negro help that came before the 1954 decision. In the deep South, Xavier University of Louisiana in New Orleans was chartered in 1918 for the education of Negroes. In 1925, its administration established Teachers College and the College of Liberal Arts and Sciences, including a premedical program; in 1927 the College of Pharmacy; in 1933 the Graduate School; in 1937 a separate library, gymnasium, and stadium. Money came from Mother Katherine Drexel and her father, Francis Anthony Drexel, as well as the contributed services of the Sisters of the Blessed Sacrament and contributions from the Catholic Mission Board and the United Negro College Fund. Also in New Orleans, the truly Catholic Archbishop, Joseph F. Rummel, by 1949 had integrated the archdiocesan Holy Name societies, sodalities, and Councils of Catholic Men and Women, and his pastoral letter of March 1953 eliminated segregation in the churches. In North Carolina, Bishop Vincent S. Waters integrated Catholic churches, schools, and hospitals in June 1953. In the archdiocese of Washington, D. C., Archbishop (later Cardinal) Patrick A. O'Boyle ended segregation in the schools in the autumn of 1948. In the Southwest, Archbishop Robert E. Lucey of San Antonio, Texas, in 1945 came out for adequate state child labor laws to protect both his Mexican and Negro minorities, in 1951 rebuked Catholics propounding segregation, and throughout these years quietly but firmly integrated all institutions under his jurisdiction. In the Midwest, Joseph Ritter, then bishop of Indianapolis, Indiana, integrated his churches and schools before his transfer to St. Louis, Missouri, in 1946; in St. Louis he ended segregation in the archdiocesan schools in 1947, just one year after his arrival. In Chicago, Illinois, Albert Cardinal Meyer, head of the archdiocese, and the Most Rev. Bernard J. Sheil, an auxiliary, also met opposition forthrightly, spoke strongly, and acted quickly to integrate all parishes, schools, hospitals, and social services. After 1954, the pace quickened, for Catholics as well as for others.

The question of coeducation must also be considered in any study of students during the period. We have seen that in 1833 Oberlin College had admitted women, and public higher education had been ready to agree that the female sex could possibly profit from higher learning. Catholic colleges moved more slowly, on moral grounds: they feared the mixing of the sexes on campus. Marquette University in Milwaukee had been the first Catholic institution to experiment with coeducation, when it opened a summer school for women in 1909. In 1914 DePaul University in Chicago had admitted women to all its regular session courses.[190] In Catholic high schools before 1929, coeducation was entered upon as a matter of economic necessity in many cases, but never as a matter of deliberate principle. On the elementary level, Catholic schools developed almost completely along coeducational lines.

Conducive to coeducation in public education above the elementary level in this country were the pervading democratic concepts of universal education, increased governmental responsibility to provide education for all, and the greater expense involved in building and maintaining separate schools for high school boys and girls. Two causes operated specifically on the level of higher education. First was the fact that in ever greater numbers, young men and women from lower socio-economic levels, as well as the well-to-do, were beginning to discover that more than a mere high school education was necessary if they were to be successful in a twentieth-century world. Secondly, women students saw advantages in coeducation, not the least of which was the provision of a market for husbands. Apologists for coeducation argued that from it resulted healthy and realistic relationships between the sexes. It provided opportunities for young men and women to work and recreate together, and thus prepared them better for life after college. Objections to coeducation were leveled mainly at the secondary school level. Critics argued that the educational needs of each sex differ so completely, especially in such areas as physical and vocational curriculum, that course planning is difficult; greater moral problems ensue; social activities, a result of the coeducational situation, detract from study. On and on the arguments went. Catholic educators held aloof from coeducation unless forced into it by economic pressures.

Pope Pius XI summed up the Church's viewpoint on the subject in the encyclical *Christian Education of Youth*:

False also and harmful to Christian education is the so-called method of "co-education." This too, by many of its supporters, is founded upon naturalism and the denial of original sin; but by all, upon a deplorable confusion of ideas that mistakes a leveling promiscuity and equality, for the legitimate association of the sexes. . . . These principles, with due regard to time and place, must, in accordance with Christian prudence, be applied to all schools, particularly in the most delicate and decisive period of formation, that, namely, of adolescence.[191]

This directive of Pius XI determined the choice between coeducational establishments and separate high schools for Catholic boys and girls during the period. Theoretically speaking, Catholic educators had no choice but to abide by the Pope's decision; practically speaking, however, in the light of the financial impossibility of providing separate schools for the sexes, parish priests were forced to apply "these principles, with due regard to time and place" and "in accordance with Christian prudence." Many pastors felt obliged to establish coeducational high schools.[192]

In 1957, the Sacred Congregation of Religious issued a detailed instruction which held that coeducation is naturally dangerous to high school youth and that no Catholic may defend the principle.[193] The encyclical of Pope Pius XI "must be considered as the 'Magna Carta' of this mixed form of education." [194] A coeducational school, however, may be tolerated for good and valid reasons, especially where the faith of youth is in serious danger by the frequenting of public schools, and there is economic stress in which it is difficult for pastors to build and maintain even one Catholic school. The Congregation imposed on bishops the obligation of investigating the possibilities of a type of school called "coinstitutional," stating:

The Apostolic See advises or favors the system of education commonly known as "coinstitution" which entails a building consisting of two separate schools, one for boys and one for girls, under a single administration, having a single library and single laboratory. Boys and girls have access to these facilities separately and at different times. Expenses would thus be considerably reduced, and this would not be coeducation in the ordinary sense.[195]

And the *Instructio* continued:

If such "coinstitution" is not possible, it is prescribed that the problem faced be included in the five-year reports by which the Holy See is kept abreast of matters regarding functioning of schools where boys and girls are educated together.[196]

The *Instructio* concerned itself exclusively with Catholic high schools. Frison observed in his commentary on the *Instructio* that

the Instruction is not concerned with universities nor elementary schools. Coeducation in Catholic centers does not generally create great moral problems on the university level. For the elementary schools, the Sacred Congregation of Religious leaves it up to the Bishops to determine up to what age boys and girls can attend school together.[197]

Concrete attempts to apply these theoretical formulations to the practical school situation in the United States have been difficult, however. In both the theoretical and practical spheres, further study is needed on sex-related differences in education.

## The Role of the Official Church in Education

The Church continued to take seriously her responsibility for the education of Catholic youth during this period. A general canonical revision of the law of the Church—the Code of Canon Law—went into effect at Pentecost, May 19, 1918.[198] The main sections of the Code are:

Persons, Sacred Things, and Canonical Trials, and under the section on Sacred Things, Part IV is "On the Teaching Authority of the Church." Here Title XXII, comprising Canons 1372 to 1383, is on "Schools." [199] The right and independence of the Church to establish schools, "not only elementary schools, but also intermediate and higher schools," is asserted in Canon 1375. This right is vindicated in Pius XI's encyclical on *The Christian Education of Youth*, in which the Pope states:

It is the inalienable right as well as the indispensable duty of the Church, to watch over the entire education of her children, in all institutions, public or private, not merely in regard to the religious instruction there given, but in regard to every other branch of learning and every regulation in so far as religion and morality are concerned.[200]

Of the Church's right to establish universities, Canon 1376 pointed up the rights of the Holy See to approve faculties of such institutions; moreover, Canon 1377 established that academic grades that have canonical recognition are to be conferred only with the authority of the Holy See. Canon 1380 imposed an obligation on local ordinaries to send fit clerical candidates for further study to educational institutions approved by the Church.

The obligations of parents for their children's education were decreed in canons interspersed throughout the Code. In a paper read by the Very Rev. William A. Galvin, J.C.D., on May 19, 1954, at the Eastern Regional Conference Meeting of The Canon Law Society of America, the speaker considered the duty of parents and guardians to give their children an education according to the law of the Church. Galvin said:

According to Canon 1113 parents are bound by the gravest of obligations to secure by all means in their power the religious, moral, physical and civil education of their children, as well as their temporal welfare. The Code further enacts in Canon 1335 that "not only parents and others that stand in their place but also masters and godparents are bound by an obligation of seeing to it that all who are subject or entrusted to them are trained by catechetical instruction." And again through the enactment of Canon 1372 the Church demands that "all the faithful are to be so reared from childhood that not only shall nothing be offered them opposed to the Catholic faith or moral propriety but also that religious and moral training shall be given the most important place." In the same canon She also decrees that "not only parents in accordance with canon 1113 but also all who stand in their place have the right and the most serious duty to ensure the Christian education of their children." [201]

The Code is explicit on the place of religion in education. Canon 1373 prescribes that courses in religion are to be provided for students in every level of schooling—elementary, secondary, and higher. To fulfill these provisions, Canon 1379 provides that "if the Catholic elementary and intermediate schools contemplated by Canon 1373 are lacking, provision shall be made, especially by local ordinaries, that they be established." Canon 1374 prohibits Catholic children from attending non-Catholic schools and gives to local ordinaries alone the right to give permission for such attendance, to be determined "in accordance with the norm of the instructions of the Apostolic See, in what circumstances and with what safeguards to overcome the danger of perversion the conducting of such schools can be tolerated." Pius XI went further in his insistence on religion in the schools when he wrote:

For the mere fact that a school gives some religious instruction (often extremely stinted), does not bring it into accord with the rights of the Church and of the Christian family, or make it a fit place for Catholic students. To be this, it is necessary that all the teaching and the whole organization of the school, and its teachers, syllabus and textbooks in every branch, be regulated by the Christian spirit, under the direction and maternal supervision of the Church; so that Religion may be in very truth the foundation and crown of the youth's entire training; and this in every grade of school, not only the elementary, but the intermediate and the higher institutions of learning as well.[202]

The religious education of every Catholic youth in all schools whatever is, according to Canon 1381, subject to the authority and supervision of the Church. Local ordinaries have the obligation to be sure that in any school within their territory nothing is taught which is contrary to faith and morals.[203]

In spite of the great amount of power that the Code of Canon Law seemed to give local ordinaries with regard to education, this power was by no means absolute—as, for example, in the case of schools conducted by religious orders. Parish schools and diocesan high schools are completely subject to his authority, since they are established and maintained by the parish and diocese. Other Catholic schools are subject to the ordinary only in matters of religious and moral training. The catechetical instruction of the faithful is completely under the authority of the local ordinary even in the schools maintained by religious, when there is a question of teaching non-exempt persons. The ordinary approves teachers and texts, and he may demand the removal of certain teachers or textbooks in the best interests of religion or morality. The Rev. Joseph A. M. Quigley, J.C.D., distinguishes three kinds of control by the local ordinary: "(1) the right of vigilance as to faith and morals; (2) direct authority regarding religious instruction; and (3) the right of canonical visitation." [204] Actually, many of the provisions of the Code of Canon Law were but a repeat of what had already been provided for by the Councils of Baltimore. The decrees of the Third Plenary Council were more detailed than the Code, but were in no way opposed to it, and therefore continued to have full force of law.[205] The Code of Canon Law made no mention of superintendents of schools, thus giving the claim on parochial schools to pastors. It is interesting to ponder, in spite of the many good aspects of this, about the possible advantages of other arrangements.

The Church also fulfilled its role in Catholic education in the United

States through its members. In Catholic educational institutions across the nation, dedicated teaching religious orders of men and women as well as devoted Catholic lay teachers implemented the rulings and advice of the American hierarchy and of the Holy See. The NCEA continued to give encouragement and practical assistance to Catholic educators through its annual meetings and quarterly bulletins.[206] The NCWC (National Catholic Welfare Conference), a voluntary association of bishops organized in 1919 at the request of Pope Benedict XV that the American hierarchy join him in working for peace and social justice, included a Department of Education. (As its Department of Education, NCWC in 1919 tried to incorporate NCEA; NCEA rejected the attempt and, as the professional association of Catholic educators, remained independent from the hierarchy.) The department exercises no administrative authority over Catholic schools, but functions in an advisory capacity. It acts as a clearing-house of information concerning Catholic education for Catholic educators, parents, and students, and for the general public.[207] It made biennial surveys of Catholic educational conditions from 1920 to 1956 and annual surveys from 1959 to the present.[208] The NCWC's Department of Education acts as a connecting link between Catholic schools and national organizations of an educational character.

In spite of all efforts, however, nearly half of the Catholic children of school age were still in public schools. To meet the need of providing catechetical instruction for these children, the Confraternity of Christian Doctrine, first organized in Europe in the sixteenth century, was brought to the United States. From small beginnings in this country in 1902 it developed into an influential mode of Catholic action during the period of 1918-1957. The earliest known record of the beginnings of the Confraternity of Christian Doctrine in the United States had been written in 1902, in the *Manual of the Confraternity of Christian Doctrine in the Archdiocese of New York*,[209] which recorded the reception of ninety-three members at the Church of Our Lady of Good Counsel in New York City on May 13, 1902. At the request of this group, the Most Rev. Michael A. Corrigan had consented to erect the Confraternity officially and to affiliate it with the Confraternity at Rome. The Confraternity's growth was neither rapid nor extensive until the 1920's, and then it was the Holy See that gave the spur to its development.[210] Pius XI published his Motu Proprio *Orbem Catholicum*, on the teaching of Christian Doctrine, in 1923. The Pope announced the establishment of an Office of Catechetics in the Sacred Congregation of the Council, which would be the instrument of the Holy See for promoting the observance of laws already enacted regarding Christian Doctrine instruction.[211] Then, on December 31, 1929, the same Holy Father in his encyclical *Christian Education of Youth*, which carried so much force in the United States for the rest of the period, stated:

We implore pastors of souls, by every means in their power, by instructions and catechisms, by word of mouth and written articles widely distributed, to warn Christian parents of their grave obligations. And this should be done not in a merely theoretical and general way, but with practical and specific applications.[212]

At first the Confraternity of Christian Doctrine was successful only in a few widely scattered dioceses in the United States. Steps were taken toward centralization of effort in 1933 by the Most Rev. Michael J. Curley, archbishop of Baltimore, and the Most Rev. Edwin V. O'Hara, then bishop of Great Falls, Montana. (From 1939, O'Hara was bishop of Kansas City, Kansas. He was, more than anyone else, founder and organizing spirit of the CCD in the United States. His guiding hand was present also in the revision of the Baltimore Catechism; in the CCD revision of the New Testament translation; and in the first permanent organization of United States biblical scholars.) The ecclesiastical center designated for the Confraternity in the United States was the National Shrine of the Immaculate Conception in Washington, D.C. The Very Rev. Francis A. Walsh, O.S.B., of the faculty at Catholic University, was appointed director. To this center, diocesan Confraternities of Christian Doctrine could apply for advice and information. Again Rome spoke through the Catechetical Office of the Sacred Congregation of the Council instituted by Pope Pius XI in 1923, and on January 12, 1935, issued a decree *Provido Sane Consilio*[213] ("On the Better Care and Promotion of Catechetical Instruction"). It commanded that the following instructions be observed:

I. In every parish . . . the Confraternity of Christian Doctrine, *as the most important of all others,* must be established . . . and it should embrace all who are capable of teaching and promoting catechetical instruction, especially teachers in schools and all who are skilled in the science of teaching children.

II. . . . Parochial classes in Christian Doctrine should be established where they do not already exist. . . . In order to overcome the indifference of parents . . . let the following be carefully observed:

a. Pastors shall not admit to the reception of the Sacraments of Penance and Confirmation . . . children who have not acquired sufficient knowledge of the catechism . . .

b. Pastors . . . shall take particular care to advise parents of the grave obligation that is theirs to see to it that "all persons subject to them or intrusted under their care shall receive catechetical instruction" . . . (Canon 1335)

c. Let pastors and their assistants endeavor so far as they can to make children eager to attend parish catechism classes. To this end the most successful and tried means shall be employed . . . and the use of suitable projects and moderate forms of amusement.

d. Let pastors prepare the children so that they may be examined by the Bishop when he makes his pastoral visitation.

III. The instruction of adults in catechetical subjects is to be treated, with indications in detail of methods and results involved in the program designed to effect the fruitful religious education of adults.[214]

The establishment of the National Center and the publication of the above decree on catechetics of the Sacred Congregation of the Council hurried the development of diocesan foundations. Organized in dioceses, it gave in particular a most effective solution to the problem of how to provide systematic religious instruction for children who attend public school. Each ordinary is free to include details of Confraternity organization which meet the needs of his particular diocese. During this period, activities stemming from Confraternity organization came to include such works as the religious vacation school program, instruction classes for children attending public elementary schools, instruction classes for public high school pupils, parent-educator discussion clubs, discussion clubs for adults, special religion classes for handicapped children, correspondence courses in religion, training centers for lay teachers of religion, high school retreats, and religious radio programs. The Publications Department of the National Center deserves special mention. We have already referred to its work of revising the Baltimore catechism. *The Proceedings of the National Catechetical Congresses* [215] published annually by the NCWC are a contribution to religious educational literature. The *Newsletter*, published monthly especially for diocesan directors, furthers the exchange of ideas and the arrangement of Confraternity programs.

## *The Supreme Court and Catholic Education*

Church-State controversies of the period as far as Catholic education was concerned centered around the two burning questions that had sparked the heated arguments between Church and State in the nineteenth century: government aid to non-public schools, and religion in public education. Certain court cases revolving around those issues showed the trend of government thought and action toward the place that, according to the views of the State, religion should hold in education. The cases chosen for study here are those of greatest importance, and even within this limited scope it is impossible to penetrate these deeply.[216] The most famous case was *Pierce* v. *Society of Sisters* which was precipitated by an Oregon state law requiring all children between the ages of eight and sixteen to be educated in *public* schools. The people passed the legislation by referendum in 1922 and it was to become effective September 1, 1926. The real purpose of the statute was to outlaw parochial and private schools. The constitutionality of the act was attacked in two actions brought by the Society of the Sisters of the Holy Name of Jesus and Mary and the Hill Military Academy. The plaintiffs based their claim on the fact that the law ran counter to the Fourteenth Amendment of the Federal Constitution, in that it would deprive them of private property without due process of law and it would deprive parents of the right to direct and control the education of their children. The decision of the Supreme Court was delivered by Justice James C. McReynolds on June 1, 1925, who ruled that private schools have the right to engage in their business and are protected in doing so by the Fourteenth Amendment. The most important paragraph of his decision, however, dealt with parents' right to educate. McReynolds declared:

> Under the doctrine of *Meyer* v. *Nebraska,* 262 U.S. 390 we think it entirely plain that the Act of 1922 unreasonably interferes with the liberty of parents and guardians to direct the upbringing and education of children under their control. As often heretofore pointed out, rights guaranteed by the Constitution may not be abridged by legislation which has no reasonable relation to some purpose within the competency of the state. The fundamental theory of liberty upon which all governments in this Union repose excludes any general power of the state to standardize its children by forcing them to accept instruction from public teachers only. The child is not the mere creature of the state; those who nurture him and direct his destiny have the right, coupled with the high duty, to recognize and prepare him for additional obligations.[217]

The *Pierce* v. *Society of Sisters* Court decision has been called the Magna Carta of parochial schools for defending their right to exist in the American school system.[218] Neil G. McCluskey, S.J., warning against its being given a superficial study with emphasis only on the causes and results, says that "the briefs and oral discussion presented by both sides in the Oregon case contain just about every argument conceivable in favor of and in opposition to non-public schools." [219] No detailed study of those arguments can be attempted here, but certain points may be highlighted because of their relevance to continuing similar arguments. The state of Oregon in presenting its case claimed that the necessity for any other kind of school than that provided by the state had ceased to exist; that the existence of the non-public schools was a fatal menace to the public school system; and that religious schools were diverse and undemocratic, creating for their students a cultural ghetto and isolating them from every-day living with their fellow Americans.[220] The Court heard the arguments and ruled on the side of educational freedom and religious liberty. In *Cochran* v. *Board of Education,* the Supreme Court in 1930 upheld the constitutionality of a Louisiana law permitting the state to supply textbooks for children whether attending public or parochial schools, on the ground that the state may act to achieve a public good even though in doing so a private end is incidentally aided. Chief Justice Charles Evans Hughes in delivering the opinion of the Court observed that "the schools, however, are not the beneficiaries of these appropriations . . . These school children and the state alone are the beneficiaries." [221] The decision expressed a "child-benefit" theory that was to appear subsequently in the *Everson* bus case and which became a rationale for advocates of federal aid to private school children. This "child-benefit theory" means, in the words of Clark Spurlock, "that the state's obligation to all the school children in the state transcends a too-literal observance of the principle of separation of church and state." [222]

*Everson v. Board of Education* was brought to the Supreme Court in 1947. The issue was the constitutionality of a New Jersey law permitting the use of public money to pay transportation costs for pupils in non-public schools. Perhaps no case holds the paramount importance of *Everson*, which read into the "due process" clause of the Fourteenth Amendment (which limited only the states) the "establishment of religion" clause of the First Amendment, which theretofore limited only the federal government. The case was judged in the light of the First Amendment, the Fourteenth Amendment, and the "child-benefit" theory. Leo Pfeffer wrote that "what in effect the court held was that where there is a clash between the prohibitions of the First Amendment and the welfare of children, the latter interest is superior," and he further commented that "both the First Amendment, guaranteeing religious freedom, and the Fourteenth, banning laws denying to any person the equal protection of the laws, preclude a state from discrimination on religious grounds in its distribution of welfare benefits." [223] The criterion for decision, then, was need, not creed. The law was declared constitutional, but the justices were sharply divided: five to four. The five who favored constitutionality argued that it satisfied both the child-benefit theory and the public welfare duty of the State. The opposing four argued that the majority decision was a subsidization of a religion. Both sides appealed to Jefferson and Madison as the true arbiters of what the First Amendment meant by the phrase, "Congress shall make no law respecting an establishment of religion." Both sides maintained that the wall of separation between Church and State was to remain impregnable. Finally, Justice Hugo Black, rendering the Court's decision, said:

We must be careful, in protecting the citizens of New Jersey against state-established churches, to be sure that we do not inadvertently prohibit New Jersey from extending its general State law benefits to all its citizens without regard to their religious belief.[224]

Justice Wiley Rutledge's dissenting view was the sum of all dissenting voices in *Everson*. Rutledge said:

Two great drives are constantly in motion to abridge, in the name of education, the complete division of religion and civil authority which our forefathers made. One is to introduce religious education and observances into the public schools. The other, to obtain public funds for the aid and support of various private religious schools. In my opinion both avenues were closed by the Constitution.[225]

The *Everson* opinion settled the bus transportation issue at the federal level, and the Supreme Court has since refused three times to consider cases involving this issue. The states, however, were left free to settle the question for themselves. Robert F. Drinan, S.J., writing in 1963, would claim that some twenty-two states were then authorizing bus rides for private-school children.[226] But many states were fearful of the "public welfare legislation" theory—for, as Pfeffer wrote:

When the *Everson* decision is coupled with the *Cochran* decision, they lead logically to the conclusion that the state may, notwithstanding the First Amendment, finance practically every aspect of parochial education, with the exception of such comparatively minor items as the proportionate salaries of teachers while they teach the catechism.[227]

Drinan wrote on the ambiguities of the *Everson* decision:

The inherent contradiction of *Everson* [lies] in the fact that judges and polemicists on both sides of the bus-ride struggle can find in all the opinions some strikingly probative sentences to support their thesis.[228]

He then showed how *Everson* stands for three principles which leave an open question of benefits to parochial schools apart from "general State law benefits." The three principles are:

1. There is no establishment of religion if a state law permits transportation of pupils to private schools;
2. The state, however, may constitutionally enact a law which would "provide transportation only to children attending public schools";
3. But the "benefits of public welfare legislation" may not be denied to individual citizens "because of their faith or the lack of it." [229]

And according to Drinan, the all-important question was not answered by *Pierce, Cochran,* or *Everson*—namely, "What is the real juridical status of the private, church-related schools?" [230] Robert Eugene Cushman in *Leading Constitutional Decisions* had also observed that *Everson* left questions unanswered. Cushman asked some of those questions:

How far may the state validly go, under the "child benefit theory," in granting benefits to parochial school children? If it may provide free textbooks and bus transportation, may it also provide free lunches, free gymnasiums and swimming pools, free school clinics, and so on? Also, if a community is not forbidden to give free bus service to all school children including parochial school children, may Catholic parents demand such service as a constitutional right from communities which now extend it only to public school children? [231]

Spurlock, commenting on some criticism of *Everson*, said that

it should be clearly understood, [*Everson*] did not sanction the use of public funds for the establishment of religion. It merely sanctioned, by the majority view, the use of public funds for a public purpose which brought no more than incidental benefit to religion.[232]

*Cochran* and *Everson* were examples of court cases seeking to provide auxiliary aids to the non-public school child. Irwin Widen wrote in 1953 that in the previous twenty-five years "the issue of public support for the parochial schools has reemerged into prominence,"[233] for which reemergence the following six factors were responsible:

(1) the expanded influence of the Catholic Church in America; (2) the assurance of continued legal protection for the non-public schools; (3) the increased need of the parochial schools for public funds; (4) the movement for Federal aid to education; (5) the trend toward providing "auxiliary services" to the school child; and (6) the reaction against the secular character of public education.[234]

"The support issue," predicted Widen, "will remain with us for a good many years to come."[235] Time has proved him right. Not all states followed *Cochran* in the distribution of free textbooks to church-related schools. Louisiana and Mississippi, for example, continued to uphold the practice, while such others as New York, New Mexico, and Oregon continued to deny its constitutionality until the U.S. Supreme Court decision in 1968 on a New York State statute to be discussed in the next chapter. The Supreme Court of Mississippi in 1940 made some interesting observations: that, for example, if the pupil fulfills his duty to the state by attending a parochial school, it is difficult to see why the state may not fulfill its duty to the pupil by encouraging him by all suitable means; and that the state, which gives the pupil the freedom to subscribe to any religious creed, should not, because of his exercise of that right, proscribe him from benefits common to all.[236] The only way at present that the public provision of textbooks may be constitutionally permissible for parochial pupils, however, is when the texts are of nonsectarian nature. As far as provision of transportaton for pupils attending parochial schools is concerned, *Everson* (as we have seen) set no hard and fast law. The United States Supreme Court *permitted* the states to put the practice into effect, but the state courts are divided as to its constitutionality. Parochial pupils have free transportation in New York, New Jersey, California, Connecticut, Kentucky, Maryland, and some parts of Massachusetts. The practice has been ruled unconstitutional in Alaska, Delaware, Missouri, New Mexico, Oklahoma, Washington, and Wisconsin.

Released-time, the history of which movement we briefly sketched in the last chapter, was the issue in the case of *McCollum* v. *Board of Education*. In 1948, a year after *Everson*, the Court dealt with the problem of released-time for religious education by endorsing (with the exception of Justice Stanley F. Reed) the theory of "separation" as developed in *Everson* and applied it to nullify an Illinois released-time plan. The appellant, Mrs. Vashti McCollum (McCluskey calls her a "secular humanist"[237] and Pfeffer labels her an "atheist"),[238] questioned the legality of the voluntary released-time religious instruction program in the Champaign, Illinois, public schools. Her suit was rejected in the courts of Illinois, and she appealed to the Supreme Court of the United States. Standing on *Everson*, the Court banned the teaching of religion *on public school property during school hours,* declaring such procedure a violation of the First Amendment. *McCollum* was a proof that *Everson* could work both ways—it gave free bus rides to parochial children and now by its "extreme separatist interpretation of the First Amendment" [239] cut the ground from under the released-time movement in thirty-seven states. But *McCollum* lived only four years. In 1952, *Zorach* v. *Clauson* brought the "released-time" issue once more before the Supreme Court. Tessim Zorach and Esta Gluck, taxpayers of New York City, whose children attended the public schools there, challenged the current ruling on released-time instruction *outside* of public school buildings. Zorach and Gluck held that in essence this program was the same as the one involved in the *McCollum* case. The Court recorded their complaints as follows:

Their argument, stated elaborately in various ways, reduces itself to this: the weight and influence of the school is put behind a program for religious instruction; public school teachers police it, keeping tab on students who are released; the classroom activities come to a halt while the students who are released for religious instruction are on leave; the school is a crutch on which the churches are leaning for support in their religious training; without the cooperation of the schools this "released time" program, like the one in the *McCollum* case, would be futile and ineffective. [240]

*Zorach* was judged in the light of the First Amendment. The Court decided that the practice of released-time is not a violation of that Amendment when pupils *leave the public school during regular school hours* to receive denominational religious instruction. Justice William O. Douglas, speaking for the majority of six justices, after enunciating that the separation of Church and State "must be complete and unequivocal," added that

the First Amendment, however, does not say that in every and all respects there shall be a separation of Church and State. Rather, it studiously defines the manner, the specific ways, in which there shall be no concert or union or dependency one on the other. . . . Otherwise the state and religion would be aliens to each other—hostile, suspicious, and even unfriendly. [241]

Douglas then reiterated the importance of religion in American traditions:

We are a religious people whose institutions presuppose a Supreme Being. . . . When the state encourages religious instruction or cooperates with religious authorities by adjusting the schedule of public events to sectarian needs, it follows the best of our traditions. . . . To hold that it may not would be to find in the Constitution a requirement that the government show a callous indifference to religious groups. That would be preferring those who believe in no religion over those who do believe.[242]

Were one to hold sentiments contrary to these, Douglas asserted, he would be reading into the Bill of Rights "a philosophy of hostility to religion." Spurlock summed up the expressed attitude of the Supreme Court toward the practice of released-time in very simple terms:

(1) where done in public schools and with particular administrative cooperation it amounts to an unconstitutional establishment of religion, but that (2) where done outside the school and with only the necessary minimum of administrative cooperation it does not amount to an establishment of religion.[243]

*Zorach* is significant because the judges of the case seemed to recognize that if state neutrality is to be interpreted as indifference to religion, the established faith becomes secularism, a radical departure from the American tradition to which Douglas alluded. *Zorach* also provided judicial recognition of parental rights of choice.

Bible reading in the public schools also remained a controversial matter during this period, and *Doremus* v. *Board of Education* in 1952 was a case in point. This case was brought before the United States Supreme Court to decide the constitutionality of a New Jersey law requiring reading from the Old Testament in public schools. The Supreme Court held that the constitutionality of the law could not be decided because the plantiffs had not shown enough direct injury by the law. The plaintiffs, Klein and Doremus, had appealed as taxpayers. McGrath, commenting briefly on the case, observed that "on appeal the United States Supreme Court held that the interests of a taxpayer in the treasury are too indeterminable, remote, uncertain and indirect to furnish a basis for court action. The court did not decide the constitutional question."[244] *Doremus* is important, however, for making observable the Court's views on the subject in 1952:

We consider the Old Testament and the Lord's Prayer, pronounced without comment, are not sectarian, and that the short exercise provided by the statute does not constitute sectarian instruction or sectarian worship but is a simple recognition of the Supreme Ruler of the Universe . . . and that, in any event, the presence of a scholar at, and his participation in, that exercise is, under the directive of the Board of Education, voluntary.[245]

The shifting sentiments of the courts and the exaggerated interpretation of the ideal of separation of Church and State as it exists in the United States brought trouble to the parochial school system in greater and lesser degrees during this period. One instance of attack on parochial schools was the case of *Zellers* v. *Huff* or, as it is sometimes referred to, the Dixon Case. It resulted from a protest made in 1947 by a group of twenty-eight citizens against the teaching of religion in the public schools of Dixon, New Mexico.[246] The main issue was that members of religious communities, teaching in the public schools of New Mexico, were said to be teaching religion in the classrooms through instruction, prayer, the distribution of religious pictures and literature, and pictures and symbols hung on classroom walls—all forbidden by the New Mexico state constitution. Plaintiffs demanded that all religious teachers be barred from the public schools because of their vows; that the wearing of religious garb by teachers in the classrooms be prohibited; that buildings owned by a church not be used for tax-supported schools; and that parochial school children not be given by the state such auxiliary services as free textbooks and bus transportation. The ruling of the lower court was handed down on March 10, 1949. One hundred and thirty-seven religious were permanently barred from teaching in the public schools of New Mexico. Parochial pupils were not to get free transportation to school; neither were they to be given free state-owned textbooks. Religion classes were not to be held before or after school, as the entire time from the moment the pupils arrived in the morning until they left in the afternoon was considered part of the school day. The case went to the Supreme Court of New Mexico, which ruled against the wearing of religious garb by teachers in public school classrooms, but recognized the fact that the vows taken by religious are not inconsistent with teaching in a public school. In the decisions handed down in *Gerhardt* v. *Heid* [247] in 1936, and as far back as *Hysong* v. *Gallitzin* [248] in 1894, the courts had agreed that to deny religious the right to contribute their salaries to their religious orders would be a denial of the right of religious liberty guaranteed by the Constitution. The question of the garb worn by Roman Catholic sisters while teaching in public schools came up again before the Supreme Court of Kentucky in 1956 in the case of *Rawlings* v. *Butler*, which stated:

While the dress and the emblems worn by these Sisters proclaim them to be members of certain organizations of the Roman Catholic Church and that they have taken certain religious vows, these facts do not deprive them of their right to teach in public schools, so long as they do not inject religion or the dogma of their church. The garb does not teach. It is the woman within who teaches. The dress of the Sisters denotes modesty, unworldliness and an unselfish life. No mere significance or insignificance of garb would conceal a teacher's character. [249]

The Court went on to render the decision, which still holds:

We find no provisions in the Federal Constitution or of the Kentucky Constitution which are violated by the Sisters teaching while wearing religious garb and emblems, or in donating to their religious order the lion's share of their salaries, or in the various school boards renting buildings from the Roman Catholic Church in which public schools are conducted. [250]

Through this period, United States Catholics continued to argue that "the principle of distributive justice entitled them to a share of the school taxes, and their financial needs necessitated it." [251] On the church-state controversy in the United States, Ellis observed in 1956 that the solution lies in "the temper in which it is discussed," specifying:

If it be in the measured terms of the Protestant, Charles C. Marshall, whose serious volume on the question followed the 1928 presidential campaign, or of the Jewish writer, Will Herberg, whose thoughtful and constructive books and articles have done much in the last few years to dissipate misunderstanding, or the Catholic publications and lectures of Father John Courtney Murray, S.J., then there is genuine hope for gain and clarification on both sides and for a calm, judicious, beneficial approach to the problem. But if the matter is left in the hands of those deep in prejudice, we can anticipate nothing better than an increase of the spirit that has divided men on this question during the past decade.[252]

Will Herberg, professor of Judaic studies and social philosophy at Drew University, Madison, New Jersey, examined, in 1957, the basic issues involved in the controversy between Church and State in the area of education. He recognized that the two major aspects of the problem were "the place of religion in public education and the propriety and limits of public support to parochial and other religious schools," [253] and that most of the larger issues come to a focus in the second. Although Herberg's article was entitled "Justice for Religious Schools," the author dealt mainly with Catholic schools, and that in a most objective manner. Justice, Herberg believed, was entirely on the side of those who were demanding public support for parochial schools, which after all perform a public function. He observed:

Parochial schools are, in fact, public institutions, though they are not governmentally sponsored and operated. They perform a public function, supplying large numbers of children with an education that is everywhere taken as the equivalent of the education given in the public schools. They have full public recognition as educational agencies; their credits, diplomas and certificates have exactly the same validity as those issued by governmental establishments. Since they are thus publicly recognized educational institutions, performing a public educational service, why should they not receive public support? [254]

The largest-scale church-state cooperative movement on a financial level during this period was occasioned by World War II and the Korean War. The Servicemen's Readjustment Act of 1944, popularly called the GI Bill of Rights, provided for one year's education with subsistence allowance. In addition, the returned soldier was eligible for a period of study equal to his years of service between September 16, 1940, and July 25, 1947. On the entrance of America into the Korean War, Congress approved new legislation for the veterans. They were granted subsidies to cover one and one-half days of schooling for each day of service, to a maximum of thirty months. A federal subsidy also guaranteed the vocational training of disabled veterans from World War II and the Korean

War.[255] Under this GI Bill of Rights, the federal government, as Herberg noted, "pays the tuitions and expenses not only of students in church-related colleges, but even of theological students in ecclesiastical seminaries." [256] Can this be called a breach of the "wall of separation between Church and State"? Herberg again had the answer:

There is no principle by which one can distinguish what is right and proper in the public mind from what is shocking and improper; it is largely a matter of prejudice, tradition, conflicting group interests, and the momentary constellation of forces.[257]

Nevertheless, some bishops, such as John Cardinal O'Hara of Philadelphia, still did not seek or want federal or state aid to Catholic schools, for fear of an ensuing loss of independence and an obligatory submission to outside control.[258]

## End of the Period

At the end of the period, in 1957, the Most Rev. Albert G. Meyer, archbishop of Milwaukee and president general of the NCEA, reviewed briefly the achievements of American Catholics in education. Moving back to the days of the new republic, he showed that when Bishop John Carroll opened Georgetown College in 1791, Catholics in the newly independent thirteen colonies were estimated to be thirty-five thousand, or 0.89 per cent of the total population of 3,939,000. Today, however, said Meyer in 1957, "according to the *Catholic Directory* for 1956, Catholics number 33,574,017 or 21.8% of the national population of 154,300,474." He continued: "There are 6,805,129 youths [in 1956] under Catholic instruction, taught by 8,995 priests, 906 scholastics, 4,168 brothers, 93,518 sisters, and 27,819 lay teachers." [259] Claiming that it was not his purpose to appraise the American Catholic school system merely by its size, Meyer remarked, after praising the quality of Catholic elementary and secondary education, that "our Catholic colleges and universities have leavened our American society with Catholic business men, dentists, engineers, journalists, nurses, physicians, teachers, and good Catholic fathers and mothers, the great majority of whom, by word and example, uphold Catholicity on an intellectual level commensurate with their stations in life." [260]

John Tracy Ellis, however, held other views on Catholic growth in intellectual maturity during this period. He claimed in 1956 that "the Catholics in posts of leadership, both clerical and lay [have failed] to understand fully or to appreciate in a practical way, the value of the vocation of the intellectual." [261] Catholic higher education, said Ellis, had failed to develop "habits of work, cherished ideals of research or a sense of dedication to an intellectual apostolate." [262] He sought reasons for the weakness and found them in such factors as anti-Catholic prejudice, the immigrant Church, "the absence of an intellectual tradition among American Catholics," [263] and an overemphasis on the school "as an agency for moral development, with an insufficient stress on the role of the school as an instrument for fostering intellectual excellence.[264] One consoling thought for Catholic educators of the period was Ellis' admission that

historically Americans have been wary of their scholars, and it is doubtful if there is a major nation in the world whose history reveals more suspicion of its academicians than our own. . . . It is our own generation that has given birth to the terms, "brain trusters" and "eggheads." . . . Catholics are, and have been, thoroughly Americans, and they have shown no more marked disposition to foster scholarship and to honor intellectual achievement than any other group.[265]

Catholics picked up Ellis' challenge, and at the NCEA meeting in 1956 following the first publication of Ellis' article "American Catholics and the Intellectual Life" in *Thought* [266] in September of 1955, faced the question, "Why is the American Catholic Graduate School Failing to Develop Catholic Intellectualism?" [267] Not least among the reasons cited as underlying Catholic lack of intellectualism was the economic one. Another thought-provoking reason was that of utilitarianism—"students interested only in credits and a degree, not in scholarly research." [268] Ellis' work definitely marked the trend of the times—the trend toward greater academic freedom evidenced in his fearlessly pointing the finger of blame at Catholic educational institutions, but even more, the trend toward a determination to clarify the issues, and to resolve the problem of increasing the "proportions of authentic scholars and trained competent intellectuals" [269] among Catholics.


## Conclusions

Social conditions between 1918 and 1957 were very tumultuous, embracing as they did two wars, the Red scares and other disturbances after both, a depression, and increasing evidences of such understandable maladjustment among the young as alcoholism, drug addiction, and delinquency. In public education at the beginning of this era, there were not many students, proportionate to the total youth population, in school; one-room schoolhouses existed in great numbers; there were many untrained and incompetent teachers, accounted for in part by low teacher salaries; and student opportunities in education were deplorably unequal. To the nation, the consequent illiteracy and lack of education was a poor basis for the type of democracy that the country's leaders envisioned; the preventable physical deficiencies of youth were expensive in peace and resulted in unfitness for military service in war; and retardation rates were making the United States a nation of sixth-graders. The situation therefore led to a reexamination of goals, curriculums, and teaching, and to a rejection of progressive education that came to a climax after World War II.

In Catholic education during this time, statistics showed a steady growth. Some reexaminations parallelled and followed those in public schools. In goals, it opposed the public-school search for social efficiency. Its declaration of the ultimate aim of education was the same as ever—the formation of the whole man, on a supernatural as well as on a natural plane. As its immediate goal, it sought the formation of a person adaptable to the contingencies of Christian living in the American democracy. The United States hierarchy touched upon it in Section XIII of their Pastoral Letter in 1919, and again in their 1950 pastoral which was entitled "The Child: Citizen of Two Worlds." It was a recurring theme at NCEA meetings in the Twenties. Pius XI dealt with it in his 1929 encyclical, *The Christian Education of Youth*. After 1938, the Commission on American Citizenship, formed that year, engaged in the matter and defined a social program. Finally, the Secondary School Department of NCEA studied it in 1939.

The Catholic school curriculum during this period, consequent upon its goals, could be given the same one-word synopsis: "social." On the elementary level, because of its concern over the dignity and the non-materiality of man, the Catholic school pattern only gradually and reluctantly accepted the testing and measurement movement which the public school pattern had immediately accepted from Edward L. Thorndike. It opposed at first the "activity program" and the utilitarian bases of curricular decisions in the public school, but then gradually adopted what was acceptable from the new theorists in the light of Catholic principles, urged on by the Rt. Rev. George Johnson of Catholic University. On the secondary level, financial strain hindered the building of laboratories and the development of vocational training, thus adding to other reasons for the retention of college preparatory courses. On this level, the introduction of social emphases to the curriculum was more gradual. Common to both levels, in catechetics there was a desire to break with the rote memorization of the past, and an attempt to make catechism come to life. Assisting in this attempt were the liturgical movement under Virgil Michel, O.S.B.; the "Munich Method," psychologically oriented and based on the Herbartian steps, introduced by the Rt. Rev. Joseph P. Baierl; Johannes Hofinger, who was writing in *Worship* in the mid-Fifties; and such efforts in catechism renewals as a return to the early Christian narrative-historical approach, Christocentrism, Bible and liturgy, the kerygmatic method, eye-catching illustrations, and the suggested use of audio-visual materials.

For teachers in the United States, the time after World War I ushered in a new era in teacher education, salaries, admission standards, and inspections. For Catholics, the Twenties added to all previous programs of teacher training some more on the diocesan level. A study in 1927 by Sylvester Schmitz indicated a superiority in some areas of sister-teachers over their public-school counterparts. At the end of the fifties, the Sister-formation program added new dimensions to the making of a sister-teacher. Throughout the period, the search for a higher level of professional training of teachers in Catholic schools was further motivated by statements of Popes Pius XI and Pius XII. The Catholic-school teacher increase was not only qualitative but quantitative, the jump during this period being more than 100%. The lay teacher was also being upgraded, in both numbers and position. He came into his own especially after World War II, becoming no longer just a substitute when a religious could not be found, receiving a better salary (always a problem because of Catholic schools' financial situation), tenure, advancement possibilities, and security.

The student, too, was becoming less the "forgotten man" of education, with the growth of child psychology. While some public educators were opting for a consideration of the "whole child" and not just statistics, Catholic educators were continuing their opposition to the current naturalism in interpreting the child to education. The Rev. Thomas Shields of Catholic University, himself a psychologist trained by Wilhelm Wundt at Leipzig, adapted the best of the growing psychological movement to Catholic education. Catholic concern for the dignity of the person continued, resulting during the Fifties in the beginnings of attention to exceptional children as well as continued attention to such minorities as Negroes. Throughout the country there was new concern for the latter because of the discovery of the Negro rejection rate for military service, the demands of the Negro returning from service for greater equality, and his greater participation in industrialization and urbanization. Attitudes continued to be different in the South than in the North; Catholics usually followed their neighbors, but are proud of the instances of Catholic action accepting Negroes prior to the Brown desegregation decision of 1954. Concerning the education of women, there were among Catholics as among others the remnants of a double standard. On the college level, Catholics moved more slowly than others in the direction of coeducation, on moral grounds. On the middle level, they joined those who voiced such objections as that each sex has very different needs, that coeducation presents moral problems to the adolescent, and that the presence of the opposite sex distracts from study. Pope Pius XI in *The Christian Education of Youth* seemed to oppose coeducation, and a further instruction from Rome on the subject in 1957 resulted in high schools that were coinstitutional rather than coeducational—i.e., presented separate classroom instruction to each sex, but had them share some facilities such as cafeteria, chapel, and library.

On the elementary level, United States Catholic schools never had any difficulty in having boys and girls together.

The Church's continuing to take seriously her role in education during this period led to several expressions. In 1918, its Code of Canon Law left no doubt about the Church's right to educate, and legislated responsibilities to education accordingly. In 1919, when the National Catholic Welfare Conference was formed as an arm of the Bishops, it included a Department of Education. In contradistinction to NCEA, which through this period continued to function as an organization related to the profession of education, NCWC's Department of Education served in an advisory capacity to the hierarchy. Several factors led to the rise to a position of importance of another organization, the Confraternity of Christian Doctrine, which had started in this country in 1902. Among these factors were further consideration of the number of Catholic children in public schools; Pius XI's statement *On the Teaching of Christian Doctrine* in 1923; the same Pontiff's encyclical on *The Christian Education of Youth* in 1929; his statement *On the Better Care and Promotion of Catechetical Instruction* in 1935; and the establishment of a national center for the Confraternity under the leadership of Bishop Edwin V. O'Hara in 1933.

Finally, the government, through its judicial branch, the Supreme Court, continued the trend of the nineteenth century. Its decisions during this period centered around two areas. The first was government aid to non-public schools, the bases for decisions of which were the First and Fourteenth Amendments to the Federal Constitution, the "child-benefit" theory, and the state's public welfare duty. The Court decided that private schools have the right to exist, and that the state can legally supply nonsectarian textbooks and transportation to children in private schools. The second area was religion in public education, wherein the Court decided that released-time programs were permissible if held off school premises and with a bare minimum of administrative cooperation. The Court refused to decide a case on Bible reading because the plaintiffs in the case were judged not to have either sufficient standing or sufficient injury to bring the suit. State courts continued to contradict one another on the legality of teaching sisters' wearing their religious garb in public schools. The greatest Church-State cooperation in education came after World War II when the Servicemen's Readjustment Act was passed in 1944. Commonly called the "GI Bill of Rights," this legislation enabled the government to pay tuition and other education expenses of "GI's" returned from World War II, and later from the Korean conflict, in any school of their choice, even schools of theology.

## CHAPTER VI

# 1958-Present: Contemporary Soul-searching and Ferment

## The Over-all Situation

### PROBLEMS

IN PUBLIC EDUCATION AND PRIVATE EDUCATION
OTHER THAN CATHOLIC

Intense criticism of all American education began with the launching of Russia's Sputnik I on October 4, 1957. A stunned American public, whose pride smarted under the humiliating sting of Russia's lead in space, questioned its educational system, and found voice in educational critics who demanded a toughening of the curriculum and a greater stress on intellectual training. The controversy was but an intensification of the assault on the schools that had, as Cremin says, "been brewing at least since the early 1940's." Directed at public education had been such publications as Mortimer Smith's *And Madly Teach*, Albert Lynd's *Quackery in the Public Schools*, and Arthur Bestor's *Educational Wastelands*.[1] Bestor, historian and educator, in an interview with *U. S. News and World Report* published November 30, 1956, had stated that the American school system had failed because of its waste of time and student brains, and that it needed a return to the three R's.[2] Among all of the country's high schools, said Bestor, one half offered no course in physics, one quarter offered neither physics nor chemistry, and nearly one quarter offered no geometry. Year after year the subjects of mathematics and science were taught to a shrinking population of students. The real crisis was one of *quality* in education, and on this point the critics of the progressive school were at one. Russian space successes in 1957 brought the

American educational issue into sharp focus. The Age of Space required emphasis on sciences, mathematics, and foreign languages without a neglect of the humanities and social sciences.

The years immediately after 1957 ushered in a revolution in quality of educational content and at the same time a battle for equality of educational opportunity. Both movements still struggle for solution. "For the Nation," said President John F. Kennedy in 1963, "increasing the quality and availability of education is vital to both our national security and our domestic well-being." [3] The new age of science and space, in the President's opinion, called for improved education "to give new meaning to our national purpose and power." [4] It became the vogue to draw comparisons between the Russian system of education and our own, to our disadvantage. Vice-Admiral Hyman G. Rickover, for example, in 1959, in his *Report on Russia* claimed that American schools fail to distinguish between training and education, and that their mistrust of "booklearning" is a carry-over from John Dewey. Rickover was disturbed by the "elective system in high school" whereby the students make decisions that "influence them for the rest of their lives." [5] In the same year, 1959, on a more professional and practical level, concern for the improvement of the American high school was evidenced in James Bryant Conant's *The American High School Today.*[6] Conant, however, made little use of comparisons with Russian education. The American educational system must be evaluated in the society which it reflects and serves. Reform was the pervasive theme—constructive, practical reform—taking its head start during the period from the National Defense Education Act of 1958 which purported in particular to strengthen education programs in mathematics, science, engineering, and modern languages.[7]

From Sputnik to today, pointing out problems in American education has assumed the proportions of a national pastime. A headline in 1965 read "America Provides Equal Educational Opportunity—For Every Fourth or Fifth Child." [8] The article cited in support the fact that South Carolina spends an average of $240 per year on each school child, with the unhappy result that only 48 per cent of those taking the relatively simple Selective Service mental test in South Carolina pass it, and only one-half of South Carolina's eighth-graders go on to finish high school. In Virginia, in the adjacent school districts of Bristol City and Buchanan County the city spends one-third more per pupil than the county and has a drop-out rate one-third of the county's; almost 98% of the city's teachers are college graduates and less than half of the county's. In central Missouri, a teacher with less than two years of college training was getting as an annual salary $3,375 for teaching all eight grades in a one-room schoolhouse with no running water, only a few textbooks, and no science equipment. One out of five teachers in the United States did not at that time meet full certification standards and nearly the same proportion were without a college degree. In 1968 three teacher strikes in New York City kept most of that city's 57,000 teachers off their jobs and 1,129,000 pupils out of class for thirty-five school days.

As for the nation's students, 200,000 out of the 600,000 who were graduating in the top third of their high school class were failing to go on to college, principally because of a lack of money. Also on the national scene, 409,000 pupils in 1964 were attending schools each day for less than the normal period of time because of the surging population in some areas. There were seventeen states with no special facilities for the education of the deaf. Only one-third of the states had sufficient classes for the mentally retarded, and the United States Office of Education statistics indicated that 150,000 more teachers were needed for the retarded and the handicapped. Relevant to this point, Michael Harrington has indicated that in 1968 children under eighteen years of age composed 42 per cent of the poor of our country, and that the average Negro who finishes high school had a mathematical ability below eighth-grade level and a reading ability not much higher.[9]

Finance was another problem; with municipal budgets overburdened, state taxing powers limited, and federal aid at a minimum, day schools were operating with extreme difficulty. Federal aid to public elementary schools during this period was in its infancy, paying for less than one-fifth of the actual total cost. Federal aid on the level of colleges and universities was more formidable, paying nearly a fourth of the cost, with the estimate that by 1975 this would increase to possibly half if present trends continued. Because of tight financing, however, in the urban slums there were antiquated school buildings that were dismal, poorly heated, and in some instances firetraps. The United States Office of Education reported that 124,300 new classrooms were needed in 1964. Even in the suburbs the cost of education stirred growing concern as taxpayers revolted against rising school costs—for example, in White Plains, New York, the superintendent of schools indicated in 1967 that "there's a fiscal crisis at our heels," and a school board member of Nassau County, New York, said that "we're in for rougher times ahead." In the same year, on Long Island forty-three school budgets for the 1967-68 school year were initially voted down in the spring.[10] In Youngstown, Ohio, the schools went so far as to close in November and December of 1968 for lack of tax money.

Fears that the Nixon Administration planned to let the states run their schools as they pleased and unassisted were laid to rest in February, 1969. For the post of United States Commissioner of Education and assistant secretary in the Department of Health, Education and Welfare, President Richard Nixon picked James E. Allen, Jr., former education commissioner of New York. The urban ghetto schools are Allen's gravest concern, and it is there that he feels federal aid can have the most impact. He was quoted as saying that "we have built a middle-class type of education taught by middle-class teachers and run by middle-class ad-

ministrators for middle-class kids. . . . But rarely have we provided the
type of teaching that a deprived child really needs." [11] And, according to
the same article, "desegregation and better teacher training are his
[Allen's] next big goals." During the same period, and boding ill for the
education of youth, was a general retreat from the home.

## IN ROMAN CATHOLIC EDUCATION

For Catholics, contemporary soul-searching and ferment in education
may be said to have had their roots in John Tracy Ellis' work on
"American Catholics and the Intellectual Life" mentioned at the end of
the last chapter. Appearing originally in the September 1955 issue of
*Thought*, it appeared in 1956 in book form, was reprinted in the same
year by Louis J. Putz, and its theme has been repeated thereafter by
such as Thomas F. O'Dea.[12] In any case, Dr. John J. Meng expressed the
contemporary situation well when he said:

American Catholic education is in disarray. Whether this disarray is the result
of decrepitude and confusion or of exuberant vitality and rapid growth is not
yet entirely clear. What is obvious is that the whole structure, from pre-school
programs through graduate school, is in flux.[13]

The process of change in Catholic education is obvious. "The comforting
feeling of security regarding Catholic Education," said C. Albert Koob,
O.Praem., in 1966, "has, indeed, been dissipated but in its place one
notices a vital and stimulating spirit of quest." [14] The 1967 meetings of
the National Catholic Educational Association were given over to "The
Role of Catholic Education in Contemporary American Society." At that
convention, the Most Rev. Ernest J. Primeau, Bishop of Manchester,
New Hampshire, and president general of the NCEA, spoke realistically
but optimistically of "The Future of Catholic Education." Admitting that
Catholic education had been "snug, content—and badly out of touch,"
and was in need of change, Primeau warned against a division into two
polarized camps—"on the one hand, those who fear and resist every
hint of departure from the old ways of doing things, and on the other
those who feel that radical uprooting is the only road to renewal." [15]
What Catholic education needs in this time of change, said Primeau, "is
a philosophy, a rationale for its own existence . . . each age needs to
work out its own rationale for what it believes and what it does." On the
same point, Dr. William H. Conley, first director of the Notre Dame
study on Catholic education, had written in 1966:

The essentials of a Catholic philosophy of education based on the nature of
God, the nature of man and his dependence upon God, the nature of truth and
man's relation to it and his ability to attain it, have, of course, not changed. But
the expansion of knowledge and the social developments which have taken
place require new emphases.[16]

The financial and personnel problems of Catholic education are so pressing that the situation has led to proposals by Catholic educators to cut back by concentrating exclusively on either the elementary or the secondary school. At present there is a continuing debate on this question—which level should be maintained and which dropped? Those in favor of Catholic elementary schools stress the argument of Catholic obligation to the child in his impressionable and formative years; [17] others claim that a student's faith is challenged and deepened in the high school years.[18] Sister Ann Virginia, I.H.M., principal of St. Mary Academy, Monroe, Michigan, spoke the mind of many Catholic educators when she said: "The question is—in a time of crisis when decisions are forced upon us, at what level can we insure the fullest Catholic education to the necessarily limited number of students we will have for a limited period of time?" [19] For Sister Ann Virginia the answer lay in terminal education which, for the vast majority, is high school.

### THE STATISTICAL PICTURE

The ferment in Catholic education is reflected in the statistics for the period. Were those statistics to end in 1964, they would be encouraging. From 1950 to 1960, for example, whereas public school growth on the elementary level was 142 per cent, Catholic schools increased 171 per cent. On the high school level in the same period, public growth was 148 per cent and Catholic school growth 174 per cent. The high point for Roman Catholic education from the point of view of quantitative attendance was the 1963-64 school year, after which a downward trend began. The rate of decrease of enrollment in all Catholic schools below college level for 1967-68 was 4.3 per cent below the previous year, that for 1968-69 was 5 per cent below that, and that for 1969-70 was estimated at 3 per cent or a total decrease of almost 156,000 pupils (nearly all at the elementary level) to a total student population of 4,860,000. Optimists hoped the smaller drop represented a leveling-off. According to Mrs. Winifred R. Long, NCEA research director and compiler of the above statistics, the Catholic school pattern "opted generally to sacrifice numbers and continue a sharp upgrading of quality. The result was a continued upgrading of teacher qualifications and of teachers' salaries, and a continued lowering of class sizes." [20] Nevertheless, the sad truth remained that over-all enrollment has been in decline, as compared with both previous Catholic enrollments and public schools. This can be accounted for only in part by a falling birth rate. Those looking to statistics for signs of optimism might perhaps find it in the approval of Catholic schools by the Catholic people which seemed to be evident in statistics released by the Department of Education of the United States Catholic Conference, indicating that Catholic schools had had to turn away 60,000 students in the two years prior to 1968. Also, there were those who saw in the closings and consolidations a process that had taken place in the public schools long before: the 283,308 public elementary schools in 1930, for example, had by 1965 been reduced to 73,260. On the high school level, optimists pointed to the advantages of reduced schools with larger student enrollments in each: whereas there were 260 more Catholic high schools in 1960 than in 1969, the average size in 1960 was 368 pupils, and that in 1969 was 504.

Catholics expressed concern, some of which was indicated in a 1967 study prepared for the Pennsylvania Catholic Conference and endorsed by a committee of civic, business, and labor leaders headed by Joseph G. Smith. Among others things, this study found that unless non-public education were subsidized in Pennsylvania there might be a massive influx of pupils into the public school system with the cost to the state being $200,000,000 in operating costs, and 1.2 billion dollars in capital costs for the construction of new schools, the provision of equipment, and the purchase of furnishings. About 600,000 pupils or 23 per cent of all children in basic education in the state were enrolled in non-public schools at that time, the saving to the taxpayers being more than $350,000,000 per year. Of the principle of the separation of Church and State, the report said:

That principle, however, also gives full and meaningful recognition of the public services rendered by Church-related institutions. . . . Thus Federal and State programs of financial support to public welfare activities carried on by Protestant, Catholic and Jewish homes for the aged have long been recognized as advancing the public interest.[21]

The St. Paul-Minneapolis Catholic schools in 1968 had a record one-year drop which reduced Catholic school enrollment by more than one-fifth as compared with four years before.[22] In St. Cloud, Minn., the 1968 enrollment in its fifty-two elementary schools went down 799 from 1967 and secondary school enrollment suffered a decrease of 967;[23] in 1969 the St. Cloud diocesan Board of Education announced the closing of nine parish schools, the combining of two others, and the dropping of grades in several schools as the first phase of a movement to consolidate the school program in the diocese. In 1969 at Baltimore, Maryland, Lawrence Cardinal Shehan termed the expenses of Catholic high school education "staggering" because of the decreasing number of teaching priests, brothers, and sisters. Though he had to phase out $900,000 of the annual archdiocesan subsidies to Catholic high schools, he pledged that all students then attending would be able to "continue through to graduation."[24] Because of staff shortages and financial problems, the archdiocese of Milwaukee, Wisconsin, in 1969 closed up eighteen schools, with St. John Cathedral School, oldest school in the archdiocese, among them. Also in 1969 in such places as Denver, Colorado, and Detroit, Michigan, announcements were made of the closings of Catholic high schools.

Not all closings or mergers, however, meant necessarily the loss of students. In 1967, for example, the diocese of Dubuque, Iowa, merged forty-nine rural schools without losing a single student. Also, although the principle of Baltimore III of "every Catholic child in a Catholic school" was becoming more and more impossible of fulfillment, more than ten per cent of the total United States school population was still in Catholic schools. A small fraction of these, it is true, was in private elementary Catholic schools, the cost of which was not a matter of any grave concern for the parents of the children enrolled. This type of convent school has been favored by parents in the diplomatic service, the armed services, and other occupations involving mobility. Among the reasons for the privileged existence of these convent schools have been smaller classes, more flexible curricula, facilities for more individual attention, frequently residence accommodations, and often their provision of a route to college.[25]

But the crises and the ferment continue. The New York State Council of Catholic School Superintendents in February 1969 issued a memorandum noting a decrease of 58,418 Catholic school students in the state during the preceding five years, more than twenty-five thousand of the decrease being in 1969 alone. While acknowledging that part of the cause can be found in a declining birth rate and efforts to reduce the pupil-teacher ratio, the memorandum attributed most of the reason to ever-rising costs. The resultant costs to taxpayers, it said, would be some $29,550,000, based on NEA statistics that per-pupil expenditure in the state's public schools was then $1,140 per year.[26] Shortly thereafter, Governor Nelson Rockefeller told a "Town Meeting" at Watertown, New York, that parents who had been both paying taxes and supporting nonpublic schools "have done a fantastic job and I think they deserve a sincere debt of gratitude from all of us in the state."[27] In Philadelphia, Msgr. Edward T. Hughes, archdiocesan superintendent of schools, noted that as of Jan. 31, 1969, parishes were $482,000 behind in payment of their educational assessments, with 75 per cent of most parish finances going for education. In March 1969, spokesmen for Connecticut's Catholic schools told legislators that unless financial assistance were provided by the state, nearly 100,000 Catholic school pupils would have to be absorbed into the public schools within about two years, at a cost of more than $56 million, not including an estimated $180 million for new buildings. The Michigan Association of Nonpublic Schools published in 1969 a booklet, *The Day the Nonpublic Schools Closed,* indicating that the closing of Michigan's nonpublic schools to their 315,000 students would cost its taxpayers immediately at least $800 million for new facilities and about $220 million in operating costs. At the same time the archdiocese of Detroit indicated that 49 schools in the archdiocese, including over 20 in Detroit's "core city," were in such dire financial straits that they would either have to close completely or drastically curtail enrollment. *Time* magazine for March 28, 1969, rating the parochial school system as "a bargain for society whatever else it may be," commented that it is no bargain for the taxpayer when a Catholic parent decides that he can no longer afford parochial school tuition. Upholding this statement, *Time* cited examples:

A Catholic-school official in New York estimated that transfers into public schools will add $30 million to the state's education bill this year, perhaps $50 million next year. If all nonpublic schools in Wisconsin were to close, the taxpayers' burden would be increased by about $230 million a year.[28]

There is indeed a fiscal crisis, with many dioceses reporting the financial squeeze publicly.[29] In 1968 the archdiocese of Omaha, Nebraska, reported that "the rising cost of operating schools within the Omaha Archdiocese is threatening the ability of the Archdiocese as a whole to maintain a balanced financial position." [30] The archdiocese of Cincinnati, Ohio, had dropped its first-grade classes before that, and a study committee of Spokane, Washington, recommended that that diocese's elementary schools close its first four grades. They said:

Our recommendation is based primarily on what psychologists and sociologists have discovered about how children develop values at various age levels. . . . These findings strongly indicate that the home is, during the preschool and primary school years, a far more influential factor than institutions such as schools, churches, youth groups, etc. Psychologists and sociologists generally agree that during the early childhood years the home is the primary agent in forming the moral, religious, social, and political values of children.[31]

The accountability of funds and the real costs of programs became major issues. The Rev. Ernest Bartell claimed, for example, that a disproportionate share of the financial burden of Catholic education was being assumed by the philanthropy of the poor rather than that of the rich and that "steadily higher tuition and fees will tend to restrict [Catholic] school attendance to an elite that can afford these costs." [32] The Rev. Joseph P. Fitzpatrick, sociologist of Fordham University, said essentially the same thing in charging that the parochial schools were not meeting the needs of minorities such as Negroes and Puerto Ricans, especially in the Manhattan and Bronx areas of the archdiocese of New York.[33] Also, Monsignor James C. Donohue, director of the U. S. Catholic Conference's Education Department, indicated in the keynote address of the NCEA 1967 convention that "we are increasingly serving a middle-class and upper-middle-class school population." [34]

### SOUL-SEARCHING, FERMENT

The problems, however, were not all financial: there was a decline in religious vocations; some religious teaching orders were conducting experimentation in other forms of the apostolate; involvement of more and more laymen as teachers, administrators, and members of diocesan parish school boards, discussed elsewhere, had its own unique problems; and

Catholic education had received a bad press, from which there seemed no way out. Such prestigious publications as *The New York Times*, when referring to Catholic education, constantly used such pejorative terms as paternalism, clericalism, ghetto, provincial, and divisive; they also referred to the anti-intellectual past of Roman Catholicism, with charges that her former intellectual giants were either converts or apostates. There may have been just enough basis in reality to some of these terms to appeal to certain segments of the population. Another problem seemed to be a growing number of ex-seminarians involved in the field of education. Psychologists often attributed the hypercriticisms and hostility of some of these to the scars of previous personal experiences rather than to objective reality or cerebral validity, and in no other field—medicine, law, or whatever—have those who did not complete their degree work or practice their profession been taken seriously as authorities to the same extent as these critics in the area of Roman Catholic education.

The problems caused a great deal of soul-searching and ferment. Some, such as the following, were based in history. The origins of Catholic schools had brought about a highly decentralized pattern: the Councils of Baltimore had exhorted and then decreed parish schools; the hierarchy had brought pressure on individual pastors to found schools; and they had also invited religious orders to establish private schools independently. Could this pattern, for the sake of efficiency, now be made more centralized? Historically, school loyalty was bound up with loyalty to the parish and the pastor; would a shift from the parish base affect parish interest in and support of schools? The establishment of Catholic schools had received impetus from the public schools' Protestant orientation and then their secularization which lacked moral training based on religion; does scientific evidence support the concept that public schools continue to be religiously harmful to Catholics? How far do the proposals for public schools to teach *about* religion answer traditional Catholic objections? From the beginning, Catholic schools emphasized securing *religious* teachers; does the fact that their number and proportion have declined substantially, change the nature of the parochial school as originally conceived and traditionally understood? Most bishops historically found it necessary to withdraw control of the schools from lay trustees; does this have any relevance to current discussions of policy-making school boards with greater lay participation? Historically, Catholics have contended that distributive justice demands public support for their schools; is there any greater hope of public agreement to this petition now than in the past? Some see in today's controversies within the Church on Catholic education another outbreak of such "liberal-conservative" fights of the past as those in the 1840's and 1890's; do those battles have any lessons for today? History shows that Protestants opted for the dual system of public schools for secular education and Sunday schools for religion; has their experience with this been satisfactory, and do circumstances suggest its application to the Catholic effort? Finally, the development of their separate school pattern has resulted in Catholic concern being focused primarily on Catholic school problems with relative indifference to those of the public schools. Today's Catholics are taught to be concerned with all the world's crises such as those of cities, and with the public schools as an integral part of those crises. Can all this be reconciled with the maintenance of the traditional separate patterns?

SUGGESTED SOLUTIONS

In spite of the problems, most fair-minded persons would agree with the statement in a United States Office of Education publication that the non-public schools of the nation have played "an enormous role in transmitting our cultural heritage [and] have exerted a tremendous influence in fashioning the American way of life." [35] Very few, therefore, would suggest as a solution the complete elimination of Catholic schools. Coming the closest, perhaps, would be Mary Perkins Ryan. The nub of her suggestion is that the

question at issue is not whether there should be *any* Catholic schools. As I have suggested, there will always be a need for Catholic schools of various special kinds. The question is whether there should be a Catholic school *system*, maintained as a part of the very structure of the Church.[36]

Her objections may be summarized into seven, which have been repeated frequently since she wrote in 1964:

1. The Catholic School system is a relic of the siege mentality.
2. General education *can* and *should* be separated from religious formation in these times and in this country.
3. Catholic schools are financial handicaps and therefore remain mediocre.
4. The manner in which Catholic schools present religious education is too formal to be effective in life.
5. In a pluralistic society they are divisive.
6. They are contrary to the spirit of ecumenism.
7. They consume time, effort and money that might better be spent upon adult formation in catechetical centers and Newman Clubs.

Among the many answers given Ryan in the heated controversy that followed the publication of her book, perhaps the arguments of the Rt. Rev. Msgr. Thomas Duffy were representative. He argued that our age is a formal one and to attempt to influence it only informally is unrealistic. He also questioned whether what exists in Catholic schools is formalism or simple order and planning. He warned against confusing ecumenism with religious emotionalism. Duffy disagreed that religion is taught adequately in the home, saying, "I do not think that the family can supply the necessary religious training of the young, nor do I think the liturgy is enough to keep the faith alive." [37] He cited France as an example of what can happen if schools are dismissed as a means of instructing youth. Others, however, were to join the Ryan bandwagon. Lee claimed that inasmuch as "the Catholic school exists far more to provide basic attitudes and values than to teach the student to read and write or to be a nuclear physicist," [38] Catholic elementary schools should be discontinued because it is an empirically proven fact that attitudes and values of children of elementary school age are almost totally parent-derived.

There were, however, many other suggestions for change, most of them for the purpose of saving money. Harriman and Wing claimed that "as professional economists we have studied the problems confronting the parochial school system on the secondary and elementary levels, and we consider these problems to be essentially, though not exclusively, economic." [39] On this basis they proposed

a restructuring of the entire Catholic parochial school system. . . . The new structure is on a 6-3-3 basis, that is, the first six grades comprise the first unit of organization; grades 7 through 9 a second unit (junior high school), and grades 10 through 12 a third (senior high school). [40]

They suggested that for economic efficiency grades 1 through 6 then be eliminated from parochial school, the classrooms to be used for junior high school purposes.

Neil G. McCluskey, S.J., suggested a similar solution, culminating in a network of junior colleges which

would mean that many tens of thousands of Catholic young men and women, at a critical stage of intellectual maturation, would have at least some access to what few of them will ever discover elsewhere, the philosophical and theological treasures of Christian humanism as well as the great documents of Catholic social thought. [41]

Many other educators, as we mentioned above, recognize the importance of the elementary school years for the formation of lifetime habits and the extreme impressionability of that age, making elementary school years extremely important. All psychologists realize, however, the importance of high school years to overcome the mental, moral, and physical difficulties connected with that transitional stage. All recognize also the intellectual commitment that is possible only at the college level and would therefore intensely dislike to have to eliminate Catholic schooling at that time.

Some would like to change the form of Catholic education, and concentrate on the teaching of religion alone. In the abandonment of Catholic schools as they have existed, they see financial advantages, a better accord with the ecumenical movement, and the opportunity of releasing increasingly scarce religious teachers and also dedicated lay teachers for other pressing needs of the Church. An experiment in this regard said to be successful is taking place at Fairport, New York. Another is at Westhampton Beach, Long Island, a summer resort with a constant population of middle-income people, where the pastor polled the 600-family parish in 1964 on the question of whether to build a parochial school. Of the minority who responded, only one out of ten was enthusiastic; a slightly larger fraction was strongly opposed; and the remainder had many reservations including satisfaction with the local public school facilities. A fifteen-member committee of real estate experts, contractors, and lawyers reported that a school and convent would cost about one million dollars, create a large debt, not guarantee a desk for every pupil, necessitate lay teachers with salaries lower than public school ones, and thus possibly invite inferior education. A religious education building, they said, would cost $400,000, have a large hall easily and quickly divisible into ten classrooms, and accommodate basketball games, dances, and Sunday Masses for the summer crowds. It was the latter suggestion that the pastor, the Very Rev. Msgr. James J. Griffin, accepted as seeming right for his particular parish in its particular circumstances. In an interview in 1967, after the building had been erected, he saw the program of Confraternity of Christian Doctrine relying mainly on laymen as teachers and creating obligations for parents. He was also of the opinion that the system eliminated the first- and second-class citizenship sometimes created in parishes with a school that was unable to accommodate all applicants.[42] In the archdiocese of St. Louis, Missouri, because of financial problems, a halt had to be placed on school building until the quality of education could be assured and the shortage of teachers rectified. Other dioceses, finding themselves in the same financial straits, had to make the same regulation.

Solutions were also sought in a re-investigation of the organization of Catholic schools. In the traditional administrative procedures as evolved in diocesan systems of education, the head of the entire system has been the bishop. His representative has been the diocesan superintendent of schools, who worked with the diocesan school board, usually comprised of diocesan clergy with the diocesan superintendent as secretary. On the level of the school itself have been the pastor and the principal, who have the immediate responsibility. Usually the pastor, who is not a trained educator, has been the head of the school. A rethinking came up with several new concepts: the diocesan superintendent of schools, as the director, should receive a stronger mandate from the bishop in order to be able to rule in truth with the principals; school boards should be given more authority; on the diocesan level, school boards should be comprised more and more of representatives of teaching communities involved, and also of laymen; and on the parish level, the school boards should supersede the autonomous rule of the pastor. According to Msgr. O'Neil C. D'Amour in 1967, nearly one out of three United States Catholic elementary schools had school boards which included laymen; almost all of these boards had been created within the previous three years. According to D'Amour, former associate secretary of the NCEA School Superintendent's Department (who for years pushed the idea of introducing school boards), this was a favorable development, providing as it did nonprofessional people from the community to form school policies that reflected the community's attitudes and wishes.[43] There were, however, indications that some priests and people still believed that "Father knows best." Still others, like Koob of NCEA, believing that modern rapid transportation and easy communication have made it unrealistic to keep confining subject specialists and administrators to many small parish schools, believed that pastors should plan jointly with others to better utilize staff through inter-parochial team teaching projects.

To discover the people's thinking, others took surveys. In a 1968 survey, for example, of some 19,000 Catholic households in Louisville, Kentucky, there were indications that many would be willing to reduce the Church's educational program. On the question whether, if the Church stepped up its efforts to provide religious education for children, "it would be less necessary for the Church to have as large a school system as it now has," 43 per cent answered "Yes," 19 per cent were undecided, and 38 per cent disagreed. On the question whether it is possible to have a strong Catholic parish without a parochial elementary school, 40 per cent answered "Yes," 43 per cent disagreed, and 17 per cent were undecided. On whether Catholic school education for the student "is narrowing because it limits children to contacts with those who have the same religious beliefs," 27 per cent answered "Yes," 59 per cent disagreed, and 14 per cent were undecided. On whether Catholics who went to public schools "turn out to be just as good Catholics as those who attend parochial schools," 44 per cent answered "Yes," 23 per cent disagreed, and 32 per cent were undecided. Contradicting all these responses, however, eight out of ten persons polled were of the opinion that Catholic schools have "a unique and desirable quality not found in public schools," and that every Catholic child should spend some time in Catholic schools.[44]

### SIGNS OF HOPE

The picture was not completely black. Concerned Catholic educators who are aware of the vital issues confronting Catholic education today hold high hopes for its continued existence. Dr. Anthony E. Seidl of the University of San Francisco sees not "the destruction of Catholic schools but their reformation and advancement." [45] Koob writes that "we can feel quite certain the Catholic schools are going to be on the scene for a long while." [46] The Rev. Roman A. Bernert, S.J., writing in 1966, claimed that what Catholic education needs is a new approach, not new objectives—a change of emphasis in which stress is given "from the beginning of instruction *to the role of the individual Christian in this world's society*," so that "the sweeping charges by such critics of Catholic education as Mary Perkins Ryan will soon disappear." [47] Bernert seems to speak the mind of the majority of Catholic educators when he contends that Catholic education needs only the flexibility to adapt to changing conditions; in his words, "the baby that Baltimore III gave birth to deserves to be saved, but its bath needs to be changed." [48]

CATHOLIC INTELLECTUAL ACTIVITY

Adding another touch of hope in the crisis in the Catholic education situation was the fact that the sophistication and intellectual status of Catholics seemed to be higher than at any other time in the history of the Church in the United States. There were several superficial but real indications of this. In publications for Catholics, for example, the editorial policy of many newspapers shifted from printing only local stories such as mere social news and parish events to those that were meaningful to "teach," especially on moral and theological topics. Although the circulations of Catholic newspapers and magazines in general declined, that of literary periodicals in some cases increased and in most cases at least held even.[49]

Another area giving evidence of and impetus to Catholic intellectual activity and higher sophistication was that of libraries. On the level of higher education, Catholic university libraries broadened their collections to serve the growing needs of scholarly research, and undergraduate libraries for instructional programs. Such universities as St. Louis, Notre Dame, Catholic, Fordham, Boston College, and Georgetown had the most comprehensive of Catholic book collections. Four college libraries qualified for the financial assistance of the Carnegie Foundation of New York—St. Catherine (St. Paul, Minnesota), Marygrove (Detroit, Michigan), Our Lady of the Lake (San Antonio, Texas), and Rosary (River Forest, Illinois)—all Catholic colleges for women. In 1963 through 1964, the grand total of library holdings in 285 Catholic institutions excluding seminaries was 19,019,147 books plus 777,042 microformat units and 150,783 periodicals. To help Catholic parochial and secondary school libraries, the Paulist Press in 1962 instituted the Catholic Library Service, which in 1966 changed its name to the American Library and Educational Service (ALESCO), serving more than 6,700 elementary, high school, and public libraries. It publishes the *Alesco Elementary School Catalogue* and the *Alesco High School Catalogue* to indicate suitable books at these levels. Covering in part these same areas, the Catholic Library Association (Haverford, Pennsylvania) sponsors the *Catholic Supplement to the Standard Catalogue for High School Libraries* and the *Catholic Book List*. On the parish level, libraries have developed unevenly, for two reasons: they are usually more adaptable to rural situations, and they depend upon the amount of enthusiasm of the local pastor.

The higher level of intellectual sophistication during this period is also witnessed by the number of programs in adult education, usually short non-credit courses sponsored by colleges and universities, dioceses, high schools, parish special centers, and libraries. In 1954, the National Catholic Educational Association had established a Commission on Adult Education which was reorganized in 1959 under the new name of the National Catholic Adult Education Commission, the purpose of which was to encourage and coordinate Catholic adult educational activities, to spread information, and to act as a clearing house for programs. Other programs were allied to adult education, such as Cana Conferences, the Rural Life Movement, the Confraternity of Christian Doctrine Study Clubs, the Catholic Family Movement, Grail programs, Te Deum forums, and the radio, television, and other programs of the National Councils of Catholic Men and Women.[50]

SCIENTIFIC RESEARCH STUDIES

Another sign of life and hope for Catholic education during this period of soul-searching and ferment was the fact that many research studies were set in motion, the end result of which will undoubtedly be to clarify solutions to the problems. Actually, the first plea for both research and experimentation in Catholic education came from one outside the establishment—Myron Lieberman—in an address to the Superintendent's Department at the 1960 NCEA convention. He claimed that Catholic education was not holding its own in either educational research or experimentation, even though in the latter regard Catholic education was freer than public.[51] Research became the theme of Catholic educators across the country. In 1962 two massive scientific studies were undertaken, and both were published in 1966. One study of Catholic elementary and secondary schools in the United States, entitled *Catholic Schools in Action*,[52] was made possible by a grant from the Carnegie Corporation and conducted at the University of Notre Dame. Under the directorship of Dr. William H. Conley at first, and then under Reginald A. Neuwien, this study was conducted under certain guide rules. The most important of these were that reliable statistical information was to be collected on a nationwide basis from all agencies that would cooperate; thirteen dioceses were to be studied in depth; the study was to be objective and informative, not evaluative; the Catholic school system was not to be compared with the public school system, although "national norms would be taken into account"; the study would pay special attention to religious and ethical education, a prime concern of Catholic education; and the editors' definition of a study in depth would involve both educational and sociological analysis.[53]

Concerning the enrollment of Catholic schools, the study dealt with such matters as eligible youth, admission policies, tuition costs, organization patterns, size, planned facilities, graduates, financial support, and academic achievement. In its treatment of staff it went into the age of teachers, their preparation and experience, school principals, the ratio of staff to students, and lay teachers. Speaking of the preparation of religious-order teachers, it provides information on Sister-formation and the training of certain specific religious-order teachers. In a large segment entitled "Inventory of Catholic School Outcomes," it dealt with three areas: the first, "Religious Understanding," treated the status of religious instruction; the second was the student attitude index, under which came religious-moral values, social-civic attitudes, family values, and educational aspirations; and the third, a student opinionnaire, dealt with student opinions on such items as the relative importance of stated Catholic school goals, the Catholic schools' success in meeting stated goals, their parents' role, sources of influence on students' religious development, and the operation of the schools. Finally, the study dealt with parental characteristics and their expectations of Catholic schooling in the areas of religion, personal and social virtue, academics, school operation, and other practical areas. The Notre Dame study was reviewed in November 1966 by Conley, its former director, who drew up the following conclusions:

1. The study was a tremendous undertaking. The collection of data from 92 percent of all elementary schools and 84 percent of the high schools is in itself a major achievement. It sets to rest for all times the charge that Catholic schools are closed operations.

2. The cooperation of the hierarchy and of the superintendents of Catholic schools was basic to the success of data collection.

3. The unfortunate delay in publishing the profile part of the study makes the factual material out-of-date in the rapidly changing situation in Catholic schools. *To be meaningful, this part of the study should be repeated immediately.*

4. The depth studies are disappointing and subject to serious misinterpretation. The instruments for the measurement of religious outcomes and student attitudes are inadequate. The sampling procedure for administration of the instruments appear to be too limited to be acceptable.

5. The visitations made and interviews conducted by staff members and consultants were not satisfactorily reported. Only casual references were made to them, yet they held the key to the most important aspects of the study.

6. The major problems of Catholic education—i.e., centralization at the diocesan level, equalization in financial support, clarification of status of the office of superintendent, long-range regional planning, development of school boards —were not identified, although they should have emerged from the depth studies.

7. The shortcomings of *Catholic Schools in Action* should set the guide lines for additional studies to be made at both the national and diocesan levels.[54]

The second major study of this era was that of Andrew M. Greeley and Peter H. Rossi, *The Education of Catholic Americans*. This study personally interviewed a representative national sample composed of 2,753 American Catholics between the ages of twenty-three and fifty-seven. In addition, the study left 1,000 self-administered questionnaires at the homes of other Catholic respondents. Where there were adolescents in these homes, another self-administered questionnaire was requested of those currently in high school. Another questionnaire was mailed to a randomly selected sample of 1,000 readers of *Commonweal*. The study was interested in four major areas, the first of which was the preservation of religious faith. The questions asked under this heading were whether Catholic schools have succeeded in providing religious education and "whether any level of education is more effective than other levels in the development of religious values." [55] The authors found that "the son of the immigrant, and the grandson of the immigrant have kept the faith (and probably would have to a considerable degree even if there had been no Catholic schools)," indicating that what was taught of religious values in the past may now be no longer equally necessary. The authors suggest:

It may be possible for Catholic schools to shift their emphasis. While taking the goals of past decades for granted, the schools may be able to emphasize new values, such as intellectual and civic competence and excellence, understanding of worship, the struggle for interracial and international justice, the quest for religious cooperation and unity.[56]

They found "that parental religiousness reinforces the effect of religious education among those from very religious families," and that

contrary to certain theoretical expectations, those highly religious Catholic families for whom no Catholic schools were available did not develop compensatory mechanisms of religious instruction which were as effective as Catholic schools.

They discovered that

those students within the system who come from very religious backgrounds become themselves even more fervent in their religious practice. Those who come from moderately religious families or nonreligious families are only influenced in a minimal way by Catholic education.[57]

They stated that "the CCD programs do not seem to be a very attractive substitute for Catholic schools, at least at the present time." Although they found "consistently strong and statistically significant relationships between Catholic education and adult behavior," they were perplexed that "no particular level is more effective than any other." In the latter connection, however, "Catholic colleges do indeed have a very powerful impact both on religious behavior and social attitudes, but only among those who have already gone to Catholic primary and secondary schools."

The authors summarize their findings in this connection by asserting first "a moderate but significant association (usually between .2 and .3) between Catholic education and adult religious behavior, an association which survives under a wide variety of socio-economic, demographic, and religious controls." They also indicate the content that has heretofore characterized Catholic religious education:

Sunday Mass, monthly Communion, Confession several times a year, Catholic education of children, financial contribution to the Church, acceptance of the Church as an authoritative teacher, acknowledgment of Papal and hierarchal authority, informality with the clergy, strict sexual morality, more detailed knowledge about one's religion—these are not only the apparent effects of Catholic education, they comprise as well a reasonable description of what the American Church has expected from its laity during the years when it was still concentrating on the preservation of the faith of the immigrant and his children and grandchildren.[58]

Contrary to their expectations, "the association is strongest among those who come from very religious family backgrounds (defined as those in which one parent went to Communion every week)." Weekly Communion by at least one parent also "indicates the presence of a 'multiplier effect.'" Thirdly, "the association between Catholic education and adult behavior is strongest for those who went to Catholic colleges (generally between .4 and .6). It is especially strong among men who went to Catholic colleges (as high as .8)"; fourthly, "family religiousness apparently does not strengthen the association between religious education and adult behavior for those who went to Catholic colleges"; and fifthly, "there are very strong relationships between Catholic education and religious behavior for teen-agers currently in school (between .4 and .6)." Finally, "the differences in the relationships between education and religious behavior found among adults and those found among adolescents are apparently due to the weaker long-run impact of Catholic education on those who do not come from very religious families or who do not marry religious persons."

The second major category was centered about the potentially divisive nature of which Catholic schools have been accused. First was the question "whether the Catholic-school Catholic is more likely to be involved in the organizational activity of his church." Secondly, inasmuch as the contacts of Catholic children while attending their Catholic schools are, for all practical purposes, limited to their school associations, a question was whether "such schools have 'divisive' effects that are manifest among Catholic adults." Finally in this connection was the query "whether Catholic schools develop a sense of social distance between their graduates and other non-Catholic members of our society." The findings, in sum, were:

No confirmation was found for the notion that Catholic schools are "divisive." . . .

In the general population there were only very weak associations (less than .11) between religious education and enlightened social attitudes.

[This] relationship . . . was slightly stronger for those who went to Catholic high schools.

Among those who were in their twenties, and among those who went to college, the relationship between religious education and social consciousness was stronger.

The strongest associations between religious education and social attitudes were found among those who went to Catholic colleges. . . .

The impact of the Catholic high school and the Catholic college on religious behavior and social attitudes apparently is the result of a cumulation of Catholic educational experience and not the result of the particular educational level operating by itself.[59]

Pertinent to the question of "divisiveness" the authors concluded:

We could find no evidence that the products of such a system were less involved in community activities, less likely to have friends from other religious groups, more intolerant in their attitudes, or less likely to achieve occupationally or academically. On the contrary, we found that they were slightly more successful in the world of study and work and—after the breaking point of college—much more tolerant.[60]

This leads to the third major category, Catholic school preparation for economic success or, as the authors put the question, "whether attendance at a Catholic school is a help or a hindrance in coming to grips with the world outside the church." Among their findings was the information that "Catholics who went to Catholic schools were more successful than Catholics who did not," and that "those in Catholic schools seemed much more academically oriented than Catholics in public schools and even more so than Protestants in public schools." The authors summed up their findings in this category thusly:

There is a weak but persistent association between Catholic education and economic and social achievement. . . .

The relationship with achievement is stronger among those from higher socio-economic status backgrounds.

This relationship apparently occurs specifically among those who belonged to Catholic friendship cliques in adolescence and even more specifically (.35) among those who had Catholic friends during adolescence and scored low on an anomie measure.

There are apparently two ways by which Catholics can succeed markedly: the path of alienation from the Catholic community and the path of integration into the Catholic subculture. The latter is somewhat more effective.[61]

Finally, the authors dealt with internal criticism of Catholic schooling, or "how its constituency views the institution." Their summary of their findings was:

There is a direct relationship between social class and sending one's children to Catholic schools. . . .

The most frequent reasons for not sending children to Catholic schools have to do with their availability; the most common criticisms of the schools have to do with their physical facilities.

Both Catholic school attendance and criticism increase with social class, suggesting that the proportion of Catholics in Catholic schools and the criticism of the schools will increase in years to come.[62]

Because readers and reviewers of these studies seem to have approached them from their own points of view, with their own particular prejudices and preconceptions, it is important to keep in mind "what we [Greeley and Rossi] take to be the major theme behind all the findings: like other American schools, Catholic schools are neither as bad as their most severe critics portray them nor as good as they might be."[63] On the other hand, the authors "hazard the guess that . . . Catholic schools . . . have not, by themselves, at least, been responsible for the very high level of religious practice to be found among all American Catholics," and find that "Catholic education was not as important as either the religiousness of parents or the social class of the respondent." Further, the authors emphasize, *"there is no evidence that Catholic schools have been necessary for the survival of American Catholicism,"* [64] and "rather than causing the comparatively high level of minimal allegiance to be found in American Catholics, the schools may be the result of it." Nevertheless, "given the goals which were operative and the obstacles to value-change through formal education, Catholic schools were probably more worth the effort than not worth it"; further, "while Catholic education is not the most important influence on adult religious behavior, it is not an unimportant influence"; and "while American Catholicism would probably have survived in reasonable health without its schools, the schools have nevertheless produced a rather fervent religious elite."[65]

The trend for scientific studies in Catholic education continued. On November 5 to 10, 1967, some 110 authorities in education gathered at Washington, D.C., to participate in a meeting sponsored by NCEA entitled "Blueprint for the Future: The Washington Symposium on Catholic Education." The participants discussed Catholic education in terms of its goals, its structures, its finances, and the growing role of the Catholic layman.[66] The Symposium called for "well designed programs of research and experiment aimed at obtaining reliable data to guide decisions about the most productive use of resources," [67] and asked for a continuing review of all existing programs. In 1967 also, the Roman Catholic Bishops of the United States acknowledged "the immediate need for more research to evaluate our present endeavors, to project our future responsibilities, and to make a thorough inventory of our resources in personnel and finance." [68] In April 1968, Archbishop Terence J. Cooke of New York City appointed a sixteen-member interdenominational Committee on Catholic Education, authorizing it "to undertake a major study of all aspects of Catholic education in the Archdiocese." [69]

In the same year the Office of Educational Research of the University of Notre Dame completed two significant studies. One was a ten-month study for the diocese of Denver, Colorado, which then had 21,980 students in its Catholic schools, representing a 7 per cent decrease in five years. For a variety of reasons, such as convenience and lower cost, 70 per cent of the Catholic students in metropolitan Denver were attending public schools. The study found Catholic schools to be far more effective in religious formation than classes in the Confraternity of Christian Doctrine. The second of these studies was of the Saginaw, Michigan, diocese, with an enrollment of 6,458 students representing a 3 per cent drop in five years. Its findings were similar to those in Denver.

Several recommendations were common to both Notre Dame studies. The first of these was the observation that the schools "could be more strongly emphasizing the commitment to the world which Vatican II so strongly urged." Secondly, both made the same concluding recommendation—i.e., increased centralization of planning, programming, and budgeting. In the area of economics, both studies recommended a consolidation and a cooperative use of elementary facilities as dictated by enrollment, continual economic evaluation of possible cost-saving teaching aids and other innovations to improve quality, the establishment of tuition and fees common to all schools, and the formation of an equalization fund to help poor parishes to support their elementary schools. In the area of teachers, the studies recommended increased teacher specialization, especially in the profusion of centralized services; improved teacher quality, through paying salaries commensurate with academic degrees; and encouraging the acquisition of advanced degrees, perhaps through a subsidization of teacher education. In the area of administration, the studies recommended the establishment of regional councils to act in an advisory capacity to school boards and as informative agencies; a shift of high schools from parish to central administration, to be financed through weighted parish assessments based on the financial ability of each parish; greater attention to the potential for cooperation between public and Catholic schools; and the development of adequate religious education for children not under formal Catholic education.

Incidental to research studies, an October 8, 1969, release from NCEA indicated the establishment of a national Data Bank on Catholic elementary and secondary schools, funded for one year by the Carnegie Corporation of New York and under the leadership of NCEA. It appeared that all 147 dioceses would take part in the Data Bank; if continued, it will not only result in more detailed statistical summaries of Catholic education in the U. S. each year, but will also enable far more accurate studies, appraisals, and planning. Corollary to research studies, it is probably advisable to observe that there is also a brighter side to the statistics that are usually interpreted pessimistically. The latest figures indicate a continuation of the trend of the past five years—

i.e., "better and better education for fewer and fewer pupils." [70] There is a greater pursuit of excellence than ever before: between 1960-61 and 1968-69, the average secondary school size has increased from 386 to 481, and the average elementary school size has decreased from 417 to 378; [71] pupil-teacher ratios are down to 19 to 1 in the high schools and 33 to 1 in the elementary schools; lay teachers, constituting an ever-increasing percentage of the whole, are better paid and better qualified than ever; and reimbursement and training of religious teachers are also up. There are even valid reasons to explain the decrease in the number of religious teachers: some missing religious are accounted for by the low-birth-rate years of the late Thirties (depression) and early Forties (World War II), and there has been a greater scarcity of young people entering professions as well. This, coupled with the hope for a smoothing of the turbulent waves in religious belief at present, lend reasonable hope to future improvement in the numbers of religious teachers. There are also statistics to prove that American citizens are becoming more concerned: one major Gallup survey in 1969 concluded that the chief complaint against public schools is lax discipline, and another Gallup poll indicated in the same year that "the nation's dual system of public and private education . . . won strong endorsement from an over-whelming majority," and that "most Americans value private schools." [72]

## VATICAN II

Another sign of hope and life for Catholic education in the United States as well as in the world was the Second Vatican Council in which from 1962 to 1965 the Roman Catholic bishops of the world participated at Rome in decision-making on all aspects of Catholic life. Relative to education, at least as important as the relatively weak and traditional *Declaration on Christian Education* [73] was the *Pastoral Constitution on the Church in the Modern World.* [74] Addressing itself "not only to the sons of the Church, . . . but to the whole of humanity," [75] the latter document evidenced a positive concern for the whole world. The Council, it said, "gazes upon that world which is the theatre of man's history, and carries the marks of his energies, his tragedies, and his triumphs," [76] and declared its "solidarity with the entire human family with which it is bound up." [77] It invited all men, including atheists, to dialogue, to examine the gospel of Christ with an open mind, and to join in working "for the rightful betterment of this world in which all men alike live." [78] It enjoined that "everyone consider it his sacred obligation to count social necessities among the primary duties of modern man, and to pay heed to them." [79] The *Constitution* urged that "the expectation of a new earth must not weaken but rather stimulate our concern for cultivating this one." [80]

Under its fourth chapter, "The Role of the Church in the Modern World," the *Constitution* presented three points. The first was the mutuality of the relationship between the Church and the world, and it indicated that the Church "goes forward together with humanity and experiences the same earthly lot which the world does." [81] The earthly and heavenly cities penetrate each other, the Church serving "as a leaven and as a kind of soul for human society." [82] Secondly, the *Constitution* pointed out the twofold help that the Church gives to the world through individuals and through society. Helping the individual means primarily opening up to him the meaning of his own existence, and this the Church seeks to do by revealing the mystery of God, since "the Church truly knows that only God, whom she serves, meets the deepest longings of the human heart, which is never fully satisfied by what the world has to offer." [83] The help the Church offers to society as a whole is based on her religious role, in this role transcending the political, economic, and social orders.[84] But the Council Fathers had strong words for those Christians who would "shirk their earthly responsibilities" because they seek the heavenly city more. They declared that "the Christian who neglects his temporal duties neglects his duties toward his neighbor and even God, and jeopardizes his eternal salvation." [85] The chapter's third point concerned the help the Church receives from the world. The Council Fathers acknowledged how richly the Church has profited by the history and development of humanity, and how progress helps to reveal the nature of man and to open new roads to the truth.[86] The Fathers declared that "from the beginning of her history, she [the Church] has learned to express the message of Christ with the help of ideas and terminology of various peoples, and has tried to clarify it with the wisdom of philosophers, too." [87]

In this *Constitution* the Fathers did not treat education specifically very often, but there were several oblique references. One comment, for example, seemed to speak to those who react with hostility and fear in the presence of new scientific theories and truths:

Therefore, if methodical investigation within every branch of learning is carried out with a genuinely scientific manner and in accord with moral norms, it never truly conflicts with faith. For earthly matters and the concerns of faith derive from the same God. . . . Consequently, we cannot but deplore certain habits of mind, sometimes found too among Christians, which do not sufficiently attend to the rightful independence of science. The arguments and the controversies which they spark lead many minds to conclude that faith and science are mutually opposed.[88]

In this connection the Council Fathers called for "the education of youth from every social background . . . so that there can be produced not only men and women of refined talents, but those great-souled persons who are so desperately required by our time." [89] In the section of this *Constitution* on "The Proper Development of Culture," the Fathers suggested that the faithful, to "keep pace" and "interpret all things in a truly Christian spirit," be encouraged to "blend modern science and its theories and the understanding of the most recent discoveries with Christian morality and doctrine." [90] The same important paragraph concluded with the observation that "all the faithful, clerical and lay, possess a lawful freedom of inquiry and of thought, and the freedom to express their minds humbly and courageously about those matters in which they enjoy competence." The Fathers had also mentioned a warning, however, "that man, confiding too much in modern discoveries, may even think that he is sufficient unto himself and no longer seek any higher realities." [91]

Although the entire Vatican Council II acknowledged that Catholic education is much wider than Catholic schooling, the *Declaration on Christian Education* by its context quite obviously refers principally to schooling. With regard to such programs as the Newman Apostolate and the Confraternity of Christian Doctrine, the Bishop of Stockton, California, Hugh A. Donohue, in an intervention before the voting on the *Declaration on Christian Education,* asked that the Church undertake with the same dedication to excellence the religious education of those not in schools belonging to the Church. The intervention of Joseph Cardinal Ritter of St. Louis, Missouri, was stronger and more precise:

It is noteworthy that the title of this declaration has been changed from *De scholis catholicis* to *De educatione christiana,* a much wider term. The Catholic school is not and must not be the only concern of the Church. Most of the Catholic children and students in the world are in State schools and must be in fact the object of the solicitude of the Church, the family, and especially the teachers in these schools for their religious education. [92]

In its Introduction to the *Declaration on Christian Education* the Council stated that "this sacred Synod enunciates certain basic principles of Christian education, especially those applicable to formal schooling." [93] Other passages leave no doubt about the special status of the Catholic school: "among all the agencies of education the school has a special importance"; [94] "the Church's involvement in the field of education is demonstrated especially by the Catholic school"; "the Catholic school retains its immense importance in our times too"; and "as for Catholic parents, the Council calls to mind their duty to entrust their children to Catholic schools, when and where this is possible, to support such schools to the extent of their ability, and to work along with them for the welfare of their children." [95]

Other documents of Vatican II also had something to say about education. Its *Declaration on Religious Freedom* vindicated freedom in education as a significant aspect of religious freedom. It stated that the "government . . . must acknowledge the right of parents to make a genuinely free choice of schools and of other means of education" without imposing unjust burdens or forcing children "to attend lessons or instruction which are not in agreement with their religious beliefs." Religious bodies also have a right to teach publicly "and witness to their faith, whether by the spoken or by the written word." They are encouraged "to hold meetings and to establish educational, cultural, charitable, and social organizations, under the impulse of their own religious sense." The Council Fathers urged "everyone, especially those who are charged with the task of educating others, to do their utmost to form men who will respect the moral order and be obedient to lawful authority." The *Declaration on Religious Freedom* clearly asserted that a single educational system "from which all religious formation is excluded" [96] imposed on all peoples is a violation of the rights of parents. Even the *Decree on Priestly Formation* is relevant. Referring as it does to the formation of those who will be dedicating their lives to the education (at least religious) of others, its spirit is one of due accommodation to civil standards in such areas as courses, hours, and degrees. It has wide application when it mentions that, for example, "doctrinal training ought not to aim at a mere communication of ideas, but at a genuine and deep formation of students." [97]

One of the tangible results of Vatican II as applied to United States Catholic education was the change in the constitution of NCEA in 1968. This put the Association at the service of *society* through Catholic education, rather than only at the service of Catholic schools. Reflecting its widened scope were its new goals, which were expanded to promote Christian ideals, encourage educational cooperation, and contribute to the national educational effort.

## Goals

In the area of public as well as private education, specific and practical goals are difficult to express and yet are an important aspect of education. A dynamic society like ours demands specific goals. The report of the President's Commission on National Goals, *Goals for Americans*, with its emphasis on equality and an education that fosters individual and national growth,[98] stated that "modern life has pressed some urgent and sharply defined tasks on education, tasks of producing certain specially needed kinds of educated talent." [99] Yet researchers at the Battelle Memorial Institute, a nonprofit research foundation in Columbus, Ohio, in 1968 concluded from a survey of school boards in Ohio that most boards do not know what kind of education the public wants or needs, and that even if they did know, they would not be certain whether they were providing it.[100] In 1969 Charles E. Silberman, author of the forthcoming "Study of the Education of Educators," the result of two and a half years of research sponsored by the Carnegie Corporation of New York, said in an interview:

What's wrong has much less to do with technique or substance than with the mindlessness of the whole enterprise. Nobody's encouraged to think about the purpose of his work. . . .

What's wrong with schools is not that teachers don't know what they're teaching, but they don't know why they're teaching it—what the relation of their subject is to the rest of knowledge as well as to life.[101]

The same report has Silberman continuing despondently:

I think they [the public schools] are the most grim, joyless places on the face of the earth. They are needlessly authoritarian and repressive—not because teachers and principals are stupid or venal, but because nobody ever asks why: why the rules, or why the curriculum?

From some ascertainable information one would wonder whether the actual, real, and practical goals of Catholic education differ from their public school counterparts, whether their difficulties have been any more resolved, and whether the children in Catholic schools reflect the goals and attitudes of suburbia or other socio-economic backgrounds more than they reflect the goals of their schools. A four-year study published in 1967 after an analysis of the attitudes of suburban children, their parents, and their teachers, found the central values to be "cleanliness and order." [102] For these people, appearance was the measure of worth. The poorly-dressed are not so because of poverty, but because they just aren't American. Goodness was the equivalent of pleasing adults and being "nice." The desires of the children, like those of their parents, were very self-centered and materialistic; their goals were things and possessions, with "good marks" being the only intrusion. In a town lopsidedly white and middle-class, the author found racial bigotry. In Catholic schools, one of the advantages of this time of soul-searching and ferment is that it forces what a more relaxed age would not accomplish: a re-examination of all aspects of education, one of the chief being aims and goals. Some writers, like Lee,[103] have continued to use the traditional Thomistic terminology, dividing goals into ultimate and proximate. Of ultimate goals, those to which all others have been subordinated and which in themselves have not been subordinated to any other, we have already spoken at some length. With regard to proximate, immediate, goals, traditional Thomism further subdivides them into primary and secondary, depending on their degree of importance. With regard to the primary proximate goals, Lee mentions that there are essentially three positions.[104] The first is the moralist position, which holds that Catholic schools exist to bring students closer to Christ. Among those holding this position (opposed to such as John Henry Cardinal Newman) have been Kevin O'Brien, C.SS.R., John D. Redden and Francis Ryan, Franz de Hovre, Msgr. George A. Kelly,[105] and others. Although this position would be attacked more and more in the Sixties by such theorists as Neil G. McCluskey, John Tracy Ellis, Thomas T. McAvoy, Leo R. Ward, and Herbert Johnston,[106] in practice both the Notre Dame and the Greeley-Rossi studies indicated that both parents and students on the elementary and middle educational levels conceived the primary proximate goal of Catholic education to be moral-religious. Lee indicates some weaknesses of the moralist position: it is unrealistic from the viewpoint of contemporary schools, most of which from elementary school through college have heavy vocational goals, and the concept of schooling as the best avenue to success; some of its proponents refuse sufficient respect to intellectual achievement; Catholic students should be trained for a dialogue with all of reality, not only that which is doctrinally "safe" or which builds moral character; and it would also seem to place an unwarranted dichotomy between the natural and the supernatural.[107] Ward points out in this last connection that "secular" or "natural" knowledge has a value and an intrinsic importance, and that God has incarnated Himself into all reality, not only into the segment of reality called "religious." [108]

Second is the intellectualist position, which emphasizes the intellectual development of the student. Aristotle and Thomas Aquinas had asserted that man's highest faculty is his intellect, wherein he most resembles God.[109] The *strict* intellectualists hold that the intellectual virtues are the only legitimate primary proximate goal of education, the *moderate* intellectualists that the intellectual virtues are the primary, but not the only, goal. Lee records certain criticisms of this position also. It does not take into account, for example, the factual situation whereby parents of children in Catholic schools, as we said, overwhelmingly showed themselves in the Notre Dame and the Greeley-Rossi studies as favoring moral-religious training. It is undoubtedly true that the hierarchy support and the clergy teach in Catholic schools because they believe them able to provide the moral-religious end better than the government schools. Secondly, both groups of intellectualists have restricted the notion of the school's function to less than that conceived by contemporary American society, in which there are schools recognized as legitimate for music, art, all sorts of vocations, for the emotionally disturbed, etc. Thirdly, inasmuch as man is more than intellect, but also will, emotions, and a body, perhaps this position overvalues knowledge. As McDowell put it, "knowledge is important, but it is not enough." [110] Fourthly, not all learning, even conceptual learning, is directly intellectual—as is shown by modern psychology. Lastly, this position is prey to vagueness. Some speak of a "Catholic atmosphere" to be supplied by Catholic schools, or of theology as an integrating factor, but fail to define their meaning precisely.

Finally, there is what Lee describes as the integralist position, a combination of the ingredients of the moralist and intellectualist positions plus new ones, so that the primary proximate purpose of Catholic schools is to be a coequal combination of understanding, action, and love.

All of the above was, as we said, in the framework of traditional Thomistic analysis. More modern statements do not confine themselves to this analysis, however, even when they enunciate the same truths: Vatican II's *Declaration on Christian Education*, for example, stated:

Its principal aims are these: that as the baptized person is gradually introduced into a knowledge of the mystery of salvation, he may daily grow more conscious of the gift of faith which he has received; that he may learn to adore God the Father in spirit and in truth (cf. John 4:23), especially through liturgical worship; that he may be trained to conduct his personal life in righteousness and in the sanctity of truth, according to his new standard of manhood (Eph. 4:22-24).[111]

The *Declaration*, aware that "the Catholic school fittingly adjusts itself to the circumstances of advancing times," [112] also juxtaposes various goals. Bishop G. Emmett Carter, of London, Ontario, commenting on it, notes that "what is most distinctive about this document, at least in general terms, is the insistence upon the integration of Christian education into the whole pattern of human life in all its aspects." [113] The education of Catholics called for by this document "should pave the way to brotherly association with other peoples" and should aim at the formation of the human person both relative to his ultimate goal and relative to "the good of those societies of which, as a man, he is a member, and in whose responsibilities, as an adult, he will share." [114] In 1968, Pope Paul VI spoke indirectly to the need for including God in education as a goal in general when he said: "To take away God as the goal of the search, God to whom man is inclined by his nature, means mortifying man himself. The so-called 'death of God' ends in the death of man." [115]

## Curriculum

### SIMILARITIES BETWEEN PUBLIC AND CATHOLIC SCHOOLS

Many areas of curricular arrangements are quite identical in Catholic and public schools: such curricular provisions for individual differences as, for example, "tracks," homogeneous grouping according to aptitude and interest; in elementary schools, ungraded primary, intermediate, and upper levels; for the gifted, accelerated programs in high schools, advanced placement programs in colleges, and on all levels enriched curricula. In such areas as mathematics it is reasonable to presume that Catholic and other schools are similar: the National Science Foundation-sponsored institutes have been available to teachers of both public

and Catholic patterns of education, and have been held at Catholic as
well as at other private and also public institutions. At least one state,
Rhode Island, has provided in-service training for its teachers from both
the public and parochial school systems. Since 1961, the same state has
offered four in-service courses, three to teachers in the larger public
schools systems and one to teachers in the Roman Catholic Diocese of
Providence. Catholic school administrators have had the choice of
modern mathematics textbooks of the type used in public schools or
could use those designed by Catholic writers.[116]

## DIFFICULTIES

All patterns of education, both public and private, are also similar,
though not identical, in their difficulties. For example, whereas a 1968
survey of fifty selected Roman Catholic dioceses of different sizes by
*U.S. Catholic Magazine* said that Catholic elementary schools were
doing a superior job in teaching the new math, reading, and spelling,[117]
in these areas public schools were sometimes failing. For the 1966-67
school year, for instance, the Board of Education of the City of New
York reported the results of standardized achievement tests that "showed
that pupils in the public schools lagged behind national norms or
standards in virtually every grade." [118] One out of three pupils in city
schools were a year or more behind in reading, and two out of three
children achieved lower than the national standard in a test of arithmetic
skills given to fourth- and sixth-graders. Not that Catholic schools can
take any consolation in this. The same report indicated also that Catholic schools were weakest in science and physical education, and not very
outstanding at current events or geography. It has long been known also
that Catholic schools have been weak in the social aspects of the curriculum—a fact perhaps responsible, in part at least, for the attitudes of
some adult Catholics. George Gallup, Jr., managing director of the
American Institute of Public Opinion, revealed on January 18, 1967, that
according to public opinion surveys conducted by his Institute, the views
of Protestant and Roman Catholic churchgoers were almost identical to
those of non-churchgoers on such issues as continuing the war in Vietnam, the death penalty for convicted murderers, the speed of integration,
open housing, and the anti-poverty program. Even though his survey
revealed that churchgoers tended to be "better informed, more socially
involved, and happier than non-churchgoers," [119] perhaps more emphasis could be placed upon Christian social virtue in Catholic school
curricula. Bernert, already cited in this chapter as advocating a new
approach to Catholic school objectives, is concerned that Catholic education has emphasized the salvation of one's soul rather than the salvation
history of God's people. The main objective which received nearly all
the effort of Catholic educators was Christ's first commandment, but
little time or thought was expended on the second, which is like the

first: "Thou shalt love thy neighbor as thyself." [120] The *Declaration on Christian Education* made very clear that much greater emphasis must be placed on the social character of education, claiming that one distinctive function of the school is "to relate all human culture eventually to the news of salvation." [121]

## SEX EDUCATION

Sex education has been an area of similarity between public and Catholic schools, in reasons and in methodology, if not in content. The reasons for the inclusion of sex education in school curricula at this time were many: urbanization, depriving children of what they were formerly able to learn through simple observation on the farm; the rising number of those in society's middle class, often protected from a rough-and-tumble knowledge "picked up in the gutter"; the alarming statistics about rising venereal disease and unwed teen-age pregnancies; and the deprivation of the defenses that once protected adolescents, on which point Dr. Mary Calderone is quoted as saying:

We have done away with chaperons, supervision, rules, close family relations, and privacy from the intrusion of the communications media. We have left our children totally vulnerable to the onslaughts of the commercial exploitation of sex, tabloid reporting of sordid sexual occurrences, wholly unsupervised after-school occupations.[122]

With regard to methodology, much is common to all: models of genitalia to be made in clay or drawing by the children themselves, or from simple materials by the instructor; plastic male and female manikins; and such movies as *Human Reproduction, Phoebe, Fertility and Birth*, and Walt Disney's *Story of Menstruation*.

The federal government in 1967 for the first time awarded two grants to help plan model courses on sex education in public schools at Bedford, Massachusetts, and New Orleans, Louisiana. Programs have been started in such disparate localities as Chicago, Illinois; Glen Cove, New York; Washington, D.C.; Detroit, Michigan; and Anaheim, California, whose program is considered one of the best in the country. In New York City, Dr. Bernard E. Donovan, then superintendent of schools, announced a program to begin in November 1967.[123] The program, entitled "Family Living, Including Sex Education," began in the pre-kindergarten classes and developed gradually through the twelfth grade. Sex education was not always placed in the curriculum with such great care, however. Dr. Alan Guttmacher, for example, voiced opinions hostile to the sensibilities of most Roman Catholics; speaking to a Manhattan audience of tenth- and twelfth-graders, he was reported as saying:

Pre-marital sex should be entered into as a faithful episode. You choose your mate carefully and remain faithful at the time. But please, you must use effective controls. There is too much trauma in a pre-marital pregancy to the girl, the boy, the parents, the unborn child.[124]

Whence this gentleman became an authority in ethics or morality is unknown, but his frequent utterances through the various communications media have been similar to this one.

In this area the Catholic schools have been at least on a par with, and in many cases ahead of, their public counterparts. At a meeting of the twenty-second annual Teachers Institute of the Archdiocese of New York, for example, on February 9, 1967, it was announced that as a result of various parish meetings with parents, children, doctors, and teachers, and due to the entreaties of parents, sex education would be introduced into the archdiocese's school curriculum.[125] In the diocese of Burlington, Vermont, planning began for the state-wide Catholic schools in May 1967.[126] It attempted to involve the whole family, and to be as complete, frank, and open as possible, adding an ethical dimension arising from the Catholic moral position. The diocese of Rockville Centre, New York, established a pilot program in September 1969 entitled "Family Life Education." [127] The Rev. James McHugh, director of the Family Life Bureau of the United States Catholic Conference, announced in August 1967 the development of a sex education program on a national level in cooperation with the USCC Education Department, NCEA, and the National Center of the CCD.[128] As a result of dialogue with physicians, psychologists, educators, and theologians, it was drawing upon existent nationwide programs of sex education for nuns and teachers, curriculum guides for different age groups, and effective materials for parents, as well as the experiences of parishes and school systems. McHugh indicated that this was the result of strong urgings from Vatican Council II and that it would involve the home, the school, and the parish.[129]

One of the differences between the public and the Catholic programs of sex education is the over-all greater care in the approaches of the latter. This care was shown in the very choice of titles for the program: "Becoming a Person," for example, or "Education for Living," and in another case, "Family Life Education." Such care was not the result only of the fear of misunderstandings by parents. It was based on a concept of the sacredness of sex which derives from the pre-Christian Hebrews; this concept, which elevated Hebrew women to a dignity higher than that accorded women in all their contemporary societies, was elaborated upon by Jesus Christ and incorporated into Christian theology. It differentiates sex education from such other subjects as biology, which is a discussion of physical processes, and anatomy, which is more analogous to geography than to proper sex education. It elaborates on the axiom that "the glory of God is man fully alive," believing that man cannot become fully alive until he accepts and has reverence for his sexuality. Motivated by directives in Pius XI's encyclical on *The Christian*

*Education of Youth* in 1929, and spurred on by the injunction in Vatican II's *Declaration on Christian Education* that children "as they advance in years . . . be given positive and prudent sexual education," [130] modern Catholic educators are careful to base their programs on moral and ethical values, and not only considerations of physical or emotional health, fear, pleasure, practical consequences, or concepts of personality development; to teach that this area does not represent a vacuum, but is related to other aspects of his life; to recognize that school sex education complements that of the family and the Church; and to point out that the greatest opportunity for personal fulfillment in this respect is sexual intercourse within marriage.

## TEXTBOOKS

There is a similarity also in textbooks. No textbook, Catholic included, can avoid revealing the basic outlook and prejudices of the author. With regard to public school textbooks, the very interesting Harris study on *The Treatment of Religion in Elementary School Social Studies Textbooks* points to a more subtle anti-religiosity that that of the nineteenth century. Motivated by a Jewish background, this study embraced one of the largest collections of social studies texts in the country, an extensive sampling consisting of "120 elementary (grades 1-6) public school social studies textbooks shelved in the Social Studies Division of the Teachers' Central Laboratory of Hunter College, New York City." [131] It came up with some thought-provoking conclusions. For example, to the question, "Are the textbooks for elementary schools sectarian in their outlook?" parts of Harris' answer were that

the Reformation is treated in a manner which unduly favors Protestantism over Catholicism. . . . Passages . . . may tend to disturb non-Christian students. . . . [They have a] tendency to treat Christianity as being synonymous with everything good, so that by implication everything not Christian is bad . . . [and a] disproportionate number of references to one religion as compared with others.[132]

To the question, "How do the textbooks present the role of religion in the past and in contemporary society?" this study answered, in part:

Generally speaking, while the texts say that religion was important in the past they imply that it is no longer a significant force in our society. . . . The Jewish group is also pictured as being outdated, having exhausted its contributions in the Biblical period.[133]

To the question, "How are religious conflicts and persecutions treated?" part of the answer was:

The Inquisition and the Reformation are presented in a way that creates the impression that Catholicism bears a far greater onus for the intolerance of the era than does Protestantism. Catholics are pictured as the agents of reaction and the Protestants are depicted as advocates of enlightenment.[134]

A damaging (undeservedly, in this author's opinion) study was made also of textbooks used in Catholic schools. When the federal government in 1961 was extending the National Defense Education Act to parochial schools, the Department of Religious Liberty of the National Council of Churches of Christ requested George R. LaNoue to examine parochial school textbooks in science, mathematics, and modern foreign languages, in order to discover whether religious teachings were included. His 192-page findings were unpublished, but are reported by him in published articles. The purpose of his study was to show that "the religious and secular aspects of education are not separated by subject matter in parochial schools." [135] LaNoue examined a non-exhaustive list of over one hundred textbooks and teaching manuals produced by major publishers. About 60 per cent of the texts were of high school or junior high school level, and "about 90 per cent of the books surveyed were Catholic texts, which is about the percentage of Catholic students in the non-public school population." [136] Among his findings were the following:

There are seven general ways in which religion is integrated into the academic material in the textbooks surveyed. . . .

1. Religious symbols and subjects used in examples for arithmetic and grammar drill. . . . *Common in mathematics and languages.*

2. Specific sectarian doctrines taught where controversial matter appears in the text. . . . *Common in science, geography, and languages.*

3. A general theistic Christian approach to all matters. . . . *Common in all subjects.*

4. Request that the children concern themselves with specific Church goals. . . . *Common in geography and language.*

5. Appeals to Church authority for proof of a point. . . . *Common in science, geography, and languages.*

6. Selective emphasis on Catholic institutions and contributions to the culture and on facts favorable to the Church and omission of institutions and contributions to the culture by non-Catholics and of facts unfavorable to the Church. . . . *Common in science, mathematics, and languages.*

7. Defense of Church social ideas and regulations. . . . *Common in science and languages.*[137]

He reported further:

The concept of a "secular" subject in a religious school is very complex. There are unquestionably variations in the amount of religious content in courses. (There is often more religion in the subjects not covered in this study: history, philosophy, psychology, government and sociology, for example.) There is more overt religious material in the textbooks for the elementary grades than for high schools.[138]

Some of LaNoue's examples contained references to mere superficialities or points of view more representative of individual authors than of the teaching Church. He cited, for example, one textbook which, under the subheading "Education is a Social Responsibility," says, "First of all they said—we will take God out of government; and they not only planned it but they did it by the complete separation of Church and State." [139] He cited pejoratively the preface of a parochial school arithmetic textbook as saying, "The teaching of arithmetic to Catholic children should not be confined only to knowledge that pertains to quantitative thinking, but should also present applications of this knowledge in situations which are normal to them," [140] and then cited textbooks that used this as an opportunity to integrate religious material. One gave arithmetic problems in terms of buying religious books, ransoming pagan babies, selling subscriptions to a Catholic magazine, and mission problems. [141] Another example unrepresentative of the teaching Church was LaNoue's Plate I, a page from a biology textbook:

One related question is now closed for Catholics. That is the question of POLYGENISM. Polygenism may mean the theory that men existed after Adam but were not directly descended from him; or the theory that Adam was a name that is merely a symbol for a multitude of parents. [142]

LaNoue seemed unmindful of the fact that another respected Catholic author has taken an opposing viewpoint:

Without doubt Pius XII, enlightened by the assistance of the Holy Spirit, has pronounced very serious words (although not infallible) against polygenesis. Nevertheless, no one is entitled to stigmatize it as a "deviation from Catholic truth," i.e., in the strict sense of the terms, to call it heresy. [143]

Plate II presented statements in another text that are also questionable from an orthodox Catholic point of view:

Our Blessed Mother chose many spots in Europe, Fatima, Lourdes, LaSalette, Beauraing, and others to remind us that she wishes us to make her Son better known and to offer us her most powerful assistance in obtaining salvation for the whole world. [144]

Not all Catholics would agree with another of LaNoue's examples, either:

In every country of the Western Hemisphere, shrines and churches have been erected in Mary's honor. The most recent and the most beautiful of these shrines is the one that has been erected in Washington, D.C., the capital of our country. [145]

Other examples cited, however, seem to be in accord not only with a Catholic philosophy of an integrated curriculum, but also with common sense—e.g., the introduction to an arithmetic text:

The authors of *Finding Truth in Arithmetic* have recognized that first and foremost, an arithmetic program designed for Catholic schools must be mathematically sound. Over and above this, they have recognized that there are innumerable situations which involve quantitative thinking, measurement, and other mathematical understandings and skills in typical social circumstances. Furthermore, they have taken advantage of the fact that these situations present opportunities for the exercise of Christian virtues. The virtues of justice, charity, honesty, liberality, prudence, and temperance often form an integral part of such situations. . . . Like a strand running through this instruction is the brightness of mathematical truth. This truth is sacred and the sacredness of this truth must be woven into the mind and heart of the child.[146]

It is difficult to see what one could criticize in the honest statement in a Catholic high school literature text quoted by LaNoue:

This book is edited from a Catholic point of view, for Catholic students. Every selection from nonsense verses to Negro spirituals is integrated with the Catholic philosophy of life. Such integration is possible because wholesome literature as a comment on life, is essentially in accord with the Christian, and therefore the Catholic outlook. As Faith does not deny but builds on nature, so necessarily literature of both natural and supernatural inspiration is taken into account in the making of this book. Catholic and non-Catholic authors will be found side by side, but in every instance their comments on life find interpretation in the light of the Catholic faith and Catholic ideals.[147]

Another citation exemplifies what may be excellent advice not only for Catholic students but for all who wish to preserve both their ability to interpret current affairs and their freedom:

There is much of it [American life], however, that is not touched with the Catholic spirit. . . . Hence it is imperative that we train ourselves to think, to read critically, for many an author with a persuasive style has only a husk of truth to offer the reader, or he may even be spreading the deadly virus of positive error.[148]

Evidently it was not only the Catholic schools that desired to establish a Christian-integrated curriculum. A Lutheran catalogue cited by La-Noue indicated:

A Lutheran elementary school teacher will insist that all areas of the curriculum reflect an adequate philosophy of Christian education. Thus he will select content and provide experiences that are consistent with such a philosophy.[149]

The National Union of Christian Schools (Christian Reformed) also indicated a desire for a Christian-integrated curriculum in mathematics, in a guide for teachers of the subject:

Appraising the student's progress toward God-centered thinking in mathematics is difficult. Periodic discussion of questions like the following may help the teacher make the proper evaluation.

Why is it important to learn mathematics? Responses should relate to the idea that mathematics reveals God.

Why should a student's work be neat, accurate, and honest? Responses should relate to the idea that mathematics is a useful tool for work and service and must be done according to God's standards.

What would be the basis on which you would establish a business? Responses should relate to Christian ethics, stewardship, and usefulness.

How are number ideas used in making things? Responses should relate to mathematics as a tool for our creative activity.

How were mathematical ideas used in the creation of the world? Responses should relate to God the Creator and indicate the observation of form and order in creation.

Where does the idea of numbers come from? Responses should relate to God as the source of mathematical principles and of all knowledge.

What part did man play in revealing God through mathematics? Responses should deal with the history of the number system.[150]

Concerning LaNoue's study, several points must be kept in mind. First, one questions whether his examples are typical. Secondly, it is necessary to remark upon the freedom of both teacher and student to disagree with certain of the examples from the viewpoint of religious orthodoxy. Finally, does one not have the right to suggest that perhaps some of the religious permeation cited may be beneficial to many students and to our country?

## THE BASIC DIFFERENCE BETWEEN PUBLIC AND
## CATHOLIC SCHOOLS: RELIGION

Although there have always been those who were interested in teaching religion in the public schools, that issue has remained confusing because of conflicting interpretations of the Constitution. After the United States Supreme Court decision in 1963, however, banning Bible reading and prayer in public schools, public school interest in including religion in curricula has taken a new slant: teaching "about" religion. In May of 1966 Harvard University sponsored a conference on the role of religion in education centering around the concept of teaching "about" religion from the educational, religious, and legal points of view.[151] In 1968 it was reported that "a campaign to increase the frequency in teaching 'about' religion in the public schools is making steady progress in both religious and educational circles."[152] The same article reported that "the Pennsylvania Department of Public Instruction is testing a pilot course in Western religious literature this year in a cross-section of thirty-one schools throughout the State," and that "the course would eventually be coupled with material on eastern religious literature."

Always basic to the United States Catholic curriculum have been the truths of faith and the formation of American Catholics with the purpose of making them productive for themselves and society, intelligent to the extent possible, and aware of their relationships to God, their fellow men, nature, and themselves. The methods of accomplishing this, however, have changed with conditions from one moment of history to another. For about fifteen centuries, there had prevailed the presentation to children of fixed formularies reflecting the *fontes revelationis* through what was known as the Catechism. Because these "official" catechisms had their origins in times of near illiteracy, they had been from the beginning committed to memory. When people did not have the Scriptures in the vernacular or did not celebrate the liturgy meaningfully, catechisms were a necessity. (Eastern churches, both those in union with Rome as well as the Orthodox, were always without catechisms except where under Western influence.) It is understandable, therefore, that in the contemporary period there have been vestiges of some ancient traditions of the catechism, such as the publication of national catechisms. This began with the German *Katholischer Katechismus* [153] at Freiburg in 1955. Intended for the upper elementary years, it followed the traditional arrangements, and was translated into twenty-two languages within five years. Austria followed with a similar one in 1960, Australia in 1963 and 1964, and England shortly thereafter. In the face of the more numerous and varied vehicles of living teaching, this kind of witness is coming to enjoy less and less favor.

The contemporary period has seen numerous changes. Koob, for example, noted in 1967 "more stress on learning about other religions, and acknowledgement that atheism should be understood and less regimentation of students in their religious duties." [154] *U. S. Catholic Magazine* in a special issue in 1968 said essentially the same thing:

A major revision has been made in Catholic school courses since the Council, particularly in the religion courses. There has been a shift in emphasis, away from the apologetical and the catechetical, toward the scriptural and ecumenical. Many of the diocesan systems have adopted new religion texts, with a different approach to belief and a much greater emphasis on scripture and liturgy. [155]

Long before Vatican II, however, there had been stirrings in the direction of a new catechetics. In the early part of the century, an attempt to formulate a theology completely independent of scholastic theology had failed because it was imprecise, of limited scope, and ambiguous. During this contemporary period, however, there were notable successes by such as Josef Jungmann, Johannes Hofinger, Sister Maria de la Cruz, Bernard Cooke, S.J., and Godfrey Diekmann, O.S.B. [156] These had in common a "kerygmatic" approach to the teaching of religion, a systematic synthesis of the data of revelation as the "good news" of salvation in Christ. Elements included in its pedagogy were salvation history, proceeding from Abraham through Jesus Christ and the New Testament to God's deepening revelation; Christocentrism; reasonableness; a climax in the Church's liturgy, where word and action joined, and which invites commitment to Christ and its dynamic actualization; and a theology of *value*. In accord with the latter, the kerygmatic approach held that the dominant value of each doctrinal truth is perceptible throughout the total theological synthesis of Christian truth and in every part thereof, especially through a thematic organization. This theology of value was concrete rather than

abstract, historical rather than scientific or speculative, and used sym-
bolism to convey value.

*Kerygma* is as old as Homer, who had used *kērux* to signify a divine
messenger. The Old Testament had used the same word in the secular
sense of a royal messenger or herald and also in connection with the
prophets Jonah and Joel. In the New Testament, Matthew and Luke [157]
had used *kērux* to signify an authorized preacher announcing the truth
that "the kingdom of God has come upon you." Peter had exemplified
the method in the speech attributed to him on the first Pentecost.[158] Paul
had revealed a formula similar to Peter's in his letter to the Romans,[159]
had spoken of the Son of God "who gave himself for our sins, that He
might deliver us from the wickedness of this present world," [160] and at
Pisidian Antioch had had a further expanded formula attributed to
him.[161] In the early Church, the Christian preacher had thought of himself as a divinely approved herald of very important news after the
manner of John the Baptist;[162] apologists of the second century had
modified the *kerygma* in their attempts to rebut their anti-Christian ad-
versaries, and finally this approach had become more generally abandoned with the growth of catechetical schools and the development of
the homily on the scriptures. Reapplied to modern catechetics, this
approach attempted a new concreteness, immediacy, relevance to life,
deep knowledge of God, and sense of mission to all the human family.[163]
Vatican II gave further impetus to changes, both with regard to its
themes and also with regard to criteria for good catechetical methodology. Some conciliar documents contained only indirect references to
religious education, but six of the official writings contained clear and
direct statements.[164]

In the attempt to discern themes from the Council for catechetics, Karl
Rahner is very helpful. He speaks of three outstanding themes—the
Church's fundamental self-understanding, inner life, and mission to
those outside—and in expanding on the theme of "mission" he describes
the Church as "considering in all expressions how she can *serve*—God,
man, the world, and her destiny." [165] Relative to *God*, this involved some
new emphases. The Council dwelled upon God's communication of Himself,[166] and indicated that revelation is a living relationship between God
and man occurring not merely in a well-protected "deposit of faith," but
in an ongoing manifestation. As Gabriel Moran put it:

> The point is frequently made these days that "salvation history" is not to be
> understood in a narrow, biblicist way. It is said that the student's whole life
> will be understood as a part of salvation history.[167]

Relative to *man*, the Council stressed his dignity, his freedom, and his
individuality. The Council reminded teachers of the scriptural respect
that God always manifested for man and encouraged them to be sensitive to findings of psychologists concerning the child's level of growth

and receptivity, his individual personality, and his social and cultural milieu. Concerning the *world*, it is "the vividness of the here-and-now" [168] that engages especially the adolescent. The Church is a Spirit-permeated community of God's people in that world, with the mission to serve it; and that is her *destiny*—to dialogue in a loving faith-relationship with a technological world.

Concerning catechetical criteria, Vatican II did not change the substance of Christian truth, but changed dramatically the ways in which that truth is to be expressed and communicated. The classic manuals based on the Aristotelian synthesis of the Scholastics prior to Vatican II (1962-1965) did not do justice to, when indeed they did not simply ignore, such biblical notions as *qahal*, covenant, word, *agapē*, *hesed*, flesh, kingdom, and a host of others. Further, after Vatican II Rahner claimed that "dogmatic theology today has to be theological anthropology." Man is the question, and Christ the answer—but we do not even know the question apart from Christ or, as Rahner put it, "in Christian dogmatic theology there is a mutual and necessary relationship between anthropology and Christology." [169] In Christ we have not only the revelation of who God is, but what man is. Rahner's anthropological stress in theology found its first specific echo in catechetics at the Bangkok Study Week on Mission Catechetics in 1962. It was then popularized in the United States by the dynamic Spanish Jesuit Alfonso Nebreda, who had spent many years in the missions of Japan, and who toured the United States in the summers of the early 60's heralding the rediscovery of "pre-evangelization." [170]

On religion texts, two over-all observations may be made with reference to all levels. First, modern religious texts and catechisms mirror the theological emphases of the post-Vatican II era: they present a meaningful treatment of the liturgy and practical discussions of such important virtues as honesty, self-control, and regard for material things. Secondly, today there is a greater blurring of boundaries between religion texts for Catholic schools on the one hand and for the use of Catholic children in public school through the Confraternity of Christian Doctrine program on the other. Formerly, texts for Catholic schools provided highly organized programs and those for CCD were short manuals with skeletal outlines usually padded with multiple-choice and completion questions. Today, on the elementary school level, new catechisms contain less religious material per page, but sound pedagogy. This pedagogy is not necessarily new—going back to St. Thomas Aquinas, for example, and his principle that "whatever is received is received in the manner of the one receiving it," and St. Paul's statement that children need milk, not meat.[171] Because their new emphases reflect the turmoil in theology, many of the elementary school texts especially have been criticized by parents who were used to a traditional presentation. All these complaints had similar patterns: pictures of the Rev. Martin Luther King, modern art illustrations, "political" issues included in the text, the recommendation of folk songs by Pete Seeger, and a de-emphasis of the question-and-answer approach.

*Come to the Father* [172] was the effort of thirty catechists, theologians, psychologists, sociologists, and teachers to write a catechism in conformity with Vatican II and simultaneously relevant to the child's experiences and child psychology. This catechism warns that "fear is a bad educator." It involves a long-playing record with basically religious themes, bright posters as "visual focal points," and a handbook for parent-teacher-priest meetings. When it presents the question "What is God?" it asks the child to look at a brightly-colored picture of the rising sun reflected in a pool of blue water. One sister using the catechism indicated an excellent response but the need for some adjustments because of some confused parents as well as children. For example, the catechism begins where the child is and with the concept of God as a "loving Father." Some children, however, were from broken homes in which they had no contact with a father. In such cases this particular sister substituted mothers, grandmothers, or even brothers or sisters, and recalled that "one child said no one loved him, but we finally decided on an Aunt." [173] Sadlier published two series that met with opposition. When Catholic laymen in New Orleans challenged the *On Our Way Series*, Thomas J. Dolan said for Sadlier Company that the main objection reported by salesmen was the illustration of Christ in which his skin is "darker than the Caucasian Christ we've had all along . . . it's a mid-eastern Christ." [174] In the Richmond, Virginia, diocese, the Emerging Catholic Laymen, Inc.—which had been formed to oppose socially oriented religious education—advertised in the *Washington Post* their objection to some of the texts: "Have you read your child's new religion book? Must we take our children out of our Catholic school to insure their Catholic education? Join our protest to throw the fraudulent text out and return to the Baltimore Catechism." [175] Some members of "Emerging Catholic Laymen" have taken their children out of parochial schools. Because of parental pressure, Benziger withdrew its *Word and Worship Series* from New Orleans in 1966.

A catechism published for use in the 435 elementary schools of the archdiocese of Chicago also ran into difficulty in 1967. One section, accompanying a picture of a civil rights march in Selma, Alabama, read:

In this picture we see Negro and white people marching together. They are marching for better homes, jobs and schools for the Negro people.

One of the leaders of the Negro people is a brave man named Martin Luther King. He is a Christian minister from Alabama. He preaches the message of Jesus, "Love one another."

Some people do not like the Rev. King. They say he is a trouble maker, but, no matter what some people may say, he continues to tell everyone to keep on seeking justice. Rev. King is a brave Christian.[176]

Richard White, president of the Concerned Catholic Parents, brought demands from his constituency to the FBI to investigate the Roman Catholic Archdiocese of Chicago. He said that illustrations depicting the Marxist clenched-fist salute appear "over thirty times in the book," and that his group had obtained signatures from more than thirteen hundred Catholic parents from over seventy parishes. In answering their arguments before the group, the Rev. James J. Kilgallon, one of the catechism's authors, said that their objections were based on ignorance of sacred scripture; they booed and told him to "shut up." The Rev. Gerard P. Weber, another of the authors, charged that the group's opinions had roots in the John Birch Society and in racism. In October 1969, Catholic school superintendents and other officials, all members of the NCEA, voted to reject attacks on modern books and curricula, and on catechetical developments.

On the high school level, one statement made of religion texts applies to other levels as well—viz., that "there is no textbook in high school religion which will meet all the needs of every teacher. There never has been such a work nor can there be." [177] Sheila Moriarty gives four criteria for evaluating such texts: open-endedness, love as central to Christian life, sex as a dimension of the human, and Christ as the person in whom God meets man.[178] Of the *Lord and King Series*,[179] Moriarty lists as positive contributions the fact that it is a first, a new moment in catechetical thinking in the United States; contains some good scriptural research; provides some pertinent information on liturgical history; and has initiated new interest in a biblical-liturgical approach. On the negative side, she lists first a stylized format; a claim that the text fails to "present" Jesus Christ, and puts religion and life far apart; that it too often makes do-goodism the substitute for love; and that the teaching on sex reflects a distrust of human values. As the positive contribution of the *Loyola Religion Series*,[180] Moriarty asserts that the theme of the text for seniors, "Man and the Modern World," is well chosen because today's questions about God are necessarily questions about man. Even this senior text, however, fails to give real understanding, borrows from pious essays, is simplistic, and leaves little room for student participation. Uniquely, the series borrows from missiology the concept of the need for pre-evangelization in religious education.

In the *Roots of Faith Series*,[181] the freshman text, which is on the Old Testament, is entitled "God Gives His Word." The second-year text, which is on the New Testament, is entitled "Encountering Christ," and the third year text is called "Servant of Peace." On the positive side, the text is free-flowing, is spiral-bound for greater versatility, and contains creative art and excerpts from poets, theologians, and philosophers who are contemporary. On the negative side, says Moriarty, the series lacks coherence; frequently there is no relation between the material and the capacity of the thirteen- or fourteen-year-old for whom the first and

second books are intended; there is an unawareness of student needs; the
authors play with psychology under the guise of Christian personalism;
and there are overextended metaphors and some false definitions of
Christian love, some of them Manichean. For the *Living With Christ
Series*,[182] Moriarty reserves nothing but praise. This series, to her, represents "perhaps the first successful attempt to express man's contemporary
experience of existence in the life of God's word." [183] Attractively bound
in pamphlet form, it recreates situations from literature, drama, and
contemporary life—e.g., Chapter One of the third-year course features
*West Side Story*, leading into questions of alienation and estrangement,
the fear of being separate, and false security in gangs. Both the third-
and fourth-year courses include in their teachers' manuals lists of appropriate novels, films, and photo posters to complement their themes.
Another work for high school, entitled *Friendship*,[184] develops the theme
of the title as a special need in the adolescent's search for maturity, the
materials being developed from the authors' experiences listening to and
working with students.

As a result of increasing criticism of religion texts on the elementary
and secondary school levels, the division of research and development of
the Department of Education of the U. S. Catholic Conference on December 15, 1969, began a nationwide study of all major books in current
use for the teaching of religion. The biggest such evaluation ever made,
it will examine about 400 volumes, including texts, teacher's manuals,
and other materials used in elementary and secondary Catholic schools
and CCD programs in the United States. Inasmuch as all these books
presumably have the *imprimatur*, which guarantees doctrinal and moral
orthodoxy, the evaluation will not approximate censorship, but will encompass rather content, teaching methods, and some emphases, possibly
resulting in suggestions for clarifications. Under the chairmanship of
Auxiliary Bishop William E. McManus of Chicago, chairman of the
USCC Department of Education, and with the encouragement of Msgr.
Raymond Lucker, director of the department, the project will be
under the charge of the Rev. Thomas C. Donlan, O.P., director of the research division. No estimate was possible at the inception of the work
on how long it would take.

On the college level, the Society of Catholic College Teachers of
Sacred Doctrine has worked in the direction of constant progress, and
in 1963 the Carton study [185] made some interesting observations. In
dogmatic theology, there have been increasing attempts to indicate its
implications to contemporary life, and a concentration on the development of dogma in order to help students to appreciate the dynamic
nature of the Church and her teaching, to recognize the freedom of
thought that has resulted in the precision of the expression of Catholic
dogmas, and to realize that one must learn to live with problems. In
moral theology, positive approaches are being developed; scriptural

foundations are stressed; there is abundant evidence of the influence of such Europeans as Emile Mersch, Bernard Häring, Gérard Gilleman, and Fritz Tillman; faith is pointed out as a personal, mature commitment to Christ, and is shown in its crisis during adolescence; there is an omission of material of a pastoral nature; and course content is related to studies of history, current literature, recent philosophy, and ecumenical problems. An attempt is made to teach an appreciation of the values of liturgy, but this subject is not integrated very much into the established curricula. The electives indicate trends in current theological thinking: ecumenism, comparative religion, patristics, theology of the layman, scripture, modern theology, and ecclesiology. Among the texts in use are the *Foundations of Catholic Theology Series*.[186]

A catechism published for adults has also received a great deal of publicity. It was first published, in Dutch, in Holland in 1966, having been commissioned by the Dutch Bishops and prepared by the Higher Catechetical Institute in Nijmegen, Holland, with the help of Dutch theologians, psychologists, church historians, and others. Intended for adults, it abandoned the question and answer method. The Most Rev. Robert F. Joyce of Burlington, Vermont, gave his *imprimatur* for an American translation, but when officials of the Vatican presented objections to the book Joyce withdrew his *imprimatur* until a subsequent edition could incorporate changes. Finally in 1967 the publishers went ahead without an *imprimatur* and published *A New Catechism: Catholic Faith for Adults*. In 1968 the Dutch Bishops agreed to put Rome's suggested changes in an appendix to future editions. On the plus side, the catechism attempted to implement the decrees of Vatican II. Like Vatican II it was essentially pastoral—not intended for professional theologians or even a highly sophisticated audience, it distilled much of the best in contemporary scholarship in biblical studies, history and theology into a readable but not superficial form; it provided understandings necessary for an intelligent participation in the liturgy; it presented a warmly human invitation to share in the privileges and the joy of Christian faith and love; and it provided a deep insight into the rich traditions of Christian contemplation and prayer. Other aspects of it, however, are questionable. On the existence of hell, this catechism said that no clear teaching is possible, and that "each of us must draw his own conclusions here." On birth control, it asserted that "the efforts to attain the greatest possible fruitfulness in love, free from all egoism, will lead in one married couple to quite a different form of family planning than in another. People must remain free in the matter." On the virgin birth, the catechism asserted:

When He [Jesus] came into the world, he was being prayed for by a whole people and promised by a whole history. He was a child of promise in a unique sense, and the profoundest desire of the whole of mankind. He was born wholly of grace, wholly of promise—"conceived of the Holy Spirit." He was *the* gift of God to mankind.

This the evangelists Matthew and Luke express when they proclaim that Jesus' birth was not due to the will of man. . . this is the deepest meaning of the article of faith, "born of the Virgin Mary." [187]

On divorce, the catechism insisted on retaining our Catholic position on the indissolubility of marriage, but also took the position that we cannot immediately refuse the practical possibilities of redemption to those divorced and remarried. On most occasions where the catechism opposed traditional orthodox interpretations it frequently did so by simply ignoring them rather than by direct confrontation.

Whether all these efforts in teaching religion were bringing about significantly different results in the products of Catholic schools as against others is, of course, extremely difficult to judge. There are too many such outside influences as parents, siblings, age, experiences, and disagreements on criteria of religiousness. Donald A. Erickson's study on the "Differential Effects of Public and Sectarian Schooling on the Religiousness of the Child" does not seem applicable. He used 212 sixth-, seventh-, and eighth-grade students who attended Fundamentalist churches and/or Fundamentalist and public day schools in the Midwest and West. Overall, he found no statistically significant differences in religiousness between Fundamentalist and public schooling. He found the variables of Church involvement, parent religiousness, and home congeniality extremely important, with "high intercorrelations among them." [188] He was careful to note in his conclusions that Fundamentalist schools are only one kind of sectarian school. He cited the conclusion of a work by Philip Pitruzello to point up a further complication relative to Catholic schools, noting "a strong tendency for such schools to limit admissions largely to the superior student, quite in contrast to the official Catholic position on education." [189]

# Agents of Education

## GOVERNMENT

Vatican II (1962–1965) repeated the Church's recognition of civil society's right and duty "to provide all citizens with an opportunity to acquire a proper degree of cultural enrichment, and with the proper preparation for exercising their civic duties and rights." [190] The *Declaration on Christian Education* cautioned against the danger of a state monopoly of education:

The state . . . ought to protect the right of children to receive an adequate schooling. It should be vigilant about the ability of teachers and the excellence of their training. It should look after the health of students and, in general, promote the whole school enterprise. But it must keep in mind the principle of subsidiarity, so that no kind of school monopoly arises. For such a monopoly would militate against the native rights of the human person, the development and spread of culture itself, the peaceful association of citizens, and the pluralism which exists today in very many societies.[191]

The over-all tone of the entire document is one of respect both for the rights of Catholic education and of public education and secular learning. In practice, both public and Catholic schools during this period were running into extreme difficulties, mostly financial. On the public school scene, in Youngstown, Ohio, a school tax increase was defeated at the polls in 1968 for the sixth time in two years, so that its 28,000 school children were out of session from Nov. 27, 1968, to Jan. 2, 1969. In Philadelphia, a disclosure was made in November of 1968 that, unless new revenues were found, schools might have to close in April 1969 instead of the usual later terminal date. In Detroit, school leaders in January 1969 warned of an extended closing of schools in the next school year unless extensive financial assistance were provided. During this period, there were other signs of voters hostile to rising school budgets: LaCrosse, Wisconsin, had to slash its school budget by 10 per cent; Danville, Illinois, had to resort to such economy measures as half-day sessions; and St. Louis voters defeated a school-bond issue three times in 1968. In 1968 the United States Commissioner of Education, Harold Howe II, and Samuel Halperin, deputy assistant secretary for legislation in the Department of Health, Education, and Welfare, formulated a document which made many recommendations such as "consolidation and coordination," organizational housecleaning, reordering of the federal role in education, raising of education to Cabinet rank, and the need to develop a consistent and coherent policy of education.

On the Catholic side, the financial difficulties were more intense. In the beginning of 1969 the diocesan school board of Richmond, Virginia, charged the State Commission on Constitutional Revision with unfairness for refusing to recommend state aid to diocesan schools, asserting that it "might well mean the death of church-related schools." [192] In early 1969 the Catholic bishops of Missouri warned that private schools could not continue without outside financial assistance. The fourteen-member Kansas City–St. Joseph School Board voted to close the schools if no aid were forthcoming. In Brooklyn, New York, a report of the diocesan school officials to the Priests' Senate in February 1969 indicated that

1. Without public assistance, Catholic schools in the Diocese cannot survive at their present level more than five to seven years.
2. Research by all major faiths shows that part-time auxiliary religious education has never been successful to date.
3. Catechetical confusion has parents and priests losing confidence in Catholic schools' ability to achieve their primary aim.
4. By next year laity will outnumber religious as teachers in local schools.[193]

On the other hand the Rev. Franklin E. Fitzpatrick, superintendent of schools, pointed out that "there is every indication that the Catholic people want Catholic schools. Last year we had to turn away 8,000 students from our elementary schools and 9,000 from our high schools."[194] He added that "religious do not leave because they don't want Catholic school teaching. In fact, many who leave apply to teach in Catholic schools." In February 1969 at Chicago, a two-million-dollar deficit in the operation of Catholic elementary schools led to the removal of tuition ceilings set by the archdiocese. At the same time in New Orleans, the operation of the archdiocese's 104 parochial schools resulted in an estimated deficit of $737,743 for the first half of fiscal 1969; if the depreciation of equipment and buildings and also the cost of contributed services were considered, the estimated deficit would have been around six million dollars.[195]

Because of the crisis aspect of the situation many impartial theorists, some of them in government, were more and more in favor of governmental aid to parochial schools, mostly for practical reasons. In Illinois in January 1969 Michael J. Howlett, auditor of public accounts, came out in favor of state aid to students of private schools in the state as "absolutely necessary now." He claimed that this was "the most economical method," and that

it makes for better sense to consider $100 for each non-public student than it does to wait until they become eligible for $600 each as public school students. The men who fought a war against "taxation without representation" never intended to set up a system in which one out of every four parents would be taxed, but not represented in the securing of funds for the education of their children.[196]

He was also of the opinion that state aid to students of private schools would help the poor to afford a better education. In Minnesota, also in January 1969, Governor Harold LeVander in his "State of the State" message stressed that, whereas private elementary school enrollments had increased steadily until 1963, now they had dropped 20 per cent in five years—with the result of "an immediate, sometimes intolerable burden on the taxpayer, who must then provide many more public facilities, teachers and administrators."[197] Theodore R. Sizer, dean of the Graduate School of Education of Harvard University, published in the same month an article on his participation in the Symposium of the Committee for Economic Development on "Education in the Ghetto: A Search for Solutions." He opted for a decentralization of schools "by persuasion rather than geography" in which

an area with a mixed population could have, cheek by jowl, several public schools—for example, one run by the city (P.S. 121), one by the Catholic Church (St. Mary's School), and one by the black community (The Martin Luther King Freedom School). Under this scheme, all would receive public financial support in varying measures and in varying ways, perhaps in patterns similar to those in use in the United Kingdom or, closer to home, in American private universities.[198]

He expressed cynical awareness that

Catholic schools are facing a financial crisis that can only be solved by some form of public aid to their system. Public aid to their schools may be cheaper in the long run than the costs of absorbing their youngsters into an expanded public system and, if this is true, the pragmatic American will willy-nilly get over his church-state hang-up. Taxes now seem to be a more telling issue than theology.[199]

He allowed for varying methodologies, among them giving money directly to the children and allowing them and their parents to choose their own school, the best known advocate of this option being economist Milton Friedman. He was of the interesting opinion that

the states will have to allow for diversity, but prevent destructive extremism. In a society made increasingly homogeneous by the mass media, education carries a new responsibility for this diversity and for nurturing cultural identities of great variety. The school should no longer be the melting pot, if it ever was. . . . The need for the common school has largely passed; television has seen to that. We need more critical, culturally dissenting, and intellectually vigorous people. . . . The public school is Mom and apple pie. The facts that it is a monopoly and that all children with few exceptions are *forced* to submit to *communal* schooling rarely dissuade July Fourth orators.[200]

In November 1969 the Education Department of the State of New York released a report of the University of the State of New York exploring the financial crisis of the more than 2,000 nonpublic elementary and secondary schools (with 872,000 pupils) in the state. It presented "six possibilities for expanding state financial assistance to nonpublic schools, ranging from subsidies to parents to direct aid to the schools involved." [201]

In the midst of the crisis situation for all contemporary education, for private schools there continued the same historical ambivalence of the United States government, especially in its judicial branch. Pertaining to the legislative branch, there had been isolated incidents of grants and loans to private schools as distinguished from programs in aid of individual students, as we have seen, throughout U. S. history. These had been on the level of higher education. The first massive program of this kind had been contained in the first Morrill Act of 1862 which formed the "land-grant colleges." [202] The Hatch Act of 1887 had provided for federal support of agricultural experimental stations at these land-grant colleges. During World War I, the National Research Council had been established and, supported partly with federal funds, it had financed research at universities. It had been made a permanent organization in 1918. During World War II, government contracts with colleges and universities had received greater importance and prominence. The Office of Scientific Research and Development, for example, had awarded many contracts, and in 1944 the Public Health Service Act had made it possible for federal funds to support research in medicine and related fields. After World War II there had been continued growth. In 1946, for example, there had been legislation establishing the Office of Naval Research, expressly providing for grants and contracts for educational institutions. The Armed Services Procurement Act of 1947, as amended, had provided a role in research and development affecting national defense to academic institutions; supplementary legislation of 1952 had conferred specific contracting authority. An amendment in 1956 to the Atomic Energy Act had permitted grants to educational, charitable, and other eleemosynary institutions for activities connected with the atomic energy program. The National Science Foundation Act of 1950 had also been very important—it had enabled the NSF to make grants for "basic scientific research" (for which phrase there is no exact definition commonly agreed upon) to educational and other organizations without many of the usual formalities connected with government contracting. In 1958, the federal government conferred upon each federal agency already having the authority to *contract* for "basic scientific research" with non-profit institutions the authority to make *grants* for similar purposes to the same institutions.[203] The National Defense Education Act of 1958 was the first major act of Congress in modern times whereby the federal government helped financially with the middle level of education, most of its aid going to improving the teaching of mathematics, the physical sciences, and modern languages. Unprecedentedly, it included loans (not grants) to fulfill its provisions in church-related middle level schools as well as colleges. On September 6, 1961, Congress renewed the NDEA for two more years. In 1964 Congress extended to teachers in private schools and all colleges the same partial remission of NDEA loan money as for those in public schools, and it broadened the original three subjects to be aided to include also English, reading, history, geography, and civics.

The two broad categories of grants and loans to private schools were in support of research, and they went directly to institutions. With or without grants or loans, legislation providing for *state control* and supervision of private schools has been at a minimum. On the level of higher education, some states regulate private trade, business, and correspondence schools which charge tuition. Even in these categories, however, a small fraction of the states having licensing requirements exempt schools that are operated by a religious or eleemosynary institution. Some states exercise *indirect* control, especially in the area of teacher training and also in regard to scholarship students whose tuition is paid wholly or partially from public funds. On the level of elementary and secondary education, state control and supervision of church-affiliated schools form a part of the compulsory education laws. In the area of curriculum, there is considerable agreement in two areas: length of the school term and the minimum elementary school curriculum. Pertaining to teachers, in a few states they must be licensed or certified like public school teachers. Some other states ask for such minimal standards as "competent" teachers or ones "capable of teaching." In the majority of states, however, there are no statutory standards. Very few states establish standards for buildings, teaching facilities, and equipment for church-affiliated schools in particular or private schools in general—they are merely subject to general regulations on fire, sanitation, and construction requirements. In the great majority of states, the compulsory education laws make no provision for home instruction. In a few states, however, case law has established that home instruction by competent tutors is sufficient if certain conditions are met; some states require administrative approval. On admission and expulsion, state regulations are at an absolute minimum. An increasingly-heard argument maintains that private schools, particularly those receiving public benefits, cannot discriminate on the basis of race with regard to admission; on expulsion, the governing principles are those of contract law.[204]

The year 1961 was a crucial one for the relationship of the federal government to church-related schools. On February 20, exactly one month after his inauguration, President John F. Kennedy, the first Roman Catholic President, sent a message to Congress with these words: "In accordance with the clear prohibition of the Constitution, no elementary or secondary school funds are allocated for constructing church schools or paying church schoolteachers' salaries." [205] In the same message Kennedy indicated that his position on higher education was different. On March 2, the Administrative Board of NCWC, through its Chairman, the Most Rev. Karl J. Alter, slightly "altered" (if we may be forgiven the pun) the traditional stand of the United States Catholic hierarchy concerning federal aid to education. It made this four-point statement:

1. The question of whether or not there ought to be Federal aid is a judgment to be based on objective, economic facts, connected with the schools of the country. . . .
2. In the event that there is Federal aid to education we are deeply concerned that in justice Catholic school children should be given the right to participate.
3. Respecting the form of participation we hold it to be strictly within the framework of the Constitution that long-term, low-interest loans to private institutions could be part of the Federal aid program. . . .
4. In the event that a Federal aid program is enacted which excludes children in private schools these children will be the victims of discriminatory legislation. There will be no alternative but to oppose such discrimination.[206]

Kennedy then directed that the Department of Health, Education and Welfare issue a brief. Secretary Abraham Ribicoff supervised it. Its principal conclusion, in sum, was:

The difficult problem is posed by the dual constitutional mandate: that the state must recognize these [parochial] schools as part of its educational system for purposes of compulsory education laws, but that it cannot support them in ways that would constitute an "establishment of religion."[207]

Also, concluded HEW, although the *Everson* ruling would seem to state that "direct grants to sectarian schools are prohibited," this does not decide whether a state, in carrying out a public purpose unrelated to religion, can distribute its benefits in the same way to religious as to secular institutions. Again, the brief concluded that tax support for church-related schools might

perhaps be extended to textbooks for the use of individual students where the books in question are common to the secular and sectarian educational systems. It might also be extended to some equipment, or possibly to facilities, designed for special purposes totally unconnected with the religious function of the schools.[208]

Along the latter line, the brief further conceded that a

program of financial aid to qualified students attending institutions of their choice to carry out a public policy of assisting unusually able students to develop their full potentialities, or to encourage study in subjects where there is a shortage of adequately trained persons to serve national needs, does not seem to raise a serious question.[209]

On March 28, HEW sent a memorandum to Congress listing forty-one federal educational programs involving grants and loans. In every program involving higher education, church-related institutions participated on a basis equal with other academically qualified institutions. Shortly after that, NCWC published a detailed analysis and reply to the HEW brief,[210] pointing out the concessions as well as the inconsistencies and ambiguities in the Kennedy administration position. On August 30, 1961, a federal aid bill excluding aid to private schools was defeated in the House, with Catholics on both sides of the issue.

After 1961, Congress many times renewed federal aid to schools in federally impacted areas, but did not include non-public schools on the elementary or secondary level. On Feb. 2, 1965, Rt. Rev. Msgr. Frederick G. Hochwalt testified as director of the Department of Education of NCWC before the Subcommittee on Education of the Senate Committee on Labor and Public Welfare. Among his remarks was a reminder of NCWC's comment when President Lyndon B. Johnson presented his education message to Congress:

Of great significance is the fact that the President calls for cooperation between the Nation's public and private schools. I have always considered the public and private school systems of this country to be partners, not competitors, in education. Our experience in many parts of the country proves the great benefit that such a partnership can be to the children in all schools.[211]

As part of the statistics he presented, Hochwalt, who had been in his position for about twenty years at that point and knew Catholic education, indicated the high percentage of non-Catholic children in Catholic elementary schools in "inner city" areas. In the same year, Congress overwhelmingly passed, and President Johnson signed in April, the Elementary and Secondary Education Act, sometimes called the Johnson Education Act.[212] In the latter connection, James Reston wrote:

The Elementary and Secondary Education Act of 1965 is probably the most significant accomplishment of his [Johnson's] Administration. For in this he found the political formula that broke through the church-state barrier and enabled the Federal Government not only to help neglected children in poverty areas, but to provide supplementary services to poor schools, regardless of religious affiliation.[213]

This was the the first federal aid bill in United States history to give such massive help to schools of less than collegiate rank—$1.3 billion to start—and the first to include private as well as public school children. With exceptional cleverness, the bill met the two arguments most frequently used up to then against federal aid to non-public schools: (1) that this would violate the First Amendment, and (2) that it would undercut the prestige and undermine the place of the public school in American life. This bill therefore gave aid for only secular subjects, and made the public school the sole recipient of public funds. The bill actually enhanced the prestige of the public school by making it the center of all programs in which non-public students may participate. Of particular significance was the federal government's recognition that all schools are an integral part of American education and that *all* children, no matter what school they attend, should benefit from the new educational opportunities. The Act was designed to recognize the special educational needs of children of low-income families and to provide financial assistance to local educational agencies in a way that would supplement and not diminish existing programs. It legislated special incentive grants for schools that increased their own efforts.

Under this legislation there are forty-four examples of the types of special programs that might be initiated by a local educational agency.[214] A few typical ones include special classes for physically handicapped, disturbed, and socially maladjusted children; preschool training; remedial programs (especially in reading and mathematics); Saturday morning special opportunity classes; home-oriented bookmobiles; a vast enlargement of library services; English for non-English-speaking children; programs for early identification and prevention of dropouts; supplemental health and food services; school health, psychiatric, and psychological services; and provision of clothing, shoes, and books where necessary. Since the funds are public, they are to be granted only to public agencies, to be channeled to the child who qualifies under the terms of the legislation. The broad language of the legislation was intended to enable public and private school administrators to devise imaginative programs that would meet the needs of the children without transgressing federal or state statutes. The state and the United States Office of Education must review each plan submitted by the local educational agency. The number of children of low-income families (earning less than $2000 per year or on "aid to dependent children") was the basis for determining the amount of money to be distributed to the states and to the local educational agencies.

The beneficiaries, as repeatedly insisted on by the legislation, are *children*, not schools. There are six titles, the last three concerning the establishment of research centers, the strengthening of state education departments, and a series of definitions. The first three are more important to our study. Title I—for the educationally deprived—amounts to about $1 billion. It presumes a high correlation between educational deprivation and economic deprivation. This Title encourages shared-time or dual enrollment for non-public school students. Under it, however, most educators want shared services and mobile equipment rather than shared time—in other words, to move the teachers, not the children, and this ordinarily during regular school hours. The most urgent need in this connection was basic remedial services—in reading, mathematics, and associated services. Title II—on books and instructional materials—required each state to use two criteria: relative need and equitability. Title III was included to create supplementary educational centers and services—e.g., mobile elementary school librarians, psychologists, and reading specialists, and also the production of educational television programs. Its basic intention was to mobilize all community resources for the education of all the children—colleges and universities, libraries, museums, the fine and performing arts, educational radio and television, and industry. In 1967, when new amendments were being considered for ESEA, Republican representative Albert H. Quie of Minnesota, with the backing of the House Republican Policy Committee, proposed to scuttle the ESEA and substitute direct grants to state school authorities. Quie led the Republican minority on the House Education and Labor Committee. While his proposal was not specifically directed at eliminating ESEA's grant to religious-operated schools, it would have had that effect, because in thirty-three states constitutional requirements would prohibit it. Nevertheless, Quie failed, and Reston pointed out the educational trends:

Despite the war in Vietnam, the expense of Federal aid to American education in the last three years has been unprecedented. The Federal commitment for education and training has risen from $4.7 billion in 1964 to $12.3 billion this year. And in the last three years Congress has passed more laws and committed more funds to education and health than in all the previous history of the Federal Government.[215]

In the area of legislation on the state level, in June 1968 Governor Raymond P. Shafer of Pennsylvania signed a bill for private and parochial school aid, making Pennsylvania the first state to authorize direct payment of public funds to private schools, most of which are Roman Catholic. This was under the "Purchase of Services" concept, whereby payment for services in non-religious subjects is to be based on the cost of teachers' salaries, textbooks, and other teaching materials. Shafer commented: "As we purchase hospital care for our sick and needy in sectarian health institutions, so we now begin a program to purchase education services for our 600,000 nonpublic school students." [216] Many looked upon the bill as a test-case device, expecting constitutionality tests from the "Friends of the Public Schools," a group of Protestant-affiliated organizations; the American Civil Liberties Union; and the statewide organization of public school officials.[217] In December 1969, a 2-1 decision of a federal panel of judges declared for the constitutionality of the Pennsylvania law; the majority pointed out that it is neither necessary nor constitutionally permissible to require that educational goals be pursued only in public institutions. In March 1970 in Connecticut, another three-judge federal court declared unanimously for the constitutionality of federal funds for church-related colleges (through the Higher Education Facilities Act of 1963) in the case known as *Tilton* v. *Finch*. Some saw the decision as the most significant one for private higher education since 1819, when the Dartmouth College Case established the right of private institutions to exist free of state interference. The Court found "no conflict between preservation of religious freedom and provision of higher education. Without both, we may end up with neither." This case, as well as most other such cases, is expected ultimately to reach the Supreme Court and have repercussions in all states of the Union.

In February 1969, the *Lutheran Witness Reporter* published a state-by-state survey of present aid to private schools.[218] The survey indicated that twenty-four states [219] give no aid whatsoever; seven [220] give such limited aid as to be, for all practical purposes, no aid at all; seven [221] provide bus transportation in various forms, but no other form of aid; thirteen states [222] provide more extensive aid; state-aid laws were involved in litigation in three states; [223] and seven states [224] possibly would be considering some form of aid during the current session of the legislature.

So it is evident that during our contemporary period government money is still being allocated to private schools in various forms. In 1968, for example, the City Council of Marlboro, Massachusetts, voted 6-4 to pay the salaries of lay teachers employed in Catholic schools. The City Council decided that it was cheaper in the long run for the city to pay $60,000 a year in this way toward the 1,000 parochial school students than to pay the estimated $750,000 to absorb the parochial students into the public schools in the likelihood of the parochial schools' having to close because of lack of funds.[225] In January 1969, a Joint Committee of the Michigan Legislature proposed a $40,000,000-a-year subsidy for private and parochial schools, recommending that a "purchase of service" approach be considered by the House of Representatives in February. Teachers of non-religious subjects were to receive their salaries from the state. George Romney, leaving as Governor of Michigan to become President Richard Nixon's Secretary of Housing and Urban Affairs, was severely criticized in many quarters for remarking publicly that church-operated schools should restrict themselves to religious instruction and leave secular education to the state. Lt. Governor William G. Milliken, however, Romney's successor, expressed sympathy with the financial plight of the non-public schools in his state and indicated a willingness to sign a bill to provide state aid, provided the bill were constitutional and there were sufficient funds.[226]

In connection with all this there was founded in 1959 a group called Citizens for Educational Freedom—a national, nonprofit, nonsectarian group of parents and others concerned with the rights of all children, whose purpose is to obtain for students in private and independent schools the same government financial support as that given those attending public schools. In April of 1959, Mae Duggan had a group of eight people meet in her living room in St. Louis because they were aroused by inequities in government educational grants. Incorporated under the laws of the State of Missouri in 1961, the group developed as their slogan, "A fair share for every child"; the slogan was intended to sum up their principles, the first of which was and is that parents have the primary and inalienable right to educate their children and to choose the kind of school their children are to attend. Parents who because of conscience or other reasons prefer independent schools should not be penalized. Through speeches and letters to government officials, the group claims credit for a change in the climate of public opinion. Specifically, it claims credit for those 1963-64 extensions to independent schools of the National Defense Education Act of 1958 that had previously been restricted; a major role in the passage of a law in Michigan that made it mandatory for local communities to provide bus service for independent as well as public schools; in 1965, responsibility for the adoption of a law in Pennsylvania requiring the transportation of private school children on publicly-owned buses over existing routes; and in Missouri the group helped bring the state to extend special services to handicapped pupils of independent schools. It publishes a monthly newspaper, *Freedom in Education,* and in 1965 there were 408 chapters and

50,000 members. In 1967 its annual national convention had over 15,000 in attendance.[227]

It is under the *judicial* branch of the government, however, that most church-state relations have taken place. Most of these were concerned first of all with the Establishment clause of the First Amendment and secondly with education, usually involving specific areas such as free textbooks for non-public students. The 1930 case of *Cochran* v. *Louisiana State Board of Education*,[228] discussed in the previous chapter, had left the basic question unanswered: may a state grant secular textbooks to *all* its students, *constitutionally*? It left other questions unanswered too. Is a state *required* to provide secular textbooks for non-public school students? If a state does so, may it constitutionally exclude students in private *sectarian* schools? *May* a state provide *religious* textbooks for non-public school students? In 1941 the Supreme Court of Mississippi had sustained a statute providing for the loan of textbooks to private school students. A brief passage of the decision was a harbinger of things to come:

If the pupil may fulfill its duty to the state by attending a parochial school, it is difficult to see why the state may not fulfill its duty to the pupil by encouraging it "by all suitable means." The state is under a duty to ignore the child's creed, but not its need.[229]

This statement gave rise to a widely publicized motto of advocates of government aid to parochial schools: "Need, not creed!" The court continued: "The state which allows the pupil to subscribe to any religious creed should not, because of his exercise of this right, proscribe him from benefits common to all." The answer to the basic question had become clear only when rereading *Cochran* in the context of *Everson* v. *Board of Education* of 1947, the school bus case.[230] Justice Hugo Black, writing for the majority and specifically affirming Cochran, had said, "It is much too late to argue that legislation intended to facilitate the opportunity of children to get a secular education serves no public purpose." [231]

Black was, however, ahead of the times in that assertion: an Oregon court 14 years later (1961) argued in just that way—*Dickman* v. *School District No. 62 C*.[232] Here the state court found inconsistent with the Oregon constitution a state statute that authorized private school students free use of the *same* textbooks prescribed for public school students. The state court was removing itself from Black's majority opinion in *Everson* and attaching to *Everson* another postulate to become the vogue: a "child safety" label. Its argument was that the "public purpose" served by the private school as defined in *Everson* was not to be found in the secular education offered, but in the physical well-being of the child. *Everson* was, in other words, not a "child education" decision, but a "child safety" decision. Intertwined throughout

*Dickman* was the related argument that in a sectarian school religion permeates the teaching of every subject including the secular. The leading case for the child-benefit theory, said the court, is *Borden* v. *Louisiana State Board of Education* [233] and the leading case rejecting the child-benefit theory *Judd* v. *Board of Education*.[234] The court said that "the classification which excludes such pupils from the State's bounty is not only reasonable, it is commanded by the Constitution itself." [235] Not only the "child safety" argument, but also the "religious permeation" argument distort the *Everson* ruling. The "permeation" argument ignores many subsequent court cases as well. There is, for example, the 1961 case of *McGowan* v. *Maryland*,[236] in which the United States Supreme Court found constitutional the concept of Sunday as a day of rest, even though the legislation satisfied the religious needs of a portion of the community as well as providing a secular purpose in a uniform day of rest. The Court thus broke a silence of almost a decade on the Establishment clause; it refused to characterize the existing Sunday laws of Maryland, Massachusetts, and Pennsylvania as establishments of the Christian religion. Only Justice William O. Douglas dissented. Justice Felix Frankfurter wrote a separate opinion: conscious of the occasional overlapping of the concerns of the state and of religion, he suggested that the Establishment clause of the First Amendment forbids both legislation whose primary purpose is religious, and legislation furthering combined secular and religious ends by means unnecessary to attain the secular end alone. This veered from absolute separation and opened the way for the neutrality principle of the *Abington* decision in 1963, about which more later.[237]

The answers to the above questions on textbooks were becoming clearer: the state may grant secular textbooks to all its students; it may limit itself to public schools; once it chooses to provide secular texts to *private* school students, however, it cannot exclude those in *sectarian* schools, because this would constitute a religious test; [238] and the state is forbidden to provide religious texts.[239] Finally in the area of textbooks was the "New York State Textbook Case." On Jan. 15, 1968, the United States Supreme Court agreed to rule on the constitutionality of a 1965 New York State law that required public school systems to lend textbooks to students in private, including parochial, schools. It granted the appeal of the School Board of East Greenbush, a suburb of Albany, New York, and other school officials in Rensselaer, Columbia, and Nassau counties who contended that the law forced them to violate both the state and federal constitutions. The law directed school districts to lend $15 in textbooks each year to each private school pupil in grades seven through twelve, requiring a total of about $25,000,000 per year. More importantly, the federal government was spending about $60,000,000 per year for textbooks and for specialized instruction to church-related school pupils in accord with the Elementary and Secondary Education Act

(ESEA). In 1967 the New York Court of Appeals had ruled in a 4-3 decision that the law did not violate either the state constitution or the First Amendment to the federal constitution,[240] and on June 10, 1968, the United States Supreme Court ruled the law constitutional by a 6-3 vote.

The majority reasoned that the program benefits students and not parochial schools, thus not constituting state support of religion. The majority opinion, written by Justice Byron R. White, adopted the "child-benefit" rationale of the 1947 *Everson* decision. He noted that the state law specifically forbade the state to purchase religious books, which would have been unconstitutional. Part of his opinion paid an interesting tribute to parochial schools and those sustaining them:

> Underlying these cases [*Pierce, Cochran,* and *Everson*], and underlying also the legislative judgments that have preceded the court decisions, has been a recognition that private education has played and is playing a significant and valuable role in raising national levels of knowledge, competence, and experience. Americans care about the quality of the secular education available to their children. They have considered high quality education to be an indispensible ingredient for achieving the kind of nation, and the kind of citizenry, that they have desired to create. Considering this attitude, the continued willingness to rely on private school systems, including parochial systems, strongly suggests that a wide segment of informed opinion, legislative and otherwise, has found that those schools do an acceptable job of providing secular education to their students. This judgment is further evidence that parochial schools are performing, in addition to their sectarian function, the task of secular education.[241]

The dissenters were Justices Hugo Black, William O. Douglas, and Abe Fortas. They reasoned that the sectarian schools choose the books, which was very different from having the state lend them the regular texts prescribed for the public school.[242] The effects were both immediate and longer range. As to the former, the New York taxpayers' case returns to Trial Court where an attempt will be made to determine whether the Federal Aid Act as applied to New York schools violates the First Amendment. The American Jewish Congress, the New York Civil Liberties Union, and the United Federation of Teachers will jointly sponsor the litigation. From the longer-range point of view, six other states with the same plan are affected.[243] In one of these states, Rhode Island, on October 28, 1968, the State Supreme Court reversed a ruling of Sept. 19, 1967, by the Superior Court that the state's 1963 statute on textbook lending violated both the federal and state constitutions, citing the June 10 United States Supreme Court decision on the New York statute.[244]

On the same date, June 10, 1968, the aforementioned taxpayers won their right to challenge federal spending, thus overturning the forty-five-year-old *Frothingham* decision.[245] In 1966, and again on April 12, 1967, the Senate had moved to permit taxpayer suits concerning the application of federal funds to church-supported schools in order to arrive at judicial guidelines as to what federal aid is consistent with the First Amendment proscriptions against the establishment of religon. In 1966 this bill had died in the House when the Judicial Committee failed to consider it, but in 1967 it had finally succeeded. On Oct. 16, 1967, the Supreme Court had granted the appeal made in June against a 2-1 decision of a special Federal District Court in New York, which had held that they lacked legal standing, of seven New York taxpayers [246] to bring a test case to challenge the constitutionality of federal aid to parochial schools under the Elementary and Secondary Education Act of 1965. There had been previous rumblings of this: cases had been introduced in federal courts in New York City; in Dayton, Ohio, where the opposed organizations were Protestants and Other Americans United for the Separation of Church and State, and twenty-two individuals; and also in the state courts in New York and in Pennsylvania, where a suit filed on Nov. 24, 1966, in the Common Pleas Court of Philadelphia directly attacked Title I of ESEA. All cases were against Titles I and II of the law, which permit public aid to private schools under the "child-benefit" theory. This particular case, brought against John W. Gardner, Secretary of Health, Education and Welfare, and Harold Howe II, Commissioner of Education, was sponsored jointly by the American Jewish Congress, the New York Civil Liberties Union, the United Federation of Teachers, and the United Parents Association. The case came to be known as *Flast* v. *Gardner*.[247]

Plaintiffs were urging the Supreme Court to hold that an exception to the *Frothingham* rule would be present when a church-state issue was involved. In 1923 Frothingham had, as a taxpayer, sought to challenge federal expenditures to fight infant mortality on the ground that Congress had no power to pass such a law. In the case of *Frothingham* v. *Mellon*, the Supreme Court had held that taxpayers lacked standing in court to challenge the way Federal funds were spent because their tax payments were too small to give them a real interest in a court decision. Now, in *Flast* v. *Gardner*, Chief Justice Earl Warren, writing the majority opinion, indicated that the new test for "standing" requires a taxpayer to contend that the statute under attack "exceeds specific Constitutional limitations imposed upon the exercise of the Congressional taxing and spending power." Warren did not say which constitutional limitations the Court had in mind, but Justice Abe Fortas in a concurring opinion argued for the establishment-of-religion clause. Warren emphasized that the ruling had nothing to do with the contentions about federal aid to parochial schools—that problem would have to be dealt with by the lower court where the argument began. Among the effects of the latter decision, the opponents of federal aid to church-related schools indicated that "the textbook ruling represented only a long skirmish in a continuing battle." Mrs. Blanche Lewis, president of the United Parents

Association, said "this [decision giving taxpayers the right to sue], we believe, will serve to apply the brakes to any rash of legislative activity that might be encouraged by the textbook decision, since every issue will now be carefully scrutinized and tested." Leo Pfeffer, contending that the "taxpayers' standing" decision was more important than the one on textbooks, stated: "The fact that the Court now allows taxpayers' suits indicates its readiness to meet the support question head on." [248] One thing was certain as a result of *Flast* v. *Gardner*: in the words of Charles M. Whelan, S.J., "there can be little doubt that the next twenty years will see a series of decisions unparalleled for church-state significance." [249] Among them will be federal programs granting millions of dollars to church-related educational and eleemosynary institutions.

Another area of judicial action was that of state-prescribed prayer. In *Engel* v. *Vitale* [250] of 1962, the Court declared unconstitutional a New York Regents' recommendation that at the beginning of each school day the students recite a non-denominational prayer which said: "Almighty God, we acknowledge our dependence upon Thee, and we beg Thy blessings upon us, our parents, our teachers, and our country." For the Court, Justice Hugo Black held that the matter was a violation of the Establishment clause because the prayer was composed by government officials. Neither the non-denominational nature of the prayer nor the fact that a pupil could refrain from reciting it changed the unconstitutionality. Justice William O. Douglas, concurring separately, considered the unconstitutionality to consist in the financial aid given to the religious exercise. Justice Potter Stewart was the sole dissenter. To many citizens it seemed that the Court was preferring nonbelief over belief, and no Supreme Court decision in connection with religious establishment ever aroused more heated opposition. Nevertheless, in the following June (1963) in *School District of Abington Township* v. *Schempp* [251] the Court declared unconstitutional any officially sponsored reading of the Bible and/or recitation of the Lord's Prayer at the beginning of the public school day. Justice Tom Clark wrote the majority opinion. He characterized Americans as a religious people, but asserted the absolute equality, before the law, of belief and non-belief. Because Clark seemed to confine religion exclusively to the individual, the home, and the church, many citizens objected that this decision did not adequately take into consideration the primary educational role and rights of parents. The Court acknowledged that the government may "not establish a 'religion of secularism' in the sense of affirmatively opposing or showing hostility to religion, 'thus preferring those who believe in no religion over those who do believe.'" It further indicated that the Bible could be studied for its literary and historical benefits in the public schools "when presented objectively as a part of a secular program of education." [252]

Several kinds of violent reactions followed upon these two decisions. There were, first, movements to amend the Constitution. With the object of permitting some such forms of religious observance in the public schools, 146 resolutions were presented in Congress by the end of 1964, the most widely publicized being the proposal of Representative Frank Becker. There were also suggestions of substitute programs—loosely speaking, four in number, all involving teaching "about" religion rather than teaching religion itself. The first suggestion was for cultural programs whereby religious writings were to be studied in various curricular offerings for their literary value. More specifically religious was the suggestion for religion-weighted cultural programs. Others suggested courses in comparative religion. Still others opted to introduce programs for the inculcation of ethical values with such subjects as "Inter-Group Relations," "Inter-Cultural Relations," and "Democratic Values"—most seeming to rely upon humanitarian, secularist, and communitarian values, frequently indistinctly enunciated. A third type of violent reaction consisted in the simple refusal of many to obey the court's ruling. In the South, where this type of devotion had been popular, violations were especially rampant; in the West and Midwest, the practice of Bible and prayer reading in school had never been widespread; in the Northeast, the ban was more meaningful. Nationwide, figures compiled by Prof. Richard B. Dierenfield in 1966 indicated that at that time nearly 13 per cent of the public schools were violating the Supreme Court's ruling; all indications after 1966 have indicated a spread of defiance rather than a containment of it.[253] Finally, the prayer decision led one wag to print posters in luminous air-raid-shelter colors for hanging in schools that read: "In the event of atomic attack all rules against praying in this school are indefinitely suspended." [254]

Another area in which the judicial branch of the government has rendered treatment is released-time. The *Zorach* decision in Spokane, Washington, only applied insofar as the program there involved the distribution of registration cards on school premises and used school time for announcements. Apart from these extrinsic elements, however, released-time as such was upheld in the *Perry* decision in 1959 [255] and in the *Dilger* decision of 1960.[256] In the last decade total registration estimates for the released-time program varied between two and three million Catholics and about 1,250,000 Protestants. A partial survey conducted by the National Center of the Confraternity of Christian Doctrine in 1964 posited a registration of 509,000 Catholics at that time. Jewish agencies estimate that the ten thousand students in the Jewish programs of New York City constitute most of their national total. All these figures are, however, estimates and not statistics. [257]

Despite Supreme Court ambiguity, inconsistency, and vagueness, grass-roots America seemed in some cases to see more clearly than the highest court of the land what they want and need. As we have seen in another connection, many areas of the country treat parochial schools as equal to other schools, parochial school students as persons with the same worth and dignity as other students, and teachers in parochial schools as being in partnership in the educational task of the community. This author was suprised to discover how numerous were such amicable and efficient situations.[258] But the rendering of judicial decisions is ongoing. A case that also caused excitement was one rendered by the Maryland Court of Appeals on June 2, 1966, at which time the Maryland Court held 4-3 that state grants to three church-related colleges were unconstitutional.[259] The decision indicated that Maryland grants for the construction of dormitories and classroom buildings at church-affiliated colleges that are "sectarian" violate the Establishment clause of the First Amendment of the United States Constitution. The Maryland Court of Appeals indicated that Hood College, an independent liberal arts college for women that is affiliated with the United Church of Christ, was not sectarian in a legal sense: its "stated purposes in relation to religion are not of a fervent, intense or passionate nature, but seem to be based largely upon its historical background"; "it welcomes students of all religious faiths"; "the administration does not represent any particular church or religious body"; "none of the courses offered . . . is geared to aiding the Protestant religions or any other"; and "there is absolutely no attempt at indoctrination in any way." The Court judged that the same could not be said of West Maryland College, which is Methodist Church-affiliated, or of Notre Dame and St. Joseph Colleges, both of which are Catholic. Sister Margaret Mary, president of the College of Notre Dame in Baltimore, testified that she was not aware of any areas in which Catholic doctrine would interfere with teaching in liberal arts courses.

Although he did not say so, it may have been the Maryland case that gave rise to John J. McGrath's study of the legal status of Catholic institutions in the United States. His "study is an examination of the juridical structures of those institutions chartered by authority of state or federal law that are conducted under the auspices of the Catholic Church. Primary emphasis thus falls upon colleges, universities, hospitals and similar charitable institutions."[260] He examined persons in law (physical and corporate), property of institutions in civil and canon law, and the legal character of the sponsoring bodies in civil and canon law. He concluded:

Charitable and educational institutions chartered as corporations under American law are not *owned* by the sponsoring body. The legal title to the real and personal property is vested in the corporation. . . . If anyone *owns* the assets of the charitable or educational institution, it is the general public.[261]

He then addressed himself to the question of "what makes the institution Catholic?," and replied:

The answer to this question lies in the influence over the institution exercised by the sponsoring body. The structure of American corporations provides four vehicles for directing and effectuating this influence: (1) the charter and by-laws; (2) the board of trustees; (3) the administration; and (4) the staff of the corporation.[262]

His last word was a request for what he called "cooperative separate-ness," wherein he stated: "The unique character of American charitable and educational corporations conducted under Catholic auspices de-mands a unique form of cooperation and separation between the insti-tution and the sponsoring body." [263] Nevertheless, the process of re-moving clergy from administrative posts in favor of laity quickens in pace. It is never stated whether the reasons for this are to be found in concern to comply with Vatican II's emphasis on the responsibilities of the emerging laity or in concern over modern interpretations of the Con-stitution in connection with continued procurement of government money.

### CHURCH

Obviously the Church has rights as an agent of education. How this agency will be exercised and how it will be looked upon has varied and will vary from age to age. After World War II a reaction set in against the rigidity of Catholic education, a reaction attributed in some quarters to the continued existence of a Thomistic synthesis of philosophy and theology that had been officially approved by Pope Leo XIII and his successors. A demand set in for pluralism, openness to contemporary science and culture, and more dialogue with the world. These demands reached a climax in Vatican II and were reflected in its *Declaration on Education*. The original draft of this document was a Constitution, the highest category of document, entitled *Constitution on Catholic Schools*. The first two texts presented in 1962 and 1963 were roundly criticized by many. When in late 1963 it became apparent that time was running out for all the Council's business, the Council Fathers reduced the schema on education from a Constitution to a *votum*, the lowest category of conciliar document. Several important figures, however, succeeded in increasing its importance, so it was revised from being a consideration of schooling to the broader notion of education, raised in status, and debated on the floor of St. Peter's November 17-19, 1964.[264] The debate was less than full, because the Fathers were then concerned with Schema Thirteen, *The Church in the Modern World*, and also with the discussions on religious liberty. Consequently Paul-Emile Cardinal Leger of Montreal made an intervention [265] indicating that, due to lack of time and the physical strains upon the Council Fathers, "we should not approve too hastily what will be the *Magna Carta* of Christian education." [266] A post-conciliar commission is expected to develop more fully Catholic positions on education.

On the national level, in the realm of theory the U. S. Bishops' statement on Catholic schools on Nov. 16, 1967, contained applications of principles of Vatican II as well as reminders of truths for our hard-pressed Catholic educators. Although the Bishops addressed themselves "largely to teachers," they wanted also "to reinforce public confidence in Catholic education and to reassure our people to whom we are profoundly grateful for their consistently generous moral and financial support of Catholic education." For truly apostolic teachers to raise their pupils "to high standards of Christian conduct," they must "have an interest in their pupils' homes and neighborhoods." This concept "is especially relevant in those areas where the poor and oppressed depend on Catholic schools for their education," where the teachers need "new and better educational techniques for fighting against the demoralizing and dehumanizing effects of poverty and injustice." The school "must be an expression of what is meant by being a Christian in today's world." [267] In the area of practice, on the elementary and middle levels there has been a tendency toward stronger diocesan control, but in higher education a tendency toward academic freedom.

On March 3, 1970, for the first time in history the President of the United States (Richard M. Nixon) paid tribute to the educational efforts of the churches in this country, in a "Message on Education Reform" to the Congress. In a section of the text (provided by the Office of the White House Press Secretary) on nonpublic schools, "most of them church-supported," he listed the advantages of the elementary and secondary institutions which "have long been an integral part of the nation's educational establishment." Among them were: "a diversity which our educational system would otherwise lack"; "a spur of competition to the public schools"; parental "opportunity to send their children to a school of their own choice"; "a wider range of possibilities for education experimentation"; "special opportunities for minorities, especially Spanish-speaking Americans and black Americans"; "a dimension of spiritual value giving children a moral code by which to live"; and the financial contribution. Concerning the last, he indicated that private elementary and secondary schools "educate 11% of all pupils— close to six million school children"; he also pointed out that "if most or all private schools were to close or turn public, the added burden on public funds by the end of the 1970's would exceed $4 billion per year in operations, with an estimated $5 billion more needed for facilities." He warned against any complete monopoly over education by any school system, public or private. Reminding his audience that "in the past two years, close to a thousand nonpublic elementary and secondary schools closed," and that they were now "closing at the rate of one a day," he

made "the specific problem of parochial schools . . . a particular assignment of the [President's] Commission [on School Finance]," which he
was then establishing. Finally, he asserted that "our purpose here is not
to aid religion in particular but to promote diversity in education."

## FAMILY

In both Catholic schooling and Catholic education, parents have an
essential role. Vatican II's *Declaration on Christian Education* called
them the "first and foremost educators of their children," a role the
Fathers considered to be so decisive "that scarcely anything can compensate for their failure in it." [268] Only through parents can an atmosphere be created in which love and reverence for God and men so
animate the family "that a well-rounded personal and social development
will be fostered among the children." It is in the family that children
are taught to know and worship God and to love their neighbor, and
through the family, the first school of those social virtues which every
society needs, that children "are gradually introduced into civic partnership with their fellow men, and into the People of God." These statements of Vatican II are substantiated by modern psychology, so that all
schools welcome the cooperation of parents. In Catholic schools there
have been greater efforts to involve the parents through such organizations as the National Home and School Service.

### COMMON TO CHURCH, STATE, AND FAMILY: SHARED TIME

Church, state, and family meet in "shared time," a compromise between the secularization of the state school as a concomitant of religious
pluralism on the one hand and concern over the rapidly rising religious
illiteracy in the United States on the other. It was defined in a 1963
bill to amend the National Defense Education Act of 1958 as

a program of instruction in academic subjects at secondary school level which
is (a) carried out under the administrative control and direction of a local
agency and (b) attended by public secondary school students and students
who are enrolled in non-public secondary schools." [269]

To avoid confusion with released-time and shared facilities, its name was
changed to "Dual Enrollment." The Department of Health, Education
and Welfare has defined this as

an arrangement whereby a child or youth regularly and concurrently attends a
public school part time and a nonpublic school part time, pursuing part of elementary or secondary studies under the direction and control of the public
school and the remaining part under the direction and control of the nonpublic
school.[270]

It was during the contemporary period that shared time had its historical development. On November 22, 1960, Protestant and Catholic officials met at the Hotel Woodner in Washington, D. C., to discuss topics of common concern such as the question of religious exercises in public schools and federal aid to religious institutions. The officials discussed the concept of shared time and almost a year later, in October 1961, the idea was discussed again at the Interchurch Center in New York. A few months later a new emphasis was provided when the magazine *Religious Education* published a symposium on the subject.[271] On May 20, 1963, Abraham Ribicoff proposed in a Senate speech that shared time be a part of general aid to public elementary and secondary schools.[272]

Arguments are presented for and against shared time. Stearns thinks the program could be adopted because of parents' rights to draw from the public school that portion of the child's education assumed to be the state's job, "and to obtain from the parochial school at their own or the church's expense only that portion of schooling which is determined to be of such religious import that it cannot be entrusted to lay public authority." [273] Such an arrangement would continue to maintain separation of church and state. Stearns points to "the chance that such a plan offers a means of assuaging the bitterness and divisiveness that is now mounting over the strife for public funds for church schools." [274] Theodore Powell of the Connecticut State Department of Education sees as an advantage "good relations among all sections of the community" [275] and views the program as constitutional under three conditions: that it have a public and not a religious purpose; that the expenditure of public funds remain under public control; and that it be available to all pupils of the same category without arbitrary discrimination.[276] Further, he sees in it "a method of constitutional cooperation to give our children a rich spiritual development and the broad social experience essential to maintain our democracy and advance our civilization." [277] One school—St. Paul's High School in Chicago—was even designed to operate as a shared-time school.

Others are strongly opposed. Walter A. Anderson opposed the program because:

1. Shared time would appear to be unconstitutional from a federal and state standpoint.
2. Shared time would undermine and impair the support of public schools and thereby weaken them.
3. Shared time would result in two inferior part-time educational programs for the children and youth of both sectarian and public schools.
4. Shared time is a concession to a limited group of sectarian schools, largely of one faith.[278]

Louis Cassels opposed the program because of problems of scheduling classes, transportation, discipline, exchange of school credits, and parochial school holy days and holidays from school.[279] A 1964 teacher-opinion poll that was reported in the *NEA Journal* indicated more than five teachers in ten opposing or tending to oppose such programs.[280] Many Catholic educators see in this program a compromise to the Catholic emphasis on the integration of religion in the curriculum. In 1965 NCEA reported 251 Catholic elementary schools and 182 Catholic high schools with shared-time programs, and in the same year NEA reported shared-time programs operating in at least 183 public school districts in 25 states. Because of its many problems shared time will probably remain sporadic.[281]

## Teachers

With teachers, as with other aspects of education, neither problems nor opportunities are confined to Catholic schools. With public school teachers, the first problem area has been shortage. An NEA survey of 1967 showed that the nations' public schools were estimated to be short about 171,300 teachers for 50.7 million elementary and high school students.[282] Many states reported they would have to employ teachers with substandard qualifications. Rural and small-town school systems faced the most severe pinch. Some of the reasons alleged for the shortage were unattractive salaries, greater opportunities in business and industry, induction into the military services, and resignations by long-time teachers. The Office of Education projections indicate hopefully that in the early 1970's small yearly reductions may occur in new school registrations because of a lower birth rate. With regard to salaries, many unionized janitors earn more than degree-holding teachers, causing many teachers to hold "moonlight" positions. Teachers are also frustrated because of outmoded bureaucracies. Today's young teachers, probably better educated and more articulate than their predecessors, are quicker to weary of the impersonal restrictions of the larger school systems and are tired of study hall duties and lunch hour and rest room patrol. Teachers are being spurred into action by two competing organizations, the million-member National Education Association and the American Federation of Teachers. The NEA, composed of classroom teachers, superintendents, and principals, regards itself as an organization of professionals rather than a union. The AFT has made no pretensions to being anything other than an AFL-CIO union. Its aggressive, militant successes, particularly in big cities, have triggered NEA into action also. Public school administrators often oppose the teachers, claiming that union demands are exorbitant, asserting that local autonomy is threatened, and resenting teachers' becoming policy makers. Under the pressure of teacher demands, some school districts are being forced into deficit financing.

With Catholic school teachers, problems also exist. Some are not so different from their public school counterparts—e.g., the matter of unions and strikes. The Association of Catholic Teachers, strong in such places as Philadelphia, Cleveland, Newark, and Chicago, has stiff competition from the nonsectarian American Federation of Teachers, whose locals in many places now have chapters of Catholic teachers, including (in Chicago, at least) nuns. The unions are very much to the fore in deciding such issues as salary and tenure, and Catholic teacher strikes took place during this period in such areas as Chicago, Philadelphia, and Newark. Other problems are different, or have a different intensity, in Catholic schools—e.g., the (praiseworthy) efforts of some state departments of education to impose more rigorous controls over accreditation requirements, an issue over which there are greater pressures in Catholic schools than in their public school counterparts. There exists a shortage of competent teachers at all levels, but especially at the elementary and middle levels. There is a pathetic shortage of religious teachers caused by lack of vocations, those leaving the sisterhoods, and religious sisters going into other fields of work. Catholic schools must face daily the need to make savings brought about by the increased faculty salaries, of lay teachers in particular. In that connection, by 1960 the number of lay teachers increased by 537% over the 7,422 lay teachers in the Catholic schools of 1948.[283] In spite of the shortages, however, some new teaching religious communities have come to the United States during these years. The Sisters of Charity of the Immaculate Conception of Ivrea, for example, founded in Piedmont, Italy, in 1828, for educatonal and other social works, came to the United States in 1961. They work in the New York archdiocese and in the Greensburg, Pennsylvania, diocese. The Daughters of Charity of Canossa, founded in Verona, Italy, by Blessed Gabriella Canossa in 1808 to run schools, provide religious instruction, and visit hospitals, also came to the United States in 1961 to teach at a school in Albuquerque, New Mexico. These and the teaching religious nuns who preceded them had to continue the spirit of dedicated sacrifice established by their forebears. Even in our time, some of the sisters have had to sacrifice further by "moonlighting" to help make ends meet. The Sisters of St. Joseph of Carondelet in the St. Louis province, for example, took salaried jobs in the summer of 1968 to help meet the cost of education. Their Provincial, Sister Joan Marie Gleason, said that any of the sisters may work, "preferably within the area of their present profession." [284]

There were, however, new evidences of awareness of the dignity and responsibilities of teachers in the Roman Catholic Weltanschauung. Vatican II's *Declaration on Education* urged teachers to be enriched with both secular and religious knowledge, to be appropriately certified, and "to be equipped with an educational skill which reflects modern-day findings." [285] Pope Paul VI in an address to the National Congress of the Italian Association of Catholic Teachers on November 4, 1968, indicated the importance and dignity of teachers when he said:

The teacher forms the man, the whole man, as the Council has frequently underlined: not one part of man, even if worthy of every attention and care, but his entirety as a person who thinks and judges, wills and loves, and develops himself in a precise social and community context, from which he cannot and ought not to feel uprooted.[286]

There are also other encouraging signs: new approaches, preparation methods, and principles for religious. For example, the Sister Formation Conference of Washington, D. C., which operated in conjunction with the Conference of Major Superiors of Women, had a two-week workshop at Woodstock, Maryland, in July 1968, to provide an opportunity for sisters to work on their own problems, but with the help of resource personnel. The latter included religious and lay specialists in psychology, psychiatry, counseling, history, and theology. Attending were sisters representing ninety-six orders from throughout the country, who made an attempt at "renewal," discussed the concept of community, the dignity of the human person, relationships with the world while remaining faithful to their role as sisters, and prayer. Many believed that such approaches are beginning to make the new teaching religious the best teachers in this country or any other at any time in history. The contrast between teacher preparation in the 1950's and that in the 1960's is astounding. The studies of Sister Mary Brideen Long, for example, illustrate this.[287] Her study in 1966 found that the percentage of sisters holding a degree before beginning to teach increased from 7.1% in 1952 to 41.9% in 1964. Essentially the same finding results from the comparison of a study by Sister Rose Matthew Mangini [288] in 1956 with the 1966 observations of Sister Mary Emil Penet in *Catholic Schools in Action.*[289] Although the direction is up, the picture is not all sunshine and roses: Sister Mary Emil says that 35% of the total teaching force in elementary and secondary schools have substandard preparation. Sister Bertrande Meyers confirmed that observation by saying in 1965: "In all honesty it must be admitted that even today some communities have not yet organized a satisfactory intellectual and professional preparation program." [290]

The formation and preparation of Catholic teachers were on the highest level, perhaps, in the area of the teaching of religion. In spite of the pre-eminence of religion in the Catholic school curriculum, it was at one time considered possible for any religious, only because he or she was a religious, to teach this subject without special preparation. Up to the scholastic year 1963-64, only two institutions had developed doctoral programs—The Catholic University of America in Washington, D. C., and the Graduate School of Theology, St. Mary's College, Notre Dame, Indiana. Others granted either a Master of Arts degree or a certificate. Recently, other needs of the Church began to motivate more Catholics to seek training in Sacred Doctrine. For lay men and women, opportunities began to open up for teaching in this field at the college level. The establishment of the Sister Formation Conference for a more profound intellectual, professional, and spiritual training of young religious women was a great help. There was growing concern for the intellectual needs of the Newman apostolate and a growing acceptance of religious scholars on secular campuses. There was at the same time recognition of a need for solidly trained leaders in the Confraternity of Christian Doctrine. The Church became increasingly aware of the growing need for the development of a catechesis specially addressed to adult members of the Church. Finally, there was growing recognition of the need for special training for the teaching of religion in high schools. On this level it became increasingly evident that a Master of Arts degree was necessary, whereas for college teaching a doctorate should be required. To meet all these needs, and for the maintenance of Roman Catholic intellectual dignity, many became increasingly aware of the need for a first-rate Roman Catholic theological school in this country.[291]

Helping to improve teacher education in Catholic schools were many more-than-willing organizations. The NCEA has national, and also six regional, units that concentrate on secondary and higher education, including teacher training. There are organizations centering around specific subject matter, such as the Catholic Business Education Association, the National Catholic Music Educators Association, and the Society of Catholic College Teachers of Sacred Doctrine. There is also a growing number of educational conferences and institutes sponsored by such teaching community organizations as the Jesuit Educational Association, the Loretto Educational Conference, the Sisters of Mercy, and the Christian Brothers.[292]

## Students

In the fast pace since World War II, youth is said to have undergone four ages: the atomic, space, computer, and DNA (deoxyribonucleic acid, carrier of the code of heredity). In all of them, as before them and after them, Catholicism retains a certain sameness, especially in its vision of the dignity of the person in Christian education. This vision was nicely summarized in a series of Pope Paul VI's addresses to general audiences in 1968 at Rome. In the first of the series, on July 10, he gave the relevant warning that "a morality without God, a Christianity without Christ and without his Church, a humanism without the true concept of man, these do not lead us to a good end." [293] On August 14 he spoke on the concept of the ideal Christian character, and asked, "Is there an existential difference between the person who is a Christian and the one who is not? Certainly." [294] After pointing out the differences made by the spiritual imprint especially of three sacraments on the Christian soul—baptism, confirmation, and priesthood—he added:

But there is more than this. There is grace, the state of grace, that quality in which the soul is enfolded, when the new, supernatural relationship into which God wishes to elevate the man who abandons himself to Him is established. . . . There is no way to define fully the state of grace; it is a gift, riches, beauty, a wonderful transfiguration of the soul associated with the life of God Himself, by which to a certain extent we share in His transcendent nature; it means being elevated to the position of adopted sons of the Celestial Father, the brothers of Christ, of living members of the Mystical Body through the animation of the Holy Spirit.[295]

On September 4th he again dealt with fundamentals, saying: "Again the question is raised: 'Who is man?' Again . . . men do not agree." He indicated that the

confrontation becomes a conflict in a double sense. The first sense concerns truth. What is the truth about man? . . . The second sense is that of inclusiveness. Who, today, has the larger concept of man, more complete in its analysis of his human components, more comprehensive in its grasp of his modern needs, more adequate in relating his actual and historical characteristics to our time?[296]

Speaking of some modern scientists who do not believe in God and who make the absolute conclusion that man is a prime being, Paul deplored "the tragic mockery implied by such a qualification, attributing infiniteness to a being which is neither its own cause nor its own finality, a being subject to limitations, weakness, infirmity and inexorable frailty." He pointed to the human dignity with which the Church considers man and recalled the Constitution of Vatican II, *Gaudium et Spes*: "An outstanding cause of human dignity lies in man's call to communion with God." Speaking of "the two aspects most relevant to the contemporary attitude towards man: the individual and the social," he said:

In regard to both of these aspects, the Church evaluates man . . . as a being of incomparable greatness. No anthropology equals that of the Church in its evaluation of the human person. This is true as regards man's individuality, his originality, his dignity; as regards the intangible richness arising from his fundamental rights; as regards his sacredness, his capacity for education, his aspiration to complete development, his immortality, etc.[297]

He reminded his audience that

the Church confers on man a stature she describes as 'creature,' but a creature made in the image of God, the Creator. This creature, elevated into the ineffable love of Christian regeneration, is raised to the level of son and of participant of the divine nature (cf. 2 Peter 1:4).

Speaking of man's social nature, he again recalled *Gaudium et Spes:* "Man's social nature makes it evident that the progress of the human person and the advance of society itself hinge on each other." In this connection the Church teaches him that

the vital, intimate and stable rapport which grows between himself and God is unfolded and developed in his charity towards his brothers (cf. I John 4:20). This includes all men without discrimination. . . . No single school of social thought arrives at such a conclusion. . . . Authentic Christian life gives rise to a social spirit, even on the natural and temporal plane, which is always progressing along the lines of respect for others, concord, collaboration and peace among men.[298]

### THE GIFTED AND THE HANDICAPPED

In the area of practice, at least one new group that had been neglected in the past has begun to receive special care at the hands of Catholic education: the superior student. Sister Mary Emmanuel, for example, observed in 1960 that "since the Second World War, we have been hearing a great deal about the superior or the gifted student." [299] For the most part, however, Catholic education continued among the poor and the outcast, the *anawim* of all faiths, as illustrated by excerpts of a letter from a school in Harlan, Kentucky:

We've had three killings recently here in Harlan! One was the brother of our bus driver. His wife shot him with a shotgun blast in self-defense, she says, as he, after a night of drunkenness and threats, was coming at her to kill her. As he was dying, she ran for aid, had to crawl under a freight train temporarily stopped so she could get to the road from the shack, then screaming and hysterical stopped a car to appeal for help to get the dying man to the hospital and was spit on by the white men in the car! She came to ask to pray in our church for a little while. . . .
Believe it or not, our kids tell us "We love our school and hate to stay home on holidays!" Bishop Sheen summed it up recently, saying that without Catholic schools, the nation will be doomed, for they are the only ones where morality is taught. I believe myself that the government is going to give the cost of a child's education to the parents and let the parents send the child to whatever school they wish. We, with our already established religious school system, will receive both the children and their support from *all* parents who want their children taught about God, religion and morality, and that's the greatest majority in the U. S. It's certainly that way here. Denominational bigotry is dissolving with prayers in Unity and parents of all faiths in our vicinity *want* their children taught about God in our Catholic school.[300]

Catholic educational procedures among the *anawim* often take advantage of all the latest scientific improvements. The Sisters of the Good Shepherd, for example, whose work among socially maladjusted girls began in 1842 at Louisville, Kentucky, with vocational training, now operate their programs through residential treatment schools in which they provide specialized education for these girls based on the girls' potentials. They have developed multiple curricula in settings which enable girls in personal, social, and/or family difficulties to meet the standards of the traditional junior and senior high school. Specifically designed programs provide individual attention in small classes. The focus of the Sisters' rehabilitative program has become more exclusively educational, and the Sisters now conduct chartered schools for their young ladies. Theirs is a very interesting combination of educational and social work.

Certainly among the *anawim* have been the handicapped of all types who, during the contemporary period as in the past, are a concern of Catholic education. Diocesan schools for handicapped children have multiplied, and practically every diocese has made provision for them in one way or another. In 1964, for example, St. Raphael's Geriatric Adjustment Center for the Blind and Visually Handicapped was established in the former residence of St. Raphael's Home for the Blind in Boston.[301] The International Catholic Deaf Association (ICDA), whose headquarters are in Brooklyn, New York, has more than 4,000 members engaged in work with the deaf as a form of Catholic action. In 1960 the ICDA census listed 20,336 Catholic deaf in the United States, 148 priests working with the deaf, and 14 schools for the deaf with an enrollment of 2,014 under Catholic auspices. ICDA also sponsors annual workshops and promotes sign-language courses in major seminaries. At Gallaudet College there is a Newman Club chapter for the Catholic students. Catholic education in these regards attempts to keep up with the latest trends, in addition to administering to the spiritual needs of students. Most schools in the United States emphasize "oralism," through the elementary and intermediate levels. At the secondary level, the combined or simultaneous method is advocated—oral speech, finger spelling, and signs are given simultaneously, in order to encourage students to absorb language patterns in logical and correct word order.[302]

Catholic education has also been as active as possible among the mentally retarded. Although classification is difficult, modern scientific usage is generally based on I.Q. and forms three functional groupings: the *educable* retarded, with what the experts term *mild* retardation, of I.Q. from about 50 to 75, comprising about 85 per cent of the retarded; the *trainable* retarded, with *moderate* retardation, ranging in I.Q. from about 25 to 50 and comprising about 13 per cent of the retarded; and the *totally dependent* children, with *severe* retardation, in an I.Q. range from a theoretical zero to 25, comprising about 2 per cent of the retarded and usually institutionalized. Education of the mentally retarded usually refers to the use of special methods and techniques to help such persons attain functional literacy and social competence. In the beginning of the contemporary period—in February 1958 to be exact—a study indicated that the United States public school system enrolled

201,406 educable and 16,779 trainable retarded children.[303] This represented only about one-fourth of the retarded who were estimated to need special educational facilities, but this proportion would grow, especially with NDEA of 1958 and the accession to the presidency of John F. Kennedy, who had first-hand experience with the problem through the affliction of one of his sisters.

Under Roman Catholic auspices, institutions for the mentally retarded are either private or diocesan. Those under private auspices are usually identified with an institutional concept, typified by such schools as St. Coletta's School for Exceptional Children, Jefferson, Wisconsin, which had been founded in 1904. Diocesan institutions are a later development and involve special day classes in parochial schools or in separate special schools either residential or day. Typical of this trend is the Department of Special Education of the archdiocese of St. Louis, Missouri, founded in 1950. The basic Catholic operative principles are an application of the regular principles of the supernatural destiny of man, basically no different from those for any other group of children: teach the children to live better for both this world and the next, use all the child's mental capacities to a maximum, and enable the child to become as far as possible a useful and contented member of society. The special emphasis for this group is the preparation of the children to receive their first holy communion.[304]

With regard to growth, the NCEA in 1965 showed seventy-two schools caring for 6,928 pupils in 171 classes.[305] As for their effectiveness, a study of 1963 indicated that the adjustment of a group of these children, with a mean I.Q. of 53, in the areas of home, community, economics, and religion was as follows: 56 per cent made a favorable adjustment, 27 per cent fair, and 17 per cent poor.[306] Neurobiologists are studying more and more how the nervous system receives, arranges, and evaluates information and translates it into action, in order to raise intelligence, to improve memory, and to control human behavior.[307]

### NEGROES

In the area of civic affairs, after the Brown desegregation decision of 1954 the northern and western states were under attack for *de facto* racial segregation in education, for such charges as discriminatory transfer practices, overcrowding of Negro schools, bias in the application of special programs and in the selection of sites for schools, and complete lack of or inadequate provisions for equipment in schools that serve primarily Negro students. The Civil Rights Act of 1964 also helped the Negro. Title IV (Desegregation of Public Education) directs the U. S. Commissioner of Education to see to desegregation in public education and empowers the Attorney General to initiate legal proceedings against offenders. Title VI (Non-Discrimination in Federally Assisted Programs) forces recipients of federal aid to give assurance that "no person shall be excluded from participation, denied any benefits or subjected to discrimination on the basis of race, color, or national origin." The Economic Opportunity Act of 1965 contributes to the improvement of Negro education, in counteracting influences basic to learning difficulties. The Elementary and Secondary Education Act of 1965 (Public Law 89-10) seeks to improve the kind of education provided for lower income families, into which category falls a high percentage of Negroes. The Higher Education Act of 1965 has helped the Negro in all its Titles.[308] On October 29, 1969, the Supreme Court helped the Negro even further. It replaced the concept of integration "with all deliberate speed" of the *Brown* decision of 1954, by ruling unanimously that school districts must end segregation "at once" and operate integrated systems "now and hereafter." The specific case at issue, *Beatrice Alexander et al.* v. *Holmes County Board of Education et al.*, immediately affected thirteen school districts in Mississippi, but will apply to all school segregation cases present and future.[309]

For Catholics, beginning after World War I, but especially after World War II, their position, as well as that of the Negroes, swiftly changed: Negroes had increasingly begun moving into northern cities and Catholics had begun to shed their minority-group characteristics and to gain acceptance. Therefore, Catholic-Negro relations entered a new phase. Nevertheless, conditions continued to vary greatly in different parts of the country; so in writing in 1967 of Catholics, William Osborne in *The Segregated Covenant* [310] selected eleven dioceses for detailed descriptions. In metropolitan New York City, this phase had begun in Harlem during the 1920's. In New York City and elsewhere, as large Negro communities supplanted white Catholic parishioners, attempts were made to care for their material and spiritual needs, most of the creative ideas coming from individual priests and laymen rather than from chancery offices. It was, for example, individual priests, nuns, brothers, and others who participated in the march on Washington (1963), Selma and Montgomery, Alabama (1965), and Chicago, Illinois (1965). Among the notable exceptions during this period were Lawrence Cardinal Shehan of Baltimore, who in his pastoral letter of March 1, 1963, on racial justice pointed out that because Catholics had been slow in the field of racial justice "we have a special obligation to place ourselves in the forefront of movements to remove the injustices and discriminations which still remain." Archbishop Joseph Rummel of New Orleans ordered the desegregation of Catholic schools in 1962. Patrick Cardinal O'Boyle of Washington, D. C., in pastoral letters of 1963 and 1967 stressed equal rights for Negroes, and at Vatican Council II asked for "forthright and unequivocal condemnation of racism in all forms." In his archdiocese, as well as in others in sensitive areas, desegregation in schools and elsewhere proceeds apace.

Among the problems of contemporary work among the Negroes is the fact that the particular conditions to which the different parts of the country had become accustomed are now changing. A massive migration from the South is going on, so that the major effort is now in the large northern, midwestern, and far-western cities. In a 1968 booklet of the Commission for Catholic Missions among the Colored People and the Indians, many diocesan leaders addressed themselves to this subject.[311] The Most Rev. Henry J. Soenneker of Owensboro, Kentucky, for example, said: "Work among the Negroes here is somewhat discouraging because many of the Catholics are moving away." Many of the difficulties are, here as elsewhere, financial. Albert L. Fletcher, bishop of Little Rock, Arkansas, made this observation:

> Our number of Catholic Negro pupils is not decreasing. But the overall enrollment in our Negro schools are [sic] decreasing perceptibly, because more non-Catholic children are going elsewhere on account of facilities which we cannot afford. The number of Catholic Negro students in our Catholic high schools is increasing.

And the vice-chancellor of Milwaukee, Wisconsin, said "rising costs and declining income have made running the schools extremely difficult."

Several new patterns have become discernible. There is, for example, a movement away from segregated schools, with the children provided for in some other way through integrated schools. This is especially true in the South. Ernest L. Unterkoefler, bishop of Charleston, South Carolina, observed:

> Due to Federal regulations, it has become necessary for us to hasten our program to eliminate dual school systems. The problem is a serious one; how not to have schools for Negroes specifically in order to elevate and instruct them, yet at the same time maintain an active and successful apostolate among the Negroes. By experience we know that many Negroes simply will not make any attempt to attend a white school, whether public or parochial.

In the view of Thomas J. Toolen, bishop of Mobile-Birmingham, Alabama, "down here there will be need for many years for Negro schools and churches." The Most Rev. Paul J. Hallinan of Atlanta, Georgia, observed in 1968:

> This year saw the closing of Drexel, our Negro high school. The students from this school now attend our two other high schools. The closing of this school became a necessary step. Drexel was opened in 1961 but because of the great distance involved, white students did not attend and so numbers have always been a problem.

Vincent S. Walters, bishop of Raleigh, North Carolina, expressed the "hope that all parishes in North Carolina will ultimately do away with personal parishes for Negroes . . . the same is true in regard to our parochial grammar school and high schools." The same process is observable in the Midwest: the Most Rev. Richard H. Ackerman of Covington, Kentucky, observed in 1968 that "the schools in . . . two parishes have been closed for several years and the Catholic Negro children have been received into the neighboring parish schools."

Another discernible pattern is consolidation, which has taken place throughout the country in Negro as well as white facilities. In the South, Bishop Vincent M. Harris of Beaumont, Texas, stated that "the Negroes of high school age who can afford tuition are attending our inter-parochial high schools." In the Midwest the Most Rev. John F. Dearden of Detroit, Michigan, explained:

> In order to provide quality education for students living in predominantly Negro areas, several parishes are consolidating their high schools. This particular problem will continue to grow as the churches in the older sections of the city continue to age.

Also in the Midwest, the Most Rev. Thomas J. McDonough of Louisville, Kentucky, observed in 1968 that "at this moment in these [almost exclusively Negro] neighborhoods, two newly-formed Catholic elementary schools are being opened to take the place of six schools which were unable to minister effectively to the educational needs of the pupils." In the East, Patrick Cardinal O'Boyle of Washington, D. C., explained that "in 1964 a consolidated school, Mother Catherine Spaulding School, was constructed in Helen, Maryland, to provide Catholic educational facilities for the large colored population in three parishes of St. Mary's County." Finally, among Negroes as among whites there is a discernible trend in the direction of catechetical centers. Robert E. Tracy, bishop of Baton Rouge, Louisiana, stated:

> These [ongoing] programs consisted mainly in the building-up of catechetical and rehabilitation centers in places where there were formerly Negro schools; the improvement of our C.C.D. program for Negro children not in Catholic schools; co-operation with governmental poverty programs among the Negroes; the care of retarded Negro children at our newly opened Christ-Child Center in Baton Rouge; and our struggle to provide the fifteen hundred Catholic Negroes attending the State Southern University, likewise in Baton Rouge, with adequate spiritual care.

We cannot fairly conclude this section on contemporary Catholic education without indicating that progress has been made in the past and there are signs of hope for the future. The aforementioned bishop of Owensboro, Kentucky, for example, has stated that "where Catholic Negro children live in their parishes their pastors are concerned to have them enrolled in the parish schools." In Seattle, Washington, the Most Rev. Thomas A. Connolly points to great activity in one of his Negro parishes that is typical of inner city parishes and schools elsewhere:

> Four Sisters of Providence are in residence at St. Peter Claver's Center and are in daily contact with the children and adults. They conduct catechism

classes, convert classes, days of recollection, boy and girl scout programs with the assistance of the priests of the Church of the Immaculate, and they have an active Legion of Mary. The Sisters visit the various homes in the area, which is in the heart of the poverty belt of the city.

In connection with the Center we have a very active and thriving Caritas and Head Start programs, which are partially subsidized by the federal government, but with their extensive work they need a great deal of assistance.

Hallinan of Atlanta, Georgia, revealed even the procurement of some new teachers: "We have received the services of four Franciscan Sisters to work exclusively in the Negro areas . . . . We are planning programs in adult education, remedial work with children and teenagers, and programs in home economics." And Schexnayder of Lafayette, Louisiana, surprised many with the statement that "proportionately, we have more Catholic schools for our colored children than for the whites."

Another typical pattern forgotten by most is that Catholic work among Negroes is for the most part a contribution to non-Catholics, many of whom perceive the value of Catholic school education. The United States Bureau of Census reported in 1960 that there were about nineteen million Negroes in the United States, nearly three-fourths affiliated with some religious body, the great majority of which were the Baptist and Methodist groups. After World War II an increase of Negro converts to Catholicism had begun, so that by 1968, there were 808,332 Negro Catholics (slightly more than one in twenty-five, versus about one in eighty in 1890), 250,000 of whom were in the South; 568 churches, 283 of which were in the South; 347 schools, 174 of which were in the South; and 108,251 pupils, many of them, as we said, non-Catholic. As for the schools, all were completely or predominantly Negro; 14 long-established schools and 17 churches for Negroes in the South were closed in the year 1968.[312] A circular letter from the Catholic Board for Mission Work among the Colored People, in October, 1969, indicated 472 Sisters, 35 Brothers, and 205 lay teachers "working in . . . the [Southern] United States to educate Negro-American children under the most trying conditions of poverty and bigotry"; stated that in one of its schools three nuns were teaching 83 children, only one of whom was Catholic; and observed that "in modest schools, dedicated sisters teach little children to grow in the Grace of God and take responsible places in their communities." [313]

The interplay between Catholic school education and non-Catholic Negroes, however, is ongoing. Many dioceses are trying desperately to prevent any further withdrawal of Catholic elementary schools from inner cities, despite the fact that parishes there are least able to afford them; financing is being provided in these cases by the dioceses. Bishop Thomas K. Gorman of Dallas-Forth Worth, Texas, testified that "we are more than happy that graduates from our Catholic schools and high schools (85), 90% non-Catholic, seem to appreciate our schools." [314] In

Milwaukee, Rt. Rev. Msgr. Francis M. Beres, vice-chancellor, stated that "in spite of the controversies concerning de facto segregation, the Catholic school is still the principal attraction for families in the inner-city."[315] And the Most Rev. Paul C. Schulte of Indianapolis synopsized the situation in many areas even outside of the South when he wrote:

> Our schools are at the disposal of non-Catholic parents who appreciate their discipline and the religious instruction they offer. We require these parents to attend an orientation course so that they will know and appreciate the value of what is being taught their children and back us up on the home front.[316]

## AMERICAN INDIANS

The over-all picture of the education of American Indians is "at best inadequate, and at worst disgraceful." [317] During 1968 the special Indian Education Subcommittee of the United States Senate studied Indian education, came up with some surprising information, and reported in early 1969. Rowan lamented:

> Only 1% of Indian elementary school children have Indian teachers or princi-pals. One-fourth of their teachers, by their own admission, would prefer not to teach Indian children. Some 9,000 Indians nine years old or younger are taken from their homes and sent away to boarding schools for nine months of the year.[318]

The dropout rate among Indian pupils is therefore twice the national average and their level of formal education (about five years) less than half the national average. In the boarding-school system, a chief target of criticism, the Indian child is separated "from family, culture and eventually from himself." Even in the public day schools, dropout rates range from forty to one hundred per cent, and "many Indians develop serious mental problems." Some interested leaders such as Dr. Robert A. Roessel, Jr., president of Navajo Community College, see malnutrition as one of the most acute obstacles for Indian children. Roessel

> charged that some public school superintendents prided themselves on virtually eliminating free lunches for Indian children. They did this . . . on the mistaken notion that they were "teaching the Navajos responsibility and helping the children adjust to the world in which they live." But they were driving away Indian children unable to pay $1.50 a week for lunches.[319]

The final report of the Indian Education Subcommittee, presented in November 1969, after two years of hearings, staff studies, and field in-vestigations, concluded that "Federal efforts to provide American Indians with quality education have been marked with near-total failure and haunted by prejudice and official ignorance." [320] The report labelled the bureaucratic system for educating the nation's 600,000 In-dians as stagnant, inefficient, and destructively paternalistic. On the issuance of the report, Senator Walter F. Mondale of Minnesota remarked on the methods of educating the Indian as being culturally insensitive at best, insulting at worst.

The Catholic picture is more optimistic. One out of five Indians is Catholic. The special apostolates to the 300,000 reservation Indians (of whom 139,554 were Catholic in 1968) are located in forty-three northern, midwestern, and western dioceses largely in Arizona, South Dakota, Montana, North Dakota, New Mexico, and Alaska. About 25,000 Indians are off their reservations in other towns and cities.[321] Of the 253 priests working among Indians in 1968, about 185 were in pastoral work, forty in educational or other activities on the reservations, and thirty with parishes that had small Indian missions to which they devoted part time. About six hundred nuns, scholastics, lay brothers, and lay teachers staffed the schools. There were 403 churches and chapels for Indians with few or no white parishioners; fifty-three schools for Catholic Indian children; and seven Indian centers in western cities or towns for counseling, social facilities, and religious services. Most of the schools were in sparsely populated areas and therefore used school buses or provided boarding accommodations—so that 8,696 Indian children from about 175 missions were thus accommodated. All offered the elementary grades and ten offered high school courses in addition. Thirty-eight were day schools, five exclusively boarding schools, and the others had both day and boarding pupils. For those attending federal or public schools (the majority), released-time or other provisions presented religious instruction. Catholic curricula do not differ very much from those in the public schools, and the mission schools differ from one another in the abilities of their teachers, facilities, and administrators.

Other than schools, the chief pattern for providing religious education is the catechetical center. The Most Rev. Francis P. Leipzig of Baker, Montana, for example, spoke of providing a Confraternity of Christian Doctrine program for the spiritual welfare of the Klamath Indians at Chiloquin as being hampered because of lack of proper facilities. But he wrote in 1968 that "during the coming year we have hope of securing means for building four classrooms for Confraternity work." [322] Of the Sioux Indians, the Most Rev. William T. McCarty, C.SS.R., of Rapid City, South Dakota, indicated the presence of "the Mother Butler Indian Center for the Indians living in Rapid City, and three large mission schools." [323] And the Most Rev. Joseph Lennox Federal of Salt Lake City, Utah, wrote:

> Work among the Indians in this diocese centers in two areas: the federal Intermountain Indian School at Brigham City and the Ute Indian Reservation at Fort Duchesne.
> The principal location of our activity is, however, at the Intermountain School, where approximately 2,200 Navaho students from their reservation in Utah and Arizona are trained.[324]

The problems among the Indians are many: for example, alcoholism, magic beliefs, materialism, mobility, indifference, and at times a scattered populace. The financial problem is as much a specter here as elsewhere. As one might also expect, old buildings constitute another problem, with the Most Rev. George A. Hammes of Superior, Wisconsin, asserting that "five of the six churches and the three schools which serve the Indian reservations are old buildings and need constant repairs." [325] Finally, as for pupils themselves, many have little or no knowledge of English and no interest in learning; the reasons are probably the same as or similar to those cited above. Nevertheless, there has been growth, and there is progress and hope. None has been uniform in either time or place. In the Southwest the Franciscans had started two schools for the Navajos. In 1901 the Pima Missions, in 1907 the Papago Missions, and by 1965 the greater part of all of these fairly large tribes, were Catholic. Also by 1965, the three day-schools for the children of the Pueblo Missions had increasing numbers of pupils. In Santa Fe, the Sisters of the Blessed Sacrament are currently sponsoring a million-dollar renovation of St. Catherine's School for Pueblo students, built originally by Mother Katherine Drexel. Also, St. Michael's boarding school for Navajos, founded by Mother Katherine in 1902, continues to offer Catholic education. The Northwest was unfavorably affected by the large-scale sale of Indian lands to incoming white settlers, but nevertheless nearly all the older schools remained in operation; in Michigan, Wisconsin, and Minnesota, the situation was similar. In these areas, among the Chippewa and Ottawas there has been a serious depletion in numbers to more prosperous towns and cities. Two Menominee missions and schools are prospering in Wisconsin, and throughout this area the sisters are teaching in six mission schools. In Oklahoma, due to the dissolution of the reservations and the consequent dispersal of their occupants, former mission schools of the early twentieth century became unnecessary, and only three small schools and missions remain.

Nevertheless, the Most Rev. Eldon B. Schuster of Great Falls, Montana, could write in 1968 that

in September, St. Labre's Mission will open a new, modern grade and high school to accommodate at least four hundred students. A heartening increase of fifty pupils was reported by St. Xavier's mission. Construction of a new school at this mission is now in progress. [326]

The Most Rev. Hubert M. Newell wrote from Cheyenne, Wyoming, that "our school enrollment is quite good and the attendance is improving," and Leipzig of Baker, Montana, that "St. Andrew's on the Umatilla reservation had done good work for the education of the children, which is reflected in the attendance of more and more adults at Sunday Masses." [327] And finally there were interesting aspects of the work that gave heart and hope to the chancellor of the diocese of Portland, Maine:

> The convents house teaching Nuns who have the responsibility of elementary education for the Indian children. Their salaries are paid by the State Department of Education.
>
> The Indian reservations in Maine are unique, in that they do not come under federal controls; that is, under the U.S. Bureau of Indian Affairs. Responsibility for the Indians has always been with the state of Maine.[328]

As a final hopeful sign, an Indian sisterhood, the Oblate Sisters of the Blessed Sacrament, has been established at St. Paul's, Marty, South Dakota, albeit as only a small group with only about fifteen professed members.

### OTHER MINORITIES

Catholic education was also caring for other minority groups during this period, as throughout its history—unobtrusively, because publicity has never been a forte of most Catholic institutions, and to the extent possible in the face of difficulties special to each case. This was true with, for example, the uncounted millions of Puerto Ricans who migrated to the large cities of the East and Midwest, and the five million Mexicans who settled (legally and illegally) mostly in the Southwest. The *Chicanos*, as the Mexicans came to be called, have only recently emerged from the stereotype of the placid peasant asleep under a sombrero, and continue to have major impediments to any type of education, Catholic or otherwise: the frequently migratory nature of their work, for instance, and their adherence to the Spanish language, which is not spoken in United States schools. The result has been that "Mexican Americans have come to average eight years of schooling, two years less than Negroes and a full four years less than whites," [329] and in some locations a high percentage of Mexicans are considered functionally illiterate. The Catholic Church has tried to help the Mexican-Americans, most of whom are at least nominally Catholic, in such ways as accepting qualified applicants into parochial schools, placing special missions among them, and allowing them the use of parish halls for functions (some of which have been to unionize for work protection and betterment). Arising out of this situation is the personification of this varied and diverse people's despairing past, restless present, and hopeful future in Cesar Chavez, their leader in a long strike against grape growers. A migrant worker's son who attended many schools but never got to the eighth grade, Chavez nevertheless received inspiration and encouragement from his study of the papal social encyclicals, especially *Rerum Novarum* and *Quadragesimo Anno*.

## Conclusions

The over-all situation of education in the contemporary era presented problems for both the public and private sectors. In the public sector, Russia's "Sputnik" in October of 1957 seemed to give all kinds of people the right to criticize United States education in comparison with Russian. Criticisms of United States Catholic education began before "Sputnik," with the Rt. Rev. John Tracy Ellis' 1955 denigration of Catholic intellectual life, a theme taken up by many others. Among Catholic problems were curriculum changes that were bound not to appeal to some, the ever-present burden of finance, the amount of personnel training, the smaller number of teaching religious, and a bad press. The soul-searching and ferment were reflected in statistics, which showed increases in the number of students to around 1964, after which there was a steady decline that seemed to become more and more precipitous. Among those suggesting solutions were Mary Perkins Ryan, who in 1964 asked "Are Catholic Schools the Answer?" and presented reasons for concentrating efforts on religious education; those who opted for completely restructuring the existing system; those who saw it as necessary for the Church to drop some levels, leaving the agonizing problem of which levels to drop; and those who attempted school mergers instead of complete closings in order to prevent, as far as possible, student loss.

There were, however, signs of hope. The Catholic level of sophistication and intellectual achievement seems to have increased, if such criteria as number and quality of publications, libraries, and adult education courses are accurate criteria. Scientific research studies, long needed to find out where we are and to provide impetus for further study, have been begun. Two massive studies lead the field, one by Notre Dame University, *Catholic Schools in Action*, and the other by Andrew Greeley and Peter Rossi under the auspices of the National Opinion Research Center at Chicago, *The Education of Catholic Americans*. Among other studies were the NCEA symposium in 1967, "Blueprint for the Future"; the study which Terence Cardinal Cooke commissioned in 1968 for the archdiocese of New York; and those done by Notre Dame's Office of Educational Research on the dioceses of Denver, Colorado, and Saginaw, Michigan. Vatican Council II, bringing the 2,500 bishops of the world together at Rome from 1963 to 1965, gave further impetus to hope through such documents as its *Declaration on Christian Education* and the *Pastoral Constitution on the Church in the Modern World*.

Goals constituted another area wherein difficulties and disagreements were common to both public and private education. For Catholics, the practical application of immutable perennial goals to the ever-changing present is an ongoing search. Granting that the definition of education involves the harmonious development of all man's potentialities, where is the emphasis? Is it to be intellectualist, in the tradition of John Cardinal Newman, the Rt. Rev. John Tracy Ellis, and the Rev. Thomas T. McAvoy, C.S.C.? Should it be moralist, the position held, according to the Greeley-Rossi study, by most United States Catholic parents? Should it be integralist, attempting some kind of rapport with all? Or should the emphasis, like Vatican II, eschew Thomistic analysis and assert a list of principal aims, differentiating Catholic education from all others by training in a specific kind of relationship to God?

Curriculum during this period, as ever, followed goals. In some ways, public and Catholic education were similar. Both, for example, in formulating curriculums had difficulties commensurate with their problems in arriving at goals. Also, both perceived the need for sex education, both introduced it, and both experienced opposition, with the difference that because of the religious Weltanschauung in Catholic schools their approach required greater care. Many of the textbooks in secular subjects were also the same, especially those provided by government. Those textbooks that were specific to each, however, like all books, contained their own particular prejudices. In this connection, the study by Judah Harris, *The Treatment of Religion in Elementary School Social Studies Textbooks*, revealed interesting biases in public school texts with particular reference to Jews although including Catholics, and the study by George R. LaNoue concerning Catholic texts on secular subjects was also interesting. The basic difference between the public and Catholic patterns remained, of course, religion. Public educators were now discerning religion's importance to the imparting of culture, and were using such subterfuges as teaching "about" religion rather than getting involved in the unconstitutionality of teaching sectarian religion. Catholic schools were now placing more stress on learning about other religions, the Bible, ecumenism, and the liturgy. On Catholic school texts in this area, two observations would seem important. First, they mirrored the theological emphases of the post-Vatican II era. This meant that they were also including some of theology's turmoil, and this very often met with parental objections. Secondly, boundaries now became blurred between texts intended for use in Catholic schools and those heretofore written for Catholic students from public schools in programs of the Confraternity of Christian Doctrine.

Among the agencies of education during this period, the government seemed to step up its activities. The financial difficulties of both public and private education have become so overpowering that governmental assistance seemed to become mandatory if both patterns are to survive. On the federal level, firmer patterns formed. The legislative branch seemed more in touch with grass-roots United States of America, and more concerned with the rights of the individual. The National Defense Education Act of 1958 unprecedentedly gave loans (not grants) to

fulfill its provisions in church-related middle level schools; it was renewed in 1961, and broadened in 1964. The Elementary and Secondary
Education Act of 1965 was the first to include private as well as public
school children in its massive aid program, which consisted of $1.3
billion to start. This "Johnson Act" very cleverly met the two most
frequent traditional objections to government aid to church-related
schools: violation of the First Amendment, and undercutting of the
prestige of the United States public school. The bill therefore gave aid
only for secular subjects and enhanced the prestige of public schools
by making them the sole recipients of the funds, through them to be
distributed to others who merited them. The beneficiaries of the act are
*children*, not schools, and the Act was intended for those who are in
one way or another underprivileged. As for state legislatures, Catholic
education fulfills compulsory education requirements, and most states
have minimal legislation on admission, expulsion, curriculum, teachers,
buildings, and equipment. Some states are currently providing more
financial assistance than in the past.

In the judicial branch of the federal government, there has been an
increase in court cases because of growth in Catholic sophistication, a
continuance of subtle and indirect hostile prejudice from pressure groups
although less direct and overt prejudice from the total population, and a
higher educational level for all. In 1959 and 1960, the United States
Supreme Court upheld the practice of released-time. In 1962, it declared
unconstitutional the public-school recitation of a state-prescribed non-
denominational prayer composed by government officials. In 1963, it declared unconstitutional the official sponsoring in public school of Bible
reading and/or recitation of the Lord's Prayer. These two decisions resulted in violent reactions from many citizens. In 1968, the Court
declared constitutional the government's provision of textbooks on secular subjects to sectarian schools. Also in 1968, the Court overturned a
1923 decision and granted individual taxpayers the right to sue to
challenge federal spending. This author, not being a constitutional
lawyer, fails to see a clear pattern in many areas of Supreme Court
decision-making, and also to understand the bases upon which the decisions are made. If the foundations are intended to be historical, some
decisions seem contrary to the minds of those Founding Fathers who
wrote the Constitution. If, as seems to be the case, the foundations are
sociological, it is difficult to understand, in the absence of statistically
valid sociological studies sponsored by the Court or available to it, how
the Court arrives at its concepts of applying the "living" Constitution to
the country's needs and/or wants, here and now. That the Court sometimes contradicts the country's wishes is evident from frequent popular
opposition to its decisions and, at times, to its entire approach. If the assumption is correct, however, that this is the Court's approach, and if
Catholics really want Catholic education, it seems that Catholics have

not used sufficiently the democratic procedures available to them to create a climate for favorable judicial decision.

In the Church, attitudes have changed regarding education, as they have in other areas, after Vatican II. Characteristic of her present attitudes are openness to the contemporary scene and modern culture, less rigidity, and more dialogue with the world. The United States Bishops' statement on Catholic education on November 16, 1967, contained applications of Vatican II as well as words of encouragement to hard-pressed Catholic educators. As for the family, in spite of Vatican II's reminder of the traditional truth that parents are "the first and foremost educators of their children," the same retreat from the home that has characterized other segments of society and caused them to give more consideration to the need for religion in education, has unfortunately applied to Catholics as well. The common concern of State, Church, and family have led to, among other things, Protestant and Catholic formation in 1960 of the concept of "shared time" to let children receive the best from religious and secular education. Inasmuch as it involves no little inconvenience, however, it engenders many arguments pro and con.

The short supply of teachers during this period for all patterns of education led—again in all patterns—to acceptance of substandard qualifications in some parts of the nation, and to strikes. The situation has been complicated by low salaries, better opportunities in business, compulsory military service, disenchantment with outmoded educational bureaucracies, retirements, resignations of the disenchanted, and abandonment by the disillusioned. Other characteristics were specifically Catholic: e.g., more rigorous controls on accreditation by some state departments of education (difficult for those religious communities that are substandard); shortage of teaching religious because of lack of vocations, the numbers leaving religious communities, and communities' entering such other work as social service in preference to teaching; financial burdens of the higher salaries required by the increased proportion of lay teachers; and the new pattern of sisters "moonlighting" to help make ends meet. Offering hope, however, are a new awareness of the dignity and importance of teachers as expressed by Vatican II and Pope Paul VI, and the higher over-all levels of formation and preparation, especially in the area of religion.

The student has continued to receive the benefit of the Church's great vision of the dignity of the person. Throughout this period, Vatican II, especially in such documents as the *Pastoral Constitution on the Church in the Modern World*, as well as statements of Paul VI and many bishops, brought this home to the modern mind. Appropriate to the times, there were new provisions for the gifted. The mission of the Church's education, however, like the mission of the Church, continued to be mainly to the *anawim:* the poor, rejected, and underprivileged, who were in most cases members of minority groups. New insights were applied, for example, to the education of the handicapped—the blind, the deaf, and the retarded. The Negro, helped by the Brown desegregation decision of 1954, the Civil Rights Act of 1964, the Economic Opportunity Act of 1965, and the Elementary and Secondary Act of 1965, continued to receive varied Catholic treatment in different parts of the country. Individual priests, nuns, and laymen came up with creative ideas, e.g., participation in the civil rights marches on Washington (1963), Selma and Montgomery (1965), and Chicago (1965). In Catholic educational provisions for the Negro, among the patterns that emerged were a huge migration from the South; a decrease of segregated schools and parishes in favor of integrated ones; and consolidation. Catholic work here continues to be mostly a contribution to non-Catholics. For the American Indian, whereas public educational provisions have been, to say the least, inadequate, the Catholic picture is more optimistic. A body of evidence indicates that much of public education has separated the Indian from his family, his culture, and himself, resulting in many dropouts and some serious mental problems. Catholics have succeeded in providing some schools and catechetical centers with more success. A small "new immigration" has comprised such other mostly Catholic minorities as Puerto Ricans and Mexicans. The Church's new legislation against the establishment of national parishes results in these persons' melting into other parishes and schools, creating difficulty in coming up with accurate statistics.

## CHAPTER VII

# Conclusions, Trends, and Prospects

THE STORY OF United States Catholic education has, it seems clear, brought certain patterns into bold relief. For example, there is in these pages a larger number of heroes to warrant admiration, and an appreciably smaller number of rogues, than in comparably-sized groups elsewhere. Secondly, the over-all effect is not a wonderment at some things that were left undone, but amazement that so much was done with so little. Also, the entire phenomenon seems from many points of view to be a miracle of American society. United States Catholic education also seems to be, however, a poor relation. Does this mean it is just a cheap imitation of other education, with only a distant relationship of which the country at large is ashamed? Or does it mean that Catholic education in the United States is a Cinderella stepchild who, if only given a chance, would blossom and realize all its potentialities? As a help in deciding, we should take this opportunity to delineate some discovered trends from the past, form some conclusions for the present, and prognosticate as to the future.

## The Past

Without repeating too much, we think it necessary to observe that many interesting patterns have emerged. For example, American Catholic education has made many contributions to our country which should not be forgotten. Evidence for this lies with, for one thing, the many "firsts" for Catholic education. The first school of *any* kind was Roman Catholic in such areas as Louisiana, Kansas, the District of Columbia, North Dakota, Ohio, Kentucky, lower California, and Baltimore. The first American textbook was the *Doctrina Breve* of Juan Zumarraga, brought into present territorial United States from Mexico. The first dictionaries and formulations of Indian languages were compiled by such educators as Frederic Baraga, Slovenian missionary in the United States,[1] and Samuel Mazzuchelli, O.P. Baraga came from Austria to Cincinnati in 1831 and devoted himself to the Christianization of the Indian in Northern Michigan, of which field of labor he became bishop in 1853; Mazzuchelli, an Italian, arrived in Cincinnati in 1830, and in the "Far Northwest" (Michigan, Wisconsin, and Iowa) gave missionary service for thirty-four years.[2] The first printing press in Michigan was that which the Rev. Gabriel Richard brought to his educational establishment at Spring Hill, which turned out textbooks in addition to a newspaper. The first normal schools in the United States, about a quarter of a century before the public ones, were those of the Sisters of Charity under Mother Elizabeth Bayley Seton and of the Sisters of Loretto in Nazareth, Kentucky. West of the Mississippi, the first literary magazine (*The Catholic Cabinet*, 1843-45) was Catholic, as was the first chartered university (St. Louis, 1832).[3] The first high school diploma awarded in the state of Colorado was given by St. Mary's Academy, Denver, founded in 1864 by the Sisters of Loretto. The Ursulines, in addition to being the first teachers of the Negro and Indian races and the first women to take care of a military hospital within the confines of the present United States, were the first to establish an orphanage (1728, enlarged in 1729 after the Natchez Indian massacre of adults in Fort Rosalie, now Natchez, Mississippi), to shelter and work for the protection of girls, to give the United States a woman who contributed a work of literary and historical merit (Madeleine Hachard), and to give the country a woman druggist (Sr. Frances Xavier Hebert, 1734).

There have been many other frequently-overlooked contributions of Catholic education to our country. The recruitments of European religious-order teachers for this country took place at a time when the United States was a cultural desert. Among these teachers were the Rev. Simon Gabriel Bruté, an M.D. from the University of Paris, whom John Quincy Adams called "the most learned man of his day in America"; Frederic Baraga, mentioned above, who had received a law degree from Vienna, and who, like Bruté, condescended to "beat the bush" educationally in this country; Theodore Schneider. S.J., who had been a lecturer in philosophy and rector of the University of Heidelberg; Andrew White, S.J., the first Jesuit missioner to Maryland, who left the posts of prefect of studies and professor of scripture, dogmatic theology, and Hebrew at the English colleges of Valladolid and Seville in Spain to take up missionary educational activity in the New World; the Rev. Demetrius Gallitzin, a Russian prince; Thomas Wilson, O.P., who had been president of the Dominican English College in Flanders; Benedict J. Flaget, S.S., one-time professor at several seminaries in France;

the Rev. John Francis Rivet of Vincennes, Indiana, who had been a professor in France; William DuBourg, S.S., who had been rector of the seminary at Issy, France; Gabriel Richard, S.S., whose accomplishments have been sufficiently recorded above; and the Most Rev. John England, who had been a professor and president of St. Mary's College in Cork, Ireland. The first Catholic schools in such areas as Maryland and Pennsylvania were priests' rooms in their rectories, with the priests as the teachers. The *School Record* of Nazareth Academy in Kentucky attests that from 1815 to 1881 fully two-thirds of the girl students were Protestant, and most from the "deep South"—a real contribution from many points of view, not the least being a consideration of the virulent anti-Catholicism in that time and place. The sisters who conducted this institution laid the groundwork in Louisville, Kentucky, for the schools to receive the tide of immigration beginning about 1845; gave free service for several years to schools in the mining sections of Ohio; maintained schools in poor urban and rural areas while refusing lucrative offers; provided free service to orphans in the Louisville area from 1831 to 1923; and performed innumerable other works for all the needy.[4]

The teaching religious often sacrificed to the point of heroism. After the first Ursuline nuns who came to New Orleans in 1727 had been on the Atlantic for three months and landed at the mouth of the Mississippi, they still had to make another long and tedious trip through mosquito- and snake-infested bayous and swamps to the town, which then contained more than its share of a rough population.[5] In gauging such natural emotions of these immigrants as homesickness, one's imagination is helped by a few lines in a letter from the Rev. Felix De' Andreis, C.M., back home to Italy:

I assure you that when I think of Italy, it appears to me an earthly paradise, in comparison with America. . . . I know that were it not for the glory of God and the salvation of souls, I would not stay where I am for all the gold in the world.[6]

The first community of American origin—the Visitation Nuns—lived in a combination convent and school whose walls were not even plastered from 1799 to 1811, at which latter date a sister lathed and plastered most of it herself. The first Sisters of Charity at Emmitsburg, Maryland, became sick from the lack of heat in their unfinished house, and from hunger. For the Sisters of Charity of Nazareth, Kentucky, the first accommodations were a log house with one room below and one above, with a hut nearby serving as a kitchen; when they went to Indiana, patronage of their schools was scanty, and they were deprived of even their most important source of spiritual sustenance, Mass and the sacraments, for weeks and sometimes months at a time. The first Sisters of St. Joseph at Carondelet, Missouri, lived in dire poverty in a wretched log cabin with only one room. The dying Father Frederic Baraga forced upon a visiting priest all the money he had in the world for the visitor's school—a total of $20. When three Sisters of Loretto and two Sisters of Charity were travelling with others to Santa Fe in 1867, some of the party contracted cholera and all were frequently attacked by Indians; so disturbing was the experience that one Lorettine, Sr. Mary Alphonsa Thompson, aged eighteen, on July 24 literally died of fright.[7] At the other end of the age scale, Philippine Duchesne was 72 years of age when she went among the Potawatomi.[8] By the time of her death in 1955, Katherine Drexel had given a financial fortune to the Catholic education of Indians and Negroes, and her death set in motion the provisions of a further fortune to Catholic education in general through her father's will.

In addition, most of the sisters faced a paucity of vocations, often took on such outside work for support as laundering, frequently undertook long journeys that gave second thoughts even to strong men, and unhesitatingly allowed their dedication to carry them into the middle of border warfare and riots. They were also prey to such external natural disasters as fire and such personal problems as mental breakdowns brought on by overwork, with the added factor that these disasters were more devastating to them than to others. Nevertheless, they invariably set up free schools for the poor, long before such was the practice elsewhere, beside their boarding schools, from which they derived necessary financial support. The Sisters of Charity in Emmitsburg were the first religious community to give their services to the cause of gratuitous education in this country. Pioneer sisters also brought their educational work to the *anawim*—the downtrodden, outcast, poor members of society —such as the Indian and the Negro, even when the Indian was savage (remember Fray De Solis' diary calling the Indians in Texas "cruel, inhuman and ferocious"),[9] and the Negro difficult to work with. In addition to eradicating religious illiteracy, they contributed to the country as well as to their Church a cultural enrichment and a fullness of life.

From all groups of Catholic teachers—religious, clergy, and lay—came outstanding teachers of whom any educational system would be proud. Most of these were unsung. Others achieved a measure of fame—Bishop John Ireland, for example, whose speeches showed him so alert to educational needs, and Bishop John Lancaster Spalding, whose interest in Catholic education and his ability to convert ecclesiastical and other leaders to its causes makes him also worthy of mention. In the classroom were such as Bishop John England, to whom education was not a matter of book learning only, but also a means for the perfecting of civilized society; the Rev. Edward Aloysius Pace, with his superb training from Wilhelm Wundt at Leipzig; the Rev. Thomas Edward Shields, whose work at The Catholic University of America brought him national attention; the Rev. George Johnson, who made "a most masterful attempt to modernize and update a statement on the philosophy of Catholic education;" [10] and many others. Modern empirical research puts into focus the value of these contributions of Catholic teachers to our country. The prestigious Coleman report, testifying in careful wording on another area, but in a matter that is applicable here, said:

It appears that variations in the facilities and curriculums of the schools account for relatively little variation in pupil achievement insofar as this is measured by standard tests. . . . The quality of teachers shows a stronger relationship to pupil achievement. Furthermore, it is progressively greater at higher grades, indicating a cumulative impact of the qualities of teachers in a school on the pupil's achievements. Again, teacher quality seems more important to minority achievement than to that of the majority.[11]

Coleman emphasizes again and again that schools have a much greater effect on the underprivileged than on the majority group in society, and that "the effect of teachers' characteristics shows a sharp increase over the years of school." [12]

As for the laity, it was from their ideals of sacrifice that the religious came when they did, and from their willingness to undergo double taxation for their schools for so long—the marvel of the world—that the American pattern of Catholic education was given birth. Further, their "new" responsibilities in education today are really age-old: the Rev. Stephen Badin left them to finish the construction of a combination school-church; [13] "from the time of the establishment of St. Peter's Free School [1800] until 1831 the students were taught exclusively by laymen"; [14] in six of the first seven schools founded between 1800 and 1860 in Savannah, Georgia, the teachers were exclusively lay; [15] towards the latter half of the nineteenth century, a college at New Windsor, Maryland, was under the supervision of Catholic laymen; [16] when the Rev. Sévéré Dumolin from Canada opened the first school at Pembina, North Dakota, it was in conjunction with a layman by the name of William Edge, a catechist and school teacher. Even the phenomenon of those honorably leaving religious life, returning to the lay state, and continuing to contribute service to the Church, is not new: ex-Jesuit novice Ralph Crouch started the first recorded Catholic school in Colonial Maryland.

Many non-Catholics as well as Catholics have paid tribute to the contributions of Roman Catholic education: non-Catholics were happy to pay tuition for their children to attend the early Catholic school at Goshenhoppen, Pennsylvania; the entire citizenry of Detroit, Michigan, elected to Congress the Rev. Gabriel Richard, S.S., who set up their city's educational system and laid the early foundations of the University of Michigan; Bishop John England's Philosophical and Classical Seminary in Charleston, North Carolina, was the only opportunity for discussions on the level of higher education in that area at that time, for non-Catholics as well as Catholics; Visitation Academy in Georgetown was recognized for many years as the best secondary-level educational opportunity

for the daughters of high governmental representatives of all denominations; Protestants went out of their way to congratulate the Jesuit Father
Leonard Neale for his educational efforts in their behalf; the Sisters of
Charity teaching in Philadelphia so distinguished themselves taking care
of the sick during the cholera epidemic of 1832 that the city council paid
them special recognition; a nineteenth-century visitor from England,
recognized as perceptive for his observations in other areas, wrote that

the education of all the first classes of Protestants seems to be entrusted to the
Catholic priests and nuns. The lads are sent to Jesuit and other colleges; the
girls to convents. The parents say that their children are better taught and
better looked after than they would be in any other schools.[17]

In 1877, Henry Kidde, superintendent of schools for New York City,
felt that the teachers in parochial schools were better prepared and
superior to teachers in public schools.[18] Because of the contributions of
the Ursuline and other nuns to education in New Orleans, that city to this
day exempts women religious from paying public transportation fares (a
privilege made difficult by the introduction of modern religious dress!).
When the Sisters of Charity of Nazareth, Kentucky, were surrounded at
Nazareth by Union forces during the Civil War and the sisters were fearful for the safety of themselves and the seventy girls then in their
charge, Mother Columba Carroll, their Superior, on Jan. 9, 1865, wrote
for protection to their Senator, L. W. Powell, who in turn on Jan. 17
appealed to President Abraham Lincoln. Lincoln, who could then have
known the sisters only from their educational work, personally wrote and
signed a safeguard which read, "Let no depradation be committed upon
the property or possessions of the 'Sisters of Charity' at Nazareth
Academy, near Bardstown, Ky." [19]
    The story was not, of course, all sweetness and light. There were
failures: the Rev. Demetrius Gallitzin's attempts to found a community
of teaching sisters, and the Rev. Joseph Rosati's to found a teaching
brotherhood for boys; the first Christian Brothers to come to these
shores, three young men who because of separation and isolation withdrew from religious life; the Ursuline Sisters from Black Rock Convent,
Cork, Ireland, at New York City in 1815; some teaching orders that were
too rigid to learn American speech or ways (Les Dames de la Retraite at
Charleston, South Carolina, in the mid-nineteenth century, and the Poor
Clares at Georgetown in 1804), or too much ahead of their time, such as
two projects of the Rev. Charles Nerinckx (a teaching religious brotherhood in 1819 and a Negro teaching sisterhood in 1824); the Trappists'
attempt to establish a boys' school in Kentucky; the Rev. Stephen
Badin's initial school on the site of what would later become the University of Notre Dame; efforts to raise the level of education through
literary magazines by Bishops Peter L. and Francis P. Kenrick, and
other periodicals and newspapers with the same purpose through the

country's entire history; the Jesuit attempts to found St. Regis Indian Seminary at St. Louis, Missouri, in 1824-30; many Catholic colleges, like other private institutions, of the nineteenth century especially, such as Laurel Hill College in Philadelphia; some early textbooks, which because of other-worldly concentration, or prejudice, or lack of awareness, sometimes failed even in Catholic schools' basic aim of personal formation; some teachers, especially the foreign-born, with respect to American ideals of patriotism; some early industrial schools for Negroes, because of engulfing prejudice; some individual schools, for one reason or another, established by many religious communities; poor administration, such as that brought about by Bishop Célestine de la Hailandère's overanxiety and inability to delegate authority in Vincennes, Indiana; and, again for a variety of reasons, in experimentation generally. An important point in connection with all this, however, is that, by and large, these dedicated individuals "stuck with it"—through failure as well as success —to make the heroic sacrifices necessary for the survival of the special kind of formation of the whole person that is Catholic education.

The history of Catholic education in the United States also shows many situations similar to today. To those, for example, who may have thought that Catholic educational policy has been completely dictated by Rome, or by the hierarchy, or by some other source "from above," history shows a surprising freedom of thought and expression. One witness for this is the number of differences of opinion that have taken place: in the midst of the flood of immigrants to Michigan from the East after the opening of the Erie Canal and the establishment of steam navigation between Buffalo and Detroit, Bishop Frédéric Résé of Detroit and the Poor Clare Sisters fought over property and administration, resulting in the closing of the sisters' schools at Detroit and Green Bay in Michigan and in Pittsburgh, Pa., and also in the breakup of the community; when in 1859 the Sisters, Servants of the Immaculate Heart of Mary fought with Bishop Peter Paul Lefevre of Detroit, they sought a clarification of the jurisdiction of bishops, which they succeeded in obtaining; factional troubles at St. Mary's parish in Philadelphia from about 1812 to approximately 1832 perturbed educational activity; through a good part of the nineteenth century, the self-assertiveness of lay trustees sometimes kept out of the schools those teachers who had been approved by local pastors; in the early part of the same century, national sensitivities prompted  Germans to stand up for their rights in such parishes and schools as Holy Trinity in Philadelphia, the Irish at St. Mary's in Charleston, and the French at St. Patrick's in Norfolk, Virginia; and, in the face of vociferous demands to the contrary, the Second Provincial Council of Baltimore had to insist that the selection of bishops remain with the hierarchy. Among the clergy themselves, the self-assertiveness was no less strong, and no less public: when the present state of Illinois was mission country, the Jesuits fought with the Canadian diocesan priests who dared cover the same territory; the independent attitude of some New Orleans clergy as well as laity did not make life easy for Bishop William Du-Bourg, who later (1826) resigned his See and returned to France; the first priest ordained in the United States, Stephen Badin, had difficulties with his bishop, Benedict J. Flaget, causing him to return to France from 1819 to 1826; Badin was succeeded in Green Bay, Wisconsin, by the pseudo-priest Jean Baptiste François Fauvel, who taught school during the week as well as acting as a priest,[20] until the arrival of the Rev. Samuel Mazzuchelli; the public fights over educational and other issues between such nineteenth-century giants as Bishops John Ireland, Bernard McQuaid, John Lancaster Spalding, and John Hughes, are well known; and the Bouquillon controversy in the 1890's was a milestone in clarifying some important educational emphases.

There were other similarities in history to modern situations. There were, then as now, pressures brought because of immediately urgent needs: when the first bishop of the United States, John Carroll, wanted an academy opened for girls, he persuaded the Carmelite Sisters, a cloistered order, to leave their cloister and enter the world to live this new form of witness; when the Rev. Charles Nerinckx departed from property that had been acquired as a novitiate for a teaching brother-hood, to go to Belgium to procure funds and candidates, Bishop Benedict J. Flaget, to keep the property in use, permitted the Rev. William Byrne to start a school and to keep it upon Nerinckx' return; and so on. There was even the incongruous—not unknown today, God knows!—such as the Dominican Sisters in one instance starting a school in an old still.

Another pattern which this story makes obvious is the inconsistency of governmental action, particularly judicial, relative to the presence of religion in public schools and to many aspects of Catholic schools. On the positive side, it must be observed that, up to the recent advent of secular-ism, religious considerations were always paramount in the public schools, even during times of prejudice and hostility to the Catholic per-suasion; fair-minded peoples' considerations of justice resulted in such plans of governmental financial assistance as those at Poughkeepsie, New York, Lowell, Massachusetts, Faribault and Stillwater, Minnesota, and Savannah, Georgia; government funds were long provided for Catholic schools in such widely-separated places as New York City, Detroit, Vir-ginia after disestablishment, and some other Southern states; and the Catholic schools even today in communities of some states, e.g., Kansas and Maine, receive full state financial support as agents of the State as well as of the Church.

On the other hand, the United States government, when Florida was ceded to the United States in 1819, unjustly took over the free school of the Franciscan Friars which had been supported by the king of Spain since 1785 at St. Augustine, Florida; her legislative actions with regard to Catholic participation in the education of the Indian and other minority groups seem shortsighted and harmful to the national interest as well as the minorities; and the different nature of the legislation for elementary and middle-level private schools on the one hand and for private institutions of higher education on the other seems an unwarranted dichotomy. Judicially, decisions seem to have been made on a pragmatic and *ad hoc* basis: the fundamental underpinnings of some of the court cases at times seem to be an unrealistic philosophy (e.g., with regard to the rights of parents and of the Church in the education of their children), a falsified history (e.g., the meaning of "disestablishment"), an amateur sociology (e.g., in some aspects of the application of the Constitution as a living document to modern needs and circumstances), and a poor notion of religion (e.g., religion as wholly private with no public purpose, and putting the religion of secularism in a special higher category than all other religions); the inconsistencies of judicial interpretation seem obvious in such specific areas as teachers wearing religious garb, the use of public school premises for religious purposes during non-school time, prayer in public schools, flag salute, right of Catholic schools to fulfill compulsory education requirements but not to share in other recognition; and the time-consuming decisions over such "major" items as textbooks and buses for Catholic school students on the one hand, with none over such areas as fire and police protection, sewage disposal, or use of public sidewalks, on the other.

Finally, the story of Catholic education in the United States suggests many areas for further research. Among these may be mentioned Catholic educational efforts among the Negro; the extent to which the goals of suburbia have been true of Catholic- versus public-school products; the extent to which attitudes and values have been, are, and can be imparted through schooling versus the home; Catholic publications of various periods as reflective of the Catholic educational level; Catholic teacher-training in various communities of religious in all the periods of United States history; a personality profile of the Catholic student versus that of his public-school counterpart in the various periods of history; in-depth monographs on individual geographical areas—dioceses, states, districts; the history of the nature and concept of the Catholic family as an agent of education; a comparison of the concepts of psychology and of papal pronouncements on sex-related differences in education; comparative studies on the preparation of teaching religious and teachers in secular schools in the various periods, to attempt a determination of which was ahead, and from what points of view; the contributions to the United States of the Catholic educational leadership pattern of travelling to Europe for money and personnel for schools; studies of the Church Fathers at the Councils of Cincinnati and Baltimore concerning education, to determine whether their intentions were only to meet an *ad hoc* situation or to provide permanent guidelines; applications of the concepts of such farsighted theorists as Isaac Hecker to modern problems; studies of the patterns and attitudes implicit in governmental procedures towards Catholic schools; etc., etc., etc.

## The Present

Precise statistics on the present status of Catholic education in the United States are contained elsewhere in this study. Suffice it to recapitulate here that this establishment involves billions of dollars, thousands of dedicated lives of lay and religious teachers and administrators, and about five million children. As with most situations and institutions that are human, one can take an optimistic or a pessimistic view about almost any aspect of it—the glass is both "half full" and "half empty." To speak of some aspects of statistics first, and to start with a world-view before coming into the United States and its pattern of Catholic education, let it be known that, according to the United States Arms Control and Disarmament Agency, the world spent a total of $182 billion for war and preparation for war in 1967, the last year for which figures are complete —40 per cent more than the world spent for education. The same agency, ACDA, indicated that from 1900 to 1969, when the figures were released, the world spent for military purposes a total of $4,000 billion—and, if the 1969 rate of increase in such spending were to continue, that total of $4,000 billion will be spent over again within the next ten years. As for our country, all-out and full development of an anti-ballistic missile system would make it possible for the United States to spend more than the 1967 world total in a few years all by itself. This puts into a cold blue light statistics on education in our country which under another light might look encouraging. In 1959, outlays for education in the United States were $24.7 billion, or 5.1 per cent of our gross national product; in 1968, the educational outlays soared to $58.5 billion, or 6.8 per cent of the gross national product—a gain of 137 per cent. Zooming our camera in further to a close-up of United States Catholic education, the statistical picture of financial straits already pointed out, on the one hand, and on-going financial discussions with our government at the various levels, on the other, are for our country speaking about relatively very small amounts.

As for her schools, Catholic education at present indicates various strengths: the local and community character of her institutions and patterns; highly trained, community-minded, and thoroughly professional administrators; and the post-conciliar awakening of lay participation and opinion. Put together, these result in a program highly in accord with the best interests of the country at large. Today's Catholic elementary school purports to be an invitation to learning, to group experience, and to seek God. Today's Catholic middle-level school adds to the continuation of religious formation and citizenship training an intensive concentration on academic subjects required for the student's future, and intensive guidance in all matters required for sound personal growth. Today's Catholic higher education broadens and deepens this venture.

Teachers in Catholic schools, as those outside them, are in turmoil. The worth of their contribution is challenged on many sides. Parents, concerned but sometimes confused, are often indulgent of their children, neglectful of their obligations, and selfish enough to want to shift serious and difficult responsibilities to teachers. Our activist society has in many instances succeeded in propagating its ideals to even the dedicated hearts of consecrated persons, with the result that many are leaving the work of forming the minds, hearts, and souls of children through teaching, for other forms of the social apostolate. Many others are not entering the ranks of teachers in the first place. Several positive factors that are at work only partly offset the general trend: among the religious communities, always having an uncommon dedication to teaching, there is beginning a higher level of competence than ever in the past, with the result that many impartial observers claim that they will constitute a teaching force in this nation that is best in every respect; lay teachers joining the religious now represent about half of the Catholic teaching population, and in many places much more; the attempts to redefine, reorganize, and reconstitute Catholic education at the diocesan level assists indirectly, if not indeed directly, to more efficient use of teaching as well as other resources; and the rapidly accelerating participation of the laity on the decision-making level is also a great help.

As for the ones for whom it all exists, and who will be its product—students—twelve per cent of the United States total remain enrolled in Catholic educational institutions, but more than half of the Catholic school-age population of approximately fifteen million is in educational institutions other than Catholic. The expectations of Catholic-school students add the dimension of a religious commitment to grow in Christ to the educational hopes of other American students, which are to receive from formal education an enabling resource for the lifetime development of the intellect, the person, and the citizen. For the intellect, through satisfying intellectual curiosity and giving expression to enthusiasm for ideas, Catholic-school students continue to seek those essential qualities that promote learning, understanding, and judgment. For the person, growth in Christ embraces qualities that will enable him to be effective in personal life, family life, social life, and civic life, so that human happiness will come as the result of the practice of virtue in these areas. Toward development of the citizen, Catholic-school students learn the freedoms which are vitally necessary for a democratic way of life, and that freedom and dignity for one are not possible without freedom and dignity for all.

## The Future

As this is written, the future of Catholic education in the United States is extremely problematic. Dependent not only on directions given by its past, but on such imponderables as outside financial help, it can go under, as some predict, or it can take one of several directions. In this section, therefore, we deem it essential to ask three questions. The first is, "Should there be Catholic schools in the United States?" The remaining questions presuppose an affirmative answer to the first. The second question is, "Should there be government aid to Catholic schools?" The third question asks, "Judging by present trends and other information at our disposal, what will future Catholic schooling be like?"

### SHOULD CATHOLIC SCHOOLS CONTINUE?

History shows that Catholic schools are not essential to or inseparable from the practice of the Catholic religion in this country. Such leaders as the first bishop in the United States, John Carroll, and many other Catholic leaders who were interested in the formation of youth, such as Bishop John Ireland, did not conceive of the form of Catholic schooling as it exists today as absolutely necessary to the worship of God or the growth of the Church. Archbishop Francesco Satolli, representing Rome to the United States in 1891 vis-à-vis the school controversy of that time, issued fourteen points which, as we have seen, did not absolutely demand strict adherence to a principle of a Catholic school in every parish and every Catholic child in a Catholic school.

Besides, there are others—sincere Catholics among them—who argue actively for eliminating Catholic schools. Their arguments take different turns. Some argue historically—but invalidly—that the Church got into education accidentally in the first place, because of the vacuum at the end of the Roman Empire, and has been trying to justify this commitment ever since. Some contend that for the religious formation of the student, the presentation of catechetics outside the school can show the child that religious education is different from the "ordinary" subjects. There are those who argue that not continuing Catholic schools would force upon some who need it a form of Christian witness to "go forth and teach all nations" outside the Church's own institutions, thus eliminating some of the "ghetto" mentality. Both the financial and manpower resources saved, claim others, would be released to support and educate the family, the most effective institution for teaching religious values. The social-minded point out that, in a world whose great problem is the growing gap between the rich and the poor, the Church would be enabled to contribute more to solve the problem. Other theorists would hope that, if parents were not able to delegate (or relegate) their responsibilities to the Catholic school, they would be forced to become more responsible and more educated themselves. There are also those who contend that, without Catholic schools, the Church, lay and clerical, would be forced to develop ecumenically. Other arguments, presented by such as Mary Perkins Ryan, have been indicated in this study.

Nevertheless, this author would present the guarded opinion that, given certain conditions, Catholic schools should be encouraged to continue, even at great sacrifice should that be necessary. The opinion is guarded, because of the realization of some sad but true facts. Not all education by Catholics is Catholic education. Not all "Catholic" education has the purposes, nature, and tradition delineated in these pages. An affirmative answer is valid only if Catholic schools be what they should be, and is given for a variety of historical reasons.

One reason is that history bears witness that this has been the ideal which the Church has most constantly taught. We have presented, for example, the declarations of the Councils of Baltimore between 1829 and 1884 and the pastoral letters of all the American hierarchy in connection with some of them; the serious direct and indirect legislation on education in the Code of Canon Law of 1918; the constant pronouncements of the Popes on the importance of forming youth according to the mind of God, not only in Pius XI's 1929 encyclical *On the Christian Education of Youth*, but in other documents to the whole world as well; and the documents of Vatican Council II. The Bishops of the United States have also expressed their interest in various other ways; in their November 1967 statement, for example, they said to Catholic teachers:

> We declare today that the Catholic elementary and secondary schools are an indispensable component of the Church's total commitment to education in the United States. We therefore will do our part to continue, improve, and strengthen these schools.[21]

Further, they said that "our schools must be, above all else, an expression of what is meant by being a Christian in today's world."

History also teaches lessons about the undesirability of monopoly in any field, including religion. Our Founding Fathers had had experiences with the evils of religion as a monopoly, and had witnessed the wars fought because of it, the heresy trials, the witch burnings, and the impositions of "establishment." In writing our Constitution, therefore, they wisely made provisions for religious freedom. In business, monopoly has been at least as bad. When because of the Industrial Revolution history witnessed for the first time the ways in which monopolistic business could trample upon the rights and dignity of persons to the extent that it did, the beginning of this century brought anti-monopolistic and anti-trust legislation. Every consumer knows that he benefits from competition, that he is the better because Hertz has Avis, Macy's Gimbel's, and General Motors Ford. The same principles on monopoly that apply to religion and to business apply, *mutatis mutandis,* to education. While it is true that Catholic education needs other patterns coexistent with it, other patterns need Catholic education too. The former is true because of such phenomena as Catholic education too often criticizing innovations, then belatedly adopting them. The latter is true because it is historically and otherwise demonstrable that Catholic education has given education in the United States a temper of wisdom, contributed a needed examination of ultimate goals and aims, provided challenging concepts of personal formation, supplied stimulation in many areas, contributed greater profundity than most other educators to true foundations of such virtues as citizenship and patriotism, and donated resources and services of countless thousands of dedicated personnel to United States communities across the land.

Such objective theorists as Peter Shrag see the advantages of competition for the public schools. He pointed out, for example, that in 1967 a very important proposal for competitive schools came from the Task Force on Economic Growth and Opportunity of the United States Chamber of Commerce. He cited this task force—headed by Erwin D. Canham, editor of the *Christian Science Monitor,* and including major corporation executives—as declaring:

If all parents, at every income level, could choose between sending their children to public schools and sending their children to approved private schools at public expense, both public and private education would improve as schools attempted to attract and hold pupils.[22]

He further cited similar proposals as having come from James S. Coleman (director of the massive United States Office of Education study, *Equality of Educational Opportunity*), "who suggested that the city of Washington operate competing public school systems," and from such as Christopher Jencks, Paul Goodman, and Edgar Friedenberg, "who feel that a diversity of educational options is the only way to provide healthy alternatives to the conformist rigidities of the established public system." Shrag made these very interesting and relevant observations:

We know, moreover, that the alternatives for education and economic advancement that existed fifty years ago—the shop, the farm, the community—are no longer adequate or available. The schools now have a monopoly that they never had before. For all but the very exceptional, they *are* the gates to success. . . . The movement to provide alternatives to these schools is therefore not only directed to the development of new educational ideas and of institutions that will be hospitable to minorities, but also toward restoring the choices that a simpler society took for granted. Dropouts become a problem only where the local public school is the only available educational resource—where there is no other place to go.[23]

What this country needs, then, in education, is diversity, albeit not divisiveness. A monolithic, monopolistic educational system helped such dictators as Adolph Hitler to acquire and maintain power. In Communism's modern struggle to achieve power in Macao, although "only a small part of the . . . population is Catholic," most parents who send their children to school "choose Roman Catholic schools," and "almost all schools except the Catholic ones have become Communist-dominated." [24] In Yugoslavia today, "it is in the field of education that Communists appear to see the greatest danger from religion." [25] People do not differ in time or in place, and such things *can* happen here. A monolithic, monopolistic educational system could help the "Big-Brotherism" that some social scientists see creeping into the United States. Mindful of the lessons of history, Ronald David Laing, British psychiatrist and author, has said: "Induce people all to want the same thing, hate the same thing, feel the same threat, then their behavior is already captive. . . . You have acquired your consumers or your cannon-fodder." [26]

Further, the deepest and most solid underpinnings of true democracy are today, as in ancient Greece, those which religion provides. If one leaves aside religious considerations, the worth of the individual doesn't amount to enough to cause concern about his welfare, particularly if he distastefully opposes one's own opinions. Our equality as men, our individual worth, and our common brotherhood, all make the most sense in the context of our being sons of God. These foundations of United States democracy are religious. They are all presented in the activities of Catholic education. Again, the very definition of democracy entails freedom of choice—true and real choice, not just radically possible choice—which would be present minimally in all the important areas of life, of which one, certainly, is education. In the present circumstances of education in the United States, there is no real choice. If one is in a good school district, he is lucky. If he is in a poor district, he is unlucky. Real, true choice is the prerogative of only the wealthy, who can send their children to private schools or move to another district. The principle to be recognized is the *acceptance* of private education, including the Catholic, not just *toleration* of it. This alone can bring about real choice in education, and nothing less represents democracy at its *best*.

History prompts an affirmative answer to the question also in the area of theology. Several approaches indicate this. As we have seen, it was the sacrifices of our forebears that made possible whatever belief in God today's generation possesses. Their sacrifices prove that they believed with their whole being, as their Master commanded them. Today's generations do not seem willing—whether because they haven't the same faith, or have simply "gone soft," or because of some other reason, is not clear—to make the same sacrifices or to put up the same fight. And yet theology is an important constituent of life, and as such should be reflected in education. Endres put it this way:

Generally, Christians agree that a way must be found to heal the breach [between the sacred and secular dimensions], to make Christianity relevant to modern life. And generally, education is regarded as vital to that objective. Prescinding momentarily from any question of methodology, it is evident that if the Church has any essential validity and if it is to have any impact on the modern world, it must remain deeply involved in education.[27]

Because this "impact on the modern world" that the churches seek is advantageous for the United States, particularly in its present condition, our country should do everything in its power to help it while simultaneously recognizing the principle of church disestablishment. This is also based upon the fundamental theological principle that grace builds upon nature and does not contradict it, in consequence of which the young, for effective personal formation, need as much good exposure as possible. For the kind of personal religious formation that is deep and long-lasting, such programs as released-time, dual enrollment, shared time, etc., are good, but are historically, empirically, and experientially demonstrable as insufficient. And this formation is an advantage not only to an individual from a religious viewpoint, or to a parish, but to the community as well, and other citizens, and the nation.

As history unfolds, it teaches that youth need, more and more, every good formative influence they can get. The Uniform Crime Reports which the Federal Bureau of Investigation releases every three months from statistics furnished by local and state police agencies have indicated not only increased crime, but more and more frequent commission of worse and worse crimes by younger and younger persons. In the report for 1967, not only did the number of serious crimes—both violent and nonviolent—increase by 16 per cent over 1966, but "the rate of arrests of juveniles ten to seventeen years old more than doubled since 1960." For the first nine months of 1968, the FBI's report indicated that crime increased 19 per cent over the corresponding period in 1967. The 1969 report indicated a further increase.

It is of historical record that daily newspapers have been substantiating the truth of these statistics. Under the headline, "Student Morals Worry Educators," one article, reporting on a meeting of the National Association of Independent Schools, began, "An official of the country's leading association of private schools asserted yesterday that students had adopted 'terrifying' attitudes toward sex." This referred to Nathaniel S. French, of Winnetka, Illinois, who, speaking of students' "lack of a moral code," observed: "There is a great discrepancy today between cultural mores and the practices of youth. Chastity is out the window at sophisticated colleges. It has been given up as a value." Under another headline, "Epidemic of V.D. in Minors Noted," a newspaper report elaborated: "The United States today is in the grip of a 'serious' epidemic of teen-age venereal disease, according to doctors attending the 22nd Clinical Convention of the American Medical Association." Still another headline read, "Use of Drugs in Grade Schools Feared by Mental Health Aides." In an article on New York City entitled, "Fear Soars with Rate of Crime," the chairman of the city Housing Authority was quoted as saying, "No society, no government, no taxpayer, can afford to spend what is needed to assure the safety of everyone." A police captain in this article was reported to have the position that "he cannot do more than 'play checkers' with the gangs of youthful muggers who are plaguing the neighborhood." In 1969, the High School Principals' Association reported that such "chaos" as outbreaks of student disorders, rallies, protest demonstrations, rule testing and violence, had reached unprecedented proportions in New York City. Also in 1969, a report of the National Commission on the Causes and Prevention of Violence said that crime by youths is the key to U. S. violence, and challenged youth, who "account for an ever-increasing percentage of crime." [28] In a national magazine an article on the spread of youth violence down to the high school level began:

In Washington, D.C., an assistant high school principal tried to stop three teen-agers from robbing the school bank; they shot him dead. In New York City, a high school chemistry teacher stepped into the hall to investigate a disturbance; three youths squirted lighter fluid on his clothing and set him aflame. In San Francisco, helmeted police dispersed teen-agers . . . after violence had flared between black and Spanish-speaking sudents for six successive days.[29]

It is logical to agree with the report of the National Commission on the Causes and Prevention of Violence that "the heavy concentration of crime . . . is among the poor, the ethnic minorities in the city slums, areas of lowest per capita income, of highest unemployment, of lowest level of average educational attainment, of poorest housing, and of highest infant mortality." [30] It is also sensible to agree with their perspective enunciated in the same article that "99 per cent of the population do not engage in crimes of violence." Nevertheless, the amount of violence and crime in the country has already produced reactions, and is likely to produce more. The 1968 political campaign was won, in part, on promises of "law and order." Not too long after it, the president of the American Bar Association, William T. Gossett, said that violence is raising the risk of "repression in this country comparable to a police force action of a police state, such as they had in Germany during the days of the Nazis and such as they have in Russia today." [31] It is not our purpose in relating the above indications of crime and violence to criticize our younger generation, who have justly been called the best in history. At the same time, however, they are also the victims of forces, pressures, and freedoms hitherto unknown, with which they need guidance to cope. Is it not just possible that *one* of the answers beneficial to our youth and to the whole country is the inclusion of religion in formal schooling?

Current history seems to be demonstrating that the fundamental principles under which our society has come to operate have resulted in a waning influence of religion. At least, Gallup polls taken five times from 1957 to 1968 indicated a rapid rise in the number of people—more young adults than their elders—who think that religion is losing its influence on American life. Here (Table I) are some of the statistics on answers to the question, "At the present time, do you think religion as a whole is increasing its influence on American life, or losing its influence?"

TABLE I

| ANSWERS | 1968 | 1957 |
|---|---|---|
| *Increasing* | *18%* | *69%* |
| *Losing* | *67* | *14* |
| *No difference* | *8* | *10* |
| *No opinion* | *7* | *7* |

Those answering "Losing" usually cited one of four reasons: young people are losing interest in formal religion; growing immorality and violence; materialism; the Church is not playing its proper role (these being divided about equally between those who said the Church was not keeping up with the times and those who thought the Church too involved in social and political issues).[32]

Are these statistics on the dangers to our youth and on the declining influence of religion *really* surprising, in view of the positive exclusion of all religions other than secularism from so many areas of our society including public schools, and the unnecessary difficulties imposed upon church-affiliated schools, under the guise of "the wall of separation between Church and State?" Do we *honestly* have the right to expect anything else? If the theological axiom that "grace builds on nature, and does not contradict it" is true, can we *realistically* expect any essential differences in this regard between our society and, say, that of Russia? Do we not, by now, have a body of historical precedents and experiential knowledge sufficient to warrant some reasonably accurate conclusions? *Isn't it just possible that the inclusion of religion in schooling would help our people and our country in many ways?*

#### GOVERNMENT AID TO CATHOLIC SCHOOLS?

That brings us to the second of our three questions: should there be government aid to Catholic schools? The difficulties delineated above make it obvious that this question is more important today than ever. The attempts to close Catholic schools that failed through the anti-Catholic legislation of Colonial times, the nativist bigotry of the early nineteenth century, the Know-Nothingism of the middle nineteenth century, the prejudice of the American Protective Association of the later nineteenth century, and the rabble-rousings of the Ku Klux Klan of the early twentieth century are now perhaps being accomplished more subtly through money. The history of action on federal aid to private education points up in both the legislature and the judiciary inconsistencies, ambiguities, and lack of a developed over-all policy, and also at times a lack of clarity on the part of some Catholics. It is a happy situation that all are youthful enough to be open to change. Even Supreme Court decisions are self-reversible: in 1952, during the heyday of Senator Joseph McCarthy, the United States Supreme Court confirmed by a 6-3 majority the validity of New York State's Feinberg law barring subversives from the public school system, but in 1967 the Court ruled by a vote of 5-4 that the law is unconstitutional; their *Plessy* v. *Ferguson* decision said in 1892 that "separate but equal" schooling and other facilities for the Negro were adequate to satisfy the demands of the Constitution, but their *Brown* v. *Board of Education* decision of 1954 was that the Constitution demanded integration; the *Minersville School District* v. *Gobitis* [33] decision of 1940 asserted that the flag salute requirement in schools was constitutional, but their *West Virginia State Board of Education* v. *Barnett* [34] decision of 1943 (only three years later!) reversed this; and in 1923 *Frothingham* v. *Mellon* declared that the individual taxpayer lacks standing in court to challenge how federal funds are spent, but *Flast* v. *Gardner* of 1968 granted that right. The discussion that follows does not have the intention of criticizing past decisions, but rather the purpose of creating a climate for democratic expression of opinion and of establishing the foundations for true choice.[35]

## Against

The prime reason ascribed against government aid to denominational schools seems to be church-state separation. As *The New York Times* editorial concerning the Supreme Court decision on New York's textbook case put it:

> The Supreme Court, in upholding the New York law that provides public funds for textbooks "loaned" to parochial school pupils, deepens the already serious inroads that have been made into the vital principle of church-state separation. . . .
> The principle at stake, as Justice Black [who presented the minority opinion] warned, is religious freedom itself—and, to protect it, the wall of separation must be kept "high and impregnable." No single decision will destroy that wall. The most significant tests are those still to come.[36]

Leo Pfeffer, special counsel for the American Jewish Congress and also attorney for the plaintiff in the New York cases against the Elementary and Secondary Education Act, sees other difficulties as well. Among these is lawlessness, whereby "the sectarian groups are impatient with constitutional restrictions in the administration of the law and exert often irresistible pressure on public school authorities to disregard such restrictions." [37] He also alleges discrimination, whereby "private interests always have stronger lobbies than the public, and the results show this," and disintegration, which he indicates may come about

in a way neither anticipated nor desired by the Church. The pressure on the part of the Negro community for public school integration in Northern cities is accelerating an exodus from the public schools to private white schools, the great majority of which are parochial schools.[38]

### For

The arguments for providing federal aid to private education if it is given to public education are built upon foundations from many areas. We shall confine ourselves to the historical. Were church-related schools not to be included, it would seem that a religious test for full citizenship is again being inserted into our national life. This would be in contradiction to the Constitution's guarantees of freedom and equality, as was obvious especially to those who fought the "religious test" concept in the drafting of the Constitution in the first place, and to those who in the early days of our Republic fought to continue to exclude religious tests for public office. William B. Ball, a constitutional lawyer, speaking of the law suits projected against ESEA, said that they had to be seen in two broader perspectives—as part of a wider campaign to dramatize the principle of church-state separation, and "as a disturbing survival of America's long history of religious prejudice." [39]

Historical developments in other countries have enabled government help to church-affiliated schools. Virgil C. Blum, S.J., believes that in the matter of education we can learn much from European democracies in that they treasure freedom and equality in the education of all children, and that "in all the democracies in which the government supports the education of children in church-related schools, there is a great deal of religious harmony, and close co-operation among religious groups for the improvement of all education." [40] Augmenting his statements by example, Blum places the picture into true and sharp focus. "In West Berlin," says Blum, "tax funds pay from 50 to 60 per cent of the operating costs of church-related schools, including teacher's salaries and free textbooks for all children." Throughout the British Commonwealth there is government aid to education. A case in point is British Honduras where "the government pays 50 per cent of the construction costs of new church-related elementary schools; 50 per cent of the cost of improvements, additions, and repairs; and 50 per cent of the cost of all school equipment." In Canada, writes Blum, "provincial laws provide that the tax-paying citizen must designate the schools of his own religion as the recipients of his school taxes." [41] In being given the choice of whether they are to be taxed for the support of the public schools or of the "separate" ones, Canadian citizens have not only meaningful and true choice; they also enjoy real separation of church and state whereby the church schools are not penalized by making their adherents also support the state schools.

Estelle Fuchs also cites the "Free Schools" (*friskoler*) of Denmark as representing a "model of public education that is flexible in the use of alternative types of public schools," and a demonstration of

how a modern nation can establish standards of education required for national life and the protection of the young, while at the same time provide for the freedom of parents with special religious, ethnic, economic, or pedagogic interests to oversee and direct the education of their children with minimal interference by the government.[42]

Again, many see federal financial aid to Catholic schools as likely under one of a number of possible concepts from history: as an extension of the *Zorach* principle which in 1952 sanctioned religious instruction off school premises; under the "child welfare" doctrine enunciated in *Cochran* in 1930 and *Everson* in 1947; as an aspect of national defense as put forward in the National Defense Education Act of 1958; under a "purchase of services" concept; or under any of numerous other titles. In this area the legal department of the National Catholic Welfare Conference made these relevant conclusions in 1961:

1. Education in church-related schools is a public function which, by its nature, is deserving of governmental support.

2. There exists no constitutional bar to aid to education in church-related schools in a degree proportionate to the value of the public function it performs. . . .

3. The parent and child have a constitutional right to choose a church-related educational institution meeting reasonable state requirements as the institution in which the child's education shall be acquired.

4. Government in the United States is without power to impose upon the people a single educational system in which all must participate.[43]

They contended that the weakening and ultimate closing of many church-related schools brought about by a massive governmental spending program solely on public schools, taken in conjunction with the compulsory education laws, would force all the children of our nation to acquire their education in the public schools. This would result in a lack of the type of freedom guaranteed by the Constitution.

They made further interesting points concerning a principle which the Supreme Court enunciated in *West Virginia State Board of Education* v. *Barnett:* "If there is any fixed star in our constitutional constellation, it is that no official, high or petty, can prescribe what shall be orthodox in politics, nationalism, religion or other matters of opinion." [44] They saw an "orthodoxy" expressed even in a curriculum for which religious "orthodoxies" are absent. They asked what, by constitutional definition, is "religion?" They cited Leo Pfeffer, an opponent, as considering non-theistic beliefs to be "religious":

In this study I shall regard humanism as a religion along with the three major faiths: Protestantism, Catholicism, and Judaism. This, I submit, is not an unreasonable inclusion. Ethical Culture is exclusively humanist but is generally considered a religion.[45]

They cited Lanier Hunt of the National Council of Churches as providing a very wide definition of religion as "simply loyalty to ultimate values." [46] They cited to the same effect Justice Hugo Black's observation in *Torcaso* v. *Watkins* that "among religions in this country which do not teach what would generally be considered a belief in the existence of God are Buddhism, Taoism, Ethical Culture, Secular Humanism, and others." [47] They then referred to a statement by the Educational Policies Commission of the National Education Association of the United States and the American Association of School Administrators that public schools inculcate values: "The development of moral and spiritual values is basic to all other educational objectives." [48] They concluded that a child compelled to attend such a school is subjected to a *de facto* denial of the free exercise of his religion, a result discountenanced by the Court in *McCollum*. They also came to the obvious conclusion of the expression of a religion in the public schools.

Some even charge that the frequent, unfounded claims that denominational schools are "divisive" suggest that there exists in the public school an orthodoxy from which non-public schools deviate: secular humanism, of course. The public school is in possession, however, and the existent establishment, like any other, has vested interests. Robert F. Drinan, S.J., called it "an empire which enrolls every fourth American as a student and which enjoys a prestige more abiding than any collective admiration given to any other American public institution," and continued with this shrewd observation:

Unanalyzed slogans about the alleged unifying effect of children of the public school are accepted as incontrovertible truths while no one really raises the question of whether and how the public school is training young persons to be dissenters from political or social orthodoxy without being disloyal to their nation.[49]

Whereas in such areas as highway and hospital construction the shift from state and local fiscal responsibility to the federal government has already taken place, in education existing policies are difficult to change. The educational opportunity for *all* children which the federal government seeks to provide in an equal measure to all places and all classes, promising as it does no "thought control" but only a routine review for accounting purposes, is proceeding rapidly nonetheless.

How?

A corollary to the question of government aid to Catholic schools is the query on how this may be accomplished. Our study has shown that Bishop John Ireland expressed some ideas on this subject to the National Education Association in 1890, that Isaac Hecker and others have addressed themselves to this question, and that certain arrangements such as the Poughkeepsie and Lowell plans actually worked it out. Modern versions are perhaps more sophisticated *vis-à-vis* the complexities of later interpretations of the Constitution. Some, for example, propose a modest federal appropriation for experimentation in "shared time." Others opt for further extensions of the 1958 National Defense Education Act. There is the so-called "Junior G. I. Bill" whereby the parents of non-public school students would apply to a federal or state educational agency for a check payable to the private school for the same amount that the public school in the same community would receive for every student. The suggestions for federal income tax deductions for parents of children in non-public schools would not seem too practical, because the majority of Catholic parents are in the lower middle class economically. Many suggestions, like that of Donald A. Erickson, are quite imaginative:

> There is no good reason . . . why parents should be required to secure their children's total education from a single source. If one agency offers the best reading program, another the best mathematics program, and another (perhaps not even called a "school") the best exposure to the fine arts, why should the parent not be free to obtain one component here, another there, and a third somewhere else? [50]

To effect this, he would have tuition vouchers in identical amounts made available to all parents of school-age children, redeemable through any state-approved school, public or non-public. He also suggested that "special incentive grants could be offered to all schools, non-public or public, that maintained student bodies that were racially, academically, and perhaps socio-economically integrated." All this would alleviate the need of the public school system for more drastic renovation, by applying "the shock treatment of being forced to compete for clients and support." He was realistic enough to see dangers in the private school sector too:

> Non-public schools, too, are often stodgy and establishmentarian. For this reason, I would be reluctant to see public aid doled out indiscriminately. We must carefully arrange the financial carrots to reward the people who are creative.[51]

RESTRICTIONS NECESSARY

That brings us to a final point on this subject: some historically demonstrable abuses of federal aid to non-public schools would make some restrictions advisable in conformity with government norms. First, there is a danger that government money thus provided may be used for the purpose of furthering segregation. At least two hundred segregated private schools were reported established in Southern states in the few years during the ideological recovery from the *Brown* desegregation decision of 1954.[52]

Secondly, there is a possibility of misuse by some religions in the direction of un-American practices. The Old Order Amish, or "Plain People," for example, view the larger society as evil, and do not want their children to be taken out of their own enclaves. Therefore, in the states where they dwell—Ohio, Iowa, Kentucky, and Pennsylvania for the most part—they violate the state's minimum standards of education. Most of their children attend primitive one-room elementary schools. Usually education beyond the eighth grade is forbidden, and the teachers have no more than that themselves. Erickson pointed out a further complication, however:

Their success in training the young to be farmers has impressed many agricultural experts. Unemployment, indigence, juvenile delinquency, and crime are surprisingly infrequent. Amish prosperity and self-sufficiency are legendary. These are not the characteristics of a preparation for adulthood that has failed.[53]

Finally, parochial schools with government aid should admit applicants with no religious test, as they have done in their past history. This is especially important now, with the incarnational emphases of Vatican Council II and with society's need for the influence of religion. If there are any Catholic educators who object, they should perhaps be reminded of the historic precedents, that the mission of their pattern of education —as of their Church—is not only for the saved but for all men, and of their need to put their convictions on the line for true tests of validity.

### PAST AND PRESENT UNFOLD THE FUTURE

In spite of financial problems, decline in enrollments, closings, bad press, shortage of teachers, lack of vocations, questionings, and ferment, Catholic schools will continue in the future. Their investment is large, and some, like George N. Shuster, believe "that American Catholic schools have been considerably better than their reputations and are doubtless here to stay." [54] The Rev. C. Albert Koob of the National Catholic Educational Association predicts that

there will be a continuing decrease in the number of Catholic schools across the country, and a slight decline in the number of students. This should settle down around 1980, when we will have a smaller operation, but one with much greater quality education and more flexibility.[55]

All of this will be taking place in what is prognosticated as a burgeoning population: the Metropolitan Life Insurance Company, for example, estimates that there will be a new high in births sometime during the 1970's.[56] The latest *Projections of Educational Statistics* of the Department of Health, Education, and Welfare corroborates this information.[57]

This does not mean, however, that Catholic education will continue in the future to be the same as it has in the past. A new order of priorities is obviously necessary, and one of the first to receive priority will be adult education. As one pastor wrote: "Catholic elementary schools, by assuming too much responsibility for the welfare of the children, have solved the problem of inadequate religious guidance at home only at the cost of perpetuating it."[58] He suggested, therefore, that some of the money theretofore used to build and maintain parochial elementary schools be used henceforth on parents: to educate them and to provide them with the necessary aids for religious instruction so the gain would be greater than the loss. Vaile J. Scott has seen adult education as important to Catholicism today because of the convergence of four factors at this point in history: Vatican II, enabling the laity to emerge; the crisis in Catholic education, reexamination of which has put things in a new light; the ecumenical movement, resulting in an interest based on inter-religious dialogue; and the changes in modern society, whereby the Church must share in the social, political, scientific, and economic revolutions if she is to preserve basic human and religious values.[59]

In the United States, adult education has been used as an umbrella term to refer to "any activity in which the main purpose is to acquire some type of knowledge, information or skill."[60] In such general education programs the Church has a definite role of Christian witness for the concerns of men and of service to the community—not, however, for proselytization. Whereas her traditional role in such broad areas as basic education, literacy training, self-improvement, family life, community issues, and job training is obvious, it is even more enhanced by Vatican II's *Constitution on the Church in the Modern World* and *Decree on the Laity*. There is in these programs a need for free and open inquiry into such areas as theology and also a need for experimentation. One excellent example of Catholic participation in this program is Catholic Adult Education in the archdiocese of Chicago. Begun in 1955 as an experiment in continuing liberal adult education, it is now organized under six divisions: Centers for Continuing Education; Summer Biblical Institute; World Peace Center; Center for Film Study; John A. Ryan Forum, offering serious discussions of social questions; and Special Projects, an open-ended experimental laboratory. The National Catholic Adult Education Commission was organized at a workshop at Catholic University in 1958 and established as a commission of NCEA in November of the same year. Its objectives are to coordinate and encourage adult education programs under Catholic auspices; to act as a clearing-house of information; to provide continuity of purpose and effort; to assist new programs needing it; and to promote training, writing, and research in the field. Its principal services are a one-day conference and annual meeting held in conjunction with the NCEA annual convention; a two-day national conference each fall; and a newsletter to members.

Also high in the order of priorities is the Confraternity of Christian Doctrine. Heretofore, because of many factors such as voluntary attendance, Confraternity programs have received a rather low priority. Teachers have not been professionals, their major qualification being their willingness to work rather than expertise. Today much thought, many books, and frequent training programs have been going into the work of Confraternity personnel. Because of the turmoil in Catholic schools it is obvious that quantitatively, at any rate, Confraternity programs will be coming more and more into the fore in the future.

Last in the order of priorities will be the continuation of the present school system as we have known it. Even there, however, we can expect changes. One of the advantages of the recent pressures has been the reexamination of all areas of the Catholic pattern of education. In administration this has revealed duplications, overlaps, and inefficiencies —which are "the product not of perfidy but of history," as Shaw put it.[61] Henceforward on all levels the watchwords will be coordination, cooperation, unification, and increased centralization of planning and budgeting—as witnessed by such studies as that of the Office of Educational Research of Notre Dame University on the archdiocesan schools of Denver, Colorado, and Saginaw, Michigan.[62] None of this will be a coordination imposed from above, but is expected to emerge from the will of the participants.

On the national level, all separate and frequently overlapping were the offices of the United States Catholic Conference, National Catholic Educational Association, Confraternity of Christian Doctrine National Center, and the Newman Office. Officials of the NCEA, the National Center of CCD, and the Education Department of USCC, announced in June 1967 the formation of an *ad hoc* committee to explore the possibilities of mutual cooperation. At a meeting of the United States Bishops in April 1968, the USCC was formally reorganized to clarify its relationship to the National Council of Catholic Bishops, to streamline its work, and to provide a greater voice for priests, religious, and laity. The reorganization consolidated the twenty-four existing offices as divisions under five major departments, the departments to be supervised by committees composed of an equal number of espiscopal and non-episcopal members, including laymen. Under the department entitled "Communications" come the divisions of National Catholic News Service, Division for Press Relations, National Catholic Office for Motion Pictures, and the National Catholic Office for Radio and Television;

under "Christian Formation," the Confraternity of Christian Doctrine, and the divisions of Elementary and Secondary Education, Youth Activities, Religious Education, Higher Education including the Newman Apostolate, and Continuing (Adult) Education; under "Health Affairs," the Bureau of Health and Hospitals and the National Association of Catholic Chaplains; under "International Affairs," Migration and Refugee Service, Foreign Visitors, Latin America, U.N. Affairs, and World Justice and Peace; and "Social Development" embraces Urban Life, Rural Life, Family Life, Spanish Speaking, and Poverty Programs. Also on the national level, but with reference to the federal government, Neil G. McCluskey, S.J., presents the reminder that "while occupying the office, Dr. Howe repeatedly stated that he considered himself the U. S. Commissioner of Education and not merely the U. S. Commissioner of *Public* Education," and the consequent interesting proposal for "the creation of the office of Assistant Commissioner for Private Education with special responsibility for the nonpublic schools." [63]

On the diocesan level of administration, heretofore the chanceries have had a superintendent of schools, a director of the Confraternity of Christian Doctrine, a Newman director, and often others, all professionally separate. The tendency now into the future is to have a director for all education, called "Vicar for Education" or "Secretary for Education," who coordinates all educational activities. Under him, the superintendent of schools will have authority over schools only. There will also be diocesan school boards, created in part to restore the balance between the three agencies of education: family, state, and Church. Both of the last two have erred in the past—the state by failing to provide the involvement of the religious community in its decision-making, and the Church by failing to involve representatives of the other two societies.[64] These boards have historical roots not only in the recent *Constitution on the Church* from Vatican II,[65] but ultimately in Baltimore III, which set up an "Education Committee" in each diocese. Although they had been set up in almost every diocese within a few years, the concentration of authority in the bishops during those years made them more nominal than effective. Adding to Vatican II such stimuli as public school reorganization, isolation-ending communications media, increased population mobility, and educational complexity, Catholic school authorities began to perceive the need for change. Under diocesan administration and the school board, McCluskey envisions "curriculum planning and experimentation, teacher accreditation, standards for promotion, advance placement, selection of textbooks, enforcement of library standards, etc." [66]

On the parish level, "the parochial school as an independent, parish-controlled, and parish-financed operation is an anachronism," [67] finding here a historical antecedent in public education, which had also tended to have schools that were isolated entities controlled almost completely

at the local level. The parish situation until now has been no less
confusing than the national and diocesan: parish educational programs
—parish school, CCD, adult discussion clubs, etc.—have all existed in
isolation, and accurate accounting programs have been difficult in the
face of such procedures as overlapping heating plants for school and
church. In the latter regard, finance, McCluskey predicts new procedures:

> Tuition is now abolished. In its place there is a school tax levied on every adult
> member of the diocese. The present system of financing Catholic school educa-
> tion is unbelievably archaic, obsolete, and inefficient. In this matter, we are a
> good one hundred years behind the public-school system.[68]

Some recommend inter-parish cooperation in financing; at any rate, the
future must see greater clarification, unification, and cooperation on
this level as on the others.

There are also an increasing number of *lay* boards of *education*, not
just *school* boards. At present there are over two thousand such boards.
These boards amplify home-school cooperation by bringing together the
religious and laity, providing the benefit of lay experience, enlisting the
talents of the laity in policy formation, and bringing about a more
dynamic school situation. The lay board does not administer, but establishes and enforces policy; recommends local criteria for admission, expulsion, and attendance at the parish school; suggests principles on textbooks and other educational materials; advises concerning tuition and
other means of financial support; counsels on school uniforms, and
fosters cooperation—between the home and the school, between the
local public schools and the parish school, between the local community and the parish school, and between the local parish and other
parishes. In its administration, the pastor, associate priests, and princi-
pal(s) are *ex officio* members of the board. Ultimately the board is
responsible to the pastor and to the parish council; the chairman of the
school board is sometimes an *ex officio* member of the parish council. The
parish board's policy decisions are largely supportive and implementative
rather than creative. Its membership is not to be confined to the parents
of children in the parish school; is to be elected, not appointed; and
should be representative of the parish. The Rev. Olin J. Murdick saw
the origins of the parish school board in Chapter IV of the *Constitution on the Church* of Vatican II, which reminded that the "individual
layman, by reason of the knowledge, competence, or outstanding ability
which he may enjoy, is permitted and sometimes even obliged to express
his opinion on things which concern the good of the Church." In the
same booklet, Murdick added:

> Certainly the Catholic school "concerns the good of the Church" and the
> present critical status of Catholic education represents the proper occasion for

the Church to set up an effective "agency" or structure for the development of Catholic school policy. A parish board of education is such a structure.[69]

We must remark parenthetically here that in addition to diocesan and parish lay boards of education, area boards are also coming into being. The area concept is comparable to that of the public school system losing its provincial idea of strictly local control and having mergers. The earlier provincial concept is no longer adequate in either case, making the area board concept realistic. The NCEA reported: "It is hoped that the very operation of Parish Boards will lead the entire community to recognize the need to abandon the parochial structure in education and replace it with an area structure."[70] Inasmuch as the area board will need an executive officer, the need will be thus created for an area or regional superintendent. Area boards and their superintendents "take on new significance as the state and federal governments increase their involvement in education."[71] As school funds from the government increase, more detailed reporting will be necessary; the present size of the diocesan systems makes this difficult if not impossible.

On the elementary school level, after the peak years of 1963-64 the quantitative trends were downward. Table II shows those trends for the immediately succeeding years of 1965 to 1968.

TABLE II

CATHOLIC SCHOOL OPENINGS AND CLOSINGS
1965-1968 *

|  | OPENINGS | | CLOSINGS | |
| --- | --- | --- | --- | --- |
|  | ELEMENTARY | SECONDARY | ELEMENTARY | SECONDARY |
| *Inner City* | *48* | *21* | *182* | *85* |
| *Suburbs* | *72* | *31* | *144* | *37* |
| *Rural* | *27* | *8* | *194* | *95* |
| TOTALS | *147* | *60* | *520* | *217* |

* NCEA Research Office, as reported in *The Tablet* (Aug. 29, 1968), p. 1.

Several points are not shown in the table. First, the quantitative decrease is expected to continue until around 1980, when a levelling-off is foreseen. Secondly, during the period immediately after the peak many schools were becoming regional; a typical example of this process was St. Mary's School, Philadelphia, Pennsylvania, which, as one of the first parochial schools in the country, was typical of the early parochial school—small, individualistic, and local—and which today is serving several "inner city" parishes. Thirdly, closings will first affect small and isolated schools, as religious communities withdraw their sisters first from locations remote from their motherhouses.

There are many other reasons why Catholic educators have been and will be more and more interested in the inner city education of the urban poor. Former United States Commissioner of Education Francis Keppel pointed out that "the public school is less a 'common' school for all classes of children than the ideals of democracy suggest," and that whereas in the aftermath of Sputnik the brilliant student received much attention, "society has come to realize that there was another area of need, and a more tragic waste, in this plight of the poor." [72] This is one of the most urgent moral problems in our society. Unless these children are given such a means of escape as a good education, they will be trapped for their entire lives—by their background, by their color, and by their draining poverty. One cannot be a Christian and remain disinterested. To help in the educational task involved, Catholic education has facilities already available in slum areas: faculties, administrators, specialists, materials, and buildings. Catholic teachers have been living in the midst of inner city persons and will continue to do so, thus becoming a part of them and available to them outside of regular hours. Catholic teachers also have been and will continue to be available over longer periods not subject to the rapid turnover currently characteristic of public school teachers in the inner city; also because of their dedication they have the potential of being among the better qualified, another factor not presently characteristic of public schools. The genuine respect, admiration, and love of inner city residents of all religious persuasions for the priests, nuns, and brothers who work among them is an observable, and almost tangible, quality. Finally, Catholic educators are relatively free of the political vulnerability of public schools. In this connection the archdiocese of Chicago, for example, has already adopted a "guest" program whereby students from the inner city are bused to suburban Catholic schools and adopted by a family which provides a hot lunch. There are similar programs in other dioceses, with the encouragement of state and federal officials who feel that because Catholic schools cut across school district and city boundaries they can more easily experiment.

*How* they are proceeding does not necessarily represent a transplantation of traditional modes. In 1968 NCEA convened a meeting of those interested in developing model programs to upgrade the education of the disadvantaged. Attending were the National Education Association's Task Force on Urban Education, the Bishops' Task Force, the Division of Elementary and Secondary Education of the United States Catholic Conference, the National Catholic Conference for Interracial Justice, the Jesuit Educational Association, the Conference of Major Superiors of Men, and the Conference of Major Superiors of Women. Out of the planning has arisen a close cooperation with other schools and educators. Among the programs of experimentation that are ongoing and beginning to delineate a picture of the future are the formation of nonprofit corporations for the purposes of education in the inner city and common efforts within the same school regardless of religious affiliation. With regard to the former, the formation of nonprofit corporations, a serious proposal to this effect was made at the first regional United States chapter of the Christian Brothers, held at Lockport, Illinois, in August 1968 concerning the Brothers' schools.[73] With regard to the latter, common efforts disregarding religious affiliation, most of these experimental programs have religious education available for those who wish it. All of these programs are open to any and every kind of experimentation and are independent of local parish control where necessary or desirable. All of this leads many who have been used to the traditional modes to concerned questioning of the degree to which these and other nominally Catholic schools will continue to remain religious.[74]

As for the future of Catholic middle-level education, past and present trends would seem to indicate that it is on the increase. Although for a variety of reasons explained in this study junior high schools never "took" in Catholic education, now the trend for Catholic middle-level education is more and more to begin at puberty. As some grades of elementary-level education are phased out, again for a variety of reasons mostly administrative and financial, it is possible to increase the number of classes dedicated to middle-level education. In the nerve-wracking and conscience-shattering procedure of having to make decisions for the survival and/or rejection of various levels of education, Catholic educators, for good or for ill, impressed by society's dangers particularly to the adolescent, have stressed the importance of this middle level. Look for Catholic middle-level institutions of education to remain constant at worst, and perhaps to increase.

In higher education, in four-year degree-granting private institutions undergraduate enrollment is expected to have over the next few years an average annual increase of about 2.5 per cent. On the faculty and administrative level, the trend is toward increasing lay facilities and decreasing clerical control. This does not necessarily, however, mean the salvation of Catholic institutions. Some studies in allied fields have findings that might spill over into Catholic education. One of them—*College and University Trustees: Their Backgrounds, Roles, and Educational Attitudes* [75]—sampled the opinions of more than five thousand trustees at 536 of the nation's colleges and universities. Its findings indicated that the trustees who are governing the nation's institutions of higher learning are predominantly white, wealthy Protestants with political leanings to conservative Republicanism. Because faculty members are considered quite different, the study therefore anticipates a continuation of difficulties.

In the area of religious training on the higher educational level, the trend of the future is for theological teaching centers to be set up near secular college campuses. Students enroll in the secular college, using its laboratories, gymnasium, and parking lots. Theology is taken care of off the secular campus. Such institutions as Harvard and the Graduate Theological Union in California already utilize these procedures. A problem could be present in whether a state university under these conditions would give credit for courses provided by the theological teaching center.

With all levels of educational experimentation and innovation, many feel that Catholic education has not done enough in the past. Michael O'Neill, for example, has observed:

Though there are encouraging recent efforts—such as the Montessori schools found on some Catholic campuses, the Webster College teacher education and curriculum development programs, and Fordham's work in teaching movies as one of the creative arts—it still seems that Catholic education generally is making little impact on the field of educational innovation.[76]

Nevertheless, Myron Lieberman holds that Catholic education should be more free here than public education, which is constrained mainly because of political vulnerability: superintendents of education feel that their positions are so precarious that they cannot afford to overrule objections, even unrepresentative ones, from parents and communities. O'Neill agrees with Lieberman's observation, stating that "Catholic education could use its relatively free and independent status to improve the quality not only of its own schools but that of public schools as well."[77]

And experimentation and innovation are continuing at a much more rapid pace in Catholic education today than in the past, boding well for the future. For example, talented teachers are engaging in team teaching with a specialist teaching upwards of 100 students, ordinary teachers leading smaller discussion groups, and assistants or clerks handling more routine chores. Because of individual differences revealed by group testing, some experimentation is being conducted in class enrichment. Programmed instruction, with both programmed texts and teaching machines, are changing traditional teaching habits, especially in educational objectives involving skills, habits, and factual knowledge. Language laboratories, with their sound recorders, microphones, and earphones, are one specialized form of this. Analogous is educational television, effective use of which is today helping the over-all planning of programs in such forward dioceses as Detroit, Miami, and Brooklyn, and tomorrow will spread to many others. Much experimentation is being carried on with grant money: the Carnegie Foundation is funding a Data Bank on studies being done, basic data, etc., in order to get a feel of how professional Catholic education is; in 1966-67, the Ford Foundation sponsored the Practicum in Educational Problems (PEP), in which a team headed by Dr. Melvin P. Heller and the Rev. C. Albert Koob helped to identify leaders in innovation in secondary schools; also in 1966-67, the Minnesota Mining and Manufacturing Company tried to identify the best elementary and secondary school teachers, study their creative techniques, and explain them to others, in what was called the Impact Teacher Program; [78] and in 1967-68, Ford sponsored the Long Range Financial Planning Project, in which Dr. Anthony Seidl worked with a staff in six large dioceses to initiate better methods for financial planning. Some experimentation breaks more violently with tradition, such as one event that took place during the 1968-69 school year: Sister Irenaeus of the Sisters of St. Joseph of Carondolet, Missouri, at that time became Miss Maureen Mashek, an English teacher at Central High School, Minneapolis, Minnesota, the first nun to be hired by the city's public school system. She had taught English, speech and drama for fourteen years, and in the public school taught sophomore English.[79]

## Conclusion

To an extent Chesterton's dictum on Christianity is true also of real Catholic education—that it has not been tried and found wanting, but has been found difficult and never tried. John Courtney Murray, S.J., said as much:

The failures of Christian education are normally multitudinous, sometimes scandalous, and occasionally spectacular. Even at its best a school is only a school, one milieu of influence among others, able to do only what a school can do. What matters in every age is the idea that inspires its efforts, and the integrity of these efforts.[80]

No matter what happens to Catholic education at this point—whether it goes under as some predict or whether it is appreciated by all the citizenry to the extent of greater support—certain it is that we will never again see the like of its past. In the decade of the 1970's—1976 to be exact—we celebrate the bicentenary of the independence of this Republic. Not too long after that, we will commemorate the bimillenary of the Christian era. By these dates, it is to be hoped that the reflected-upon ideals of Christian democracy will be fully operative in the direction of Catholic education. Meanwhile—as well as thereafter—we fervently hope that Catholic education, and also public education with which it is a partner in a great work, will take to heart the words that Pope Leo XIII spoke on January 10, 1890: "Where the right education of youth is concerned, no amount of trouble or labor can be undertaken, how great soever, but that even greater still may not be called for." [81]

# Notes

## Introduction

1 *Webster's Third New International Dictionary*, 1961, p. 1073f.
2 Oscar Handlin, and others, *Harvard Guide to American History* (Cambridge, Mass.: The Belknap Press of Harvard University, 1963), p. 8.
3 Henri-Irénée Marrou, *The Meaning of History* (Baltimore, Md.: Helicon Press, Inc., 1966), p. 228.
4 Pope Leo XIII, *Saepenumero*, Par. 93, in the Benedictine Monks of Solesmes, *Papal Teachings: Education* (New York: St. Paul Editions, 1960), p. 94. Cicero had written (*De oratore*, 11, 15 [62]), "The first duty of history is to say nothing false, the second being to dare to say all that is true" (Ne quid falsi dicere audeat, deinde ne quid veri non audeat.).
5 *Webster's Dictionary of Synonyms*, p. 825.
6 Psalm 118:96. This verse is appropriately a part of the Entrance Hymn of the "Me expectaverunt" Mass for Holy Virgin Martyrs.
7 See Roger J. Connole, *A Study of the Concept of Integration in Present-Day Curriculum Making* (Washington, D.C.: The Catholic University of America Press, 1937); George Johnson, *The Curriculum of the Catholic Elementary School* (Washington, D.C.: The Catholic University of America Press, 1919); Michael J. McKeough (ed.), *The Curriculum of the Catholic Secondary School: Proceedings of the Workshop on the Curriculum of the Catholic Secondary School Conducted at the Catholic University of America from June 11 to June 22, 1948* (Washington, D.C.: The Catholic University of America Press, 1949).
8 T. S. Eliot, "Burnt Norton," *Four Quartets* in *The Complete Poems and Plays* (New York: Harcourt, Brace and Co., 1943), p. 117.
9 John D. Hicks, *The American Nation* (Cambridge, Mass.: The Riverside Press, 1941), p. xi.
10 R. G. Collingwood, *The Idea of History* (London: Oxford University Press [Reprint], 1967), p. 10.
11 Marrou, *The Meaning of History*, p. 282
12 Edgar W. Knight, "In Darkness Dwells," *School and Society*, LXV, No. 1692 (May 31, 1947), 388. Knight's title is part of the sentence, "In darkness dwells the people which knows its annals not," which is found on front of the William L. Clements Memorial Library at the University of Michigan.
13 John Lancaster Spalding, "Normal Schools for Catholics," *The Catholic World*, LI, No. 301 (April, 1890), 96.
14 *Ibid.*, p. 94.
15 "Report of the Sub-Committee on the Training of Teachers," *Journal of the Proceedings and Addresses of the National Education Association*, Session of the year 1895, held at Colorado (St. Paul, Minn.: National Education Association, 1895).
16 John Gilmary Shea, *The History of the Catholic Church in the United States* (4 vols; New York: John G. Shea, 1886–1892); Peter Guilday, *A History of the Councils of Baltimore (1791–1884)* (New York: The Macmillan Company, 1932); John Tracy Ellis, *American Catholicism* (2nd ed.; Chicago: University of Chicago Press, 1969); Thomas T. McAvoy,

*History of the Catholic Church in the United States* (Notre Dame, Ind.: University of Notre Dame Press, 1969).

[17] Neil G. McCluskey, *Catholic Education in America: A Documentary History* (New York: Teachers College, Columbia University, 1964); *Woodstock Letters: A Record of Current Events and Historical Notes Connected with the Colleges and Missions of the Society of Jesus in North and South America* (Woodstock, Md., 1872); Henry Foley, *Records of the English Province of the Society of Jesus* (London: Burns and Oates, 1877–1883); *Acta et decreta concilii plenarii Baltimorensis tertii* (Baltimore: Typis Joannis Murphy Sociorum, 1886); Peter Guilday (ed.), *National Pastorals of the American Hierarchy, 1792–1919* (Washington, D.C.: National Catholic Welfare Council, 1923); Raphael M. Huber (ed.), *Our Bishops Speak: National Pastorals and Annual Statements of the Hierarchy of the United States, 1919–1951* (Milwaukee: Bruce Publishing Co., 1952); Henry F. Brownson (ed.), *The Works of Orestes A. Brownson* (20 vols; Detroit: Thorndike, Nourse, 1882–1887); Orestes A. Brownson, *Brownson's Quarterly Review* (New York); John England, *The Works of the Right Reverend John England* (7 vols; Cleveland: Arthur H. Clark Co., 1908); John Ireland, *The Church and Modern Society: Lectures and Addresses* (2 vols; Chicago: D. H. McBride and Co., 1897); John Lancaster Spalding, *Education and the Future of Religion* (Notre Dame, Ind.: The Ave Maria Press, 1901); Spalding, *Means and Ends of Education* (Chicago: A. C. McClurg and Co., 1897); Thomas Bouquillon, *Education: To Whom Does It Belong?* (Baltimore: John Murphy and Co., 1892); Renée I. Holaind, *The Parent First* (New York: Benziger Brothers, 1891); Pius XI, *On the Christian Education of Youth* (New York: The America Press, 1936); and Walter M. Abbott and Joseph Callagher (eds.), *The Documents of Vatican II* (New York: Guild Press, etc., 1966).

[18] Thomas T. McAvoy, "Public Schools vs. Catholic Schools and James McMaster," *The Review of Politics*, XXVIII, No. 1 (January, 1966), 19-46; Francis P. Cassidy, "Catholic Education in the Third Plenary Council of Baltimore," *The Catholic Historical Review*, XXXIV, No. 1 (January, 1949); Henry J. Browne, "The American Parish School in the Last Half Century," *National Catholic Educational Association Bulletin*, L, No. 1 (August, 1953); James A. Burns, "The Development of Parish School Organization," *The Catholic Educational Review*, III, No. 5 (May, 1912); and William B. Ball, "The Constitutionality of the Inclusion of Church-Related Schools in Federal Aid to Education," *Georgetown Law Journal*, L (1961), 387-455.

[19] John Tracy Ellis, *John Lancaster Spalding* (Milwaukee: Bruce Publishing Co., 1961); Ellis, *The Life and Times of James Cardinal Gibbons* (2 vols; Milwaukee: Bruce Publishing Co., 1952); Sister M. Salesia Godecker, *Right Reverend Simon William Gabriel Bruté de Remur, First Bishop of Vincennes* (Washington, D.C.: The Catholic University of America Press, 1929); Annabelle M. Melville, *Elizabeth Bayley Seton, 1774–1821* (New York: Charles Scribner's Sons, 1951); Sister Mary Agnes McCann, *The History of Mother Seton's Daughters, the Sisters of Charity of Cincinnati, Ohio* (New York: Longmans, Green & Co., 1917); Anna B. McGill, *The Sisters of Charity of Nazareth, Kentucky* (New York: Encyclopedia Press, 1917); Louise Callan, *The Society of the Sacred Heart in North America* (New York: Longmans, Green and Co., 1937); Edward M. Connors, *Church-State Relationships in Edu-*

*cation in the State of New York* (Washington, D.C.: The Catholic University of America Press, 1951); William H. Jones, *The History of Catholic Education in the State of Colorado* (Washington, D.C.: The Catholic University of America Press, 1955); Sr. M. Salesia Godecker, *History of Catholic Education in Indiana: A Survey of the Schools, 1702–1925* (St. Meinrad, Ind.: St. Meinrad Abbey Press, 1926); Louis L. Walsh, *The Early Irish Catholic Schools of Lowell, Mass.* (Boston: Thomas A. Whalen & Co., 1901); *ibid., A Historical Sketch of the Growth of Catholic Parochial Schools in the Archdiocese of Boston* (Newton Highlands, Mass.: Press of St. John's Industrial Training School, 1901); George Johnson, *The Curriculum of the Catholic Elementary School* (Washington, D.C.: The Catholic University of America Press, 1919); Judah J. Harris, *The Treatment of Religion in Elementary School Social Studies Textbooks* (New York: Anti-Defamation League of B'nai B'rith, 1963); Sister Marie Léonore Fell, *The Foundations of Nativism in American Textbooks, 1783–1860* (Washington, D.C.: The Catholic University of America Press, 1941).

20 All three published in New York City by Benziger Brothers.

## Chapter I

1 Herbert Eugene Bolton, *Rim of Christendom* (New York: The Macmillan Company, 1936).

2 Fred Rippy, *Historical Evolution of Hispanic America* (New York: F. S. Crofts and Co., 1940), p. 64.

3 Herbert Eugene Bolton and Thomas Maitland Marshall, *The Colonization of North America: 1492–1783* (New York: The Macmillan Company, 1920), p. 22.

4 Herbert Eugene Bolton, *Wider Horizons of American History* (New York: D. Appleton-Century Company, 1939), pp. 98-100.

5 See Juan Escobar, *Vida del B. Sebastián de Aparicio* (Mexico City: Fr. Juan Escobar, 1958).

6 Juan Zumárraga, *Doctrina Breve* (Tenochtitlan, Mexico: privately printed, 1544), title page. Facsimile by the United States Catholic Historical Society, New York, 1928.

7 "El parecer de algunos señores sobre los indios" (*s.a., circa* 1516), *Colección de documentos inéditos relativos . . .* , VII, 11-12. Cited in Pius J. Barth, *Franciscan Education and the Social Order in Spanish North America (1502–1821)* (Chicago, Ill.: University of Chicago Press, 1945), p. 111.

8 In this connection, many archives and collections are valuable. In Spain, the important holdings would be the Archivo General de Indias, Sevilla (Archives of the Indies in Seville); el Escorial; and in Madrid, the National Library and the Instituto Hispánico. In Mexico, there are the archives of such Franciscan monasteries as Celaya, Guanaquato; Queretaro; and Mexico City; also, the Biblioteca Nacional de México. In the United States, good sources are the Peabody Museum at Harvard University; Yale University Library; Bancroft Library, University of California at Berkeley; San Francisco Public Library; St. Louis University Library; Newberry Library, University of Chicago; Coronado Library, University of New Mexico; Ritch Collection, Huntington Library, San Marino, Calif. There are also such primary source materials as José

Arlegui, *Crónica de la Provincia de N. S. P. S. Francisco* (Mexico City: Cumplido, 1851, reprinted from original 1737 ed.), which presents a chronicle of the Franciscan province in Mexico from 1546 to 1736. The first Franciscan monastery in northern Mexico was Zacatecas; from this provincial headquarters, the Franciscans proceeded to Durango, El Paso del Norte, and on to Santa Fe.

[9] Zephyrin Englehardt, O.F.M., "Florida's First Bishop, Rt. Rev. Juan Juarez, O.F.M.," *The Catholic Historical Review*, IV (1919), 479-485.

[10] Herbert Eugene Bolton, *Spanish Borderlands* (New Haven: Yale University Press, 1921), pp. 158-160.

[11] John Gilmary Shea, *The History of the Catholic Church in the United States* (New York: John G. Shea, 1886–1892), I, 152.

[12] Maynard Geiger, *The Franciscan Conquest of Florida, 1573–1618* (Washington, D.C.: The Catholic University of America Press, 1937), pp. 265-268. The existence of a "golden age" has, however, been put in serious doubt by Charles W. Spellman, "The 'Golden Age' of the Florida Missions, 1632–1674," *The Catholic Historical Review*, LI (October, 1965), 354-372.

[13] Juan de las Cabezas de Altamirano, O.P., "Carta del obispo de Cuba para su majestad," St. Augustine, Florida, June 24, 1606, *Archivo General de Indias*, Sevilla, Simancas, Eclesiástico, Audiencia de Santo Domingo, ed. Rev. V. F. O'Daniel, O.P., printed in the *Catholic Historical Review*, II (1917), 450-459.

[14] Diego Davila, "Relación presentada a s. m. en su consejo de Indias, de la visita pastoral qui hizo a las provincias de la Florida el obispo de Cuba 26 de junio, 1606," *Archivo General de Indias*, Sevilla, Est. 54-5-20, Simancas, Eclesiástico, Audiencia de Santo Domingo. *Cartas y expedientes de personas eclesiasticas de la Florida vistas en al consejo desde el año de 1573 a 1700.* As photostated from the Woodbury Lowery Papers, MMS Florida, 1605–1607, Vol. V, "The Spanish Settlements within the Present Limits of the United States," in the Department of Manuscripts, Library of Congress, Washington, D.C.

[15] "Relación presentada a su majestad en su consejo de Indias, 26 de junio de 1606," *Archivo General de Indias*, Section V, Audiencia de Santo Domingo, leg, 235. Cited in John Tate Lanning, *The Spanish Missions of Georgia* (Chapel Hill, North Carolina: The University of North Carolina Press, 1935), p. 152. See also Michael V. Gannon, *The Cross in the Sand: The Early Catholic Church in Florida, 1513–1870* (Gainesville: University of Florida Press, 1965), p. 46.

[16] Verne E. Chatelain, *The Defenses of Spanish Florida 1566–1763* (Washington, D.C.: Carnegie Institute of Washington, Publication 511), p. 25.

[17] Shea, *History of Catholic Church*, pp. 469-470.

[18] "Reglamento para las peculiares obligaciones de el presidio de San Augustín de la Florida," Mexico, April 8, 1753, *Regulations for Religious Teachers*, fol. 362 (V.) 6. MSS of Vice-Royal Papers in the John Carter Brown Library, Providence, Rhode Island. Cited in Barth, *Franciscan Education and Social Order*, pp. 143-145.

[19] Claude Vogel, *The Capuchins in French Louisiana 1722–1766* (Washington, D.C.: The Catholic University of America Press, 1928), pp. 69-83.

[20] See France V. Scholes, *Church and State in New Mexico, 1610–1650* (Albuquerque: University of New Mexico Press, 1937); *ibid., Troublous Times in New Mexico, 1659–1670* (*ibid.*, 1942); and the same author's many articles in the *New Mexico Historical Review*.

[21] *The Memorial of Fray Alonso de Benavides,* trans. Mrs. Edward E. Ayer (Chicago: privately printed; 1916), p. 19. A better edition, however, is *Benavides' Memorial of 1630,* trans. Peter P. Forrestal, introduction and notes Cyprian J. Lynch (Washington, D.C.: Academy of American Franciscan History, 1954). For the second memorial, see *Fray Alonso de Benavides' Revised Memorial of 1634,* with numerous supplementary documents, elaborately annotated by Frederick Webb Hodge, George P. Hammon, and Agapito Rey (Albuquerque: University of New Mexico Press, 1945).

[22] Ayer, *Memorial of Fray Alonso de Benavides,* p. 20.

[23] John Tracy Ellis, *Catholics in Colonial America* (Baltimore: Helicon Press, 1965), p. 58.

[24] See Eleanor B. Adams and Fray Angelico Chavez, *The Missions of New Mexico, 1776* (Albuquerque, N.M.: University of New Mexico Press, 1956), and Fray Angelico Chavez, *Archives of the Archdiocese of Santa Fe 1678–1900* (Washington, D.C.: Academy of American Franciscan History, 1957). In the latter, see especially "Education" and "Catechetics" in the index.

[25] See Charles Wilson Hackett, *Richardo's Treatise on the Limits of Louisiana and Texas* (4 vols.; Austin, Tex.: The University of Texas Press, 1931).

[26] Catholic Archives of Texas, North Congress and 16th Streets, Austin, Texas, under "Texas, Education in General (Catholic)."

[27] Thomas P. O'Rourke, *The Franciscan Missions in Texas* (Washington, D.C.: The Catholic University of America Press, 1927), p. 22.

[28] Catholic Archives of Texas.

[29] Marion A. Habig. O.F.M., *San Antonio's Mission San José* (San Antonio: The Naylor Co., 1968), p. 61.

[30] *Diary of a Visit of Inspection of the Texas Missions made by Fray Gaspar José de Solis in the Year 1767–1768,* trans. Margaret Kenney Kress in *The Southwestern Historical Quarterly,* (Austin, Tex.: The Texas State Historical Association, 1932), XXXV (July, 1931 to April, 1932), 42-43.

[31] *Ibid.,* pp. 39-40.

[32] *Ibid.,* p. 40.

[33] Bartholomé Garcia, O.F.M., *Manual para administrar los santos sacramentos* (Mexico: Imprenta de dos herederos de Doña Maria de Rivera, 1760). Lenox Collection, New York Public Library, cited in Barth, *Franciscan Education and Social Order,* p. 150.

[34] James A. Burns, *The Catholic School System in the United States* (New York: Benziger Brothers, 1908), p. 48.

For further information on Texas, the classic work is Carlos E. Castañeda, *Our Catholic Heritage in Texas 1519–1936* (7 vols.; Austin, Tex.: Von Boeckmann-Jones Co., 1936–1958). Among lesser works on limited areas are Robert Neal Blake, "A History of the Catholic Church in El Paso" (unpublished M.A. thesis, Graduate School of the College of Mines and Metallurgy [now the University of Texas], El Paso, 1948), esp. Chapter VI, pp. 124-152, entitled "Catholic Schools in El Paso"; David Murray McCleskey, "The Attitude of the Sixteenth-Century Spanish Missionaries toward the Religion of the Indians of New Spain" (unpublished M.A. thesis, University of Texas [Austin], 1959); Sr. M. Beatrice Jaks, "The Educational Work of the Congregation of the Incarnate Word and Blessed Sacrament of San Antonio" (unpublished M.Ed. thesis, University of Texas [Austin], 1951; and Genevieve Tarlton Alexander, "An Historical Analysis of Catholic Educational Integration in Texas" (unpublished M.A. thesis, University of Texas [Austin],

1959). There are also very interesting archival holdings. Sr. M. Claude Lane, O.P., "Catholic Archives of Texas: History and Preliminary Inventory" (unpublished M.A. thesis, University of Texas, 1961, and mimeographed by the Dominican Sisters in Houston, Tex., in 1961) records, in addition to the indications of its title, holdings that are original and those which have been copied. Among the holdings of these archives, which unfortunately have not yet been sufficiently catalogued, is a very interesting and personal account of a missionary college and seminary for Franciscans founded by Fr. Anton Margil: Fr. Juan Domingo Arricivita, *Crónica Seráfica y Apostólica del Colegio De Propaganda Fide de la Santa Cruz de Querétaro en la Nueva España* (Mexico: Por Don Felipe de Juniga y Ontiveros, 1792). The Alamo Research Library at San Antonio contains interesting first editions and limited editions. There is, for example, Fray Juan Augustín Morfi, *History of Texas 1673–1779*, Carlos E. Castañeda trans. and annotator (2 parts; Albuquerque, N.M.: The Quivira Society, 1935. Critical ed., limited to 500 copies). Morfi, who died in 1783, gathered thousands of documents on the Franciscans in the Southwest and even in the Philippine Islands, and "though avowedly undertaken for the purpose of defending the work of the missionaries, the account is fair on the whole" (p. 36). The Alamo also contains *Documentos para la Historia Ecclesiástica y Civil de la Provincia de Texas o Nuevas Philipinas 1720– 1779* (Madrid: Ediciones Jose Porrua Turanzas, 1961. Limited edition). This is Vol. XII of Colección Chimalistac de Libros y Documentos Acerca de la Nueva España, and contains maps, dispatches, representations of the religious personnel to the government, petitions, requests, and letters. Also, Nicholas de Lafora, *Relación del Viaje que Hizo a Los Presidios Internos Situados en la Frontera de la America Septentrional Perteneciente al Rey de España*, ed. Vito Alessio Robles (Mexico, D.F.: Editorial Pedro Robredo, 1939); and Vargas Rea (ed.), *Razón de la provincia de Texas* (Mexico: Biblioteca de Historiadores Mexicanos, 1955; limited edition of 75 copies), which gives very brief accounts of various aspects of the spiritual and temporal condition of the missions from the documents of a visit by Raymundo Luna Olmedo to Texas in 1765. There are also the Laredo Archives in St. Mary's University, San Antonio; the Bexar Archives, Barker Historical Center, University of Texas, Austin (for which see Chester V. Kielman, *The University of Texas Archives* [Austin: University of Texas Press, 1967] and *ibid.*, *Guide to the Microfilm Edition of the Bexar Archives, 1717– 1803* [Austin: National Historical Publications Commission, 1967]); and the Nacogdoches Archives, State Library, Austin. A consortium of 14 U. S. universities are currently microfilming relevant Mexican archival holdings.

[35] Edward W. Heusinger, *Early Explorations and Mission Establishments in Texas* (San Antonio: The Naylor Co., 1936), p. 176.

[36] Zephyrin Englehardt, O.F.M., *The Franciscans in Arizona* (Harbor Springs, Mich.: The Holy Childhood Indian School Press, 1899), p. 25.

[37] Hubert Howe Bancroft, *Arizona and New Mexico (1530–1888)* (*History of the Pacific States of North America*, Vol. XII [San Francisco: The Historic Company Publishers, 1888]), p. 352. Bancroft lamented the futility of his research in bringing anything to light on the Arizona missions. He despaired that no chronologic narrative of early Arizona annals could be found with even approximate accuracy and complete-

ness (*ibid.*, p. 372). Bolton gave new meaning to the history of the Spanish American colonies by his "adventures in archives and on the trail" (Bolton, *Rim of Christendom*, p. vii). In 1915 he discovered the "Favores celestiales," a manuscript history in Kino's own hand in which the Jesuit described his work and that of his associates in Pimeria Alta.

[38] *Kino's Historical Memoir of Pimeria Alta, A Contemporary Account of the Beginnings of California, Sonora, and Arizona by Father Eusebio Francisco Kino, S.J., 1683–1711*, ed. H. E. Bolton (Cleveland: Arthur H. Clark Co., 1919), II, 234-253. Cited in Ellis, *Documents of American Catholic History* (Milwaukee, Wis.: Bruce Publishing Co., 1962), p. 26.

[39] Bolton, *Rim of Christendom*, p. 589.

[40] For primary sources here see, for example, Ernest J. Burrus (ed., trans., and notes), *Kino Reports to Headquarters. Correspondence of Eusebio F. Kino, S.J., from New Spain with Rome, 1682–1704* (Rome: Institutum Historicum Societatis Jesu, 1954); also Ernest J. Burrus (ed.), *Kino's Plan for the Development of Pimeria Alta, Arizona and Upper California: A Report to the Mexican Viceroy (1703)* (Tucson, Arizona: Arizona's Pioneers' Historical Society, 1961). In the former work, footnote 2 on page 14 states that the King granted 300 *pesos* annually to missionaries (350 for some), plus 35 *pesos* annually for a mission school.

[41] See Arthur L. Campa, "The Churchmen and the Indian Languages of New Spain," *Hispanic American Historical Review*, XI, No. 4 (November, 1931), 542-550.

[42] Englehardt, *The Missions and Missionaries of California* in Vol. I, *Lower California* (4 vols.; San Francisco, Calif.: The James S. Barry Co., 1908–1915), p. 74. The latest work on this subject is Francis J. Weber, "The United States versus Mexico: The Final Settlement of the Pious Fund of the Californias," *Southern California Quarterly*, LI, No. 2 (June, 1969), 97-152, which as of this writing is due to be published in book form.

[43] Hubert Howe Bancroft, *History of the North Mexican States and Texas* (San Francisco: A. L. Bancroft & Co., 1884–1889), I, 279.

[44] Englehardt, *The Missions and Missionaries of California*, I, 124.

[45] Francis J. Weber, *The Missions and Missionaries of Baja California* (Los Angeles: Dawson's Book Shop, 1968), p. 30.

[46] Englehardt, *The Missions and Missionaries of California*, III, 515. Englehardt calls the secularization of the missions of California the "crime of the nineteenth century." The mission despoilers called it "secularization," but it was a brutal confiscation which resulted in the annihilation or dispersion of the Indian converts. See also Gerald Geary, *The Secularization of the California Missions (1810–1946)* (Washington, D.C.: The Catholic University of America Press, 1934).

[47] John A. Berger, *The Franciscan Missions of California* (New York: G. P. Putnam's Sons, 1941), p. vii.

[48] Englehardt, *The Missions and Missionaries of California*, II, 272-273.

[49] In addition to the sources cited, see Zephyrin Englehardt, "Catholic Educational Work in Early California," *National Catholic Educational Association Bulletin*, XV, No. 1 (November, 1918), 359-374; James A. Burns, "Early Mission Schools of the Franciscans," *Catholic University Bulletin*, XIII (January, 1907), 33-43; William E. Nicholl, "The Early Mission Schools of California," *Pomona College Bulletin* (May, 1937), pp. 14-19; Daniel D. McGarry, "Educational Methods of the Fran-

ciscans in Spanish California," *The Americas*, VI, No. 3 (January, 1950), 335-338; James T. Booth, *Church Educational Problems in the State of California* (Rome: Catholic Book Agency, 1960), for which there is an excellent review by Francis J. Weber in *The Americas*, XIX, No. 4 (April, 1963), 439-441; Mark J. Hurley, *Church-State Relationships in Education in California* (Washington: The Catholic University of America Press, 1948); William E. North, *Catholic Education in Southern California* (Washington, D.C.: The Catholic University of America Press, 1936); Francis J. Weber, *Documents of California Catholic History (1784–1963)* (Los Angeles: Dawson's Book Shop, 1965); *ibid.*, *A Historical Sketch of Pioneer Catholicism in the Californias: Missions and Missionaries* (Van Nuys, Calif.: California Historical Publications, 1961). More listings may be found in Francis J. Weber, *A Select Guide to California Catholic History* (Los Angeles: Westernlore Press, 1966).

[50] Oliver Perry Chitwood, *A History of Colonial America* (New York: Harper & Bros., 1948), p. 32.

[51] David Hawke, *The Colonial Experience* (New York: The Bobbs-Merrill Co., 1966), p. 27.

[52] Sr. Mary Doris Mulvey, *French Catholic Missionaries in the Present United States* (Washington, D.C.: The Catholic University of America Press, 1936), pp. 7-12.

[53] Ellis, *Catholics in Colonial America*, p. 132.

[54] "Letter from Father Sébastien Rasles, Missionary of the Society of Jesus in New France to Monsieur his Brother," trans. Reuben Gold Thwaites in *Jesuit Relations and Allied Documents*, LXVII (Cleveland: Burrows Brothers, 1896–1901), 229.

[55] "Letter from Father de la Chasse, Superior-General of the Missions in New France, to Father ***, of the same Society," *Jesuit Relations*, LXVII, 241 and 237.

[56] Other reliable secondary sources for this history of the Catholic Church in Maine, in addition to those cited elsewhere in this work, are: Sr. Mary Céleste Léger, *The Catholic Indian Missions in Maine (1611–1820)* (Washington, D.C.: The Catholic University of America, 1929); William L. Lucey, *The Catholic Church in Maine* (Francestown, N.H.: Marshall Jones Co., 1957); and Annabelle M. Melville, *Jean Lefèbvre de Cheverus, 1768–1836* (Milwaukee: Bruce Publishing Co., 1958), esp. Ch. IV, "Missionary to Maine."

[57] *Jesuit Relations*, LXIV, 241-245.

[58] Mulvey, *French Catholic Missionaries*, pp. 42-43.

[59] Claude Dablon, S.J., to Mon Révérend Père, Québec, August 29, 1690, cited in Pierre Margry, *Découvertes et Etablissements des Français dans l'Ouest et dans le Sud de l'Amérique Septentrionale, 1614–1698* (Paris, 1879), I, 63.

[60] *Jesuit Relations*, LXX, 235-237, 281.

[61] Gibault to Briand, Vincennes, June 6, 1786. "Correspondence between the Abbe Gibault and Bishop Briand 1768–1788," from the Archdiocesan Archives at Quebec, with notes by the Abbe Lionel St. George Lundsay. *Records of the American Catholic Historical Society of Philadelphia*, XX (1909), 426.

[62] Margry, *Découvertes*, V, 154-156.

[63] George Paré, *The Catholic Church in Detroit, 1701–1888* (Detroit: The Gabriel Richard Press, 1951), pp. 194-195. (The Journals of Chausse-

gros de Léry are published in the *Report of the Archivist of the Province of Quebec for 1926–27* [Quebec, 1927], pp. 334-504; *Report . . . 1927–28*, pp. 335-439. This quotation from Chaussegnos is taken from the second *Report*, p. 416).

[64] *Jesuit Relations*, LXX, 9.

[65] Ellis, *Catholics in Colonial America*, pp. 198-200; J. G. Rosengarten, *French Colonists and Exiles in the United States* (Philadelphia, J. B. Lippincott Company, 1907), pp. 35-36; Roger Baudier, *The Catholic Church in Louisiana* (New Orleans: A. W. Hyatt Stationery Mfg. Co., Lt., 1939), pp. 13-18.

[66] Marcel Giraud, *Historie de la Louisiane Française* (3 vols.; Paris: Presses Universitaires de France, 1953, 1958, and 1966), II, 122. In this monumental work, Giraud says on the page cited: "Il va de soi que cet échelon inférieur comporte une majorité d'illetrés. L'instruction des enfants est elle-même singulièrement négligée. Aucun ordre religieux n'a encore entrepris d'oeuvre éducatrice dans la colonie, et rien n'indique que les missionaries s'adonnent à cette tâche. Seule, Françoise de Boisrenaud, la 'conductrice' des émigrantes de 1704, dispense un enseignement élémentaire aux 'filles d'habitants,' tout en faisant l'instruction des Indiennes destinées au baptême. Mais elle est âgée, 'accablée d'infirmités,' et, ayant longtemps appartenu à l'abbaye de Fontevrault, à la communauté de l'Annonciation, et vécu dans l'entourage de Mme. de Montespan, elle en éprouve trop de fierté pour supporter le séjour dans la colonie. Elle solicite en conséquence l'autorisation de regagner la France."

[67] Pierre F. X. de Charlevoix, S.J., *Journal d'un Voyage fait par ordre du Roi dans l'Amérique septentrionale, addressé à Madame la Duchesse de Lesdiguières* (Paris, 1744), VI, 192. Written in New Orleans, January 10, 1722.

[68] *Ibid.*, p. 193.

[69] Claude L. Vogel, O.F.M. Cap., *The Capuchins in French Louisiana (1722–1766)* (Washington, D.C.: The Catholic University of America Press, 1935); Martin Luther Riley, "The Development of Education in Louisiana Prior to Statehood," *The Louisiana Historical Quarterly*, Vol. XIX, No. 7 (Aug., 1936). (The materials in this article were collected as a byproduct of the research in preparation for a doctoral dissertation at the Louisiana State University, June, 1936); Lena Lopez Emanuel, "Education in Colonial Louisiana" (unpublished master's thesis, Tulane University, New Orleans, Louisiana, 1931).

[70] Baudier, *The Catholic Church in Louisiana*, p. 103.

[71] Henry Churchill Semple (ed.), *The Ursulines in New Orleans, 1727–1925* (New York: P. J. Kenedy & Sons, 1925), p. 10. The "Supplement" section of this volume is composed of archival material from the Ursuline Convent in New Orleans. One finds there, for example, on pp. 167-176, the "Treaty of the Company of the Indies with the Ursulines" and the "Commission of Louis XV, King of France, in Favor of the Ursulines." Definitive on the early history of the Ursulines in New Orleans, however, is the lengthy work of Sr. Jane Frances Heaney, "A Century of Pioneering: History of the Ursuline Nuns in New Orleans (1727–1827)" (unpublished Ph.D. dissertation, St. Louis University, 1949). Sr. Jane Frances used archival material in this country from the New Orleans convent (which archives, as well as a museum, are now at the Ursuline Academy, 2635 State St., New Orleans, La., 70118,

although the old convent, now a state museum, remains in the Vieux Carré), and from Baltimore; in Quebec, Canada; and in Santiago de Cuba. At Ursuline Academy there is also a museum containing artifacts, early texts, examples of needlework, corner stones, and handwritten books.

[72] Sr. Marie Magdeleine Hachard de St. Stanislaus' letter to her father, October 27, 1727, in Semple, *Ursulines in New Orleans*, p. 184. An account of the voyage of the Ursulines from France to New Orleans is contained in Sister's diary, which is really a series of letters to her parents in France. The diary was published as *Relation du Voyage des Dames Religieuses Ursulines* (Paris: Maisonneuve et Cie., 1872), of which two copies are extant, as far as is ascertainable—one at Ursuline Academy in New Orleans, the other in Paris. There is, however, a complete English translation in a supplement to: Anonymous, *The Ursulines in New Orleans and Our Lady of Prompt Succor: A Record of Two Centuries, 1727–1925* (New York: P. J. Kenedy & Sons, 1925), 177-282.

[73] Ellis, *Catholics in Colonial America*, p. 249.

[74] Shea, *History of Catholic Church*, I, 571.

[75] *Réglemens des Religieuses Ursulines de la Congregation de Paris, divisée en trois livres* (Paris: chez Louis Josse, Rue St. Jacques à la Couronne d'Epines, 1705). Typewritten copy forwarded to the author from the Archives of the Ursuline Convent, New Orleans, La.

[76] *Constitutions of the Ursuline Order*, New Orleans. Cited in Sr. Catharine Frances, S.S.J., *The Convent School of French Origin in the United States, 1727 to 1843* (Philadelphia: The University of Philadelphia, 1936), p. 24.

[77] *Réglemens*. Livre Premier: *Des Pensionnaires* (Chapitre I–Chapitre XV); Seconde Partie: *Des Ecolières Externes* (Chapitre I–Chapitre V).

[78] The dutes of the *dixainières* are given special place in the Ursuline Rule: pp. 31-32.

[79] Baudier, *The Catholic Church in Louisiana*, p. 323. Also not to be overlooked on Louisiana are Jean Delanglez, S.J., *The French Jesuits in Lower Louisiana 1700–1763* (Washington, D.C.: The Catholic University of America, 1935), and Charles Edwards O'Neill, S.J., *Church and State in French Colonial Louisiana, Policy and Politics to 1732* (New Haven: Yale University Press, 1966).

[80] Charles M. Andrews, *The Colonial Period of American History* (New Haven: Yale University Press, 1936), II, 278-289.

[81] *Ibid.*, p. 291.

[82] John Tracy Ellis, *American Catholicism* (2nd ed.; Chicago: University of Chicago Press, 1969), p. 25.

[83] William T. Russell, *Maryland: The Land of Sanctuary* (Baltimore: J. H. Furst Co., 1908), pp. 518-529.

[84] William H. Browne (ed.), *The Archives of Maryland* (67 vols.; Baltimore: Maryland Historical Society, 1883–1956), XXVI, 340-341.

[85] Thomas Bacon, *Laws of Maryland: 1638–1763* (Annapolis: Jonas Green, 1765), Art. 1715, Chap. XXXIX.

[86] *Archives of Maryland*, L, 198-204.

Russell in *Maryland: The Land of Sanctuary*, pp. 412-414, summarizes the Committee of Grievances' report, which was signed by Episcopalian ministers. As it touches on education, we read that a Papist kept a school for the education of youth within six miles of Annapolis. This fact was apparently reported by one Benjamin Wright, who, as the report states, held that "a certain James Elston, a papist, keeps a school near his house which is about 7 miles from Annapolis; that he has heard Elston say that he would educate such of the people's children in the Romish religion as approved of it, and such as did not he would educate in the Protestant way. That he (Elston) told him (Wright) that he was a Papist and went to Mass." The charge was also made that papists sent their children into foreign Popish seminaries for education—to St. Omer's—and that they influenced Protestants to do the same.

87 J. Thomas Scharf, *History of Maryland* (3 vols.; Baltimore: John P. Piet, 1879), II, 511.

88 Neil G. McCluskey, *Catholic Education in America: A Documentary History* (Richmond, Virginia: William Byrd Press, Inc., 1964), p. 3.

89 Ellis, *Catholics in Colonial America,* p. 349.

90 J. Moss Ives, *The Ark and the Dove* (New York: Longmans, Green and Co., 1936), p. 110.

Bernard U. Campbell, in "Sketches of the Early Missions in Maryland," *United States Catholic Historical Magazine,* VII, No. 10 (October, 1887), 529, claims that two lay brothers accompanied the expedition. He writes: "With the first colonists of Maryland, came two Jesuit priests, Fathers Andrew White and John Altham; and two lay brothers, or temporal coadjutors, as they are designated, of the same society, whose names were John Knowles and Thomas Gervase.

91 Henry Foley, *Records of the English Province of the Society of Jesus* (7 vols.; London: Burns and Oates, 1877–1883), III, 334.

92 *Ibid.;* Russell, *Maryland: The Land of Sanctuary,* p. 93.

93 Thomas Hughes, *The History of the Society of Jesus in North America* (2 vols.; New York: Longmans, Green and Co., 1908), I, p. 346.

94 *Maryland Will Book,* Hall of Records, Annapolis, Liber I, pp. 46-48. Cited in Leo Joseph McCormick, *Church-State Relationships in Education in Maryland* (Washington, D.C.: The Catholic University of America Press, 1942), p. 6.

95 *Ibid.* Guilday claims that in Colonial Maryland "Catholic interest in elementary education is evidenced by no less than forty-two legacies for school purposes left between 1650 and 1685." Peter Guilday, *The Life and Times of John Carroll* (New York: The Encyclopedia Press, 1922), p. 9.

96 Edwin W. Beitzell, *The Jesuit Missions of St. Mary's County, Maryland* (privately printed by photo offset, 1959), p. 28. Available in Jesuit Provincial Archives, Baltimore.

97 Henry S. Spalding, *Catholic Colonial Maryland* (Milwaukee: The Bruce Publishing Co., 1931), p. 133.

98 *Maryland Will Book,* Liber I, p. 183.

99 Foley, *Records of the English Province,* XII, 593.

100 William T. Treacy, *Old Catholic Maryland* (Swedesboro, New Jersey: St. Joseph's Rectory, 1889), pp. 72-73.

101 Hughes, *History of Society of Jesus in North America,* II, p. 136.

102 Shea, *History of the Catholic Church,* I, 345.

Bernard C. Steiner, *History of Education in Maryland,* Circular of Information, No. 2, United States Bureau of Education, 1894, p. 16, claims that the Jesuits established a preparatory and elementary school at Newtown which was directed successively by two lay brothers, Ralph Crouch and Gregory Tuberville, until the death of the latter in 1684.

103 Beitzell, *The Jesuit Missions of St. Mary's County,* p. 65, indicates that

under the Rev. Peter Atwood, S.J., who was stationed at Newtown
from 1730 to 1734, the circulating library—one of the earliest in
Maryland—flourished, books being lent to non-Catholics as well as
Catholics. This, he claims, is but one example of extensively-used libraries at Jesuit residences at the time, and cites "one ffaire Library
of Books," valued at 150 pounds, lost during the Ingle invasion in
1645 by the Rev. Thomas Copley, S.J., apparently the first missionary
to serve at Newtown.

At Newtown today, there is the old church (St. Francis Xavier),
manor house, other outlying buildings, and archeological remains. The
church is still in use, but unfortunately, for lack of money, the manor
house is in bad repair and the archeological remains unexplored—see the
*Catholic Standard*, Weekly Newspaper of the Archdiocese of Washington, June 26, 1969, p. 11.

[104] *Archives of Maryland*, XIX, 49.

[105] Elihu S. Riley, *A History of the General Assembly of Maryland* (Baltimore: Nunn and Co., 1905), p. 96.

[106] Bacon, *Laws of Maryland*, Art. 1696, Sec. 2, Chap. 17.

[107] Elsie Worthington Clews, *Educational Legislation and Administration of
the Colonial Governments* (New York: The Macmillan Company,
1899), pp. 423-429.

[108] William Kilty, *Laws of Maryland* (2 vols.; Annapolis: Frederick Green,
1779), Art. 1723, Sec. 2, Chap. 19, cited in McCormick, *Church-State
Relationships in Education in Maryland*, p. 26.

[109] Richard J. Purcell, "Education and Irish Teachers in Maryland," *The
Catholic Educational Review*, XXXII (March, 1934), 152.

[110] Guilday, *Life and Times of John Carroll*, p. 15.

[111] Edward I. Devitt, S.J., "Bohemia," *Records of the American Catholic Historical Society*, Vol. XXIII, No. 2 (June, 1913), 98.

[112] Spalding, *Catholic Colonial Maryland*, p. 138.

[113] Hughes, *History of Society of Jesus in North America*, Text II, 123, 520.

[114] Fragment of the Account Book of Bohemia Manor School, Georgetown
University Archives. Reproduced in Devitt, "Bohemia," p. 107.
    According to Shea, *History of Catholic Church*, II, p. 27, and Guil-
day, *Life and Times of John Carroll*, p. 14, John Carroll entered Bohemia when he was twelve years of age, and this date coincides with
the year 1747.

[115] Devitt, "Bohemia," p. 105.

[116] Shea, *History of Catholic Church in America*, I, 405.

[117] Hughes, *History of Society of Jesus*, Text II, 520; Shea, *History of Catholic
Church in America*, I, 404.

[118] Guilday, *Life and Times of John Carroll*, p. 12.

[119] Scharf, *History of Maryland*, I, 192.

[120] Beitzell, *The Jesuit Missions of St. Mary's County*, p. 61.

[121] *Maryland Gazette*, Dec. 13, 1764. Cited in McCormick, *Church-State Relationships in Education in Maryland*, p. 32.

[122] Oliver Perry Chitwood, *A History of Colonial America* (New York: Harper
and Brothers, 1958), pp. 250-251.

[123] Wayland F. Dunaway, *A History of Pennsylvania* (New York: Prentice-
Hall, Inc., 1948), p. 24.

[124] Ellis, *Catholics in Colonial America*, p. 370.

[125] Theodore Thayer, *Pennsylvania Politics and the Growth of Democracy,
1740–1776* (Harrisburg: Pennsylvania Historical and Museum Com-

mission, 1953), p. 1.

[126] Pennsylvania Archives, Colonial Records, Series I, p. 144, as found in Jesuit Provincial Archives, Baltimore.

[127] "Rev. Joseph Greaton, S.J.: Planter of the Faith in Philadelphia and Founder of Old St. Joseph's Chapel," *American Catholic Historical Researches*, XVI, No. 2 (April, 1899), 72-74.

[128] Joseph L. Kirlin, *Catholicity in Philadelphia* (Philadelphia: John J. McVey, 1909), pp. 23-29.

In May, 1689, Jacob Leisler, a Calvinist, overthrew the government of New York. The Catholic governor, Thomas Dongan, was hunted like a criminal. A reign of terror for Catholics began. The Church of England became the Established Church and the Jesuits were forced to flee. (Ellis, *American Catholicism*, p. 31).

[129] Martin I. J. Griffin, *William Penn: The Friend of Catholics* (Philadelphia: Press of the I.C.B.U. Journal, 1886), p. 7.

Griffin was the first vice president of the American Catholic Historical Society of Pennsylvania. He read his paper, "William Penn, The Friend of Catholics," before the Friends' Evening Hour Club of Germantown, Pennsylvania, December 7, 1885, and before the American Catholic Historical Society on February 1, 1886. It was then published in pamphlet form.

[130] *Ibid.* For further early history of St. Joseph's in Willing's Alley, see *Catalogus Provinciae Marylandiae Societatis Jesu* (Georgetown: Langtree and O'Sullivan, annually in early nineteenth century), and *Woodstock Letters*, vol. 3, pp. 94-111.

[131] John Gilmary Shea, *The Catholic Church in Colonial Days* (New York: John G. Shea, 1886), pp. 386-387.

[132] *Woodstock Letters: A Record of Current Events and Historical Notes Connected with the Colleges and Missions of the Society of Jesus in North and South America* (Woodstock, Md.: 1872), VII, 830.

[133] Foley, *Records of the English Province*, XLV, 18of.

[134] "The Story of Old Saint Mary's Church, Lancaster," *Diocese of Harrisburg, 1863–1968*, centennial volume published by the Diocese of Harrisburg, 1968, p. 15.

[135] James Pyle Wickersham, *A History of Education in Pennsylvania* (Lancaster, Pa.: Inquirer Publishing Co., 1886), p. 115.

[136] Foley, *Records of the English Province*, XLV, 18.

[137] Jesuit Provincial Archives, Baltimore, citing Perry, *Historical Collections, Pennsylvania*, p. 216.

[138] *Woodstock Letters*, V, 203, 313.

[139] "Archives of Old St. Joseph's—Philadelphia—List of Deeds and Documents from 1689 to 1851," *American Catholic Historical Researches*, XIV, No. 4 (October, 1897), 169.

[140] "Rev. Ferdinand Farmer, S.J., of Philadelphia, 1758–86," *American Catholic Historical Researches*, XIV, No. 1 (January, 1897), 2-3; Shea, *The Catholic Church in Colonial Days*, p. 448.

The University of Pennsylvania held a unique position among early American colleges as a nondenominational school.

[141] Jesuit Provincial Archives, Baltimore.

[142] Hugh L. Lamb, "Catholicism in Philadelphia," *Records of the American Catholic Historical Society*, LXII, No. 1 (March, 1951), 6-7.

[143] Kirlin, *Catholicity in Philadelphia*, p. 110.

[144] *Ibid.*

[145] "Minute Book of St. Mary's Church, Philadelphia, Pa., 1782–1811," *Records of the American Catholic Historical Society,* IV (September, 1893), p. 255. The Minute Book is reproduced in its entirety in the above volume, pp. 253-443.

[146] *Ibid.,* p. 254.

[147] *Ibid.,* p. 268.

[148] "Report of the Overseers of the Poor on the Condition of the Exiled Acadians in Philadelphia," *American Catholic Historical Researches,* XVIII, No. 3 (July, 1901), 141.

[149] Herbert Ingram Priestley, *The Coming of the White Man, 1492–1848* (New York: The Macmillan Company, 1950), pp. 158, 159.

[150] H. E. Bolton, "The Mission as a Frontier Institution in the Spanish American Colonies," *The American Historical Review,* XXIII (October, 1917), 57.

[151] *Ibid.,* p. 61.

[152] *Jesuit Relations,* XII, 123.

[153] Reuben Gold Thwaites (ed.), *Louis Hennepin, A New Discovery of a Vast Country in America* (Chicago: A. C. McClure & Co., 1903), p. 462. Also cited in Ellis, *Documents of American Catholic History,* pp. 76-77.

[154] *Jesuit Relations,* LXVI, 231.

[155] *Ibid.,* p. 241.

[156] *Ibid.,* p. 3.

[157] *Ibid.,* p. 117.

[158] *Ibid.,* p. 243.

[159] *Jesuit Relations,* VIII, 83.

[160] Priestley, *Coming of the White Man,* p. 246.

[161] *Ibid.,* p. 247.

[162] Ellis, *Catholics in Colonial America,* p. 179.

[163] John Francis McDermott and others (eds.), *Old Cahokia: A Narrative and Documents Illustrating the First Century of its History* (St. Louis: St. Louis Historical Documents Foundation, 1949), pp. 68-69, 72.

[164] John Francis McDermott, "The Library of Father Gibault," *Mid-America,* New Series, VI (May, 1935), 274.

[165] William Bennett Munroe, *Crusaders of New France* (New Haven: Yale University Press, 1920), pp. 131-132.

[166] Ellis, *Catholics in Colonial America,* p. 132.
    The five principal areas wherein the Spanish missions occupied a major role in American colonial history, and to which Ellis refers were: Florida, New Mexico, Texas, Arizona and California.

[167] Ellis, *American Catholicism,* p. 11.

[168] Herbert Eugene Bolton, "The Missions in the Spanish American Colonies," *The American Historical Review,* XXIII, No. 1 (Oct., 1917), 51.

[169] Thomas Hughes, "Educational Convoys to Europe in the Olden Time," *American Ecclesiastical Review,* XXIX (January, 1903), 25.

[170] Ellis, *American Catholicism,* p. 40.

## Chapter II

[1] See Charles H. Metzger, *Catholics and the American Revolution: A Study in Religious Climate* (Chicago: Loyola University Press, 1962).

[2] Isaac T. Hecker, *The Catholic Church in the United States* (New York: The Catholic Publication Society Company, 1879), pp. 13-15.

3 Peter Guilday, *The Life and Times of John Carroll, Archbishop of Baltimore, 1735–1815* (New York: Encyclopedia Press, 1922), p. 223. Carroll sent to Rome a report on the state of religion in the United States in 1785. Guilday claimed that it is among the most treasured first-hand sources for the history of the Church in this country. In *The Life and Times of John Carroll,* Guilday printed in full the *Relation of the State of Religion in the United States* from a photostat copy from the Propaganda Archives. (The rough draft is in the Baltimore Cathedral Archives, Case 9 A-F1.) Carroll had obtained his information on the Catholic population through correspondence with his fellow priests between November, 1784, and March 1, 1785.

4 John Tracy Ellis, *American Catholicism* (Chicago: University of Chicago Press, 1955), p. 53.

5 This would remain true for some time to come, even though there is some evidence—e.g. in Wilfrid Parsons, S.J., *Early Catholic Americana: A List of Books and Other Works by Catholic Authors in the United States, 1729–1830* (New York: The Macmillan Company, 1939)—to show that the number of publications would increase.

6 Cited in Ellis, *Documents of American Catholic History* (Milwaukee: Bruce Publishing Company, 1955), p. 150. *The First American Report to Propaganda on Catholicism in the United States, March 1, 1785.* The translation is taken from John Gilmary Shea, *History of the Catholic Church in the United States* (New York: John G. Shea, 1888), II, pp. 257-261.

7 Peter Guilday (ed.), *The National Pastorals of the American Hierarchy, 1792–1919* (Washington, D.C.: National Catholic Welfare Conference, 1923), p. 3.

8 Shea, *History of the Catholic Church,* pp. 399-400.

9 Guilday, *The Life and Times of John Carroll,* p. 115. See also Anson Phelps Stokes, *Church and State in the United States* (3 vols.; New York: Harper and Bros., 1950).

10 Ray Allen Billington, *The Protestant Crusade, 1800–1860* (New York: Columbia University Press, 1943).

11 Gerald Shaughnessy, S.M., *Has the Immigrant Kept the Faith?* (New York: The Macmillan Company, 1925), p. 114.

12 Philip Gleason, "Immigration and American Catholic Intellectual Life," *The Review of Politics,* XXVI (April, 1964), 150-159.

13 Shaughnessy, *Has the Immigrant Kept the Faith?* pp. 61-62.

14 Jerome E. Diffley, *Catholic Reaction to American Public Education* (Notre Dame, Indiana: University of Notre Dame, 1959), pp. 209-210.

15 Guilday, *The Life and Times of John Carroll,* p. 227.

16 "Archbishop Maréchal's Report, 1818," cited in Ellis, *Documents of American Catholic History,* p. 208. The fifty-two priests "have come from various nations, namely, Italians 1, Germans 3, English 4, Belgians 7, American 12, Irish 11, and French 14."

17 See Guilday, *The Life and Times of John Carroll,* p. 567, and Shea, *History of the Catholic Church,* II, 386. The bishops appointed for these Sees were: for Boston, the Rt. Rev. John Cheverus; for New York, the Rt. Rev. Luke Concanen, O.P.; for Philadelphia, the Rt. Rev. Michael Egan, O.F.M.; for Bardstown, the Rt. Rev. Benedict Joseph Flaget, S.S. Concanen was consecrated in Rome upon appointment to the bishopric but never did return to New York. Napoleon had enforced his Continental Blockade and had imprisoned Pope Pius VII. Concanen died

two years after his consecration. Archbishop Carroll sent Anthony Kohlmann, S.J., as administrator to the diocese of New York.

[18] Francis T. Furey, "Our Debt to France," *American Catholic Historical Society*, I, No. 2 (June, 1892), 8.

[19] Guilday (ed.), *National Pastorals of the American Hierarchy, 1792–1919*,
p. 4.

[20] Letter of the First Council of Baltimore to Pope Pius VIII, October 24,
1829. Quoted from Shea, *History of the Catholic Church*, III, 417-418.

[21] Shea, *History of Georgetown College: Memorial of the First Centenary* (New
York: Published for the College by P. F. Collier, 1891), p. 9.

[22] Thomas Hughes, S.J., *The History of the Society of Jesus in North America,
Colonial and Federal Documents* (New York: Longmans, Green & Co.,
1910), I, Part II, 665-666.

[23] *The Laity's Directory*, 1822, p. 84.

[24] John M. Daley, S.J., *Georgetown University: Origin and Early Years* (Washington, D.C.: Georgetown University Press, 1957), p. 220.

[25] *The Laity's Directory*, 1822, pp. 84-85.

[26] *Prospectus of Georgetown College, 1798*. Georgetown University Archives,
62.9.

[27] *Prospectus of Georgetown College, 1814*. Georgetown University Archives,
62.10.

[28] Daley, *Georgetown University*, p. 221.

[29] *Ibid.*, pp. 221-222.

[30] *Prospectus of Georgetown College, 1820*. Georgetown University Archives,
62.10.

[31] *Regulations of 1829*. Georgetown University Archives, 1.3.

[32] *Order of Time for Georgetown Students, 1831*, MS, Georgetown University
Archives, 1.5 This order of time came into effect from January 1, 1831.

[33] *Prospectus*, May 1, 1814, Georgetown University Archives, 62.10.

[34] *Reminiscences of the Reverend Francis Barnum, S.J.*, p. 31. Georgetown
University Archives, 222.4.

[35] Shea in his *History of Georgetown College* devotes pp. 82-89 to a commentary on the *Ratio Studiorum*. One paragraph, in particular, sums
up the *Ratio's* aims:

> After the religious and moral training of the student, the chief aim
> of the method prescribed by the *Ratio* is twofold: first, to stimulate,
> develop and train the powers of the mind, so as to give their pos-
> sessor full and skilled control of their highest efficiency. The memory,
> the imagination and fancy, the understanding, the reflective and
> reasoning powers are all in turn exercised and disciplined. The sec-
> ondary purpose is to impart to the student such knowledge as will
> secure to him an intelligent mastery of all the fundamental lines of
> mental culture, and will constitute a firm basis for highly specialized
> training in any branch he may afterwards choose to adopt.

[36] *Ibid.*, p. 89.

[37] The sixty-six students of 1791 would grow by 1968 to 7,479 in the College
of Arts and Sciences, Graduate School, Medical and Dental Schools,
Law School, School of Foreign Service, School of Nursing, School of
Languages and Linguistics, and School of Business Administration.
(*Register of Faculties and Students, 1967–1968*, [Washington, D.C.:
Georgetown University]).

[38] Lloyd P. McDonald, *The Seminary Movement in the United States: Projects,
Foundations and Early Development, 1784–1833* (Washington: The
Catholic University of America Press, 1927), pp. 13-14.

[39] *Memorial Volume, Centenary of St. Mary's Seminary of St. Sulpice* (Baltimore, 1891), p. 8.

[40] Joseph William Ruane, *The Beginnings of the Society of St. Sulpice in the United States (1791–1829)* (Washington, D.C.: The Catholic University of America, 1935), p. 43.

[41] *The Laity's Directory*, 1822, p. 86.

[42] St. Mary's College, *Foundation, Government, Assemblies. Written over 4th June 1818*, pp. 2-3.

[43] *Rules for Day Scholars, 1809.* St. Mary's Seminary Archives.

[44] *The Rule. St. Mary's College, Baltimore.* St. Mary's Seminary Archives.

[45] *Ibid.*

[46] *Ibid.*

[47] Charles G. Herbermann, *The Sulpicians in the United States* (New York: The Encyclopedia Press, 1916), p. 122.

[48] *The Rule.* St. Mary's Seminary Archives.

[49] Ruane, *Society of St. Sulpice*, p. 141.

[50] *Mount Saint Mary's College Catalogue 1900–1901* (Baltimore: Press of the Sun Printing Co., 1901), p. 51.

[51] *Mount Saint Mary's College and Seminary 1808–1958* (Emmitsburg, Md.: Mt. St. Mary's, 1958), p. 14.

[52] F. X. McSweeney, *The Story of the Mountain* (2 vols.; Emmitsburg, Md.: 1911), I, 232.

[53] *The Rule of Mt. St. Mary's College, 1810.* Mt. St. Mary's Archives.

[54] *Day Book of Mt. St. Mary's College, 1811.* Mt. St. Mary's Archives.

[55] *Diary of William Seton, 1809.* Mt. St. Mary's Archives.

[56] *College Account for 1822.* Mt. St. Mary's Archives.

[57] *The Laity's Directory*, 1822, p. 89. The historical resume prepared by the college for its Sesquicentennial Year of 1958 spanned fifteen decades of scholarly work and attributed Mount St. Mary's success to its past: see *Mount St. Mary's College and Seminary 1808–1959: A Glorious History of One Hundred Fifty Years*, p. 63.

[58] Adrian M. Dupuis and Robert C. Craig, *American Education: Its Origins and Issues* (Milwaukee: The Bruce Publishing Co., 1963), p. 229.

[59] George Parsons Lathrop, *A Story of Courage: Annals of the Georgetown Convent of the Visitation* (Boston: Houghton-Mifflin Company, 1895), p. 150.

[60] Archives of the Georgetown Visitation Convent.

[61] *Ibid.* Original document intact.

[62] *The Laity's Directory*, 1836, p. 137.

[63] The esteem in which the Georgetown Visitation Academy was held is shown by the following letter, written October 13, 1833, by the Governor of Michigan, Steven Mason, to his two sisters, who were then attending Mrs. Willard's Seminary at Troy, N.Y., urging their attendance at the school of the Poor Clares in Detroit and offering as a recommendation in its favor its comparable standing with the Visitation Academy in Georgetown:

> In the event of your returning I think you would find St. Clare Seminary a school sufficiently good for all your purposes. The institution is thought well of, and the instructresses are said to be as well qualified for their station as any females in the country. Indeed I think that the school if properly managed will be second to none west of Troy. Of course I do not expect that you could find any institution equal to the one you are at, but I do think that for girls who are anxious to learn, that as much useful knowledge could be

obtained at this institution as at any other. It is conducted precisely
after the Catholic Female Seminary in the District of Columbia,
where you recollect your father spoke of sending you to school. The
school in Georgetown is said not to be surpassed if equalled by
Mrs. Willard's.

(Sr. M. Rosalita, *Education in Detroit Prior to 1850* [Lansing: Michigan Historical Commission, 1928], p. 364.)

⁶⁴ Hélène de Barbarey Bailly, *Elizabeth Seton*, trans. and adapted from the
6th French edition by the Rev. Joseph B. Code (New York: The Macmillan Company, 1927), p. 196.
⁶⁵ Annabelle Melville, *John Carroll of Baltimore* (New York: Charles Scribner's
Sons, 1955), p. 182.
⁶⁶ Agnes Sadlier, *Elizabeth Seton* (New York: D. & J. Sadlier and Company,
1905), p. 98.
⁶⁷ *Ibid.*, p. 116. This is considered the first American community because it
was the first to be formally organized, although the "Pious Ladies" had
initiated their work in Georgetown at an earlier date.
⁶⁸ Guilday, *The Life and Times of John Carroll*, p. 497.
⁶⁹ Charles I. White, *Life of Mrs. Elizabeth A. Seton* (New York: P. J. Kenedy),
p. 384. See also Sr. Mary Regis Hoare, *Virgin Soil: Mother Seton from
a Different Point of View* (Boston, Mass.: The Christopher Publishing
House, 1942), p. 49; Annabelle M. Melville, *Elizabeth Bayley Seton,
1774–1821* (New York: Charles Scribner's Sons, 1951); and Joseph
I. Dirvin, *Mrs. Seton, Foundress of the American Sisters of Charity*
(New York: Farrar, Straus and Cudahy, 1962).
⁷⁰ Copied from the Archives of the Motherhouse at Emmitsburg.
⁷¹ *Regulations of the School at St. Joseph's, 1812.* Archives of St. Joseph's
Central House, Emmitsburg.
⁷² Report Card in Museum, St. Joseph's Central House, Emmitsburg, Md.
Report Card of N_____, April 29, 1826.
⁷³ *The Catholic Almanac, 1822.*
⁷⁴ Council Book 1813–1829, Secretariat, St. Joseph's Central House, Emmitsburg, p. 38.
⁷⁵ Archives, St. Joseph's Central House, Mother Seton, V.
⁷⁶ J. Thomas Scharf, *The History of Maryland* (Baltimore: John B. Prett, 1879),
p. 374.
⁷⁷ *The Laity's Directory*, 1822, p. 83.
⁷⁸ *Catholic Almanac* for 1835 and 1838 as cited in James A. Burns, *The
Principles, Origin and Establishment of the Catholic School System in
the United States*, p. 254.
⁷⁹ *American Catholic Historical Researches*, XIII, 82.
⁸⁰ George Paré, *The Catholic Church in Detroit, 1701–1888* (Detroit: The
Gabriel Richard Press, 1951), p. 265.
⁸¹ Letter to Bishop Carroll from Father Michael Levadoux, September 10,
1796. Baltimore Chancery Archives, 4E2. Also quoted in Paré, p. 270.
⁸² Stanley Pargellis, *Father Gabriel Richard* (Detroit: Wayne University Press,
1950; Lewis Cass Lecture before the Detroit Historical Society, June 7,
1948, marking the 150th anniversary of Richard's arrival in Detroit),
p. 9.
⁸³ Frank B. Woodford and Albert Hyma, *Gabriel Richard* (Detroit: Wayne
State University Press, 1958), p. 42.
⁸⁴ Bishop Joseph-Octave Plessis, who traveled extensively throughout his vast
diocese, kept a journal, written in the third person, and preserved in

the Quebec Chancery Archives. There is a copy of the portion relating to Detroit in the Burton Historical Collection in the Public Library in Detroit. Quoted in Paré, *Catholic Church in Detroit*, p. 317.

[85] *Ibid.*

[86] Pargellis, *Father Gabriel Richard*, pp. 18-19.

[87] Pargellis, *Gabriel Richard, Second Founder of Detroit* (Detroit: Catholic Study Club, 1958), p. 11.

[88] Pargellis, *Father Gabriel Richard*, pp. 14, 17.

[89] Chase S. Osborn, *Detroit's Own Father Gabriel Richard* (Detroit: Van Antwerp Library, 1936), p. 5.

[90] Registres de la Paroisse de Ste. Anne, Detroit, 1704-1848. Quoted in Sr. M. Rosalita, *Education in Detroit Prior to 1850*, p. 20.

[91] *Historical Records and Studies*, VIII, 70.

[92] Letter of Richard to Carroll, dated March 14, 1805, in Baltimore Chancery Archives, 7C8.

[93] *American Catholic Historical Researches*, XV, 87. In 1822 Elizabeth Williams entered a religious house in Montreal. Two years later she was back in Detroit, and in 1825 we find her teaching for Father Déjean at Mt. Clemens. When he was transferred to L'Arbre Croche in 1829, she took charge of his Indian school. In 1837 she was in Detroit as the superintendent of the "French Female Charity School," a position which she held presumably until her death in 1843. Elizabeth Lyons likewise left Detroit, and entered the Ursuline Convent at New Orleans. On account of failing health she returned in 1824, and probably resumed her work for Father Richard. Four years after his death, she was still maintaining a private school in a residence which she owned. Angélique Campeau apparently remained in the service of Richard until 1830, when she accompanied Badin to the Potawatomi mission near Bertrand. She died in 1838, but the place of her death is uncertain. Monique Labadie was the only one of the four teachers who married, but the effect of her years of association with Richard was evident throughout her life. As the wife of Antoine Beaubien, one of the wealthiest French citizens of old Detroit, she became the most devoted patroness of Catholic education and charities in the city. (Paré, *Catholic Church in Detroit*, pp. 624-625.)

[94] Original in the Baltimore Chancery Archives. Quoted in Paré, p. 619.

[95] In the Burton Historical Collection, Detroit. Askin Papers, Vol. 457, 204. Quoted in Paré, p. 619.

[96] Original in the State Department at Lansing, Box 777. Quoted in Paré, pp. 621-622.

[97] The original of the "Outline," dated January 20, 1809, is in the Library of Congress.

[98] Sr. M. Rosalita, "The Spring Hill Indian School Correspondence," *Michigan History Magazine*, XIV (1930), 140.

[99] Letter of Richard to the President of the United States, dated October 12, 1810. There is a photostat copy of this letter in the Burton Historical Collection, Detroit. Quoted in Paré, *Catholic Church in Detroit*, pp. 311-312.

[100] Paré claims that the farm included the land running back from the river between Twentieth and Twenty-second Streets.

[101] No researcher seems to have seen any but the first issue of *The Michigan Essay*.

[102] Albert H. Greenly, *A Selective Bibliography of Important Books, Pamphlets*

*and Broadsides Relating to Michigan History* (Lunenberg, Vt.: The
Stinehour Press, 1958), p. 79f.

[103] The only extant copy known of the *Michigan Instructor* is in the Burton
Historical Collection, Detroit. The preface is quoted in Paré, *Catholic
Church in Detroit*, p. 678. Paré remarks that the phraseology and style
of the preface are unmistakably Richard's.

[104] Greenly, *A Selective Bibliography*, p. 80.

[105] Pons Augustin Alletz, *Les Ornemens de la Mémoire; ou les Traits Brillans
des Poètes François le Plus Célèbres; Avec des Dissertations sur chaque
Genre de Style, Pour perfectionner l'éducation de la Jeunesse* (Detroit:
A. Coxshaw, 1811). Albert H. Greenly, *A Bibliography of Father
Richard's Press in Detroit* (Ann Arbor: University of Michigan, 1955),
pp. 21-30, contains an extremely interesting translation into English of
the comments of Richard on the contents of this little book of old
French literary selections. Also, the reader will note in the bibliographi-
cal data that Richard did not use the name of his press, which was
frequently the case.

[106] Woodford and Hyma, *Gabriel Richard*, pp. 70-71.

[107] The original is in the Church Archives, Diocesan Chancery, Detroit, and a
copy, with a translation, may be found in the Burton Historical Collection, Detroit. Quoted in Sr. M. Rosalita, *Education in Detroit Prior
to 1850*, pp. 100-102.

[108] Paré states the Act was written by Judge Woodward. A draft in Woodward's handwriting is preserved in the University of Michigan Library.

[109] Pargellis, *Father Gabriel Richard*, pp. 21-22.

[110] Documents of the appointments may be found in the Detroit Chancery
Archives.

[111] The University of Ann Arbor in Michigan is a direct descendant of the
corporation of 1817. Paré, *Catholic Church in Detroit*, pp. 631-632.

[112] The Burton Historical Collection contains, in addition to the estate inventory, an abundance of primary and other source material on Richard,
plus photocopies of Detroit Archdiocesan Chancery archival holdings
(those at the Chancery being uncatalogued). There are, for example,
two boxes of "Gabriel Richard Papers" containing, in the form of
typewritten transcripts, photocopies, and microfilms of originals in the
Burton Collection or other repositories: correspondence; a memorandum
book (1792–1806); marriage certificates, deeds, and other papers relating to Richard's ministry at St. Anne's parish and Indian missions; his
scholarly activities with the University of Michigan and the Richard
press; his term in Congress; letters; biographical sketches; genealogical
material; papers on the slander suit of *Labadie* v. *Richard;* and Richard's will. There are also two boxes of Edward John Hickey Papers,
containing notes and drafts of writings on Richard by this authority.
There is one wallet of Joseph-Octave Plessis Papers, containing an
English translation of the Journal of the pastoral visitation of Mon-
seigneur Joseph-Octave Plessis, Bishop of Quebec, made June 19–July
8, 1816. There are books that issued from his press, as well as many
books on Richard. Among his publications, in addition to those already
mentioned, are *Fables choisies de La Fontaine* (Detroit: Printed by
A. Coxshaw, 1811); *La Journée du Chrétien, Sanctifiée par la Prière
et la Méditation* (Detroit: Printed by A. Coxshaw, 1811); M. Berquin,
*La Livre de famille ou Journal des enfans—The Family Book; or Chil-
dren's Journal, Consisting of Moral and Entertaining Stories, with*

*Instructive Conversations on those Subjects which daily occur in Nature and Society* (Detroit: Printed by Theophilus Mettez, 1812); *Neuvaine à l'honneur de St. François Xavier* . . . (Detroit: Printed by A. Coxshaw, 1811); Bishop Chalenor (*sic*), *The True Principles of a Catholic. To which is added, An Exposition of the Commandments* (Detroit: J. M. Miller, 1810); *Epitres et évangiles pour tous les dimanches et fêtes de l'année* (Detroit: Gabriel Richard Press, Printed by T. Mettez, 1812); Barthelemi Baudrand [?], *L'Ame pénitente ou le nouveau Pensez-y-bien* (Detroit: Gabriel Richard Press, Imprimé par Jacques M. Miller, 1809). Among those about Richard, in addition to those already mentioned, are: Norman E. Clarke, *The Richard Press, 1809–1823* (Detroit: Privately Printed Limited Edition of 100 copies, 1951); Andrew A. Polscher, *Father Richard: Notes on his Printing in Early Detroit* (Detroit Club of Printing House Craftsmen, n.d.g.); and Dolorita Mast, *Always the Priest: the Life of Gabriel Richard* (Baltimore: Helicon, 1965).

113 Sr. Mary Denis Marcelle, "Catholic Education in the Diocese of Louisville, 1812–1926" (unpublished Master's dissertation, The Catholic University of America, 1926).

114 Benjamin J. Webb, *The Centenary of Catholicity in Kentucky* (Louisville: Charles A. Rogers, 1884), p. 27. *The United States Catholic Miscellany* of Wednesday, Dec. 1, 1824, mentions the fact that about 20 Catholic families reached Kentucky in the year 1785.

115 Letter of Carroll to Badin, dated August 2, 1794. A copy of this letter is in the Nazareth Archives, Nazareth, Ky.

116 By agreement of certain of the more prominent emigrants, Whelan was to receive an annual salary of $280, and for this sum six heads of families bound themselves in writing. Whelan, not taking into account the poverty of his debtors, insisted upon their compliance with the letter of their bond, and when the money was not forthcoming he became indignant. (Webb, *Catholicity in Kentucky*, pp. 156-157.)

117 J. Herman Schauinger, *Cathedrals in the Wilderness* (Milwaukee: The Bruce Publishing Company, 1952), p. 14.

118 Baltimore Cathedral Archives, 8GB5.

119 Badin to Neale, Sept. 2, 1808. Baltimore Chancery Archives. Quoted in Schauinger, *Cathedrals in the Wilderness*, p. 29.

120 Quoted in James M. Graham, *Dominicans in Illinois* (Springfield, Illinois: Ed. F. Hartman Co., 1923), p. 14.

121 Camillus P. Maes, *The Life of Rev. Charles Nerinckx* (Cincinnati: Robert Clark & Co., 1880), p. 169.

122 Martin J. Spalding, *Sketches of the Early Catholic Missions of Kentucky, from their Commencement in 1787 to the Jubilee of 1826–7.* (Baltimore: John Murphy Co., 1844), p. 160.

123 From Flaget's *Relatio* sent to Rome under the date of April 10, 1815, we have the following authentic information regarding the state of Catholicity in the several divisions of his diocese. Kentucky counted some 10,000 Catholics with nineteen churches, fourteen of which were mere log chapels, seven built by Nerinckx. Ten priests counting the bishop were ministering to them. In the Seminary, which had been opened with three students brought from France, young boys had been admitted who had to be taught even reading and writing, "such (was) the great and almost barbaric ignorance of this district"; they were imbued with veneration for the Holy See. The two religious communi-

ties of women were progressing: Loretto had twelve nuns, and Nazareth ten. Although some of the churches had properties attached to them, they yielded no revenues, and some difficulty had arisen between the bishop and Fr. Badin regarding the ownership of ecclesiastical property. Tennessee counted twenty-five Catholic families destitute of every help of the Church, since they had been visited only once and years ago by Badin and Flaget himself. Many Catholics scattered in Ohio "had almost forgotten their religion." In Poste Vincennes, Ind., which had been his own charge twenty years before, there were some 130 families, mostly French, to whom a priest was sent twice a year. Illinois had three parishes for the 120 families, also mostly French, looked after by a very old priest, Donatien Olivier, and the Canadian priest, Fr. Savine. Detroit in Michigan had 1,500 souls attached to St. Ann's Church and in the charge of Fr. Gabriel Richard, to whom the parishioners faithfully paid tithes. In upper Louisiana, which belonged to the diocese of New Orleans, there were six parishes, but only one priest, a Trappist, Fr. Marie-Joseph Dunand. The Protestant sects were Presbyterians, Baptists, Methodists, and Quakers, and there were among them many ignorant people. Flaget ends his Report with the mention of numerous Indian tribes that had never been evangelized. Those barbarous nations, scattered as far as the Pacific, would offer a great field for the restored Society of Jesus. From Flaget's *Relatio*, given in Latin and English in the *Catholic Historical Review*, I, No. 3 (October, 1915), 305-310. See also the "Kentuckiana" collection donated to Bellarmine-Ursuline College, Louisville, Ky., by Rt. Rev. Msgr. Felix N. Pitt, from 1925 to 1968 superintendent of schools of the Louisville diocese; also, Brother Evan Enos, C.F.X., "A Study of the Development of Negro Education under Catholic Auspices in Kentucky" (unpublished Master's thesis, Boston College, 1951).

[124] It was not until August, 1812, that Flaget in his diary called the ladies of St. Charles "the Sisters." ("Bishop Flaget's Diary," *Records of the American Catholic Historical Society*, XXIX, 156-165.)

[125] Archives of the Loretto Academy, Nerinckx, Ky. These archives contain other interesting material. There is, for example, a copy of the Holy Rule in Nerinckx' own handwriting, covering 77 pages of a small copybook. These "Rules of the Society and School of Loretto" prescribe the smallest details for "The Little Society of the Friends of Mary under the Cross of Jesus" under such headings as dress, furniture, wills, punishments, visits, meals, silence, letter-writing, and manners. Under "Rules of the School," (pp. 25-28), Number One (p. 25) is: "No Denomination is refused, if willing to observe the Rules of the School." This Holy Rule was presented to the Sacred Propaganda at Rome on April 1, 1816. The subsequently published edition (London: Keating and Brown, 1820) did not incorporate the changes recommended for the Society by Rome and subsequently adopted.

Also, Sr. Matilda Barrett had begun composing a well-documented history of the Religious before she died on June 25, 1968. Her notes for Vol. I, from 1812 to 1890, comprise about 200 interesting pages preserved in the archives. They present background from Europe, the United States, and Kentucky; material on Nerinckx, such as his views on education, his entry on the missions, and his founding the Society; some "firsts" in the Society; the establishment of schools, teacher training; and prominent members.

Sr. Edwarda Ashe is at this writing continuing the work of putting the archives in order.

126 Martin J. Spalding, *Sketches of the Life, Times, and Character of the Rt. Rev. Benedict Joseph Flaget, First Bishop of Louisville* (Louisville, Ky.: Webb and Levering, 1852). See also Anna C. Minogue, *Loretto, Annals of the Century* (New York: The America Press, 1912), and Sister M. Celestine Casey and Sister M. Edmond Fern, *Loretto in the Rockies* (Denver, Colo.: Loretto Heights College, 1943).

127 Anna B. McGill, *The Sisters of Charity of Nazareth, Kentucky* (New York: Encyclopedia Press, 1917), pp. 19-20.

128 David to Bruté, July 12, 1813. Quoted in Schauinger, *Cathedrals in the Wilderness*, pp. 81-82. The first vow day of Mother Catherine and the other three Sisters was Feb. 2, 1816.

129 Dates of expansion during this period supplied by Sr. M. Ramona Mattingly, archivist at Nazareth Generalate, Ky., and author of *The Catholic Church on the Kentucky Frontier (1785–1812)* (Washington, D.C.: The Catholic University of America Press, 1936). Further information in "List of Branch Houses, When Opened, Closed," Nazareth Archives; Chapters 8, 11, and 14 of Sr. Columba Fox, *The Life of the Right Reverend John Baptist Mary David* (New York: The United States Catholic Historical Society, 1925); Sr. Mary Rosalia O'Leary, "The History of Catholic Education in Nelson County, 1805–1934" (Unpublished Master's thesis, University of Kentucky at Lexington, 1934); Sr. Berenice Greenwell, "Nazareth's Contribution to Education, 1812–1933" (Unpublished Ph.D. dissertation, Fordham University, 1933); Sr. Mary Loyola Graves, "A Subject Bibliography of the Works of the Sisters of Charity of Nazareth and A Bibliography of Works Containing Information about the Sisters of Charity of Nazareth," (unpublished Master's thesis, The Catholic University of America, 1954), which has a supplement in the Nazareth Archives updating it to 1960; Sr. Agnes Geraldine, "Educational Ideals of Jean Baptiste Marie David, S.S.," *The Messenger* (diocesan newspaper of Covington, Ky.), XIV, No. 7 (September 19, 1939), in Nazareth Archives, "Clippings," XXXV, 136; and Sister James Maria Spillane, *Kentucky Spring* (St. Meinrad, Ind.: Abbey Press, 1968), a historical novel of Mother Catherine Spalding and the Sisters of Charity of Nazareth, Ky., from 1812 to 1858, for high-school level.

130 All from the *Catholic Almanac*, 1833–1835.

131 Although the original intent had been to form a cloistered group enclosed from the world, the need for the education of young ladies in the area and the group's financial requirements brought about their beginning an academy. See Anna C. Minogue, *Pages from a Hundred Years of Dominican History* (New York: Frederick Pustet & Co., 1921), p. 43.

132 Webb, *Catholicity in Kentucky*, pp. 261, 263-264; also Spalding, *Sketches of Kentucky*, p. 106. For further information, see also Sr. Mary Damian Carty, O.P., "Educational Contribution of the Dominican Sisters of Saint Catharine, Kentucky 1823–1953" (unpublished master's thesis, De Paul University, 1955). A proposed history is now being written by Henry C. Mayer with the tentative title *Witnesses to the Light* and the envisioned publication date of 1972 for the 150th anniversary of the founding of the community. Unfortunately, archival holdings were destroyed by fire in 1904 (Minogue, *ibid.*, p. 186).

133 Quoted in Maes, *Rev. Charles Nerinckx*, p. 385.

134 Spalding, *Life of Bishop Flaget*, p. 297.

135 *Ibid.*

136 *Ibid.*, p. 34.

137 *Ibid.*, p. 47.

138 The *Bulletin of Kentucky Department of Education* for July, 1914, VII, No. 4, 303, gives further information on St. Joseph's College of Bardstown.

139 Flaget to Maréchal, Archives of Baltimore. Quoted in Sr. Columba Fox, *The Life of the Right Reverend John Baptist Mary David (1761–1841)* (New York: The United States Catholic Historical Society, 1925), p. 94.

140 Webb, *Catholicity in Kentucky*, p. 278.

141 Spalding, *Life of Bishop Flaget*, p. 299.

142 Webb, *Catholicity in Kentucky*, p. 341.

143 *Ibid.*, p. 342.

144 *Abridgement of the Debates of Congress, From 1789–1856* (New York: D. Appleton and Co., 1860), XI, 639.

145 Webb, *Catholicity in Kentucky*, pp. 282-283.

146 *Bulletin of Kentucky Department of Education*, July, 1914, p. 317.

147 Spalding, *Life of Bishop Flaget*, p. 301.

148 Maes, *Rev. Charles Nerinckx*, p. 390. In a letter of David to Bruté, dated October 4, 1831, David comments on Byrne's compliance with Flaget's request. David wrote that Byrne gave "the plantation of 31-acres, a good estate, with all the utensils of work, all the animals, and the college, with all his household goods, and all that without asking a single compensation . . . then, he will go to join his family and his compatriots in Jackson's Purchase near the junction of the Ohio and the Tennessee with the intention of starting there another establishment like the one he leaves. . . . This is a man of truly extraordinary composition." (Quoted in Schauinger, *Cathedrals in the Wilderness*, p. 266.)

149 Spalding, *Life of Bishop Flaget*, p. 302.

150 Robert H. Lord, John E. Sexton, and Edward T. Harrington, *History of the Archdiocese of Boston in the Various Stages of Its Development, 1604–1943.* (3 vols.; New York: Sheed and Ward, 1944), I, 479.

151 Matignon's *Account Book*, p. 119, in Boston Diocesan Archives. Quoted in Lord, Sexton, and Harrington, *ibid.*, p. 597.

152 *Ibid.* Mrs. Sarah Torpey died Dec. 7, 1806, according to the Church Register in the Boston Diocesan Archives.

153 Letter from Stephen C. Blyth to the President of the Massachusetts Senate. Quoted in Lord, Sexton, and Harrington, *Archdiocese of Boston*, pp. 597-98.

154 *Account Book*, p. 253. Quoted in Lord, Sexton, and Harrington, p. 599.

155 Letter from Matignon to Carroll, Nov. 25, 1806, in Baltimore Diocesan Archives. Quoted in Lord, Sexton and Harrington, p. 599.

156 *Account Book*, p. 261.

157 Letter from Matignon to Carroll, dated July 15, 1805, in Baltimore Diocesan Archives. Quoted in Lord, Sexton and Harrington, pp. 602-603.

158 John J. McCoy, *A History of the Catholic Church in the Diocese of Springfield* (Boston: Hurd and Evarts Co., 1900), p. 9.

159 Robert H. Lord, "Religious Liberty in New England: The Burning of the Charlestown Convent," *Historical Records and Studies*, XXII (1932), 30.

160 *The Laity's Directory*, 1822 (New York: William H. Creagh, 1822), p. 103.

[161] *Ibid.*, p. 104.
[162] *The Metropolitan Catholic Almanac or Laity's Directory*, 1839 (Baltimore: Fielding Lucas), p. 120.
[163] Robert H. Lord, "Religious Liberty in New England: The Burning of the Charlestown Convent," *Historical Records and Studies*, XXII (1932), 10.
[164] *The United States Catholic Almanac or Laity's Directory*, 1834 (Baltimore: James Myres, 1834), p. 97.
[165] *Ibid. The Prospectus of the Ursuline Academy, 1828* is preserved in the Boston College Archives.
[166] "An account of Life in the Ursuline Convent at Mt. Benedict, Charlestown, Massachusetts, and of the Events of the Night on which the Convent was Destroyed," manuscript account in the treasure room, Harvard College Library, written by a former pupil, Miss Lucy White Thaxter, January, 1843. Presented to the Harvard College Library in 1920, by Professor Roland B. Thaxter. Quoted in Sr. M. Xaveria Sullivan, *The History of Secondary Education in the Archdiocese of Boston* (Washington, D.C.: The Catholic University of America Press, 1946), p. 88.
[167] *Ibid.*, pp. 88-89.
[168] The convent was destroyed on August 11, 1834. Lord, Sexton and Harrington (*Archdiocese of Boston*, II, 220) write of the event:
> The assault on the convent was, apparently, launched a little after 11:30 P.M. Soon a door was battered in and the rioters burst into the building. The nuns and their pupils had barely time to escape to the garden in the rear, where a high board fence barred their further flight. With torches brought, or at least with fire obtained, from Engine No. 13, "the party" ranged through the building, accompanied by various sympathizers or even curious persons who stole in under cover of darkness, while outside several hundred of their friends formed a covering force to ward off any possible interference. The rioters, after first assuring themselves that the inmates had all departed—the one thing that can be said to their credit—ransacked the house from top to bottom, smashing or ruining whatever they did not care to steal. Next combustible materials were piled in the middle of the rooms. Amid cheers and jeers, the Bible, the ornaments of the altar, the cross were tossed upon the pyre. And then, sometime around half-past twelve, the fire was started, and the beautiful convent—the first fruits of Catholic educational enterprise in New England—went up in a roar of flame.
[169] Shea, *History of the Catholic Church*, pp. 144, 159.
[170] Orestes A. Brownson, "The Right Reverend Benedict Joseph Fenwick, Second Bishop of the Diocese of Boston," *Brownson's Quarterly Review*, III (1846), 526.
[171] Louis L. Walsh, *The Early Irish Catholic Schools of Lowell, Mass.* (Boston: Thomas A. Whalen & Co., 1901), p. 7.
[172] *Ibid.*, p. 10. When application was made for financial assistance for these schools, they were formally adopted into the school system of the town and supported at public expense with the provision that the schoolrooms or buildings were to be provided by the Catholic people of the town. Certain conditions were agreed upon by the school committee and Father Connelly, the assistant at St. Patrick's, who represented the Catholics of the town. Textbooks, exercises, and studies were to be prescribed and regulated by the committee. Catholic schools were ac-

cepted as on a basis of equality with the other schools of the town. The plan, approved by Fenwick, worked till 1852. The difficulties it ran into at that time are discussed in Chapter III.

[173] John Talbot Smith, *The Catholic Church in New York* (New York and Boston: Hall and Locke Co., 1908), I, 25-28.

[174] Michael J. Considine, *A Brief Chronological Account of the Catholic Educational Institutions of the Archdiocese of New York* (New York: Benziger Bros., 1894), p. 9. (The Rev. Michael J. Considine was inspector of parochial schools in New York.) See also Leo Raymond Ryan, *Old St. Peter's, the Mother Church of Catholic New York (1785–1935)* (New York: The U. S. Catholic Historical Society, 1935), originally a Ph.D. dissertation at Fordham University.

[175] *Laws of New York*, 1805, Chapt. 108. Quoted in Edward M. Connors, *Church-State Relationships in Education in the State of New York* (Washington, D.C.: The Catholic University of America Press, 1951), 1.

[176] *New York City Education Pamphlets, Document No. 41.* Quoted in Burns, *The Principles, Origin and Establishment of the Catholic School System,* 171.

[177] *Laws of New York*, 1826, Chapt. 25. Quoted in Connors, *Church-State Relationships in Education in the State of New York,* 2.

[178] Henry DeCourcy, *The Catholic Church in the United States* (New York: Edward Dunigan and Bro., 1856), 367.

[179] *Woodstock Letters: A Record of Current Events and Historical Notes Connected with the Colleges and Missions of the Society of Jesus in North and South America* (Woodstock, Md.: 1872), IV, 143.

[180] Considine, *Catholic Educational Institutions of the Archdiocese of New York,* p. 11. See also Mother Mary Peter Carty, "Old St. Patrick's, New York's Oldest Cathedral," (unpublished Master's thesis, The Catholic University of America, 1948).

[181] Information in Shea, *History of the Catholic Church,* III, p. 180; and in Emmitsburg Archives (Archives of the Motherhouse of the Sisters of Charity).

[182] *United States Catholic Historical Magazine,* I, No. 3, 300.

[183] Information in Shea, *History of the Catholic Church,* III, 203-204; and in the *Truth Teller* (New York City Catholic newspaper), V, pp. 103, 174, 212, 228, 238, 245, 260. Quoted in Burns, *The Principles, Origin and Establishment of the Catholic School System in the United States,* pp. 274-275.

[184] Shea, *History of the Catholic Church,* III, 260.

[185] Coleman Nevils, *Miniatures of Georgetown* (Washington, D.C.: Georgetown University Press, 1934), p. 123. St. Mary's School was not attached to St. Mary's Church, but was back of Walnut Street, next to the old chapel of St. Joseph's.

[186] Minutes of the Board Meeting, Sept. 1, 1783, in *Records of the American Catholic Historical Society of Philadelphia,* IV, 268.

[187] *American Catholic Historical Researches,* VIII, 19.

[188] *A Memoir of the Very Rev. Michael Hurley, O.S.A.,* in *Records of the American Catholic Historical Society,* I (1884–1886), 211-212. The first volume of the *Records* covered activities during the years 1884–87.

[189] List of the establishments founded by the Sisters of Charity of Emmitsburg; also in Shea, *History of the Catholic Church,* III, 217.

[190] "Constitution of the Roman Catholic Sunday School Society of Philadelphia, 1816," *American Catholic Historical Researches,* VII (1890), 156-157.

[191] James Pyle Wickersham, *A History of Education in Pennsylvania* (Lancaster, Pa.: Inquirer Publishing Co., 1886), p. 117.

[192] Sarah M. Brownson, *Life of Demetrius Augustine Gallitzin* (New York: Frederick Pustet Co., 1873), p. 189.

[193] Facsimile in (Mother Therese Wolfe), *The Ursulines in New Orleans and Our Lady of Prompt Succor: A Record of Two Centuries, 1727–1925* (New York: P. J. Kenedy, 1925), opposite p. 60. One of the Ursuline letters is in the National Archives, State Department, Misc. Letters: ALS, and is printed in Clarence Edwin Carter (comp. and ed.), *The Territorial Papers of the United States*, IX, *The Territory of Orleans, 1803–1812* (Washington, D.C.: U. S. Printing Office, 1940), pp. 231-232; the other is in the Library of Congress, Papers of Thomas Jefferson, 141:2447-2448. A polygraph copy of Jefferson's reply is in the Library of Congress, Papers of Thomas Jefferson, 142:24602. All three letters appeared in *Le Moniteur de la Louisiane* (New Orleans), Sept. 13, 1804.

[194] Information in Shea, *History of the Catholic Church*, I, 670; II, 356-365. Also in Richard H. Clarke, *Lives of the Deceased Bishops of the Catholic Church in the United States* (3 vols.; New York: 1888), I, 228-231.

[195] Shea, *ibid.*, III, 366.

[196] Quoted in John E. Rothensteiner, *History of the Archdiocese of St. Louis* (2 vols.; St. Louis: Blackwell, Wielandy Co., 1928), I, 298. See also Frederick J. Easterly, C.M., *The Life of the Rt. Rev. Joseph Rosati, First Bishop of St. Louis. 1789–1843* (Washington, D.C.: The Catholic University of America Press, 1942).

[197] Walter H. Hill, *Historical Sketch of St. Louis University* (St. Louis: Patrick Fox, Publisher, 1879), p. 2.

[198] The archival holdings at St. Mary's Seminary, the institution still remaining in "the Barrens," now Perryville, Mo., are precious, but uncatalogued. They contain, in addition to many property deeds, letters of such men as DuBourg and Rosati, their libraries, and many early textbooks and other volumes.

[199] DuBourg had returned from Europe with, in addition to dedicated personnel, many beautiful and precious things for his cathedral, and its interior excited much wonderment. For the words of the first St. Louis directory, issued in 1821, on this subject, see Rothensteiner, *History of the Archdiocese of St. Louis*, I, 273.

[200] *Ibid.*, pp. 275-276. DuBourg's college was built in 1820 on the site of the old Catholic log church, on Second below Market. Rothensteiner, who was archivist of the Catholic Historical Society of St. Louis, claims that, in connection with St. Louis College, mention must be made of DuBourg's valuable library, containing 8,000 volumes.

[201] Letter of DuBourg to Francis Neale, S.J., Nov. 27, 1823. Quoted in Rothensteiner, pp. 354-355.

[202] *Ibid.*, p. 359. See William Faherty, *Better the Dream: St. Louis University and Community* (St. Louis University Press, 1968).

[203] *Catholic Almanac*, 1833, p. 80.

[204] Louise Callan, R.S.C.H., *Philippine Duchesne, Frontier Missionary of the Sacred Heart, 1769–1852* (Westminster, Md.: Newman Press, 1957).

[205] *Laity's Directory*, 1822.

[206] Marjorie Erskine, *Mother Philippine Duchesne* (New York: Longmans, Green and Co., 1926), p. 211.

[207] Mother Marie Paméla Doizé, R.S.C.H., "Educational Work of the Society

of the Sacred Heart of Jesus in Lower Louisiana 1821–1930" (unpublished Master's thesis, St. Louis University, 1930). See also Jeanne de Charry, *Sainte M. Sophie* (Paris: Casterman, 1965); Mae Duval, *Religeuses du Sacré Coeur* (Paris: De Gigard, 1924); M. O'Leary, R.S.C.H., *Education with a Tradition* (New York: Longmans, Green and Co., 1936); Ana L. Vila, *Bibliography of Writings of the Religious of the Sacred Heart in the U. S. (1914–1960)* (Washington, D.C.: The Catholic University of America, 1961); Margaret Williams, *Ste. M. Sophie—Life and Letters* (St. Louis: Herder, 1965); and Louise Callan, *Society of the Sacred Heart in North America* (New York: Longmans, Green and Co., 1937).

[208] See Juliana Wadham, *The Case of Cornelia Connelly* (New York: Pantheon, 1958).

[209] Archives of the Motherhouse, Loretto Academy, Nerinckx, Ky. List of institutions established by the Loretto Society quoted in Burns, *The Principles, Origin and Establishment of the Catholic School System in the United States*, p. 234.

[210] Shea, *History of the Catholic Church*, III, 306-317; John O'Brien, *John England, Bishop of Charleston* (New York: The Edward O'Toole Co., 1934), pp. 12-13.

[211] Shea, III, 317. Guilday writes that *The Michigan Essay*, begun by Father Gabriel Richard at Detroit on August 31, 1809, was not issued professedly in the interests of Catholics and of the Catholic religion, although it was in close sympathy with the Catholic religion. Guilday, *The Life and Times of John England* (2 vols.; New York: The America Press, 1927), I, 463.

[212] Guilday, p. 485.

[213] Shea, *History of the Catholic Church*, III, 318-319.

[214] Letter of Bishop England to Gaston dated Sept. 21, 1822, in *American Catholic Historical Society*, XVIII. Quoted in Guilday, *The Life and Times of John England*, p. 486.

[215] Letter of England to Maréchal, dated June 26, 1823, in the Baltimore Chancery Archives, Case 16-J10. Quoted in Guilday, p. 487.

[216] *Time* (April 21, 1967), p. 26.

[217] "Establishment," *Encyclopedia Britannica*, 14th ed., VIII, 726.

[218] Charles James Antieau, Arthur T. Downey, and Edward C. Roberts, *Freedom from Federal Establishment* (Milwaukee: The Bruce Publishing Company, 1964), pp. 1-2.

[219] Wilfrid Parsons, S.J., *The First Freedom* (New York: J. J. Little and Ives Company, 1948), p. 27.

[220] Joseph Story, *Commentaries on the Constitution of the United States* (Boston: Little and Brown, 1833).

[221] Edward S. Corwin, *A Constitution of Powers in a Secular State* (Charlottesville, Va.: Michie Co., 1951).

[222] *McCollum v. Board of Education*, 333 U. S. 203, 68S, Ct. 461, 92 L. Ed. 649 (1948). Appellees' Brief, p. 31.

[223] *Ibid.*

[224] Annals of Congress, I, 730.

[225] Antieau, Downey, and Roberts, *Freedom from Federal Establishment*, p. 208.

[226] Parsons, *The First Freedom*, p. 42.

[227] Sanford H. Cobb, *The Rise of Religious Liberty in America* (New York: The Macmillan Company, 1902), pp. 70-71.

[228] Antieau, Downey, and Roberts, *Freedom from Federal Establishment,* pp. 30-61. The entire second chapter deals with disestablishment in the states.

[229] Ray A. Billington, "American Catholicism and the Church-State Issue," *Christendom,* V, No. 3 (1940), 365.

[230] Information in Antieau, Downey, and Roberts, *Freedom from Federal Establishment,* Chapt. I, "Establishment in Colonial America," pp. 1-29, and in Pfeffer, *Church, State and Freedom,* (Boston: The Beacon Press, 1953), pp. 68-70.

[231] John J. McGrath, *Church and State in American Law* (Milwaukee, Wis.: Bruce Publishing Co., 1962), p. 359.

[232] *Ibid.,* p. 388.

[233] *Ibid.,* p. 389.

[234] *Writings of Thomas Jefferson* (20 vols.; Libscomb and Berg, eds. (Washington, D.C.: The Thomas Jefferson Memorial Association of the United States, 1903), XVI, pp. 281-282.

[235] Pertaining to judicial reference to this metaphor, the initial quotation appeared in 1878 in the opinion of Chief Justice Waite in the case of *Reynolds* v. *United States,* 98 U. S. 145 (1878). The metaphor played no role in the decision of that case, but assumed a role as a constitutional rule in a citation by Justice Hugo Black in *Everson* v. *School Board,* 330 U. S. 1, 1618 (1947). It gained even wider acceptance in *McCollum* v. *Board of Education,* 333 U. S. 203, 212 (1948), and was cited by all the justices in the rendering of their opinions in *Zorach* v. *Clauson,* 343 U. S. 306 (1952).

[236] Jefferson, like most of his contemporaries, was willing to use public funds, and government funds specifically, to send Christian missionaries to the Indians. In 1803, for instance, he proclaimed a treaty with the Kaskaskia Indians which, in recognizing that the great part of the tribe had already been baptized and received into the Catholic Church "to which they are much attached," provided that $100 would be given annually for seven years to a priest designated to "perform for the said tribe the duties of his office and also instruct as many of their children as possible in the rudiments of literature." In addition, the treaty provided that $300 be given to the tribe to assist it in erecting a church (Antieau, Downey, and Roberts, *Freedom from Federal Establishment,* p. 201).

[237] McGrath, *Church and State in American Law,* pp. 380-387. Madison's last citation was from the Virginia Declaration of Rights. Justice Hugo Black used Madison's *Memorial and Remonstrance* in the *Everson* case of 1947 to interpret the "establishment of religion" clause of the First Amendment. It means, Black said in what appears to this author an extremist interpretation out of context, at least this: "Neither a State nor the Federal Government can . . . pass laws which aid one religion, *aid all religions* or prefer one religion over another," (*Everson* v. *Board of Education,* 330 U. S. 1, 67 S. Ct. 504, 91 L. Ed. 711 [1947]. Italics mine.)

[238] Charles A. and Mary R. Beard, *The Rise of American Civilization* (New York: The Macmillan Company, 1947), p. 65; Pffeffer, pp. 71-75.

[239] James M. O'Neill, *Catholicism and American Freedom* (New York: Harper and Brothers, 1952), p. 10.

[240] Stephen B. Weeks, "The Church and State in North Carolina," *Johns Hopkins Studies,* XI (Baltimore, 1893), pp. 234-235.

430 *Of Singular Benefit*

Evarts B. Greene, *Religion and the State* (New York: University Press, 1941), pp. 33-35.
242 *Acts and Resolves, Public and Private, of the Provisions of the Massachusetts Bay* (21 vols.; Boston, 1869–1922), I, pp. 423-424, Chapt. I, "1700 Laws." Quoted by Arthur J. Riley, *Catholicism in New England to 1788* (Washington, D.C.: The Catholic University of America Press, 1936), pp. 327-328.
243 Pfeffer, p. 79.
244 Most Rev. James P. Butler, *Catechism of Christian Doctrine* (Philadelphia, 1821); Most Rev. Richard Challoner, *The Catholic Christian Instructed* (Philadelphia: Eugene Cumminsky, 1824); and *The Catechism of the Council of Trent* (Baltimore: Murphy, 1829). This last-named catechism became the principal source for catechisms throughout the Catholic world—including, of course, the Baltimore catechism. This particular one is a translation by the Rev. J. Donovan and is considered by many as the best English translation up to the present time. The volume cited here is the first American edition. A large number of catechisms of Christian Doctrine published from 1788 to 1900 are in the Archives of St. Charles Seminary, Philadelphia.
245 This information on the text of Molyneux is found in "Sketches of Father Molyneux" in the *United States Catholic Magazine*, IV (April, 1845), 249. No copy of the textbook can be found.
246 Selections from *Correspondence of Mathew Carey* in *Records of American Catholic Historical Society*, Vols. IX (1898), pp. 352-359; X (1899), pp. 102-111, 222-225, 345-353, 457-463; XI (1900), pp. 67-69, 213-214, 338-350.
247 *Freeman's Journal*, New York, Nov. 22, 1862, cited in John K. Sharp, *History of the Diocese of Brooklyn 1853–1953* (2 vols.; New York: Fordham University Press, 1954), I, 201. Studies of teachers through newspaper advertisements of any period would be very revealing and interesting.
248 Letter of Father Stephen Dubuisson, S.J., to Father A. Young, S.J., March 3, 1827. Quoted in Daley, *Georgetown University: Origin and Early Years*, p. 249.

## Chapter III

1 Nelson Manfred Blake, *A History of American Life and Thought* (New York: McGraw-Hill Book Company, Inc., 1963), pp. 128-134.
2 Ray Allen Billington, *American History after 1865* (Ames, Iowa: Littlefield Adams and Co., 1950), p. 25.
3 *Ibid.*, p. 83.
4 Arthur M. Schlesinger, *A Critical Period in American Religion, 1875–1900* (Philadelphia: Fortress Press, 1967), p. 1.
5 Horace Mann, *Life and Works of Horace Mann* (5 vols.; Boston: Lee and Shepard, 1891), III, 230-419.
6 Ellis Ford Hartford, *Education in These United States* (New York: The Macmillan Company, 1964), p. 155:
> The Department of Education, established by Congressional act in 1867, changed its title to Office in 1869, to Bureau in 1870, and to Office again in 1929. The U. S. Office of Education was in the Department of the Interior from 1869 to 1939 when it became part of the Federal Security Agency. In 1953, it became one of the three components of the Department of Health, Education, and Welfare.

[7] John S. Brubacher and Willis Rudy, *Higher Education in Transition* (New York: Harper and Brothers, 1958), p. 58.

[8] Frederick Rudolph, *The American College and University* (New York: Random House, Inc., 1962), pp. 253-254.

[9] Charles W. Eliot, *Educational Reform* (New York: The Century Co., 1898), p. 12.

[10] Brubacher and Rudy, *Higher Education in Transition*, p. 111.

[11] John Gilmary Shea, "The Progress of the Church in the United States, from the First Provincial Council to the Third Plenary Council of Baltimore," *American Catholic Quarterly Review* IX, no. 35 (July, 1884), 477.

[12] *Ibid.*, p. 495. *Sadlier's Catholic Directory Almanac and Ordo* (New York: D. & J. Sadlier & Co., 1890), p. 408, estimates the Catholic population of the year at 8,277,039, according to incomplete returns at hand. *Sadlier's Directory* for 1884 did not total diocesan tabulations.

[13] Carl Wittke, *We Who Built America* (New York: Prentice-Hall, Inc., 1939), p. 131. Wittke claims that from 1820 to 1920 over four and a quarter million Irish immigrants came to the United States.

[14] John F. Maguire, *The Irish in America* (New York: D. & J. Sadlier & Co., 1868), p. 540.

[15] John Lancaster Spalding, *The Religious Mission of the Irish People and Catholic Colonization* (New York: The Catholic Publication Society Co., 1880), Preface, p. 13.

[16] Colman J. Barry, *The Catholic Church and German Americans* (Milwaukee: The Bruce Publishing Company, 1953), p. 7.

[17] *Ibid.*

[18] Albert B. Faust, *The German Element in the United States* (New York: The Steuben Society of America, 1927), I, 581.

The ten American cities with largest German populations were: New York, Chicago, Philadelphia, St. Louis, Milwaukee, Cleveland, Cincinnati, Buffalo, San Francisco, and Baltimore.

[19] Barry, *The Catholic Church and German Americans*, p. 7.

[20] Wittke, *We Who Built America*, p. 210.

[21] *Ibid.*, p. 147.

[22] Barry, *The Catholic Church and German Americans*, pp. 3-4.

[23] *Ibid.*, Preface, p. vii. Wittke, too, discusses at length our debt to the German immigrants—e.g., the celebration of Christmas as a Church festival day and the introduction of the German Christmas tree; the influence upon American speech; the role of the German element in American industry, science, and fine arts; etc. (pp. 215-260). But more germane to our study is the author's discussion of the German gift of the kindergarten to the United States (p. 235). Faust states that as early as 1882 there were 500 kindergartens in the United States. (Faust, *The German Element in the United States*, II, 238.) Germany influenced the rest of American education as well.

[24] Ray Allen Billington, *The Protestant Crusade, 1800–1860* (New York: Rinehart and Company, Inc., 1938), p. 1.

[25] Victor F. O'Daniel, *The Right Reverend Edward Dominic Fenwick, O.P.* (Washington, D.C.: The Dominicana, 1920), p. 243.

[26] Fenwick to Cardinal-Prefect of Propaganda, January 25, 1821 (Propaganda Archives, America Centrale, VII, No. 1), cited by John H. Lamott, *History of the Archdiocese of Cincinnati* (New York: Frederick Pustet Company, Inc., 1921), p. 48.

[27] *Liberty Hall and Cincinnati Gazette*, March 30, 1822, p. 2. Quoted in Lamott, p. 51.

[28] O'Daniel, *Edward Dominic Fenwick*, p. 261.

[29] Eliza Rose Powell was born in 1801 in Woodford County, Ky. She was converted in 1817 by Fenwick and sent to the academy of the Sisters of Charity at Nazareth, Ky., to complete her education. After Fenwick became bishop of Ohio, he requested her to come to take any school which most needed her services. She came to Cincinnati and was probably the "neophyte" who assisted Sr. St. Paul, 1825–1826. In 1832 she was teaching school at Caton, Ohio. Seeing the delicate state of the health of the bishop in 1832, and that he was alone, she determined to accompany him to Cincinnati. After his death, she returned to her home in Kentucky, where she died on August 20, 1872, in Midway. (*Catholic Telegraph*, January 9, 1879, quoted in Lamott, *Archdiocese of Cincinnati*, p. 68).

[30] Letter of Fenwick to Badin in *Annales de la Propagation de la Foi*, III, 289. Quoted in O'Daniel, *Edward Dominic Fenwick*, p. 312. O'Daniel states that the letter is undated.

[31] *Ibid.*

[32] *U. S. Catholic Miscellany*, February 24, 1827, VI, 246. Quoted in Lamott, *Archdiocese of Cincinnati*, p. 63.

[33] O'Daniel, *Edward Dominic Fenwick*, p. 319.

[34] Sr. Mary Agnes McCann, *The History of Mother Seton's Daughters, The Sisters of Charity of Cincinnati, Ohio* (New York: Longmans, Green and Co., 1917), I, 162.

[35] Letter of Fenwick To Abbé Rigagnon, France, dated Feb. 25, 1830, in *Annales*, IV, 532. Quoted in O'Daniel, *Edward Dominic Fenwick*, p. 371.

[36] O'Daniel, pp. 427-28.

[37] Edward A. Connaughton, *A History of Educational Legislation and Administration in the Archdiocese of Cincinnati* (Washington, D.C.: The Catholic University of America Press, 1946), Chapt. III, pp. 44-76.

[38] Peter Guilday, *A History of the Councils of Baltimore (1791–1884)* (New York: The Macmillan Company, 1932), p. 273.

[39] John F. Spalding, *The Life of the Most Reverend M. J. Spalding* (New York: Catholic Publication Society, 1873), p. 202.

[40] *Pastoral Letter of the First Provincial Council of Cincinnati to the Clergy and Laity* (Cincinnati: John P. Walsh, 1855), p. 8.

[41] John Baptist Purcell, *Pastoral Letter on the Decrees of the First Provincial Council of Cincinnati, with Instructions to Pastors and People* (Cincinnati: John P. Walsh, 1858), pp. 9-10.

[42] Sr. Mary Agnes McCann, *Archbishop Purcell and the Archdiocese of Cincinnati* (Washington, D.C.: The Catholic University of America Press, 1918), p. 103.

The financial failure of 1878 caused great strain to Archbishop Purcell and broke his health. In 1879 he retired to the Ursuline Convent in Brown Bounty and died there on July 4, 1883. Throughout the nation's financial panics of 1837 and 1857, the people of his diocese had deposited their savings with Purcell, and the archbishop's brother Edward acted for the archbishop in all financial matters. The treasury of Edward Purcell was hard hit in 1878. When the crowds clamored for their money at the cathedral residence, it had to be announced that there was no money with which to pay. (Lamott, *Archdiocese of Cincinnati*, pp. 180-207.)

[43] Sr. Helen Louise Nugent, *Sister Louise, American Foundress of the Sisters*

*of Notre Dame de Namur* (New York: Benziger Brothers, 1931), pp. 70, 78-79.

44 *Catholic Almanac*, 1842, pp. 93-94.

45 John Gilmary Shea, *The History of the Catholic Church in the United States* (New York: John G. Shea, 1888), IV, 541.

46 Lamott, *Archdiocese of Cincinnati*, p. 274.

47 *Ibid.*, p. 278. Lamott's sources for this information were the *Catholic Almanac*, 1854, p. 104; *First Annual Report of Superintendent of Parish Schools of the Archdiocese of Cincinnati* (1907–08).

48 Shea, *History of the Catholic Church*, III, 642.

49 *Ibid.*, p. 645; Sr. M. Salesia Godecker, *Right Reverend Simon William Gabriel Bruté De Remur, First Bishop of Vincennes* (Washington, D.C.: The Catholic University of America Press, 1929), pp. 108-109. See also James Roosevelt Bayley, *Memoirs of the Right Reverend Simon William Gabriel Bruté, D.D., First Bishop of Vincennes, with Sketches Describing his Recollections of Scenes Connected with the French Revolution and Extracts from his Journal* (New York: P. O'Shea, 1865), pp. 77 and 79. This is contained in the Old Cathedral Library, 205 Church St., Vincennes, Ind. 47591. This same collection, sponsored by the Lilly Endowment, Inc., also contains such other items in connection with Indiana Catholic history as early documents and, especially, much of Bruté's very interesting library which reveals the man, the teacher, and the reason why John Quincy Adams called him "the most learned man of his day in America."

50 Godecker, p. 109.

51 *Catholic Almanac*, 1841, pp. 133-35. St. Gabriel's College, according to Erbacher, closed in 1847 when the Eudist Fathers left the diocese of Vincennes. Sebastian Anthony Erbacher, *Catholic Higher Education for Men in the United States* (Washington, D.C.: The Catholic University of America Press, 1931).

52 Herman J. Alerding, *A History of the Church in the Diocese of Vincennes* (Indianapolis: Carlon and Hollenbeck, 1883), p. 149. Alerding was consecrated bishop of Fort Wayne on November 30, 1900. He is the first Catholic historian of Vincennes and Fort Wayne.

53 Shea, *History of the Catholic Church*, IV, 198.

54 Robert F. Trisco, *The Holy See and the Nascent Church in the Middle Western United States, 1826–1850* (Rome: Gregorian University Press, 1962), pp. 158-163.

55 Shea, *History of the Catholic Church*, III, 650; IV, 199. See also Arthur J. Hope, *Notre Dame, One Hundred Years* (Notre Dame, Ind.: University of Notre Dame, 1943).

56 *Catholic Almanac*, 1845, p. 107.

57 Elinor Long Dehey, *Religious Orders of Women in the United States* (Hammond, Indiana: W. B. Conkey Co., 1930), pp. 249-253.

58 Sr. Mary Carol Schroeder, *The Catholic Church in the Diocese of Vincennes, 1847–1877* (Washington, D.C.: The Catholic University of America Press, 1946), pp. 4-5.

59 Tombstones in the Old Cathedral, Vincennes.

60 Sr. M. Salesia Godecker, *History of Catholic Education in Indiana: A Survey of the Schools, 1702–1925* (St. Meinrad, Indiana: St. Meinrad Abbey Press, 1926), p. 39.

61 Alerding, *History of the Church in Vincennes*, pp. 207-208.

62 Godecker, *History of Catholic Education in Indiana*, p. 32.

[63] Shea, *History of the Catholic Church*, IV, 594.

[64] *Ibid.*, III, 634. Pope Gregory XVI erected the See of Detroit on March 8, 1833, making the bishop a suffragan of the archbishop of Baltimore. The diocese embraced the state of Michigan and the Northwest Territory, which had hitherto been administered by the bishop of Cincinnati. (*Ibid.*, III, 633.)

[65] George Paré, *The Catholic Church in Detroit, 1701–1888* (Detroit: The Gabriel Richard Press, 1951), pp. 423, 633-634.

[66] Chrysostomus Verwyst, *Life and Labors of Bishop Baraga* (Milwaukee: M. F. Wiltzius and Company, 1900), p. 118.

[67] *United States Catholic Almanac*, 1837. Quoted in Sr. M. Rosalita, *Education in Detroit Prior to 1850* (Lansing: Michigan Historical Commission, 1928), pp. 301-303.

[68] Paré, *Catholic Church in Detroit*, p. 638.

[69] Sr. M. Rosalita, *Education in Detroit Prior to 1850*, pp. 305-307.

[70] Julius McCabe, *Directory of Detroit*, 1837. Quoted in Sr. Mr. Rosalita, p. 310.

[71] Sr. M. Rosalita, p. 315.

[72] Paré, *Catholic Church in Detroit*, pp. 423-424. See also Trisco, *The Holy See and the Nascent Church*, pp. 344-384.

[73] *Ibid.*, p. 470.

[74] *Catholic Almanac*, 1846, pp. 96-98.

[75] *Catholic Almanac*, 1847, p. 96. See Paré, *Catholic Church in Detroit*, p. 640.

[76] *Catholic Almanac*, 1857, p. 104.

[77] Paré, *Catholic Church in Detroit*, p. 440.

[78] *Ibid.*, pp. 645-646.

[79] Shea, *History of the Catholic Church*, III, 139.

[80] Robert H. Lord, John E. Sexton, and Edward T. Harrington, *History of the Archdiocese of Boston* (3 vols.; New York: Sheed and Ward, 1944), II, 310.

[81] Louis S. Walsh, *Historical Sketch of the Growth of Catholic Parochial Schools in the Archdiocese of Boston* (Newton Highlands, Mass.: Press of St. John's Industrial Training School, 1901), p. 19.

[82] Louis L. Walsh, *The Early Irish Catholic Schools of Lowell, Mass.* (Boston: Thomas A. Whalen & Co., 1901), pp. 7-10.

[83] Centennial Program, *Academy of Notre Dame, Roxbury, Massachusetts, 1854–1954* (privately printed, 1954), pp. 20-21; International Federation of the Notre Dame Alumnae Associations, *The Sisters of Notre Dame de Namur in the United States 1840–1940* (printed by the Federation, 1940), pp. 55-56.

[84] Francis X. Weiser, *Holy Trinity Parish, 1844–1944, Boston, Massachusetts* (Boston: Holy Trinity Rectory, 1944), pp. 27-29.

[85] Richard J. Quinlan, "Growth and Development of Catholic Education in the Archdiocese of Boston," *The Catholic Historical Review*, XXII, No. 1 (April 1936), 33-34; William F. Kenney, *Centenary of the See of Boston* (Boston: J. K. Waters Company, 1909), p. 120.

[86] Lord, Sexton, and Harrington, *History of the Archdiocese of Boston*, II, 588-608. These pages give a detailed account of the proceedings of the Eliot School case.

[87] Sr. M. Xaveria Sullivan, *The History of Catholic Secondary Education in the Archdiocese of Boston* (Washington, D.C.: The Catholic University of America Press, 1946), p. 18.

Sr. M. Xaveria Sullivan cites the "Annals of the Sisters of Notre

Dame," Archives of the Sisters of Notre Dame, Lowell, Mass., as the source of her information. She also claims that the Sisters of Notre Dame de Namur conducted 83 per cent of the parochial secondary schools established between 1854 and 1885. Thirty parochial secondary schools were established between 1854 and 1907. Six of these were for boys, seventeen were for girls, and seven were coeducational. The reason that girls' schools predominate was that the Sisters of Notre Dame de Namur were restricted by rule to the teaching of girls and young boys. (*Ibid.*, p. 45.)

88 *Metropolitan Catholic Almanac and Laity's Directory*, 1856, p. 112.

89 Louise Callan, *The Society of the Sacred Heart in North America* (New York: Longmans, Green and Company, 1937), p. 612.

90 William Byrne, *History of the Catholic Church in the New England States* (2 vols.; Boston: Hurd and Everts Company, 1899), I, 179. The Sisters of St. Joseph came to Boston in 1873 but did not conduct secondary schools during this period. (Sullivan, *History of Catholic Secondary Education*, pp. 28-29). The Sisters of Charity of Nazareth, Ky., established in 1882 their first foundation in Boston—in the Newburyport section of East Boston. They opened the Immaculate Conception parochial school in 1882, and in December 1883 organized a high school which functioned satisfactorily for some years. (Anna B. McGill, *The Sisters of Charity of Nazareth, Kentucky* [New York: The Encyclopedia Press, 1917], p. 213.) Sullivan claims that the Archives of the Immaculate Conception Convent, Newburyport, Mass., state that the high school of the Sisters of Charity closed in 1905.

91 *Sadlier's Catholic Almanac and Ordo*, 1866, p. 104.

92 W. E. Murphy, S. J., "The Story of Boston College," *The Catholic Contribution to Religion and Education*, V, Constantine E. McGuire, ed., *Catholic Builders of the Nation* (5 vols.; Boston: Continental Press, Inc., 1923), p. 254.

93 Lord, Sexton, and Harrington, *History of the Archdiocese of Boston*, III, 85.

94 Hugh J. Nolan, *The Most Reverend Francis Patrick Kenrick, Third Bishop of Philadelphia, 1830–1851* (Philadelphia: American Catholic Historical Society, 1948), Foreword, p. vii.

95 Shea, *History of the Catholic Church*, III, 550.

96 John R. G. Hassard, *Life of the Most Rev. John Hughes, First Archbishop of New York* (New York: D. Appleton & Co., 1866), p. 90.

97 Taken from the list of establishments founded by the Sisters of Charity of Emmitsburg, Maryland, in the Archives of the Motherhouse at Emmitsburg.

98 *Catholic Almanac*, 1833, p. 107.

99 Nolan, *Francis Patrick Kenrick*, p. 292. When Les Dames de la Retraite left Charleston is also not definitely known. The last we hear of them is a notice of their educational activity in Florida in 1839 where they conducted an academy in St. Augustine. (Peter Guilday, *The Life and Times of John England, First Bishop of Charleston, 1786–1842*, (2 vols.; New York: America Press, 1927), II, 171.

100 Nolan, *ibid.*, p. 292; and Joseph J. L. Kirlin, *Catholicity in Philadelphia* (Philadelphia: John J. McVey, 1909), p. 341.

101 Nolan, p. 315.

102 Sr. Maria Alma, *Standard Bearers* (New York: P. J. Kenedy & Sons, 1928), p. 65; Nolan, p. 388.

103 Daniel H. Mahony, *Historical Sketches of the Catholic Churches and In-*

436 *Of Singular Benefit*

stitutions of Philadelphia (Philadelphia: Daniel H. Mahony, 1895),
p. 119.
104 *Metropolitan Catholic Almanac and Laity's Directory*, 1845, p. 79. Nolan
writes thus of Villanova College: "There was also for young men the
Manual College established in 1842 at Villanova." (*Francis Patrick
Kenrick*, p. 293).
105 Nolan (p. 434) states that the *Catholic Directory* for 1850, pp. 43-44,
advertised the following productions of Bishop Kenrick: *The Primacy
of the Apostolic See Vindicated; Theologia Dogmatica* (4 vols.); *Treatise
on Baptism; The Catholic Doctrine on Justification; The Four Gospels*,
translated from the Latin vulgate and compared with the original
Greek text: being a revision of the Rhemish translation, with critical
and explanatory notes.
106 Shea, *History of the Catholic Church*, IV, 67. The present dioceses of Philadelphia, Altoona, Erie, Harrisburg, Pittsburgh, and Scranton in Pennsylvania; Camden and Trenton in New Jersey; and Wilmington, Delaware, were all in the territory once governed by Kenrick. (Nolan, p.
434.)
107 James Pyle Wickersham, *A History of Education in Pennsylvania* (Lancaster, Pa.: Inquirer Publishing Co., 1886), p 117.
108 Andrew A. Lamling, *A History of the Catholic Church in the Dioceses of
Pittsburgh and Allegheny* (New York: Benziger Bros., 1880), p. 45;
Nolan, *Francis Patrick Kenrick*, p. 103; Trisco, *The Holy See and the
Nascent Church*, pp. 297ff.
109 *Thirty-eighth Annual Report of the Catholic Schools in the Diocese of Pittsburgh* (Pittsburgh: Diocesan School Board, 1943), p. 8. This report is
a centenary issue commemorating one hundred years of Catholic education in Pittsburgh. The Rev. Thomas J. Quigley had been appointed
superintendent of schools in Pittsburgh in 1939, and in the *Thirty-eighth
Annual Report* he made "The History of One Hundred Years of Catholic Education" a special feature. His sources are worth citing: Reports
of the Superintendent of Pittsburgh Catholic Schools, published annually 1905 to 1942; James R. Cox, *History and Development of the
Parochial Schools of the Roman Catholic Diocese of Pittsburgh* (unpublished Master's thesis, University of Pittsburgh, 1923); Andrew A.
Lamling, *History of the Catholic Church in the Diocese of Pittsburgh
and Allegheny* (New York: Benziger Bros., 1880); Andrew A. Lamling,
*Foundation Stones of a Great Diocese*, I (Pittsburgh: Republic Bank
Note Co., 1914); *Official Catholic Directories;* parish and diocesan
archives; questionnaires to school principals, supervisors, and superiors
of religious communities; and questionnaires to pastors of existing
schools as a final check.
110 *Thirty-eighth Annual Report*, p. 9.
111 *Ibid.*, p. 10.
112 *Ibid.*, pp. 11-12. Philadelphia, too, made tremendous strides in Catholic
educational development after 1850: Bishops John Nepomucene Neu-
mann and James Frederic Wood were alive to educational needs. Some
of the statistics for 1895 (Mahony, *Catholic Churches and Institutions
of Philadelphia*, p. 2) show remarkable progress since 1830 (see statistics, pp. 268-269): colleges, 3; brothers, 88; religious orders of
women, 16; religious women, novices, and postulants, 1,601; academies
and parochial schools taught by brothers, 11; academies and select
schools for young ladies taught by religious women, 14; high schools

for boys, 1; parochial schools, 98; children attending parochial schools, 32,579; young ladies attending academies and select schools, about 1,510; orphan asylums, 10, with 2,332 orphans; industrial school for boys, 1, and for girls, 1; protectory for girls, 1; houses for homeless boys, 2; and Catholic population, about 415,000.

For further information on Catholic education in the archdiocese of Philadelphia, Brother Thomas J. Donaghy, F.S.C., is now working on a manuscript tentatively titled *Philadelphia's Finest: Education in the Catholic Archdiocese,* publication date estimated as 1971. There are also several archives. Those at St. Charles Seminary, Overbrook, contain many materials, mostly uncatalogued, including a very fine catechism collection from the late eighteenth century on, from Europe as well as the U.S.; individual parish histories; *Records of the Catholic Historical Society* and its predecessor, *American Catholic Historical Researches;* some of Prince Gallitzin's library, with his marginal notations in some books; some Mother Seton letters; collections of some early American publishers, such as Mathew Carey; one of the largest newspaper collections of the nineteenth century, including a file of the *Catholic Star Herald,* which started in 1832; notes of Martin I. J. Griffin; and a large collection of old U. S. Catholic books, and Maria Monk and other anti-Catholic literature. The diocesan archives at the Chancery Office, 1712 Summer St., include the Kenrick diary, diocesan synodal statutes of 1832 and 1842, and Kenrick-Frenaey correspondence. The archives of the Office of the Superintendent of Schools, 19th and Wood Streets, contains correspondence from ordinaries, early curricula, reports of the school office, reports on school projects, and information on the beginnings of parish schools. Villanova College also contains good archives.

[113] New York was erected by Pope Pius IX on July 19, 1851, into an Archiepiscopal See, with Metropolitan powers, and with the bishops of Boston, Hartford, Albany, and Buffalo as suffragans. Hughes was promoted to the office of archbishop (Shea, *History of the Catholic Church,* IV, 122).

[114] Henry A. Brann, *Most Reverend John Hughes, First Archbishop of New York* (New York: Benziger Bros., 1892), p. 62.

[115] John R. Hassard, *Life of the Most Reverend John Hughes, D.D., First Archbishop of New York* (New York: D. Appleton & Co., 1866), pp. 212, 229.

[116] Sr. Marie Léonore Fell, *The Foundations of Nativism in American Textbooks, 1783–1860* (Washington, D.C.: The Catholic University of America Press, 1941), p. 148.

[117] Hassard, *John Hughes,* p. 227.

[118] Lawrence Kehoe (ed.), *Complete Works of the Most Reverend John Hughes* (New York: L. Kehoe Publisher, 1866), I, 63.

[119] For a discussion of Seward's motives in participating in this controversy, both pro and con, see Vincent P. Lannie, "William Seward and Common School Education," *History of Education Quarterly,* IV (September, 1964), 181-192, and John W. Pratt, "Religious Conflict in the Development of the New York City Public School System," *History of Education Quarterly,* V (June, 1965), 110-120.

[120] Hassard, *John Hughes,* p. 251. The Public School Society of New York City merged its properties with those of the Board of Education in 1853. The value of the real estate and personal property that it turned

over to the Board totaled $605,221.85. Andrew S. Draper, *Origin and Development of the New York Common School System* (Albany: James B. Lyon, 1890), p. 20.

[121] Louise Callan, *The Society of the Sacred Heart in North America* (New York: Longmans, Green & Co., 1937), p. 315.

[122] *Sadlier's Catholic Almanac and Ordo*, 1864, pp. 85-90.

[123] Shea, *History of the Catholic Church*, IV, 475.

[124] Brother James D. Boylan from Ireland, mentioned in the preceding chapter, had attempted a secondary school for boys in 1829 which failed because of Boylan's inefficiency. Bishop John Dubois had founded at Nyack, on the Hudson River, in 1833, "a classical and ecclesiastical seminary." Nyack College, as this institution was called, was destroyed by fire. *Catholic Almanac*, 1837, p. 105.

[125] Hassard, *John Hughes*, p. 189.

[126] *Ibid.*, p. 252. The seminary remained at Fordham until 1860 when it was removed to Troy.

[127] Edward P. Tynan, S.J., "The Story of Fordham," *The Catholic Contribution to Religion and Education*, V, Constantine E. McGuire, ed. *Catholic Builders of the Nation* (5 vols.; Boston: Continental Press, Inc., 1923), pp. 285-287.

[128] James Cardinal Gibbons, *Retrospect of Fifty Years* (Baltimore: John Murphy Co., 1916), II, 39. This is also the opinion of Vincent P. Lannie, *Public Money and Parochial Education: Bishop Hughes, Governor Seward, and the New York School Controversy* (Cleveland: The Press of Case Western Reserve University, 1968). For further information on the controversy over the New York Public School Society, see: Henry J. Browne, "Public Support of Catholic Education in New York, 1825–1842: Some New Aspects," *Catholic Historical Review*, XXXIX (April, 1953), 1-27; Joseph J. McCadden, "Bishop Hughes versus the Public School Society of New York," *Catholic Historical Review*, L (July, 1964), 188-207; "Governor Seward's Friendship with Bishop Hughes," *New York History*, XXIV (April, 1966), 160-184; "New York's School Crisis of 1840–1842: Its Irish Antecedents," *Thought*, XLI (Winter, 1966), 561-588; David J. O'Brien, "American Catholicism and the Diaspora," *Cross Currents*, XVI (Summer, 1966), 307-323.

[129] Peter Guilday, *A History of the Councils of Baltimore, (1791–1884)*, p. 183.

[130] *Catholic Almanac*, 1854, p. 282, reproduced in Guilday, p. 183.

[131] For some of the educational growth, see Brother Jerome de la Salle Beck, "Educational History of the Christian Brothers in the Elementary Schools of St. Louis and Vicinity, 1849–1925" (unpublished Master's thesis, St. Louis University, 1946); Sr. Mary Eustacia Stansell, "Early Catholic Education in the Archdiocese of St. Louis from Citations in the Catholic Press," (unpublished Master's thesis, St. Louis University, 1953); John J. O'Brien, "History of Catholic Education in the Mississippi Valley, 1704–1866," (unpublished Ph.D. dissertation, St. Louis University, 1951); Henry Archambeault, "History and Educational Program of Christian Brothers College, St. Louis, Mo.," (unpublished Master's thesis, St. Louis University, 1947); Sr. M. Sylvana Houser, "The Catholic Church in East St. Louis to 1900," (unpublished Master's thesis, St. Louis University, 1937); William J. Windelmann, "Beginnings of Catholic Education in the City of East St. Louis," (unpublished Master's thesis, St. Louis University, 1947); Sr. Mary Afra White, "Catholic Indian Missionary Influence in the Development of

Catholic Education in Montana, 1840–1903," (unpublished Ph.D. dissertation, St. Louis University, 1940); Brother Hubert Gerard (ed.), *Mississippi Vista: The Brothers of the Christian Schools in the Mid-West, 1849–1949* (Winona, Minn.; St. Mary's College Press, 1948); and Brother Angelus Gabriel, *The Christian Brothers in the United States 1848–1948* (New York: Declan X. McMullen Co., 1948).

[132] Shea and O'Connell differ only on this point. Shea, *History of the Catholic Church*, III, 580, claims that England gave them the Rule of St. Vincent de Paul, and O'Connell (J. J. O'Connell, O.S.B., *Catholicity in the Carolinas and Georgia, 1820–1878* [New York: D. & J. Sadlier and Co., 1879], p. 42) that the rule was that of the Presentation Order.

[133] Shea, III, p. 580; O'Connell, pp. 64-65. The school is mentioned for the first time in the *Catholic Almanac*, 1840, pp. 73-74.

[134] O'Connell, p. 71. O'Connell laments the lack of sources for research. He writes: "Most of the records of the diocese perished with the *U. S. Catholic Miscellany* in the conflagration of Charleston; the parochial registers were, in some instances, destroyed during the Civil War," (p. x).

[135] John England, *The Works of the Right Reverend John England*, edited by Sebastian Messmer, *et al.* (7 vols.; Cleveland: Arthur H. Clark Co., 1908), IV, 354.

[136] Joseph L. O'Brien, *John England—Bishop of Charleston* (New York: The Edward O'Toole Co., Inc., 1934), p. 36:
In 1880, a school for boys was opened by the Brothers of the Sacred Heart, who remained in Charleston until the earthquake of 1886.

[137] *Works of John England*, IV, 374.

[138] Guilday, *The Life and Times of John England, 1786–1842* (2 vols.; New York: America Press, 1927), II, 553.

[139] Shea, *History of the Catholic Church*, IV, 99-100.

[140] Sr. M. Columba Cummins, R.S.M., *One Hundred Years of Service* (Savannah: privately printed, 1945), p. 9.

[141] *Metropolitan Catholic Almanac and Laity's Directory*, 1850, p. 118.

[142] O'Connell, *Catholicity in the Carolinas and Georgia*, pp. 624-625.

[143] John Tracy Ellis, *The Life and Times of James Cardinal Gibbons* (Milwaukee: Bruce Publishing Company, 1952), I, 653-654.

[144] Haygood S. Bowden, *Two Hundred Years of Education* (Richmond, Va.: Press of the Dietz Printing Co., 1932), p. 257; also Michael V. Gannon, *Rebel Bishop: The Life and Era of Augustin Verot* (Milwaukee: Bruce Publishing Co., 1964), Chapt. VII: "The Catholic Public School."

[145] Sr. M. Felicitas Powers, R.S.M., "A History of Catholic Education in Georgia, 1845–1952" (unpublished Master's thesis, The Catholic University of America, 1956), p. 12. Powers claims that this system of financing was revived and in use in 1956.

[146] Reginald Zyendoorn, SS.CC., *History of the Catholic Mission in the Hawaiian Islands* (Honolulu: Star-Bulletin, Ltd., 1927), p. 26. See also Benjamin O. Wist, "Education in Hawaii: the Historic Setting," *The Teachers College Journal*, XVII (January, 1946), 51-55.

[147] Constitutions and Laws of Kamehameha III, p. 61, cited in Daniel J. Dever, "The Legal Status of Catholic Schools under the Constitutional and Statutory Laws of Hawaii" (unpublished Master's thesis, The Catholic University of America, 1952).

[148] Eugene Paulin and Joseph A. Becker, *New Wars* (Milwaukee: Bruce Publishing Co., 1959), pp. 10-12.

149 *Concilia Provincialia Baltimori habita ab anno 1829 usque ad annum 1849* (Baltimore: Typis Joannis Murphy et Sociorum, 1851), Decretum XXXIV, p. 84.

150 *Ibid.*, Decretum XXXV, p. 84.

151 "Pastoral Letter to the Laity, 1829," *The National Pastorals of the American Hierarchy (1792–1919)*, ed. Peter K. Guilday (Washington, D.C.: National Catholic Welfare Council, 1923), pp. 24-25.

152 *Ibid.*, p. 28.

153 Peter K. Guilday, *A History of the Councils of Baltimore* (New York: The Macmillan Company, 1932), p. 106.

154 Guilday, *National Pastorals*, p. 74.

155 *Pastoral Letter of the Most Reverend the Archbishop of Baltimore and the Right Reverend the Bishops of the Roman Catholic Church in the United States of America Assembled in Third Provincial Council of Baltimore, 1837* (Baltimore: Fielding Lucas, 1837), p. 43.

156 Guilday, *National Pastorals*, pp. 152-153.

157 *Concilium Plenarium Totius Americae Septentrionalis Foederate, Baltimori Habitum Anno 1852* (Baltimore: Apud Joannem Murphy et Socios, 1853), Decretum XIII, p. 47.

158 Guilday, *National Pastorals*, p. 191.

159 John L. Spalding, *The Life of the Most Reverend M. J. Spalding* (New York: Catholic Publication Society, 1873), p. 304.

160 *Concilii Plenarii Baltimorensis II* (Baltimore: Joannis Murphy, 1868), Titulus IX, Caput I, numbers 423-424.

161 *Ibid.*, number 430, p. 221.

162 Guilday, *History of the Councils of Baltimore*, pp. 211-212.

163 Spalding, *Life of the Most Reverend M. J. Spalding*, p. 315.

164 *Pastoral Letter of the Most Reverend Archbishop of Baltimore on the Eve of His Departure for Rome, 1867* (Baltimore: Kelly and Piet, 1867), p. 6.

165 "A Special Report of the Commissioner of Education, District of Columbia, 1868" (Washington, D.C.: Published by the District of Columbia, 1869), p. 239.

166 *Ibid.*, p. 217.

167 *Ibid.*, p. 218.

168 Francis P. Cassidy, "Catholic Education in the Third Plenary Council of Baltimore," *The Catholic Historical Review*, XXXIV (January, 1949), 430.

169 Thomas T. McAvoy, C.S.C., "Public Schools vs. Catholic Schools and James McMaster," *The Review of Politics*, XXVIII, No. 1 (January, 1966), 19-46.

170 "Minutes of the Roman Meeting Preparatory to the Third Plenary Council of Baltimore, Chapter X, Parochial Schools," *The Jurist*, XI, No. 3 (July, 1951), 423.

171 *Ibid.*, p. 424.

172 *Acta et decreta concilii plenarii Baltimorensis tertii* (Baltimore: Typis Joannis Murphy et Sociorum, 1886), Titulus VI, Caput I, no. 199, p. 104.

173 *Ibid.* Titulus 6, no. 202, p. 107.

174 Guilday, *History of the Councils of Baltimore*, p. 239.

175 Religious tests had been a means of controlling education in Colonial times and of keeping it under the Established Church. They were still a source of conflict during the early national period, as we observed.

Each state prohibited religious tests during the period 1829–1884. Burton Confrey, *Secularism in American Education* (Washington: The Catholic University of America, 1931).

[176] William Oland Browne, *History of the Public School Society of New York* (New York: William Wood and Co., 1870), p. 496.

[177] Billington, *The Protestant Crusade, 1800–1860*, p. 156.

[178] Henry F. Brownson (ed.), *The Works of Orestes A. Brownson* (20 vols. Detroit: Thorndike, Nourse Publishers, 1882–1887), XIX, p. 210.

[179] Orestes A. Brownson, *Brownson's Quarterly Review*. New York Series 11 (July, 1854), 372.

[180] *Ibid.* "Catholic Schools and Education," quoted by Neil G. McCluskey, *Catholic Education in America: A Documentary History* (New York: Teachers College, Columbia University, 1964), p. 96.

[181] *Ibid.*, pp. 102-103.

[182] Isaac T. Hecker, *The Catholic Church in the United States* (New York: The Catholic Publication Society Co., 1879), p. 16. Hecker was a famous convert, founder of the Paulist Fathers, and long-time editor of *The Catholic World*.

[183] *Ibid.*, p. 17.

[184] *Donahoe v. Richards*, 38 Me. 376 (1854).

[185] *Billington*, pp. 315-316.

[186] *Federal Relations to Education*. Report of the National Advisory Committee on Education, 2 parts. Washington, D.C.: 1931, 11, 76-77. Quoted in Richard J. Gabel, *Public Funds for Church and Private Schools* (Washington, D.C.: The Catholic University of America Press, 1937), p. 518.

[187] Brubacher and Rudy, p. 76. When the Congregationalists founded Howard University in Washington, D.C., they did so under the authorization of the Freedmen's Bureau, and the institution was named for General Oliver O. Howard, head of the Bureau.

[188] *Annals of the Bureau of Catholic Indian Missions* of 1878 contain a "Tabulated Statement of Indian Agencies in the U.S. Assigned to the Catholic Church and of Agencies which, Under the Peace Policy, Should Have Been Assigned to Said Church." On Catholic agencies for the Indians, see Peter J. Rahill, *The Catholic Indian Missions and Grant's Peace Policy, 1870–1884* (Washington, D.C.: The Catholic University of America Press, 1953).

[189] *The Constitution of the United States* (New York: Barnes and Noble, 1966), p. 52.

[190] Horace E. Flack, *The Adoption of the Fourteenth Amendment* (Baltimore: Johns Hopkins Press, 1908), p. 94.

[191] *Meyer v. Nebraska*, 262 U. S. 390 (1923). The Court held as unconstitutional a Nebraska statute forbidding the teaching of foreign languages to school children. Of importance to the history of Catholic education was also the case of *Pierce v. Society of Sisters* of 1925, which was also resolved in the light of the Fourteenth Amendment and which invalidated an Oregon statute outlawing private schools.

[192] "The President's Speech at Des Moines," *The Catholic World*, XXII, 434-435.

[193] *The Congressional Record*, IV, Part 1, p. 175. Relevant parts of the texts of Grant's speech to the Army of the Tennessee and of his message to Congress may also be found in John Tracy Ellis, *Documents of American Catholic History* (Milwaukee, Wis.: The Bruce Publishing Co., 1969), pp. 392-393.

[194] *The Congressional Record,* IV, Part 1, p. 205.

[195] "The President's Speech at Des Moines," *The Catholic World,* XXII, No. 130 (January, 1876), 440-441.

[196] *The Congressional Record.* IV, Part 6, p. 5595.

[197] For the application of the Blaine philosophy to one of these states, New York, see my article, "Historical Perspectives on New York's 1967 Constitutional Convention and Article XI, Section 3 (The 'Blaine' or 'Know-Nothing' Amendment)," *Catholic Educational Review,* LXV, No. 3 (March, 1967), 145-175, and Charles E. Rice," The New York State Constitution and Aid to Church-Related Schools," *The Catholic Lawyer,* XII (Autumn, 1966), 272-329. For Blaine on the national level, see also Marie Carolyn Klinkhamer, "The Blaine Amendment of 1875: Private Motives for Political Action," *Catholic Historical Review,* XLII (April, 1956), 15-49, and Laurence R. Gardner, "The Blaine Amendment of 1876: A Proposal to so Extend the Constitution as to Prohibit Indirect Aid to Sectarian Institutions" (unpublished Master's dissertation, The Catholic University of America, 1947).

[198] Arthur J. Hefferman, *A History of Catholic Education in Connecticut* (Washington, D.C.: The Catholic University of America Press, 1937), pp. 33-36.

[199] *Annual Report of the School Visitors of Hartford* (1866), pp. 9-10. Quoted in Hefferman, p. 37.

[200] *New Haven Board of Education Report* (1869), p. 41. Quoted in Hefferman, p. 58.

[201] Louis L. Walsh, *The Early Catholic Schools of Lowell, Massachusetts* (Boston: Thomas A. Whalen and Co., 1901), pp. 9-10.

[202] MS Records, St. Peter's Church, Poughkeepsie, New York. Cited in Connors, pp. 110-11.

[203] MS Records, St. Peter's Church, Poughkeepsie, New York. Report of the special committee to the Board of Education of the City of Poughkeepsie in 1873, relating to Schools No. 11 and No. 12, copy. Cited in Connors, p. 111.

[204] Patrick F. McSweeny, "Christian Public Schools," *The Catholic World,* XLIV, No. 262 (March, 1887), 796.

[205] Connors has the best definitive study of the Poughkeepsie Plan. He cited the *Annual Reports of the Board of Education,* 1873–1875, 1875, 1876, 1882–1890, 1892, and 1895 to show the financial aid given to Schools No. 11 and No. 12 during the Plan's implementation.

[206] The report incorporating the entire decision may be found in *Forty-Fifth Annual Report of the State Superintendent of Public Instruction, 1899* (Albany: Wynkoop, Hallenbeck, Crawford Co., 1899), pp. 110-112. Cited in Connors, p. 120.

School No. 11 was reopened on January 3, 1899, as a parochial school. School No. 12 was rented to the Board of Education for the annual sum of $1,000, which arrangement continued until 1903.

Michael J. Considine, *A Brief Chronological Account of the Catholic Educational Institutions of the Archdiocese of New York* (New York: Benziger Brothers, 1894), pp. 38-44.

## Chapter IV

[1] Charles William Eliot, "Undesirable and Desirable Uniformity in Schools," *National Education Association Journal of Proceedings and Addresses,*

Session of the year 1892, Saratoga Springs, New York (New York: NEA, 1893), pp. 82-95.

2 Edgar W. Knight, *Fifty Years of American Education* (New York: The Ronald Press Co., 1952), pp. 110-113.

3 John W. Cook, "Professionally Prepared Teachers," *National Education Association Journal of Proceedings and Addresses*, Fifty-second annual meeting held at St. Paul, Minn., July 4-11, 1914 (Ann Arbor, Michigan: N.E.A., 1915), pp. 113-115.

4 Grenville Stanley Hall, *The Contents of Children's Minds on Entering School* (New York: E. L. Kellogg & Co., 1893).

5 Gerald Shaugnessy, *Has the Immigrant Kept the Faith?* (New York: The Macmillan Company, 1925), p. 262.

6 John Tracy Ellis, *American Catholicism* (Chicago: The University of Chicago Press, 1955), p. 81.

7 Shaugnessy, *Has the Immigrant Kept the Faith?* p. 33.

8 *Official Catholic Directory* (1890) (New York: P. J. Kennedy), p. 987.

9 *Ibid.*, p. 1011.

10 Carl Wittke, *We Who Built America* (Wisconsin: Wisconsin Cunes Press, Inc., 1964), pp. 407-408.

11 Thomas Edward Green, *Immigration and its Effect upon the Present and Future Condition of the United States* (unpublished address delivered to the Maryland Society, Sons of the American Revolution, on April 19, 1922), p. 3.

12 John Higham, *Strangers in the Land* (New Jersey: Rutgers University Press, 1955), pp. 62-63.

13 The *A.P.A. Magazine* was published in San Francisco, Calif., from 1895 to 1897. Editions may be found in the Stanford University Library. The A.P.A., however, operated a "patriotic press" and published 95 newspapers of varying titles in 29 states, Washington, D.C., and Ontario, Canada. Information on the A.P.A. press is found in Donald L. Kinzer, *An Episode in Anti-Catholicism* (Seattle: University of Washington Press, 1964), pp. 95-96, 255-258.

14 *Patriotic American*, a Detroit weekly organ of the A.P.A.

15 *Patriotic American*, Detroit, April 8, 1893. (William J. H. Traynor, the A.P.A.'s president, was its editor and publisher.)

16 Humphrey J. Desmond, *The A.P.A. Movement: A Sketch* (Washington: The New Century Press, 1912), pp. 9-11. Desmond's monograph on the A.P.A. carries an authoritative account of the factors in this anti-Catholic situation. The work includes letters from the founder of the A.P.A., Henry F. Bowers (who was re-elected its national president in 1898), to the author, and is the most exhaustive and reliable over-all source that we possess on the causes for and the dealings of the organization from 1892 until 1911.

17 *Ibid.*, p. 13. Cf. Higham, *Strangers in the Land*, p. 157.

18 Charles De Garmo, *Herbart and the Herbartians* (New York: Charles Scribner's Sons, 1896), pp. 57-66.

19 Francis W. Parker, *Talks on Pedagogics* (New York: E. L. Kellogg and Co., 1894), p. 191.

20 William Torrey Harris, "Religious Instruction in the Public Schools," *The Independent*, LV (August 6, 1903), 1841.

21 John Dewey, *The School and Society* (Chicago: University of Chicago Press, 1899), p. 4.

22 Henry J. Browne, "The American Parish School in the Last Half Century,"

*National Catholic Education Association Bulletin,* L, No. 1 (August, 1953), p. 323.
[23] John Ireland, *The Church and Modern Society: Lectures and Addresses* (2 vols.; Chicago: D. H. McBride & Co., 1897), I, 197-214.
[24] Daniel F. Reilly, *The School Controversy (1891-1893)* (Washington, D.C.: The Catholic University of America Press, 1943), p. 48.
[25] The controversy should be rewritten to include the Corrigan papers in the Archives of the Chancery of the Archdiocese of New York as well as with more intense perusal of the Baltimore Cathedral Archives and the St. Paul, Minn., Archdiocesan Archives.

The Baltimore Cathedral Archives contain (88 F 8), for example, a very long letter from Ireland to Gibbons dated "Dec. '90," defending his speech. In it, he said, among other things:
I cannot bring myself to believe, that those in Rome, finding fault with me, could have had my whole discourse before their eyes. . . . I admitted in principle the State School. . . . I am most plain & strong, in declaring that the right [to educate] belongs primarily to the parent. . . .
"Free Schools! Blessed indeed is the nation whose vales & hillsides they adorn, and blessed the generations upon whose Souls are poured their treasures!" A fearful cry went out against those words, as if I extolled the present free-schools of America, as being perfect. . . .
"The free-Schools of America! Withered be the hand raised in sign of their destruction!"—Another sentence, for which I was threatened with excommunication. . . .
The necessity for parish schools is hypothetical—the necessity being not a direct result of the Church's mission, but a provision in certain cases for the protection of the faith. The Church is not established to teach writing & ciphering: but to teach morals & faith, & she teaches writing & ciphering only when otherwise morals & faith could not be taught. . . .
Now, what is required in the State School to make it acceptable to us, I develop in two-thirds of my discourse. I am sure you will find this part ultra-orthodox. I demand positive Catholic dogmatic teaching—rejecting mere moral teaching, rejecting totally the so-called "common Christianity" theory. . . .
Indeed, since our own schools are neither numerous enough, nor efficient enough, for our children, and many of these must attend the public school, have we not done immense harm to souls by our anathemas? . . .
I repeat—I have read all the objections to the discourse, & they come either from partial reading of my words, or from hatred of the American state.
In a letter to Gibbons on Dec. 17, 1890 (88 E 4), Ireland states, "I rather enjoy the predicament into which I have got. . . . The 'address' which brings out from Your Eminence such an elaborate defence of me may well be called—'Felix Sermo.' . . . Any reproof from Rome . . . would be taken as a censure of my Americanism, and as a proof of the hopeless foreignism of the Church."
In St. Paul, Minn., the Seminary Archives contain Archbishop Ireland papers; microfilm copies of the *Catholic Telegraph,* the *Northwestern Chronicle,* and the *Catholic Bulletin,* plus periodicals from the early

decades of this century. The Chancery Office Archdiocesan Archives contain two boxes of Ireland correspondence from the 1890's.

A good recent article is John R. Gilbert, "Archbishop Ireland and Thomas Bouquillon: The State's Right to Educate," *Catholic Educational Review*, LXVI, No. 9 (December, 1968), 566-591.

26 Thomas Bouquillon, *Education: To Whom Does It Belong?* (Baltimore: John Murphy & Co., 1892), p. 3.

27 *Ibid.*, p. 31.

28 *Ibid.*, p. 16.

29 René I. Holaind, *The Parent First: An Answer to Dr. Bouquillon's Query* (New York: Benziger Brothers, 1891).

30 Archbishop John Ireland's *Memorial* cited in Reilly, *The School Controversy (1891–1893)*, pp. 250-266. This defense was addressed to Cardinal Ledochowski, prefect of the Sacred Congregation for the Propagation of the Faith. The other cardinals who heard the defense were: Rampolla, Vanutelli, Serafini, Zigliara, and Parocchi. The defense is not dated. It was probably presented about April, 1892.

31 *Ibid.*, p. 251.

32 *Ibid.*, p. 255.

33 *Ibid.*, p. 266.

34 No condemnation of Bouquillon's efforts ever came from Rome.

35 Francesco Cardinal Satolli, *For the Settling of the School Question and the Giving of Religious Education* (Baltimore: J. Murphy & Co., 1892). Quoted in Reilly, *The School Controversy (1891–1893)*, p. 272.

36 *Ibid.*

37 For the Latin original of the Propositions see Francesco Satolli, *Ad scholasticum questionem dirimendam et educationem religiosam impertiendam* (New York, 1892). The English translation used here is taken from Appendix G of Reilly's *The School Controversy (1891–1893)*, pp. 271-276.

38 Frederick James Zweierlein, *Letters of Bishop McQuaid*, (3 vols.; Rochester, N. Y.: The Art Print Shop) III, 187.

39 *Ibid.*, pp. 187-188.

40 This letter from Pope Leo XIII to James Cardinal Gibbons, both in the Latin original and in the English translation, is in *The American Catholic Quarterly Review*, XVIII, No. 71 (July, 1893), 642-649.

41 Walter Eliott, *Life of Father Hecker* (New York: Columbus Press, 1891).

42 John J. Wynne, S.J. (ed.), *The Great Encyclical Letters of Pope Leo XIII* (New York: Benziger Bros., 1903), pp. 441-453. Cited in John Tracy Ellis, *Documents of American Catholic History* (Milwaukee: The Bruce Publishing Company, 1956), pp. 553-562.

43 Ellis, p. 554.

44 *Ibid.*, p. 558.

45 Ellis, *The Life of James Cardinal Gibbons, Archbishop of Baltimore, 1834–1921* (Milwaukee: The Bruce Publishing Company, 1952), II, 71.

46 Ellis, *Documents of American Catholic History*, p. 514.

47 See Thomas T. McAvoy, C.S.C., *The Great Crisis in American Catholic History, 1895–1900* (Chicago: Henry Regnery Co., 1957).

48 *People v. Board of Education*, 92 N.E. 25 (1910).

49 *Herold v. Parish Board of Education*, 136 La. 1034, 68S. 116 (1915).

50 Colorado, Georgia, Iowa, Kansas, Maine, Massachusetts, Michigan, Minnesota, Ohio, Pennsylvania, and Texas.

[51] *Commonwealth* v. *Herr*, 229 Pa. 132, 78 Att. 68 (1910).

[52] *O'Connor* v. *Hendrick*, 184 N.Y. 421, 77 N.E. 612 (1906).

[53] *Hysong* v. *Gallitzin*, 164 Pa. 629, 30 Att. 482 (1894).

[54] John J. McGrath, *Church and State in American Law* (Milwaukee: The Bruce Publishing Company, 1962), pp. 271-272.

[55] J. A. W. Haas, "Week-day Religious Instruction and the Public Schools," *Religious Education*, IX, No. 1 (February, 1914), 26-27; Austin Kennedy De Blois and Donald R. Gorham, *Christian Religious Education: Principles and Practice* (New York: Fleming H. Revell Company, 1939), pp. 301-302. The "released-time" movement was slow in starting. It had its practical beginnings in religious instruction on released time in Gary, Ind. The initiative came from William Wirt, superintendent of public schools in Gary, who in the fall of 1913 offered to release pupils from the public schools for religious instruction. De Blois and Gorham, p. 302.

[56] Donald R. Gorham, *A Study of the Status of Weekday Church Schools in the United States* (Philadelphia: The University of Pennsylvania, 1934), p. 10.

[57] *McCollum* v. *Board of Education*, 333 U.S. 203, 68S. Ct. 461, 92L. Ed. 649 (1948).

[58] Neil G. McCluskey, *Catholic Viewpoint on Education* (Garden City, New York: Doubleday & Company, Inc., 1962), p. 130.

[59] *Zorach* v. *Clauson*, 343 U.S. 306, 72S. Ct. 679, 90L. Ed. 954 (1952).

[60] John Ireland, *The Church and Modern Society* (Chicago: D. H. McBride & Company, 1896), p. 203.

[61] *Ibid.*, pp. 205-206.

[32] John J. Wynne, S.J. (ed.), Encyclical Letter "Longinque Oceani," January 6, 1895, in *The Great Encyclical Letters of Pope Leo XIII: Translated from Approved Sources* (New York: Benziger Brothers, 1903), p. 324.

[63] George D. Wolff, "Our Parochial School—The Progress It Has Made and Is Making," *American Catholic Quarterly Review*, XVII (December, 1892), 866.

[64] McCluskey, *Catholic Viewpoint on Education*, p. 80.

[65] Michael H. Lucey, "Administration of the Parish Schools," *The Catholic World*, XCIV, No. 547 (October, 1911), 63.

[66] Henry J. Browne, "The American Parish School in the Last Half Century," *National Catholic Education Association Bulletin*, L, No. 1 (August, 1953), 330. Another example of the fact that not all these improvements began with Baltimore III was Archbishop John Hennessy, head of the archdiocese of Dubuque, Ia., from 1866 to 1900. Under him, approximately 160 schools were started; he helped found ten communities of religious sisters in the archdiocese and was instrumental in bringing other religious communities into the archdiocese, and on March 18, 1868, signed the official document of the "Catholic Pay and Free School Association of the City of Dubuque," the See City's constitution concerning Catholic education. See Rt. Rev. Msgr. Justin A. Driscoll, *With Faith and Vision: Schools of the Archdiocese of Dubuque 1836–1966* (Dubuque, Iowa: Bureau of Education, Archdiocese of Dubuque, 1967), pp. v and xii.

[67] Louis S. Walsh, "Unity, Efficiency, and Public Recognition of Catholic Elementary Schools," *American Ecclesiastical Review*, XXV, No. 6 (December, 1901), 486-487.

[68] Browne, "The American Parish School," p. 324.

[69] *Report of the Proceedings and Addresses of the First Annual Meeting of*

*the Catholic Education Association,* St. Louis, Mo., July 12, 13, and 14, 1904 (Columbus, Ohio: 1905), pp. 18-24.

[70] *Report of the Proceedings and Addresses of the Twenty-fourth Annual Meeting of the National Catholic Education Association,* Detroit, Mich., June 27, 28, 29, and 30, 1927. The Report stated (p. 7):
> The word, National, by vote of the Executive Board and of the Association, has now been added to the title to indicate the scope of the influence of the Association.

[71] See Edgar P. McCarren, "The Origin and Early Years of the National Catholic Educational Association" (unpublished doctoral dissertation, The Catholic University of America, 1966); James Howard Plough, "Catholic Colleges and the Catholic Educational Association: The Foundation and Early Years of the CEA, 1899–1919" (unpublished Ph.D. dissertation, University of Notre Dame, 1967).

[72] *Report of the Proceedings and Addresses of the First Annual Meeting of the Catholic Education Association,* July 12, 13, and 14, 1904, pp. 9-10.

[73] *Ibid.,* p. 10.

[74] *Report of the Proceedings and Addresses of the Fourteenth Annual Meeting of the Catholic Education Association.* Buffalo, New York, June 25, 26, 27, and 28, 1917, (Columbus, Ohio, 1917), p. 3.

[75] The NCEA quarterly *Bulletin* and the published annual reports of the Proceedings of the Association are excellent sources for the study of the Catholic history of education in the United States since 1904.

[76] At the first meeting of the CEA, there was a registration of 769 names, and "all sections of the country were represented and a number of religious communities sent official delegates." (Francis W. Howard, "Educational Association: The Catholic," *The Catholic Encyclopedia* [New York: Robert Appleton Co., 1909], V, 305.) At the 1965 New York Convention of the NCEA there were more than 26,000 delegates. *Report of the Proceedings and Addresses of the Sixty-second Annual Meeting of the National Catholic Educational Association.* New York, April 19, 20, 21, and 22, 1965. (Washington, D.C., 1965), p. xvi.

[77] H. G. Good, *A History of American Education* (New York: The Macmillan Company, 1964), p. 239.

[78] *Report of the Committee of Ten on Secondary Education* (Washington, D.C.: U.S. Bureau of Education, 1893), pp. 46-47.

[79] James A. Burns, "Catholic Secondary Schools," *American Catholic Quarterly Review,* XXVI, No. 102 (July, 1901), 497.

[80] Joseph L. J. Kirlin, *Catholicity in Philadelphia* (Philadelphia: John Jos. McVey, 1909), p. 445.

[81] "The Roman Catholic High School, Philadelphia," *First Report of the Proceedings and Addresses of the Annual Meeting of the Catholic Educational Association,* St. Louis, Missouri, July 12, 13, and 14, 1904 (Columbus: 1904), p. 62.

[82] "Report of the Joint Committee on High Schools," *ibid.,* p. 39. The members of the Committee on High Schools appointed in 1903 were: the Rev. James A. Burns, president of Holy Cross College, Washington; Rev. Read Mullin, S.J., vice president of Georgetown University—both representing the College Conference; the Rev. Hugh T. Henry, president of the Roman Catholic High School, Philadelphia; and the Rev. Morgan M. Sheedy, rector of the Cathedral, Altoona, Pa.—the last two representing the Parochial School Conference.

[83] *Ibid.,* pp. 40-41.

84 "Report of the Committee on High Schools," *Report of the Proceedings and Addresses of the Eighth Annual Meeting of the Catholic Educational Association,* Chicago, Illinois, June 26, 27, 28 and 29, 1911 (Columbus: 1911), p. 45f.

85 *Ibid.,* p. 49.

86 *Ibid.,* p. 50.

87 *Ibid.,* p. 53.

88 *Ibid.,* p. 62.

89 "The Condition of Catholic Secondary Education in the United States: Report of the Advisory Board to the Executive Board of the Catholic Educational Association," *The Catholic Educational Review,* VI, No. 7 (October, 1915), p. 216.

90 *Ibid.,* p. 219. In 1915 there were 1,276 Catholic secondary schools—preparatory departments, high schools containing boys, and girls' high schools. The combined attendance amounted to 74,538. Of this number, 34,798 were boys, and 39,740 were girls ("Condition of Catholic Secondary Education," *The Catholic Educational Review,* No. 7 [October, 1915], p. 206). Of the curriculum in the Catholic high school for girls, the Advisory Board had this to say (*ibid*):

> There are, in fact, two distinct types of secondary schools for girls—the school that aims at culture and distinctly womanly accomplishment, and the school that aims primarily, after religious and moral training, at teaching a girl how readily to earn her own living. Both types are needed—in fact, indispensable, but the second answers better to the general popular demand at present.

91 John S. Brubacher and Willis Rudy, *Higher Education in Transition* (New York: Harper and Row, 1958), p. 239.

92 *Ibid.,* p. 240; Frederick Rudolph, *The American College and University* (New York: Random House, Inc., 1962), p. 436.

93 Brubacher and Rudy, *Higher Education in Transition,* p. 251.

94 Peter Guilday, *A History of the Councils of Baltimore, 1791–1884* (New York: The Macmillan Company, 1932), pp. 211-212.

95 Peter Guilday, *The National Pastorals of the American Hierarchy, 1792–1919* (Washington, D.C.: National Catholic Welfare Council, 1923), p. 226.

96 John Lancaster Spalding, *Means and Ends of Education* (Chicago: A. C. McClurg and Co., 1897), p. 220; cited in Ellis, *Documents of American Catholic History,* p. 432. See also Ellis, *John Lancaster Spalding* (Milwaukee, Wis.: Bruce Publishing Co. and National Catholic Educational Association, 1961).

97 Ellis, *The Formative Years of the Catholic University of America* (Washington, D.C.: American Catholic Historical Association, 1946), p. 7. Ellis, "Catholic University of America, The," *New Catholic Encyclopedia,* (New York: McGraw-Hill Book Company, 1967), III, 332.

98 Patrick Henry Ahearn, *The Catholic University of America 1887–1896: The Rectorship of John J. Keane* (Washington, D.C.: The Catholic University of America Press, 1948), p. 2.

99 Ellis, "Catholic University of America, The," *New Catholic Encyclopedia,* III, 333.

100 Ellis, *Documents of American Catholic History,* p. 479.

101 John Lancaster Spalding, *Education and the Higher Life* (Chicago: A. C. McClurg and Co., 1891), pp. 178-179; 193, 195-198. Quoted in Ellis, *Documents of American Catholic History,* p. 481.

102 Leo XIII, *Magni Nobis Gaudii,* quoted in Rita Watrin, "The Founding and Development of the Program of Affiliation of the Catholic University of America: 1912 to 1939" (unpublished Master's dissertation, Catholic University of America, 1964), p. 2.

103 An account of the first session of the Summer School at The Catholic University of America may be found in *The Catholic Educational Review,* II, No. 2 (September, 1911, 648-661. The session was officially opened on Sunday, July 2, 1911, and closed Sunday, August 8, 1911. The School was opened only to the teaching sisterhoods and to women teachers in public or private schools. The total registration was 284 and of this number 255 were religious.

104 Colman J. Barry, *The Catholic University of America 1903–1909: The Rectorship of Denis J. O'Connell* (Washington, D.C.: The Catholic University of America Press, 1949), pp. 150-153.

105 Leo XIII, *Magni Nobis Gaudii,* quoted in Watrin, "The Program of Affiliation of the Catholic University of America," p. 2.

106 ———, "For the Affiliation of Colleges and High Schools to the University," *The Catholic Educational Review,* III, No. 5 (May, 1912), 445-449. These pages present the conditions required for colleges and high schools desiring to affiliate, and the University's procedures. In 1968, the director of the Program of Affiliation would define the program as a service operation. He would record that the 1967 Directory of the Program included 709 affiliated institutions: 426 secondary schools and 283 higher educational institutions, in 34 states and 13 foreign countries. From 1912, when the program was founded, the trend had been constantly upward to 1965, when it reached almost 800 institutions. About 80 institutional evaluation consultants were listed in 1968. (Rev. Thomas J. Taylor, "Program of Affiliation is Reviewed by New Director," *The Catholic University of America Bulletin,* II, No. 2 (February, 1968), 4. The Academic Senate would recommend to the Board of Trustees at their meeting of December 6-8, 1968, that the Program of Affiliation be phased out as no longer filling the same need. The Board of Trustees approved this recommendation, voting to have the phasing out completed not later than January 1, 1970 (The Catholic University of America, *Administrative Bulletin,* I, No. 11 (December 16, 1968). The action was probably long overdue.

The statutes of Catholic University would also change in the course of time. After a revision in 1937, the most radical changes were made in new statutes drafted by a committee under Lawrence Cardinal Shehan of Baltimore, and approved on September 13, 1969, by the Board of Trustees and on January 23, 1970, by the Sacred Congregation for Catholic Education, in Rome. The new bylaws and statutes give the Board of Trustees, instead of the Vatican, full control of all schools of the university except those of theology, philosophy, and canon law; remove the presence of cardinals on the Board of Trustees "ex officio," and limit their number on the board to five; make the choice of president no longer subject to Vatican approval; make unnecessary Rome's accreditation for degrees except those in philosophy, theology, and canon law; make mandatory an even division between laymen and clergy on the thirty-member board of Trustees; and make more vague the role of chancellor. The new regulations are intended to modernize the university's administrative design to become more like that of other American universities, but not to secularize it or make it any less Catholic. See The Catholic University of America, *Administrative Bulletin*, II, No. 15 (February 11, 1970), p. 1; *Tower*, undergraduate student publication of The Catholic University of America, Vol. 48, No. 14 (February 6, 1970), pp. 6-7; *The New York Times*, February 6, 1970, p. 41.

[107] Walter D. Agnew, *The Administration of Professional Schools for Teachers* (Baltimore: Warwick and York, 1924), p. 98.

[108] Archbishop Francesco Satolli, "Fourteen Propositions Presented November 17, 1892, to the Archbishops of the United States for the Settling of the School Question," cited in Daniel F. Reilly, *The School Controversy, 1891–1893* (Washington, D.C.: The Catholic University of America Press, 1943), p. 275 (Proposition XIII).

[109] *Ibid.* (Proposition XIV).

[110] *Acta et decreta concilii Baltimorensi tertii* (Baltimore: Typis Joannis Murphy et Sociorum, 1886), Titulus VI, Caput I, Number 203, p. 108.

[111] James A. Burns, "The Development of Parish School Organization," *The Catholic Educational Review*, III, No. 5 (May, 1912), 432.

[112] John Lancaster Spalding, "Normal Schools for Catholics," *The Catholic World*, LI, No. 301, (April, 1890), 95.

[113] *Ibid.*, pp. 95-96.

[114] Thomas Edward Shields, *Philosophy of Education* (Washington, D.C.: The Catholic Education Press, 1917), pp. 391-393.

[115] Thomas J. Keane, "The Catholic Universities of France," *The Catholic World*, XLVII, No. 279 (June, 1888), 295.

[116] Ninth Annual Report of the Rector, October, 1898, p. 25f. (Archives, The Catholic University of America.) Quoted in my article, "The Teaching of Education at The Catholic University of America, 1889–1966," *The Catholic Educational Review*, LXV, No. 1 (January, 1967), 3.

[117] Tenth Annual Report of the Rector, October, 1899, p. 31. (Archives, The Catholic University of America.) Quoted in Buetow, p. 3.

[118] *Year Book*, 1914–1915, p. 102. (Archives, The Catholic University of America.) Quoted in Buetow, p. 8. See also Sr. M. Augustine O'Connor, "The Influence of Very Reverend Doctor Thomas E. Shields on Catholic Education in the United States" (unpublished Master's dissertation, Department of Education, The Catholic University of America, 1941), p. 71.

[119] *Year Book*, 1923–1924, p. 9. (Archives, The Catholic University of America.) Quoted in Buetow, p. 10.

[120] Spalding, "Normal Schools for Catholics," p. 96.

[121] Sr. Bertrande Meyers, *The Education of Sisters* (New York: Sheed and Ward, 1941), pp. 20-21.

[122] Sr. Maria Concepta McDermott, *The Making of a Sister-Teacher* (Notre Dame: University of Notre Dame Press, 1965), Preface by George N. Shuster, p. vii.

[123] *Ibid.*, p. 106.

[124] Sr. Mary Antonia Durkin, *The Preparation of the Religious Teacher: A Foundational Study* (Washington, D.C.: The Catholic University of America Press, 1926), p. 14.

[125] Robert D. Cross, "Origins of the Catholic Parochial Schools in America," *The American Benedictine Review*, XVI, No. 2 (June, 1965), 203.

[126] Willard S. Elsbree, *The American Teacher* (New York: The American Book Company, 1939), p. 334.

[127] Meyers, *The Education of Sisters*, p. 21.

[128] Henry D. Hervey, "The Rating of Teachers," *Journal of the Proceedings and Addresses of the National Education Association*, Session of the year 1921 (St. Paul: National Education Association, 1921), pp. 825-827.

[129] *Ibid.*

[130] McDermott, Preface, p. viii.

[131] *School Manual for the Use of the Sisters of St. Joseph of Carondelet* (St. Louis: Ev. E. Carreras, Printer, Binder and Publisher, 1883-84).

[132] *Ibid.*, p. 14.

[133] *Ibid.*, pp. 49, 16, 17, and 44.

[134] *Ibid.*, p. 68.

[135] *Ibid.*, p. 82. This is the form which the sister-directress used:

### TEACHER'S GRADE CARD

| Name ........... | Neatness | Order | Ability to Command Attention | Method | Manner | Interest | Profit from Suggestions | General Remarks | Average Teaching Capacity |
|---|---|---|---|---|---|---|---|---|---|
| Month | | | | | | | | | |
| September | | | | | | | | | |
| October | | | | | | | | | |

[136] Thomas Edward Shields, *Philosophy of Education* (Washington, D.C.: The Catholic Education Press, 1917), p. 393.

[137] Shields, "Catholic Teachers and Educational Progress," *The Catholic World*, LXXXIII, No. 493 (April, 1906), 97.

[138] *Ibid.*, p. 98.

[139] "Report of the Committee of Fifteen," *Journal of the Proceedings and Addresses of the National Education Association*, Session of the year 1895, held at Colorado (St. Paul: National Education Association, 1895), p. 240.

[140] *Ibid.*, p. 289.

[141] *Ibid.*, pp. 356-357.

[142] Sarah Louise Arnold and Charles B. Gilbert, *Stepping Stones to Literature* (Newark: Silver Burdett & Co., 1899).

[143] Ida Coe and Alice J. Christie, *Story Hour Readers* (New York: American Book Co., 1913).

[144] Harry Pratt Judson and Ida C. Bender, *Graded Literature Readers* (New York: Merrill Co., 1899).

[145] Margaret Free and Harriett T. Treadwell, *Reading Literature Series* (Evanston, Illinois: Row, Peterson & Co., 1910-1916).

[146] Van Sickle, Seegmiller and Jenkins, *The Riverside Readers* (Boston: Houghton Mifflin Co., 1907).

[147] Edward G. Ward, *The Rational Method in Reading* (Newark: Silver, Burdett & Co., 1894).

[148] Frank E. Spaulding and Catherine T. Bryce, *The Aldine Readers* (New York: Newson & Co., 1907).

[149] James H. Fassett, *The Beacon Readers* (Boston: Ginn & Co., 1912).

[150] *The New Century Catholic Series* (New York: Benziger Brothers, 1905).

[151] Brothers of the Christian Schools, *De La Salle Series* (New York: La Salle Bureau of Supplies, 1906).

[152] Thomas E. Shields, *Catholic Education Series* (Washington, D.C.: The Catholic University of America Press, 1915).

[153] *De La Salle Second Reader*, Preface, p. 1.

[154] Thomas E. Shields, *Teacher's Manual of Primary Methods* (Washington, D.C.: The Catholic Education Press, 1912), p. 95f.

[155] Richard Gilmour, *Catholic National Series* (New York: Benziger Brothers, 1889).

[156] Mother Angela Gillespie, *Metropolitan Readers* (New York: Sadlier House, 1871).

[157] P. O'Shea, *The Graded Catholic Education Series* (New York: P. O'Shea, 1881).

[158] *The McBride Readers* (Chicago: D. H. McBride & Co., 1898).

[159] Gillespie, *Metropolitan Second Reader*, p. 6.

[160] O'Shea, *Fourth Reader*, p. 2.

[161] Thomas J. O'Brien, "Textbooks in Catholic Schools," *Report of the Proceedings and Addresses of the Second Annual Meeting* (New York: Catholic Educational Association, 1905), p. 199f.

[162] A Catechism of Christian Doctrine, Prepared and Enjoined by Order of the Third Plenary Council of Baltimore (New York: Benziger Brothers, 1886). A German-English edition was also published: *Katholischer Katechismus, Hergestellt und ambefohlen von dem Dritten Plenar Concil von Baltimore* (New York: F. Pustet & Co., 1886).

[163] Quoted in John K. Sharp, "How the Baltimore Catechism Originated," *The American Ecclesiastical Review*, LXXI (December, 1929), 576.

[164] *Ibid.*, p. 577.

[165] *Ibid.*, p. 580.

[166] *Ibid.*

[167] Baltimore Cathedral Archives, 79 E 15.

[168] *Ibid.*

[169] *Ibid.*, 84 01.

[170] Sharp, "How the Baltimore Catechism Originated," p. 584.

[171] Bishop Hay, *An Abridgment of the Christian Doctrine* (Philadelphia: Mathew Carey, 1803).

[172] Richard Gilmour, *Bible History* (New York: Benziger Brothers, 1890).

[173] Thomas L. Kinkead, *An Explanation of the Baltimore Catechism* (New York: Benziger Brothers, 1891), p. 4.

[174] Peter C. Yorke, *Textbooks of Religion for Parochial and Sunday Schools* (San Francisco: The Text-Book Publishing Co., 1898), p. 3.

[175] Pierre Ranwez, S.J., "General Tendencies in Contemporary Catechetics," in *Shaping the Christian Message*, ed. Gerard S. Sloyan (New York: The Macmillian Company, 1948), p. 112.

[176] Thomas E. Shields, "The Method of Teaching Religion," *Report of the Proceedings and Addresses of the Fifth Annual Meeting of the Catholic Educational Association*, Cincinnati, Ohio, July 6, 7, 8, and 9, 1908 (Columbus, Ohio: 1908), pp. 142-143.

[177] *Ibid.*, p. 201.

[178] *Ibid.*, p. 209.

[179] *Ibid.*, p. 225.

[180] *Ibid.*, pp. 233-234.

[181] Philip Gleason, "American Catholic Higher Education: A Historical Perspective," *The Shape of Catholic Higher Education*, ed. Robert Hassenger. (Chicago: The University of Chicago Press, 1967), p. 28.

[182] *Ibid.*, pp. 28-29.

[183] Charles W. Eliot, *More Money for the Public Schools, Because of the Failures and Shortcomings in American Education* (New York: Doubleday, Page & Co., 1903), p. 36.

[184] Merle Eugene Curti, *The Social Ideas of American Educators* (Paterson, N. J.: Pageant Books, 1949), p. 255.

[185] Ellwood P. Cubberley, *Public Education in the United States* (New York: Houghton Mifflin Company, 1919), p. 489. See also, however, Colin Greer, "Public Schools: the Myth of the Melting Pot," *Saturday Review* (November 15, 1969), 84-86, 102. This article was adapted from Greer's forthcoming book, *Cobweb Attitudes: Essays in American Education and Culture*, to be published by Teachers College Press, Columbia University. Greer claims in his article (p. 84): "The public schools have always failed the lower classes—both white and black."

[186] George H. Martin, *Evolution of the Massachusetts Public School System* (New York: D. Appleton & Co., 1894), p. 233. It is also Martin who wrote that in Massachussetts in 1894 the parochial school contained 10.6 per cent of the whole school attendance.

[187] Wolff, "Our Parochial School," p. 876.

[188] Thomas C. Harte, "Racial and National Parishes in the U. S.," *The Sociology of the Parish*, ed. C. Joseph Nuesse and Thomas C. Harte (Milwaukee: The Bruce Publishing Co., 1951), p. 156.

[189] John J. Harbrecht, *The Lay Apostolate: A Social Ethical Study of Parish Organization for Large City Parishes* (St. Louis: B. Herder Book Co., 1929), p. 98.

[190] James A. Burns quotes these words of James Cardinal Gibbons from *The Catholic Standard and Times*, Dec. 21, 1907. The writer found that the periodical was a Philadelphia production not available in the libraries. (James A. Burns, *The Growth and Development of the Catholic School System in the United States* [New York: Benziger Brothers, 1912]), pp. 298-299.

[191] Fergus MacDonald, "A Development of Parishes in the United States," *Sociology of the Parish*, ed. C. Joseph Nuesse and Thomas C. Harte (Milwaukee: The Bruce Publishing Co., 1951), p. 69.

[192] Coleman J. Barry, *The Catholic Church and German Americans* (Milwaukee: The Bruce Publishing Co., 1953), Appendix IV, p. 315. John Tracy Ellis in *Documents of American Catholic History* (pp. 496-499) reproduced the petition of American immigrants to Pope Leo XIII: "The St. Raphaelsverein Protests the Neglect of Immigrant Catholics in the United States, February, 1891." Ellis writes that the St. Raphaelsverein was an organization founded in 1871 for the care of German Catholic immigrants, and that from an international conference of the organization held in Lucerne, Switzerland, on Dec. 9-10, 1890, there emerged a document to be sent to Pope Leo XIII. The document was signed by officials of the society from seven different countries. Concerning Catholic schools for immigrants in America, the document stated (Ellis, p. 498):

It will be necessary to establish parochial schools wherever Christian public schools are not available, and these schools should be separate, as far as possible, for each nationality. The curriculum of these schools should always include the mother tongue as well as the language and history of the adopted country.

[193] Angelo Patri, *A Schoolmaster of the Great City* (New York: The Macmillan Company, 1917), pp. 78-79.

[194] *Ibid.*, p. 218.

[195] *Ibid.*, p. 120.

[196] Raymond G. Fuller, *Child Labor and the Constitution* (New York: Thomas Y. Crowell Company, 1923), p. 2.

[197] *Ibid.*, pp. 3 and 126.

[198] H. G. Good, *A History of American Education* (New York: The Macmillan Company, 1956), p. 381.

[199] Edward Reisner, *Nationalism and Education Since 1789* (New York: The Macmillan Company, 1922), p. 547.

[200] Browne, "The American Parish School in the Last Half Century," p. 324.

[201] "The Catholic Church and the Colored People," *The Catholic World* (June, 1883), 374.

[202] John T. Gillard, *Colored Catholics in the United States* (Baltimore: The Josephite Press, 1941), pp. 95, 39.

[203] *Ibid.*, pp. 42-43.

[204] Guilday, *A History of the Councils of Baltimore*, p. 192.

[205] *Acta et Decreta Concilii Plenarii Baltimorensis II* (Baltimore: Typis Joannis Murphy et Sociorum, 1868), Caput IV, "De Nigrorum Salute Procuranda," nos. 488, 490.

[206] *Acta et Decreta Concilii Plenarii Baltimorensis Tertii* (Baltimore: Typis Joannis Murphy et Sociorum, 1886), Caput II, no. 238.

[207] *Ibid.*, nos. 240, 243.

[208] Mother M. Agatha, *Catholic Education and the Negro* (Washington, D. C.: The Catholic University of America Press, 1942), p. 8.

[209] Gillard, *Colored Catholics in the United States*, p. 124.

[210] Elinor Long Dehey, *Religious Orders of Women in the United States* (Hammond, Indiana: W. B. Conkey, 1930), p. 467.

[211] Mother M. Agatha, *Catholic Education and the Negro*, pp. 8-9.

[212] Joseph Butsch, "Negro Catholics in the United States," *The Catholic Historical Review*, III, No. 1 (April, 1917), 49. Mother Katherine Drexel's congregation would establish the first and only Catholic University for Negroes in the U. S.—Xavier University of Louisiana in New Orleans, which opened in 1915.

[213] Dehey, *Religious Orders of Women*, p. 268. In the research on the Catholic education of the Negro that came to my attention, more seems to center around Louisiana than any other area. See, for example: Loretta M. Butler, "A History of Catholic Elementary Education for Negroes in the Diocese of Lafayette, Louisiana" (unpublished Ph.D. dissertation, The Catholic University of America, 1963); Sr. Mary Josephina Kenny, S.B.S., "Contributions of the Sisters of the Blessed Sacrament for Indians and Colored People to Catholic Negro Education in the State of Louisiana" (unpublished Master's thesis, The Catholic University of America, 1942); Sr. Mary David Young, S.B.S., "A History of the Development of Catholic Education for the Negro in Louisiana" (unpublished Master's thesis, Louisiana State University, 1944); Marie Dejan, "Education for Negroes in New Orleans Prior to 1915" (unpublished Master's thesis, Xavier University, New Orleans, 1941); and Myrtle Rosabella Banks, "The Education of the Negro in New Orleans," (unpublished Master's thesis, Xavier University, New Orleans, 1935); Robert Smith Shea, "The Development of Catholic Facilities for

Negro Education in the State of Louisiana with Special Reference to the Work of Sisters of the Blessed Sacrament for Indians and Colored People," (unpublished Master's thesis, Tulane University, 1949); etc. But see also Sr. Mary Edna Kilroy, "History of Catholic Education of the Negro in Texas, 1886–1934," (unpublished Master's thesis, St. Mary's University, San Antonio, Tex., 1944).

[214] Dehey, p. 819.

[215] Butsch, "Negro Catholics in the United States," p. 43.

[216] John Tracy Ellis, *The Life of James Cardinal Gibbons* (2 vols.; Milwaukee: The Bruce Publishing Co., 1952), pp. 369, 399. Between 1889 and 1894 five Negro Catholic congresses also met to further the welfare of the Negro—see David Spalding, "The Negro Catholic Congresses, 1889–1894," *The Catholic Historical Review*, LV, No. 3 (October, 1969), 337-349.

[217] Butsch, "Negro Catholics in the United States," p. 51.

[218] Mother M. Agatha, *Catholic Education and the Indian* (Washington, D.C.: The Catholic University of America Press, 1942), p. 10; this is an off-print from Roy J. Deferrari (ed.), *Essays on Catholic Education in the United States* (Washington, D.C.: The Catholic University of America Press, 1942), pp. 523-552.

[219] *Annals of the Catholic Indian Missions of America*, I, No. 1 (Washington, D. C.: Bureau of Catholic Indian Missions, 1877), in Mother M. Agatha, *Catholic Education and the Indian*, p. 12. The *Annals of the Catholic Indian Missions of America* was a semi-annual magazine of the Catholic Indian Bureau, which was also published in German in July, 1877. The main purpose of the *Annals* was to solicit funds for the Indian missions. It succeeded in this, for the January, 1878, edition of the *Annals* showed that almost $12,000 had been given to the Bureau in about thirteen months (Peter J. Rahill, *The Catholic Indian Missions and Grant's Peace Policy, 1870–1884* [Washington, D. C.: The Catholic University of America Press, 1953], p. 168).

[220] Charles Warren Currier, "Our Indian Schools," *Report of the Proceedings and Addresses of the Fourth Annual Meeting of the Catholic Educational Association*, Milwaukee, Wisconsin, July 8, 9, 10, and 11, 1907 (Columbus: 1907), p. 58.

[221] *Ibid.*, p. 59.

[222] *Sadliers' Catholic Directory*, (New York: D. J. Sadlier & Co., 1890), p. 406.

[223] *Journal of the Senate*, 53rd Cong., 2d Sess., 1893–94, March 13, 1894, as cited in Sister Mary Claudia Duratschek, O.S.B., Ph.D., *Crusading Along Sioux Trails, A History of the Catholic Missions of South Dakota* (Yankton, S.D.: Grail Publications, 1947), p. 148.

[224] *Quick Bear* v. *Leupp*, 210 U.S. 80-81 (1908), as cited in Duratschek, p. 150.

[225] "Appeal in Behalf of the Negro and Indian Missions in the United States," *Catholic Church in the U.S.: Commission for Catholic Missions among the Negroes and Indians* (Clayton, Delaware: St. Joseph's Industrial School for Colored Boys, 1902), pp. 1-2. The signatures to the appeal were: James Cardinal Gibbons, archbishop of Baltimore; P. J. Ryan, archbishop of Philadelphia; and J. J. Kain, archbishop of St. Louis. Currier claims that in 1906, the Bureau spent $176,392.72 for Indian schools. These funds, he said, came from the following sources (Currier, pp. 65-66):

Mother Katharine Drexel gave $86,882.85. From the tribal funds were received $44,339.17. The allotment from the Lenten collection was $26,270.70. The income from the Preservation Society was $17,900. Besides her donations through the Bureau, Mother Katharine sent directly to some of the schools $32,077.25. She also supplied the entire support of two schools. It will thus be seen that without her aid it would be impossible to meet the requirements of the schools.

[226] This and the following quotations in this section are from the unnumbered pages of the "Diary of Sr. Mary Meinrada, O.S.F.," in her possession at St. Mary's Home, Bryn Mawr, Pa.

[227] John Lancaster Spalding, *Means and Ends of Education* (Chicago: A. C. McClure & Co., 1909), pp. 113, 152.

[228] Spalding, *Education and the Future of Religion* (Notre Dame, Ind.: The Ave Maria Press, 1901), p. 25.

[229] Michael J. Curley, "The Aim of Catholic Education," *The Catholic Educational Review*, VII, no. 1 (June, 1916), 20.

[230] John L. Spalding, "Normal Schools for Catholics," pp. 90-91.

[231] Shields, *Philosophy of Education*, p. 171.

[232] *Ibid.*, p. 180.

[233] Cross, "Origins of the Catholic Parochial Schools in America," p. 204.

[234] Archives, Notre Dame University, Bishop McDevitt papers, McDevitt to S. Edwin Megargee, Esq., Box No. 5.

[235] *Ibid.*, Box No. 5. For the formation of the "Catholic Archives of America" at the University of Notre Dame toward the end of the nineteenth century, see Sister Damien Tambola, O.S.B., "James F. Edwards, Pioneer Archivist of Catholic Church History of America," *Records of the American Catholic Historical Society of Philadelphia*, Vol. LXXII, Nos. 1 & 2 (March and June, 1961), 3-32. The Catholic Archives of America are now called the Archives of the University of Notre Dame, and are housed on the sixth floor of the library of that university.

## Chapter V

[1] Arthur S. Link and William B. Catton, *American Epoch: A History of the United States Since the 1890's* (3 vols.; New York: Alfred A. Knopf, 1963), I, 231.

[2] John D. Hicks, *The American Nation* (Cambridge, Mass.: The Riverside Press, 1941), p. 457.

[3] *Ibid.*, pp. 457-458. By the middle of the 1920's the Ku Klux Klan counted perhaps four million members. In due time, however, the many scandals attributed to the organization, including murder, speeded its decline. (Hicks, pp. 458-459.)

[4] Carl Wittke, *We Who Built America* (New York: Prentice-Hall, Inc., 1940), p. 516.

[5] *Ibid.*

[6] Hicks, *The American Nation*, p. 526.

[7] Nelson Manfred Blake, *A History of American Life and Thought* (New York: McGraw-Hill Book Company, Inc., 1963), p. 487.

[8] Merle Curti, *The Social Ideas of American Educators* (Patterson, New Jersey: Pageant Books, Inc., 1959), p. 573.

[9] Blake, *History of American Life and Thought*, p. 510.

[10] *The Four Freedoms*, from President Roosevelt's annual message to Congress, January 6, 1941. Quoted in full in Blake, Appendix, p. xxii.

[11] Ernest Hemingway, *For Whom the Bell Tolls* (New York: Charles Scribner's Sons, 1940).

[12] Hicks, *The American Nation*, p. 763.

[13] Link and Catton, *American Epoch*, III, 635.

[14] Walter Lippmann, "Education without Culture," *Commonweal*, XXXIII, No. 13 (January 17, 1940), 323. This was an address delivered Dec. 29, 1940, before the American Association for the Advancement of Science. *Commonweal's* comment on the article was: "The prevailing education's career of ruin is traced with threatening clarity" (p. 322).

[15] Hicks, *The American Nation*, p. 771.

[16] Link and Catton, *American Epoch*, III, 609.

[17] Fulton J. Sheen, *Peace of Soul* (New York: Whittlesey House, 1949).

[18] Norman Vincent Peale, *The Power of Positive Thinking* (New York: Prentice-Hall, Inc., 1952).

[19] Lawrence A. Cremin, *The Transformation of the School* (New York: Alfred A. Knopf, 1961), p. 347.

[20] Link and Catton, *American Epoch*, III, 656.

[21] The source here cited is in the Archives of the University of Notre Dame, McDevitt papers, Box 32. The source McDevitt cited is the *Research Bulletin* of the National Education Association, I, No. 4 (September, 1923).

[22] Commission on the Reorganization of Secondary Education, *Cardinal Principles of Secondary Education* (Washington: U. S. Government Printing Office, 1918). Quoted in Ellis Ford Hartford, *Education in These United States* (New York: The Macmillan Company, 1964), p. 235.

[23] Herbert Spencer, *Education: Intellectual, Moral and Physical* (New York: D. Appleton Co., 1866).

[24] Hartford, *Education in These United States*, p. 235.

[25] Joy Elmer Morgan, "Restating our National Goals," *NEA Journal*, XXIII, No. 1 (January, 1934), 5. The NEA created the Committee on Social-Economic Goals of America in July, 1931.

[26] Frank J. Kelley, "Social-Economic Goals of America," *NEA Journal*, XXIII, No. 1 (January, 1934), 6-12.

[27] *Ibid.*, p. 8.

[28] *The Reports of the White House Conference on Education, Washington, D.C., November 28–December 1, 1955* (Washington, D.C.: U.S. Printing Office, 1955), pp. 1-2.

[29] Willard E. Givens, "The Released-Time Decision," *NEA Journal*, XXXVII, No. 4 (April, 1948), 209.

[30] "The Principles of Progressive Education," *Progressive Education*, I, No. 1 (April, 1924), 2.

[31] Cremin, *The Transformation of the School*, p. 306.

[32] *Ibid.*, p. 307.

[33] *Ibid.*, p. vii.

[34] Link and Catton, *American Epoch*, III, p. 655.

[35] H. G. Good, *A History of American Education* (New York: The Macmillan Company, 1956), p. 395.

[36] Gerard S. Sloyan, "The Curriculum in Transition," *Report of the Proceedings and Addresses of the Fiftieth Annual Meeting of the National Catholic Educational Association*, Atlantic City, New Jersey, April 7, 8, 9, and 10, 1953 (Washington, D.C.: August, 1953), L, No. 1, 343.

[37] Thomas Edward Shields, *Philosophy of Education* (Washington: The Catholic Education Press, 1921), p. 97.

[38] Henry J. Browne, "The American Parish School in the Last Half Century," *National Catholic Educational Association Bulletin*, L, No. 1 (August, 1953), p. 323.

[39] *The Official Catholic Directory*, 1917, p. 1101. Detailed summaries on

Catholic school enrollments do not begin until 1920, under the Department of Education of the National Catholic Welfare Conference, Washington, D.C.

[40] *The Official Catholic Directory,* 1957, General Summary, p. 1.

[41] John Dewey, *Moral Principles in Education* (Boston: Houghton Mifflin, 1909), p. 11.

[42] William Chandler Bagley, "An Essentialist's Platform for the Advancement of American Education," *Educational Administration and Supervision,* XXIV, No. 4 (April, 1938), 250.

[43] Bagley, *Education and the Emergent Man* (New York: Thomas Nelson and Sons, 1934), p. 63.

[44] Pope Pius XI, *Christian Education of Youth* (New York: The America Press, 1936).

[45] "The Pastoral Letter of 1919," *The National Pastorals of the American Hierarchy, 1792–1919,* ed. Peter Guilday (Washington, D.C.: National Catholic Welfare Council, 1923), pp. 332-339.

[46] Guilday, *The National Pastorals of the American Hierarchy,* p. xii. The remaining citations in this paragraph are from pp. 332-335.

[47] Rev. Patrick J. McCormack, "Standards in Education," *Report of the Proceedings and Addresses of the Fourteenth Annual Meeting of the Catholic Educational Association,* Buffalo, New York, June 25, 26, 27, and 28, 1917 (Columbus, Ohio: November, 1917), XIV, No. 2, 83.

[48] Br. Albert L. Hollinger, S.M., "Getting Full Value Out of Catholic Education," *Report of the Proceedings and Addresses of the Seventeenth Annual Meeting of the Catholic Educational Association,* New York, N.Y., June 28, 29, 30 and July 1, 1920 (Columbus, Ohio: November, 1920), XVII, No. 2, p. 267.

[49] Rev. Joseph Wehrle, "Education for Citizenship," *Report of the Proceedings and Addresses of the Eighteenth Annual Meeting of the Catholic Educational Association,* Cincinnati, Ohio, June 27, 28, 29, 30, 1921 (Columbus, Ohio: November, 1921), XVIII, No. 2, p. 201.

[50] Rev. Daniel Feeney, "Safeguarding the Religious Spirit in Catholic Education," *Report of the Proceedings and Addresses of the Twenty-Sixth Annual Meeting of the National Catholic Educational Association,* Toledo, Ohio, June 24, 25, 26, and 27, 1929 (Washington, D.C.: November, 1929), XXVII, No. 2, 327.

[51] Pius XI, *Christian Education of Youth* (New York: The America Press, 1936).

[52] Very Rev. Paul C. Reinert, S.J., "American Educators Face New Responsibilities," *Report of the Proceedings and Addresses of the Forty-ninth Annual Meeting of the National Catholic Educational Association,* Kansas City, Missouri, April 15-18, 1952, (Washington, D.C.: August, 1952), XLIX, No. 1, p. 57.

[53] Rev. Raymond A. Lucker, "The Aims of Religious Education in the Early Church and in the American Catechetical Movement" (unpublished S.T.D. dissertation. Rome, Italy: Pontificia Studiorum Universitas a S. Thoma Aq. in Urbe, Facultas S. Theologiae), Chapter VIII, pp. 263-325.

[54] Pius XI, *Christian Education of Youth,* pp. 35-36.

[55] *Ibid.,* pp. 37, 4-5.

[56] George Johnson, *The Curriculum of the Catholic Elementary School* (Washington, D.C.: The Catholic University of America, 1919), vii.

[57] George Johnson, "The Aim of Catholic Elementary Education," *The Catholic Educational Review,* XXIII, No. 5 (May, 1925), 257-268.

[58] Sr. Mary Joan, O.P. and Sr. Mary Nona, O.P., *Guiding Growth in Christian*

*Social Living* (Washington, D.C.: The Catholic University of America Press, 1944), Preface, p. v.

[59] Johnson, *Better Men for Better Times* (Washington, D.C.: The Catholic University of America, 1943).

[60] George Johnson, "Education for Life," In Sr. Mary Joan and Sr. Mary Nona, *Guiding Growth in Christian Social Living*, p. 14. The plan of Christian social living drawn up by the Commission on American Citizenship was mirrored in catalogued aims of Catholic colleges and universities across the nation. Interesting studies have been made of such statements of aims, including the following: Lavina C. Wenger, "An Analysis of the Aims of Catholic Women's Colleges in the United States," *The Catholic Educational Review*, XLII, No. 5 (May, 1944), 276-286; Frank A. Solari, "An Analysis of the Aims of Catholic Colleges for Men as Expressed in Their Catalogs" (unpublished Master's thesis, The Catholic University of America, 1953); Sr. Mary Incarnata Smith, R.S.M., "A Study of the Aims and Objectives of Catholic Colleges for Women in the United States" (unpublished Master's thesis, The Catholic University of America, 1954); and Sr. Mary Mariella Bowler, *A History of Catholic Colleges for Women in the United States of America* (Washington, D.C.: The Catholic University of America Press, 1933), in which Chapter VII deals with aims. Effective November 1, 1969, the Commission on American Citizenship was transferred to the School of Education as a center for the development of curriculum materials (The Catholic University of America, *Administrative Bulletin*, II, No. 8 [October 29, 1969]).

[61] "A Tentative Statement of the Objectives of Catholic Secondary Education in the United States," *Catholic School Journal*, XL, No. 5 (1940), 148-149.

[62] All from Pius XI, *Christian Education of Youth*, pp. 4-5, 36, 23-24.

[63] Raphael M. Huber (ed.), "The Child: Citizen of Two Worlds," *Our Bishops Speak* (Milwaukee: The Bruce Publishing Company, 1952), pp. 161-169. The remaining citations are from pp. 108, 113, and 114.

[64] Neil G. McCluskey, S.J. (ed.), *Catholic Education in America: A Documentary History* (New York: Teachers College, Columbia University, 1964), p. 193.

[65] John Courtney Murray, S.J., "Towards a Christian Humanism: Aspects of the Theology of Education," in *A Philosophical Symposium on American Catholic Education*, ed. Hunter Guthrie, S.J., and Gerald G. Walsh, S.J. (New York: Fordham University Press, 1941), p. 115. The other citations in this paragraph in the text are from pp. 108, 113, and 114.

[66] Hartford, *Education in These United States*, p. 513.

[67] Edward Lee Thorndike, *Human Learning* (New York: The Century Co., 1931), p. 112.

[68] Walter T. Pax, *A Critical Study of Thorndike's Theory and Laws of Learning* (Washington, D.C.: The Catholic Education Press, 1938), p. 153.

[69] William J. McGucken, *The Catholic Way in Education* (Milwaukee: The Bruce Publishing Co., 1934), Preface, p. ix.

[70] Mybert E. Broom, *Educational Measurements in the Elementary School* (New York: McGraw Book Company, Inc., 1939), pp. 3, 10, 11.

[71] Thomas G. Foran, "The Usefulness of Educational Tests," *Report of the Proceedings and Addresses of the Twenty-first Annual Meeting of the National Catholic Educational Association*, Milwaukee, Wis., June 23, 24, 25, and 26, 1924, (November, 1924), XXI, No. 2, p. 333.

[72] Rev. Maurice S. Sheehy, "The Use of Personality Rating Scales in Educa-

tional Guidance," *Report of the Proceedings and Addresses of the Twenty-sixth Annual Meeting of the National Catholic Educational Association*, Toledo, Ohio, June 24, 25, 26, and 27, 1929 (Washington, D.C.: November, 1929), XXVI, No. 1, 531-539.

[73] Rev. John M. Cooper, "Diagnosis and Treatment of the Factors in Moral Conduct," *Ibid.*, pp. 566-567.

[74] Rev. Maurice S. Sheehy, "Use of Personality Rating Scales in Educational Guidance," p. 539.

[75] Curti, *The Social Ideas of American Educators*, p. 468.

[76] Franklin Bobbitt, *What Schools Teach and Might Teach* (Cleveland, Ohio: The Survey Committee of the Cleveland Foundation, 1916); *The Curriculum* (Boston: Houghton Mifflin Company, 1918); *How to Make a Curriculum* (Boston: Houghton Mifflin Company, 1924); and *The Curriculum of Modern Education* (New York: McGraw-Hill Company, Inc., 1941).

[77] William James, *Talks to Teachers on Psychology, and to Students on Some of Life's Ideals* (New York: Henry Holt & Co., 1906), pp. 25-29.

[78] John Dewey, *Ethical Principles Underlying Education* (Chicago, Ill.: Chicago University Press, 1897), p. 8.

[79] George Johnson, "The Activity Curriculum in the Light of Catholic Principles," *Education*, LXI, No. 7 (March, 1941), p. 416.

[80] Thomas Edward Shields, *Philosophy of Education* (Washington, D.C.: The Catholic Education Press, 1921), pp. 407-408.

[81] *Ibid.*, p. 412.

[82] Johnson, "The Activity Curriculum in the Light of Catholic Principles," p. 9.

[83] Johnson, *The Curriculum of the Catholic Elementary School* (Washington, D.C.: The Catholic University of America, 1919), p. 114.

[84] Johnson, *Better Men for Better Times* (Washington, D.C.: The Catholic University of America Press, 1943).

[85] *Ibid.*, pp. 109-113; Sister Mary Joan, O.P. and Sister Mary Nona, O.P., *Guiding Growth in Christian Social Living* (3 vols.; Washington, D.C.: The Catholic University of America Press, 1944), I, 22-63.

[86] *Ibid.*

[87] Johnson, "The Elementary School Curriculum," *The Catholic Educational Review*, XXII, No. 8 (October, 1924), 449-456.

[88] Under Dr. George Johnson's direction Sister Mary Marguerite, a Sister of Notre Dame, wrote all the readers for the primary grades; Dr. Mary Synon in collaboration with Sister Thomas Aquinas, O.P., wrote the intermediate readers, and the advanced readers were written by Dr. Mary Synon, Sister M. Charlotte, R.S.M., and Mrs. Katherine Rankin. *Faith and Freedom Series* (Boston: Ginn and Company, 1941).

[89] Shields, *Catholic Education Series* (Washington, D.C.: The Catholic Education Press, 1915).

[90] Brothers of the Christian Schools, *De La Salle Fifth Reader* (New York: La Salle Bureau, 1929), Preface, p. vii.

[91] Rev. John A. O'Brien, *Cathedral Basic Readers* (New York: Scott, Foresman & Co., 1931).

[92] Rev. John A. O'Brien, *Teacher's Guide Book for the Cathedral Basic Readers* (New York: Scott, Foresman & Co., 1931), p. 14.

[93] Sr. M. Marguerite, S.N.D., "The Catholic Approach to Citizenship through Reading," *Report of the Proceedings and Addresses of the Thirty-ninth Annual Meeting of the National Catholic Educational Association*, Chicago, Ill., April 7, 8, and 9, 1942 (Washington, D.C.: August, 1942), XXXIX, No. 1, 437-438.

[94] Br. Francis de Sales O'Neil, F.S.C., *The Catholic High School Curriculum* (Washington, D.C.: The Catholic University of America, 1930), pp. 53-54. All but six states were included in this study (the exceptions being Wyoming, Nevada, North Carolina, South Carolina, Arizona, and Arkansas). The number of schools studied in each of the 42 states ranged from 1 to 30.

[95] John R. Rooney, *Curricular Offerings of Catholic Secondary Schools: An Examination of 283 Institutions* ("The Catholic University Educational Research Monographs" [Washington, D.C.: The Catholic University Press, May 15, 1931]), VI, No. 4, 46-47. Two other studies carried out in the 1940's on the Master's level dealing with the curriculum in Catholic secondary schools and reaching the same conclusions as O'Neil and Rooney were: Brother Leroy Flynn, C.F.X., "A Study of the Vocational and Prevocational Content in the Curricula of the Catholic Secondary Schools in the States West of the Mississippi River" (unpublished Master's dissertation, Department of Education, The Catholic University of America, 1947); and Brother Richard Kerressey, C.F.X., "A Study of the Vocational and Prevocational Content in the Curricula of the Catholic Secondary Schools of New England and the Middle Atlantic States" (unpublished Master's dissertation, Department of Education, The Catholic University of America, 1947).

[96] Edward F. Spiers, *The Catholic Central High School* (Washington, D.C.: The Catholic University of America Press, 1951), pp. 127-128.

[97] Sr. Alexius Wagner, O.P., *Improvements in Secondary Business Education Since 1900* (Boulder, Col.: University of Colorado Press, 1949), pp. 334-336.

[98] Sr. M. Therese, O.S.F., *Encyclical Dictation* (2 parts; New York: Gregg Publishing Division, McGraw-Hill, 1953).

[99] Br. Louis J. Faerber, S.M., "The Curriculum and Human Rights in Education," *Report of the Proceedings and Addresses of the Forty-eighth Annual Meeting of the National Catholic Educational Association,* Cleveland, Ohio, March 27, 28, 29, and 30, 1951 (Washington, D.C.: August, 1951), XLVIII, No. 1, 285.

[100] *Ibid.*, p. 279.

[101] Rev. Stephen Aylward, *Catechism Comes to Life* (Saint Paul, Minnesota: Catechetical Guild, 1942), p. 16.

[102] *Ibid.*, Introduction by Rev. Joseph Thorning, p. 6.

[103] Rudolph G. Bandas, *Catechetical Methods* (New York: Joseph F. Wagner, Inc., 1929), p. 294.

[104] Rudolph G. Bandas, *Catechetics in the New Testament* (Milwaukee: The Bruce Publishing Company, 1935); *Modern Problems in the Light of Christian Principles: A Manual for Classes, Study Clubs, and Open Forums of College and University Students* (Chicago, Ill.: Loyola University Press, 1937); and *Catechetical and Confraternity Methods* (Saint Paul, Minnesota: North Central Publishing Company, 1957).

[105] Sr. Jane Marie, O.P., *The Life of Our Lord* ("The Christian Religion Series," I [Milwaukee: The Bruce Publishing Company, 1942]), Preface, p. v. The first volume of the series made its appearance three years after Father Virgil Michel's death but "he is the person chiefly responsible for *The Christian Religion Series*," says Sr. Jane Marie in the Preface of the above volume.

[106] Dom Virgil Michel, *The Christ Life Series* (Minneapolis, Minn.: Burgess Publishing Co., 1934).

[107] Sr. Jane Marie, O.P., *The Christian Religion Series* (6 vols.; Milwaukee, Wis.: The Bruce Publishing Co., 1942-1945).

[108] Joseph J. Baierl, S.T.D., *The Creed Explained* (Rochester, N.Y.: The Seminary Press, 1919).

[109] Baierl, *The Sacraments Explained* (Rochester, N.Y.: The Seminary Press, 1922) and *The Commandments Explained* (Rochester, N.Y.: The Seminary Press, 1934).

[110] Johann Friedrich Herbart outlined certain formal steps in method: (1) clearness, (2) association, (3) system, and (4) method. These steps were amplified by his followers, particularly by Tuiskon Ziller at Leipzig, and designated as follows: (1) preparation, (2) presentation, (3) association, (4) systematization, and (5) application.

[111] Baierl, *The Commandments Explained*, Preface, p. 14.

[112] Gerard S. Sloyan, *Speaking of Religious Education* (New York: Herder and Herder, 1968), p. 8.

[113] *Ibid.*

[114] Gerard S. Sloyan, "Catechetics," *The New Catholic Encyclopedia*, III, p. 225.

[115] Sloyan, *Speaking of Religious Education*, Foreword, p. 8.

[116] Francis J. Connell, C.SS.R., "The Forthcoming Revision of the Baltimore Catechism," *Report of the Proceedings and Addresses of the Thirty-Seventh Annual Meeting of the National Catholic Educational Association*, Kansas City, Mo., March 27, 28, 29, 1940 (Washington, D.C.: August, 1940), XXXVII, No. 1, p. 549.

[117] Confraternity of Christian Doctrine, *A Catechism of Christian Doctrine, Revised Edition of the Baltimore Catechism, No. 2* (New York: Benziger Brothers, Inc., 1941).

[118] Michael McGuire, *Father McGuire's The New Baltimore Catechism No. 1* (New York: Benziger Brothers, Inc., 1942).

[119] Francis J. Connell, C.SS.R., *Father Connell's The New Baltimore Catechism No. 3*, (New York: Benziger Brothers, Inc., 1943), Preface, pp. iii-iv.

[120] Clarence Edward Elwell, *Our Quest for Happiness* (4 vols.; Chicago: Mentzer, Bush and Company, 1945–1958).

[121] *Ibid.*, IV, *Toward the Eternal Commencement*, p. 11.

[122] *Ibid.*, pp. 337-448 are devoted to social justice.

[123] John M. Cooper, *Religious Outlines for Colleges* (2nd revised ed.; Washington, D.C.: The Catholic Education Press, 1924-1930, 1935–1946).

[124] Sloyan, "Catechetics," *The New Catholic Encyclopedia*, III, p. 225.

[125] Cooper, *The Content of the Advanced Religion Course* (Washington, D.C.: The Catholic Education Press, 1924).

[126] Cooper, "The Moral Content of the Advanced Religion Course," *The Catholic Educational Review*, XXI, No. 1 (January, 1923), 1-13; "The Dogmatic Content of the Advanced Religion Course," XXI, No. 2 (Feb., 1923), 80-88; "The Historical Content of the Advanced Religion Course," XXI, No. 3 (March, 1923), 153-160; "The Apologetic Content of the Advanced Religion Course," XXI, No. 4 (April, 1923), 207-213; "The Ascetic Content of the Advanced Religion Course," XXI, No. 5 (May, 1923), 349-356.

[127] Cooper, *The Content of the Advanced Religion Course*, p. 7.

[128] Irvin Shepard, "Continuous Sessions in Normal Schools," *Journal of the Proceedings and Addresses of the Thirty-Eighth Annual Meeting of the National Education Association*, Los Angeles, California, July 11-14, 1899 (Chicago: The University of Chicago Press, 1899), p. 893.

[129] Sr. Maria Concepta McDermott, *The Making of a Sister-Teacher* (Notre Dame, Indiana: University of Notre Dame Press, 1965), p. 134.

130 Sr. Bertrande Meyers, *The Education of Sisters* (New York: Sheed and Ward, 1941), p. 21.

131 W. C. Bagley, "Training of Teachers," *The Journal of the National Education Association*, III, No. 9 (May, 1919), 575.

132 Meyers, *The Education of Sisters*, p. 25.

133 Rev. Edward Jordan, "The Evaluation of Credits," *Report of the Proceedings and Addresses of the Twenty-second Annual Meeting of the Catholic Educational Association*, Pittsburgh, Pa., June 29, 30, July 1, 2, 1925 (Columbus, Ohio: November, 1925), XXII, No. 2, 493.

134 Sylvester Schmitz, A.M., *The Adjustment of Teacher Training to Modern Educational Needs* (Atchison, Kansas: The Abbey Student Press, 1927), p. 24. The above study showed the extent of preparation of elementary and high school sister-teachers and public school teachers in 36 states. The study included more than 500,000 teachers employed in the elementary and secondary public schools and likewise more than 10,000 sisters employed in Catholic schools.

135 John Raphael Hagan, *The Diocesan Teachers College* (Washington, D.C.: The Catholic University of America Press, 1932), p. 16.

136 Sr. Mary Antonia Durkin, *The Preparation of the Religious Teacher* (Washington, D.C.: The Catholic University of America, 1926), p. 16. Sr. Mary Antonia Durkin listed those colleges offering credits towards degrees for Catholic teachers from data gathered by National Catholic Welfare Conference in 1921.

137 Rev. Francis J. Macelwane, "A Diocesan Normal School," *Report of the Proceedings and Addresses of the Twentieth Annual Meeting of the Catholic Educational Association*, Milwaukee, Wis., June 23, 24, 25, 26, 1924 (Columbus, Ohio: November, 1924), XXI, No. 2, p. 424.

138 Sylvester Schmitz, *The Adjustment of Teacher Training to Modern Educational Needs*, pp. 96, 103.

139 Rev. Leon A. McNeill, "The Diocesan Normal School," *Report of the Proceedings and Addresses of the Twenty-Seventh Annual Meeting of the National Catholic Educational Association*, New Orleans, La., June 23, 24, 25, 26, 1930 (Washington, D.C.: November, 1930), XXVII, No. 2, 382.

140 Meyers, *The Education of Sisters*, pp. 40-47.

141 The NEA *Research Bulletin*, XXXV, No. 1 (February, 1957), entitled "The Status of the American Public-School Teacher," claimed that in the previous 25 years the levels of teacher preparation rose greatly. There was an increase in elementary teachers with Master's degrees from 0.6 per cent in 1931 to 12.8 per cent in 1956. For secondary teachers the corresponding figures were 12.9 and 43.7 per cent (p. 13).

142 National Catholic Welfare Conference, *Summary of Catholic Education, 1949–1950* (Washington, D.C.: NCWC, Department of Education, 1952), pp. 34-35.

143 National Catholic Welfare Conference, *Summary of Catholic Education, 1959* (Washington, D.C.: NCWC Department of Education, 1960), p. 41. NCWC issued no educational summary in 1957 or 1958. From 1920 to 1956 biennial surveys had been made for every level of Catholic education. In 1958 it was decided that the need for *annual* figures on the schools was imperative. Questionnaires were sent out in the fall of 1958 asking for statistics as of October 31, 1958. The returns were not complete enough to publish in the spring; therefore, it was decided not to publish them, but only to use them as comparative

figures in the 1959 annual survey. (The above information was found on p. 9 of the *Summary of Catholic Education 1959* issued by NCWC, and by an interview with Mrs. Mildred K. Kehoe of the United States Catholic Conference Department of Education).

[144] Sr. Marie Theresa, S.C., "The Principal and the Lay Teacher," *Report of the Proceedings and Addresses of the Fiftieth Annual Meeting of the National Catholic Educational Association*, Atlantic City, N.J., April 7, 8, 9, and 10, 1953 (Washington, D.C.: August, 1953), L, No. 1, p. 363.

[145] *Ibid.*

[146] *Ibid.*

[147] Rt. Rev. Msgr. Carl J. Ryan, "The Lay Teacher in the Catholic School," *The Homiletic and Pastoral Review*, XLVIII, No. 8 (May, 1948), p. 577.

[148] *Ibid.*, p. 578.

[149] *Ibid.*, p. 575. See the Rev. Thomas A. Quigley's "The Lay Teacher in the American Catholic School System" (unpublished Master's dissertation, The Catholic University of America, Washington, D.C., 1938), for a detailed history of the lay teacher in Catholic schools. For the lay teacher's status during the period see the Rev. William F. McKeever, "The Present Status of the Lay Teacher in Selected Catholic High Schools," (unpublished Master's dissertation, Department of Education, The Catholic University of America, 1948); and the Rev. William Novicky, "Lay Teachers in Catholic High Schools in Certain Cities of Ohio," (unpublished Master's dissertation, Department of Education, The Catholic University of America, 1949).

[150] Pius XI, *Christian Education of Youth*, p. 34.

[151] Sr. Mary Emil, I.H.M., "The Sister-Formation Movement and the Pastoral Outlook," *Sister-Formation Bulletin* I, No. 2 (December, 1954), p. 9.

[152] Sr. Mary Emil, I.H.M., "Progress Report—Sister-Formation Conference," *Report of the Proceedings and Addresses of the Forty-third Annual Meeting of the National Catholic Educational Association*, St. Louis, Missouri, April 3-6, 1956 (Washington, D.C.: August, 1956), LIII, No. 1, p. 42.

[153] Sr. Mary Emil, I.H.M., "The Sister-Formation Movement and the Pastoral Outlook," p. 12.

[154] Sr. Mary Emil, I.H.M., "Progress Report—Sister-Formation Conference," p. 42.

[155] Pope Pius XII, "Apostolic Exhortation to the First International Convention of Teaching Sisters" given on Sept. 13, 1951. Quoted in Joseph F. Gallen, S.J., "Statements of the Holy See on the Education and Formation of Sisters," *Sister Formation Bulletin* I, No. 3 (March, 1955), p. 14.

[156] The six geographical regions where Conferences are held by the SFC (Sister-Formation Conference) are: East, Northwest, South, Midwest, Southwest, and New England.

[157] Sr. Mary Emil, I.H.M., "Progress Report—Sister-Formation Conference," p. 43.

[158] *Ibid.*

[159] *Ibid.*, pp. 43-44.

[160] Sr. Mary Jerome Keeler, O.S.B., "Letter from Everett," *Sister Formation Bulletin* III, No. 1 (Autumn, 1956), 10-13.

[161] Pius XI, *Christian Education of Youth*, pp. 33-34.

[162] Joseph F. Gallen, S.J., "Statements of the Holy See on the Education and

Formation of Sisters," *Sister Formation Bulletin* I, No. 3 (March, 1955), 14.

163 Pius XI, *Christian Education of Youth,* p. 23.

164 *Ibid.,* p. 24.

165 *Ibid.*

166 Horace S. Tarbell, "Report of the Sub-Committee on the Training of Teachers," *Journal of Proceedings and Addresses of the NEA,* Session of the year 1895, Denver, Colorado (St. Paul, Minn.: Pioneer Press Co., 1895), p. 242.

167 Lawrence A. Cremin, *The Transformation of the School,* p. 103.

168 Jean-Jacques Rousseau, *Emile,* trans. Barbara Foxley (New York: E.P. Dutton & Co., 1933).

169 Johann Heinrich Pestalozzi, *Extracts from Letters on Early Education* (Liverpool: G. Smith Publishers, 1828).

170 Friedrich Wilhelm Froebel, *The Education of Man,* trans. from the German and annotated by W. N. Hailmann (New York: D. Appleton and Company, 1892).

171 Edwin G. Boring, *A History of Experimental Psychology,* (2nd ed., New York: Appleton-Century-Crofts, Inc., 1950), p. 522.

172 Grenville Stanley Hall, *The Contents of Children's Minds on Entering School* (New York: E. L. Kellogg & Co., 1893).

173 Grenville Stanley Hall, *Adolescence: Its Psychology and Its Relations to Physiology, Anthropology, Sociology, Sex, Crime, Religion, and Education* (2 vols.; New York: D. Appleton and Company, 1904).

174 Boring, *A History of Experimental Psychology,* pp. 568, 570.

175 *Ibid.,* p. 570.

176 Edward A. Fitzpatrick, "The 'Forgotten Man' of Education," *The Catholic School Journal,* LII, No. 10 (December, 1954), 312.

177 Shields, *Philosophy of Education,* p. 401.

178 *Ibid.,* Introduction, pp. 31, 32.

179 Willard S. Elsbree, *Pupil Progress in the Elementary School* (New York: Teachers College, Columbia University, 1943), pp. 33, 46.

180 Joseph Roemer, Charles Forrest Allen, and Dorothy Atwood Yarnell, *Basic Student Activities* (New York: Silver, Burdett and Company, 1935), pp. 14-15.

181 Sr. Mary Joan and Sr. Mary Nona, *Guiding Growth in Christian Social Living* III, 18.

182 Stephen J. Landherr, C.SS.R., "Are Catholics Doing Enough for the Deaf and the Blind?," in *Essays on Catholic Education in the United States,* ed. Roy J. Deferrari (Washington, D.C.: The Catholic University of America Press, 1942), p. 555.

183 Rev. William F. Jenks, C.SS.R., "Realizing our Philosophy of Special Education," *Report of the Proceedings and Addresses of the Fifty-second Annual Meeting of the National Catholic Educational Association,* Atlantic City, N.J., April 12-15, 1955 (Washington, D.C.: August, 1955), LII, No. 1, 403.

184 Rev. Elmer H. Behrmann, "The Archdiocesan Program for the Exceptional Child in St. Louis," *Report of the Proceedings and Addresses of the Fifty-first Annual Meeting of the National Catholic Educational Association,* Chicago, Illinois, April 19-22, 1954 (Washington, D.C.: August, 1954), LI, No. 1, p. 469.

185 *Ibid.,* p. 570. In another article, "The Education of Retarded Children," the same author stated that by 1955, Catholic schools for exceptional

children numbered 54. (*Catholic Education: A Book of Readings*, ed. Walter B. Kolesnik and Edward J. Power [New York: McGraw-Hill Book Company, 1965], p. 261).

[186] Rev. William F. Jenks, C.SS.R. (ed.), *Special Education of the Exceptional Child* (Proceedings of the Workshop on Special Education of the Exceptional Child conducted at The Catholic University of America, June 13-24, 1952, [Washington, D.C.: The Catholic University of America Press, 1953]), Foreword, p. iii.

[187] Mother M. Agatha, *Catholic Education and the Negro* (Washington, D.C.: The Catholic University of America Press, 1942), p. 21; John T. Gillard, S.S.J., *Colored Catholics in the United States* (Baltimore: The Josephite Press, 1941), p. 204.

[188] John T. Gillard, S.S.J., *Colored Catholics in the United States* (Baltimore: The Josephite Press, 1941), pp. 204, 211.

[189] See *Pearson v. Murray*, 169 Md. 478 (1936); *State of Missouri ex rel. Gaines v. Canada*, 305 U.S. 337 (1938); *Sipuel v. Board of Regents*, 332 U.S. 631 (1946–1947); *Sweatt v. Painter*, 339 U.S. 629 (1949); *McLaurin v. Oklahoma State Regents*, 339 U.S. 637 (1949); and *Brown v. Board of Education*, 347 U.S. 483 (1954).

[190] Edward J. Power, *Education for American Democracy* (2nd ed.; New York: McGraw-Hill Book Company, 1965), p. 220.

[191] Pius XI, *Christian Education of Youth*, pp. 26-27.

[192] Sr. Mary Angela, "The Separation of Boys and Girls in High School Classes," *The Catholic School Journal*, XLIX, No. 9 (November, 1949), 296.

[193] Basil Frison, C.M.F., *Coeducation in Catholic Schools: A Commentary on the Instruction on Coeducation* (Boston: Printed by the Daughters of St. Paul, 1959), p. 15. Frison gives a full translation and detailed commentary on "Instructio de Juvenum Utriusque Sexus Promiscua Institutione" as issued by the Sacred Congregation of Religious. Latin text is included.

[194] *Ibid.*, p. 18.

[195] *Ibid.*, p. 20.

[196] *Ibid.* An excellent article appeared in *The Catholic School Journal* of September, 1960, on "Administrative Patterns in the Coinstitutional High School." The author was the Rev. Anthony H. Dorn, special consultant for *The Catholic School Journal's* high school section. Dorn claimed that during the 1959-1960 school year, 51 Catholic constitutional high schools were operating in the United States (LX, No. 7, p. 38). He also wrote that a survey of teachers working in these schools showed almost 75 per cent convinced of the schools' superiority over separate or coeducational schools from the viewpoint of solving the problems of social adjustment for boys and girls without harming the advantages of separate education. He admitted, however (and indeed that was the primary purpose of the article), that the coinstitutional school was a headache to administrators. The article proposed to find a solution to some administrative problems. Also pointing out the administrative problems of coinstitutional high schools is the Rev. Paul F. Curran, "An Evaluation of Administrative Devices for Effectual Operation of Coinstitutional High Schools" (unpublished Ph.D. dissertation, The Catholic University of America, 1965), which was summarized and published by the *NCEA Bulletin* as "The Coinstitutional High School—A Study of the Problems and the Rewards," in November, 1965.

[197] Frison, *Coeducation in Catholic Schools*, p. 42.

[198] Peter Guilday, *A History of the Councils of Baltimore, 1791–1884* (New York: The Macmillan Company, 1932), p. 253.

[199] John A. Abbo and Jerome D. Hannan, *The Sacred Canons: A Concise Presentation of the Current Disciplinary Norms of the Church* (2nd revised edition; St. Louis, Mo.: B. Herder Book Co., 1960), pp. 605-613.

[200] Pius XI, *Christian Education of Youth*, p. 9.

[201] Very Rev. William A. Galvin, J.C.D., "Ecclesiastical Legislation on Christian Education with Special Application to Current Problems," *The Jurist*, XIV, No. 4 (October, 1954), 468-469. The part-title of Galvin's article "With Special Application to Current Problems" is of interest since the talk was given during the period under present discussion—in 1954. Galvin was very clear as to the purpose of the paper. He observed (p. 463):

> When we consider the Catholic training given in many of our homes, we are cognizant of the lack of interest shown by many parents with regard to the religious training of their children. We have to be realistic about this and face the fact that our Catholic children are being spiritually neglected in our homes. In view of this negligence our duties are increased almost a hundredfold and the entire obligation seems to devolve upon us. This we must be ready to assume to the best of our ability, namely by providing the facilities for this education in accordance with the Instructions and Encyclicals of our Supreme Pontiffs, the decrees of the Plenary Councils of Baltimore and the prescriptions of the Code of Canon Law.

[202] Pius XI, *Christian Education of Youth*, p. 21.

[203] *Ibid.*, p. 611.

[204] Joseph A. M. Quigley, J.C.D., "The Authority of the Local Ordinary Over Schools Conducted by Religious," *The Jurist*, XXI, No. 1 (January, 1961), 48-49.

[205] John Daniel Barrett, S.S., *A Comparative Study of the Councils of Baltimore and the Code of Canon Law* (Washington, D.C.: The Catholic University of America Press, 1932), pp. ix, 180.

[206] The *NCEA Bulletins* are excellent sources for studying the Catholic history of education in the United States since 1904.

[207] Michael Williams, *American Catholics in the War* (New York: The Macmillan Company, 1921), pp. 90-94. This book is the record of Catholics in World War I, but it is of use for the early history of the NCWC. The early history and work of the NCWC is summarily sketched in John Tracy Ellis, *American Catholicism* (Chicago: The University of Chicago Press, 1955), pp. 139-142.

[208] National Catholic Welfare Conference, *Summary of Catholic Education 1959* (Washington, D.C.: NCWC, 1960), p. 5.

[209] *Manual of the Confraternity of Christian Doctrine in the Archdiocese of New York* (New York: Printed by the Press of M. A. O'Connor, Oct. 6, 1902).

[210] Rev. William S. Stone, "The History of the Confraternity of Christian Doctrine in the United States" (unpublished master's thesis, Department of Education, The Catholic University of America, Washington, D.C., 1948), p. 7.

[211] Pius XI, *Orbem Catholicum* (Rome, June 29, 1923), trans. by NCWC (Washington, D.C.: NCWC Press, 1944), p. 12; Stone, "The History of the Confraternity of Christian Doctrine in the United States," pp. 7-8.

[212] Pius XI, *Christian Education of Youth*, pp. 28-29.

[213] Catechetical Office, Sacred Congregation of the Council, *Provido Sane Consilio* (Rome, Jan. 12, 1935), trans. by NCWC (Washington, D.C.: NCWC, 1946). Quoted in Stone, "The History of the Confraternity of Christian Doctrine in the United States," p. 12-13.

Part-time religious instruction should not, however, be considered an unqualified success. Westerhoff, a Protestant, believes that Roman Catholics' "present alternative to religious education in parochial schools —the Confraternity of Christian Doctrine school of religion—looks frightfully like a Saturday version of our traditional Protestant Sunday school." Asserting that "we have had a long experience with the one-hour-a-week religious education class taught by volunteer teachers," he adds: "It has failed. It is not a viable instrument for church education." He sees the failure in many places:

> Even today most of our parishioners lack a serious commitment to quality education. Few of our clergymen are adequately prepared to offer the leadership necessary to assure education in our parishes. We lack paid professional teachers, so we enlist lay volunteers . . . often they settle for anyone willing to help out. . . . Traditionalism prevails. . . . Everything within our society, community and public school, as well as within the life of so many of our churches, works against even that education in the Sunday church school that might be considered superior.

Therefore, he begs us not "to waste several decades of time and many human and material resources on a mistake that you can avoid." (All from John H. Westerhoff III, "A Protestant Insight: Does CCD Have a Future?," *The Catechist*, January, 1970, p. 12.)

[214] *Ibid.* (Stone). No. III differs, however, from the translation of Stanislaus Woywod of the Decree of the Sacred Congregation of the Council on the Promotion of Catechetical Instruction, found in "Catechetical Instruction," *The Catholic School Journal*, XXXVI, No. 1 (January, 1936,) 3-4, which reads:

> But lest the religious instruction received in childhood should be forgotten with the advancement of age, . . . let the local Ordinaries guard sedulously that the precept of Canon 1332 shall be observed sacredly by the pastors, by which the latter are bound "on Sundays and other feasts of obligation" to give catechetical instructions to the adult faithful in discourses adapted to their capacity.

[215] The First National Congress was held at Rochester, New York, in 1935.

[216] These cases are *Pierce* v. *Society of Sisters*, 268 U.S. 510 (1925); *Cochran* v. *Louisiana State Board of Education*, 281 U.S. 370 (1930); *Everson* v. *Board of Education*, 330 U.S. 1 (1947); *McCollum* v. *Board of Education*, 333 U.S. 203 (1948); *Zellers* v. *Huff*, 55 N.M. 501 (1951); *Doremus* v. *Board of Education*, 342 U.S. 429 (1952); *Zorach* v. *Clauson*, 343 U.S. 306 (1952); and *Rawlings* v. *Butler*, Ky. 290 S.W. 2nd 801 (1956).

[217] John J. McGrath, *Church and State in American Law: Cases and Materials* (Milwaukee: The Bruce Publishing Company, 1962), p. 80. *Meyer* v. *Nebraska*, 262 U.S. 586 (1923), dealt with the rights of teachers and parents in the matter of foreign language instruction. The Court held that foreign language may be taught as a parent's right to educate and a teacher's duty to follow his chosen occupation.

[218] *Ibid.*, p. 70.

[219] Neil G. McCluskey, S.J., *Catholic Viewpoint on Education* (New York: Doubleday and Company, Inc., 1959), p. 114.

[220] *Ibid.*, pp. 114-116. The briefs and proceedings of *Pierce* v. *Society of Sisters* (the "Oregon School Case") may be found in *Oregon School Cases: Complete Record* (Baltimore: Belvedere Press, 1925), 943 pp.; further information in M. Paul Holsinger, "The Oregon School Bill Controversy, 1922–1925," *Pacific Historical Review* (August, 1968), 327-342; and a convenient summary in Lloyd P. Jorgenson, "The Oregon School Law of 1922: Passage and Sequel," *Catholic Historical Review*, LIV (October, 1968), 455-466.

[221] McGrath, *Church and State in American Law*, p. 102. Important court cases dealing with religious instruction in public schools and governmental aid to parochial schools are dealt with in the above volume. Other books used by the writer to find the text of the court cases were: Joseph Tussman (ed.), *The Supreme Court on Church and State* (New York: Oxford University Press, 1962); and Clark Spurlock, *Education and the Supreme Court* (Urbana: University of Illinois Press, 1955). And for commentaries on the court cases: Neil G. McCluskey, S.J., *Catholic Viewpoint on Education* (New York: Doubleday and Company, Inc., 1959); Robert F. Drinan, S.J., *Religion, the Courts, and Public Policy* (New York: McGraw-Hill Company, Inc., 1963); and Leo Pfeffer, *Church, State, and Freedom* (Boston: The Beacon Press, 1953).

[222] Clark Spurlock, *Education and the Supreme Court*, p. 76.

[223] Leo Pfeffer, *Church, State and Freedom*, pp. 476f.

[224] Tussman (ed.), *The Supreme Court on Church and State*, p. 211.

[225] *Ibid.*, p. 233.

[226] Drinan, *Religion, the Courts, and Public Policy*, p. 140.

[227] Pfeffer, *Church, State and Freedom*, p. 476.

[228] Drinan, *Religion, the Courts and Public Policy*, p. 141.

[229] *Ibid.*

[230] *Ibid.*, p. 146.

[231] Robert Eugene Cushman, *Leading Constitutional Decisions* (New York: Appleton-Century-Crofts, 1950), p. 145.

[232] Spurlock, *Education and the Supreme Court*, p. 92.

[233] Irwin Widen, "Public Support for Parochial Schools: Why the Issue has Re-emerged," *History of Education Journal*, IV, No. 2 (Winter, 1953), p. 72.

[234] *Ibid.*, p. 59.

[235] *Ibid.*, p. 72.

[236] *Chance* v. *Mississippi State Textbook Rating and Purchasing Bd.*, 190 Miss. 453 (1940), pp. 467-468. Quoted in Chester James Antieau, S.J.D., Phillip Mark Carroll, L.L.M., and Thomas Carroll Burke, L.L.B., *Religion under the State Constitutions* (Brooklyn, New York: Central Book Company, Inc., 1965), p. 30.

[237] McCluskey, *Catholic Viewpoint on Education*, p. 129.

[238] Pfeffer, *Church, State and Freedom*, p. 343.

[239] McCluskey, *Catholic Viewpoint on Education*, pp. 129f.

[240] McGrath, *Church and State in American Law*, p. 199. Complete texts of court decisions are cited in McGrath.

[241] *Ibid.*, pp. 200-201.

242 *Ibid.*, pp. 201-202.
243 Spurlock, *Education and the Supreme Court*, p. 133.
244 McGrath, *Church and State in American Law*, p. 241, footnote 1.
245 *Ibid.*, pp. 240-241.
246 Sr. Clare Mary McGee, S.B.S., "The Causes and Effects of the Dixon Case" (unpublished Master's thesis, Department of Education, The Catholic University of America, Washington, D.C., 1955), p. 1. This dissertation gives a detailed study of the case and relates the historical background. The extensive use of primary source material makes it an invaluable reference.
247 *Gerhardt v. Heid*, 66 N.D. 444, 267, N.W. 127 (1936).
248 *Hysong v. Gallitzin*, 164 Pa. 629 Atl. 482 (1894).
249 *Rawlings v. Butler*, Ky., 290 S.W. 2nd 801 (1956).
250 *Ibid.*, as the case is cited in McGrath, *Church and State in American Law*, p. 270.
251 Sr. Raymond McLaughlin, O.S.B., *A History of State Legislation Affecting Private Elementary and Secondary Schools in the United States, 1870–1945* (Washington, D.C.: The Catholic University of America Press, 1946), p. 17.
252 John Tracy Ellis, *American Catholicism* (Chicago: The University of Chicago Press, 1955), p. 156.
253 Will Herberg, "Justice for Religious Schools," *America*, XCVIII, No. 7 (Nov. 16, 1957), p. 190.
254 *Ibid.*, p. 191.
255 John A. Hardon, S.J., "Co-operation of Church and State," *The Homiletic and Pastoral Review*, LVII, No. 5 (February, 1957), p. 529.
256 Herberg, "Justice for Religious Schools," p. 192.
257 *Ibid.*
258 Thomas T. McAvoy, C.S.C., *Father O'Hara of Notre Dame: The Cardinal-Archbishop of Philadelphia* (Notre Dame, Ind.: University of Notre Dame Press, 1967), esp. pp. 314 and 401.
259 Most Rev. Albert G. Meyer, S.T.D., "Education and Communication," *Report of the Proceedings and Addresses of the Fifty-fourth Annual Meeting of the National Catholic Educational Association*, Milwaukee, Wisconsin, April 23-26, 1957 (Washington, D.C.: August, 1957), LIV, No. 1, pp. 40f.
260 *Ibid.*, p. 40.
261 John Tracy Ellis, *American Catholics and the Intellectual Life* (Chicago, Illinois: The Heritage Foundation, Inc., 1956), p. 31.
262 *Ibid.*
263 *Ibid.*, p. 21.
264 *Ibid.*, p. 46.
265 *Ibid.*, pp. 19-20.
266 Ellis, "American Catholics and the Intellectual Life," *Thought*, XXX, No. 118 (Sept., 1955), 351-388.
267 Rev. Arthur A. North, S.J., "Why is the American Catholic Graduate School Failing to Develop Catholic Intellectualism?," *Report of the Proceedings and Addresses of the Fifty-third Annual Meeting of the National Catholic Educational Association*. St. Louis, Mo., April 3-6, 1956, (August, 1956), LIII, No. 1, 179.
268 *Ibid.*, p. 184.
269 John J. Wright, D.D., Prefatory Note in Ellis, *American Catholics and the Intellectual Life*, p. 6.

# Chapter VI

[1] Lawrence A. Cremin, *The Transformation of the School* (New York: Alfred A. Knopf, 1961), p. 338; Mortimer Smith, *And Madly Teach* (Chicago: H. Regnery Co., 1949); Albert Lynd, *Quackery in the Public Schools* (Boston: Little, Brown, 1953); and Arthur Bestor, *Educational Wastelands* (Urbana: University of Illinois Press, 1953).

[2] "Interview with Professor Arthur Bestor, University of Illinois," *U. S. News and World Report*, XLI, No. 22 (November 30, 1956), 68, 71.

[3] President John F. Kennedy, "Message on Education from the President of the United States," The White House, January 29, 1963. To the Congress of the United States. 88th Cong., 1st sess. Reported in full in Francis Keppel, *The Necessary Revolution in American Education* (New York: Harper & Row, 1966), Appendix A, p. 165.

[4] *Ibid.*, p. 166.

[5] Hyman G. Rickover, USN, *Report on Russia*. U. S. Congress. Hearings before the Committee on Appropriations. House of Representatives. 86th Cong., 1st sess. (U. S. Government Printing Office, Washington, D.C., 1959), pp. 35-36.

[6] James Bryant Conant, *The American High School Today* (New York: McGraw-Hill, 1959).

[7] H. G. Good, *A History of American Education* (3d printing; New York: The Macmillan Company, 1964), p. 589.

[8] *The Washington Post* (January 15, 1965), p. 1.

[9] Michael Harrington, *Toward a Democratic Left* (New York: The Macmillan Company, 1968).

[10] *The New York Times* (Sept. 4, 1967), pp. 1, 22.

[11] *Time* (February 14, 1969), 59.

[12] John Tracy Ellis, "American Catholics and the Intellectual Life," *Thought*, XXX, No. 118 (September, 1955), 351-388; Ellis, *American Catholics and the Intellectual Life* (Chicago: Heritage Foundation, 1956); Louis J. Putz (ed.), *The Catholic Church, U.S.A.* (Chicago: Fides, 1956); and Thomas F. O'Dea, *American Catholic Dilemma: An Inquiry into the Intellectual Life* (New York: Sheed and Ward, 1958).

[13] Dr. John J. Meng, in a symposium on Catholic education in Washington, D.C., in November, 1967, as reported in *The New York Times* (January 12, 1968), p. 73.

[14] C. Albert Koob, O.Praem. (ed.), *What Is Happening to Catholic Education?* (Washington, D.C.: National Catholic Educational Association, 1966), p. xi.

[15] *The Role of Catholic Education in Contemporary American Society: Report of the Proceedings and Addresses at the Sixty-Fourth Annual Convention of the National Catholic Educational Association*. Atlantic City, New Jersey, March 27-30, 1967, pp. 17-21.

[16] William H. Conley, "Renewal of Catholic Education," *The Catholic School Journal*, LXVI, No. 7 (September, 1966), 4.

[17] Daniel D. McGarry, "The Crisis in Education: Will Christian Schools Survive?" *Social Justice Review*, LV, No. 9 (October, 1962), 188.

[18] Sr. Ann Virginia, I.H.M., "The Cruel Choice Facing Catholic Education," *The Catholic World*, CXCV, No. 1 (September, 1962), 170, 343.

[19] *Ibid.*, p. 346.

[20] This statement and most of the statistics in this paragraph, from NCEA News Release of Sept. 4, 1969.

[21] *The New York Times* (August 20, 1967), p. 72.

[22] The drop was from 78,300 to 70,600, a loss of 7,700. In 1964–65 the enrollment was 89,100.

[23] *National Catholic Reporter* (November 13, 1968), p. 6.

[24] *The Tablet* (Feb. 13, 1969), p. 1.

[25] *The New York Times* (Feb. 10, 1965), p. 1.

[26] *The Tablet* (Feb. 27, 1969), p. 10.

[27] *Ibid.* (March 6, 1969), p. 9.

[28] "Catholic Schools," *Time* (March 28, 1969), p. 42.

[29] A financial report from early in this period is Robert B. Binswanger, "The Dilemma Facing Roman Catholic Schools in the United States with Respect to Current Financial Considerations," (unpublished doctoral dissertation, Harvard University, 1961).

[30] *National Catholic Reporter* (October 30, 1968), p. 3.

[31] Report of the Schools Committee of the Diocese of Spokane, Wash., "Planning for the Future," *NCEA Bulletin*, LXIV, No. 4 (May, 1968), 10-11.

[32] *The New York Times* (Nov. 8, 1967), p. 50. Bartell also wrote a doctoral dissertation at Princeton University on Catholic education.

[33] *The New York Times* (Sept. 25, 1967), p. 34.

[34] Msgr. James C. Donohue, "Catholic Education in Contemporary American Society," *NCEA Bulletin*, Vol. LXIV, No. 1 (August, 1967), 15.

[35] *The State and Non-Public Schools* (Washington, D.C.: U. S. Government Printing Office, misc. #28, 1958), p. 1.

[36] Mary Perkins Ryan, *Are Parochial Schools the Answer?* (New York: Holt, Rinehart & Winston, 1964), p. 173.

[37] Rt. Rev. Msgr. Thomas P. Duffy, "A Positive View of Catholic Education in the Light of Today's Crisis," *NCEA Bulletin*, LXI, No. 1 (August, 1964), 254.

[38] James Michael Lee, *Catholic Education in the Western World* (Notre Dame, Ind.: University of Notre Dame Press, 1967), p. 307.

[39] Gerald Harriman and George Wing, "Restructuring Elementary and Secondary Education," *Ave Maria*, XCI, No. 2 (Feb. 19, 1966), 12.

[40] *Ibid.*, p. 13.

[41] Neil G. McCluskey, S.J., "The Dinosaur and the Catholic School," *Catholic Mind*, LVIII, No. 1150 (July–August, 1960), 330.

[42] *The New York Times* (Aug. 20, 1967), p. 63.

[43] *National Catholic Reporter* (Sept. 27, 1967), p. 5.

[44] All as reported in *The Long Island Catholic* (July 25–Aug. 1, 1968), p. 20.

[45] Anthony E. Seidl, *Focus on Change—Management of Resources in Catholic Schools* (New York: Joseph F. Wagner, Inc., 1968), Preface, p. v.

[46] Koob, *What Is Happening to Catholic Education*, p. xiv.

[47] Roman A. Bernert, S.J., "Catholic School Objectives: Do We Need a New Approach?," *The Catholic School Journal*, LXVI, No. 7 (September, 1966), p. 53.

[48] *Ibid.*, p. 49.

[49] See the annual editions of the *Catholic Press Directory* (New York: Catholic Press Association, 432 Park Ave. South, New York City, 10016).

[50] For further information on adult education see Clinton H. Grattan, *In Quest of Knowledge: A Historical Perspective on Adult Education* (New York: Association Press, 1955); Sr. Mary Jerome Keeler (ed.), *Handbook of Catholic Adult Education* (Milwaukee: Bruce Publishing Co., 1959); Malcolm S. Knowles, *Informal Adult Education* (New York: Association Press, 1950); The Catholic University of America, *Princi-*

*ples and Problems of Adult Education: Proceedings of the Workshop on Principles and Problems of Catholic Adult Education, 1953,* ed. Sebastian Miklas (Washington, D.C.: The Catholic University of America Press, 1959); Gustav Weigel, "The Challenge of Adult Education," *NCEA Bulletin,* LVI, No. 1 (August, 1959), 406-414; Paul J. Hallinan, "Adult Education for Catholics: The Necessity and the Challenge," *NCEA Bulletin,* LIX, No. 1 (August, 1962), pp. 513-517.

[51] Myron Lieberman, "Parochial Schools and Public Leadership," National Catholic Educational Association Bulletin, LVII, No. 1 (August, 1960), 242.

[52] *Catholics Schools in Action,* The Notre Dame study of Catholic elementary and secondary schools in the United States, ed. Reginald A. Neuwien (Notre Dame, Ind.: University of Notre Dame Press, 1966), p. 420.

[53] *Ibid.,* p. x.

[54] William H. Conley, "Catholic Schools in Action—A Critique," *The Catholic School Journal,* LXVI, No. 9 (November, 1966), 30. Dr. William H. Conley, as we observed in the text, was the first director of the Notre Dame study. The study was planned and organized during his service from May, 1962 until May, 1963. He resigned from the study at the end of its first year to accept the presidency of Sacred Heart University, Bridgeport, Conn. In 1966, he was also editor of *The Catholic School Journal.*

[55] Andrew M. Greeley and Peter H. Rossi, *The Education of Catholic Americans* (Chicago: Aldine Publishing Co., 1966), pp. 9, 10, 13.

[56] *Ibid.,* pp. 74-75.

[57] *Ibid.,* pp. 112-113.

[58] *Ibid.,* pp. 181, 197, 219, 222.

[59] *Ibid.,* pp. 10-12, 219, 220, 223.

[60] *Ibid.,* p. 229.

[61] *Ibid.,* pp. 12, 156, 198, 220.

[62] *Ibid.,* pp. 12, 221.

[63] *Ibid.,* p. 231.

[64] *Ibid.,* pp. 110, 112-113, 228, 227 (italics theirs).

[65] *Ibid.,* p. 111.

[66] "Washington Symposium on Catholic Education," Dr. William H. Conley interviews Rev. C. Albert Koob, O.Praem., *The Catholic School Journal,* LXVII, No. 9 (November, 1967), 5.

[67] *News* from the National Catholic Educational Association, February 13, 1969, p. 2.

[68] "Statement by U.S. Bishops on Catholic Schools," *Catholic Mind,* LXVI, No. 1219 (January, 1968), 3.

[69] *National Catholic Reporter* (August 28, 1968), p. 2.

[70] Winifred R. Long, "A Time of Transition," *Catholic Education 1969: An Overview* (Washington, D.C.: NCEA Office of Information, 1969), n.p.g.

[71] Winifred R. Long, Bureau of Research, NCEA, personal interview.

[72] *The New York Times* (June 30, 1969), p. 1; *ibid.,* (August 17, 1969), p. 1.

[73] *Declaration on Christian Education* in *The Documents of Vatican II,* ed. Walter M. Abbott, S.J., and Very Rev. Msgr. Joseph Gallagher (New York: America Press, 1966), pp. 637-651.

[74] *Pastoral Constitution on the Church in the Modern World* in Abbott and Gallagher (eds.), *The Documents of Vatican II,* pp. 199-308.

[75] *Ibid.,* Para. 2.

[76] *Ibid.*
[77] *Ibid.*, Para 3.
[78] *Ibid.*, Para. 21.
[79] *Ibid.*, Para. 30.
[80] *Ibid.*, Para. 39.
[81] *Ibid.*, Para. 40.
[82] *Ibid.*
[83] *Ibid.*, Para. 41.
[84] *Ibid.*, Para. 42.
[85] *Ibid.*, Para. 43.
[86] *Ibid.*, Para. 44.
[87] *Ibid.*
[88] *Ibid.*, Para. 36.
[89] *Ibid.*, Para. 31.
[90] *Ibid.*, Para. 62.
[91] *Ibid.*, Para. 57.
[92] Mark J. Hurley (ed.), *The Declaration on Christian Education of Vatican Council II* (Glen Rock, N.J.: Paulist Press, 1966), pp. 154-155, 157.
[93] *Declaration on Christian Education* in Abbott and Gallagher (eds.), *The Documents of Vatican II*, Introduction, p. 639.
[94] *Ibid.*, Para. 5.
[95] *Ibid.*, Para. 8.
[96] *Declaration on Religious Freedom* in Abbott and Gallagher (eds.), *The Documents of Vatican II*, pp. 675-696, Paras. 4, 5, and 8.
[97] *Decree on Priestly Formation*, Vatican Council II, Para. 17.
[98] The President's Commission on National Goals, *Goals for Americans* (New York: The American Assembly, Columbia University, 1960), pp. 1-23.
[99] John W. Gardner, "Goals in Education," *Goals for Americans*, the Report of the President's Commission on National Goals (Englewood Cliffs, N.J.: Prentice-Hall, 1960), p. 100.
[100] *The New York Times* (July 18, 1968), p. 37.
[101] *The New York Times* (Jan. 26, 1969), p. 22.
[102] Alice Miel with Edwin Kiester, Jr., *The Shortchanged Children of Suburbia* (New York: Institute of Human Relations Press, The American Jewish Committee, 1967), p. 51.
[103] James Michael Lee, *The Purpose of Catholic Schooling* (Dayton, Ohio: NCEA Papers, 1968).
[104] *Ibid.*, p. 19.
[105] Kevin O'Brien, C.SS.R., *The Proximate Aim of Education* (Milwaukee: The Bruce Publishing Co., 1958); John D. Redden and Francis A. Ryan, *A Catholic Philosophy of Education* (Milwaukee: The Bruce Publishing Co., 1942); Franz de Hovre, *Catholicism in Education*, trans. Edward B. Jordan (New York: Benziger Bros., 1934); and George A. Kelly, *The Catholic Family Handbook* (New York: Random House, 1959).
[106] Herbert Johnston, *A Philosophy of Education* (New York: McGraw-Hill, 1963).
[107] Lee, *Purpose of Catholic Schooling*, pp. 37-42.
[108] Leo R. Ward, C.S.C., *New Life in Catholic Schools* (St. Louis: Herder and Herder, 1958), p. 24.
[109] See Thomas Aquinas *Ethics*, X, and an analysis of this text in Pierre Conway, O.P., *Principles of Education: A Thomistic Approach* (Washington, D.C.: Thomist Press, 1960), pp. 71-74.
[110] John B. McDowell, "The Encyclicals on Education and the Catholic Sec-

ondary Schools," *National Catholic Educational Association Bulletin*, LVI, No. 1 (August, 1959), 219.

[111] *Declaration on Christian Education*, Para. 2.

[112] *Ibid.*, Para. 8.

[113] Abbott and Gallagher (eds.), *Documents of Vatican II*, p. 635.

[114] *Declaration on Christian Education*, Para. 1.

[115] Pope Paul VI, "The Continual Ardent Search for God," to the General Audience on November 20, 1968, as reported in *L'Osservatore Romano* (Weekly English Edition), No. 35 (November 28, 1968), p. 1.

[116] A book designed to teach mathematics to children in the elementary grades is that of the Most Rev. Clarence E. Elwell, Superintendent of Schools, Diocese of Cleveland, *New Ways in Numbers* (Boston, Mass.: D. C. Heath & Co., 1964).

[117] *The Long Island Catholic* (Sept. 12, 1968), p. 2.

[118] *The New York Times* (Nov. 2, 1967), p. 1.

[119] *The New York Times* (Jan. 19, 1967), p. 10.

[120] Roman A. Bernert, S.J., "Catholic School Objectives: Do We Need a New Approach?" *The Catholic School Journal*, LXVI, No. 7 (Sept., 1966), 50.

[121] *Declaration on Christian Education*, paragraph 8.

[122] *Time* (June 9, 1967), p. 37.

[123] *The New York Times* (Sept. 27, 1967), p. 32.

[124] *Time* (June 9, 1967), p. 37.

[125] *The New York Times* (Feb. 10, 1967), p. 42.

[126] *The Tablet* (May 18, 1967), p. 22.

[127] *The Long Island Catholic* (Feb. 27, 1969), p. 1.

[128] *The Tablet* (August 3, 1967), p. 18.

[129] Such works as Henry V. Sattler, *Parents, Children, and the Facts of Life* (Paterson, N.J.: St. Anthony Guild, 1952) were becoming classics in this field. Further bibliography and more information may be obtained from the Family Life Bureau, USCC, 1312 Massachusetts Ave., N.W., Washington, D.C., 20005.

[130] *Declaration on Christian Education*, Paragraph 1.

[131] Judah J. Harris, *The Treatment of Religion in Elementary School Social Studies Textbooks* (New York: Anti-Defamation League of B'nai B'rith, 1963), p. 5.

[132] *Ibid.*, pp. 15-16.

[133] *Ibid.*, pp. 31-32.

[134] *Ibid.*, p. 50.

[135] George R. LaNoue, "Religious Schools and 'Secular' Subjects," *Harvard Educational Review*, XXXII, No. 3 (Summer, 1962), 257.

[136] *Ibid.*, p. 262.

[137] George R. LaNoue, "The National Defense Education Act and 'Secular' Subjects," *Phi Delta Kappan*, XLIII, No. 9 (June, 1962), 384-386.

[138] LaNoue, "Religious Schools and 'Secular' Subjects," p. 289.

[139] Sr. Mary Annetta and Sr. Mary Leonard, *Preparing for the Woman's Apostolate in Society* (New York: Wm. H. Sadlier, Inc., 1956), p. 135, as cited by LaNoue, "Religious Schools and 'Secular' Subjects," p. 269.

[140] William A. Brownell and others, *Teachers' Manual for Finding Truth in Arithmetic* (Boston, Mass.: Ginn & Co., 1959), p. 1, as cited by LaNoue, "Religious Schools and 'Secular' Subjects," p. 272.

[141] Sister M. Paulita Campbell, *Progress in Arithmetic, Grade 4*, (New York: Wm. H. Sadlier, Inc., 1957), p. 85.

[142] Dale C. Braungart and Sr. Rita Buddeke, *Biology—The Study of Living*

*Things* (Garden City, N.Y.: Doubleday and Company, Inc., 1957), as cited by LaNoue, "Religious Schools and 'Secular' Subjects," p. 267.

[143] Jean de Fraine, S.J., *The Bible and the Origin of Man* (New York, Tournai, Paris, Rome: Desclée Co., 1962), p. 82. Further, polygenism may be interpreted in a monophyletic sense, in which case it would not necessarily have the meaning mentioned by the authors of the biology text.

[144] Sr. Mary Xaveria, I.H.M., *Europe and the Mediterranean World* (Garden City, N.Y.: Doubleday & Co., Inc., 1960), p. 362, as cited by LaNoue, "Religious Schools and 'Secular' Subjects," p. 268.

[145] Sr. Mary Veronica, *Lands of the Western Hemisphere* (Teachers' ed.; Garden City, N.Y.: Doubleday & Co., Inc., 1961), p. 43, as cited by LaNoue, "Religious Schools and 'Secular' Subjects," p. 271.

[146] Brownell and others, *Teachers' Manual*, as cited by LaNoue, "Religious Schools and 'Secular' Subjects, p. 274.

[147] Julian S. Maline and Joseph F. Downey, *Prose and Poetry for Enjoyment* (St. Thomas More ed.; Syracuse, N.Y.: L. W. Singer, 1955), as cited by LaNoue, "Religious Schools and 'Secular' Subjects," p. 279.

[148] Julian S. Maline and Frederick Manion, *Prose and Poetry of America* (St. Thomas More ed.; Syracuse, N.Y.: L. W. Singer Co., 1955), p. 3, as cited by LaNoue, "Religious Schools and 'Secular' Subjects," pp. 279f.

[149] *Catalogue of Instructional Materials for Lutheran Elementary Schools* (St. Louis, Mo.: Concordia Publishing House, 1961), p. 5, as cited by LaNoue, "Religious Schools and 'Secular' Subjects," p. 281.

[150] Sidney Dykstra, *Mathematics Curriculum Guide* (Grand Rapids, Mich.: National Union of Christian Schools, 1958), p. 38, as cited by LaNoue, "Religious Schools and 'Secular' Subjects," pp. 281, 284.

[151] Based on the papers presented at this conference is Theodore R. Sizer (ed.), *Religion and Public Education* (Boston: Houghton Mifflin Company, 1967).

[152] Edward B. Fiske, "Now the Teaching is 'About' Religion," *The New York Times* (Jan. 12, 1968), p. 73.

[153] *Katholischer Katechismus der Bistümer Deutschlands* (New York: Herder and Herder, 1955).

[154] *The New York Times* (Jan. 12, 1968), p. 73, speaking of the Nov. 1967 Symposium on Catholic Education held at Washington, D.C.

[155] As cited in *The Long Island Catholic* (Sept. 12, 1968), p. 1.

[156] Josef Andreas Jungmann, S.J., *The Good News Yesterday and Today*, ed. & trans. W. A. Huesman (New York: W. H. Sadlier, 1962); Johannes Hofinger, *The Art of Teaching Christian Doctrine* (2d ed.; Notre Dame, Ind.: University of Notre Dame Press, 1962); Josef Andreas Jungmann, S.J., *Handing on the Faith*, ed. & trans. Anthony N. Fuerst (New York: Herder and Herder, 1959); Sr. Maria de la Cruz, H.H.S., and Sr. Mary Richard, H.H.S., *On Our Way Series* (New York: W. H. Sadlier, 1959).

[157] Matt. 12:28; Luke 11:20.

[158] Acts 2:14-39.

[159] Rom. 1:1-4; 2:16; 8:34; 10:8-9.

[160] Gal. 1:4.

[161] Acts 13:16-41.

[162] Matt. 3:1-2; Mark 11:30-33.

[163] See Kendig B. Cully (ed.), *The Westminister Dictionary of Christian Education* (Philadelphia, Pa.: Westminister Press, 1963), and Johannes

Hofinger (ed.), *Teaching All Nations,* trans. Clifford Howell (New York: Herder and Herder, 1961).

164 *The Dogmatic Constitution on Divine Revelation,* Para. 24; *Pastoral Constitution on the Church in the Modern World,* Para. 48; *Decree on the Bishops' Pastoral Office in the Church,* Paras. 13, 14 and 30; *Decree on Priestly Formation,* Para. 19; *Decree on the Apostolate of the Laity,* Paras. 10, 11 and 29; and the *Declaration on Christian Education,* Paras. 4 and 7. Numbers pertain to paragraph references in Abbott and Gallagher, *The Documents of Vatican II.* Statements in these documents touch on such areas as the basis for catechetics, the use of scripture, methodology, the duties of parents, pastors and bishops, and the use of contemporary media.

165 Karl Rahner, *The Church After the Council* (New York: Herder and Herder, 1966), p. 19.

166 *The Dogmatic Constitution on Divine Revelation,* Abbott and Gallagher, *The Documents of Vatican II,* pp. 111-128.

167 Gabriel Moran, *Vision and Tactics* (New York: Herder & Herder, 1968), p. 60.

168 Sr. Mary Antonina, "Salvation History and the Adolescent," *Catholic Education Today,* I (Sept.–Oct., 1967), 24.

169 Karl Rahner, "Theology and Anthropology," *The Word in History,* ed. T. Patrick Burke (New York: Sheed & Ward, 1966), pp. 1-2.

170 See Alfonso M. Nebreda, *Kerygma in Crisis* (Chicago: Loyola University Press, 1965).

171 I Cor. 3:2.

172 *Come to the Father* (New York: Paulist Press, 1967).

173 *The New York Times* (Feb. 10, 1967), p. 40

174 *The National Catholic Reporter* (Sept. 27, 1967), p. 5.

175 As cited *ibid.*

176 As quoted in *The Washington Post* (August 6, 1967), p. A-5.

177 "Religion in the Catholic High School," *Catholic High School Quarterly Bulletin,* XXII, No. 4 (Jan., 1965), 13.

178 Sheila Moriarty, "Current Directions in High School Catechetics," *Worship,* XLI, No. 7 (Aug.–Sept., 1967), 386-405.

179 *Lord and King Series* (New York: Holt, Rinehart & Winston Co., 1964, 1965 and 1966).

180 *Loyola Religion Series* (Chicago, Ill.: Loyola University Press, 1964, 1965, 1966 and 1967).

181 *Roots of Faith Series* (New York: Harcourt, Brace & World, 1966, 1967 and 1968).

182 *Living With Christ Series* (Winona, Minn.: St. Mary's College Press, 1966, 1967).

183 Moriarty, "Current Directions in High School Catechetics," p. 399.

184 Nancy Hennessy, Carol White and Joan Lark, *Friendship* (New York: Herder & Herder, 1967).

185 M. F. R. Carton, "An Inquiry Into the Study of Catholic Doctrine and Faculty Preparation in Sixty-Three Catholic Colleges," (unpublished doctoral dissertation, Washington, D.C., The Catholic University of America, 1963). This work is valuable for its bibliography as well as other content.

186 Gerard S. Sloyan (ed.), *Foundations of Catholic Theology Series* (12 vols.; Englewood Cliffs, N.J.: Prentice-Hall, 1963). Further bibliography may be found in J. F. Riley, "College Fundamental Theology: Lower Divi-

sion Curriculum in the Light of Student Needs and Happiness," (unpublished doctoral dissertation, Washington, D.C., The Catholic University of America, 1964).

[187] *A New Catechism: Catholic Faith for Adults* (New York: Herder and Herder, 1967), pp. 74-75.

[188] Donald A. Erickson, "Differential Effects of Public and Sectarian Schooling on the Religiousness of the Child" (unpublished Ph.D. dissertation, University of Chicago, 1962), p. 86.

[189] *Ibid.*, p. 9, citing Philip Pitruzello, "Admission Policies of Selected Catholic Secondary Schools and the Characteristics of Students and Parents" (unpublished Ph.D. dissertation, University of Chicago, 1962). Erickson's bibliography cites further works useful for studying differences between public and private school products, such as: Gordon W. Allport, *The Individual and His Religion: a Psychological Interpretation* (New York: The Macmillan Co., 1950); J. Milton Yinger, *Religion, Society, and the Individual: an Introduction to the Sociology of Religion* (New York: The Macmillan Co., 1957); Edward R. Bartlett, "Measurable Moral and Religious Outcomes of Week-day Religious Instruction," *Religious Education*, XXIX (January, 1934), 25-34; Miller M. Cragon, Jr., "The Religious Influence of the Parochial School," *Religious Education*, LVI (May–June, 1961), 180-184; Peter H. Rossi and Alice S. Rossi, "Background and Consequences of Parochial School Education," *Harvard Educational Review*, XXVII (Summer, 1957), 171-172; W. Cody Wilson, "Value Differences between Public and Private School Graduates," *Journal of Educational Psychology*, L (October, 1959), 213-218.

[190] *Declaration on Christian Education* in Abbott and Gallagher, *Documents of Vatican II*, Para. 6.

[191] *Ibid.*

[192] *The Tablet* (Jan. 23, 1969), p. 1.

[193] *The Tablet* (Feb. 20, 1969), p. 1.

[194] *Ibid.*, p. 3.

[195] *The National Catholic Reporter* (Feb. 26, 1969), p. 5.

[196] *The Tablet* (Jan. 23, 1969), p. 1.

[197] *Ibid.*

[198] Theodore R. Sizer, "The Case for a Free Market," *Saturday Review* (Jan. 11, 1969), p. 36.

[199] *Ibid.*, p. 38.

[200] *Ibid.*, p. 42.

[201] *The New York Times* (November 21, 1969), p. 55.

[202] Congress had granted to the states some public lands, whose sale then produced money to constitute a perpetual fund to establish and support colleges; inasmuch as public operation was not a prerequisite, some states provided land-grant funds for private schools—e.g., Brown University, a Baptist institution in Rhode Island.

[203] Alice M. Rivlin, *The Role of the Federal Government in Financing Higher Education* (Washington: Brookings Institution, 1961); Harold Orlans, *The Effects of Federal Programs on Higher Education* (Washington: Brookings Institution, 1962).

[204] See Fred Francis Beach and Robert F. Will, *The State and Nonpublic Schools* (Washington, D.C.: Dept. of Health, Education and Welfare, 1958); Sr. Raymond McLaughlin, *A History of State Legislation Affecting Private Elementary and Secondary Schools in the United States, 1870–1945* (Washington, D.C.: The Catholic University of America

Press, 1946); Edmond G. Drouin, F.I.C., *The School Question: A Bibliography on Church-State Relationships in American Education, 1940–1957* (Washington, D.C.: The Catholic University of America Press, 1963).

[205] President John F. Kennedy, "Education—Message from the President of the United States," The White House, February 20, 1961, *Congressional Record*, Proceedings and Debates of the 87th Cong., 1st Sess. (H. Doc. No. 92), p. 2430.

[206] Robert F. Drinan, "Federal Aid to Education," *The New Catholic Encyclopedia*, V, 871-892.

[207] *Memorandum of the Impact of the First Amendment to the Constitution upon Federal Aid to Education*, Senate Doc. No. 29, 87th Cong., 1st Sess., 7 [1961] (Washington, D.C.: U. S. Government Printing Office, May 1, 1961), p. 9; See also Joseph F. Costanzo, "Ribicoff on Federal Aid to Education," *Thought*, XXXVI, No. 143 (December, 1961), 489.

[208] *Memorandum*, pp. 17-18.

[209] *Ibid.*, p. 19.

[210] See *The Georgetown Law Journal*, L, No. 2 (1961), 399-455.

[211] Testimony of Rt. Rev. Msgr. Frederick G. Hochwalt, Director, Department of Education, National Catholic Welfare Conference, before the Subcommittee on Education of the Senate Committee on Labor and Public Welfare, February 2, 1965 (privately mimeographed by NCWC, n.d.g.), p. 1.

[212] Public Law 89-10. See *Federal Register*, Part II, XXX, 178 (Wash., D.C.: Office of Education, 1965). See also Edgar P. McCarren, "What the Informed Public Should Know about ESA 1965," *Catholic Educational Review*, LXIII, No. 8 (Nov., 1965), 505-523.

[213] James Reston, "Washington: President Johnson and Education," *The New York Times* (Nov. 8, 1967), p. 46.

[214] *Understanding the Elementary and Secondary Education Act* (Wash., D.C.: Dept. of Education, National Catholic Welfare Conference, 1965), pp. 1-19.

[215] *Ibid.*

[216] *The Tablet* (June 27, 1968), p. 1.

[217] *The National Catholic Reporter* (June 26, 1968), p. 1.

[218] *Ibid.*, (Feb. 26, 1969), p. 5.

[219] Alabama, Alaska, Arkansas, California, Colorado, Florida, Georgia, Idaho, Iowa, Minnesota, Missouri, Mississippi, Nebraska, Nevada, North Carolina, South Carolina, Oklahoma, Tennessee, Texas, Utah, Virginia, Washington, West Virginia, and Wyoming.

[220] Maryland, Montana, Arizona, Maine, North Dakota, South Dakota, and Vermont.

[221] Delaware, Illinois, Kentucky, New Jersey, Oregon, Indiana, and Kansas.

[222] Connecticut, Hawaii, Louisiana, Michigan, Massachusetts, Mississippi, New Hampshire, New Mexico, New York, Ohio, Pennsylvania, Rhode Island, and Wisconsin.

[223] Hawaii, Pennsylvania, and Wisconsin.

[224] Connecticut, Michigan, Massachusetts, Nebraska, New Hampshire, Wisconsin, and Maine.

[225] *The National Catholic Reporter* (Dec. 4, 1968), p. 1.

[226] *The Tablet* (Jan. 23, 1969), p. 1.

[227] Citizens for Educational Freedom has its Executive Offices in Washington, D.C.

[228] *Cochran* v. *Louisiana State Board of Education*, 281 U.S. 370 (1930).

229 *Chance* v. *Mississippi State Textbook Rating and Purchasing Board*, 200 So. 706 (1940). Quoted in Chester James Antieau, Phillip Mark Carroll, and Thomas Carroll Burke, *Religion Under the State Constitutions* (Brooklyn, N.Y.: Central Book Company, Inc., 1965), p. 30.

230 *Everson* v. *Board of Education*, 330 U.S. 1 (1947).

231 *Ibid.*, in John J. McGrath, *Church and State in American Law: Cases and Materials* (Milwaukee: The Bruce Publishing Company, 1962), p. 117.

232 *Dickman* v. *School District No. 62 C*, 366 P. 2d 533 (1961).

233 *Borden* v. *Louisiana State Board of Education*, 168 La. 1005, 123 So. 655.

234 *Judd* v. *Board of Education*, 278 N.Y. 200 15, NE 2d 576, 118 ALR 789 (1938).

235 Quoted in Antieau, Carroll, and Burke, *Religion Under the State Constitutions*, p. 31.

236 *McGowan* v. *Maryland*, 366 U.S. 420.

237 Less than a month later the Court unanimously rejected a Maryland statute requiring all office-holders to declare a belief in the existence of God: *Torcaso* v. *Watkins*, 367 U.S. 488 (1961). Black, speaking for the Court, held that Maryland had imposed a requirement preferring belief over nonbelief.

238 *Sherbert* v. *Verner* 374 U. S. 398 (1963).

239 *Engel* v. *Vitale* 370 U.S. 4S1 (1962); and *Abington*, above, in 1963. For further bibliography see Edmond G. Drouin, *The School Question* (Wash., D.C.: The Catholic University of America, 1963); Neil G. McCluskey, *Catholic Viewpoint on Education* (rev. ed.; New York: Image Books, 1962; Robert F. Drinan, *Religion, the Courts and Public Policy* (New York: McGraw-Hill, 1963); Philip B. Kurland, *Religion and the Law of Church and State and the Supreme Court* (Chicago: Aldine Publishing Co., 1962); Richard J. Regan, *American Pluralism and the Catholic Conscience* (New York: The Macmillan Company, 1963); also Richard J. Regan, "The Dilemma of Religious Instruction and the Public Schools," *Catholic Lawyer*, X (1964), 42-54, 82; Paul G. Kauper, *Civil Liberties and the Constitution* (Ann Arbor, Mich.: University of Michigan Press, 1962); John Courtney Murray, *We Hold These Truths* (New York: Sheed and Ward, 1960); Leo Pfeffer, *Church, State, and Freedom* (Boston: The Beacon Press, 1953); John Cogley (ed.), *Religion in America* (New York: Sheed and Ward, 1958); Fund for the Republic, *Religion and the Free Society*, by William Lee Miller and others (N.Y.: Fund for the Republic, 1958); also Fund for the Republic, *Religion and the Schools* by Robert Cordis and others (N.Y.: Fund for the Republic, 1959); and Wm. B. Ball, "The Constitutionality of the Inclusion of Church-Related Schools in Federal Aid to Education," *Georgetown Law Journal*, L (1961), 397-455.

240 *The New York Times* (Jan. 16, 1968), p. 20.

241 Charles M. Whalen, "Textbooks and the Taxpayer." *America*, CXIX, No. 1 (July 6, 1968), 9; *Our Sunday Visitor*, LVII, No. 10 (July 7, 1968), 16.

242 *The New York Times* (June 11, 1968), pp. 1, 39.

243 Louisiana, Mississippi, Rhode Island, West Virginia, Indiana, and Kansas.

244 *The New York Times* (Oct. 29, 1968), p. 20.

245 *Frothingham* v. *Mellon*, 43 Sp. Ct. 597 (1923).

246 Mrs. Florence Flast, president of the United Parents Association; Mrs. Helen D. Henkin, former president of the United Parents Association; Albert Shanker, president of the United Federation of Teachers; Frank

Abrams and C. Irving Dwork, officials of the American Jewish Congress; Mrs. Florence Levin, a taxpayer; and Mrs. Helen D. Buttenwieser, a lawyer and member of the New York Civil Liberties Union.

247 *Flast* v. *Gardner*, 390 U.S. 977 (1968).

248 All from *The New York Times* (June 11, 1968), p. 38.

249 Rev. Charles M. Whelan, S.J., "Textbooks and the Taxpayer: the Future of the First Amendment," *Trends and Issues in Catholic Education*, ed. Russell Shaw and Richard J. Hurley (New York: Citation Press, 1969), p. 187.

250 *Engel* v. *Vitale*, 370 U.S. 421.

251 *School District of Abington Township* v. *Schempp*, 377 U.S. 203 (1963).

252 Justices Wm. O. Douglas, Wm. J. Brennan, Jr., and Arthur J. Goldberg filed separate concurring opinions. Justice John M. Harlan joined Goldberg's opinion, and Justice Potter Stewart again constituted the sole dissent.

253 *The New York Times* (March 26, 1969), pp. 1, 20.

254 For some further bibliography, see Franklin H. Littell, *From State Church to Pluralism* (Garden City, N.Y.: Doubleday & Co., 1962); Vivian T. Thayer, *Religion in Public Education* (New York: The Viking Press, 1947); American Association of School Administrators, *Religion in the Public Schools* (New York: Harper & Row, 1964).

255 *Zorach* v. *Clauson*, 343 U.S. 306 (1952); *Perry* v. *School District No. 8*, 54 Wash. 2d 886 (1959).

256 *Dilger* v. *School District No. 24 . . .*, 222 Ore. 108 (1960).

257 Further bibliography: Richard B. Dierenfield, *Religion in American Public Schools* (Washington, D.C.: Public Affairs Press, 1962), pp. 75-82; Edmond G. Drouin, *The School Question: A Bibliography* (Washington, D.C.: The Catholic University of America Press, 1963), pp. 131-150.

258 "Americans United" (formerly "Protestants and Other Americans United for the Separation of Church and State") claims of public parochial schools (which they term pejoratively "captive schools") that "several hundred presently [1967] operate in 22 states" (J. Eugene White, *America's Captive Schools* [Washington, D.C.: Americans United, n.d.g., n.p.g.]). They define "captive school" as "a public school, totally supported by taxes levied for the public school system, but controlled by the local Roman Catholic diocese." They state that these schools were captured by the Church not through "any dark conspiracy," but "because peculiar circumstances may cause the arrangement to seem expedient." They cite as an example Antonito, Colo., where during the depression in the early 1930's "the Benedictine sisters volunteered to staff the schools . . . for a fraction of the previous cost," the townspeople accepted as the best "way to keep their schools open," and even in the better times that followed the situation continued. Americans United indicate that they participated in legal action against this situation in Fort Recovery, Ohio, in 1965, in Missouri, and in New Mexico, and that "the mere threat of action by this organization a few years ago eliminated captive schools" in Sterling, Colo., and Bremond, Tex. They also had a part in the decommissioning of all of the 11 southern Indiana parochial-public elementary schools in 1969 for alleged substandard conditions (Religious News Service release, April 22, 1969). Mr. Edd Doerr of Americans United, in a cover letter to this author of June 18, 1969, indicated of the above pamphlet that "it is the only

thing we have available that would not require extensive digging and research."

This author's research trip through the country added further information. In the diocese of Wichita, Kansas, for example, there are at least five such schools: at the towns of St. Marks, Andale, Colwich, and Ost, all staffed by the Precious Blood Sisters whose motherhouse is in Wichita, and in Garden Plain, staffed by the Dominican Sisters of Great Ben, Kans. In southern Colorado, in the Pueblo diocese, where the school district was run by Masons, the latter refused to oust the sisters when they had an opportunity to do so, because when they needed someone to staff the schools and no one else was available, the sisters had volunteered. In New Mexico, they existed to about 1949 in Las Vegas and Bernalillo; up to *Zellers* v. *Huff*, mentioned elsewhere in the text, in Dixon; and today at least at Mora and Peñasco. In Texas, they exist in at least the towns of Tours, Westphalia, and Fayetteville; in Ohio, at least in the towns of Botkins, Burkettsville, Coldwater, Russia, Minster, Maria Stein, McCartyville, St. Peters, Temperanceville, Churchtown, Caldwell, Ottoville, Kalida, Glandorf, and New Riegel; and in Maine, in many French-Canadian towns of the St. John's River Valley. (Another of the ways in which this type school originated, incidentally, was with immigrant Catholic communities of French, Italian, and German origin.) In Kentucky, a headline of the *Courier-Journal* of Louisville on July 28, 1953 (p. 2) read: "The Catholic Church now operates 24 public schools in Kentucky, along with 111 of its own institutions." The same newspaper ran a series (Ora Spaid, "A Reporter Goes to Church") on the controversy over the subject at that time, in which the town of Bradfordsville closed its school for one year rather than have nun-teachers (Archives, Nazareth Academy, Nazareth, Ky.). Because of the controversy and for other reasons—lack of vocations, for example, and the parishes buying back their schools from the public school districts in good times—the number of parochial-public schools in Kentucky dwindled from about fifteen to a mere few. Ironically, at this writing the dearth of teachers and other educational crises in Kentucky have prompted that state to welcome teaching sisters, who because of their present fewness of numbers are unable to accept.

Among the reasons presented by "Americans United" and other opposing groups to this type of arrangement are the following: the school is often owned by the Church and then leased to the public school district, thus segregating students by religion; the religious name attached to the parish is applied to the public school; children are sometimes permitted to leave school for such reasons as to serve Mass, sing religious songs, or attend church services; such schools are listed in the Official Catholic Directory; sectarian religious instructions are given in these schools which are supported by public funds; there are Catholic-oriented texts; sectarian art is often presented as part of the curriculum; there is a place on report-cards for a grade in religion; religious articles are given as prizes for achievement in other subjects; teachers escort children to church; the students are released for Church holidays; parish priests and diocesan authorities make visitations of the premises; the Sister-teachers are assigned by a Mother Superior, and the school board abdicates its hiring prerogative; the teachers wear religious garb; and parochial schools use public buses for their own purposes.

259 *Horace Mann League of the United States* v. *Board of Public Works*, 242 Md. 645 (1966), 220 A. 2d 51.

260 John J. McGrath, *Catholic Institutions in the United States: Canonical and Civil Law Status* (Washington, D.C.: The Catholic University of America Press, 1968), p. vii.

261 *Ibid.*, p. 33.

262 *Ibid.*

263 *Ibid.*, p. 36.

264 See Mark Hurley, *Declaration on Christian Education of Vatican Council II: A Commentary* (Glen Rock, N.J.: Paulist Press, 1966).

265 A speech by an official Council Father in debate at St. Peter's.

266 Cited in Xavier Rynne, *The Third Session: The Debates and Decrees of Vatican Council II, Sept. 14 to Nov. 21, 1964* (New York: Farrar, Straus, and Giroux, 1965), p. 226; see also Edward L. Heston, C.S.C., "Session No. 3, News Bulletin No. 46, General Congregation No. 125," *Concilio Ecumenico Vaticano II* (Rome: Ufficio Stampa, privately mimeographed and circulated, Nov. 18, 1964), p. 2.

267 "Statement by U. S. Bishops on Catholic Schools," *Catholic Mind*, LXVI, No. 1219 (January, 1968), 2, 5-6.

268 *Declaration on Christian Education*, Para. 3.

269 U. S. 88th Congress, 1st Session H. R. 6074; A Bill to Amend the National Defense Education Act of 1958, Washington, D.C. (1963), p. 6.

270 Department of Health, Education, and Welfare, *Dual-Enrollment in Public and Nonpublic Schools* (Washington, D.C.: U. S. Government Printing Office, 1965), p. 1.

271 Harry Stearns and others, "Shared Time: A Symposium," *Religious Education* (January–February, 1962), pp. 3-35.

272 Abraham Ribicoff, "The Religious Controversy in Education—It Must be Resolved," *Congressional Record* (May 20, 1963), p. 8500.

273 Stearns, "Shared Time," p. 154.

274 *Ibid.*, p. 155.

275 Theodore Powell, *Shared Time in Hartford*, A report of the Connecticut State Department of Education, Sept. 6, 1961.

276 Theodore Powell, "The Constitutional Position," *Teacher Educational Quarterly*, XVIII (Fall, 1960), 21.

277 *Ibid.*, p. 23.

278 Walter A. Anderson, "Opinions Differ," *NEA Journal* (March, 1964), p. 28.

279 Louis Cassels, "A Way Out of Our Parochial-Public School Conflict," *Look* (Aug. 28, 1962), 58.

280 "Reaction to Shared Time," *NEA Journal* (Dec., 1964), p. 49.

281 For further bibliography see G. S. Reuter, Jr., "Shared Time: A New Approach in American Education," *Congressional Record* (Thursday, Feb. 1, 1962).

282 *The New York Times* (Sept. 27, 1967), p. 26.

283 William H. Conley, "The Layman in Catholic Education," *Catholic School Journal*, LXII (June, 1962), 21.

284 *The National Catholic Reporter* (Feb. 21, 1968), p. 5.

285 *Declaration on Education*, Para. 8, in Abbot and Gallagher, *Documents of Vatican II*.

286 *L'Osservatore Romano* (English edition) (Nov. 14, 1968), p. 3.

287 Sr. Mary Brideen Long, *An Evaluation of Catholic Elementary School Teachers' Pre-Service Education* (Washington, D.C.: The Catholic University of America Press, 1952); *ibid.*, "An Evaluation of Catholic Elementary School Teachers' Pre-Service Education—A Follow-Up," *Sister Formation Bulletin*, Vol. XIII (Autumn, 1966).

288 Sr. Rose Matthew Mangini, I.H.M., "Sister-Teachers in the United States: A Study of Their Status and Projected Role," *Planning for the Formation of Sisters*, ed. Sister Ritamary Bradley (New York: Fordham University Press, 1958), 162.

289 Sr. Mary Emil Penet, "The Preparation of Religious for Teaching: Sister Formation," *Catholic Schools in Action*, ed. Reginald A. Neuwien (Notre Dame: University of Notre Dame Press, 1966), pp. 117-118.

290 Sr. Bertrande Meyers, *Sisters for the 21st Century* (New York: Sheed & Ward, 1965), p. 39.

291 See J. M. Egan, "Preparation of Theology Teachers," *Theology in the Catholic College*, ed. Reginald Masterson (Dubuque, Iowa: Priory Press, 1961).

292 For further information on Catholic Teacher Education see *Bulletin of the National Catholic Educational Association*, a quarterly (Washington, D.C.): *The Catholic Educational Review*, a monthly except June through August (Washington, D.C.); *Catholic Educator*, a monthly except June through August, containing general articles on elementary and secondary education; and the official organ of The Catholic Audio-Visual Education Association (CAVE) (New York); *The Catholic School Journal*, a monthly except July and August (Milwaukee, Wisc.); see also *Catholic Colleges and Schools in the United States: Summary of Catholic Education* (Washington, D.C.); and *The Official Guide to Catholic Educational Institutions*, published annually (New York).

293 *L'Osservatore Romano* (English edition) (July 18, 1968), p. 8.

294 *Ibid.* (Aug. 22, 1968), p. 1.

295 *Ibid.*

296 *Ibid.* (Sept. 12, 1968), p. 1.

297 *Ibid.*

298 *Ibid.*

299 Sr. Mary Emmanuel, "Continued Excellence in Education," *National Catholic Educational Association Bulletin*, LVII, No. 1 (August, 1960), 261.

300 Letter received by the author Dec. 18, 1968, from the Rev. Mallory Dugan, S.T., at Holy Trinity Church, Harlan, Ky.

301 For bibliography on the blind and visually handicapped see Thomas J. Carroll, *Blindness, What It Is, What It Does, and How to Live With It* (Boston: Little, Brown, 1961); Merle E. Framton and Ellen Kerney, *The Residential School, Its History, Contributions and Future* (New York: The New York Institution for Education of the Blind, 1953).

302 See S. C. Henderson and S. P. Stein (eds.), "A Special Report Based on a Workshop for Catholic Personnel Conducted at Gallaudet College, Washington, D.C., March 15, 16, 17, 1961," *American Annals of the Deaf*, CVI (1961), 294-341.

303 Romaine P. Mackie and P. P. Robbins, *Exceptional Children and Youth: . . . Special Education Enrollments in Public Day Schools . . .* (Washington, D.C.: U. S. Office of Education, 1961), p. 3.

304 For this purpose such specialized works are published as *Come, An Illustrated First Communion Catechism of Minimum Requirements* (St.

Louis, Mo.: School Sisters of Notre Dame); see also G. Breitenbeck, "May a Retarded Child Receive Holy Communion?" *Liguorian*, LII (1964).

305 National Catholic Educational Association, Special Education Department, *Directory of Catholic Special Facilities and Programs in the United States for Handicapped Children and Adults* (Washington, D.C.: NCEA, 1965).

306 Helen Mary Gieb, S.S.N.D., *A Survey of the Post-School Adjustment of 50 Mentally Retarded Children Who Have Participated in the St. Louis Archdiocesan Special Education Program* (Milwaukee, Wisc.: Cardinal Stritch College, 1963).

307 *The New York Times* (Dec. 30, 1968), p. 1; see also U. S. President's Panel on Mental Retardation, *A Proposed Program for National Action to Combat Mental Retardation* (Washington, D.C.: U. S. Government Printing Office, 1962), and Merle E. Frampton and Elena D. Gall (eds.), *Special Education for the Exceptional* (3 vols.; Boston: P. Sargent, 1955-56).

308 See W. Dunne, "The Roman Catholic Church: The Rationale and Policies Underlying the Maintenance of Higher Institutions for Negroes," *Journal of Negro Education*, XXIX (Summer, 1960), 307-314; and W. A. Low, "The Education of Negroes Viewed Historically," *Negro Education in America: 16th Yearbook of the John Dewey Society*, ed. Virgil A. Clift (New York: Harper and Brothers, 1962).

309 *The New York Times* (October 30, 1969), pp. 1, 34.

310 William Osborne, *The Segregated Covenant* (New York: Herder and Herder, 1967).

311 Commission for Catholic Missions Among the Colored People and the Indians, *Our Negro and Indian Missions: 1968* (Wash., D.C.: The Commission, 1968). Inquiries for further information may be addressed to the Rev. J. B. Tennelly, S.S., D.D., Secretary, 2021 H. St., N.W., Washington, D.C., 20006.

312 *Ibid.*, p. 22. See also Edward Franklin Frazier, *The Negro Church in America* (New York: Schocken Books, 1964); Gunnar Myrdal, *An American Dilemma* (2 vols., rev. ed.; New York: Harper and Brothers, 1944); Willis D. Weatherford, *American Churches and the Negro: An Historical Study from Early Slave Days to the Present* (Boston: Christopher Publishing House, 1957); Carter G. Woodson, *The History of the Negro Church* (Washington, D.C.: Associated Publishers, 1921).

313 Letter from the Rev. Benjamin M. Horton, Director, The Catholic Board for Mission Work Among the Colored People, 335 Broadway, New York, N.Y. 10013.

314 *Our Negro and Indian Missions: 1968*, p. 14.

315 *Ibid.*, p. 17.

316 *Ibid.*

317 Carl T. Rowan, *The Washington Star* (Dec. 1, 1968), p. B-4.

318 *Ibid.* See also: Special Subcommittee on Indian Education, Senate Committee on Labor and Public Welfare, *Indian Education: A National Tragedy —A National Challenge* (Washington, D.C.: U. S. Government Printing Office, 1969).

319 *The New York Times* (Feb. 19, 1969), p. 29.

320 *The New York Times* (November 13, 1969), p. 20.

321 Commission for Catholic Missions Among the Colored People and the Indians, *Our Negro and Indian Missions: 1968*, pp. 22-23, 33.

[322] *Ibid.*, p. 26.
[323] *Ibid.*, p. 28.
[324] *Ibid.*, pp. 29-30.
[325] *Ibid.*, p. 27.
[326] *Ibid.*, p. 24.
[327] *Ibid.*, p. 26.
[328] *Ibid.*, p. 32. See also John Gilmary Shea, *History of the Catholic Missions Among the Indian Tribes in the United States, 1529-1854* (New York: J. G. Shea, 1855); Sr. Claudia Duratschek, *Crusading Along Sioux Trails: A History of Catholic Indian Missions of South Dakota* (St. Meinrad, Ind.: St. Meinrad's Press, 1947); R. L. Wilken, *Anselm Weber: Missionary to the Navaho, 1898-1921* (Milwaukee, Wis.: Bruce Publishing Co., 1955); Bureau of Catholic Indian Missions, *The Indian Sentinel,* organ of the Catholic Indian Missions (Washington, D.C.: 1916 to date); also Bureau of Catholic Indian Missions, *Reports of the Director* (Washington, D.C.: 1883-1910).
[329] *Time* (July 4, 1969), p. 20.

## Chapter VII

[1] See *Frederic Baraga: A Portrait of the First Bishop of Marquette Based on the Archives of the Congregatio de Propaganda Fide* (New York, Washington: Studia Slovenica, 1968).
[2] See the Rev. Chrysostomus Verwyst, O.F.M., *Life and Labors of the Rt. Rev. Frederic Baraga, First Bishop of Marquette* (New York: Benziger Bros., 1900); Joseph Gregorich, *The Apostle of the Chippewas: The Life Story of the Most Reverend Frederic Baraga* (Lemont, Illinois: Franciscan Fathers, 1932); Sr. Rosemary Crepeau, O.P., *Le Père Samuel-Charles-Gaétan Mazzuchelli* (Paris: DeGigord, 1933); Samuel Mazzuchelli, *Memoirs Historical and Edifying of a Missionary Apostolic* (Chicago: W. F. Hall, 1915). This last volume was published originally in 1844 and first translated into English in 1915 by Sr. M. Benedicta Kennedy. It does not include material on the last twenty years of Mazzuchelli's life, 1844-1864.
[3] General Assembly of Missouri, *Laws of the State of Missouri* (St. Louis: E. Charles, for the State, 1825), I, 77; William B. Faherty, *Better the Dream: St. Louis University and Community, 1818-1968* (St. Louis University, 1968).
[4] Sr. Berenice Greenwell, "Nazareth's Contribution to Education, 1812-1933" (unpublished Ph.D. dissertation, Fordham University, 1933), pp. 571b-d.
[5] It is interesting that the greatest sympathy of today's nun-successors of the original band goes automatically to the early nuns' having to cope with the many mosquitoes. This is corroborated by the present population's recollections of their childhood (experienced before insecticides), by the many dissertations on various aspects of mosquitoes at nearby Tulane University, by the number and variety of insects in today's rural sections of the region, and by the frequency with which one witnesses airplane sprayings.
[6] Giovanni Battista Semeria, *Sketches of the Life of the Very Rev. Felix De Andreis, First Superior of the Congregation of the Mission in the United States* (Baltimore: Kelly, Hedian, and Piet, 1861), p. 153.
[7] Anna C. Minogue, *Loretto: Annals of the Century* (New York: The America

Press, 1912), pp. 143-144. John M. Moeder, *History of the Diocese of Wichita* (Wichita, Kans.: Father John M. Moeder, 1963), p. 10, says that the Sisters of Loretto, on about Sept. 20, 1847, were also "the first white women to venture this far [Westport, now Kansas City, then the western end of civilization] into the prairie country, the habitation of the Red men and of wild beasts."

8 Louise Callan, *The Life and Times of Philippine Duchesne: Frontier Missionary of the Sacred Heart, 1769–1852* (Westminster, Md.: Newman Press, 1957), pp. 623-659.

9 *Diary of a Visit of Inspection of the Texas Missions Made by Fray José de Solis in the Year 1767–1768*, trans. Margaret Kenney Kress in *The Southwestern Historical Quarterly*, XXXV (July, 1931 to April, 1932) (Austin, Texas: The Texas State Historical Association, 1932), pp. 42-43.

10 Most Rev. John B. McDowell, "Spell Out Why Our Schools Exist," *The Catholic Educator*, XXXIX, No. 5 (January, 1969), 19.

11 James S. Coleman, *Equality of Educational Opportunity* (Washington, D.C.: U. S. Office of Education, 1966), p. 22.

12 *Ibid.*, p. 317.

13 Sr. M. Josine Prindaville, "History of Catholic Education in Diocese of Green Bay" (unpublished Master's thesis, The Catholic University of America, 1952), p. 10.

14 Leo Raymond Ryan, *Old St. Peter's, the Mother Church of Catholic New York (1785–1935)* (New York: The U. S. Catholic Historical Society, 1935; origanally a Ph.D. dissertation at Fordham University), p. 255.

15 Sr. M. Felicitas Powers, R.S.M., "A History of Catholic Education in Georgia, 1845–1952" (unpublished Master's thesis, The Catholic University of America, 1956), p. 121.

16 Francis P. Cassidy, *Catholic College Foundations and Development in the United States (1677–1850)* (Washington, D.C.: The Catholic University of America Press, 1924), pp. 72 and 96.

17 Mother Mary Peter Carthy, *English Influences on Early American Catholicism* (Washington, D.C.: The Catholic University of America Press, 1959), p. 106, citing Richard J. Beste, *The Wabash: or Adventures of an English Gentleman's Family in the Interior of America* (London, 1855), I, 302.

18 "The Improvement of Parochial Schools," *American Catholic Quarterly Review*, IX, No. 36 (October, 1884), 249.

19 The Sisters are proud to still have the originals of Senator Powell's letter and Lincoln's statement in their archives.

20 Robert F. Trisco, *The Holy See and the Nascent Church in the Middle Western United States, 1826–1850* (Rome: Gregorian University Press, 1962), pp. 384-386.

21 "Statement by U. S. Bishops on Catholic Schools," *Catholic Mind*, LXVI, No. 1219 (January, 1968), 2.

22 Peter Shrag, "Competition for the Public Schools," *Saturday Review* (April 15, 1967), p. 75.

23 *Ibid.*

24 *The New York Times* (Oct. 27, 1967), p. 2.

25 *Ibid.* (July 13, 1969), p. 11.

26 *Time* (Feb. 7, 1969), p. 66.

27 Michael E. Endres, "Why Catholic Schools Today?" *Catholic High School Quarterly* (April, 1968), p. 11.

[28] All from *The New York Times* (Aug. 27, 1968, p. 16; Dec. 17, 1968, p. 1; March 10, 1969, p. 24; March 4, 1966, p. 21; Dec. 4, 1968, p. 35; Dec. 10, 1968, p. 14; Dec. 11, 1968, p. 41; Jan. 28, 1969, p. 29; and Jan. 31, 1969, p. 1).

[29] *Time* (Feb. 7, 1969).

[30] *The New York Times* (Jan. 31, 1969), p. 79; (Nov. 24, 1969) pp. 1, 51.

[31] *Ibid.* (Nov. 25, 1968), p. 26.

[32] All from *The National Catholic Reporter* (June 5, 1968), p. 6.

[33] *Minersville School District* v. *Gobitis*, 310 U.S. 586 (1940).

[34] *West Virginia State Board of Education* v. *Barnett*, 319 U.S. 624 (1943).

[35] For further bibliography see Leo R. Ward, C.S.C., *Federal Aid to Private Schools* (Westminster, Md.: Newman Publishing Co., 1964); John B. Cross, "Student Grants and Separation of Church and State, *Syracuse Law Review*, XII (May 1962), 387-394; Virgil C. Blum, S.J., *Freedom in Education: Federal Aid for ALL Children* (Garden City, N.Y.: Doubleday and Co., 1966); Niels C. Nielsen, Jr., *God in Education: A New Opportunity for American Schools* (New York: Sheed & Ward, 1966); William W. Brickman and Stanley Lehrer (eds.), *Religion, Government, and Education* (New York: Society for the Advancement of Education, 1961); Brother Leo R. Downey, C.F.C., "The Windfall of Federal Aid: Suppose Parochial Schools Receive Federal Aid," and Rev. C. Albert Koob, O.Praem, "The Windfall of Federal Aid: Where is ESEA Leading Catholic Education?" *The Catholic School Journal* LXVII, No. 3 (March, 1967), 43-52. These companion articles discuss the effects upon Catholic education of federal funds as they are available today and as they might become more available in the future.

[36] *The New York Times* (June 12, 1968), p. 46.

[37] Leo Pfeffer, "What Price Federal Aid?" *Saturday Review* (Jan. 21, 1967), p. 60.

[38] *Ibid.*, p. 80.

[39] William B. Ball, "Church and State: The Absolutist Crusade," *Saturday Review* (Jan. 21, 1967), p. 58.

[40] Blum, *Freedom in Education*, p. 176.

[41] *Ibid.*, pp. 185, 187, 188.

[42] Estelle Fuchs, "The Free Schools of Denmark," *Saturday Review* (Aug. 16, 1969), p. 44.

[43] Legal Department, National Catholic Welfare Conference, "The Constitutionality of the Inclusion of Church-Related Schools in Federal Aid to Education," *The Georgetown Law Journal*, L, No. 2 (Winter, 1961), 437.

[44] 319 U.S. 624 (1943).

[45] Leo Pfeffer, *Creeds in Competition*, V (1958), as cited *op. cit.*, p. 439.

[46] Lanier Hunt, *Religion in Education*, 332 Annals of the American Academy of Political Science, XCIX (1960) as cited *ibid.*

[47] *Torcaso* v. *Watkins*, 367 U.S. 488, 495 n. 11 (1961), as cited *op. cit.*, p. 440.

[48] National Education Association and American Association of School Administrators, *Moral and Spiritual Values in Publc Schools*, VII (1951), as cited *ibid.*

[49] Robert F. Drinan, S.J., "Public Aid to Private Schools—What Next?," address to the annual School of Law Conference at Miami University, Oxford, Ohio, reprinted in *The Long Island Catholic* (June 24, 1965), p. 13.

[50] Donald A. Erickson, "Public Funds for Private Schools," *Saturday Review* (Sept. 21, 1968), p. 67.

[51] *Ibid.*, p. 67.

[52] *The New York Times* (Aug. 28, 1967), p. 26.

[53] Donald A. Erickson, "The Plain People vs. the Common Schools," *Saturday Review* (Nov. 19, 1966), p. 86.

[54] George N. Shuster, *Catholic Education in a Changing World* (New York: Holt, Rinehart & Winston, 1968), p. 10.

[55] *The Long Island Catholic* (Sept. 5, 1968), p. 3.

[56] *The New York Times* (April 11, 1967), p. 28.

[57] U. S. Dept. of Health, Education, and Welfare, *Projections of Educational Statistics* (Washington, D.C.: U. S. Government Printing Office, latest edition.)

[58] John C. Moore, "Quantity and Quality," *Commonweal*, LXXII (Sept. 23, 1960), p. 514.

[59] Vaile J. Scott, *Catholic Adult Education* (Dayton, Ohio: National Catholic Educational Association, NCEA Papers, 1968), pp. 5, 6.

[60] *Ibid.*, p. 8.

[61] Russell Shaw, "Breaking Down Walls Within Catholic Education," *America* (Jan. 20, 1968), p. 72.

[62] Office for Educational Research, University of Notre Dame, *The Denver Metropolitan Area Catholic Schools of The Archdiocese of Denver: Research Study, 1967–1968* (Notre Dame, Ind.: University of Notre Dame, 1968).

[63] Neil G. McCluskey, *Catholic Education Faces Its Future* (Garden City, N.Y.: Doubleday & Co., 1969), pp. 273-274.

[64] NCEA, *Voice of the Community: The Board Movement in Catholic Education* (Washington, D.C., 1967), p. 3.

[65] *Constitution on the Church* in Abbott and Gallagher, *Documents of Vatican II* (New York: The America Press, 1966), pp. 60, 64.

[66] McCluskey, *Catholic Education Faces Its Future*, p. 264.

[67] *Ibid.*, p. 263.

[68] *Ibid.*, p. 264.

[69] Rev. Olin J. Murdick, *The Parish School Board* (Washington, D.C.: National Catholic Educational Association, 1967), p. 7.

[70] NCEA, *Voice of the Community: The Board Movement In Catholic Education*, p. 36.

[71] *Ibid.*, p. 37.

[72] Francis Keppel, *The Necessary Revolution in American Education* (New York: Harper & Row, 1966), pp. 7, 54.

[73] *The Tablet* (Aug. 15, 1968), p. 9.

[74] See The National Catholic Educational Association, *What is Happening to Catholic Education?* (Washington, D.C.: NCEA, 1966). This work has a chapter by Neil G. McCluskey, "The Catholic School Looks at its Future," pp. 13-23.

[75] Educational Testing Service, *College and University Trustees: Their Backgrounds, Roles, and Educational Attitudes* (Princeton, N.J.: 1969).

[76] Michael O'Neill, "The Parochial School Question," *America* (Feb. 4, 1967), p. 184.

[77] *Ibid.*, p. 185.

[78] Raymond H. Reno, *The Impact Teacher* (St. Paul, Minn.: 3M Education Press, 1967).

[79] *The Tablet* (June 13, 1968), p. 2.

[80] John Courtney Murray, S.J., "The Christian Idea of Education," *The Christian Idea of Education* (New Haven: Yale University Press, 1957), p. 162.

[81] Leo XIII, *Sapientiae Christianae. (On The Chief Duties of Christians as Citizens)* in John Joseph Wynne, S.J., *The Great Encyclical Letters of Pope Leo XIII* (New York: Benziger Bros., 1903), p. 206.

# A Selective Bibliography

*For annotation beyond the brief notes provided here, the reader is referred to appropriate sections of the text, especially the footnotes.*

## General

### PRIMARY SOURCES

### Archives

Catholic Archives. There are many specifically Catholic archives—national, diocesan, school, seminary, community, provincial, etc.—the chief difficulty with which is that, in some cases, due to lack of resources both in money and personnel, they are not sufficiently catalogued for easy use.

Among Catholic institutional archives are such as: The Catholic University of America; Commission for Catholic Missions Among the Colored People and the Indians, Washington, D.C.; Georgetown University, Washington, D.C.; Mt. St. Mary's, Emmitsburg, Md.; Notre Dame University; Old Cathedral Library, Vincennes, Ind.; St. Charles Seminary, Philadelphia, Pa.; St. Louis University; and St. Mary's Seminary, Perryville, Mo.

Among diocesan archives are such as: Austin, Tex., on which see Lane, M. Claude, Sister, "Catholic Archives of Texas: History and Preliminary Inventory" (unpublished Master's thesis, University of Texas, 1961, and mimeographed by the Dominican Sisters in Houston, Texas, in 1961); Baltimore, Md.; Cincinnati, Ohio; Detroit, Mich.; New York, N.Y.; Richmond, Va.; Rochester, N.Y.; St. Paul, Minn.; and Santa Fe, N.M. (about which see Chavez, Fray Angelico. *Archives of the Archdiocese of Santa Fe 1687–1900.* Washington, D.C.: Academy of American Franciscan History, 1957).

Among noteworthy religious community archives are: Academy of American Franciscan History, Washington, D.C.; Georgetown Visitation Convent, Washington, D.C.; Jesuit Provincial Archives, Baltimore, Md.; Oregon Province of the Jesuits at Gonzaga University, Spokane, Wash.; St. John's Abbey, Collegeville, Minn. (Benedictine); St. Vincent Archabbey, Latrobe, Pa. (Benedictine); Sisters of Charity at Emmitsburg, Md.; Sisters of Charity, Nazareth, Ky.; Sisters of Loretto at Loretto Academy, Nerinckx, Ky.; Sisters of Notre Dame de Namur, Lowell, Mass; Ursuline Academy, New Orleans, La.; and Woodstock College, Woodstock, Md. (Jesuit).

National Archives. U. S. State Department.

Such university libraries and museums as the Peabody Museum at Harvard University; Yale University Library; Bancroft Library, University of California at Berkeley; San Francisco Public Library; Detroit Public Library (esp. Burton Historical Collection); Newberry Library, University of Chicago; Coronado Library, University of New Mexico; Ritch

Collection, Huntington Library, San Marino, Calif.; University of Texas (on which see Kielman, Chester V. *Guide to the Microfilm Edition of the Bexar Archives, 1717–1803.* Austin: National Historical Publications Commission, 1967, and *ibid., The University of Texas Archives.* Austin: University of Texas Press, 1967).

### Other

*American Catholic Historical Researches.* Philadelphia: Catholic Historical Association, 1884–1913.

Benedictine Monks of Solesmes. *Papal Teachings: Education.* New York: St. Paul Editions, 1960.

Ellis, John Tracy. *Documents of American Catholic History.* 2d ed. Milwaukee, Wisconsin: The Bruce Publishing Company, 1962.

Foley, Henry. *Records of the English Province of the Society of Jesus.* London: Burns and Oates, 1877–1883.

Guilday, Peter (ed.). *National Pastorals of the American Hierarchy, 1792–1919.* Washington, D.C.: National Catholic Welfare Council, 1923.

Huber, Raphael M. (ed.). *Our Bishops Speak: National Pastorals and Annual Statements of the Hierarchy of the United States, 1919–1951.* Milwaukee: The Bruce Publishing Company, 1952.

McCluskey, Neil G. *Catholic Education in America: A Documentary History.* New York: Teachers College, Columbia University, 1964.

McGrath, John J. *Church and State in American Law.* Milwaukee, Wis.: The Bruce Publishing Company, 1962.

*National Catholic Educational Association Bulletin* is an excellent source for materials since 1904, among whose memorable articles have been such as Browne, Henry J., "The American Parish School in the Last Half Century," L, No. 1 (August, 1953), 323-334; Shehan, Lawrence J., Most Rev., "Christian Education: Our Commitments and Our Resources," LVI, No. 1 (August, 1959), 38-46; Lieberman, Myron, "Parochial Schools and Public Leadership," LVII, No. 1 (August, 1960), 239-248; Mary Emmanuel, Sister, "Continued Excellence in Education," LVII, No. 1 (August, 1960), 260-266; Ong, Walter J., "Academic Excellence and Cosmic Vision," LVI, No. 1 (August, 1961), 37-50; Duffy, Thomas P., "A Positive View of Catholic Education in the Light of Today's Crisis," LXI, No. 1 (August, 1964), 253-260.

*Official Catholic Directory.* New York: P. J. Kenedy Co., each year. This had numerous predecessors (e.g., *The Laity's Directory, The United States Catholic Almanac or Laity's Directory, The Metropolitan Catholic Almanac or Laity's Directory,* and *The Metropolitan Catholic Almanac and Laity's Directory*), and from 1920 has contained detailed summaries on Catholic school enrollments.

*Records of the American Catholic Historical Society.*

*Records of the American Catholic Historical Society of Philadelphia.*

*Report of the Proceedings and Addresses of the Annual Meeting of the National Catholic Educational Association,* published annually since 1904 by the Association, is a valuable reflection; among its more memorable items are O'Brien, Thomas J., "Textbooks in Catholic Schools," 1905; Currier,

Charles Warren, "Our Indian Schools," 1907; Shields, Thomas E., "The Method of Teaching Religion," 1908; McCormack, Patrick J., "Standards in Education," 1917; Wehrle, Joseph, "Education for Citizenship," 1921; Cooper, John M., "Diagnosis and Treatment of the Factors in Moral Conduct," 1929; McNeill, Leon A., "The Diocesan Normal School," 1930; Connell, Francis J., "The Forthcoming Revision of the Baltimore Catechism," 1940; M. Marguerite, Sister, "The Catholic Approach to Citizenship through Reading," 1942; Maria Theresa, Sister, "The Principal and the Lay Teacher," 1953; Sloyan, Gerard S., "The Curriculum in Transition," 1953; and Penet, Mary Emil, Sister, "Progress Report—Sister-Formation Conference," 1956.

Weber, Francis J. *Documents of California Catholic History (1784–1963)*. Los Angeles: Dawson's Book Shop, 1965.

*Woodstock Letters. A Record of Current Events and Historical Notes Connected with the Colleges and Missions of the Society of Jesus in North and South America*. Woodstock, Maryland: 1872.

SECONDARY SOURCES

Books

Agatha, M., Mother. *Catholic Education and the Indian*. Washington, D.C.: The Catholic University of America Press, 1942.

———. *Catholic Education and the Negro*. Washington, D.C: The Catholic University of America Press, 1942.

American Association of School Administrators. *Religion in the Public Schools*. New York: Harper and Row, 1964.

Antieau, Charles James; Downey, Arthur T.; and Roberts, Edward C. *Freedom from Federal Establishment*. Milwaukee: The Bruce Publishing Company, 1964.

Confrey, Burton. *Secularism in American Education*. Washington: The Catholic University of America, 1931.

Ellis, John Tracy. *American Catholicism*. Chicago: The University of Chicago Press, 1956.

———. *A Guide to American Catholic History*. Milwaukee: The Bruce Publishing Company, 1959.

Gabel, Richard J. *Public Funds for Church and Private Schools*. Washington, D.C.: The Catholic University of America Press, 1937.

Hughes, Thomas. *The History of the Society of Jesus in North America*. 4 vols. New York: Longmans, Green and Co., 1907–1917.

Kerwin, Jerome G. *Catholic Viewpoint on Church and State*. Garden City, New York: Hanover House, Doubleday and Co., 1960.

McLaughlin, Raymond, Sister, O.S.B. *A History of State Legislation Affecting Private Elementary and Secondary Schools in the United States, 1870–1945*. Washington, D.C.: The Catholic University of America, 1946.

Pfeffer, Leo. *Church, State, and Freedom*. Boston: The Beacon Press, 1953.

Spurlock, Clark. *Education and the Supreme Court*. Urbana: The University of Illinois Press, 1955.

Stokes, Anson Phelps. *Church and State in the United States*. 3 vols. New York: Harper and Bros., 1950.

## Articles

Burns, James A. "The Development of Parish School Organization," *The Catholic Educational Review*, Vol. III, No. 5 (May, 1912), 419-434.
Holsinger, M. Paul. "The Oregon School Bill Controversy, 1922–1925," *Pacific Historical Review*, Vol. 37 (August, 1968), 327-342.
Murray, John Courtney, S.J. "The Christian Idea of Education," *The Christian Idea of Education*. New Haven: Yale University Press, 1957.

## Reference Works

Monroe, Paul (ed.). *Cyclopedia of Education*. 5 vols., 2d ed. Detroit: Gale Publishing Co., 1968.
*The New Catholic Encyclopedia*. 15 vols. New York: McGraw-Hill Book Company, 1967.

# To 1783: Colonial Period of Transplantation

PRIMARY SOURCES

## Archives

In addition to the archival material cited above, see the following: France: Archives Nationales, Paris; Mexico: Biblioteca Nacional de México; Franciscan monasteries at such places as Celaya, Guanaquato; Querétaro; and Mexico City; Spain: Archivo General de Indias, Seville; El Escorial; Instituto Hispánico, Madrid; and National Library, Madrid; Quebec, Canada: Chancery Archives; Rome, Italy: Propaganda Fide Archives, and others.

## Other

Bacon, Thomas. *Laws of Maryland: 1638–1763*. Annapolis: Jonas Green, 1765.
*Benavides' Memorial of 1630*. Trans. Peter P. Forrestal. Introduction and Notes by Cyprian J. Lynch. Washington, D.C.: Academy of American Franciscan History, 1954.
*Fray Alonso de Benavides' Revised Memorial of 1634*. Annotated by Frederick Webb Hodge, George P. Hammond, and Agapito Rey. Albuquerque: University of New Mexico Press, 1945.
*Diary of a Visit of Inspection of the Texas Missions Made by Fray Gaspar José de Solis in the Year 1767–1768*. Trans. Margaret Kenny Kress in *Southwestern Historical Quarterly*, XXXV (July, 1931 to April, 1932). Austin, Texas: The Texas State Historical Association, 1932.
Kino, Eusebio Francisco. *Kino's Historical Memoir of Pimería Alta, A Contemporary Account of the Beginnings of California, Sonora, and Arizona by Father Eusebio Francisco Kino, S.J., 1683–1711*. Ed. H. E. Bolton. 2 vols. Cleveland: Arthur H. Clark Co., 1919.
———. *Kino Reports to Headquarters: Correspondence of Eusebio F. Kino, S.J., from New Spain with Rome, 1682–1704*. Ed., trans. and notes by Ernest J. Burrus. Rome: Institutum Historicum Societatis Jesu, 1954.
*Règlemens des Religeuses Ursulines de la Congrégation de Paris. Divisé en trois livres*. Paris: Louis Josse, 1705.

Thwaites, Reuben Gold (ed.). *Jesuit Relations and Allied Documents: Travels and Explorations of the Jesuit Missionaries in New France, 1610–1791.* 73 vols. Cleveland: The Burrows Brothers, 1896–1901.

Zumárraga, Juan. *Doctrina Breve.* New York: United States Catholic Historical Society, 1928. Monograph Series, 10.

### SECONDARY SOURCES

## Books

Bancroft, Hubert Howe. *History of the North Mexican States and Texas.* San Francisco: A. L. Bancroft & Co., 1884–1889.

———. *History of the Pacific States of North America.* San Francisco: The Historic Company Publishers, 1888.

Barth, Pius Joseph. *Franciscan Education and the Social Order in Spanish North America (1502–1821).* Chicago, Illinois: The University of Chicago Press, 1945.

Baudier, Roger. *The Catholic Church in Louisiana.* New Orleans: A. W. Hyatt Stationery Mfg. Co., Ltd., 1939.

Berger, John A. *The Franciscan Missions of California.* New York: G. P. Putnam's Sons, 1941.

Bolton, Herbert Eugene. *Rim of Christendom.* New York: The Macmillan Company, 1936.

Castañeda, Carlos E. *Our Catholic Heritage in Texas 1519–1936.* 7 vols. Austin, Tex.: Von Boeckmann-Jones Co., 1936–1958.

Charlevoix, Pierre F. X. de, S.J. *Journal d'un Voyage fait par ordre du Roi dans l'Amérique septintrionale; addressé à Madame la Duchesse de Lesdiguières.* 6 vols. Paris: Chez la veuve Ganeau, 1744.

Ellis, John Tracy. *Catholics in Colonial America.* Baltimore: Helicon Press, 1965.

Galvin, Catharine Frances, Sister. *The Convent School of French Origin in the United States, 1727–1843.* Philadelphia: University of Pennsylvania, 1936.

Giraud, Marcel. *Histoire de la Louisiane Française.* 3 vols. Paris: Presses Universitaires de France, 1953, 1958, and 1966.

Griffin, Martin I. J. *William Penn: The Friend of Catholics.* Philadelphia: Press of the I.C.B.U. Journal, 1886.

Heaney, Jean Frances, Sister. "A Century of Pioneering: A History of the Ursuline Nuns in New Orleans (1727–1827)." Unpublished Ph.D. dissertation, St. Louis University, 1949.

Mulvey, Mary Doris, Sister. *French Catholic Missionaries in the Present United States.* Washington, D.C.: The Catholic University of America Press, 1936.

Vogel, Claude. *The Capuchins in French Louisiana 1722–1766.* Washington, D.C.: The Catholic University of America Press, 1928.

Weber, Francis J. *A Historical Sketch of Pioneer Catholicism in the Californias: Missions and Missionaries.* Van Nuys, Calif.: California Historical Publications, 1961.

———. *A Select Guide to California Catholic History.* Los Angeles: Westernlore Press, 1966.

## Articles

Campa, Arthur L. "The Churchmen and the Indian Languages of New Spain," *Hispanic American Historical Review*, XI, No. 4 (November, 1931), 542-550.

Campbell, Bernard U. "Sketches of the Early Missions in Maryland," *United States Catholic Historcal Magazine*, VII, No. 10 (October, 1887).

McGarry, Daniel D. "Educational Methods of the Franciscans in Spanish California," *The Americas*, VI, No. 3 (January, 1950), 335-338.

Nicholl, William E. "The Early Mission Schools of California," *Pomona College Bulletin* (May, 1937), pp. 14-19.

## 1783–1828: Formative Foundations

### PRIMARY SOURCES

*The Constitution of the United States*

Jefferson, Thomas. "Bill for Establishing Religious Freedom," in Boyd, Julian P. (ed.). *The Papers of Thomas Jefferson*. Princeton, New Jersey: Princeton University Press, 1950, pp. 350f.

Madison, James. "Memorial and Remonstrance Against Religious Assessments," in Padover, Saul Kussiel (ed.). *The Complete Madison; His Basic Writings*. 1st ed. New York: Harper, 1953.

### SECONDARY SOURCES

Callan, Louise. *The Life and Times of Phillippine Duchesne: Frontier Missionary of the Sacred Heart, 1769–1852*. Westminster, Md.: Newman Press, 1957.

Graves, Mary Loyola, Sister. "A Subject Bibliography of the Works of the Sisters of Charity of Nazareth and A Bibliography of Works Containing Information About the Sisters of Charity of Nazareth." Unpublished Master's thesis, The Catholic University of America, 1954. Supplement in the Nazareth Archives updating work to 1960.

Greenly, Albert H. *A Bibliography of Father Richard's Press in Detroit*. Ann Arbor: University of Michigan, 1955.

Greenwell, Berenice, Sister. "Nazareth's Contribution to Education, 1812–1933." Unpublished Ph.D. dissertation, Fordham University, 1933.

Guilday, Peter. *The Life and Times of John England*. 2 vols. New York: The America Press, 1927.

Lathrop, George Parsons. *A Story of Courage: Annals of the Georgetown Convent of the Visitation*. Boston: Houghton-Mifflin Company, 1895.

McGill, Anna B. *The Sisters of Charity of Nazareth, Kentucky*. New York: Encyclopedia Press, 1917.

Mattingly, M. Ramona, Sister. *The Catholic Church on the Kentucky Frontier (1785–1812)*. Washington, D.C.: The Catholic University of America Press, 1936.

Melville, Annabelle M. *Elizabeth Bayley Seton, 1774–1821.* New York: Charles
Scribner's Sons, 1951.

Minogue, Anna C. *Loretto, Annals of the Century.* New York: The America
Press, 1912.

————. *Pages from a Hundred Years of Dominican History.* New York: Frederick Pustet & Co., 1921.

Pargellis, Stanley. *Father Gabriel Richard.* Detroit: Wayne University Press,
1950.

Parsons, Wilfrid, S.J. *Early Catholic Americana: A List of Books and Other
Works by Catholic Authors in the United States, 1729–1830.* New York:
The Macmillan Company, 1939.

Rosalita, M., Sister. *Education in Detroit Prior to 1850.* Lansing, Michigan:
Lansing Historical Commission, 1928.

Woodford, Frank B., and Hyma, Albert. *Gabriel Richard.* Detroit: Wayne
State University Press, 1958.

## 1829–1884: Transition

### PRIMARY SOURCES

### Books

*Acta et decreta concilli plenarii Baltimorensis tertii.* Baltimore: Typis Joannis
Murphy et Sociorum, 1886.

*Acta et decreta concilii plenarii Baltimorensis II.* Baltimore: Typis Joannis
Murphy et Sociorum, 1868.

Brownson, Henry F. (ed.). *The Works of Orestes A. Brownson.* 20 vols. Detroit: Thorndike, Nourse Publishers, 1882–1887.

Brownson, Orestes A. *Brownson's Quarterly Review.* 24 vols. New York: E.
Dunigan & Bros. etc., 1856–75.

England, John. *The Works of the Right Reverend John England.* Sebastian
Messmer and others (eds.). 7 vols. Cleveland: Arthur H. Clark Co.,
1908.

Kehoe, Lawrence (ed.). *Complete Works of the Most Reverend John Hughes.*
2 vols. New York: L. Kehoe Publisher, 1866.

*Pastoral Letter of the First Provincial Council of Cincinnati to the Clergy and
Laity.* Cincinnati: John P. Walsh, 1855.

*Pastoral Letter of the Most Reverend the Archbishop of Baltimore and the
Right Reverend the Bishops of the Roman Catholic Church in the
United States of America Assembled in Third Provincial Council of
Baltimore, 1837.* Baltimore: Fielding Lucas, 1837.

*School Manual for the Use of the Sisters of St. Joseph of Carondelet.* St. Louis:
Ev. E. Carreras, Printer, Binder and Publisher, 1883–1884.

### Articles

"Minutes of the Roman Meeting Preparatory to the Third Plenary Council
of Baltimore, Chapter X, Parochial Schools," *The Jurist*, XI, No. 3
(July, 1951), 417-424.

"The President's Speech at Des Moines," *The Catholic World*, XXII, No. 130 (January, 1876), 433-443.

SECONDARY SOURCES

Books

Connaughton, Edward A. *A History of Educational Legislation and Administration in the Archdiocese of Cincinnati.* Washington, D.C.: The Catholic University of America Press, 1946.

Diffley, Jerome E. *Catholic Reaction to American Public Education.* Notre Dame, Indiana: University of Notre Dame, 1959.

Fell, Marie Léonore, Sister. *The Foundations of Nativism in American Textbooks, 1783–1860.* Washington, D.C.: The Catholic University of America Press, 1941.

Guilday, Peter. *A History of the Councils of Baltimore (1791–1884).* New York: The Macmillan Company, 1932.

Hassard, John R. G. *Life of the Most Reverend John Hughes, First Archbishop of New York.* New York: D. Appleton and Co., 1866.

Lannie, Vincent P. *Public Money and Parochial Education: Bishop Hughes, Governor Seward, and the New York School Controversy.* Cleveland: The Press of Case Western Reserve University, 1968.

Walsh, Louis S. *Historical Sketch of the Growth of Catholic Parochial Schools in the Archdiocese of Boston.* Newton Highlands, Mass.: Press of St. John's Industrial Training School, 1901.

Articles

Cassidy, Francis P. "Catholic Education in the Third Plenary Council of Baltimore," *The Catholic Historical Review*, XXXIV, No. 3 (October, 1948), 257-305; cont'd. XXXIV, No. 4 (January, 1949), 414-436.

Gleason, Philip. "Immigration and American Catholic Intellectual Life," *The Review of Politics*, XXVI (April, 1964), 150-159.

Klinkhamer, Marie Carolyn. "The Blaine Amendment of 1875: Private Motives for Political Action," *Catholic Historical Review*, XLII (April, 1956), 15-49.

McAvoy, Thomas T., C.S.C. "Public Schools *vs.* Catholic Schools and James McMaster," *The Review of Politics*, XXVIII, No. 1 (January, 1966), 19-46.

McCadden, Joseph J. "Bishop Hughes versus the Public School Society of New York," *Catholic Historical Review*, L (July, 1964), 188-207.

———. "New York's School Crisis of 1840–1842: Its Irish Antecedents," *Thought*, XLI (Winter, 1966), 561-588.

Pratt, John W. "Religious Conflict in the Development of the New York City Public School System," *History of Education Quarterly*, V (June, 1965), 110-120.

Sharp, John K. "How the Baltimore Catechism Originated," *The American Ecclesiastical Review*, LXXXI (December, 1929), 573-586.

## 1885–1917: Further Growth

PRIMARY SOURCES

### Books

Bouquillon, Thomas. *Education: To Whom Does It Belong?* Baltimore: John Murphy and Company, 1892.

Holaind, R. I., S.J. *The Parent First: An Answer to Dr. Bouquillon's Query, "Education: To Whom Does It Belong?"* New York: Benziger Brothers, 1891.

Ireland, John. *The Church and Modern Society: Lectures and Addresses.* 2 vols. Chicago: D. H. McBride and Co., 1897. Another edition was published as *The Church and Modern Society.* St. Paul: The Pioneer Press Manufacturing Departments, 1904.

Satolli, Francesco Cardinal. *For the Settling of the School Question and the Giving of Religious Instruction.* Baltimore: John Murphy and Company, 1892.

Shields, Thomas Edward. *Catholic Education Series.* Washington, D.C.: The Catholic Education Press, 1915.

———. *Philosophy of Education.* Washington, D.C.: The Catholic Education Press, 1917.

Spalding, John Lancaster. *Education and the Future of Religion.* Notre Dame, Ind.: The Ave Maria Press, 1901.

———. *Education and the Higher Life.* Chicago: A. C. McClurg and Company, 1891.

———. *Means and Ends of Education.* Chicago: A. C. McClurg and Company, 1897.

Zwierlein, Frederick James. *Life and Letters of Bishop McQuaid.* 3 vols. Rochester, New York: The Art Print Shop, 1925–27.

### Articles

Harris, William Torrey. "Religious Instruction in the Public Schools," *The Independent,* LV (August 6, 1903), 1841–1843.

McSweeney, Patrick F. "Christian Public Schools," *The Catholic World,* Vol. XLIV, No. 262 (March, 1887), 788-797.

Spalding, John Lancaster. "Normal Schools for Catholics," *The Catholic World,* Vol. LI, No. 301 (April, 1890), 88-97.

Wolff, George D. "Our Parochial School—The Progress It Has Made and Is Making," *American Catholic Quarterly Review,* XVII (December, 1892), 866-872.

SECONDARY SOURCES

### Books

Ellis, John Tracy. *John Lancaster Spalding.* Milwaukee, Wis.: The Bruce Publishing Company and the National Catholic Educational Association, 1961.

McAvoy, Thomas T., C.S.C. *The Great Crisis in American Catholic History, 1895–1900.* Chicago: Henry Regnery Co., 1957.

McCarren, Edgar P. "The Origin and Early Years of the National Catholic Educational Association." Unpublished doctoral dissertation, The Catholic University of America, 1966.

Reilly, Daniel F. *The School Controversy: 1891–1893.* Washington, D.C.: The Catholic University of America Press, 1943.

Schlesinger, Arthur M. *A Critical Period in American Religion, 1875–1900.* Philadelphia: Fortress Press, 1967.

### Articles

Butsch, Joseph, S.S.J. "Negro Catholics in the United States," *The Catholic Historical Review,* III, No. 1 (April, 1917), 33-51.

"Catholic Teachers and Educational Progress," *The Catholic World,* LXXXIII, No. 493 (April, 1906), 93-101.

Curley, Michael J. "The Aim of Catholic Education," *The Catholic Educational Review,* XII, No. 1 (June, 1916), 18-26.

Lucey, Michael H. "Administration of the Parish Schools," *The Catholic World,* XCIV, No. 547 (October, 1911), 59-72.

## 1918–1957: *Maturing Process*

### PRIMARY SOURCES

### Books

Bandas, Rudolph G. *Catechetical Methods.* New York: Joseph F. Wagner, Inc., 1929.

Mary Joan, Sister, O.P., and Mary Nona, Sister, O.P. *Guiding Growth in Christian Social Living.* 3 vols. Washington, D.C.: The Catholic University of America Press, 1944.

Johnson, George. *Better Men for Better Times.* Washington, D.C.: The Catholic University of America, 1943.

*Oregon School Cases: Complete Record.* Baltimore: Belvedere Press, 1925.

Pius XI, Pope. *Christian Education of Youth.* New York: The America Press, 1936.

### Articles

Ellis, John Tracy. "American Catholics and the Intellectual Life," *Thought,* XXX, No. 118 (Autumn, 1955), 351-388; published under the same title: Chicago, Ill.: Heritage Foundation, 1956.

Hierarchy of the United States. "The Child: Citizen of Two Worlds," Pastoral Letter of November 17, 1950. Cited in Huber, Raphael M. (ed.). *Our Bishops Speak: National Pastorals and Annual Statements of the Hierarchy of the United States, 1919–1951.* Milwaukee: The Bruce Publishing Company, 1952, pp. 161-169.

SECONDARY SOURCES

## Books

Barrett, John Daniel, S.S. *A Comparative Study of the Councils of Baltimore and the Code of Canon Law.* Washington, D.C.: The Catholic University of America Press, 1932.

Drinan, Robert J., S.J. *Religion, the Courts, and Public Policy.* New York: McGraw-Hill, 1963.

Drouin, Edmond G. *The School Question: A Bibliography on Church-State Relationships in American Education, 1940–1957.* Washington, D.C.: The Catholic University of America Press, 1963.

Durkin, Mary Antonia, Sister. *The Preparation of the Religious Teacher: A Foundational Study.* Washington, D.C.: The Catholic University of America Press, 1926.

Frison, Basil, C.M.F. *Coeducation in Catholic Schools: A Commentary on the Instruction on Coeducation.* Boston: Printed by the Daughters of St. Paul, 1959.

Hagan, John Raphael. *The Diocesan Teachers College.* Washington, D.C.: The Catholic University of America Press, 1932.

Johnson, George. *The Curriculum of the Catholic Elementary School.* Washington, D.C.: The Catholic University of America Press, 1919.

Long, Mary Brideen, Sister. *An Evaluation of Catholic Elementary School Teachers' Pre-Service Education.* Washington, D.C.: The Catholic University of America Press, 1952.

McAvoy, Thomas T., C.S.C. *Father O'Hara of Notre Dame: The Cardinal-Archbishop of Philadelphia.* Notre Dame, Ind.: University of Notre Dame Press, 1967.

McKeough, Michael (ed.). *The Curriculum of the Catholic Secondary School.* Proceedings of the Workshop on the Curriculum of the Catholic Secondary School conducted at The Catholic University of America from June 11 to June 22, 1948. Washington, D.C.: The Catholic University of America Press, 1949.

Meyers, Bertrande, Sister. *The Education of Sisters.* New York: Sheed and Ward, 1941.

O'Connor, M. Augustine, Sister. "The Influence of Very Reverend Doctor Thomas E. Shields on Catholic Education in the United States." Unpublished Master's dissertation for the Department of Education, The Catholic University of America, Washington, D.C., 1941.

O'Neill, Francis de Sales, Brother, F.S.C. *The Catholic High School Curriculum.* Washington, D.C.: The Catholic University of America, 1930.

Quigley, Thomas A., Rev. "The Lay Teacher in the American Catholic School System." Unpublished Master's dissertation, The Catholic University of America, Washington, D.C., 1938.

Redden, John D., and Ryan, Francis A. *A Catholic Philosophy of Education.* Milwaukee: The Bruce Publishing Company, 1942.

Rooney, John R. *Curricular Offerings of Catholic Secondary Schools: An Examination of 283 Institutions.* "The Catholic University Educational

Research Monographs," Vol. VI, No. 4. Washington, D.C.: The Catholic University Press, May 15, 1931.

Schmitz, Sylvester, A.M. *The Adjustment of Teacher Training to Modern Educational Needs.* Atchison, Kansas: The Abbey Student Press, 1927.

Stone, William S., Rev. "The History of the Confraternity of Christian Doctrine in the United States." Unpublished Master's thesis, Department of Education, Catholic University of America, Washington, D.C., 1944.

Vila, Ana L. *Bibliography of Writings of the Religious of the Sacred Heart in the U. S. (1914–1960).* Washington, D.C.: The Catholic University of America, 1961.

## Articles

Galvin, William A., Very Rev., J.C.D. "Ecclesiastical Legislation on Christian Education With Special Application to Current Problems," *The Jurist,* XIV, No. 4 (October, 1954), 463-480.

Herberg, Will. "Justice for Religious Schools," *America,* XCVIII, No. 7 (Nov. 16, 1957), 190-193.

Johnson, George. "The Activity Curriculum in the Light of Catholic Principles," *Education,* LXI, No. 7 (March, 1941), 414-419.

————. "The Aim of Catholic Elementary Education," *The Catholic Educational Review,* XXII, No. 5 (May, 1925), 257-268.

Jorgenson, Lloyd P. "The Oregon School Law of 1922: Passage and Sequel," *Catholic Historical Review,* LIV (October, 1968), 455-466.

Long, Mary Brideen, Sister. "An Evaluation of Catholic Elementary School Teachers' Pre-Service Education—A Follow Up," *Sister Formation Bulletin,* XIII (Autumn, 1966), 1-9.

Murray, John Courtney, S.J. "Towards a Christian Humanism: Aspects of the Theology of Education." Cited in Guthrie, Hunter, S.J., and Walsh, Gerald G., S.J. (eds.). *A Philosophical Symposium on American Catholic Education.* New York: Fordham University Press, 1941, pp. 106-115.

Penet, Mary Emil, Sister, I.H.M. "The Sister-Formation Movement and the Pastoral Outlook," *Sister-Formation Bulletin,* I, No. 2 (December, 1954), 9-12.

Ranwez, Pierre, S.J. "General Tendencies in Contemporary Catechetics," *Shaping the Christian Message.* Edited by Gerard S. Sloyan. New York: The Macmillan Company, 1958, pp. 112-117.

Widen, Irwin. "Public Support for Parochial Schools: Why the Issue Has Re-emerged," *History of Education Journal,* IV, No. 2 (Winter, 1953), 58-72.

## *1958–Present: Contemporary Soul-searching and Ferment*

### PRIMARY SOURCES

Abbott, Walter M., S.J. (ed.). *Documents of Vatican II.* New York: The America Press, 1966.

Hurley, Mark J. (ed.). *The Declaration on Christian Education of Vatican Council II.* Glen Rock, N.J.: Paulist Press, 1966.

Jungmann, Josef Andreas, S.J. *Handing on the Faith*. Edited and translated by Anthony N. Fuerst. New York: Herder and Herder, 1959.
United States Bishops. "Statement by U. S. Bishops on Catholic Schools," *Catholic Mind*, LXVI, No. 1219 (January, 1968), 1-7.

SECONDARY SOURCES

## Books

Blum, Virgil C., S.J. *Freedom in Education*. Garden City, New York: Doubleday and Company, 1965.
*Catholic Educational Institutions and Religious Communities in the United States*. Rockville Centre, N. Y.: Catholic Institutional Directory Co., 1967.
Commission for Catholic Missions Among the Colored People and the Indians. *Our Negro and Indian Missions*. Washington, D. C.: The Commission, published annually.
Dierenfield, Richard B. *Religion in American Public Schools*. Washington, D.C.: Public Affairs Press, 1962.
Greeley, Andrew M., and Rossi, Peter H. *The Education of Catholic Americans*. Chicago: Aldine Publishing Co., 1966.
Koob, Albert, O.Praem. *What is Happening to Catholic Education?* Washington, D.C.: National Catholic Educational Association, 1966.
McCluskey, Neil G. *Catholic Education Faces Its Future*. Garden City, N. Y.: Doubleday and Company, 1969.
———. *Catholic Viewpoint on Education*. Garden City, New York: Doubleday and Company, 1962.
McDermott, Maria Concepta, Sister. *The Making of a Sister-Teacher*. Notre Dame: University of Notre Dame Press, 1965.
McGrath, John J. *Catholic Institutions in the United States: Canonical and Civil Law Status*. Washington, D.C.: The Catholic University of America Press, 1968.
Meyers, Bertrande, Sister. *Sisters for the Twenty-first Century*. New York: Sheed and Ward, 1965.
Murdick, Olin J., Rev. *The Parish School Board*. Washington, D.C.: National Catholic Educational Association, 1967.
National Catholic Educational Association. *Voice of the Community: The Board Movement in Catholic Education*. Washington, D.C.: NCEA, 1967.
Neuwien, Reginald A. (ed.). *Catholic Schools in Action*. Notre Dame, Ind.: University of Notre Dame Press, 1966.
Nielsen, Niels C., Jr. *God in Education: A New Opportunity for American Schools*. New York: Sheed and Ward, 1966.
Ryan, Mary Perkins. *Are Parochial Schools the Answer?* New York: Holt, Rinehart and Winston, 1964.
Seidl, Anthony E. *Focus on Change—Management of Resources in Catholic Schools*. New York: Joseph F. Wagner, Inc., 1968.
Shuster, George N. *Catholic Education in a Changing World*. New York: Holt, Rinehart & Winston, 1968.

Sizer, Theodore R. (ed.). *Religion and Public Education.* Boston: Houghton-Mifflin, 1967.

Sloyan, Gerard S. *Speaking of Religious Education.* New York: Herder and Herder, 1968.

*The State and Non-Public Schools.* Washington, D.C.: U. S. Government Printing Office, misc. No. 28, 1958.

U. S. Department of Health, Education and Welfare. *Projections of Educational Statistics.* Washington, D.C.: U. S. Government Printing Office, latest edition.

Ward, Leo R., C.S.C. *Federal Aid to Private Schools.* Westminister, Md.: Newman Publishing Co., 1964.

———. *New Life in Catholic Schools.* St. Louis: Herder and Herder, 1958.

## Articles

Ball, William B. "Church and State: The Absolutist Crusade," *Saturday Review,* January 21, 1967, pp. 58-59, 77.

Bernert, Roman A., S.J. "Catholic School Objectives: Do We Need a New Approach?" *The Catholic School Journal,* LXVI, No. 7 (September, 1966), 49-53.

Conley, William H. "Renewal of Catholic Education," *The Catholic School Journal,* LXVI, No. 7 (September, 1966), 4.

Erickson, Donald A. "Public Funds for Private Schools," *Saturday Review,* September 21, 1968, pp. 66-68 and 78-79.

Koob, C. Albert, O.Praem. "The Windfall of Federal Aid: Where is ESEA Leading Catholic Education?" *The Catholic School Journal,* LXVII, No. 3 (March, 1967), 44-48.

LaNoue, George R. "Religious Schools and 'Secular' Subjects," *Harvard Educational Review,* XXXIII, No. 3 (Summer, 1962), 254-291.

National Catholic Welfare Conference, Legal Department. "The Constitutionality of the Inclusion of Church-Related Schools in Federal Aid to Education," *The Georgetown Law Journal,* L, No. 2 (Winter, 1961), 399-455.

O'Neill, Michael. "The Parochial School Question," *America,* February 4, 1967, pp. 183-187.

Pfeffer, Leo. "What Price Federal Aid?" *Saturday Review,* January 21, 1967, pp. 59-60, 80.

Quigley, Joseph A. M., J.C.D. "The Authority of the Local Ordinary Over Schools Conducted by Religious," *The Jurist,* XXI, No. 1 (January, 1961), 47-56.

Regan, Richard J. "The Dilemma of Religious Instruction and the Public Schools," *Catholic Lawyer,* X (1964), 42-54, 82.

"Religion in the Catholic High School," *Catholic High School Quarterly Bulletin,* XXII, No. 4 (January, 1965).

Reuter, G. S., Jr. "Shared Time: A New Approach in American Education," *Congressional Record,* Thursday, February 1, 1962.

Ryan, Carl J., Rt. Rev. Msgr. "The Lay Teacher in the Catholic School," *The Homiletic and Pastoral Review,* XLVIII, No. 8 (May, 1948), 575-81.

Shaw, Russell. "Telling the Story of Catholic Education," *The Catholic Educator*, XXXVIII, No. 8 (April, 1968), 87-89.

Shrag, Peter. "Competition for the Public Schools," *Saturday Review*, April 15, 1967, p. 75.

Sizer, Theodore R. "The Case for a Free Market," *Saturday Review*, January 11, 1969, pp. 34-36.

Stearns, Harry, *et al.* "Shared Time: A Symposium," *Religious Education*, January-February, 1962, pp. 3-35.

# Index